for
Katie
and
Megan
two prospective readers who are a source of
unending insight into political techniques

Marian D. Irish
Professor Emerita
American University

James W. Prothro
Alumni Distinguished Professor
University of North Carolina

Richard J. Richardson
Burton Craige Professor
University of North Carolina

Prentice-Hall, Inc., Englewood Cliffs, New Jersey 07632

THE
POLITICS
OF
AMERICAN
DEMOCRACY

7 th edition

Library of Congress Cataloging in Publication Data

Irish, Marian Doris.
    The politics of American democracy.

    Includes index.
      1. United States—Politics and government.
I. Prothro, James Warren (date) joint author.
II. Richardson, Richard J., joint author.
III. Title.
JK274.I7 1981   320.973   80–17663
ISBN 0–13–685156–8

THE POLITICS OF AMERICAN DEMOCRACY, seventh edition
Marian D. Irish, James W. Prothro, Richard J. Richardson

© 1981, 1977, 1971, 1968, 1965, 1962, 1959 by Prentice-Hall, Inc., Englewood Cliffs, N.J. 07632

Printed in the United States of America

10 9 8 7 6 5 4 3 2 1

This is a Special Projects book,
edited, designed, and supervised *by*
Maurine Lewis, *director*
Ray Keating, *manufacturing buyer*
Stan Wakefield, *cover photos*
Don Martinetti, *cover design*

PRENTICE-HALL INTERNATIONAL, INC., *London*
PRENTICE-HALL OF AUSTRALIA PTY. LIMITED, *Sydney*
PRENTICE-HALL OF CANADA, LTD., *Toronto*
PRENTICE-HALL OF INDIA PRIVATE LIMITED, *New Delhi*
PRENTICE-HALL OF JAPAN, INC., *Tokyo*
PRENTICE-HALL OF SOUTHEAST ASIA PTE. LTD., *Singapore*
WHITEHALL BOOKS LIMITED, Wellington, *New Zealand*

preface

The basic objective of this seventh edition of our book is the same as the first: to meet "the need for a reasonably short book realistically portraying the way American government works." That was a bold assertion at the time of the first edition, for most textbooks on American government were encyclopedic in their factual detail, formal in their focus on the official aspects of government, and idealized in their treatment. Our effort through every edition has been to present facts not for their own sake but as a route to explanatory generalizations. We have tried to achieve a realistic view by including data and insights from other disciplines and by considering informal no less than formal institutions and activities. And we have avoided the sterility of an idealized interpretation by considering the functions or consequences of institutions and policies, which always turn out to help some and hurt others.

The encyclopedic, formal, and idealized approach has pretty much disappeared, its demise hastened at least partly, we like to think, by our efforts. The danger in reacting to those deficiencies is that overreaction may lead to treatments that are unsystematic, journalistic, and strained to fit some theme or gimmick. We hope we have not succumbed to these tendencies. The concept of politics as a system of interrelated activities offers an approach that gives some assurance of a balanced coverage. We begin with the concepts of politics and political system and with the context of the American political system. Part 2 examines the inputs of individuals, of unofficial agencies such as political parties, pressure groups, and the mass media, and of the official electoral system. Part 3 analyzes the work of official decision-making agencies. Part 4 considers policy outputs of the system.

Although we adopted the systems framework from the outset, we have always treated it simply as a useful organizing device, not as a theory. Our approach is thus open to the insights and findings of any theory that sheds light on how the American political system actually works. The guiding analytic concept is that every political institution, activity, and policy helps some people and hurts others. Hence the recurrent questions: Who gets helped, who gets hurt? By such a focus, we hope students will emerge with a way of looking at politics that will help them understand it long after the current facts have changed.

As in every edition, we have tried to make the best scholarship on American politics understandable and interesting to students. We hope we have synthesized the findings of that scholarship in simple and direct English, free of jargon or pretense. We also hope we have done so without patronizing or writing down to our readers. We think they can understand anything political scientists have learned about American politics. Rather than including a glossary, we avoid technical terms when they are unnecessary. When they are needed, we explain them as they are used. By the same token, controversial issues are neither introduced for the sake of controversy nor avoided for the sake of approval.

A list of all the changes in this edition is impossible because almost every chapter has been substantially rewritten (the two concluding chapters are the only exceptions). The most significant theoretical advance is probably in the treatment of the semi-sovereign pressure groups (chapter 6), where we analyze the inability of conventional scholarship to account for recent developments. As a corrective to the tendency of political scientists to call attention to the average citizen's misconceptions about government, chapter 1 calls attention to political scientists' misconceptions about the average citizen. The emphasis of the systems approach on the interrelatedness of political institutions was most helpful in rewriting the material on political parties, pressure groups, nominations and elections, Congress, the presidency, the bureaucracy, and the Supreme Court (chapters 5 through 11). Fragmentation of power, resulting from the further decline in American political parties, is seen to have ramifications for every political institution. The treatment of individual liberties (chapter 12) includes problems in this area presented by recent rulings on pornography, capital punishment, and affirmative action. Chapter 7 offers an analysis of the strange election of 1980 and its implications for the American system.

We are, of course, immensely pleased that many people have found our book helpful enough to make them call for seven editions. We have even found gratification in some rejections of the book, as in the case of a few professors who have ruefully admitted relying on it for their lectures but assigning dull texts to their students. Outright attacks have been rare, but they form an interesting pattern. In the 1960s, a John Birch group cited the adoption of our book as one ground for attacking the political science department of a California college; the Birchers were exercised about our unpatriotic treatment of Senator Joseph McCarthy's use of the congressional power of investigation. Later in the 1960s a graduate student member of the SDS (Students for Democratic Society) in Minnesota issued a mimeographed article charging the book with being a conservative "whitewash" of the system. Early in the 1970s columnist George Will denounced the book as slanted in an antisystem direction. The present edition will no doubt appear to some viewers as having each of these defects. We trust that most readers will once again view it as an effort to encourage students to think realistically and systematically about how the American political system works.

A principal source of encouragement in the preparation of this book has been the students who have read earlier editions, especially those at other institutions who have gone to the trouble of writing to us. If we succeed in stimulating new undergraduates in this book, much of the thanks must go to a rarely astute editor, Maurine Lewis, who treats authors and manuscripts with equal thoughtfulness and expertise, to the great benefit of both. Working with her has been a joy. Betsy Taylor and Louisa Allen efficiently typed the manuscript and unobtrusively improved its content, all with patience and good humor. Among our colleagues, particular assistance in this revision has been given by professors John Quincy Adams, Millsaps College; Charles S. Bullock III, University of Georgia; Richard Fleisher, Fordham University; Kirk L. Johnson, Fisk University; Steven Kincaid, University of Illinois; Eugene A. Mawhinney, University of Maine; Patrick McAfee, Syracuse University; Lewis E. Moore, Jr., Columbia State Community College; David C. Saffell, Ohio Northern University; William C. Spragens, Bowling Green University; Tom Uhlman, University of Missouri; Mark Weinberg, Ohio University. Finally, we continue to be grateful for Marian Irish's work on the first five editions and the indelible impression she left on this book. We happily share credit for the merits of the book with all these people; we unhappily share responsibility for its deficiencies only with each other.

Our deepest thanks and continued intellectual respect go to our wives, without whom Maurine Lewis would have had a much more difficult task.

J.W.P.
R.J.R.

Chapel Hill, North Carolina

contents

part } **DECISION-MAKING AGENCIES AND ACTIVITIES: WHO DECIDES WHAT AND HOW?**

THE CONTEXT OF AMERICAN POLITICS

part 1

misconceptions
and
concepts
of
American
politics

1

Americans apparently do not like their government—76 percent think it wastes a lot of their tax money, 71 percent think a few big interests run it for their own benefit, and 65 percent say they cannot trust it most of the time.[1] The American colonists' feelings about His Majesty's government of Great Britain in 1776 were probably no more negative than this. Indeed, with just this information about public attitudes toward the leaders of any country, most observers would conclude that the country was on the brink of revolution. What about the United States? Are Americans ready to revolt again, this time against Washington instead of against London? Not at all. Negative feelings about leaders may or may not be a cause for alarm, but they have not produced negative feelings about the political system. Only 25 percent of American adults think a big change in our form of government is needed. When specifically asked if lack of trust in the government is because of the individuals in office or because of "something more seriously wrong with government in general," 67 percent say it is just because of the individuals in office.

MISCONCEPTIONS ABOUT AMERICAN POLITICS

Americans must have good reasons for liking their system of government and disliking the way it is run. But each feeling is sometimes unrealistic and extreme. Respect for the system often leads to the idea that the men who set it up (the founding fathers) were almost gods, that the Constitution they wrote should be revered almost as if it had been carved in stone. Disappointment with current politics sometimes leads to the opposite extreme, with every politician regarded as unworthy.

Reverence for the founding fathers

The men who wrote the United States Constitution—the people we now call founding fathers—were in fact young politicians of great but varied ability. They managed to devise, through a series of compromises, a remarkably enduring plan of government. Not one of them regarded it as ideal, so why should we? On balance, the mere survival of the system they started some two hundred years ago demonstrates that the founders did their work well. On the other hand, they can be blamed for some of the difficulties their successors have faced in keeping the system alive. For example, if they had outlawed slavery at the start, the country would not have been devastated by one of

[1] References to public opinion in this paragraph are from Warren E. Miller and Arthur H. Miller, *The CPS 1976 American National Election Study* (Ann Arbor, Michigan: Inter-University Consortium for Political and Social Research, 1977), vol. 1. Henceforth it will be referred to simply by title. For a debate on the "crisis of confidence" see Patrick H. Caddell, "Trapped in a Downward Spiral," and Warren E. Miller, "Misreading the Public Pulse," *Public Opinion,* October–November 1979, pp. 2–15, 60.

America's founding fathers are usually deified in paintings, but they were actually politicians.

the worst civil wars in history. And if they had trusted ordinary citizens enough to give them the right to vote, blacks, women, and young adults would have been voting all along, without the necessity of later amendments protecting their rights.

Disrespect for current politicians

The unrealistically idealized view of the founding fathers leads almost inevitably to equally unrealistic contempt for today's political leaders. If they are expected to live up to an impossible ideal—one not achieved even by those thought to have set it—ordinary politicians will look terrible, and even good ones will look mediocre. Disrespect for politicians is, of course, sometimes very appropriate. In recent years the misconduct of our highest political leaders has ranged all the way from putting a mistress on the congressional payroll to criminal misuse of presidential power. As shocking as such events are, two points help put them in perspective. First, they are not typical of American politicians; second, such acts are probably less common in government than in private life. Bert Lance was forced to resign as Director of the Office of Management and Budget in 1977 because of dubious practices when he had been a bank executive in private life. The Lance case illustrates both our points. No one accused him of improper conduct in his government position. People in high public office are watched so closely by budget and accounting officers, congressional committees, and investigative journalists, and the procedures they must follow are so carefully spelled out that they clearly see the need to resist temptations to misuse their offices. Mr. Lance the banker could use a company airplane for personal purposes more easily than Mr.

"Well, lots of success back in government or in private business, whichever the case may be."

Lance the politician could use a government airplane for personal purposes. Oddly enough, many people would not object to such use of the bank's plane, not stopping to realize that it would involve ripping off stockholders, just as use of a government plane would be unfair to taxpayers. What is common practice in the private sector would be scandalous in government.

To demand a higher standard in politicians is appropriate, for they are supposed to be public servants. But we might remember that politicians are the only public servants we have, the only holders of power who are either elected by the general public or appointed by someone who was elected. No one else with power to shape our lives—whether journalist, educator, business executive, or union leader—has the special relationship of the politician to the general public, getting power from the people and keeping it only if the people approve. To hold politics in lower esteem than private spheres, from which we cannot demand any concern for the public welfare, seems unduly harsh. After all, if extreme misconduct were not rare among politicians, it would not create a scandal when it does occur.

Misconceptions as a special problem in studying politics

Extreme reverence or disrespect are inappropriate in studying American politics, whether we are examining the records of James Madison and Alexander Hamilton or of Jimmy Carter and Ronald Reagan. An objective approach to the founding fathers will show, we think, that most of them deserve great respect for keen political thinking and foresight; but it will also show that their reservations about democracy produced a constitutional system that has discouraged citizen participation in, and control of, government. The same approach to today's politicians suggests that most of them also deserve respect, despite the well-publicized abuse of office by a few.

We must thus lay to rest or at least seriously modify the misconceptions that the founding fathers approached perfection and that all later politicians are demagogues. If readers of this book were not exposed to these myths about politics before they came to college, they were undoubtedly exposed to a lot of others. Because politics deals with public affairs, it is everybody's business, and people begin to pick up ideas about it at very early ages. Beginning students of political science therefore come to their first course already knowing a lot about the subject. Moreover, what they "know" typically includes value judgments that are hard to change. Beginning students of chemistry, on the other hand, probably have few ideas in advance about the subject, and any they do have involve factual judgments that are easily changed.

Common misconceptions about politics tend to simplify or distort the real political world so much that they impede understanding. We will now look at some misconceptions we hope the readers of this book have resisted or will have abandoned by the time they finish this book. We shall briefly examine the myths at this point and return to them at the end of the book when we are in a better position to appraise them.

Popular misconceptions of American politics

The most common views of politics are those that are picked up in the family, taught in the public schools, and reinforced by the mass media. Along with much that is accurate, they contain a number of misconceptions, many of which carry an idealized view of American government. As noted earlier, the image of the founding fathers is one such idealized notion. Other myths of this type include:

The American Way is the only democratic way. "Democracy" is such an appealing symbol that although it did not become common as the term for the American government until the twentieth century, we sometimes claim not only to be democratic but also to be the model that all democratic countries should emulate.

Ours is a government of laws and not of men. Pride in the Constitution sometimes leads people to think it can solve political questions without human intervention, that all we have to ask of a policy is whether or not it fits the Constitution.

Free elections ensure majority control of public policy. Competitive elections give the citizens a chance to choose their leaders. We often assume that this means the citizens will have direct control over what public policies will be adopted.

Policy reflects consensus. Public policies coming out of a democracy do not reflect a conflict with losers as well as winners, but rather broad general agreement in the society.

Government is neutral. The ultimate stance of government, as the servant of all the people, should be unbiased. It should neither favor nor neglect anyone.

These views are sometimes taken to describe what American government actually is and sometimes to describe what it should be. Our purpose here is not to say whether these views should or should not be held as ideals—that's a question of differing individual preferences. We are saying that if the myths are accepted as reality, they will make it difficult to understand politics in the United States or anywhere else.

A second set of common myths tends to look down on politics and politicians ("politicians are dirty"). Other examples: *Government is inherently evil; The national government is worse (more evil) than state or local governments; Tyranny of the majority is a threat to freedom; The incapacity of the people causes any malfunctions of American government.* These are arguments that were once used against the idea of democracy itself. People who have accepted the symbols but not the substance of popular government still find them useful as arguments against any reform that would promote majority control.

We think they are at least as misleading as the idealistic myths and more opposed to the possibility of increasing popular control over public policy.

All these conventional notions have vaguely conservative implications. The first set of misconceptions suggests an American superiority that implies a lack of problems or need to learn from other countries. The antigovernment myths suggest that we should not look to government as the principal tool for dealing with social or economic problems. Taken together, they cast an aura of patriotism around those who boast about how many bathtubs and refrigerators Americans have and an aura of disloyalty about those who point out our need for a more equitable distribution of medical care and other prerequisites of a satisfactory life.

MISCONCEPTIONS FROM RIGHT AND LEFT

By definition, myths outside the mainstream of public thought are less widely shared. But some extremist myths enjoy great popularity in certain restricted circles. We shall first note one from the conservative or right side of the political spectrum and then one from the liberal or left side.

Capitalism is the cornerstone of democracy. This is a particularly appealing myth for the "haves" (or wealthy) of society, those who exercise most of the power and enjoy most of the benefits of a corporate economy. If they can convince the "have-nots" to believe that political freedom depends on the power or profits of major corporations, they can rest secure in their advantages. This notion enjoyed wide support, even from the Supreme Court of the United States, early in the century. Today it is probably heard most often in the "public service" advertisements of petroleum industries. The tax advantages and staggering profits of these huge corporations are presented as no less essential to democracy than is the right to vote.

A ruling few dictate policy in America. The imbalances of influence on public policies and the rewards received from those policies are so great that this notion enjoys considerable currency among political scientists. As people who study such things as voting turnout and tax advantages, they cannot help but be impressed by the inequities that exist. If the notion of a ruling few means only that all interests in the United States do not have equal influence on policy, we think it is correct (for the United States and for every other country we know about). If it means that a small conspiratorial group of the same individuals dictates every political decision, we think it is false.

We have raised all of these misconceptions about the political system to warn the reader that we shall not support them in their pure form. By the time we have examined the actual conduct of American government, we hope the reader will be able to replace a misconception with an understanding more rooted in reality.

All the misconceptions we have noted to this point are about politics, politicians, and the political system. And they are misconceptions that result mostly from never having studied American or other political systems.

Another type of misconception may be harder to deal with, because it is about people, rather than about the political system. Misconceptions of this type are encouraged, either directly or implicitly, by the very people who have studied the subject. What we have in mind here is *the tendency to assume that whenever people don't act or think the way we expect, something must be wrong with them, rather than with our expectations*. This assumption deserves special emphasis as we begin to look at American politics, for it is probably the most common mistake among social scientists. At least three misconceptions that put down ordinary people are encouraged by this assumption.

A distorted view of the working-class poor

Lower-status people tend to have "authoritarian personalities" more often than do people of higher status. This conclusion was supported in a monumental study of fascist beliefs, a study that was begun during World War II by a group of white, upper middle-class psychologists. They devised a measure of fascist or authoritarian personality that defined authoritarianism as including a "tendency to be on the lookout for, and to condemn, reject, and punish people who violate conventional moral values" and a focus on "power and toughness," a "preoccupation with the dominance-submission, strong-weak, leader-follower dimension. . . ."[2] The assumption was that either tendency was unrealistic. But how can a concern for protecting moral values and a preoccupation with "power and toughness" be unrealistic for people exposed daily to thefts, muggings, and brutality? By the 1970s, Louis Harris reported that 62 percent of the women in the United States "admitted they were deeply worried about violence and safety on the streets when they went out of their homes in the day or night."[3] A majority (56 percent) of all adults felt it was "very important" that they lock their doors "when out for brief periods."[4] People living in the tougher neighborhoods could be regarded as truly foolish if they were not concerned with such problems. But in the 1950s, such a preoccupation was counted as authoritarian, and the implication was that to be authoritarian was to be psychologically disturbed. An alternative and better conclusion, we think, is that the greater tendency of poor people to feel untrusting or unsafe was evidence not of disturbed psyches but of the unpleasant realities of their environment.

[2] T. W. Adorno et al., *The Authoritarian Personality* (New York: Norton, 1969), pp. 248–49. The theory of working-class authoritarianism is found in Seymour M. Lipset, *Political Man* (Garden City, New York: Doubleday, 1963), chap. 4.

[3] *The Anguish of Change* (New York: Norton, 1973), p. 168.

[4] Angus Campbell, Philip E. Converse, Willard L. Rodgers, *The Quality of American Life: Perceptions, Evaluations, and Satisfactions* (New York: Russell Sage Foundation, 1976), p. 239.

In California, Howard Jarvis led a tax revolt, one of the ways in which citizens express dissatisfaction with government.

The idea that trust is a mark of good citizenship

Good citizens trust their government to do what's right. A large body of research shows that the feelings of Americans about their political leaders and institutions have shifted from trust to cynicism. We began this chapter by noting that 65 percent of the people (in 1978) distrusted their government. This is more than twice the level of distrust (23 percent) that existed when the subject was first examined in 1958. The implication drawn from these findings is that the decline in trust is very unhealthy for the political system. And for most students of public opinion, the big question is: can our form of government survive without public trust? Ronald Inglehart, a noted authority on the subject, says in reference to 1974 findings, "If these levels of distrust persisted for long, it probably *would* undermine support for the present form of government. . . . Fortunately, however, we can probably assume that 1974 represented a low point. . . ."[5] Even without agreeing with Thomas Jefferson's radical idea that all governments should be overthrown and reshaped at least once every 20 years, the findings on distrust can be differently interpreted. In view of the performance of American leaders during the Vietnam War, the Watergate scandal, and the Korean bribery program, could one not conclude with equal reason that a decrease in trust was very healthy, that the unhealthy condition would have been one of continued trust—a sad commentary on the ability of the people to evaluate the world around them? And rather than worrying about whether the system can persist in its established form, perhaps the concern should be about how long people should put up with a system they can't trust.

[5] *The Silent Revolution: Changing Values and Political Styles Among Western Publics* (Princeton, N.J.: Princeton University Press, 1977), p. 307.

The taxpayers revolt of 1978 may have been the beginning of just that sort of revolution. Voters in California approved, by a two-to-one margin, a constitutional amendment reducing their property tax by 60 percent. Fifteen school bond issues failed in Ohio and antitax candidates won party nominations in several states for governor, senator, and representative. Tax reduction became the issue of 1978, and voters expressed lack of confidence in government leaders and policies by seeking to withhold large amounts of tax dollars from them.

Interpreting the failure of Americans to participate in politics

Most people are too uninterested and too ignorant about public affairs to get involved. This is a third notion that seems to be supported by research on public opinion, but we regard it as a distorted emphasis if not an outright misconception. In a 1978 national survey, for example, only 34 percent of American adults could identify Cyrus Vance as the secretary of state, and only 30 percent knew that the term of a member of the House of Representatives is two years. On the other hand, 69 percent knew that Democrats outnumbered Republicans in the House, and 79 percent could name Walter Mondale as Vice-President.[6] To the degree that some of the questions reveal lack of information, this may reflect on political leaders and institutions rather than on the people. Perhaps we should emphasize the failure to interest the people, rather than the people's failure to become interested.

A smaller percentage of citizens vote in American elections than in those of any other democracy. We have no evidence that Americans are inherently dumber or more apathetic than other people, so perhaps their failure to vote means that the choices they are given are not good enough, not relevant enough to their needs.

Just as we hope this book will help clear up misconceptions about the American political system, we also hope it will help clear up these misconceptions about the American citizen. If any terrible defects exist in one or the other, we would prefer to find them in the system rather than in the people. Institutions may not be easy to change, but they are at least a more inviting target for reform than human nature itself.

SOME BASIC CONCEPTS OF POLITICS

Power, politics, and/or government are terms that we all use in everyday conversation. We also talk, from time to time, about business, religion, sex, and sports, and everyone recognizes when the subject is being changed from one of these topics to another. To be sure, they sometimes overlap—tennis is a sport for most players, but it is business for Chris Evert. Sex is usually

---

[6] These findings are from a March 1978 national survey conducted by the National Opinion Research Center of the University of Chicago. The data were supplied by Professor John Sullivan of the University of Minnesota, a principal investigator for whom the survey was conducted.

The American political system stimulates fewer citizens to vote than does any other democracy.

for recreation or procreation, but it is also "the world's oldest profession." Without expecting to draw a firm line between politics and other activities, we can identify those activities that are political in nature, and we can specify the circumstances under which a normally nonpolitical act becomes political.

Power

The following exchange took place between President Nixon *(P)* and presidential counsel John W. Dean III *(D)* in the Oval Office of the White House on September 15, 1972:

P. This is a war . . . I wouldn't want to be on the other side right now. Would you?

D. Along that line, one of the things I've tried to do, I have begun to take notes on a lot of people who are emerging as less than our friends because this will be over some day and we shouldn't forget the way some of them have treated us.

P. I want the most comprehensive notes on all those who have tried to do us in . . . they are asking for it and they are going to get it. We have not used the power in these first four years as you know. We have never used it. We have not used the Bureau [the Federal Bureau of Investigation] and we have not used the Justice Department but things are going to change now. And they are either going to do it right or go.

D. What an exciting prospect.

P. Thanks. It has to be done. We have been [adjective deleted] fools. . . .[7]

The above conversation is unmistakably about *power,* and it highlights several important aspects of that concept:

First, power is not something that can be handed to a politician at the swearing in ceremony. Rather, it is a relationship. Someone must wield it; someone must respond to it. In the conversation above, Nixon and Dean are talking about the power of the President and his staff in relation to two other sets of people: those on "the other side" in the 1972 campaign and the officials of the Department of Justice (including the FBI).

Second, a power relationship is asymmetric in that the parties involved are unequal. One of the parties (the superordinate) controls while the other (the subordinate) is controlled. In this case, we have the "exciting prospect" of Nixon's ability to influence the behavior of lots of others—"they are . . . going to do it right. . . ."

Third, the power relationship disappears if the subordinate person in the relationship refuses to behave as directed. Therefore, some sanction (reward or punishment) must be available to enforce the desired behavior. Those who had emerged as "less than our friends" were "going to get it." And the mechanism for seeing that they got it was available in the FBI and the Department of Justice as a whole. Officials in these agencies could be expected to comply; otherwise, they would "go."

Fourth, those being controlled or punished for resisting control often become restless in their subordinate status. Power relations, therefore, are often characterized by struggle. In its most unadulterated form, as Nixon put it, "this is a war."

Power is thus a relationship supported by positive and negative sanctions in which one person can control the behavior of another.[8] Differences over who should exercise power and who should receive the rewards and punishments are what politics is all about.

Government

The power relations of "politics" or "government" are those in which some people fix policies or rules of behavior that others are obligated to follow. Government is thus synonymous with politics. In its broadest sense, *government* or *politics* is the process by which rules of behavior are set up and enforced. For our purposes, this definition is too broad—it takes in such institutions as the family, business corporations, labor unions, churches, and social

[7] *The New York Times, The White House Transcripts* (New York: Bantam, 1974), p. 63.

[8] See H. D. Lasswell, *Power and Personality* (New York: Norton, 1976), p. 10; and H. H. Gerth and C. W. Mills, trans. and eds., *From Max Weber: Essays in Sociology* (New York: Oxford University Press, 1946), p. 180; Robert A. Dahl, *Modern Political Analysis,* 3rd ed. (Englewood Cliffs, N.J.: Prentice-Hall, 1976), chap. 3. For the concept of power as persuasion, see Richard Neustadt, *Presidential Power: The Politics of Leadership with Reflections on Johnson and Nixon* (New York: Wiley, 1976).

clubs as well as the formal government. When club members tell newcomers how to behave, they are exercising governing power in the broad sense. But clubs rules and regulations are certainly not what we have in mind when we speak of "the government." So we shall have to narrow the definition down to the process by which rules or laws are made and applied to society as a whole.

Our definition of formal or *public* government, then, might read like this: *Government* or *politics* consists of structures and processes through which rules or policies are authoritatively determined for society as a whole.[9] These rules may be directed toward realizing such contradictory goals as achieving peace or military victory, widespread prosperity or class privilege, freedom of press or government censorship. But whatever its goals, public government differs from private governing agencies in that it can legitimately rely on physical compulsion, which means that its rules are *authoritatively* prescribed. Furthermore, only the policies of the government apply to *society as a whole.* If a man loses faith in the creed of his church, even its power to excommunicate him no longer operates as a punishment; but if he loses faith in the policies of his government, its power to put him in jail remains very much in force.

If you are in the habit of thinking about government as nothing more than official agencies and the legal decisions they make, you may need to reread the above definition. We are using the term in a more comprehensive sense, to include all the interactions that influence public policy or its enforcement. We use *politics* and *the political system* to mean the same as *government* because it is easier to think of these terms as referring to more than formal institutions and legal codes.[10] Our analysis will include not only official agencies like Congress, but also informal structures like political parties, the media of communication, business corporations, and social classes. We shall be concerned with laws as formal policies, but we shall also be concerned with popular values that informally govern our behavior. The political system includes all the activities that shape public policy and that determine how it is enforced.

POLITICAL ACTIVITIES AS A POLITICAL SYSTEM

We have focused thus far on the *political* aspect of the concept "political system." But what is meant by *system?* The notion of "system" is common to all of us; we talk easily about such things as a stereo system or a school system and have at least a vague notion of what the term means. Let us look at the concept of "political system" more carefully.

[9] David Easton, *The Political System: An Inquiry into the State of Political Science* (New York: Knopf, 1953), chap. 5. For a critique of Easton and an alternative view, see Harry Eckstein, "Authority Patterns: A Structural Basis for Political Inquiry," *American Political Science Review,* 67 (December 1973), 1142–61.

[10] Gabriel A. Almond and James S. Coleman, eds., *The Politics of the Developing Areas* (Princeton, N.J.: Princeton University Press, 1960), pp. 5–9.

The concept of a political system

Political theorist Carl J. Friedrich has offered this definition of a system:

When several parts that are distinct and different from each other compose a whole, bearing a defined functional relation to each other which establishes a mutual dependence of these parts upon each other so that the destruction of one entails the destruction of the whole, then such a constellation shall be called a system.[11]

This definition is broad enough to apply to any sort of active system—a solar system, the human body, an economic system, or of course, a political system. Like any system of activity, the American political system has certain basic attributes simply by virtue of the fact that it is a system.

First, a system has identifiable parts or elements of which it is composed. The elements of a political system are *political actions*—all those activities that bear on the formation and enforcement of policies. These activities tend to structure themselves in political roles and political groups. In the United States, for example, our elaborate system of courts settles disputes in the application of public policy to particular individuals. In more primitive cultures, these activities are less elaborately developed, but even so, they are carried out. Political structure appears to exist in all human societies, despite differences in the nature of the structures.[12]

Second, a system constitutes an identifiable whole. It has recognizable boundaries, and the different activities of the system are to some degree integrated or coordinated. For example, when a church endorses a given code of behavior, it is normally engaged in religious activity. But if the endorsement calls for legislation to prohibit the sale of contraceptives or alcoholic beverages, it has directly entered the political system. In addition to recognizable boundaries, the idea of an identifiable whole also implies some measure of cooperation among the different units of the system. Even though they may be performing different kinds of activities, one element of a system cannot operate in complete disregard of the activities of other elements without disrupting or destroying the system. The American constitutional system might have been threatened when President Nixon ordered the Office of Economic Opportunity abolished in 1973, despite statutes by Congress providing for it. When the courts ruled that the congressional provisions could not be ignored, Nixon accepted the court decision. Had he refused to abide by the court ruling, the American political system would have been significantly modified.

Third, the units of a system are interdependent—each part affects and is affected by all the other parts. Although some division of labor exists in all systems, the performance of each part is to some extent a function of the performance of the other parts. Yet Friedrich's stipulation that the destruction of one part of a system entails the destruction of the whole seems to go too

[11] *Man and His Government: An Empirical Theory of Politics* (New York: McGraw-Hill, 1963), p. 25.
[12] See Gabriel A. Almond, "A Functional Approach to Comparative Politics," in Almond and Coleman, eds., *The Politics of the Developing Areas*, pp. 10–11.

far.[13] Systems tend to persist and to adapt to changes both in their environment and within themselves. If the planet Venus were destroyed, every other part of the solar system would be affected, but the system itself would persist in a modified form. The American political system might similarly survive the loss of the Senate. The loss of both houses of Congress, however, would probably lead to the creation of an entirely different political system. The interdependence of all elements within a system does not mean, then, that every element is equally vital to its survival.

General characteristics of a political system

What are the other consequences of viewing American politics as a system? Some of the more important are illustrated in Fig. 1 · 1, which diagrams the preliminary features of a political system. (See p. 18.)

To begin with, the area in white represents a political system. It indicates that political life is separable, at least analytically, from other activities and systems. Second, in viewing politics as a system, we are forced to recognize that "the operation of no one part can be fully understood without reference to the way in which the whole itself operates."[14] Figure 1 · 1 therefore shows the entire political system as linked together in a pattern of interrelated activities. Third, the operation of the entire political system (and therefore of its parts) can be understood only in terms of the environment in which it operates. The shaded area around the political system suggests that it is a part of a broader culture by which it is influenced, and which it, in turn, influences. Fourth, the system's ungeometric shape and its irregular boundaries mean that, although it is identifiable, the area of society occupied by the system varies with circumstances and with the activities of other systems. Before 1965, for example, payment for health care was a private matter between doctor and patient. Within 10 years, however, the national Medicare program was paying about half the health bills of people over 65. The national-state Medicaid program was helping about one-third of the poor to cover their medical bills. Although the United States was the last industrialized democracy to bring medical insurance into the political system, the rising costs of medical care suggest that the overlap between the political system and health-care system will increase.

Figure 1 · 1 is also designed to suggest the basic processes of government. As a system of activities, American government—any government, for that

[13] Professor Friedrich is aware of this: despite the unqualified nature of the statement of mutual dependence in his definition, in his book he immediately thereafter distinguishes between constitutive elements, which are necessary for survival of the system, and supplementary elements, which may play important roles but which could be lost without the entire system necessarily being destroyed.

[14] David Easton, "An Approach to the Analysis of Political Systems," *World Politics,* 9 (April 1957), 383. Although our diagram of a political system departs from Professor Easton's, this entire discussion has benefited greatly from his work. His concept of the political system is further elaborated in *A Framework for Political Analysis* (Englewood Cliffs, N.J.: Prentice-Hall, 1965) and *A Systems Analysis of Political Life* (New York: Wiley, 1965).

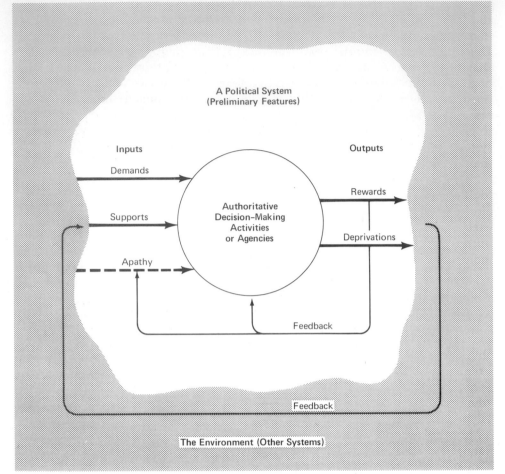

A Political System
(Preliminary Features)

Inputs

Demands

Supports

Apathy

Authoritative
Decision–Making
Activities
or Agencies

Outputs

Rewards

Deprivations

Feedback

Feedback

The Environment (Other Systems)

FIG. 1 · 1

matter—is made up of an interrelated set of activities, all bearing on the making
and carrying out of policies. This broad function is what we mean by *governance,* or the act of governing. But this is such a general statement that it
offers few clues to analysis of American politics. Figure 1 · 1 attempts to break
up this all-encompassing function into different stages of political activity.
(In the next section, we shall add more specific functions to the diagram.)

At the core of the governmental process is *authoritative decision making,*
performed by identifiable political agencies or structures. This is represented
by the "charmed circle" at the center of the political system. In a tribe ruled
largely by custom, these official decision-making activities may not be highly
structured; decisions are made by a few elders who define and interpret the
tribe's customs. In the United States, on the other hand, the highest levels
of political leadership are occupied by full-time politicians with distinctive
titles, office buildings, seals of office, and all the other paraphernalia of authority.
They are visibly engaged in the decision-making activities by which we **are**
governed.

But keep in mind that the boundary lines between the environment and the political system and between the political system and its authoritative decision-making activities are designed to identify activities, not people. Despite the constant attention of the mass media, even a President can hope that part of his life will remain purely private and therefore outside the area of the political system. Similarly, some of his political activity will represent not *authoritative* decision making but efforts to influence other decision makers, as it does when he appeals for public support of legislation he has proposed to Congress. Thus the official decision makers act partly outside the political system, mostly within it, and partly in the core area of authoritative decision making itself.

We must remember that Fig. 1 · 1 oversimplifies complex realities in order to draw attention to the principal features of the system. The decision-making circle could be broken up into a number of "departments" and "agencies," each connected to the others by crisscrossing arrows representing *inputs* and *outputs*. No matter what their internal relationships, however, all these departments and agencies are engaged in authoritative decision making.

Inputs

The term *input* refers to activities that keep the system going. The most obvious forms of inputs are *demands* on the decision makers—protest demonstrations, letters to congressmen, lawsuits challenging local ordinances, applications from college professors seeking research grants. These and countless other citizens' demands are often channeled through interest groups and political parties. Such demands may be generated outside the political system. A hurricane in Texas or an earthquake in Alaska will dramatically demonstrate how nonpolitical events create conditions that are translated into political demands. Political demands may also be generated within the political system. For example, the President urges Congress to pass a particular bill. In recognition of this pattern of influence, the diagram includes feedback arrows to represent inputs on decision makers from within the political system as well as from the nonpolitical environment.

Supports are another form of input. These include attitudes and behavior supporting the political system at four different levels: (1) the political community, (2) the form or structure of government, (3) the current administration or "authorities," and (4) particular governmental policies. Lack of support is most serious at the first level. Lacking widespread support at this basic level, a political system can hardly exist, as has been demonstrated by the turmoil in some new African states where tribal loyalties were still stronger than national awareness. Americans learn to support "America the Beautiful" so early that support at this level is largely taken for granted in the United States. But an occasional exception reminds us that the American system does not enjoy universal support even at the level of the political community. Rejecting the "nation-state mentality," a protest leader of the 1960s said, "I despise any flag, not just the American flag. It's a symbol of a piece of land

Political demands are sometimes voiced in mass demonstrations.

that's considered more important than the lives on it. . . . You see, it's not a change of government we want but a new kind of society. . . ."[15]

At the second level, the form (structure) of government also enjoys broad support in the United States. As noted earlier, the founding fathers and the constitutional system they established are held almost in awe. Most citizens don't really know much about either the founding fathers or the Constitution, of course, but they patriotically revere them all the same. Disrespect for current officeholders may someday turn into the search for a form of government that might produce better results, but no trend in that direction has been discerned.

Truly major drop-offs in support in the United States apply only to the third level—the current administration. The small minority (32 percent) who approved of the way Harry Truman was performing as President in 1946,

[15] Joan Baez, as quoted in *Playboy,* June 1970, pp. 56, 60.

contrasted with his election to a new term in 1948, demonstrates that support of officeholders varies widely over short periods of time. During their first year in office, Gerald Ford and Jimmy Carter each dropped from approval by 71 percent to approval by a small majority.[16] These ups and downs do not necessarily induce similar changes in the more basic attitudes toward the political community and the form of government.

Support for new policies, the fourth level, may not be widespread, although most Americans at least accept official decisions as legitimate. But the input of supports at this fourth level goes beyond acceptance. It usually includes belief that the policies are *needed* and that they will *work*. The most obvious exceptions are attempts to regulate individual behavior on moral grounds: prohibition of the manufacture, transportation, or sale of alcoholic beverages during the 1920s; prohibitions on contraceptive devices in a number of states; and prohibition today not only of the manufacture, transportation, or sale, but also of the possession or use of marijuana and various other drugs. The national ban on alcoholic beverages was ended by constitutional amendment, and the state bans on contraceptives were abolished by court decisions. The attempt to impose prohibition of alcohol on a large minority that flatly refused to have its private behavior dictated by law produced an increase in crime and disrespect for law but not an end to drinking. Because laws against "soft" drugs are having the same effects today, these laws have been modified or repealed in a number of states.

The third input identified in our diagram is *apathy*. It operates in more indirect fashion than the demand and support inputs, and we recognize this by using a broken line to indicate its linkage to decision-making activities. Nevertheless, widespread apathy may be almost as important as active demands on government in shaping public policy. In recent presidential elections, for example, the following percentages of eligible voters said they didn't care very much who won the election: 42 percent (in 1976); 38 percent (in 1972); 40 percent (in 1968); 31 percent (in 1964).[17] This apathy is not the same as support, although it implies passive acceptance of basic governmental arrangements. With respect to particular policies, it is entirely neutral; but it gives decision makers freedom to act without concern for public reactions, and that freedom increases in proportion to the number of apathetic citizens. In an indirect fashion, then, the degree of apathy is important to the way a political system performs. Conversely, the way a system performs is an important determinant of the level of apathy among its citizens.

The *outputs* of a political system are authoritative decisions or public policies. The substance of these policy outputs may be identified, as in Fig. 1 · 1, as *rewards* and *deprivations*. Rewards are the satisfactions, whether tangible or psychological, that individuals get from policies. These may vary from a farmer's gratification for a thousand-dollar subsidy to a veteran's pleasure

---

[16] "Opinion Roundup," *Public Opinion,* March–April 1978, p. 28. Also see George H. Gallup, *The Gallup Poll, 1935–1971* (New York: Random House, 1972), I, 604.

[17] *The CPS 1976 American National Election Study,* I, 16. For earlier elections, see CPS codebooks of the appropriate years.

over the official observance of Veterans' Day. Deprivations are, obversely, the dissatisfactions, both tangible and psychological, that people experience as a result of governmental policies. They may range from a criminal's sentence to life in prison to an atheist's disgust with "In God We Trust" on coins. Simply put, the decision makers translate demands, supports, and apathy (inputs) into rules and policies (outputs). The objective of the rewards and deprivations contained in these policies is to maintain order and promote the survival of the system.

The effects of inputs show up in the way the political system operates. The effects of outputs show up in the impact of its operation on the environment. National tax policies, for example, deeply affect the economic system. The arrow in our diagram representing the rewards and deprivations of public policy, therefore, moves from the system into the general environment. Policies do more, however, than spill rewards and deprivations into the society. Every reward and deprivation affects someone, and those who are affected may respond with new demands or supports (inputs). A Supreme Court decision approving the busing of children to achieve racial integration of public schools, for example, quickly led to demands for a constitutional amendment to prohibit busing.[18] This translation of policy outputs into new inputs is called feedback.

Feedback may also operate more directly from one government agency to another. An arrow in Fig. 1 · 1 shows that direct feedback inside the political system goes from outputs back to the decision-making circle. When the Supreme Court interprets an act of Congress—and most dramatically, on the rare occasions when it rules an act of Congress unconstitutional—the decision has a direct effect on Congress.

Every government decision carries both rewards and deprivations. When an irate citizen seeks a court order to prevent her neighbor from practicing his trombone at 2:00 A.M., the court's decision will please one of the parties and displease the other. If the judge grants the order, the trombone player will lose the freedom to practice when he chooses; if the citizen's petition is denied, she loses not only the case but undisturbed sleep. The rewards to the winner, whatever the decision, are equally obvious. But what if the judge refuses for some reason to give a decision? Even then a decision has been reached, so far as the citizens are concerned, in favor of music and against sleep.

That the failure of government to act involves a decision (which is viewed as a deprivation by some and as a reward by others) is obvious when we are talking about a lawsuit. But it is not so obvious that the same reasoning applies to the refusal of *any* government agency to decide a question put to it. Under the rules of the United States Senate, for example, a minority of members (40 percent plus one) may prevent a majority from bringing a proposal to a vote. Because a minority can block action, it has at least negative control over policy. Such *a refusal to decide involves a decision itself*—a decision to continue the status quo, which is rewarding to some but not to others.

---

[18] *Swann v. Charlotte-Mecklenburg Board of Education*, 402 U.S. 1 (1972).

Functions of the political system

Up to this point, we have talked about the basic elements of politics. We have not been concerned about the *functions* that make a given set of activities recognizable as a political system. Nor have we explained what we mean by *function*. Like so many words, this one is used with a variety of meanings. We refer to a college dance or a cocktail party as a "social function." But when we talk of the "functions of government," we certainly do not have public gatherings of this sort in mind.

Another usage identifies functions with *motives* or *purposes*. From this point of view, the function of an act of Congress could be determined by finding out what Congress intended to accomplish when it passed the act. But from the point of view of political science, the *function* of a law is not necessarily the same as its *purpose*. The function of anything is understood in terms of its *effect*. We may undertake an activity with a clear purpose in mind, only to find that the final effect or outcome of the activity is quite different from what we had expected. Thus our *purpose* in going to college may simply be to get a college degree or to kill time between leaving high school and entering the family business. However, the effect—that is, the *function*—of going to college may be the stimulation of permanent intellectual curiosity or the development of new career plans. To determine the real function of college for an individual, we ask, "What would the student's life have been without such an experience?" To clarify the primary functions of government we may ask the very same sort of question, "What would our lives be without government?"

In the broadest sense, then, *functions* refers to the effects or consequences of an activity. We shall view functions less broadly: they will refer only to effects or consequences that promote the survival of the system. *Dysfunctions* refers to consequences that tend to disrupt or destroy the system.[19] The basic output functions of the political system are fairly obvious; it must

1. *Furnish some general rules* or policies to maintain order and satisfy demands on the system.
2. Carry out its rules or policies; *apply them* in actual practice.
3. *Settle disputes* among citizens, as the one between the late-night trombonist and his neighbor.

Figure 1 · 2, with these and other basic functions added, represents a more complete diagram of a political system than does Fig. 1 · 1. The three functions we have mentioned—rule making, application of rules, and settlement of disputes—are outputs or consequences of decision-making activity. They are easy concepts for Americans to grasp, because each tends to be centered in a highly visible political agency—the Congress, the President and the bureaucracy he heads, and the Supreme Court and lower courts. Whatever the form of government, these three output functions will somehow be performed. By adding these functions to our diagram of a political system,

[19] See Robert K Merton, *Social Theory and Social Structure* (New York: Free Press, 1949), p. 50.

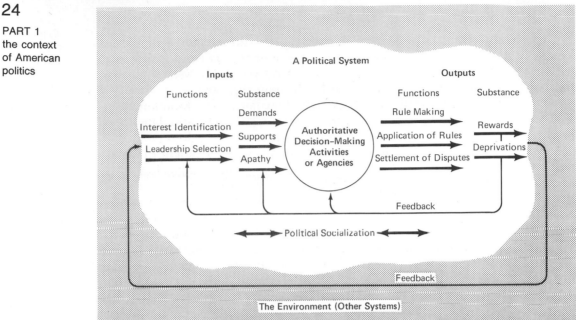

FIG. 1 · 2

we identify another dimension of the system's outputs. The decisions of a political system will thus be viewed as carrying the substance of rewards and deprivations and as performing the functions of rule making, application of rules, and settlement of disputes. Other dimensions of output might also be identified; for example, the kinds of goals toward which policy is aimed. The diagram should therefore be regarded as a representation of only some of the key features of a political system, not as a complete model.

The function of *political socialization* is presented in Fig. 1 · 2 at the base of the political system, between outputs and inputs. It is there because political socialization is, in some respects, an output of the system and, in other respects, an input. (All aspects of the system are interrelated, but political socialization is so much a part of both inputs and outputs that it cannot be identified with one over the other.)

Political socialization is the training of people in ways of thinking, feeling, and behaving that are characteristic of a political culture.[20] Political training is, of course, mixed in with broader learning experiences through which people acquire the whole range of values and practices of their society, from what and how they eat to what and how they worship. The early literature on political socialization regarded it as "the process of induction into the political system."[21] But this implies that the socialization process ends when a person reaches adulthood and is "inducted" into the political system. In fact, political

[20] The literature on political socialization from which this definition is derived is considered more fully in chap. 4.

[21] Gabriel A. Almond, "A Functional Approach to Comparative Politics," in Almond and Coleman, eds., *The Politics of the Developing Areas,* p. 27.

socialization continues throughout life. Americans who were adults at the time of the Great Depression in 1929, for example, were profoundly influenced in their political views—politically socialized—by depression experiences. As we shall see in chapter 3, the socializing experiences of Americans under colonial rule transformed people who had grown up as "His Majesty's Loyal and Obedient Servants" into revolutionary "Americans."

From this perspective, political socialization is an output function of the political system. Political systems tend to perpetuate their values and practices. They do this by developing new members who share these values and follow those practices. In all political systems, children are somehow taught the political processes and beliefs of their society. In Plato's *Republic*, political socialization can easily be recognized as an output function of government because children are to be brought up by an official agency of government rather than by their parents. In real political systems, the process is considerably more informal. Children learn the normal way of doing things (including political things) from observation and imitation in informal contacts with others. The process begins in the family, is continued with playmates, and—in more highly developed countries—is furthered by formal schooling, television programs, reading, and other contacts with the world far beyond the family.

Patriotism is encouraged by teaching children about major institutions such as Congress.

Irene Springer.

We continue to acquire political attitudes as adults through job contacts, marriage, and other experiences. Except for the public schools, these socializing agencies are not part of the official structure of government. But even the family is acting as a part of the political system when it imparts political knowledge and attitudes.

Although political socialization is thus an output of every political system, it can also be viewed as part of the input activities of the system. The kinds of demands and supports that enter the system, the general level of apathy, and the aspects of the system toward which citizens are indifferent—all these are heavily influenced by political socialization. Most American children grow up with the idea that American government is democratic and that democracy is the best system of government. Beyond this general set of facts and values, however, they may learn quite different things. A child whose parents never discuss politics will probably be a different sort of citizen from another whose parents insist that all politicians are crooked, and both will be different from a third child whose parents pin campaign buttons on his or her diaper.

Two other broad functions are essential features of a political system: *identification of interests* in the population and *selection of leaders* or official decision makers. These are more exclusively input functions than is political socialization.

Every political system must somehow identify the basic interests that unite and divide its citizens.[22] This function is performed in quite different ways and by quite different kinds of political structures from one country to another. In the United States, it is difficult for a member of Congress to identify the needs and desires of constituents, partly because of the flood of conflicting demands made on Congress. The member gets a steady flow of mail from individual constituents; hears from scores of pressure groups in and out of the home district; receives advice from local and national party organizations; and reads about his or her duty in the newspapers. The massive census program carried out every 10 years by the government may also be viewed as a way of identifying the interests to which government must respond. In a dictatorship, the flow of communication from individuals and groups to the decision makers may not be so free as in a democracy. Nevertheless, every government, if it is to remain viable, must somehow identify the conditions in society on which it must act.

The second input function—selection of leaders—is equally universal. The process is very simple in some societies: the eldest male of a particular family may be designated to hold the highest office. In such a system, leader-

---

[22] Our discussion of functions has benefited greatly from Gabriel A. Almond, "A Functional Approach to Comparative Politics," in Almond and Coleman, eds., *The Politics of the Developing Areas,* pp. 3–64. We differ in four respects. Almond treats "political recruitment" as a specialized form of political socialization; we use instead the broader and separate concept of "leadership selection." He regards political socialization as an input function; we think it cannot be properly understood without also recognizing its importance as an output function. We omit one of his input functions, "political communication," because communication is inherent in both the substance and the functions of all political activities. Moreover, communication is as much a part of output activities as it is of input activities. Finally, Almond talks of "interest articulation" and "interest aggregation" as two separate functions. Since some combination of interests has occurred in virtually every expression of interests, and since aggregated interests are articulated, this does not seem to be a meaningful distinction. Hence we use the broader concept, "interest identification."

ship positions are ascribed by one's status rather than achieved through competition. In modern democracies, millions of people, not just one, are technically eligible for the highest office. The informal norms of the system usually reduce the active prospects to a mere handful, but the surviving candidates have passed a lengthy series of tests that many more have failed. More people are elected to more offices in the United States than in any other democracy, and lower-level positions are frequently available to almost anybody who will take them. Political parties perform the central tasks in selecting American leaders; but pressure groups, government agencies, the media, and the voting public all play important parts.

AN ANALYTICAL FRAMEWORK FOR EXPLAINING AMERICAN POLITICS

We promised to try to replace myths with explanations of American politics. Scholars occasionally distinguish explanation from "mere description"; but when you stop to think about it, *mere* description is impossible. If we started out to describe rather than explain American politics, what would we describe? You might say that an entirely descriptive work would simply present "facts" with no interpretation. But a "fact" is simply one particular characteristic chosen by the observer from an infinite number of characteristics of the concrete social world. The very act of deciding which facts to present therefore requires an interpretation of what's important and what's unimportant. Once you begin making decisions on what's important, you have entered into the task of explanation.

Explanation as theory

Explanation reaches the level of *theory* when it becomes precise and applicable to a number of different facts. Notice that we are not talking here about "theory" as the word is sometimes used in popular conversation. In the statement "that's the theory, but here's how the fraternity system really works," *theory* is used to mean an official or accepted but misleading explanation. This is not what physicists, economists, chemists, or political scientists have in mind as they work to develop explanatory theory. We would be horrified to think that college students might complete a course on American politics with the lament that their reading was "good in theory but inapplicable in practice." In the search for understanding of the world we live in, theories that fail to explain actual practices are simply bad theories.

The systems framework as "near-theory"

Despite great strides by political scientists in explaining an ever-increasing range of political phenomena, the discipline has not yet arrived at a single, unifying theory that can account for the vast range of political activities. But it has developed the concept of system as a "near-theory," an analytical framework that helps us decide which facts are important and which relationships among facts bear examination.

This book is organized around the view that American politics comprise a system of activities. We have already employed the concept to specify which "facts" we need to examine—those that affect authoritative decision making for American society. Because any system of activities responds to the environment in which it operates, we shall consider next the context of American politics. The second part of the book is specifically concerned with the entry of demands, supports, and apathy into the system—who wants and needs what? Third, we shall focus on decision making as the central activity of the system, the process by which inputs are converted into policy outputs—who decides what and how? Throughout, we shall consider the outputs of rewards and deprivations that accompany every decision—who gets helped, who gets hurt? In analyzing these substantive activities, we shall focus in each case on the structures, both formal and informal, through which they are carried out and on their consequences for the political system. The final part of the book will examine individual rights and liberties as outputs of the system, consider different kinds of policies, and then return to the misconceptions noted earlier in this chapter.

The analytic focus will be on the central question of politics: Who gets helped, who gets hurt?

SUMMARY

Americans hold many misconceptions about their government. They revere the "founding fathers" who created the government and wrote the Constitution, for example, but distrust today's politicians. Other popular misconceptions range from "The American way is the only way" and "Capitalism is the cornerstone of democracy" to "Government is evil" and "The ruling few dictate policy in America."

The misconceptions of political scientists are more about the people than about the political system. When people don't behave as expected, the suggestion is that something is wrong with them, rather with than the expectation. And when people are fearful, distrusting, or uninterested, scholars sometimes forget that this may simply mean those people have something to fear and distrust but nothing worthy of their interest.

Actual concepts of American government are not as well known as are the misconceptions. The concepts include *power*—an unequal relationship in which one party controls and one is controlled. *Politics* involves differences in the control of power. *Government* and politics are one and the same—each party wants the power to make laws that apply to society. Authoritative decision making is a basic process that makes up what we call a *political system*, and that system is kept going by activities called inputs. Outputs take the form of decisions or public policies. These policies always help some and hurt others. The functions of the political system can be seen in the actual effects of laws, rather than in their original purpose.

American
culture and
ideas
of
democracy

Every government policy helps some people and hurts others. And each policy is arrived at through difficult decisions made in what we have identified as a political system. The nature of such a system is enormously influenced by all the features of the broader society of which it is a part. We can't look at all these other features—economic, religious, social, artistic, recreational, educational—but we can at least look at the broad environment of American politics. We can understand American politics better if we place it in the context of the American culture and ideas about democracy.

POLITICS AS A CULTURAL HERITAGE

In a Mr. Universe contest, we know in advance that American judges would not award first prize to a young man with extremely long fingernails, with an elaborately powdered wig, or with dainty and unmuscled limbs. Although each of these attributes has been looked upon as appealing in some times and places, Americans value huge biceps and rippling muscles. Similarly, in a Miss America contest, we can safely forecast that American judges will not vote for the young lady with the most elaborate tattoos, the most elongated lips, or the most elegantly deformed feet. Although each of these attributes is essential to true "beauty" among some people, Americans value different abnormalities, such as large breasts in combination with unusually small waists.

If beauty, which seems at first thought to be an inherent and universally recognizable quality, is subject to such extreme variations, surely political values must also be molded by culture. If we know that someone has been brought up as an American, we should therefore know some of that person's political values. The probability of distinctively American political ideas suggests that we ought to take a closer look at the relationship of culture to politics.

Culture and the way we view the world

Attitudes and habits that seem natural and "right" to us may seem strange or even "wrong" to people in other cultures. These peculiarities are part of a country's culture.

By *culture* we mean the habitual ways of thinking and behaving that characterize a given society—a *way* of thinking, feeling, believing. In other words, the culture of any society is its *social heredity*, the man-made part of the environment, the ideas and habits that are acquired by all normal people in the process of growing up—or of being "socialized"—in that society.[1] Culture therefore includes political behavior no less than sex practices and

---

[1] Among the good general treatments of culture, see Carol R. Ember and Melvin Ember, *Anthropology*, 2nd ed. (Englewood Cliffs, N.J.: Prentice-Hall, 1977); Conrad P. Kottak, *Anthropology: The Exploration of Human Diversity*, 2nd ed. (New York: Random House, 1978).

funeral customs. In a study focused on the government of only one country, this is an important point to bear in mind. It will help us to be more objective in our discussion and will remind us that our way of governing is not the only "natural" one.

Anthropologist Ruth Benedict, on the basis of her long study of different cultural patterns, concluded, "The life history of the individual is first and foremost an accommodation to the patterns and standards traditionally handed down in his community."[2] Our political expectations, hopes, and activities are shaped by the simple fact that most of us have been reared as members of the American society. Journalist Walter Lippmann painfully discovered the meaning of this truth for politics. After an early career in which he had vainly tried to convince Americans of the need for reforms, he concluded that we do not approach politics with an open mind:

For the most part we do not first see, and then define; we define first and then see. In the great blooming, buzzing confusion of the outer world we pick out what our culture has already defined for us, and we tend to perceive that which we have picked out in the form stereotyped for us by our culture.[3]

Opinions are not always built in a neutral fashion, then, on the basis of observation. We have attitudes toward many things we may never observe, from British socialized medicine to capital punishment. And we acquire attitudes toward many other things long before we have direct contact with them. This being the case, we tend later to notice anything that supports the thoughts we have already formed. If we expect college professors to be absent-minded, we see any absent-minded act by a professor as typically professorial. But we might not think anything of these acts when performed by doctors or lawyers. When we have strong feelings about a subject, like capital punishment, we find it hard to accept facts or arguments contrary to those feelings. Our culture not only shapes our *opinions* but also helps determine which *facts* we will notice and how we will interpret them.

When a familiar way of thinking and acting seems to be the right way, and that outlook is reinforced by patriotism, it tends to produce *ethnocentrism* (belief that one's own culture and nation are superior to others). Americans have long ranked high in ethnocentrism.[4] Indeed, despite the fact that only pure Indians can claim to have no immigrants among their ancestors, the people in every new wave of immigration have been regarded as backward and somehow inferior. The most conspicuous failure to respect another culture was, of course, in the enslavement of black Africans and the attempt to eradicate their culture. Less discussed in American history books is the largely successful effort to eliminate not merely the culture of American Indians but these native Americans themselves. Other "different" groups were also treated with disdain. For generations, the epithet "dumb Irish cop" rolled off the tongues of Americans so easily that one might have thought "dumbirish" to

[2] Ruth Benedict, *Patterns of Culture* (New York: Mentor Books, 1934), p. 2.
[3] Walter Lippmann, *Public Opinion* (New York: Macmillan, 1922), p. 81.
[4] See V. O. Key, Jr., *Public Opinion and American Democracy* (New York: Knopf, 1961), p. 42.

be one word. Chinese, Italians, Scandinavians, Poles, Puerto Ricans, and, most recently, Vietnamese have each in their turn been greeted with varying degrees of prejudice and misunderstanding. America was the land of opportunity and progress and the term *un-American* meant both "alien" and "bad." Newcomers needed to become "assimilated," that is, to become like the original white immigrants, in order to win respect and to share in the American dream. These ideas have had tremendous influence in American politics.

Differences and changes in the American culture

In talking about culture and "national character," we sometimes get the impression of a single set of beliefs and traits shared by everybody in a society. The notion of culture should suggest instead a set of *dominant* beliefs and traits. All those immigrants could hardly have agreed that they were less worthy than their predecessors. Perhaps the most striking indication of the power of the dominant beliefs is that so many of the blacks, Irish, and other immigrants *did* agree that the United States offered the assurance of opportunity and progress. Hence they could join earlier immigrants in trying to be-

Despite prejudice against newcomers, America still offers
freedom and opportunity for the oppressed, as it does for these Cubans.   UPI

Celebration of the United States' Bicentennial glorified
the past while the future appeared less promising.

come 100 percent American and in looking down on more backward societies.
The assimilation was never as complete as the "melting pot" image of the
United States suggested, but the belief in America as a land of progress did
seem to be almost universal.

In the late 1960s and early 1970s, however, Americans were suddenly
in disagreement on the true "facts" about American life and on what those
facts meant. Most Americans presumably saw the country in the traditional
way, as "one nation under God, indivisible, with liberty and justice for all."
But many young Americans felt differently. At the extreme they saw "one
police state under the military-industrial complex, deeply divided, with power
in the establishment and injustice for the masses." At a lesser extreme, many
people were becoming aware of continued injustice toward blacks, Hispanics,
and Indians; of widespread poverty, increasing pollution, unlivable ghetto conditions, and increasing criminal violence. On the first Fourth of July in the
Seventies, it was a leading news magazine rather than a radical journal that
reported,

We have become more painfully conscious of what pulls us apart than of what holds
us together, and some of our most sober public and private men are concerned for
our common future. This Independence Day finds the nation in a recession of the
spirit—a psychic downturn so pronounced that the mood may in itself constitute a
kind of American crisis.[5]

[5] *Newsweek,* July 6, 1970, p. 19.

The bicentennial celebration brought a surge of patriotism and a sense of history to Americans. In a display of good will, foreign ships paraded up the Hudson River as thousands watched. The magic and significance of the day kept the tremendous crowds orderly—even reverent—as spectacular fireworks and patriotic music at night ended the festivities.

By the mid1970s, the nation's celebration of its bicentennial brought a greater appearance of unity. Reminders that the country's independence went back 200 years helped maintain faith in its future. In 1975, the Gallup Poll found 76 percent of Americans had a high degree of confidence in the future of the country.[6] But the *quality* of that future no longer looks so bright.

Until the discontent of the 1960s, Americans were always described as optimistic; the culture was said to emphasize progress as inevitable. In 1959, Hadley Cantril, a leading student of public opinion, began to ask questions designed to get specifically at attitudes on national progress. And just as earlier commentators had said on the basis of their intuitive impressions, Cantril's data found that Americans thought their country had improved during the last 5 years and would improve even more during the next 5 years.[7] Cantril asked Americans where they would place their country on a 10-step ladder, with the bottom of the ladder representing "the *worst* possible situation for our country" and with the top rung representing "the *best* possible situation." In 1959, as Fig. 2·1 shows, the responses averaged out to a rating of 6.7, considerably above the midpoint but with room for improvement. Respon-

[6] *The New York Times,* July 13, 1975.

[7] Hadley Cantril, *The Pattern of Human Concerns* (New Brunswick: Rutgers University Press, 1965), pp. 38–39.

dents were also asked, "On which step would you say the U.S. was *about five years ago?*" Then: "Just as your best guess, if things go pretty much as you now expect, where do you think the U.S. will be on the ladder, let us say, *about five years from now?*" In the original 1959 study, the United States was rated at a lower point (6.5) five years earlier and respondents expected it to be at a much higher point (7.4) five years later.

This is the way "the American dream" is supposed to look: a country better off than most and getting better all the time, at an accelerating rate. But findings for the other years in the figure show dramatic changes. By 1971, *the present no longer looked better than the past.* The American assumption of progress was no longer as certain as it had been. Even so, the future was expected to be better, at least as good as the past. By 1978, the pattern had completely changed: not only did the present seem worse than the past, but *the future was expected to be even worse.* The American dream of progress had become the American nightmare of decline.

How can this reversal be explained? As we indicated in chapter 1, public opinion can be used to tell us about political realities rather than about the oddities of popular thinking. The circumstances of Americans, therefore, can be said to have deteriorated over the last two decades. As the findings in Fig. 2 · 1 show, the sharp drop in Americans' view of their country's situation began between 1964 and 1971, a period when the United States became committed to a costly, destructive, unpopular, and unsuccessful war in Vietnam. The lowest point in the ratings of the present situation came in 1974, immedi-

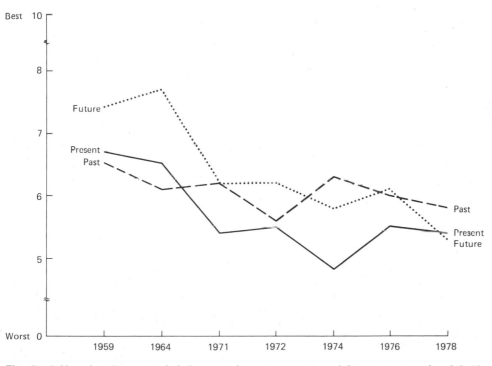

Fig. 2 · 1 How Americans rated their country's past, present, and future, on a scale of 0–10.

ately after Richard Nixon had been forced to resign from the presidency to avoid impeachment and conviction for criminal acts.

Continued inflation, energy crises, pollution problems, and similar concerns also justify as realistic a less optimistic outlook for the future. Note that the ratings do not suggest a nostalgia that makes the past look increasingly good. On the contrary, ratings of the country's past situation have also dropped, although less sharply than ratings of the present and expectations for the future. Americans are not on some nostalgia kick; they are simply experiencing a decreasingly satisfactory situation and being given less reason to be hopeful for the future.

The interpretation of these ratings as realistic and the idea of the American culture as having different meanings for different groups of Americans are both supported by Fig. 2 · 2. In 1978, blacks and whites separately rated the U.S. situation—past, present, and future. Both racial groups see their country at present as more or less midway between the worst and best possible

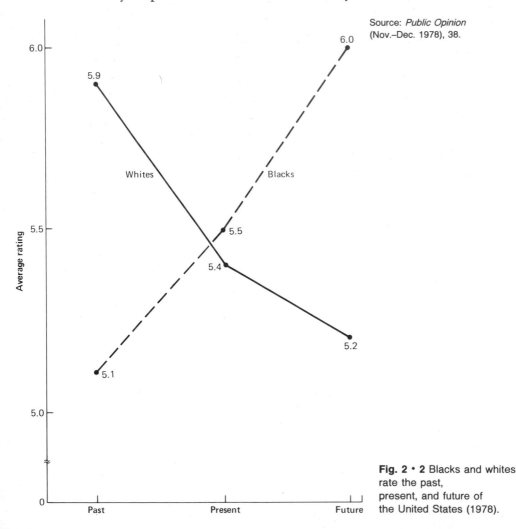

Source: *Public Opinion* (Nov.–Dec. 1978), 38.

Fig. 2 · 2 Blacks and whites rate the past, present, and future of the United States (1978).

situations. But on the past and future, they diverge completely. The stark "X" of the figure is a startlingly clear sign that white and black Americans have been living in different worlds. As the majority racial group, whites fit the new national pattern: they view the past as better than the present and expect the future to be even worse. Blacks have exactly opposite ideas about the past and future situations of the United States: *their* country was worse in the past, and they expect it to be better in the future. The progressive ideal that once characterized all Americans is now characteristic of blacks but not of whites.

The new pessimism of white Americans about their country has not destroyed their basic optimism about their personal situations, at least not yet.[8] But they have become more negative about their leaders. As strange as it seems today, most Americans used to assume that their elected leaders, especially the President, told the truth. Presidents might exaggerate or even lie in political campaigns, but as spokesmen for the nation they could be trusted. In 1960, however, an airplane called the U-2 was shot down on an "intelligence" (spying) flight for the United States over the Soviet Union. When Soviet authorities announced their capture of the U-2 and denounced the United States for violating international law by the flight, President Eisenhower blandly responded that the United States government had nothing whatsoever to do with the flight. Most Americans apparently believed their President; after all, the United States leaders were the "good guys," and they certainly would not violate international law. Unfortunately for Eisenhower's credibility, the pilot of the U-2 failed to take the poison pill that the government had provided for his suicide in the event of capture; the embarrassing survival of the pilot shattered the story fabricated by the Eisenhower administration.

We think this was the point at which America began to lose its innocence. The story was flimsy, but it did not appear so at the time. Even by 1972, when Richard Nixon's staff was ensuring his reelection by means fair and foul, only 38 percent of American adults agreed with the statement, "Over the last few years this country's leaders have consistently lied to the American people." By 1975, the proportion agreeing had reached 68 percent.[9] The period between these surveys saw both the President and Vice-President driven from office for illegal activities that they originally denied. One is therefore tempted to conclude that the minority who failed to agree that their leaders had "consistently lied" must have viewed American leaders as inconsistent liars rather than as truthful. These attitudes are a far cry from the trust of the 1950s; they point to the changing nature of American culture.

The "American character"

The influence of culture on politics is especially obvious to the foreigner, to whom the politics of a new country appears fresh and alien rather than inevitable and natural. The American "national character" has been analyzed

---

[8] See "Opinion Roundup," *Public Opinion*, November–December 1978, p. 39.

[9] The findings are those of Cambridge Survey Research, cited by Anthony Lewis, in *The New York Times*, July 14, 1975.

by an endless series of foreign commentators, and some of them—for example, Alexis de Tocqueville, an early nineteenth-century French visitor[10]—have given us insight into our national peculiarities.

The basic value that has always shaped and confused American social character is the *assertion of equality* coupled with *inequality in practice*. We began with the bold declaration that "all men are created equal." This was in stark contrast to the inequalities of the aristocratic social order in Europe. But obvious class distinctions in America, even among the free population, made the declaration untrue from the outset. In colonial Virginia, the Court of York County fined a tailor for racing his horse against that of a gentleman because it was "contrary to law for a labourer to make a race, being a sport only for gentlemen."[11] At Yale University the student directory listed students by social rank rather than alphabetically until 1765.[12] "Class standing" did not refer to academic status! Thomas Jefferson, a slaveowner, condemned slavery in the original draft of the Declaration of Independence, but the denunciation was deleted from the final version. Examining dictionaries of the period, E. E. Schattschneider concluded that the expression "We, the people of the United States" in the Constitution did not include slaves or "common People" in general. An 1815 dictionary defines *vulgar* as "plebeian, mean, low, the common people." *Villain* meant "plebeian, mean, low, the common people." As Schnattschneider said, "The ladies and gentlemen of the good old days have left us a rich legacy of contempt, a vocabulary of insults once used to express their low opinion of the people."[13]

America's stress on equality and its practice of inequality lead to three basic social characteristics that have long been noted by foreign visitors: *competition or individual achievement, status uncertainty,* and *conformity.* Let us look at each of these. If "station in life" is not fixed by a rigid class system, people must establish it themselves. That is, they must *compete* for it. In America we tend to measure achievement primarily in terms of money. As one anthropologist puts it, "Money comes closer with us than with any other people to being the universal standard of value."[14] "Worth" in the United States, even the worth of a human being, refers to cash value more often than to class position, religious standing, artistic merit, knowledge, or political or social contributions.

Americans are consistent in displaying their worth to the very end. Anthropologists look at burial practices as indicators of cultural values; and in the United States they find that we mix religion, patriotism, and money in competing for status in burial rituals. In 1963, Jessica Mitford's best seller,

[10] See his classic, *Democracy in America* (New York: Vintage Books, 1954), vols. 1, 2. First published in 1835.

[11] Douglas Southall Freeman, *George Washington: A Biography* (New York: Scribner's, 1948), I, 119.

[12] Robert A. Dahl, *Who Governs?* (New Haven, Conn.: Yale University Press, 1961), p. 18. Garry Wills notes the same practice at Harvard in *Inventing America: Jefferson's Declaration of Independence* (Garden City, N.Y.: Doubleday, 1978), p. 35.

[13] E. E. Schattschneider, *Two Hundred Million Americans in Search of a Government* (New York: Holt, 1969), p. 48.

[14] Clyde Kluckhohn, *Mirror for Man: The Relation of Anthropology to Modern Life* (New York: McGraw-Hill, 1949), p. 241.

he has waged cruel war against human nature itself, violating it's most sa-
-cred rights of life & liberty in the persons of a distant people who never of-
fended him, captivating & carrying them into slavery in another hemi-
-sphere, or to incur miserable death in their transportation thither. this
piratical warfare, the opprobrium of infidel powers, is the warfare of the
Christian king of Great Britain. determined to keep open a market
where MEN should be bought & sold he has prostituted his negative
for suppressing every legislative attempt to prohibit or to restrain this
execrable commerce: and that this assemblage of horrors might want no fact
of distinguished die, he is now exciting those very people to rise in arms
among us, and to purchase that liberty of which he has deprived them,
by murdering the people upon whom he also obtruded them: thus paying
off former crimes committed against the liberties of one people, with crimes
which he urges them to commit against the lives of another.]

Jefferson's respect for ordinary people ran contrary to the conventional wisdom of his day.

The American Way of Death, exposed the high costs and deceptive practices of the American funeral industry. In 1976, federal agencies required the funeral industry to be more open and honest in dealing with customers, but American funerals continue to be mind-blowing in costs. The industry is only partially self-serving when it claims to be merely giving the people what they want. High pressure tactics aside, many Americans willingly spend lavishly on final rites in their eternal quest for status by the dollar. A coffin called "George Washington at Valley Forge" competes with one called the "Last Supper." We can buy innerspring mattresses for the "dearly beloved" as well as high fashion negligees, hostess gowns, and brunch coats. And if we have anything left, we can put the deceased in burial shoes with "cushioned soles, but true shoe smartness." John Denver captures it all in his song "Forest Lawn," when he sings of the simple American funeral he desires, including topless dancers with golden wings, fireworks spelling out "Rest in Peace," while he reposes 'neath plastic grass with piped-in tapes of Billy Graham.

The fact that Americans must themselves achieve whatever rank they claim—that they cannot assume it as their birthright—may lead to a sense of *insecurity and uncertainty* about their status. Early foreign observers of American society insisted that our emphasis on equality and opportunity actually led to greater awareness of status than was found among the aristocracies of Europe. Recent research supports this early impression: American school children are more aware of status differences than are school children in England.[15] Status uncertainty has expressed itself in an addiction to titles,

[15] Alan Stern and Donald Searing, "The Stratification Beliefs of English and American Adolescents," *British Journal of Political Science,* 7 (April 1976), 177–201.

"exclusive" resorts, and fraternities and sororities. Commenting on these efforts to create badges of superiority, D. W. Brogan, a British political scientist, explains,

It is only an apparent contradiction in terms to assert that the fundamental democratic and egalitarian character of American life is demonstrated by the ingenuity and persistence shown in inventing marks of difference and symbols of superiority. In a truly class-conscious and caste-dominated society, the marks of difference are universally recognized even if resented. In America, they must be stressed, or they might easily be forgotten. . . .[16]

The conspicuous display of wealth is, of course, the most simple and direct way of advertising one's status, whether dead or alive.[17]

Status uncertainty leads to *conformity*. Europeans have found security in following the standards of earlier generations, but Americans tend to feel insecure unless they are "up-to-date" in clothing, slang, furniture, and child-rearing practices. Conformity usually leads to anxiety, for what is "up-to-date" changes from day to day. The person who misses the cues or who hasn't enough money to buy the latest fashions is in constant danger of being left behind. An English visitor to the America of 1830 said, "[Americans] may travel over the world, and find no society but their own which will submit to the restraint of perpetual caution, and reference to the opinions of others."[18]

Despite wide agreement on the dominant traits of "American character," America has had dissenters in life-style and in ideas throughout its history. In the 1960s, a vocal minority of college youths rejected the "establishment" values so completely and self-consciously that they could be described as representing a counter-culture. Although the political radicalism of the New Left was always confined to a small minority of college students, opposition to the Vietnam War stimulated widespread criticism of all the traditional American values. By the end of the decade, 78 percent of all college students agreed that "the real trouble with U.S. society is that it lacks a sense of values—it is conformist and materialistic." Equally shocking to parents who had sent their children to college expecting them to become financially successful was the fact that 65 percent thought "our troubles stem from making economic competition the basis of our way of life."[19] Continuing studies of American youth found sharp contrasts between the late 1960s and the 1970s. New life-styles and radical politics went together in the '60s: long hair, love beads, crunchy granola, a more open approach to sex, casual living arrangements, and pot smoking all went with radical politics. By the early 1970s the campus rebellion

[16] D. W. Brogan, *U.S.A.: An Outline of the Country, Its People and Institutions* (London: Oxford University Press, 1941), p. 116.

[17] The classic treatment of conspicuous consumption is in Thorstein Veblen, *The Theory of the Leisure Class: An Economic Study of Institutions* (New York: Macmillan, 1899).

[18] Harriet Martineau, *Society in America* (New York: Sanders and Otlan, 1837), III, 14. Quoted in Seymour M. Lipset, "A Changing American Character?" in Seymour M. Lipset and L. Lowenthal, eds., *Culture and Social Character* (New York: Free Press, 1961), p. 143.

[19] These findings are from a 1970 Louis Harris survey of undergraduates in 4-year colleges; the data are in the Louis Harris Political Data Center, University of North Carolina, Chapel Hill. See also Harris's book, *The Anguish of Change* (New York: Norton, 1973).

Conflicts over changing life-styles are found even among members of the same religion.

had died down, and new life-styles no longer implied radical politics.[20] As the 1980s began, whatever minority of nonconformist students remained had once again been submerged; they had returned to the status of outsider-as-loser, without the 1960s' glamour of outsider-as-revolutionary. Financial security was the chief goal of 75 percent of the freshmen in the Class of 1984. High-status positions and peer approval ranked close behind.

The traits of national character help to explain the *style* of a nation's politics, but they are not really very helpful in explaining the *content* of public policy. On the style side, the notion of social equality is so deeply held that when U.S. Army General George Patton slapped a soldier during World War II, an uproar of public protest resulted. Similarly, Americans can be counted on to feel that anyone in a position to control others—whether in labor unions, business corporations, or the government—has "too much power."[21] But this does not lead to any systematic ideas about how to equalize power; in fact, lower-status individuals who would presumably benefit from complete equality seem to feel uncomfortable when asked about such a prospect.[22] The value placed on individual achievement and on materialism leads Americans to think in terms of personal advancement rather than general improvement through the political system. Conformity shows up in the tendency for everyone, even opponents, to "rally 'round the winner" of an election.

The values of national character shed little light on the content of public policy, because the values are so broad and varied that they fit almost any policy. If the government were to redistribute wealth through a genuinely progressive tax system, we could say that the policy was in keeping with the commitment to equality. In practice, the tax laws of the United States have so many exemptions and loopholes for the truly rich that they help perpetuate extreme inequalities. But this, too, can be said to be in keeping with a basic value of American culture—materialistic achievement. "National character" is simply too vague and rubbery a concept to explain particular policies. Regardless of particulars, however, one value on which Americans all agree is the desirability of democracy.

DEMOCRACY AS IDEAS AND ACTIVITIES

Democracy has no fixed creed. The whole notion of democracy revolves around the belief that each generation can fix its own goals.[23] Today democracy

---

[20] Daniel Yankelovich, *The New Morality: A Profile of American Youth in the 70's* (New York: McGraw-Hill, 1974).

[21] V. O. Key, *Public Opinion,* p. 44. See also Arthur H. Miller, "Deepening Distrust of Political Leaders Is Jarring Public's Faith in Institutions," *ISR Newsletter,* 7 (Autumn 1979), 4–5.

[22] Robert E. Lane, *Political Ideology* (New York: Free Press, 1962).

[23] Thomas L. Thorson argues that the ultimate "must" of a democracy is that it must have no barriers to social goals. See *The Logic of Democracy* (New York: Holt, 1962), p. 139.

is an ideal for so many people all over the world that the word has great propaganda value. As a result, all kinds of different systems claim to be democratic.

Norms of traditional democratic theory

The central norms of democratic government, as the concept has developed in the Western world, are *majority rule and minority rights.* This simple phrase can only hint at the complex attitudes and habits that support democracy; but taken together, these principles constitute one of the briefest definitions of democracy. (A still briefer definition, outside of the Western tradition, will be offered later.)

The principle that "all men are created equal" leads directly to the idea of *majoritarianism* in the conduct of government. If people are basically equal, and if each has an inherent moral worth by virtue of his humanity, no individual or group can have a monopoly on truth. Thus it follows that the only way we can approach truth is through the free flow of ideas, through the process of give-and-take by which a wide variety of special "truths" are compromised. This implies that each individual must enjoy the freedom to work out and contribute his own version of truth. And since self-development requires self-government, the democratic theory of government is firmly based on the concept of popular consent or majority rule.

The ambiguity of democratic theory stems largely from an apparent conflict between *majority rule* and the equally basic principle of *minority rights.* In its extreme form, majoritarianism holds that the majority view is always right. In less extreme form, it holds that the majority view must always be followed, right or wrong. But democracy, if it is to be self-perpetuating, must hold certain freedoms to be "unalienable rights," rights that even the majority cannot take away. Since absolute truth is revealed to no one, even the majority can make mistakes. And the individual who is temporarily in a minority need not give up personal beliefs and adopt the majority opinion. He is simply asked to accept the majority decision as binding while retaining the right to work for a new majority that will change the decision to his liking.

The possibility of extreme conflict between majority rule and minority rights raises difficult questions. In an election, minority acceptance of the majority's victory reflects the realization that it is outnumbered and that defiance would be rightfully suppressed. But for the winners, who exercise the power of government, respecting the rights of the losers requires self-restraint rather than simply a sense of being restrained. What if the majority were to deny the minority the right to oppose the new government or even the right to enjoy such other basic freedoms as the right to a fair trial? In this situation does democratic theory favor majority rule or minority rights?

Absolute majoritarianism says the majority decision must be followed. But democratic theory has generally argued that minority rights are an essential restraint on the majority if majority rule itself is to work in the long run. The Declaration of Independence placed somewhat more emphasis on majority rule, and the Constitution somewhat more on minority rights, but both principles are clearly present in both documents. The belief underlying this view of democracy is that no individual or group can have absolute power. Not even the majority can speak perfectly or permanently for all. If such a privilege were granted—which would have to be at the cost of minority rights—majority rule itself could not survive. For majority rule to exist as a *continuing* principle, today's minority must have a chance to become tomorrow's majority. Majoritarianism thus requires the principle of minority rights.

Norms of egalitarian democratic theory

Majority rule and minority rights relate primarily to the *procedures* of government. But the idea of democracy comes from commitment to the *goal* of *egalitarianism* or *equality*. As we shall see in the next chapter, the belief in democracy was viewed as highly radical and dangerous in the early years of this nation. Liberals argued for democracy because they wanted equal political power. Conservatives opposed democracy because they feared that equal political power would be used by those less well off, to gain equal economic rewards and privileges. Their idea of democracy, then, did not stop with equal political power. Political equality was a *means* to the *end* of equal enjoyment of rewards and privileges. As Gerhard Lenski says in the most far-ranging study to date of *Power and Privilege:*

Wherever democratic theory has become institutionalized, a dramatic new possibility has arisen: *now the many can combine against the few, and even though individually the many are weaker, in combination they may be as strong or stronger.*[24]

This emphasis on equality as a goal leads to egalitarian democratic theory, defining democracy as any political system that maximizes the goal of equality. The only norm is equality itself. This definition poses the serious problem of deciding just what we mean by equality and how to measure it. But it does emphasize the *results of government for the people* rather than *procedures*. It shifts the focus from process to policy and from inputs to outputs.

Lenski examined the degree to which democracies have attained the ideal of equality in both policy inputs and outputs. He found that Sweden and the United States stand out:

In fact, one must conclude that *in the United States, unlike Sweden, the propertied classes and their allies still remain the dominant political force.* Among the more advanced industrial societies with democratic regimes, the United States and Sweden appear to represent the two extremes with respect to the pattern of political control. Most other industrialized democracies stand somewhere in between.[25]

Granted the emphasis on social equality in American culture, most middle-

[24] Gerhard Lenski, *Power and Privilege: A Theory of Social Stratification* (New York: McGraw-Hill, 1966), p. 318 (emphasis his).
[25] *Ibid.*

class Americans would be surprised to learn that their country ranks as *least* egalitarian among democracies in political power and economic privilege. But Professor Lenski's conclusion applies only to *democracies.* The United States is much closer to equality in political power than are all the many dictatorships of the world, and it is closer to equal economic rewards than are many dictatorships. Indeed, if accurate current data were available, France or Japan might replace the United States as the least egalitarian democracy.[26] The ranking of countries on various measures of equality is probably much more valid than the ranking, let's say, of beauty in a Miss Universe contest. But no ranking should be accepted as absolutely valid. Although the criteria for judging political and economic equality are clearer than those for judging beauty, they are still subject to considerable dispute.

Our first concern here is not to locate the United States or any other country very precisely in terms of equality but simply to recognize the idea of *using equality as one way of defining democracy.* A second concern is to get at least a rough idea of *how the United States compares with other countries* on measures of equality. For example, on equality of income, the United States ranks eighth out of 52 countries—7 countries have greater equality and 43 have less.[27] In 29 of 76 countries, social welfare programs are more highly developed than they are in the U.S.[28] One measure of the effectiveness of social services—including data on life expectancy, literacy, and infant mortality—ranks the United States slightly above midpoint among 27 industrialized societies: below Sweden, Iceland, Japan, Norway, Denmark, Netherlands, Canada, and Switzerland, it was tied with New Zealand, United Kingdom, France, and Finland. It was above 14 other countries that could be called advanced in development.[29] But the U.S. ranks at or near the top on measures of *total* wealth and industrial advancement. Although America is fantastically effective in the production of wealth, it has not been particularly effective in the distribution of that wealth.

Democracy: a way of governing and of getting equality

Deciding on The Most Democratic Country may be as much fun for scholars as selecting Miss Universe is for male judges; but as we have remarked, confidence in either decision cannot be great. Traditional democratic theory emphasizes the input features of the political system and therefore focuses on the *way* of governing. Egalitarian democratic theory emphasizes the output

[26] This statement is based on personal communication with Professor Lenski, March, 1979.

[27] Charles L. Taylor and Michael C. Hudson, *World Handbook of Political and Social Indicators,* 2nd ed. (New Haven, Conn.: Yale University Press, 1972), pp. 263–65.

[28] Philips Cutright, "Political Structure, Economic Development and National Social Security Programs," in C. F. Cnudde and D. E. Neubauer, eds. *Empirical Democratic Theory* (Chicago: Markham, 1969), pp. 443–45.

[29] Austria, Australia, Belgium, Bulgaria, Czechoslovakia, East Germany, Hungary, Ireland, Italy, Poland, Rumania, Spain, U.S.S.R., and West Germany. See the index developed by the Overseas Development Center as reported in *Time,* March 13, 1978, pp. 26–27.

features and therefore focuses on the *results* of governing. The first task, then, would be to agree on which theory to apply.

We think the two theories are not competing interpretations. Each emphasizes an important aspect of democracy, and both can therefore be usefully employed in describing governments. This is essentially what Professor Lenski did in classifying the United States as the least egalitarian democracy: he recognized it to be democratic, but he also recognized that political power (the input focus) and economic privilege (the output focus) were less widely shared than in other democracies at the time of his study. In practice, both aspects of democracy tend to go together. Shared political power leads to more widely shared economic benefits. That was what the early opponents of democracy feared. Political power is a means to the goal of economic and other benefits.

The traditional and the egalitarian theories seem (to some people) to conflict because of a twentieth-century development: the emergence of dictatorial systems with mass appeal and mass benefits. If the military in a Latin American country throws out the ruling oligarchs and begins a program of distributing land to the poor, has the country become democratic? Our answer is no and yes: it has not become democratic in the way its rulers achieved power and in the lack of individual rights; it has become more democratic in the sense that economic privileges are being more equally distributed. This interpretation permits us to say, for example, that Cuba is more democratic in various respects under the dictatorship of Castro than it was under that of Batista.

The trouble with the mass-based dictatorship is, of course, that irresponsible power is typically used for the benefit of the powerful rather than the powerless. While we can call Castro's Cuba more democratic on the output dimension than the old-style dictatorship it replaced, the people have no assurance that Castro's egalitarian impulses will continue. A country that is democratic on both dimensions has the assurance of *institutionalized* popular control. The Communist "dictatorship of the proletariat" was, in Karl Marx's theory, supposed to "wither away." But, in fact, the dictatorship in the Soviet Union is not made up of the proletariat, nor does it show signs of withering away. Shared political power is expressed through certain basic institutions without which a reasonably complete democracy appears to be impossible.

Basic institutions of democratic government

Political parties and a free election system are the most essential institutions for majority rule on a continuing basis. Political parties, made up of a combination of interests, enable citizens to join forces in their attempt to win control of government and to get what they want through political action. The party system thus performs the key input functions necessary to any political system: identification of basic interests in society and leadership selection. Equally crucial to the democratic performance of these functions is a system of popular elections. Through elections, opposing parties compete peaceably for control of the government. Democracy counts ballots instead of bullets. Political parties and elections, rather than conspiracies and assassina-

"IT COULD BE A BIGGER THREAT THAN ANY DEMOCRAT. WHAT IF WOMEN'S LIB PUTS UP A CANDIDATE FOR PRESIDENT?"

tions, give citizens of a democracy a means of expressing their support or disapproval of government policies and personnel.

Because the precise forms taken by these institutions vary widely from time to time and from place to place, we cannot say that they must exist in some "ideal" form in order for a government to be regarded as democratic. The perfect democracy is just as unattainable as the perfect dictatorship. Even imperfect and erratic responses to majority opinion indicate that democratic processes are at work, though perhaps at a crude, immature level. But to say that democratic institutions vary widely in form does not mean that we have no way of evaluating them. Specifically, we can evaluate any political institution in terms of how good a job it does in promoting *majority control* on a *continuing* basis; that is, with respect for the right of today's minority to become tomorrow's majority. We can say, for example, that pure one-party politics is *un*democratic because it fails to keep rulers accountable to changing public opinion. And even if party leaders are chosen by popular vote, we can say that a one-party system is *less* democratic than a two-party system. Because competition in one-party politics is merely between personalities, group responsibility for the conduct of government is lacking.

Other basic institutions of democracy are the schools, the press, and pressure groups. Perhaps American educators are not completely free in the pursuit of truth. Perhaps freedom of the press is diluted for newspaper readers by the decline in the number of competing newspapers. Perhaps some pressure groups have a loud voice in public affairs while others are scarcely heard. Still, these institutions enjoy enough freedom to place the United States in the democratic camp. The search for truth does go on, information about public affairs is widely circulated, and many groups can present their viewpoints. There is room for improvement, but these institutions operate far differently here from the way they operate, for example, in China. On rare occasions, Chinese schools, newspapers, or special groups may deviate from the opinions of the dominant group, but it is always at some risk to life and freedom.

The loose organization and lack of discipline in American political parties leave legislators free to vote against their party's platform without fear of being punished by party leaders. We might conclude that American parties are less democratic than the more united and disciplined British parties, because unified parties can better carry out their pledges to the majority who put them in office. But even our loosely organized parties give us a measure of majority control that makes our system greatly different from that of South Africa, with its one-party rule.

Just because we judge one form of an institution to be *more* democratic than another, the latter does not automatically become *un*democratic. Somewhere between universal suffrage and the complete absence of popular elections, for example, democracy as we know it is lost. But it does not make sense to suppose that there is an *exact point* at which democracy ceases to exist.

At one extreme in political theory is the model of the perfectly democratic system, in which political power and economic privilege are both equally shared by all adults. At the other extreme is the model of the perfect dictatorship, in which political power and economic privilege are both concentrated in the hands of a small group. All governments fall somewhere between these two extremes.

In Fig. 2 · 3 we have located several countries according to these two criteria. The figure should not be accepted as a precise location of nations in terms of democracy or dictatorship; it presents our guesswork in order to suggest *how* the criteria may be applied. The location of countries along the horizontal line represents the degree to which political power is shared or concentrated. (We have talked about the political power aspect of democracy in terms of two features, majority rule and minority rights; because the two tend to go together, we combine them in Fig. 2 · 3 to represent a single dimension—shared political power.) The United States is clearly closer to the democratic than the dictatorial end of that continuum. Sweden and the United Kingdom outdo us on this aspect of democracy, but countries such as China, Iran, the USSR, Brazil, and Yugoslavia are so much farther from equal political power that they fall on the nondemocratic side of the dividing line. The location of Japan represents more guesswork than information, but it suggests that some democracies may be farther from equal political power than is the U.S.

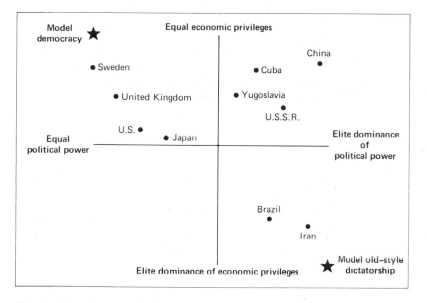

Fig. 2 · 3 Location of selected countries on two dimensions of democracy.

Shifting to the vertical dimension (economic privileges), we again find the U.S. on the democratic side of our dividing line. But on this dimension, a number of *non*democracies (by the traditional theory) are closer to the top, the democratic end of the line, than is the U.S. Even so, the old theory seems to work rather well: political equality leads to some degree of economic equality. Every country that looks democratic in terms of political power looks at least somewhat democratic in terms of economic privilege. And in the old-style dictatorships such as Brazil and Iran, political inequality is found with economic inequality. What complicates the picture is that some countries (such as Cuba, China, Yugoslavia, and the USSR) now have some degree of economic equality without political equality. Should they be called democracies? We do not think so. Historically, the concept of democracy developed around the idea of shared political power as a means to shared power in general. That is a rich and complex concept that cannot be satisfied merely by equality in economic rewards. Moreover, the lack of shared political power gives the mass of the people no assurance that equality in other matters will continue. For us, then, democracy refers to both means and ends, and it requires the sharing of both power and privilege.

What is the public ideology?

For a long time, the nature of the American ideology or basic political beliefs was thought to be so evident that people spoke confidently of "the American Creed." Thus Swedish economist Gunnar Myrdal stated:

America, compared to every other country in Western civilization, large or small, has the *most explicitly expressed* system of general ideals in reference to human interrelations. This body of ideals is more widely understood and appreciated than similar ideals are anywhere else. The American Creed is not merely—as in some other countries—the implicit background of the nation's political and judicial order as it functions. To be sure, the political creed of America is not very satisfactorily effectuated in actual social life. But as principles which *ought* to rule, the Creed has been made conscious to everyone in American society.[30]

The creed that Myrdal believed to be so "widely understood and appreciated" in the United States included the ideals first stated in the Declaration of Independence and later made official when the Bill of Rights was added to the Constitution. Equality, majority rule, minority rights, and all of the rights associated with these ideals—freedoms of speech, press, and religion; the right to assemble and make demands on government; equal treatment before the law; protection of life, liberty, and property—all of these were part of the American Creed from the outset. Although the ideals were not invented in America—they are part of the heritage of the entire Western civilization—Americans seemed even more confident than Myrdal that they were uniquely recognized in the United States. Even those aware of how frequently the Creed was violated in practice had no doubt of its existence as a recognized, if unachieved, standard.

Do Americans actually accept their Creed as widely as has been thought? The answer to this question from public opinion surveys was startling. Consensus—agreement approaching 100 percent—exists on the abstract idea of majority rule and minority rights. But no consensus is found on even such a statement as the following: "A professional organization like the AMA (American Medical Association) has the right to try to increase the influence of doctors by getting them to vote as a bloc in elections." Researchers have failed to find consensus on a whole series of such statements, all similarly derived from the principles of majority rule and minority rights.[31] They conclude that consensus disappears when democratic principles are put in concrete terms and that citizens are closer to complete discord (a 50–50 split) than to perfect consensus (a 100–0 split) on many such questions.

The essential point of commitment to the *ideal* of democracy is valid. What Americans disagree about is what those ideals mean in particular situations and how they should be achieved. Perhaps the lack of consensus below

[30] *An American Dilemma: The Negro Problem and Modern Democracy* (New York: Harper, 1944), p. 3.

[31] James W. Prothro and Charles M. Grigg, "Fundamental Principles of Democracy: Bases of Agreement and Disagreement," *Journal of Politics,* 22 (May 1960), 276–94.

the abstract level should be gratifying—democracy is characterized more by freedom to argue about differences than by total agreement.[32] The picture of thousands of people shouting approval looks more like a dictatorship than a democracy.

SUMMARY

Our political system is part of our culture—the way our society thinks, feels, and behaves. Our political views and activities are shaped by the simple fact that we are Americans. As a nation of immigrants who are particularly proud of their nationality, Americans tend to see their country as superior; foreign ways, as inferior.

The American belief in inevitable national progress disappeared in response to the harsh realities of the 1960s and 1970s. As a whole, Americans now see their country's past as better than the present and expect things to get worse. Blacks are an exception, holding an exactly opposite view. Cultural outlooks are thus not unchanging. Nor are they universally held by all groups within the culture.

The basic value that has always shaped and confused American social and political character is the assertion of equality coupled with inequality in practice. Although the Declaration of Independence states that "all men are created equal," equality has been honored more in words than in practice in America. The emphasis on equality has led to competition (or individual achievement), status uncertainty (especially in terms of money), and conformity in American life.

One value on which most Americans agree is the desirability of democracy. According to traditional theory, democratic government is based on majority rule and minority rights. In contrast, egalitarian theory sees democracy simply in terms of the goal of equality. The traditional theory focuses on inputs—a way of governing; the egalitarian theory focuses on outputs—the results of governing. Both should be used in examining democracy. Political parties and a free election system, the basic institutions of democratic government, are necessary for majority control on a continuing basis. Other institutions of democracy include schools, the press, and pressure groups.

No country is a perfect democracy (or a perfect dictatorship). The United States is clearly a democracy, more so than some countries, less so than others.

[32] For an argument that Americans have become more consistent in their beliefs, see Norman H. Nie, Sidney Verba, and John R. Petrocik, *The Changing American Voter* (Cambridge, Mass.: Harvard University Press, 1976); for contrary findings and interpretations, see John L. Sullivan, James E. Piereson, and George E. Marcus, "Ideological Constraint in the Mass Public: A Methodological Critique and Some New Findings," and "The More Things Change the More They Stay the Same: The Stability of Mass Belief Systems," *American Journal of Political Science,* 22 (May 1978), 233–49, and 23 (February 1979), 139–75.

the constitutional framework

3

As the world's oldest written Constitution, the U.S. document has been studied, imitated, and praised. But there is nothing magical or sacred about it. It was written as a series of compromises, as a practical solution to the difficulties people faced in living with each other as fellow countrymen. The men who wrote it were politicians who, as Benjamin Franklin said, brought "all of their prejudices, their passions, their errors of opinion, their local interest, and their selfish views" to the task of drafting the Constitution. Fortunately, they also brought insight, patriotism, intelligence, and understanding of human nature.

The road to the Constitutional Convention was neither predictable nor easy. The American Constitution was not part of the baggage carried off the Mayflower in 1620, although, in some ways, it reflected the hopes and desires of those who first arrived in the new land. Other features would go far back into English history for their beginnings. But the Constitution was, in the end, in its formulation and design, an American product. It came out of crises and struggles to create nationhood and a common identity. Its authors sought to construct a political system around which this identity and purpose could grow.

The men who wrote the Constitution did not expect to create a fully-developed governmental system with one legal document. They recognized the futility of trying to speak to all problems, of seeking to write out the solutions to all future political struggles. Indeed, the greater part of their wisdom may have been in what they left unsaid. We should recognize, with them, that the nature of the national union, federalism, individual rights, and national-state powers could not be decided at one point in time. Although we continually search for our roots and explore what the framers "meant" by this or that phrase or word, the surest thing that we can say about their intent is that they wanted and expected the system to change. Their expectations were realized immediately. In the few years after the document was approved, rapid changes in the organizational structure occurred—in national government powers, the Bill of Rights, and political parties. Some of these changes, the framers would resist. Others they would sponsor and encourage. But they were not surprised that writing a Constitution for a changing vital social system was a never-ending task. Thus, as we look at the beginnings of our constitutional framework, it is useful to remember that the Constitution is not something *they* did. Rather, it is something *we* are still doing.

The fact that the founding fathers did not fix the meaning of the Constitution for all time should not be misinterpreted to underestimate the tremendous degree to which we are influenced today by what they did 200 years ago. The shaping of the Constitution is a continuing process, but the options and possibilities for radically different arrangements were almost infinitely greater in the 1780s than in the 1980s. During most of the Constitutional Convention, for example, the plan accepted for choosing the President was selection by Congress; only in the waning days of the Convention was a different plan adopted. The ease with which that decision could have gone either way differs immeasurably from the difficulty one would face today in trying to change the way we choose our President.

The first generation of officeholders under the new Constitution was almost like a continuing Constitutional Convention, for much discretion remained in determining how things would actually work. The second generation of officeholders enjoyed less discretion (and suffered less torment) in deciding how things would work. And so on through the generations, until a twentieth-century descendant of James Madison would find his chances of shaping the system incomparable to those of his ancestor, but he could still have some influence. In this chapter we consider the work of the framers of the Constitution and of the first officeholders under it; many of the same people were in both groups, and all clearly deserve to be called founding fathers.

New York Public Library.

The first Cabinet, 1789 (left to right: Knox, Jefferson, Randolph, Hamilton, Washington). In determining the meaning of the Constitution, the first Cabinet enjoyed much more discretion than did any Cabinet that followed.

As is true of all political systems, certain processes of *socialization* or political learning had to occur before a new political community was possible. Many forces were at work to create a sense of American identity. Among the most important were the Declaration of Independence, the Revolutionary War, the experience with state governments and state constitutions, and finally the Articles of Confederation. Each contributed to the possibility of a constitutional government by helping to socialize and transform English subjects into American citizens.[1]

The shift in identity: from colonists to Americans

When can we first locate an "American people"? When did the new nation emerge? Most people date the beginning of the United States from the Declaration of Independence, July 4, 1776:

When in the Course of human events, it becomes necessary for one people to dissolve the political bands, which have connected them with another, and to assume among the powers of the earth, the separate and equal station to which the Laws of Nature and of Nature's God entitle them. . . .

These words marked the final breakdown of British authority within the boundaries of thirteen North American colonies. Great Britain did not, of course, recognize this fact until the Treaty of Peace in 1783. Constitutionally, the thirteen independent states were not joined as the United States of America until the Articles of Confederation had been ratified by all the states, which did not occur until 1781. The "more perfect union" was not achieved until 1788, when the new Constitution, written in Philadelphia in 1787 by delegates from twelve of the states, was ratified by nine state conventions. And the government under this Constitution did not really go into operation until after George Washington was inaugurated as the first President of the United States in April, 1789.

Formal documents cannot tell us when British authority began to disintegrate or when the American community began to assume a separate political identity. Even before the Declaration of Independence, shared interests and experiences gradually transformed British colonists into American nationalists. The French and Indian Wars, for example, represented common dangers and

---

[1] Seymour Martin Lipset views the United States in historical and comparative perspective in *The First New Nation* (New York: Basic Books, 1963). See also Richard L. Merritt's essay, "Nation Building in America: The Colonial Years," in Karl W. Deutsch and William J. Foltz, eds., *Nation-Building* (New York: Atherton, 1963), pp. 56–81. Three paperback editions of value are Daniel J. Boorstin, *The Americans: The Colonial Experience* (New York: Vintage Books, 1958); Charles M. Andrews, *The Colonial Background of the American Revolution* (New Haven, Conn.: Yale University Press, 1972); Forrest McDonald, *The Formation of the American Republic 1776–1790* (Baltimore: Penguin Books, 1970).

Library of Congress.

What would be considered "cruel and unusual punishment" today
was common in seventeenth-century American colonies.

stimulated various plans for common defense. The Stamp Act and the Sugar
Act (taxation and regulation of trade without representation) and other acts
of the British Parliament in the 1760s and '70s provoked common resentment
throughout the colonies. The Quartering Act (requiring the colonists to house
British troops) and the Intolerable Acts (petty, punitive acts against patriots)
prompted a spirited defense of American rights.

Although we cannot say exactly when the colonists came to identify themselves as more American than English, the transformation apparently came
before the Declaration of Independence. Through examination of the colonial
press, Richard Merritt traces the terms used to refer to the people in the
American colonies between 1735 and 1775. His research tentatively identifies
some time during 1763 as the crucial date when the colonists assumed a common American identity.[2] In other words, had it been possible to make annual
surveys of prerevolutionary American opinion, 1763 was probably the first
year in which a majority of colonists would have called themselves Americans
rather than colonials.

For most Americans, it was easy to assume a new national identity, because
they already had so much in common. John Jay made this point in supporting
the idea of a strong federal union in 1788:

Providence has been pleased to give this one connected country to one united people—
a people descended from the same ancestors, speaking the same language, professing
the same religion, attached to the same principles of government, very similar in their
manners and customs.[3]

[2] *Symbols of American Community 1735–1775* (New Haven: Yale University Press, 1966), p. 126.
[3] *The Federalist* (also known as *The Federalist Papers*), No. 2.

Colonists tarred and feathered British loyalists.

To enslaved blacks who were involuntary members of the "one united people," however, Mr. Jay's statement must have sounded odd.

In stressing the prerevolutionary American community, we do not want to leave the impression that the United States of America emerged to full nationhood in 1776. Americans had found a common identity, but they still had a long way to go—well past the middle of the nineteenth century and through a long and bloody civil war—before the concept of "Union" evolved. In these early years, the notion of union was vague and tentative, a child of necessity, a strained cooperation required to fight a war and to deal with the consequences of victory. There was great uncertainty about the form the union was to take, and many were skeptical of its permanence. Like the initial documents and ideals of self-government, the concepts of "union" and "United States" were to change and mature and to become, in the words of Daniel Webster, "the all-absorbing topic of the day." It was not so in 1776. Then, unity was only a hopeful experiment.[4]

[4] Paul C. Nagel, *One Nation Indivisible: The Union in American Thought 1776–1861* (New York: Oxford University Press, 1964), pp. 13–23.

The Declaration of Independence

The Declaration of Independence did not cause the War of Revolution. As we have deified the founding fathers, so have we created such mythology about the Declaration that we obscure its origin and purpose. It did not produce armed opposition to Britain; it justified the fighting that had already begun. A small group of activists, deeply dissatisfied with our treatment as colonists, caused the war. The Declaration was, on one level, no more than a statement to justify and legitimize our separation from Great Britain. Jefferson sought to persuade those skeptics, both inside the country and out, that the break with the mother country was rational and necessary. Most of the Declaration is about specific acts of a specific king. Jefferson's stroke of genius came, not in spelling out these complaints against King George, but in making a more radical argument, lifting the Declaration to a higher level with universal appeal.

We hold these truths to be self-evident, that all men are created equal, that they are endowed by their Creator with certain unalienable Rights, that among these are Life, Liberty and the pursuit of Happiness.—That to secure these rights, Governments are instituted among Men. . . .

Imagine how different the impact would have been had this central proposition been put more conservatively and narrowly:

We hold this truth to be self-evident, that it is a right of British subjects not to be taxed except by their own consent.[5]

What has inspired oppressed people all over the world is not the specific case against George III, but the general ideals justifying revolution and popular government. This enduring appeal springs from five propositions in the Declaration:

1. There is *a higher law*, found in the "laws of nature and of nature's God," that embodies self-evident truths against which institutions and practices can be judged.
2. Society must recognize that *"all men are created equal,"* with the right to enjoy equality under the law and in the chance to influence the law.
3. All men have *"certain unalienable Rights,"* including those of "Life, Liberty and the pursuit of Happiness," by virtue of their common humanity and equality.
4. *Government is an instrument of the people*, to be used as they see fit for the twofold purpose of protection and service or, in the words of the Declaration, of "Safety and Happiness."
5. *"Consent of the governed"* is the only legitimate basis of power, a proposition which implies the *right of revolution* when government "becomes destructive of these ends."

[5] This rephrasing comes from the definitive study of the declaration: Carl Becker, *The Declaration of Independence: A Study in the History of Political Ideas* (New York: Alfred A. Knopf, 1951).

These are the high standards against which we have come to measure ourselves and our policies. Vernon Parrington, one of the great interpreters of American ideas, had this to say about the influence of the Declaration of Independence:

The humanitarian idealism of the Declaration has always echoed as a battle-cry in the hearts of those who dream of an America dedicated to democratic ends. It cannot be long ignored or repudiated, for sooner or later it returns to plague the council of practical politics. It is constantly breaking out in fresh revolt. . . . Without its freshening influence our political history would have been much more sordid and materialistic.[6]

The central propositions we have just set forth appear in the writings of the English theorist John Locke as well as in the Declaration—a reminder of our indebtedness to the entire Western civilization of which America is only a part. American ideals are the general ideals of democracy, and no nation has a monopoly on them. As a noted Swedish scholar puts it, "The American creed is older and wider than America itself."[7]

The Revolutionary War

Even though the Revolutionary War was to some extent a civil war that divided families and villages, fighting and winning it was the major event in uniting the American people into a political community. Those who preferred to keep their ties with the British Empire considered themselves loyalists; those who chose to fight for independence called themselves patriots.[8] Historian Samuel Eliot Morison estimated that no more than 10 percent of the white population of the United States was actively loyalist, that about 40 percent was actively patriot, and that the other 50 percent was either neutral or apathetic. To Morison, "the significant fact is that nowhere, except in Georgia and in occupied seaports, were the British able to organize a Loyalist civil government."[9]

As John Adams had predicted, the American revolution was "a long, obstinate, and bloody war." Even in the middle of revolution, the patriots conspicuously tried to create a "government of law," a constitutional government with specific and limited power. Almost immediately after its Declaration of Inde-

---

[6] *Main Currents in American Thought* (New York: Harcourt, 1930), III, 285. See also Alan P. Grimes, "Conservative Revolution and Liberal Rhetoric: The Declaration of Independence," *Journal of Politics,* 38 (August 1976), 4. For contemporary views of Jefferson's role see Ross Lence, "Thomas Jefferson and the American Declaration of Independence: The Power and Natural Rights of a Free People," *The Political Science Reviewer,* 6 (Fall 1976), 1–34 and Robert J. Morgan, " 'Time Hath Found Us': The Jeffersonian Revolutionary Vision," *Journal of Politics,* 38 (August 1976), 20–36.

[7] Gunnar Myrdal, *An American Dilemma* (New York: Harper, 1944), p. 25. A two-volume paperback edition was published by McGraw-Hill in 1964.

[8] William Allen Benton, *Whig-Loyalism: An Aspect of Political Ideology in the American Revolutionary Era* (Rutherford: Fairleigh Dickinson University Press, 1969).

[9] Samuel Eliot Morison, *The Oxford History of the American People* (New York: Oxford University Press, 1965), p. 236.

Library of Congress.

The Revolutionary War solidified the identification of Americans with their new country.

pendence, the Second Continental Congress began to consider the Articles of Confederation, the new nation's first constitution.

Directing the war was such a time-consuming activity that debate on the details of the proposed constitutional union of the states was delayed nearly a year. But in November 1776, Congress formally adopted the Articles and submitted them to the state legislatures for their approval. Although the revolutionary government was poorly financed and inadequately supported, although sacrifices were unevenly and unfairly distributed and many problems were simply put aside, fewer than three million Americans successfully defied the world's greatest colonial power and took the first steps, however faltering, toward union and self-government.

However powerful a socializing force, the Revolutionary War did not establish a political system. Indeed, the most severe test was not in getting rid of one political order but rather in replacing it with another. One of the most remarkable aspects of the American revolution was that its leaders engaged in constructive political efforts in the midst of their war activities. Twelve of the thirteen states had adopted new constitutions by 1777, and the thirteenth, Massachusetts, adopted hers in 1780.

The new state constitutions made no clear break with the past. Most borrowed their ideas from seventeenth- and eighteenth-century English and French political philosophers.[10] A bill of rights protecting basic freedoms was attached to nearly all of the state documents. All of the new constitutions were *republican;* that is, they recognized the principle of popular representation and provided for government by officials who answered to the public and who held office for a fixed term or "during good behavior."

Popular sovereignty, or "consent of the governed," did not, however, mean that everyone in the eighteenth century had the right to vote. When the first Americans demanded the "rights of free men," most of them really meant *free men.* Jefferson's denunciation of slavery in the first draft of the Declaration of Independence was deleted by his fellow delegates at the Continental Congress. The idea that slaves might have rights was unthinkable to a majority. And the concept "man," whatever the claim today that it encompasses both females and males, certainly did not include women when most revolutionists spoke of the "rights of man." No slaves or women were permitted to vote in the new state governments. Property and tax-paying qualifications further reduced the size of the electorate. The requirements were not high enough to restrict the vote to the wealthy, but they were enough to keep poor people from voting. On the eve of revolution, one-half to three-fourths of the male adults are estimated to have possessed the vote in most of the colonies.[11]

The state constitutions and state governments helped the movement toward nationhood in several ways:

1. They provided a transition from revolution to stable government without the total chaos that often follows a national revolt.

2. Within each state, the people were drawn together and given the experience of working within the confines of a written constitution.

3. State constitutions let the people try out different notions of government, which could be incorporated later into the federal union.

4. State documents provided a yardstick against which to measure future federal constitutional proposals.

---

[10] The debt to English thinkers, especially to John Locke, was very great. There is, however, scholarly controversy about the direct influence of French writers in the American colonies.

[11] Robert A. Dahl, *Democracy in the United States: Promise and Performance* (Chicago: Rand McNally, 1976), p. 70. Religious qualifications were an additional restriction in a number of the states.

This state experience was especially important for establishing the idea of a "bill of rights," but it was also important for the concepts of separation of powers, checks and balances, and the distribution of powers among government officers. Thus, the early state governments and state constitutions were important teachers in the training and socialization of American citizens. For the time, they helped to make proud "Virginia citizens" and "Massachusetts citizens." In time, however, they were to help lead the state citizenry and the state polities into a national government.

The Articles of Confederation

Finally adopted by the last of the state legislatures in 1781, the nation's first formal constitution proclaimed "a firm league of friendship" and protected each state's "sovereignty, freedom, and independence, and every power, jurisdiction, and right, which is not by this confederation expressly delegated to the United States, in Congress assembled." The Articles represented a pact among states, not a government "of the people, by the people, and for the people." The United States under the Articles was more comparable to an international organization than a nation state. Even so, they were the first effort toward a national political system.

Under the Articles, Congress was the center of governmental organization. But Congress merely represented the states. Like the General Assembly of the United Nations today, it could not make laws directly governing the people of the member states. Delegates to Congress were chosen by the state legislatures, and each state had only one vote in Congress. Such power as the national government had was concentrated in Congress. Oddly enough, this did not follow the example of the state constitutions, which made much of the principle of *"separation of powers,"* an attempt to avoid misuse of government powers by distributing them among different branches of government. But the Articles did not provide for an independent President or for national courts. Instead of a President independent of Congress, a "committee of the states," consisting of one member of Congress from each state, managed the general affairs of the government when the whole Congress was not assembled. This committee appointed one of its members to act as President. Instead of a national court system, Congress had the power to settle some disputes between states.

Possible misuse of power under the Articles was prevented by a more direct solution: the general government was not given enough power to worry about. In ratifying the Articles, the states agreed to accept certain limitations on their independence and power—in areas of foreign affairs, treaties, and warfare. But it became clear that if a state disregarded any of these restrictions, the Congress would not be able to bring that state back into line. This inability was most deeply felt in economic affairs. Congress had exclusive power over coinage, but the states were free to issue paper money which they did in great quantities. The resulting monetary confusion worsened the business depression that followed the revolution. Since Congress could not regulate interstate commerce (trade among the states), economic "cold war" developed among the states. Finally, because the central government could not levy taxes, it had to depend on "donations" from the states, and the flow of funds became less and less.

With economic rivalry among the states reaching a high pitch of tension and frustration, merchants, planters, and businessmen became unhappy with the Articles of Confederation. Money lenders were particularly hurt by the widespread inflation produced by state issuance of paper money. People in debt were presumably happy with "cheap money," but they were less influential. Groups who expected to benefit most from more power over the national economy began to demand a change in the Articles.

One of the leading authorities on the Articles argues that economic matters were not as bad during this period as we are led to believe.[12] Despite difficulties, business, agriculture, banking, and shipping continued to grow. While it is true that the Articles did not bring economic growth to a standstill, it is equally true that they provided too weak and loose a government. Insulated and removed from the people, powerless and fractured, the political system created by the Articles was simply not adequate for the problems at hand. Yet, they were important in the transition to nationhood. It is difficult to imagine going from the revolution to the Constitutional Convention without the intervening experience of the Articles.

The first efforts to cope with the inadequacy of the Articles were unsuccessful. In 1785, delegates from Virginia and Maryland met to work out an agreement on problems of navigation and commerce on the Potomac River and Chesapeake Bay. Because the conference was unsuccessful, the Virginia legislature called a general economic conference to meet in Annapolis, Maryland, in 1786. The Annapolis Conference was also a failure, for only twelve delegates appeared to represent five states. The report of these delegates, under the leadership of Alexander Hamilton of New York, observed that the situation of the United States under the Articles had become "delicate and critical." It recommended that all the states appoint commissioners to meet in Philadelphia "to devise such further provisions as shall appear to them necessary to render the Constitution of the Federal government adequate to the exigencies of the Union."

Immediately after the Annapolis Conference, several of the states began to name delegates to the meeting. In 1787, Congress itself finally endorsed the movement for a convention,

. . . for the sole and express purpose of revising the Articles of Confederation and reporting to Congress and the several legislatures such alterations and provisions therein as shall when agreed to in Congress and confirmed by the states render the federal constitution adequate to the exigencies of Government and the preservation of the Union.

All the states except Rhode Island eventually responded by appointing delegates to the Constitutional Convention that was to meet in Philadelphia in May 1787.

[12] Andrew C. McLaughlin, *The Confederation and the Constitution 1783–1789* (New York: Collier Books, 1971).

The critical issue in 1787 was how to fit the thirteen states into the greater context of one nation. The issue was *how to* and not *whether to*. The delegates were in basic agreement on the need to strengthen the national government and were nearly all in favor of retaining the separate states' identities in the federal union.[13] The second issue, less critical at the time but more basic if the new government was to last, was how to provide for popular participation in the new system of rule making.

A base of popular support

If the new government were to succeed, it would have to establish some direct relationship with the people. Otherwise, it would simply be the creature of the states, as Congress was under the Articles. But who should be allowed to participate? How should their involvement be structured, and to what degree should they be allowed to touch the decision making of the leaders? These questions demanded early answers from the Convention delegates.[14] Madison's view was that the central purpose of government is to settle conflicts—to filter opposing interests of those who owned property and those who did not into a larger national interest. Clearly, the delegates did not want government by *faction,* their term for any political interest group. With only a dim and negative awareness of political parties, they feared that factional battles would tear the new nation apart. At the same time, they did not want a government so distant from the people that legitimacy of the rulers would be questioned and participation of the people would not really exist.

How were the demands and supports in the system to be defined? How could popular support be gained without permitting direct popular control? The delegates agreed that the national government should be established under a stronger constitution, but several pressing problems remained. How should they count the slaves who then comprised nearly one-fifth of the population? Should frontier farmers participate in the national government on equal terms with eastern commercial interests? Should national elections be based on national voting requirements, and if so, should the *electorate*

[13] Martin Diamond argues that the critical issue was not the division between large and small state interests, but between advocates of a small republic and an extended republic; Martin Diamond, "What the Framers Meant by Federalism," in Robert Goldwin, ed., *A Nation of States* (Chicago: Rand McNally, 1963). Argument against the Diamond thesis is given by Christopher Wolfe, "On Understanding the Constitutional Convention of 1787," *Journal of Politics,* 39 (February 1977), 97–118.

[14] See Clinton Rossiter, *1787: The Grand Convention* (New York: Macmillan, 1966); also John P. Roche, "The Founding Fathers: A Reform Caucus in Action," *American Political Science Review,* 55 (December 1961), 799.

(those eligible to vote) include all citizens or be limited to "freeholders" (property-owners)?

For the purpose of determining the number of representatives a state could send to Congress, the delegates decided that "the people" would include the free inhabitants and three-fifths of the slaves in each state. (It was also part of the final compromise to count three-fifths of the slaves in figuring the amount of taxes each state would pay and to guarantee that Congress not prohibit importation of slaves prior to 1808.)[15] The idea that each slave was three-fifths of a person could not be defended morally or logically. It was simply a formula to which the free and the slave states were willing to agree. Northerners generally thought that the number of free inhabitants was the proper basis of representation (northern states had the largest number). White southerners generally thought that wealth, particularly wealth invested in slaves, should be counted (southerners had the most slaves).

In deciding who should participate in the new government, a few of the framers yearned to establish an *aristocracy,* rule by a small clique of the "best" citizens. In debates on the makeup of the legislature, Gouverneur Morris of Pennsylvania argued almost plaintively, "The second branch ought to be composed of men of great and established property—an aristocracy. . . . Such an aristocratic body will keep down the turbulence of democracy."[16] Morris's claim for aristocracy was intended to give greater weight in the government to the eastern commercial interests. He was opposed to any plan of representation based on mere numbers, for this would give too much power to the western people. His opposition to counting slaves in determining representation can similarly be interpreted as a reluctance to give the southern states too much power. Although the Morris plea fell on some responsive ears, his hope for a government of eastern aristocracy was unacceptable. The framers recognized that if the government were to be truly national in scope, it would have to incorporate the demands of the whole nation. The three-fifths compromise and popular participation in the House of Representatives were the Convention's negative responses to Mr. Morris's aristocratic yearnings.

The Convention attempted to meet the problem of popular participation first by providing for direct representation in one branch of Congress, then by giving Congress the power to impose or levy and collect taxes from all the people. The individual with a pocketbook interest in his government (whose leaders he helps to choose) is not so likely to be indifferent to how that government operates. When it came to determining the basis of representation and taxation, everyone agreed that at least all the free inhabitants should be counted. But disagreement arose over what the qualifications of the electorate should be. Only a few of the delegates were willing to trust all free men with the vote. John Dickinson of Delaware urged that the right of suffrage

---

[15] Calvin Jillson and Thornton Anderson, "Realignments in the Convention of 1787: The Slave Trade Compromise," *Journal of Politics,* 39 (August 1977), 712–29.

[16] Unless otherwise noted, the many quotations in this chapter from the debates in Philadelphia are taken from Max Farrand, *The Records of the Federal Convention of 1787* (New Haven, Conn.: Yale University Press, 1911), 3 volumes.

(voting) be limited to property owners. He felt that such a limitation was a "necessary defense against the dangerous influence of those multitudes without property and without principle, with which our country like all others will in time abound." James Madison was inclined to agree with Dickinson, for he, too, feared the time when "the great majority of the people will not only be without land, but any other sort, of property." Such people, he argued, were bound to become "the tools of opulence and ambition." Franklin objected, reminding the Convention that "our common people" had displayed much virtue and public spirit during the revolution, and that he would not disfranchise them for their pains.

The delegates to the Constitutional Convention showed little feeling for democracy in the modern sense. In protesting against the popular election of legislators, Elbridge Gerry of Massachusetts declared, "The evils we experience flow from the excess of democracy." No doubt Shays' Rebellion (small farmers protesting the many foreclosures in Massachusetts on the eve of the Convention) had intensified the gentleman's fear of "the levilling spirit." On the other hand, James Wilson of Pennsylvania argued that the legislators in the lower house should be chosen by the people, because "he was for raising the federal pyramid to a considerable altitude and for that reason wished to give it as broad a base as possible." When the work of the Convention was finally done, the delegates had indeed raised the federal pyramid to a considerable height above the general citizenry. "The people" were given a direct part only in the election of the lower branch of the legislature, the House of Representatives.

The delegates failed to reach a compromise on voting qualifications, however, and simply returned the problem to the states. The Constitution provided that whoever has the qualifications to vote for the most numerous house of the state legislature could also vote for United States representatives.

Republicanism: filtering the demands of the public

Giving voters in the states the power to elect members of the House of Representatives was as far as the framers were willing to go in the direction of direct popular control. "Democracy" was universally scorned at the Constitutional Convention, but "republicanism" was warmly praised. Thus, no mention is made of democracy in any of our fundamental documents—Declaration of Independence, Constitution, or Bill of Rights—but a "republican" government is guaranteed in the Constitution for each of the states.

Madison offers this view of what the framers meant by a republic in *Federalist 39:*

We may define a republic to be . . . a government which derives all its powers directly or indirectly from the great body of the people, and is administered by persons holding their offices during pleasure for a limited period, or during good behavior. It is *essential* to such a government that it be derived from the great body of the society. . . . It is *sufficient* for such a government that the persons administering it be appointed, either directly or indirectly, by the people.

Madison appears to say that a government is republican if it is representative, responsible, and popular.[17] For him, at least, this stood somewhere between democracy (direct rule by the people) and monarchy (rule by a single individual). Today, democracy is not interpreted to require direct rule by the people or to suggest the probability of mob rule. As we saw in chapter 2, it now means just about what Madison meant by republicanism and what the Declaration of Independence required of any just government: that it be an instrument of the people, with its power based on consent of the governed.

The desire for "republicanism" in the Constitutional Convention came from the necessity to avoid a monarchy. Some may have felt privately that the British monarch was the best model, for this was, after all, the age of monarchy. The complaints against the British king spelled out in the Declaration of Independence, however, had made a deep impression on public opinion. The people were bound to be against any plan for a hereditary ruler.

Gouverneur Morris opposed the proposal for the national executive to be chosen by the national legislature because he thought it would tend to make the President a mere creature of the legislature. He preferred election-at-large by the freeholders of the country. But Mr. Pinckney of South Carolina objected to election by the people on the practical ground that the most populated states could join in support of one candidate and manage to carry every election. Colonel Mason of Virginia expressed his contempt for the judgment of the general public by saying that it would be "as unnatural to refer the choice of a proper character for chief magistrate to the people, as it would, to refer a trial of colours to a blind man." Not until near the end of the Convention was a compromise reached: The President and Vice-President were to be selected by electors appointed by the states in whatever manner their legislatures might direct. James Wilson of Pennsylvania insisted that this device favored aristocracy, for it meant that the people would have no more than an indirect part in the election. Most of the other members were better pleased with it, though probably none of them was completely satisfied.

Governor Edmund Randolph of Virginia had initially proposed that the President's term of office run for seven years. Dr. McClurg of Virginia moved that the President be permitted to serve "during good behavior"; Morris seconded the motion, announcing that he was indifferent to how the executive was chosen so long as good behavior determined length of time in office. Colonel Mason thought that to base tenure on good behavior was but a step away from hereditary monarchy. The final compromise set the President's term at four years, with no restrictions concerning successive terms. This was later to be changed by the Twenty-second Amendment limiting the President to two terms.

The President and the House of Representatives would thus be selected by different procedures, would represent different groups of voters, and would

---

[17] Martin Diamond, "Democracy and *The Federalist:* A Reconsideration of the Framers' Intent," *American Political Science Review,* 53 (March 1959), 52–68. For discussion of Madison's view of "republican" see Alexander Landi, "Madison's Political Theory," *The Political Science Reviewer,* 6 (Fall 1976), 90–99.

serve for terms of different lengths. The choice of a President approached elitist or aristocratic procedures. In each state, gentlemen were selected by whatever means the state legislatures chose, and at first the legislators, themselves, made the choice. The selected gentlemen then cast ballots for some notable figure they deemed worthy of the presidency. The framers assumed that few states would name the same person, and therefore no candidate would normally receive a majority of all the electoral votes. The House of Representatives would then select a President from the *five* persons receiving the most electoral votes. In the House, each state would cast only one ballot, regardless of the number of representatives it had by virtue of the state's population. This complicated procedure was far removed from direct popular choice of representatives.

For the other branches of the new national government—the Senate and the Supreme Court—the framers also provided procedures more republican than democratic. The Senate, as the "upper" house of Congress, was formed as a small, aristocratic body exerting a conservative check on the popular House. Rather than being based on population, representation in the Senate was based on the states themselves. Each state had two senators regardless of population. If representation of mere numbers in the House involved rejection of aristocracy, representation in the Senate involved acceptance of it—especially since the two senators from each state would be chosen by the state legislature rather than by the voters. Moreover, the senators were given terms of 6 years, in contrast to 2 years for representatives and 4 years for the President. This small, elite body—originally of only 26 members—was expected to cool the hot passions of the House. As George Washington put it, the Senate would cool the popular sentiments of the House just as, in sipping coffee, he employed the saucer to cool the steaming brew from the cup. As we shall see in the chapter on Congress, the Senate is no more aristocratic today than is the practice of slurping one's coffee from a saucer. But both were so viewed by the framers.

For the Supreme Court and other courts that Congress might create, no thought was given to popular election. If the framers would not allow the people to elect senators and Presidents, they would certainly establish a court structure far removed from popular control. Justices of the Supreme Court were to be appointed by the President with the advice and consent of the Senate. And, instead of 2-, 4-, or 6-year terms, they were to serve for "good behavior," which in the absence of impeachment meant for life.

Overall, then, the structure of citizen inputs was intended to be mixed, with a little democratic liberalism enlivening a lot of republican moderation and aristocratic intransigence.

Popular support without majority control

The framers of the Constitution were outspokenly antimajority. Inputs from the majority were more to ensure their *support* than to ensure response to their *demands*. Even so, the doubts of most of the framers about the average citizen were moderated by concerns about the selfishness of the very people Alexander Hamilton flatteringly described as the "rich, well-born, and able." To what extent was the Constitution a reaction against the equal rights ideals of the Declaration of Independence? To what extent was it, for its time, a bold new venture in popular government?

In his classic study, *An Economic Interpretation of the Constitution,* Charles Beard analyzed the personnel of the Constitutional Convention in terms of their economic interests and professional pursuits. He found that a majority of the members were lawyers by profession. Not one represented the small farming or mechanic class. The overwhelming majority held government bonds, which they were eager to protect. Many were land speculators, anxious for a strong government which would protect their interests. Many were wealthy merchants who hoped to advance their commercial interests. Many were slaveholders who wanted specific guarantees of their right to own slaves.

Beard's thesis was shocking when it was first published in 1913. He charged that the Constitution was "an economic document drawn with superb skill by men whose property interests were immediately at stake" and that "as such it appealed directly and unerringly to identical interests in the country at large."

Today's historians and political scientists question Beard's view that only economic interests shaped the main outlines of the Constitution.[18] On the basis of what was said and how the voting went—not only at the Philadelphia Convention but also in the state ratifying conventions—the conflicts appear too numerous and complicated to attribute them to any single factor. No doubt some of the framers looked askance at what they considered economic radicalism in the state governments. Others were alarmed by what they believed to be suicidal foreign policies of the states ruining the credit of Congress and putting the whole country in military danger. Still others, out of power in state politics, may have sought to advance their own political interests in a stronger national government.

In assessing the democratic—or elitist—intentions of the framers of the Constitution, the fact that they were acting in a pre-democratic era needs to be kept in mind. Certainly they were opposed to democracy as we think of it today. On the other hand, they did provide for some popular participation in the national government, and they did give exclusive power to originate tax bills to the popular body of Congress, the House of Representatives. They did enlarge the powers of the national government while limiting those powers by enumerating them; furthermore, they carefully restricted the authority of those who were to exercise such powers. As hardheaded politicians, they recognized the seductive appeal of power. Even Hamilton believed in some balance:

Men love power. . . . Give all power to the many, they will oppress the few. Give all power to the few, they will oppress the many. Both therefore ought to have power, that each may defend itself against the other.

From this reasoning came the people's restricted access to the government. One branch of Congress, chosen directly by popular votes, would represent "the many." The other branch of Congress, the President, and the Supreme Court—all chosen by more indirect methods—would represent "the few." The same concern for a balance between "the excesses of democracy" and "the mischief of aristocracy" was to structure the powers of the official decision-making agencies.

THE STRUCTURE OF OFFICIAL DECISION MAKING

The major concerns of the Constitution's framers were the structure of the new government and the powers it should exercise. Skillfully pushing

[18] Charles Warren, *The Making of the Constitution* (Boston: Little, Brown, 1937) offers a legalist interpretation that takes sharp issue with Beard's economic thesis. Later attacks on the Beard version include Forrest McDonald, *We the People* (Chicago: University of Chicago Press, 1958), pp. 350, 357; and Robert E. Brown, *Charles Beard and the Constitution* (Princeton, N.J.: Princeton University Press, 1956). For an assessment according to modern social science, see Lee Benson, *Turner and Beard: American Historical Writing Reconsidered* (New York: Free Press, 1960).

for major constitutional reform rather than settling for temporary patching of the Articles of Confederation, the nationalists were to build their system out of two sets of major proposals offered to the Convention—the Randolph Plan and the Paterson Plan.

A strong national government or a confederation of states?

Governor Edmund Randolph presented fifteen resolutions at the opening session of the Constitutional Convention. These Virginia Resolutions proposed a strong consolidated union which, Governor Randolph admitted, was intended to be stronger than any confederation. His plan was to establish a national legislature with two branches: the first branch to be elected directly by all the people, the second to be chosen by the first from a list of persons nominated by the state legislatures. Representation of the states in both houses would be determined by their population or the amount of taxes they paid. The national legislature would have vastly greater power under this plan than under the Articles of Confederation. Rather than being unable to touch individual citizens without going through the states, the national legislature would have the power to act directly on individuals. Indeed, it would even have the authority to do away with any law passed by the states if it felt that the law went against the Constitution. It could also call out the full force of the Union against any state that failed to meet its obligations under the Constitution.

The Randolph Plan would have focused power in the legislature, much in the manner of the British government today (a form that has come to be known as parliamentary government). The national legislature was to choose the national executive for a fixed term. It would also choose the members of the national judiciary, who would hold office "during good behavior." The executive and the judiciary would comprise a "council of revision," with the power to veto all laws that it judged to be contrary to the intent of the Constitution.

For several weeks the delegates at Philadelphia debated the Randolph Plan. It was attacked by delegates from the small states, for it threatened a drastic reduction in their power. Under the Articles, all states, whether large or small, enjoyed equal representation in Congress. Under the Randolph Plan the more populous states and the wealthier states would have greater representation in both houses.

William Paterson of New Jersey offered contrasting proposals that had been worked up by delegates from Connecticut, New York, New Jersey, and Delaware. Whereas the Randolph Plan proposed to scrap the Articles in order to set up a strong national government, Paterson wanted to preserve and strengthen the existing Confederation. The Paterson Plan would add to the powers of Congress the authority to regulate commerce among the states, to raise government income by tariff, and to obtain financial contributions from the states in proportion to their populations. It would also give Congress the power to choose a President who would serve a single term. It would establish a court system, the judges to be appointed by the President and to serve during good behavior. The "kingpin clause," later to appear in the Constitution, appeared first in the Paterson Plan. It provided that the laws and treaties of the national government would be the "supreme law" of the nation, making any conflicting state laws invalid.

The Randolph Plan and the Paterson Plan presented the Convention with two clear-cut alternatives. The Randolph Plan sought to construct a new and strong consolidated union. The Paterson Plan sought to continue a fairly loose association of states—a confederation. Under the Randolph Plan, Congress was to be composed of two houses and each state's representation was to be determined by its population or the amount of taxes it paid to the national government. Under the Paterson Plan, the Congress would remain unicameral (one house), the state legislatures would choose the representatives, and the states would be represented equally. The Randolph Plan would give Congress full power to legislate in all matters of national concern affecting the general welfare. The Paterson Plan would give Congress only certain powers. Both plans were calculated to strengthen the national government; they differed only in the degree to which it would be strengthened.

Federalism: the Great Compromise

The text of the Constitution reveals the "Great Compromise" that was finally worked out between the large and small states. From the Randolph and Paterson plans and scattered proposals from the floor, the "more perfect union" was proposed. It was neither a consolidated national government nor a confederation of sovereign states. By mixing some features of a consolidated national government with some features of a confederation, Americans developed a new, mixed system. Neither the national nor the state governments would be creatures of, or dependent on, the other for existence. Both levels of government would receive their powers from the same Constitution. This new American system has come to be called *federalism* or a *federal* system of government. The original framers didn't know what to call it, but they did know that some imaginative compromise was necessary if they were to reach agreement.

How far should the United States go from its confederation of states toward a national union? Colonel George Mason of Virginia declared that "notwithstanding his solicitude to establish a national government, he never would agree to abolish the state governments or render them absolutely insignificant." Luther Martin of Maryland agreed with Colonel Mason on the importance of the state governments: "He would support them at the expense of the general government which was instituted for the purpose of that support."

James Wilson of Pennsylvania took a more national view; he did not think "state governments and state sovereignties to be so much the idol of the People that they are averse to receive a national government." Alexander Hamilton was the most outspoken in denouncing the idea of a mere confederation. He felt that "great economy might be obtained by substituting a general government" for the state governments, though he admitted he would not shock public opinion by pressing for such a drastic measure. James Madison reviewed the history of ancient and modern confederations and found in all of them "the same tendency of the parts to encroach on the authority of the whole;" he begged the smaller states to drop their "pertinacious adherence" to the Paterson Plan.

From these divergent points of view, federalism emerged. Over the years, by usage, judicial interpretation, and congressional statute, the meaning of federalism has developed. Federalism today is regarded as *any system of government in which there is a common national government for all the people in the country, and in which the country is divided into provinces (for us, "states") each of which has its own government for handling at least some provincial (state) problems.* A federation has a national government that directly governs all the people, whereas a confederation is restricted to governing through the member governments. A federation differs from a unitary government in that a federation has provincial or state governments that exist independently and exercise some powers on their own; a unitary government has no such provincial or state governments with independent authority. The particular distribution of powers and responsibilities between the national government and the state or provincial governments varies among such federal systems as those of Switzerland, the Soviet Union, Brazil, Canada, and the United States.[19]

In the United States of America, the title of the new government created by the Constitution accurately describes what the framers were trying to achieve. The *states* remained as governing bodies in their own right, but the people were also *united* under a single national government. Official decision making in the United States is therefore structured by the federal system. Among the key elements of this structure are:

1. The Constitution, treaties, and all acts of the national government (in keeping with the Constitution) are the supreme law of the land, taking precedence over any contrary state decisions.

2. Nevertheless, the states are an integral part of the political structure of the union. The states are the units, for example, through which all elections of national officials are carried out.

3. All of the states, old and new, are on an equal footing within the union.

4. The union is indestructible, that is, no state has the right to withdraw from the union, for the constitutional bonds are considered permanent and firm.

5. The states have certain obligations to each other. For example, each must give full faith and credit to the public acts of other states, and each must refrain from discriminating against the "privileges and immunities" (rights and liberties) of citizens of other states.

---

[19] For discussions of federalism see K. C. Wheare, *Federal Government* (New York: Oxford University Press, 1964); Valerie Earle (ed.), *Federalism: Infinite Variety in Theory and Practice* (Itasca, Ill.: F. E. Peacock, 1968); Carl J. Friedrich, *Trends of Federalism in Theory and Practice* (New York: Praeger, 1968); Ivo D. Duchacek, *Comparative Federalism* (New York: Holt, Rinehart & Winston, 1970); William Riker, *Federalism: Origin, Operation, Significance* (Boston: Little, Brown, 1964).

6. The national government has certain obligations to the states, such as guarantee-ing each a republican form of government, providing equal representation for each state in the Senate, and protecting states against invasion or domestic violence.

7. The powers of government are distributed by the Constitution, with some being given to the national government and others being reserved to the states.

The basic outline of American federalism can be read in the Constitution, but its real meaning has developed through interpretation and practice. The framers did not know where federalism would take the society. They hoped that it was a plan ingenious enough to be politically acceptable to the states and at the same time strengthening to the national level of government. But many serious political battles, including a civil war, had to be fought before power relationships between the nation and the states were defined. Nor are they fully defined even now. Federalism is new in the sense of posing new problems, because its changing definition is central to the question of who gets helped and who gets hurt.

The evolution of federalism has been closely tied to the expansion of governmental activities and powers. In the federal structure, the Constitution spells out both obligations and powers of the national and state governments. It limits the authority of both levels of government. Moreover, it guarantees some individual rights against any governmental intervention.

The care with which the framers distributed and limited the powers of both the national and state governments is suggested by the following pattern:

1. Certain powers are assigned to the national government and belong only to it—the conduct of foreign affairs, for example, or the control of currency.

2. Certain powers are assigned to the national government but are also held by the states—taxation or regulation of commerce.

3. Certain powers are specifically denied to the national government—for example, Congress may not tax exports or give preference to the ports of one state over those of another.

4. Certain powers are specifically denied to the states—for example, no state may enter into any treaty, alliance, or confederation, or lay any duties on imports or exports.

5. All other powers belong to the states or to the people—that is, those powers that are neither delegated to the national government nor denied to the states.

Although these power assignments in the federal system appear specific and concrete, they became subjects of change and interpretation almost from the outset. The principal conflict has been between proponents of national power and champions of states' rights. Those who stress national power point to Article VI, Section 2. It explicitly states that the Constitution and the laws and treaties of the United States shall be the supreme law of the land. Those who favor states' rights point to the Tenth Amendment, which provides that "The powers not delegated to the United States by the Constitution, nor prohibited by it to the States, are reserved to the States, respectively, or to the people." What the Tenth Amendment added to the original intentions of the 1787 framers, however, is not at all clear. When the Amendment was drafted in 1789, Congress rejected a proposal to insert the word "expressly" before the word "delegated." Nevertheless, to this day, some advocates of states' rights continue to claim that the national government is limited to powers *expressly* delegated to it.

The Articles of Confederation plainly held that each state retained "every power, jurisdiction, and right" not *expressly* delegated to the United States. The Constitutional Convention was well aware of this wording; so was the First Congress, which rejected similar wording for the Tenth Amendment. In the case of *McCulloch v. Maryland,*[20] Chief Justice Marshall declared that the framers, both of the Constitution of 1787 and of the Tenth Amendment in 1789, had experienced "such embarrassments" from this restrictive wording that they "probably omitted it to avoid those embarrassments."

It was in this case, *McCulloch v. Maryland,* that the Supreme Court first determined that Congress had powers beyond those expressly delegated. In question was the power to establish a National Bank even though the Constitution does not specifically mention banking as one of the national government's powers. The Court pointed out that the enumeration of powers in Article I, Section 8, ends with a blanket clause giving the Congress power "to make all laws which shall be necessary and proper for carrying into execution the foregoing powers, and all other powers vested by this Constitution in the government of the United States, or in any department or officer thereof." This clause is placed with the *powers* of Congress—not among the *limitations* on its powers. It is intended to grant additional power, not to restrict those already granted. Chief Justice Marshall therefore interpreted "necessary and proper" to mean that Congress could choose whatever means it believed convenient, useful, or essential to perform its legislative functions. Had the Court not interpreted the "necessary and proper" clause to grant powers beyond those specifically delegated to Congress, the national government would have been severely handicapped in meeting new problems.

The doctrine of "implied powers," first recognized by Chief Justice Marshall in *McCulloch v. Maryland,* has been an important concept in justifying the growth of national powers to meet the changing and increasing needs of the American people. The framers of the Constitution could not have anticipated such bold expansions of governmental activities as commissions to regulate atomic energy and television broadcasting. But they were farsighted enough to give Congress power to make all laws that would prove "necessary and proper" to the future "Welfare of the United States." Demands on the system called for expansion of powers and the flexible Constitution permitted it.

Separated, checked, and balanced powers

The framers of the Constitution mixed democratic, republican, and aristocratic ideas in establishing input structures, and they mixed aspects of both confederation and unitary government in establishing a federal system.

[20] Wheaton 316 (1819).

This willingness to compromise demonstrates their great political skill, for if each of them had stubbornly held out for the exact principles he preferred, they could never have come to agreement.

But the mixing of different principles meant more than willingness to compromise. The dominant view of the eighteenth century was of a universe in neat if delicate balance, governed by the laws of physics demonstrated by Sir Isaac Newton's work on the forces of gravity. With such a view of the natural laws of the universe, the idea of a mixture of opposed forces, each affecting the others and all held in place by the interaction, had powerful appeal. Hence the idea of combining contrary views appeared to be in harmony with natural laws governing the entire universe. *Separation of powers* among decision-making agencies and the exercise of *checks and balances* were thus viewed as desirable principles in their own right. The tasks of decision making—rule making, application of rules, and settlement of disputes—were accordingly given to separate bodies (separation of powers) and each was given some control over the others' use of powers (checks and balances).

Separation of powers combined with checks and balances was a barricade against the supposed dangers of majority rule. All the state constitutions, including those written at the peak of the revolutionary fervor, embodied the principle of separated, checked, and balanced powers. The Massachusetts Constitution, adopted in 1780, spells it out most clearly, because the Massachusetts voters had rejected an earlier draft that did not provide adequate checks and balances. Federalists and Antifederalists agreed on the principle of separation of powers—both Adams and Jefferson vigorously defended it. Most delegates to the Convention of 1787 seem to have taken the principle for granted. Among the few opposing the principle were Benjamin Franklin and Alexander Hamilton, Franklin because he was not afraid of majority rule and Hamilton because he favored monarchy. The common view was that of James Madison, who refers to separation of powers in *The Federalist* as "this essential precaution in favor of liberty" and as "the sacred maxim of free government."

The delegates were so committed to the concepts of separation of powers and checks and balances that they spent far more time debating procedures and structure of government than they spent on governmental powers. Separation of powers as well as the need for settling the conflicts of the large and small states led the delegates into bicameralism. The bicameral legislature was made up of two houses, each with separate organizations and different constituencies. The House of Representatives was the popular body with the people directly electing representatives in proportion to their population. The Senate was the body of the states, with each state represented by two delegates chosen by the state legislature.

Of the three branches of government, the federal judiciary was the least discussed at the convention. There was agreement on the need for a supreme national court; the establishment of lower courts was left to the discretion of Congress. The Convention did not accept the Randolph proposal for a council of revision in which the executive and the judges both had the power to declare national and state laws unconstitutional. Elbridge Gerry of Massachusetts objected to the idea of "making statesmen of the judges; and setting them up as the guardians of the rights of the people; he relied for his part on the representatives of the people as the guardians of their rights and interests." James Madison argued that since experience showed the powerful tendency of the legislature "to absorb all power," it was necessary to give "every defensive authority to the other departments that was consistent with republican principles." Whether the Convention meant to give the courts the power of judicial review—the power to declare acts of the legislature or of the executive unconstitutional—is uncertain, for they did not write their intentions regarding this matter into the document itself.

The checks and balances written into the Constitution were thus viewed as a major feature of free government. They were numerous and complex, and in the operation of the government they have been both a blessing and a burden. Bicameralism—a Congress with two branches—allows either house to block legislation. The President is given legislative responsibility in the provision that, "He shall from time to time give Congress Information on the State of the Union, and recommend to their Consideration such Measures as he shall judge necessary and expedient." The President's power to approve or disapprove ("veto") legislation is actually spelled out in the Constitution's Article I on *legislative powers*. Presidential veto and the power of Congress to override the veto thoroughly mix executive and legislative powers in a double-check designed to ensure balance between them. To compound the mixture, Article II on *executive power* directs the Senate to give the President "Advice and Consent" on appointments and treaties, with the "advice" including the possibility of refusing "consent." Although basically separated along functional lines—Congress makes policies and the President applies them—legislative and executive powers were also deliberately mixed to ensure that each branch could check the other in the interest of the same sort of balance Newton saw in the universe. Article III of the Constitution starts, "The judicial Power . . . shall be vested in one supreme Court and in such inferior Courts as the Congress may from time to time ordain and establish." Although the meaning of "the judicial power" is not spelled out, the Supreme Court early interpreted it to include the power of judicial review, that is, of courts ruling on the constitutionality of acts by other decision-making agencies. With judges appointed by presidential nomination and Senate approval, and with Congress having authority to create and abolish courts below the Supreme Court, separated powers were once again mixed in the interest of checks and balances.

Although the complexities of checks and balances preoccupied the framers of the Constitution and have since preoccupied authors of texts on American politics, they have rarely been a matter of great interest to the public. This was dramatically changed in 1974 when impeachment proceedings were begun against President Richard M. Nixon. The framers referred to the impeachment power in their Articles on each of the three branches of the new national government. They gave Congress the power to impeach, and they named "the President, Vice President, and all civil Officers of the United States" as the subjects of that power. To remove an unfit President or other official, the framers returned to their English heritage and adopted a system in which a majority of the House would be able to impeach; and after a trial

Public awareness of the impeachment process reached unprecedented levels in 1974.

in the Senate, a two-thirds vote of the senators could convict. Impeachment was to be for "treason, bribery, or other high crimes and misdemeanors." In this context "crimes and misdemeanors" were not merely ordinary crimes against the person, such as murder, but also included offenses against the state, such as political crimes. Originally, George Mason proposed that "maladministration" be the basis for impeachment, but Madison objected because of the vagueness of the term and suggested that it be replaced with "high crimes and misdemeanors."[21] In the first Congress, Madison amplified the meaning of "high crimes and misdemeanors": in defending the President's power to appoint executive subordinates, he pointed out that such appointees would not be beyond congressional control, because a President could be impeached and convicted for improper acts on the part of his subordinates. In the impeachment inquiry of 1974, Nixon argued against Madison's interpretation, claiming that a President could be impeached only for a criminal act of his own. Demonstrating anew the importance of checks and balances, the

---

[21] See Raoul Berger, *Impeachment: The Constitutional Problems* (Cambridge, Mass.: Harvard University Press, 1973).

House Committee on the Judiciary rejected Nixon's view and recommended articles of impeachment.

ADOPTION AND CHANGE OF THE NEW DOCUMENT

Finished with the tasks of defining governmental powers and establishing the agents who would exercise them, the delegates were faced with one final set of nagging questions. How was the new government to be established? Could the people be persuaded to accept it? What arguments would opponents bring against it, and how powerful would be their attacks? From secret deliberations, the Constitution was now to emerge into the full glare of public deliberation and debate.

The fight for ratification

The work of the Convention ended on September 17, 1787. Benjamin Franklin rose to urge all "for our own sakes and for the sake of posterity" to act "heartily and unanimously" in recommending the Constitution. Three members who stayed to the end, though they confessed that they were "painfully embarrassed," declined to sign the document—Governor Randolph, Colonel Mason, and Mr. Gerry. Thirty-nine delegates, representing twelve states, did sign. On September 28, 1787, without making any recommendation of its own, Congress submitted the proposed constitution to the states.

How to justify the result of the Philadelphia Convention was a rather delicate problem. In writing a new constitution, the delegates had clearly gone beyond their authority, which was simply to recommend changes in the Articles of Confederation. Since the members of Congress and of the state legislatures were sworn to the "perpetual union" under the Confederation, they could hardly vote to scrap the Articles. Even before the Convention had met, James Madison had written to Thomas Jefferson that he felt it best "to lay the foundation of the new system in such a ratification by the people themselves as will render it clearly paramount to their legislative authority." Madison recognized that approval of the Constitution by the people would give it greater authority than would approval by state legislatures.

In the Convention itself, some of the members objected to departing from the amending procedure outlined in the Articles, which demanded the unanimous consent of the state legislatures. The complete absence of a Rhode Island delegation at the Convention, however, made unanimity out of the question. Moreover, as Madison pointed out, because the powers that the Constitution granted to the general government had been taken mainly from the state legislatures, the legislatures might decide to reject the document. The solution was to refer the document to state conventions elected for the express purpose of considering the new Constitution. The Convention decided that the Constitution would be "ordained and established" when nine state conventions had ratified it. Certainly the legitimacy of the proposed new government could only be enhanced by popular participation in the ratification procedure.

Conventions called by the state legislatures in Delaware, Pennsylvania, New Jersey, and Georgia swiftly and unanimously adopted the new Constitution. The debate in other states was more prolonged, and the voting, in some instances, was very close. It is hard for us now, looking back, to analyze the climate of public opinion during the fight for ratification. Propaganda for and against the new Constitution took many forms: pamphlets, editorials, letters to newspapers, caricatures, handbills, and platform lectures. Probably the most important single contribution to the literature of American political theory and also the most effective piece of propaganda favoring the proposed Constitution was *The Federalist (The Federalist Papers)*, which first appeared as a series of letters in the newspapers of New York. The three authors, Alexander Hamilton, John Jay, and James Madison (writing under the name *"Publius"*), while careful not to reject the popular doctrines of natural rights, individual freedom, and popular participation, argued a skillfully wrought case for a strong national government, limitations on the powers of the states, and "stability in government." Madison wrote to his father that *The Federalist* was "the best commentary on the principles of government which was ever written."

The Federalist certainly had an influence on the New York convention. Later, when the letters were collected in book form, they were effectively used in the Virginia campaign as well. They made a particularly strong impression on John Marshall, who was fighting for ratification in the Virginia convention. A few years later, as Chief Justice of the United States, Marshall referred frequently to *The Federalist* in citing the intentions of the framers of the Constitution. *The Federalist* was not impartial toward the Constitution, however, for it was first published as a piece of electioneering. During the campaign for ratification, a great deal was also said and written in opposition to the proposed Constitution. Because most of this material never found its way into book form, and because it championed the losing side, it has disappeared. *The Federalist* has lived on.

The demand for a bill of rights

As arguments against *The Federalist* "Agrippa" (James Winthrop) wrote in the *Massachusetts Gazette:*

The question before the people is whether they will have a limited government or an absolute one. . . . It is the opinion of the ablest writers on this subject that no extensive empire can be governed upon republican principles and that such a government will degenerate to a despotism unless it be made of a confederacy of smaller states each having the full powers of internal regulation.

And "Cato" (Governor Clinton) warned the people of New York to beware "the proffered constitution of Caesar" which denies separation of powers and gives authority to the President that is too vast and important for any one man without limited tenure. "Sidney" (Robert Yates) argued in the *New York Journal* that the new Constitution would "destroy the rights and liberties of the people."[22]

The opponents of the proposed Constitution hammered away at its most obvious weakness: it had no bill of rights. This omission was especially glaring in view of the fact that eight of the new state constitutions contained separate bills of rights, and three guaranteed basic liberties within the main text. And yet, until the very end of the Philadelphia Convention, no one had mentioned the idea of a bill of rights. Even after it had been suggested, none of the members showed much interest. Later, Charles C. Pinckney told the South Carolina ratifying convention that the framers had hesitated to list specific rights because some might think the government could take away any rights that were not listed. But he also admitted that a bill of rights generally begins with a declaration that all men are born free and equal. The members of the Philadelphia Convention felt they could not honestly make such a statement in that "a large part of our property consists in men who are actually born slaves."

The framers considered the issue of individual liberties important. This is shown in the original text by the following provisions: the individual was protected against being

- held for a crime without cause (writ of habeas corpus)
- punished for an act that was not illegal when it was performed (ex post facto law)
- singled out for punishment by an act of Congress (that is, being punished by bill of attainder)
- convicted of treason except for offenses and by procedures spelled out in the Constitution

True, the Constitution did not grant national suffrage, but neither did it impose suffrage restrictions, as some members had urged. And the Constitution, as approved, did prohibit religious tests for any national office, though such tests were common in the state governments. It seems fair to conclude that the failure to form a more complete bill of rights was simply an error in judgment, not an effort to undermine individual liberties.

The arguments of the framers, however logical, were not convincing. The framers had thought that separation of powers, checks and balances, and the enumeration of the powers of the national government were enough protection against the abuse of power. But the majority of citizens believed they were entitled to a bill of rights. The New York, Massachusetts, and Virginia conventions agreed to ratify the new Constitution only after receiving the solemn promise that it would immediately be amended to include a bill of rights as part of the supreme law of the land.

[22] The primary source for the fight over ratification is Jonathan Elliot, *The Debates in the Several State Conventions and the Adoption of the Federal Constitution* (Philadelphia: Lippincott, 1888). Also see Ann Diamond, "The Anti-Federalist 'Brutus,'" *The Political Science Reviewer,* 6 (Fall 1976), 249–81; Richard Crosby, "The New York State Ratifying Convention: On Federalism," *Polity,* 9 (Fall 1976), 97–116.

The fight over ratification was in part a regional one. The Eastern Seaboard and the Tidewater South were generally in favor; westerners were inclined to be suspicious and doubtful. Economic lines were rather roughly drawn: merchants, bankers, slaveholders, and persons of property were more often in favor of ratification than were the small farmers, shopkeepers, mechanics, and debtors. These were not, of course, solid blocs. There were some advocates and opponents of the proposed constitution in every state, in every community, among all classes.

At the level of practical politics, the supporters of the Constitution seemed to have more effective leaders. With the same political skill that secured them their delegations to the Philadelphia Convention in the first place, the proponents of the Constitution succeeded in gathering support. On the other hand, except for pointing out the need for a bill of rights, the opponents had little to offer of constructive value. Their objections were vague suspicions rather than specific dissents. However it was achieved, the important fact is that a majority of the conventions in 9 states were persuaded to approve the new Constitution.

When the Constitution was written and adopted, the framers were worried about the magnitude of their task. A gigantic task it was: designing a federal union for 13 distinct and independent states; setting up a republican government for nearly 4 million people; ruling a "vast territory" outlined by 1,500 miles of coastline and stretching all the way from the Atlantic Ocean to the Mississippi River. The framers could not possibly have imagined that the instrument of government they fashioned would be operating 200 years later, for more than 200 million people in 50 states, from Florida to Alaska, from Maine to Hawaii.

In this chapter, we have focused on the constitutional text of 1787. But it should be clearly understood that the present-day Constitution is always changing. It has grown and matured since 1787, not only by 26 formal amendments but also by statutory enactments, presidential interpretations and executive orders, administrative rules and regulations, judicial decisions, popular attitudes and opinions, and customary behavior, official and unofficial. The Constitution is not merely a historical document. It is rooted in the experience of the nation. It retains its vitality and validity because it is both input and output in the ongoing political process. All policy making is conditioned by the Constitution. In short, the Constitution sets the outer limits of permissibility for all governmental activities. In this broad sense of constitutional law, all the following chapters may be seen as fuller development of what Americans regard to be "the supreme law of the land."

Although many people identified themselves as American citizens rather than British subjects even before the Declaration of Independence, fighting and winning the Revolutionary War was the major event that united Americans into a political community. The Articles of Confederation were formulated during the revolution and were the new nation's first Constitution. They represented a pact among the states, rather than a strong central government; indeed, they proved too weak for the problems at hand.

Congress finally endorsed movement for a convention to work out some of the problems the new government was facing. The Constitutional Convention met in Philadelphia in 1787 and after much compromise wrote the Constitution, which is still our basic law. There was much debate over whether to have a strong national government or a loose confederation of states. A compromise allowed for a combination of both: one unifying national government and individual state governments. It has come to be called *federalism*. The framers of the Constitution also provided for separation of powers (to prevent direct popular control of the government) and a system of checks and balances (to give each branch of the government some measure of control of the others' powers).

The new government was far from democratic by today's standards. To prevent easy public control of policy, it was designed to mix, separate, balance, and check powers. Inputs from the majority were more to ensure their *support* than to guarantee response to their *demands*.

part 2

INPUTS
OF THE
POLITICAL
SYSTEM:
WHO
WANTS
AND
NEEDS
WHAT?

political opinions and participation

What do people want from their government? How much public support do government policies and leaders enjoy? To what extent do citizens simply not care about politics? These questions get to the substance of what we have called the "input" activities of the political system.

THE NATURE OF POLITICAL OPINIONS

Public opinions are the foundations on which all governments, democratic or dictatorial, ultimately rest. Some understanding of public opinion is accordingly central to any understanding of government.

What is public opinion?

Public opinion is the *expression of attitudes on a social issue.* Notice that this definition includes three parts. First, unless an attitude is *expressed,* it is neither public nor opinion. Attitudes are internal feelings that cannot be directly observed, and opinions are the expressions of those feelings. Suppose that most of the people in a country hate their rulers but fail to express their dislike in talking with friends, in behavior at political meetings, in voting, in responses to interviewers, or in any other way. Such attitudes would not be part of public opinion, although they would constitute a highly important potential or latent public opinion.

Second, public opinion requires an *issue* on which people take different positions. An opinion is always pro or con. If people have neither favorable nor unfavorable feelings about an issue—government support for medical care, for example—we say they have no opinion on the subject.

Third, public opinion deals with *social* rather than purely private questions. A hypochondriac's operation, however enthusiastically the patient expresses opinions about it, is not a social issue. It becomes a social issue and an object of public opinion only if others are stimulated to form opinions on the subject. Public opinion refers, then, to the preferences of a number of people, rather than to those of a single person. Despite our tendency to assume that the only real issues are those we are interested in, public opinions exist on a tremendous range of questions—from Pam Shriver's ability as a tennis player to problems of world peace. Any question on which people have favorable or unfavorable attitudes can, in other words, become an object of public opinion.

We started with a deliberately broad definition of public opinion as a reminder that every question of public concern is not necessarily political. Some sort of public opinion is created and expressed by every change in the weather. But these opinions become political only as they acquire relevance for government—if they deal with the need to subsidize heating costs for low income groups, for example. If we use *public opinion* to mean the expression of attitudes on a social issue, then *political opinion* refers somewhat more narrowly to the expression of attitudes on a political issue. The issue may concern candidates, parties, or anything else that affects public policies.

The functions of opinions for the individual

Opinions perform at least three basic functions for the individual: object appraisal, social adjustment, and externalization of inner requirements.[1] *Object appraisal* helps us understand and respond to our world. We appraise, or size up, an object, categorize it, form an opinion, and store the opinion in our memory. Later, when we come across something similar, we respond to it in the light of our previously formed opinion. If we were reared in a loyal Republican family, for example, we inherited a clue for evaluating candidates and proposals. Republicans make favorable first impressions; others do not. Although the dangers and disadvantages of this instant judgment are apparent, without such convenient categories for quick response the many things that confront us would make the world appear to be a great, buzzing confusion. Each event cannot be approached with genuine innocence—no opinions at all—or we would never cope with the multitude of things around us. Voters reacting to names undifferentiated by party labels—as in party primaries—show unstable preferences and high responsiveness to influence by the mass media.

Social adjustment refers to how opinions improve, disrupt, or maintain an individual's relations with others. In the family, the child discovers early that some opinions win approval, others disapproval. Family and friends make up "reference groups"—groups with which we feel a sense of identity or kinship and from which we derive standards for judging ourselves and others. But a reference group may also be quite impersonal, involving no face-to-face contact, and it may be negative as well as positive. A young woman who is a lonely intellectual in a small town may willingly and even eagerly look for the disrespect of her neighbors in order to enjoy the feeling that she is acting in ways that would satisfy the editors of *The American Scholar*. In this case, her immediate neighbors are a negative reference group (her self-esteem is increased by their disapproval). The editors of *The American Scholar* are a positive reference group (her self-esteem is increased by the feeling that she conforms to their standards). We tend to find our social identity and self-esteem by relating our opinions to those of others. We like to have the "right" opinions about politics as much as we like to wear the "right" clothes or hair style.

---

[1] M. Brewster Smith, Jerome S. Bruner, and Robert W. White, *Opinions and Personality* (New York: John Wiley, 1956), pp. 39–46. These 3 broad functions of opinions cannot be considered exhaustive, but they appear as useful as any others that have been offered. Psychologists have listed "basic irreducible needs" ranging from 2 (Freud—gratification of the libido and the death wish) to more than 50. See E. L. Thorndike, *The Original Nature of Man* (New York: Teachers College of Columbia University, 1913). In an effort to unravel this complex subject, Robert Lane comes up with 10 needs served by political ideas, but he shifts to 6 in trying to explain the political ideas of 24 college students. *Political Thinking and Consciousness* (Chicago: Markham, 1969).

88

PART 2
inputs of the
political
system: who
wants and needs
what?

Berry's World

"Put me down as having a deeply felt sense of powerlessness and disengagement, which has led to a profound crisis of confidence."

Reprinted by permission. © 1979 NEA, Inc.

Externalization of inner requirements simply means that it helps to get things off your chest. Expressing an opinion may reduce anxiety produced by some unresolved psychological problem. An early study discovered, for example, that people who are insecure and afraid of the future tend to be conservative. This may be because conservative philosophy suggests stability, the wisdom of the past, and the dangers to society that social experimentation would bring.[2] Robert Lane, a pioneer in the study of political psychology, found that people unable to tolerate ambiguity showed some tendency to vote for a candidate who offered simple solutions to difficult problems.[3] The externalization of inner requirements is not associated more with one political party, however, than with another. As much as politicians might like to think all the "crazies" are on the other side, the facts don't support such a view.

Occasionally, an event will have such clear political meaning that it will influence opinions held by almost everyone. The scandalous revelations of the "Year of Watergate" from 1973 to 1974, for example, had disastrous effects on opinions about President Nixon, even among those who had previously thought highly of him. In one study, a group of college students who said in 1973 that Nixon was "one of the best recent Presidents" had mostly come to an opposite view in April of 1974, four months before Nixon was forced

[2] Herbert McClosky, "Conservatism and Personality," *American Political Science Review,* 52 (March 1958), 27–45.

[3] Robert E. Lane, "Political Personality and Electoral Choice," *American Political Science Review,* 49 (March 1955), 181.

to resign.[4] Even strongly held opinions may be changed by the strength of forceful events. Although the core of Nixon support in 1974 came from those who in 1973 were pro-Nixon, *most of the students with those earlier pro-Nixon views did change.*

POLITICAL SOCIALIZATION

Where do political opinions come from? In chapter 1 we discussed political socialization as a basic function of every political system. Now we are ready to examine it in more detail. In this and the following section, our focus will be on the output aspects of socialization—how the system shapes political opinions. In the third section we shift to the input aspects of political socialization—how the expression of political opinions affects the system.

The family

Most parents do not think of themselves as performing a function for the political system when they train their children. Politics is not important enough in most families for parents to think about teaching it to their offspring. We would be surprised, for example, to discover that neighbors took their children to every meeting of the family's political party and encouraged them to study the party's platform. But we are not surprised when neighbors take their children to Sunday School and church and encourage them to study their catechism. Nevertheless, most parents somehow convey to their children a general feeling of patriotism, giving them a sense of identity as "Americans" and of pride in the U.S.A. In fact, little children are uncritically patriotic: at first they think of the Stars and Stripes simply as *the* flag, *the* symbol that stands for *the* (good) country; later, as they learn a little about foreign lands, they come to recognize the existence of strange looking flags representing lesser countries. In passing on these ideas about politics, Mom and Dad are acting as informal agents in the political system, whether they realize it or not. And most parents probably do have some special sense of responsibility when they have to answer a question related to patriotism, such as why July the Fourth is celebrated.

That children pick up favorable images of their country and its symbols is not surprising. Most parents give their children an idealized, sugar-coated view of almost everything, feeling that youngsters should not be disturbed by unpleasant, threatening, or complex realities. They may think the neighborhood kindergarten is abysmal; but if the children have to go there, it will be pictured as a wonderland of joy and learning. With such sugar-coating for institutions that the parents don't like, the ones they do like—such as their country—are naturally presented in an overwhelmingly favorable light.

[4] Robert Entman, James W. Prothro, and Edward Sharp, "Watergate and Political Trust: A Panel Study," Study No. W4–23, November 1974, Institution for Social and Policy Studies, Yale University.

Children learn the symbols of patriotism from family and friends.

Cues as to which political party represents the "good guys" are passed on much more casually, often unintentionally. Even so, the first systematic studies of political socialization in the 1960s emphasized how early and how well the parents' party identifications was picked up by children. When grade school children were asked about their party choice, they referred to it as a family characteristic rather than as an individual choice. "All I know," said one ponytailed ten-year-old, "is *we're* not Republicans."[5] Even by the second grade, 36 percent of the children in a large-scale study in the Chicago area claimed a party preference; by the fifth grade, the proportion had risen to 55 percent.[6]

The most thorough study of the way children learn political values comes from a nationwide survey of high-school seniors and their parents. This survey has the advantage of offering direct information from both parents and their children, rather than relying on only one or the other to report the opinions

[5] Fred I. Greenstein, *Children and Politics* (New Haven, Conn.: Yale University Press, 1965), p. 73.

[6] Robert D. Hess and Judith V. Torney, *The Development of Political Attitudes in Children* (Chicago: Aldine, 1967), p. 90.

of both. Moreover, it deals with pre-adults at an important age, just as they are completing their secondary education and preparing to leave home. By the time they have reached their senior year in high school, as many readers of this book can no doubt attest, young people tend to be more critical of—and perhaps even rebellious against—the preferences of their parents. The function of externalization of inner needs, particularly the need for autonomy or independence, could lead to rejection of the parental party preference. And the political ideas of friends or teachers might outweigh those of parents in performing the functions of social adjustment and object appraisal. But the rebellion is not strongly political; rather, it appears to focus on matters more central to young people, principally questions of personal life-style such as control over one's time, appearance, and behavior.

No wholesale desertion of the family's party identification occurs. The following is the distribution of student-parent agreement and disagreement:

Child same as parents (Democrat, Independent, or Republican). 59%

Child Independent, parents partisan 23

Child partisan, parents Independent 11

Child and parents partisan, for different parties . . . . __7__

100%[7]

Findings like these gave rise to the early emphasis on party identification being inherited from parents, but the actual inheritance of a *family* partisan position is far less than the above percentages indicate. These figures on child-parent agreement are based only on families in which both parents have the same partisan position—Democrat, Independent, or Republican. In fact, however, about a fourth (24 percent) of all parents differ from each other in their choices among these three positions.[8] This means that a fourth of all families are necessarily left out of calculations such as those above on child-parent agreement. The frequency of family homogeneity—that is, both parents and their child in the same partisan position—is thus reduced to less than half (45 percent) of all families.

If the family is not as homogeneous a political unit as it was once thought to be, neither is it as marked by disagreement as our interpretation might suggest. Most of the husband-wife differences are minor, with one spouse being Independent while the other identifies with a party. In only 7 percent of the families was one parent a Republican and the other a Democrat. Most of the child-parent disagreement similarly represents combinations of an Independent position on the one hand with a partisan position on the other. This underscores the degree to which politics is a low-key concern in most families; partisan positions are not passed on especially well, but neither are they rebelled against.

[7] M. Kent Jennings and Richard G. Niemi, *The Political Character of Adolescence: The Influence of Families and Schools* (Princeton, N.J.: Princeton University Press, 1974).

[8] Richard G. Niemi, Roman Hedges, and M. Kent Jennings, "The Similarity of Husbands' and Wives' Political Views," *American Politics Quarterly,* 5 (April 1977), 136–137.

92

PART 2
inputs of the
political
system: who
wants and needs
what?

The most conspicuous difference between parents and their offspring is the greater tendency of the children to call themselves Independents. In the national study of high-school seniors and their parents, 36 percent of the students, compared to 24 percent of their parents, were Independents. Parents of both parties "lost" children to an independence of party, with Republicans losing even more (36 percent) than Democrats (27 percent). Nor was the greater number of Independents in the younger generation merely a reflection of the uncertainties of people inexperienced in politics. Were that the explanation, more of them could be expected to take on a party identification after the experience of taking part in several elections. A follow-up study of these same parents and offspring 8 years later permits a direct test of this idea: rather than remaining stable in their partisanship, as their parents did, or shifting toward a party identification, as earlier studies suggested they would, the offspring became even more Independent, with the proportion rising from the already high level of 36 percent to 48 percent.[9]

Increasing disenchantment of young adults with both political parties indicates that the high proportion of Independents among the young is not, as many have believed, merely an indication of uncertainty or lack of interest in politics. Many Independents are uninformed and uninterested, but they are increasingly being joined by people whose independence is based on an informed and concerned dissatisfaction with both parties. As we shall see in the next chapter, the most dramatic shift in partisanship in the last generation has been the increase in the ranks of the Independents. Young people have been in the vanguard of this move toward the rejection of the American party system.

On balance, the transmission of political opinions in most families is very weak. Aside from general feelings of patriotism, few political beliefs are directly passed on by parents. We have focused on party identification because it comes closer than other political beliefs to being inherited. But even there, parent-child agreement is hardly impressive, and it is getting weaker. What parents mightily influence is the basic personality of their offspring. And students of political psychology insist that the psychic condition has enormous importance for one's outlook on life and that this general orientation has an indirect impact on political beliefs. The person whose basic psychological needs are met is seen as becoming a "self-actualizer," a healthy person who will be more interested in politics and more likely to get involved.[10] But no one has convincingly shown that people with these healthy traits take political positions that are different from the positions of people who were psychologically deprived as children. Moreover, a different research tradition

[9] M. Kent Jennings and Richard G. Niemi, "Continuity and Change in Political Orientations: A Longitudinal Study of Two Generations," *American Political Science Review,* 69 (December 1975), 1324–25.

[10] Jeanne N. Knutson, *The Human Basis of the Polity* (Chicago/New York: Aldine-Atherton, Inc., 1972), p. 224. This study is based on the pioneering work of Abraham Maslow; see, for example, his *Toward a Psychology of Being* (Princeton: Van Nostrand, 1962). Also see Steven H. Chafee et al., "Family Communication Patterns and Adolescent Political Participation," in Jack Dennis, ed., *Socialization to Politics* (New York: Wiley, 1973).

emphasizes that people extremely active in politics are often "externalizing" some unresolved inner problem.[11] Personality no doubt shapes—or is—a person's general orientation to life; but with so many influences at work on political opinions, personality can have no more than an indirect influence.

Learning from political realities and from school

Although the school is the agency with the job of educating children, what school children learn doesn't all come from teachers and books. When children start going to school, the world they experience is tremendously enlarged. In keeping with our emphasis on recognizing the role of political realities in studying public opinion, we recognize that political events no less than the schools can influence children after their first years in the family.

The schools supported by any society can be expected to teach children the important values of that society. The effort of American schools is clearly to produce loyal, supportive, law-abiding citizens. Most studies indicate that the effort is successful.[12] The response of a second-grade boy, when asked if he would rather be an Englishman or an American, is instructive:

Well, I wouldn't like to be an Englishman because I wouldn't like to talk their way, and I'd rather be an American because they have better toys, because they have better things, better stores, and better beds and blankets, and they have better play guns, and better boots, and mittens and coats, and better teachers and schools.[13]

The ethnocentrism and materialism we noted in discussing American culture are already present in this second grader, who sounds ready to join his local Chamber of Commerce. Not surprisingly, he was a white, nonghetto respondent.

Urban white children, as the ones in a position to enjoy the better things of America, really like the system. Nearly 95 percent of all urban whites from the second through the eighth grade agree that "the American flag is the best flag in the world" and that "America is the best country in the world." The American child's earliest awareness of the political system is the President of the United States. And especially in grammar school, children idealize the President and his office. After studying 12,000 children, David Easton and Jack Dennis observed, "In all our testing and interviewing, we were unable to find a child who did not express the highest esteem for the President."[14] With more schooling, children come to focus less on the personal figure of the President as best showing "what the government is" and shift to institutions (Congress) and finally to political processes (voting). More realistic and critical

[11] The seminal work in this tradition is Harold D. Lasswell, *Psychopathology and Politics* (Chicago: University of Chicago Press, 1930). See also Smith, Bruner, and White, *Opinions and Personality*.

[12] David Easton and Jack Dennis, *Children in The Political System: Origins of Political Legitimacy* (New York: McGraw-Hill, 1969). Also see Charles F. Adrian, *Children and Civic Awareness* (Columbus, Ohio: Charles E. Merrill, 1971).

[13] Hess and Torney, *The Development of Political Attitudes*, p. 27.

[14] Easton and Dennis, *Children in the Political System*, p. 177.

94

PART 2
inputs of the
political
system: who
wants and needs
what?

opinions begin to appear among older children, but attitudes as a whole remain highly supportive.

These strongly positive feelings about government were so common in the first studies of children's attitudes that they seemed to be part of a child's natural outlook, in which "God's in His heaven and all's right with the world." But these studies were carried out before the United States became mired in a war in Vietnam and in subsequent turbulence and violence at home. They were also based mostly on urban white children. More recent research reports, based on data collected from the late 1960s to the late 1970s and including disadvantaged groups, present a different picture. The basic pattern is one of greater realism, with the idealized view of "the benevolent leader" replaced by a recognition of fallibility in public figures.[15] In the first chapter of this book we proposed that people's opinions could tell us about the realities of their lives no less than about their psychological needs and tendencies. This "reality explanation" applies to children no less than to adults.

The influence of political events on children's outlooks was first demonstrated in a study of people who are now about the age of most readers of this book. In 1966 and 1968 Roberta Sigel and Marilyn Brookes interviewed children in grades four, six, and eight in a middle-sized city near Detroit.[16] When asked about the "two most important events that have happened in the United States during the last two years," the children showed that they did not ignore current events: 90 percent were able to respond, and of these all except one answered in political terms. Moreover, every important event they mentioned was something bad, such as the war in Vietnam, the Detroit race riot, and the assassination of Martin Luther King, Jr. (Senator Robert Kennedy was assassinated a couple of months after the interviews.) These negative events did not reduce the children's positive feelings about the system in general, but they did decrease confidence in the government's performance and in its responsiveness to the people. These findings were directly contrary to two lines of earlier speculation: (1) that children have a psychological necessity to view public authorities favorably, or (2) that a negative feeling about government performance cannot coexist with positive feeling about the system.

The unravelling of the Watergate scandal from 1973 to 1974 presented another chance to test the "reality oriented" versus the "psychic necessities" view of the presidency. The white children's once overwhelmingly favorable view of the President was replaced, even in high-status suburban schools, with an overwhelmingly unfavorable view. Whereas 58 percent of fourth graders in 1962 had rated President Kennedy as "my favorite (or almost my favorite) of all [people]" only 7 percent in 1973 rated Nixon so highly.[17] Not only did

[15] See Roberta S. Sigel and Marilyn Brookes, "Becoming Critical About Politics," in Richard G. Niemi and associates, *The Politics of Future Citizens* (San Francisco: Jossey-Bass, 1974), pp. 103–25. Also see R. Sigel, *Adolescence and Political Involvement* (North Scituate, Mass.: Duxbury Press, 1973); H. Tolley, Jr., *Children and War* (New York: Teachers College Press, 1973).

[16] In 1968 they also reinterviewed the children from the 1966 survey, but those findings are not essential to our point here. See the note immediately above for the citation.

[17] See F. Christopher Arterton, "The Impact of Watergate on Children's Attitudes Toward Political Authority," *Political Science Quarterly,* 89 (June 1974), 272, 285–86.

During Kennedy's presidency, children had overwhelmingly favorable views of the President.

school children show an ability to reject the President when the facts seemed to call for rejection, but they also showed an ability to tell the difference between the *incumbent*—the person in the office—and the capabilities of the *office* itself. They were highly negative toward Richard Nixon but not toward the office of the President. Watergate thus proved that children are more flexible, accurate, and discriminating in their perceptions than most researchers had given them credit for.

Studies of children from disadvantaged groups support the "reality explanation" from a different perspective. Just as children's attitudes respond to political events, they also respond to the social status of the students. As would be expected from the reality explanation, the disadvantaged children have less positive feelings than their luckier age peers. White children from a poverty-stricken county in Appalachia, Mexican-American youngsters from Texas, and black ninth graders from Pennsylvania, for example, all turned out to be much less favorable in their images of the President than were

95

96

PART 2
inputs of the
political
system: who
wants and needs
what?

children from the "mainstream" culture.[18] Compared with "most men," the President did not come off especially well among these children. Whereas 1 percent of white urban children thought the President might be less honest than most men, for example, 27 percent of the Appalachian children thought so.

In feelings about the President, the policeman, and the fairness of laws, black and white children differ from the earliest grades—whites being more positive—and the difference is maintained as both become less positive in their views. The decrease in favorable views proceeds in parallel fashion, so that blacks of every age have less favorable views than do whites. Figure 4 · 1 illustrates this trend for responses to the idea that "all laws are fair." Such a simplistic view is decreasingly common among all the children as they move to higher grades, but more whites than blacks accept it at every grade level.

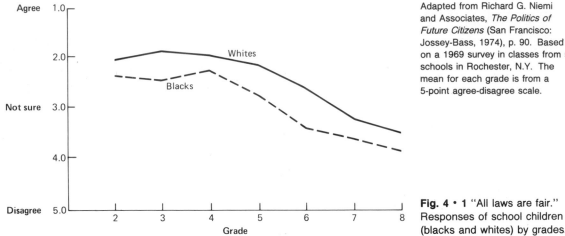

Adapted from Richard G. Niemi and Associates, *The Politics of Future Citizens* (San Francisco: Jossey-Bass, 1974), p. 90. Based on a 1969 survey in classes from 5 schools in Rochester, N.Y. The mean for each grade is from a 5-point agree-disagree scale.

Fig. 4 · 1 "All laws are fair." Responses of school children (blacks and whites) by grades.

In contrast, feelings of political efficacy (confidence that one can get things done through the political system) follow a divergent path for blacks and whites. As Fig. 4 · 2 shows, they start off close together in the third grade, but blacks come to feel less and less efficacious, while whites come to feel more and more so. By the eighth grade, most of the blacks rate their effectiveness as low, while most of the whites rate theirs as high. The childish view of the political process is not, then, automatically favorable. Instead, it seems to reflect with some accuracy the reality experienced by the children and their parents.

As to the specific influence of school itself, the findings are mixed. One study found that middle-class schools teach pupils to become active participants, while working-class schools encourage them to become conforming,

[18] See Robert Weissberg, *Political Learning, Political Choice, and Democratic Citizenship* (Englewood Cliffs, N.J.: Prentice-Hall, 1974), pp. 51–52; Edward S. Greenberg, "Black Children and the Political System," in Jack Dennis, ed., *Socialization to Politics: A Reader* (New York: Wiley, 1973), p. 265.

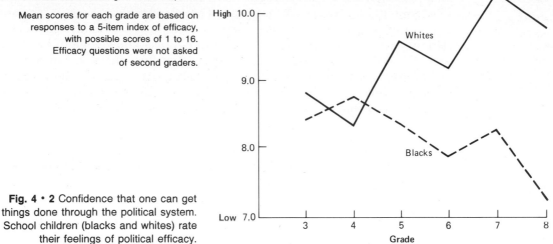

Source: Same as Fig. 4–1: Niemi, p. 91.

Mean scores for each grade are based on responses to a 5-item index of efficacy, with possible scores of 1 to 16. Efficacy questions were not asked of second graders.

Fig. 4 · 2 Confidence that one can get things done through the political system. School children (blacks and whites) rate their feelings of political efficacy.

"loyal" citizens.[19] But what appeared to be caused by the school and its type of instruction may have resulted simply from social class differences. Even when both groups have the same teachers, middle-class students are more interested in politics, more critical of government policies, and more inclined to participate than are their schoolmates from working-class families.[20] The effect of formal courses in civics seems to be minimal, whether one looks at students' information or attitudes. Any effect they have seems to be influenced heavily by the social status of the students and by what the real world of politics is like at the time the courses are taken.

A 1965 study reported civics courses to have no effect on white students, but it seemed that they taught blacks "that a good citizen is above all a *loyal* citizen rather than an *active* one."[21] This was at a time when the civil rights movement was making progress. Black and white school children in general felt about the same trust in political leaders, even though blacks felt less effective politically. Few political gains were won by blacks after the high point of the Civil Rights Act of 1964, and black discontent flared up in widespread riots by the summer of 1967.[22] Black trust dropped sharply in this period of disappointment. By 1974, researchers were reporting, "There is no evidence

[19] Edgar Litt, "Civic Education, Community Norms, and Political Indoctrination," *American Sociological Review,* 28 (February 1963), 69–75.

[20] Sigel and Brookes, "Becoming Critical About Politics," p. 122.

[21] Kenneth P. Langston and M. Kent Jennings, "Political Socialization and the High School Civics Curriculum in the United States," *American Political Science Review,* 62 (September 1968), 864.

[22] Paul R. Abramson, "Political Efficacy and Political Trust Among Black School Children," *Journal of Politics,* 34 (November 1972), 1265. Also see Charles S. Bullock, III, and Harrell R. Rodgers, Jr., *Racial Equality in America: In Search of an Unfulfilled Goal* (Santa Monica, California: Goodyear, 1975), and John S. Jackson, "The Political Behavior and Socio-Economic Backgrounds of Black Students: The Antecedents of Protest," *Midwest Journal of Political Science,* 15 (November 1971), 662–63.

98

PART 2
inputs of the
political
system: who
wants and needs
what?

that black students are taught nonparticipation in the public schools."
The content of a course did not promote such attitudes; instead, "the analysis
revealed the most substantial support for the political reality explanation."[23]
Although civics courses may increase the political knowledge of black adolescents, the students become more cynical as they become more knowledgeable.
As another research group put it, "Ironically, then, . . . a curriculum can
have a noteworthy effect on minority group children but . . . it does so by
instilling in them a more realistic, and not necessarily more positive, appraisal
of the American political system."[24]

Although some researchers claim that the public school outranks the family
as the source of children's political ideas,[25] the comparison is hardly worth
making, since neither really seems to have much influence on what children
say about specific policies. The family undoubtedly shapes an individual's personality, and the school certainly crams a student (at least momentarily) with
information. However important these influences on a child's personality and
state of knowledge, why should that lead children to the same opinion on
political issues, the same evaluation of candidates, or even the same partisan
identification as their parents, their teachers, or their fellow students?
People who are well informed, ill informed, well adjusted, or maladjusted
can all be found, in every possible combination, on both sides of every issue
and campaign. The changing political environment and other agents of socialization are too important for the family or school to dominate the socialization
process.

Class status

In looking at the school as an agent of socialization, we saw that what
appeared to be an influence of different kinds of schools turned out, on closer
inspection, to be a result of differences in social status among the children.
Even when they are youngsters in the same grade, at the same school, with
the same teachers, children from working-class families show less interest in
politics than do those from middle-class families. When they get old enough
to take part in actual elections, this contrast persists.

Lower-status people in the United States participate in politics less than
those of higher status. In the 1976 presidential election, for example, 63 percent of the people who called themselves "average working class" reported
no campaign activity, while only 36 percent of the "upper middle class" reported none (see Table 4 · 1). Only 10 percent of the average working class,
compared to 29 percent of the upper middle class, engaged in more than
one activity. These are sizable class differences in political participation, and

[23] Harrell R. Rodgers, Jr., "Toward Explanation of the Political Efficacy and Political Cynicism of
Black Students: An Exploratory Study," *American Journal of Political Science,* 18 (May 1974),
278–79.

[24] Sarah F. Liebschutz and Richard G. Niemi, "Political Attitudes among Black Children," in *The
Politics of Future Citizens,* p. 102.

[25] Hess and Torney, *The Development of Political Attitudes,* p. 101.

TABLE 4·1

99

CHAPTER 4
political
opinions and
participation

Number of activities	Average working	Upper working	Average middle	Upper middle
0	63%	51%	48%	36%
1	27	32	34	35
2	7	12	11	14
3	2	3	4	8
4	1	1	2	5
5	0	1	1	2
Respondents = 2,290	100%	100%	100%	100%

Campaign activity in 1976 according to class identification

Source: *The CPS 1976 American National Election Study.* Campaign activities were: try to influence the vote of others, attend political meetings, work for a party or candidate, exhibit a campaign button or bumper sticker, give money to a candidate.

they appear even larger when compared with class differences in other countries. Although Americans take pride in their social equality, the United States has a greater difference in political participation by social class than does any European democracy. Indeed, the central question to emerge from the most thorough study of political participation ever conducted in America is: "Why should class, in its relationship to American politics, appear at once so weak and so strong?"[26]

The importance of this question cannot be overemphasized, for it gets to what is probably *the* most distinctive feature of American democracy. Among the industrialized democracies, the United States is alone in its peculiar combination: in *participation,* there are strong class differences; in *organized politics,* class differences are weakly expressed. The combination seems paradoxical, but the weakness of class differences in organized politics actually contributes to the strong differences in participation.

The concept of social equality has been a basic American myth. This myth of equality discourages class appeals in politics. Lower-status people, without appeals to their needs as "have-nots," have little motivation to participate. The United States is the only industrialized democracy in the world that does not have a socialist or labor party to mobilize the working class.[27] Sidney Verba and Norman Nie, from their study of *Participation in America* submit, "If there were more class-based ideologies, more class-based organizations, more explicit class-based appeal by political parties, the participation disparity between upper- and lower-status citizens would very likely be less."[28]

[26] Sidney Verba and Norman H. Nie, *Participation in America: Political Democracy and Social Equality* (New York: Harper, 1972), p. 340.

[27] We go into this more fully in chapter 5, "Political Parties." The contrast between the U.S. and Norway in these regards is sharply drawn by Angus Campbell and Henry Valen, "Party Identification in Norway and the United States," in Campbell et al., *Elections and the Political Order* (New York: Wiley, 1966), chap. 13.

[28] *Participation in America,* p. 340.

100

PART 2
inputs of the
political
system: who
wants and needs
what?

Thus the apparent paradox: by de-emphasizing class, the American system increases class differences in participation. The lack of recognition of classes and lack of organization along class lines leaves lower-status people without the stimuli needed for equal participation.

The myth of America as a "classless" society was created when the privileged classes realized that they could become less privileged if all the newly franchised lower classes voted against them. It is a story that well illustrates our theme of politics as a competition to determine who gets helped and who gets hurt.

America's first politicians disagreed about the role of class in politics, but in a fashion that would seem most peculiar today: the conservatives talked about class hostility, while the liberals stressed class harmony. In the early years of the Republic, when the vote was limited by property and tax-paying qualifications, conservative leaders of the Federalist and Whig parties (men like Alexander Hamilton and Daniel Webster) stoutly emphasized the inherent antagonism between classes, while Jeffersonian and Jacksonian Democrats denied that class conflict was inevitable. Thus an arch-conservative Federalist, Chancellor Kent, argued in New York's Constitutional Convention of 1821 that "the tendency of universal suffrage is to jeopardize the rights of property," while an unknown liberal opponent replied, "Let us not, sir, disgrace ourselves in the eyes of the world, by expressing such degrading opinions of our fellow citizens."[29] When virtually all free adult males won the vote in the 1820s and 1830s, conservative leaders began to use less insulting terms to describe them, while liberal leaders borrowed discarded conservative arguments about class differences.

Why the switch in arguments? If we recognize that politics is the pursuit of power, the change of positions is easy to understand. Before the Jacksonian Democrats extended the right to vote, conservatives had tried to restrict the suffrage. They warned worthy citizens of the hostility of the lower classes. Liberals, on the other hand, tried to extend the suffrage by glossing over class differences, assuring those same worthy citizens that poor people were only rich people without money—friendly and harmless. With suffrage extended, however, the desire of each group to win elections produced a different emphasis: conservatives wooed the new and poorer voters by maintaining that all Americans were really "one big happy (and classless) family"; liberals sought the poor man's vote by insisting that the interests of the "rich, wellborn, and able" were opposed to those of the "common man."

To some extent, the conservative forces lost the battle (against the lower classes getting the vote) but won the war (by preventing American politics from being organized explicitly among class lines).

What are the effects of class in political socialization? The pervasive influence of class is found in the fact that it helps determine the things we think *about*, no less than *what* we think. The great Irish playwright and socialist

[29] From debates in the New York Constitutional Convention of 1821, as quoted in Alpheus Thomas Mason, *Free Government in the Making: Readings in American Political Thought* (New York: Oxford University Press, 1949), pp. 400–405.

George Bernard Shaw submitted, "Man does not philosophize on an empty stomach."[30] Poor people worry about basic needs such as food, clothing, and shelter; about not being able to pay for a visit to the doctor; and—at the extreme of poverty—about their children being bitten by rats. These concerns are quite different from those of the wealthy matron who has to worry about overeating, avoiding high taxes, and getting her children into the best schools. Because the wealthy are much more active and influential than the poor, the concerns of the "haves" are likely to become public issues, while the concerns of the "have-nots" are likely to remain nonissues. "Participation," as Verba and Nie put it, "makes some problems more visible and others less so."[31]

Class not only helps determine what issues are raised, it also influences feelings about those issues. People who think of themselves as working class are much more likely than middle-class people to favor government actions to help the underprivileged and reduce economic inequality. From the first systematic sampling of public opinion in the 1930s to the present, more of the working class than of the middle class have been found to support measures such as the adoption (and, later, expansion) of a government program of retirement benefits (known as social security), national aid to education in the states, government guarantee of a job and decent standard of living for all, heavier taxes on corporations and on corporate stock dividends, and a government program of medical insurance.[32] Table 4 · 2 shows that class differences on such issues were still found during the 1976 presidential election. A large majority (66 percent) of the upper middle class rejected the idea of the government seeing to it that everybody has a job and good standard of living, whereas a much smaller proportion (42 percent) of the average working class took the same negative view. Half of the average working class, compared to only a third of the upper middle class, support a government plan to cover all medical and hospital expenses.

These problems of economic equality and social welfare—"bread-and-butter" issues—have divided "liberals" and "conservatives" for half a century. Because people who call themselves working class are so much more liberal on these questions than are those in the middle class, one is tempted to conclude that the working class is more liberal in general. Liberalism as a general outlook includes at least three dimensions:

1. Approval of government action to promote economic equality and social welfare
2. Belief in social experimentation rather than acceptance of the *status quo*
3. Support of the rights of dissenters, minorities, and champions of unpopular causes

---

[30] The psychologist Abraham Maslow develops this insight into a more elaborate hierarchy of human needs. See the works cited in note 10.

[31] *Participation in America,* p. 274.

[32] For a summary of trends in public opinion on such issues, see Robert S. Erikson, Norman R. Luttbeg, and Kent Tedin, *American Public Opinion,* 2nd ed. (New York: Wiley, 1980), chap. 2.

TABLE 4·2 | Social classes' opinions of government help in employment and medical care

"The government should see to it that every person has a job and good standards of living" *versus*
"The government should just let each person get ahead on his own."

	CLASS IDENTIFICATION			
	Average working	*Upper working*	*Average middle*	*Upper middle*
Government should see to it	36%	34%	25%	19%
In the middle	22	18	24	15
Each on his own	42	48	50	66
Total	100%	100%	99%	100%

Respondents = 2,184

"There should be a government medical plan covering all medical and hospital expenses" *versus*
"Medical expenses should be paid by individuals and through private insurance like Blue Cross."

	CLASS IDENTIFICATION			
	Average working	*Upper working*	*Average middle*	*Upper middle*
Government plan	50%	43%	42%	33%
In the middle	13	14	12	12
Private insurance	37	44	46	55
Total	100%	101%	100%	100%

Respondents = 2,174

Source: *The CPS 1976 American National Election Study.*

But people with a working-class identification are not especially prone to think of themselves as "liberals" in any general sense.[33] They accordingly feel free to respond to different issues on an individual basis, without concern for how they fit into any general scheme of liberalism or conservatism. Working-class views actually turn out to be *less* liberal than those of the middle class on the second and third dimensions of liberalism.

Social change and innovation are much more acceptable to upper-status people than to those at lower levels, who are likely to cling to ways of the past.[34] Two-thirds of the people with college training are liberal in their atti-

[33] In the 1976 national election survey on which we are principally relying here, 46 percent of the average working class respondents said either that they did not know whether they were liberal or conservative or that they had not thought much about it; in contrast, only 13 percent of the upper middle class gave such responses.

[34] Herbert McClosky, "Conservatism and Personality," *American Political Science Review,* 52 (March 1958), 35. Also see Glenn D. Wilson, ed., *The Psychology of Conservatism* (New York: Academic Press, 1973).

In times of unemployment, the working class has especially
good reasons for supporting social welfare measures.

tudes toward change, while less than a fourth of those with only grade-school
training are liberal.

On a third measure of liberalism—tolerance toward the rights of dissenters—lower-status individuals once again rank low. People with low levels of
education tend to be uneasy about ideas that are strange, new, or "different,"
and their unease shows up in a greater willingness to deny free speech and
other civil liberties to groups like communists, alleged communists, atheists,
and socialists.[35] As education increases, so does tolerance of such unpopular

[35] For an excellent analysis of this subject and of prior findings, see John L. Sullivan et al., "An
Alternative Conceptualization of Political Tolerance: Illusory Increases 1950s–1970s," *American
Political Science Review*, 73 (September 1979), 781. The classic study is Samuel A. Stouffer,
Communism, Conformity, and Civil Liberties (New York: Doubleday, 1955).

Middle-class people have demanded equal rights for women more than have those of lower status.

groups. Cultural intolerance among white Americans has been tabulated as follows:[36]

Education	Culturally intolerant (%)
Eighth grade or lower	52
High school	39
Some college	28
College degree	12

People of lower status express their greater resistance to social change, to unpopular ideas, and to issues of all kinds, from public nudity to the right to resist laws regarded as unjust. In 1980, the working class lagged behind the middle class in favoring gun control, legal use of marijuana, racial desegregation, and equal rights for women.[37]

Whether class is determined subjectively by the choice of the individual or objectively by such criteria as occupation, income, or education, the differences between the middle and working classes are much the same. Class is

[36] Seymour M. Lipset and Earl Raab, *The Politics of Unreason* (New York: Harper, 1970), p. 447. Studies of status differences usually eliminate nonwhites because they are concentrated in the lower status levels and tend to be distinctly liberal.

[37] *The CPS 1980 American National Election Study.*

a sufficiently vague concept in the United States, however, that about a fourth of Americans are "misidentifiers" (blue-collar workers who think of themselves as middle class or white-collar people who think of themselves as working class). Generally, these misidentifiers think and act like hybrids; on "bread-and-butter" issues (such as medical care, social security, aid to the unemployed) they are neither as liberal as the blue-collar, working-class identifiers nor as conservative as the white-collar, middle-class identifiers.[38] But these are the exceptions: three-fourths of all adults identify with a class that objective observers would call appropriate to their occupations.

Class position affects voting choices even more clearly than it affects attitudes on issues. In every national election that has been studied, regardless of whether the Democrats or the Republicans won, the working class has been consistently more Democratic than the middle class. In bad years for the Democrats, even the working class may give a majority of their votes to the Republicans. They gave 61 percent in the 1972 choice between President Richard Nixon (R) and Senator George McGovern (D), but that was less than the 65 percent Republican vote of the middle class. Conversely, 1964 was a bad year for Republicans. President Lyndon Johnson (D) ran against Senator Barry Goldwater (R). Then, a majority of the middle class (56 percent) voted for the Democratic incumbent, but that was below the level of Democratic support (77 percent) from the working class. In the close contest of 1976, a majority of the middle class voted for President Gerald Ford (R), and a majority of the working class voted for Jimmy Carter (D). As Table 4·3 shows, if those who think of themselves as upper middle class had been the only voters, Ford would have won a landslide victory (with 63 percent of the vote). Jimmy Carter became President only because the average working class outnumbers the upper middle class.

What conclusions can we draw from the findings on class as an influence on political opinions and behavior? The most compelling is that class, whether determined by personal feelings or by education and occupation, is an essential

TABLE 4·3

Working-class and middle-class vote preferences in 1976

Preference	Average working class	Upper working class	Average middle class	Upper middle class
Democratic (Carter)	64%	46%	41%	37%
Republican (Ford)	34	52	56	63
Other, don't know, refused	2	1	2	—
Total	100%	99%	99%	100%
Respondents	622	146	620	223

Source: *The CPS 1976 American National Election Study.*

[38] See Campbell et al., *The American Voter,* pp. 102, 106–7.

106

PART 2
inputs of the
political
system: who
wants and needs
what?

concept for understanding political differences. Equally significant, class-related opinions do not constitute a highly structured ideology. Although more liberal on bread-and-butter issues than those of higher status, working-class Americans are more conservative toward social change and nonconformity. Accordingly, we cannot characterize the relationship of social class to political liberalism without first specifying the issue or dimension of liberalism involved.

Like other factors that shape people politically, the influence of class varies with the real political situation. We noted earlier that American political parties are not organized to emphasize class differences to the degree that parties do in most democracies—with some kind of socialist or labor party. Hence the choices offered the voters in the United States give them less of a stimulus to think in class terms. Just as class differences in politics vary from one country to another, so do they vary from time to time in any particular country. During an economic depression, class differences are more acute because widespread unemployment increases resentment over the uneven distribution of wealth.[39] Whatever the variations in its importance, the concept of class is essential for an understanding of political opinions.

Residence: region and size-of-place

Where a person lives was once thought to be as important as class status for understanding public opinion. Most Americans are familiar with the image of the South as conservative and of the East as liberal. Although such regional differences may once have been sizable, they have largely disappeared. Erikson and Luttbeg analyzed opinions on 10 current issues and found regional differences to be almost nonexistent.

Since . . . each of the four regions (East, Midwest, South, West) shows up as the most liberal on at least one issue and as the most conservative on at least one other, clearly it does not make much sense to stereotype any one region as a center of unusual liberalism or conservatism.[40]

The chief exception to the leveling off of regional distinctiveness in political opinions is the South, but even its uniqueness is often exaggerated. On most issues, southerners divide just about the way people do in the rest of the country. Only on issues involving race relations do southerners differ sharply from other Americans. Although racism is certainly not confined to the South, white southerners remain much more resistant to policies promoting racial equality. Even on civil rights issues, southern resistance has declined since the 1950s, but it still remains a stronger force than in other regions.

Except for the special case of the South,[41] size of place is now more impor-

---

[39] On both these points, see Sidney Verba and K. L. Schlozman, "Unemployment, Class Consciousness, and Radical Politics: What Didn't Happen in the Thirties," *Journal of Politics,* 39 (May 1977), 291–323.

[40] Erikson and Luttbeg, *American Public Opinion,* pp. 199–200.

[41] John Reed, *The Enduring South: Subcultural Persistence in Mass Society* (Lexington, Mass.: Heath, 1972); George B. Tindall, "Beyond the Mainstream: The Ethnic Southerners," *Journal of Southern History,* 40 (February 1974), 3–18.

tant than region for predicting political opinions. People who live in the suburbs and the country tend to be more Republican and conservative on "bread-and-butter" social welfare issues. People who live in central cities, on the other hand, tend to be Democratic and liberal on such issues. These differences are useful in telling us where people with particular opinions are most likely to be found. This may be all a candidate for office needs to know—where supporters are most concentrated. But the student of public opinion wants to know *why*, rather than simply *where*, opinions exist. Opinions are shaped less by living in the country, the suburbs, or the central city than by the status and ethnic characteristics of the people who live there.[42]

Ethnic groups

By definition, ethnic groups are large groups of people identified by common customs and traits, such as religion, race, or national origin. In practice, in the United States, the word *ethnic* is applied to *minority* groups with common customs, race, religion, or national origins. Contrary to the old myth of the United States as a "melting pot" in which different ethnic groups are molded into indistinguishable "Americans," ethnic consciousness persists.

As the only ethnic group in the United States that has experienced official repression to the point of being enslaved, blacks have long had greater reason than any other group to favor reform. Logically, then, they are more liberal than whites. Particularly impressive in black liberalism is its consistency across every dimension of liberalism-conservatism. Working-class whites are thought to be distinctively liberal, too, but their liberalism is confined to bread-and-butter issues. Blacks are distinctively liberal not only on bread-and-butter issues but on questions of social innovation and the rights of dissenters as well. Moreover, race consciousness among blacks is the *only* force we know of that helps reduce the large status difference in American political participation. Despite lower average levels of education and income, blacks participate in politics almost as much as whites. And blacks who express some degree of group consciousness are *more* active than whites of the same status.[43]

Long deprived of both status and welfare, blacks have emerged as perhaps the most distinctive political group in the United States. In 1976, for example, blacks gave Jimmy Carter 88 percent of their votes, a greater proportion by far than he got from any other group.[44] Nor was this simply a matter of overwhelming support for a winner. Four years earlier, when Senator George McGovern was defeated as the Democratic nominee, blacks gave him 86 percent of their votes, *more than twice* the proportion (37.5 percent) he received from the electorate as a whole. Although only 11 percent of the electorate,

[42] Erikson and Luttbeg, *American Public Opinion*, p. 203. Also see Ada W. Finifter and Paul R. Abramson, "City Size and Feelings of Political Competence," *Public Opinion Quarterly*, 39 (Summer 1975), 189–98.

[43] Verba and Nie, *Participation in America*, chap. 10.

[44] Robert Axelrod, "1976 Update," *American Political Science Review*, 72 (June 1978), 623. Also see his "Where the Votes Come From: An Analysis of Electoral Coalitions, 1952–1968," *ibid.*, 66 (March 1972), 11–20.

108

PART 2
inputs of the
political
system: who
wants and needs
what?

blacks nevertheless furnished 22 percent of the total vote received by the Democrats in 1972 and 16 percent in 1976.

Black votes are unusually oriented toward issues, with keen commitment to social welfare and civil rights. Black leaders, in their early criticism of Carter, showed that their support of the Democratic party does not reflect blind loyalty but the choice of the best available route to possible reforms.

Claiming over 70 percent of the population as members, Protestants in the United States are not thought of as an ethnic group. Because the ethnic minorities are all distinctively Democratic, white Protestants as a whole are relatively pro-Republican by definition. They are also more conservative on bread-and-butter issues. But religion, as such, is not thought to be important for the political tendencies of Protestants. The generally accepted view is that Protestant distinctiveness can be explained by the group's generally high status without regard to religion itself.

When the general category of "Protestant" is classified into different denominations, however, the impression of homogeneity quickly disappears. When they are divided into 9 major groups, as in Table 4 · 4, white Protestants turn out to vary greatly in their identification with the Republican party. The range is from 50 percent for Episcopalians all the way down to 21 percent for Baptists. The proportion of Republicans among *all* white Protestants (about 33 percent) is certainly greater than among all non-Protestants (15 percent) or even in the total population (about 23 percent), but the differences *within* the Protestant camp are equally impressive.[45] Republicans are at least twice as frequent among Episcopalians as among Baptists or members of such fundamentalist sects as Churches of God, Pentecostal, Seventh Day Adventists, and Jehovah's Witnesses. In fact, the Baptists are closer to the general population than to other Protestants in their partisan orientation.

Although such extreme differences among members of different Protestant churches are not usually noted, let alone examined in detail, every observer knows that some variation exists in such a large group. But the usual interpretation is to attribute any intra-Protestant differences to status rather than to church membership as such. Episcopalians, Presbyterians, and Congregationalists, for example, rank at the top of Table 4 · 4 in proportions of Republican identifiers, and they also rank at or near the top in the median family incomes of their members. The Methodists, Lutherans, and Pietistic churches rank in the middle on both Republicanism and income. To complete the neat correspondence, Baptists and the various fundamentalist sects rank low on both Republicanism and income.[46] Hence the belief developed that political differences among Protestant denominations reflect the influence of status differences rather than of religion. In specific terms, rich Baptists were thought to be as Republican as rich Episcopalians; the only difference was supposed to lie in the fact that fewer Baptists were rich.

[45] These figures are all from *The CPS 1976 American National Election Study.*

[46] Galen Gockel, "Income and Religious Affiliation: A Regression Analysis," *American Journal of Sociology,* 74 (May 1969), 632–47; Bruce L. Warren, "Socioeconomic Achievement and Religion: The American Case," *Sociological Inquiry,* 40 (Spring 1970), 130–55.

TABLE 4·4 | Republican identification and family income
of white Protestants, by denomination (1976)

Denomination	Republican (%)	Median* family income	Respondents
Episcopalian	50	$14,848	62
Presbyterian, Congregationalist, Reformed, United Church of Christ	44	12,006	199
Nontraditional (Mormon, Christian Science, Unitarian, Quaker)	40	12,677	64
Methodist	38	11,587	280
Lutheran	36	11,652	233
Pietistic (Disciples of Christ, "Christian," etc.)	32	11,315	47
General Protestant (no denomination given)	29	10,092	132
Fundamentalist (Churches of God, Pentecostal, Seventh Day Adventist, Jehovah's Witnesses)	26	7,884	195
Baptist	21	10,457	367

Source: *The CPS 1976 American National Election Study.*

* Income is the mean value derived from reported income coded in 20 categories, with the last an open-ended ($35,000 and over) category; it is thus closer to a true median than to a true mean.

A close look at the family income figures in Table 4 · 4 throws some doubt on this neat interpretation. Baptists are far *ahead* of fundamentalists in income, but they are *less* likely to be Republicans; similarly, compared with people who have a nondenominational Protestant identification, Baptists are somewhat *ahead in income* but far *less likely to be Republicans.* Nor is the political distinctiveness of Baptists explained by their geographical concentration in the South. Fifty-two percent of all white Baptists actually live outside the South. And when the comparison is confined to nonsouthern states, Baptists are *still* less Republican than any other Protestant denomination. This looks like ethnicity, with religious factors having an influence independent of income.[47]

A study of the partisanship of religious groups for the entire decade of the 1960s supports our conclusion that Protestant churches have an influence independent of status. To the 9 Protestant groups, David Knoke added Catholics, Jews, members of other (non-Christian, non-Jewish) religions, and people with no religion. With the status characteristics (income, education, occupa-

---

[47] In view of Jimmy Carter's candidacy in 1976 and his Baptist church membership, Baptists' Republican identification in that year might be thought to have been temporarily decreased, but data from earlier years show similar results.

110

PART 2
inputs of the
political
system: who
wants and needs
what?

tion) of their members controlled, Knoke then examined partisan preferences of all 13 groups. Status was "controlled" in the sense that it was held at the same level in order to compare the partisanship of people from *different denominations* but of the *same status*. Figure 4·3 displays the results. With possible scores ranging from 1 for Strong Democrats to 5 for Strong Republicans, the average scores of Protestant denominations vary greatly. Unlike the partisan ranking in Table 4·4, the location of religious groups in Fig. 4·3 removes the influence of status. Nevertheless, the ranking of Protestant groups is remarkably similar. Whether rich or poor, college educated or high school drop-outs, business executives or blue-collar workers, Episcopalians, Presbyterians, and most other Protestants from older churches of the Reformation Era are more Republican than is the general population. Oddly, fundamentalists, people with no religion, and people of non-Christian or non-Jewish religions are closest to the average position of all Americans. Baptists, however, remain distinctively Democratic with all three status variables taken into account.

We cannot fully explain these differences, but we can say that the old idea of status overpowering religion as an influence among Protestants does not hold up. Although these differences could result from church doctrine, Professor Knoke is probably prudent in concluding that "a more likely explanation would involve nondoctrinal sources—tradition, socialization, peer-group and work-group interactions among coreligionists."[48] Distinctive traditions, social experiences, and group interactions are all features of ethnic groups. The implication of these findings, then, is that church affiliation of Protestants has been falsely assumed to have no influence in and of itself only because the diverse Protestant denominations were not separately examined.

The clearest demonstration that religious affiliation can outweigh other influences is found in the overwhelmingly Democratic identification of Jews. Reporting family incomes that averaged $12,953 in 1976, Jews were below only the Episcopalians among the Protestant denominations; nevertheless, with only 7 percent calling themselves Republicans, Jews were the least Republican of all religious groups. When status variables are held constant, as in Fig. 4·3, Jews are far and away the most Democratic of all groups.

One explanation for the Democratic orientation of Jews is that they do not rank high in religious status itself; on the contrary, they have often been a persecuted minority. Aware of anti-Semitism as a long-standing prejudice, even upper-status Jews may feel deprived of status in a predominantly Christian society. Only within the last generation have Jews felt free, regardless of their status, to make reservations at any hotel of their choice without worrying about the possibility of being turned away because of their religion. With this background, Jews have reasons similar to those of groups with lower economic and educational status for identifying with whatever political party speaks for the disadvantaged. Moreover, the Jewish creed encourages a liberal political view with its stress on learning, humane values, and social welfare.

[48] David Knoke, "Religion, Stratification and Politics: America in the 1960s," *American Journal of Political Science,* 18 (May 1974), 345.

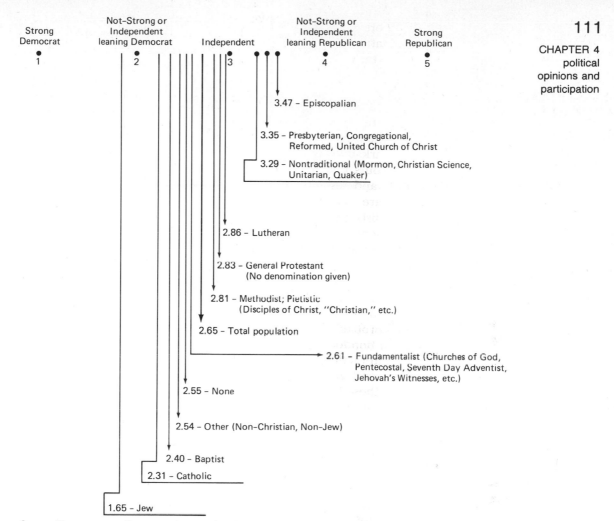

Source: The scores are the mean of scores for 1960, 1964, and 1968 for each religious group in David Knoke, "Religion, Stratification and Politics: America in the 1960s," *American Journal of Political Science*, 18 (May 1974), 343.

Fig. 4 · 3 Average partisan location of 12 religious groups, with status factors controlled.

For generations after the Civil War, Jewish voters identified with the Republicans as the party of emancipation, but they shifted in the 1930s as the Democrats began to emerge as the stronger champions both of civil rights and social welfare reform. The shift was solidified before World War II when the Democratic party earlier and more actively opposed Nazism (which was responsible for acts of genocide against European Jews) than did the Republican party.[49]

[49] See Lawrence E. Fuchs, *The Political Behavior of American Jews* (New York: Free Press, 1956). Also see his "American Jews and the Presidential Vote," in Fuchs, ed., *American Ethnic Politics* (New York: Harper, 1968), pp. 144–62.

Hispanic Americans today
identify predominantly with
the Democratic party, as did
earlier Catholic immigrants.

Catholics are between Protestants and Jews in several respects. Outnumbered by Protestants almost 3 to 1, they are nevertheless much more numerous (claiming 25 percent) than Jews (with only 3 percent). With annual family incomes of $12,119, white Catholics on the whole are slightly less affluent than Jews but better off than most Protestant denominations. With status controlled, as Fig. 4 · 3 shows, Catholics are closer in partisanship to Baptists than to any other church group, but they lean even more in the Democratic direction than do Baptists. In 1976, only 16 percent of all white Catholics thought of themselves as Republicans. Similarly, Catholics are more liberal than Protestants but less liberal than Jews on domestic political issues.[50]

The relatively liberal stance of American Catholics does not appear to come from religious doctrine. In countries where Catholics are in the majority,

[50] On the attitudes of Catholic ethnic groups, see Andrew M. Greeley, "Political Attitudes Among American White Ethnics," *Public Opinion Quarterly,* 36 (Summer 1972), 213–21.

they generally support conservative rather than liberal parties. Thus their minority status rather than their religious beliefs is probably the key to the liberal orientation of American Catholics. Immigrants to the United States have suffered the pains of adjustment with acute awareness that they were "different" and were regarded by many native Americans as inferior. As more and more Irish came to the Northeast in the nineteenth century, proper Bostonians learned to distinguish between "Shanty Irish" and "Lace-Curtain Irish," but phrases such as "dumb Irish cop" were a reminder that all "Micks" were beneath Yankees (which meant Protestants). Italian, Polish, and other Catholic immigrants from southern and eastern Europe followed the Irish immigrants and were similarly dubbed with derisive names to remind them of their marginality. Whatever political party the Yankees opposed would naturally attract these despised immigrants. At that time, deprived economic status reinforced the tendency of their deprived social status to identify them with the Democratic party.

In addition to these social and economic forces, a specifically political factor helps account for the Democratic preferences of Catholics. Irish, Italian, and Polish immigration to the United States was heaviest at a time when the Democratic party controlled most of the eastern cities where these immigrants settled. Predominantly Catholic, they developed into good Democrats at the same time they developed into good Americans. And they may have passed on their party identification to their children, along with their new nationality. Party identification may itself shape behavior. In this case, the descendants of these immigrants seem to be voting simply as Democrats, not as Catholics.

When a religious issue is injected into politics, however, religious preference becomes highly relevant. Members of some Protestant denominations regard the consumption of alcoholic beverages as sinful, for example, and many Catholics regard the use of birth-control devices similarly. Given a chance to vote on such questions, members of the churches concerned will tend to vote according to their religious beliefs. The important question, then, is this: How salient is religion in politics? Catholics who had voted for Eisenhower, a Republican, in 1956, returned in overwhelming numbers in 1960 to vote for Kennedy, a Democrat—and a Catholic under fire because of his religion. Since Nixon's Protestantism was not under fire, religion played a much smaller role for many Protestants in that election. Even so, Protestants who attend church most regularly were much likelier than infrequent attenders to vote against Kennedy.[51]

The 1976 election demonstrates that religion does not always have as much importance for voters as it does for the mass media. This election offered the usual choice between two Protestants—Jimmy Carter, a Baptist, and Gerald Ford, an Episcopalian. With this choice, religion did not become particularly salient to the voters, despite emphasis by the media on Carter's active role as deacon, Sunday School teacher, and door-to-door missionary worker for

[51] Philip E. Converse et al., "Stability and Change in 1960: A Reinstating Election," *American Political Science Review,* 55 (June 1961), 269–80.

114

PART 2
inputs of the
political
system: who
wants and needs
what?

his church. Carter received twice as many votes, proportionally, from white Baptists (45 percent) as from white Episcopalians (22 percent), but this pretty much corresponded to their normal vote. If white Baptists had been the only voters, the Episcopalian candidate would have won.[52] Though a white Baptist, Carter gained his margin of victory mostly from white Catholics (55 percent), white Jews (70 percent), and blacks, regardless of their religion (88 percent).

National origins and race influence political opinions in much the same way as do religion and other ethnic characteristics. When members of any ethnic group are deprived of political rewards—or even of prestige alone— because of their ethnicity, they tend to support policies or candidates that recognize their interests. The desire for recognition in the form of public office, appointive jobs, and improved services heavily influences the votes of people who are hungry for acceptance, but who have also been just plain hungry.

THE CONTINUING SOCIALIZATION OF ADULTS

Most students of socialization think the political learning of adults is somehow less influential than the initial political learning of children. We think that the case for such a view is weak. For one thing, childhood learning doesn't have as great an influence in adulthood as was once thought.[53] Adult socialization through one's job or marriage may outweigh the earlier socialization in one's neighborhood or family. The ideas acquired in adult socialization may, moreover, be more politically relevant than the vague notions acquired in childhood. Let us look more closely at some of the forces that shape adult political thinking.

The most continuous influences on political opinions are the mass media of communication—television, newspapers, magazines—and the issues, candidates, and political parties about which they report. These influences are such important parts of the political system that they will be given detailed treatment in separate chapters (5, 6, and 7). Here we will briefly look at the role of college, family, and friends.

College

Of all the agents of political learning, the one that exists specifically to promote advanced learning is the system of higher education. Young adults who go to college have, of course, already acquired lots of facts and values

---

[52] Contrary to popular impression, even in the South, *white* Baptists gave Carter only 50 percent of their votes.

[53] Donald J. Searing, Joel J. Schwartz, and Alden E. Lind, "The Structuring Principle: Political Socialization and Belief Systems," *American Political Science Review,* 67 (June 1973), 415–32; Donald Searing, Gerald Wright, and George Rabinowitz, "The Primacy Principle: Attitude Change and Political Socialization," *British Journal of Political Science,* 6 (January 1976), 83–113.

from their families, school, class, residence, and ethnic associations. These may be so firmly implanted that they can go through college with no change in political opinions. But contrary to the feeling professors occasionally get in reading exam papers, college does make a difference. College campuses all over the world are a prime source of critical, anti-establishment ideas, whether the "establishment" is the right-wing regime of Brazil or the Communist regime of the Soviet Union.

Although American college students are by no means as radical as is often imagined, college clearly has a liberalizing influence. As Table 4 · 5 shows, college students who place themselves on the "left" outnumber their classmates on the "right" almost 3 to 1. (Talking in terms of "right" and "left" is rare in the United States, but Gallup asked for it in this college study.) This is in marked contrast to the general public, among whom self-designated conservatives outnumber liberals (34 to 26 percent). A more telling indication of the impact of college is the increase in the proportion of liberals from the Freshman year, when it is about the same as in the general population, to the high level of later years. And the liberal bent becomes overwhelming among graduate students (from whose ranks come college professors).

TABLE 4·5 | Ideological self-placement of college students, by year in school (1971)

	Far left, left (%)	Middle-of-road(%)	Right, far right (%)	Can't say (%)
Freshmen	28	56	14	2
Sophomores	31	52	15	2
Juniors	41	43	14	2
Seniors	40	46	9	5
Graduate students	63	24	11	2
All students	35	49	13	3

Source: *Gallup Opinion Index*, February 1972, p. 7.

As a staging ground between adolescence and adult responsibilities, college is an ideal time for developing opinions that do not necessarily mirror those of parents; for assessing one's self, society, and one's place in that society; for exposure to new people, new ideas, and new patterns of behavior.[54] In the United States, these processes produce a distinctively liberal orientation to politics.

What is it about college that produces liberal attitudes? Studies of the effect of particular courses always find that they have little impact either on attitudes toward political participation or on substantive political values.[55] Political opinions come from the cumulative experience of college—more from peers (college classmates) and from the general college atmosphere (including what happens in courses) than from the study of particular subjects.

[54] See James J. Best, *Public Opinion: Micro and Macro* (Homewood, Ill.: Dorsey, 1973), pp. 103–9.
[55] Dean Jaros, *Socialization to Politics* (New York: Praeger, 1973), pp. 116–20.

116

PART 2
inputs of the
political
system: who
wants and needs
what?

The general atmosphere of college, in which all sorts of ideas are explored fairly objectively, is what makes the liberalism of college students. Just as attitudes may vary on campus—with more liberal students drawn to the arts and sciences and less liberal ones to engineering and business administration—so do they vary from campus to campus. Graduates of the more prestigious colleges have been consistently found to take more liberal positions than those from other colleges. All of the things about college that have a liberalizing influence seem to exist in stronger form in the arts and sciences division within a university and in high-prestige colleges as a whole.

A conservative businessman may ridicule the liberal ideas of his college daughter and her favorite professor, remarking that neither has ever "had to meet a payroll." His daughter may join her professor in thinking that her father's commitment to material success blinds him to broader social needs. These contrasts are more likely if the young woman is studying political theory or philosophy than if she is studying business administration or advertising; they are also more likely if she is studying at Oberlin or Swarthmore than if she is enrolled at a technical institute. Perhaps the distinguishing feature is that these subject matters and colleges are farther removed from specific occupational training and hence from the profit-and-loss concerns of the business world.

As to whether the liberal ideas acquired in college disappear after one enters the "real world," the answer is not clear. Disregarding both age and the era in which one's schooling took place, the college educated are more likely than others to label themselves as liberals *and* as conservatives—that is, they are more inclined than others to use ideological terms; and when invited to do so, they are less inclined than others to choose a middle-of-the-road position.[56] But among all people with college degrees, in marked contrast to current college students, conservatives (with 47 percent) vastly outnumber liberals (with 30 percent). Unless colleges have recently come to have a more liberalizing effect than they once did or unless that effect is more permanent than it used to be, some drift toward conservatism can be expected. The critical factor seems to be whether the people they associate with in postcollege years, especially the people they marry, reinforce their college beliefs.

Primary group influences: home, friends, co-workers

Just as a person's earliest view of politics comes from parents, so are later opinions molded by an adult's own family, friends, and co-workers. The pressure to conform to primary (face-to-face) group judgments is so great that people are influenced even in their perception of physical objects. Psychological experiments have shown that when all other members of a group pretend to perceive the longer of two objects as shorter, experimental subjects tend to reject what they see with their own eyes and give in to the group judgment. If people adjust perceptions of purely physical objects to the norms of their

---

[56] Every national survey that includes questions on liberal-conservative orientation supports these statements. We rely here on *The CPS 1976 American National Election Study.*

group, consider how easily they can adjust attitudes on the much more vague subject of politics. Through group experiences, individuals develop not only their definition of themselves—their social identity—but also their picture of the outside world.

Primary group members tend to agree more on matters they consider important than on passing concerns or trivial questions. As we say in discussing children's socialization, politics is not a central concern in most families. Nevertheless, a husband and wife are more likely to vote the same way than are any other pair; about 90 percent have been found to agree in their presidential votes.[57]

Spouse agreement results in part, of course, from the fact that most people who marry are of similar racial, religious, and class backgrounds. And whatever their backgrounds, people tend to marry others who agree with them. Even though political agreement must rarely be a factor in the selection of spouses, general similarity in viewpoints could be expected to lead to at least a moderate degree of political accord. A survey of high school sophomores and a follow-up 15 years later, when the people from the original sample were about 31 years old, offers support for both the *background similarity* and the *selective mating* explanations.[58] According to the reports of married respondents, the parents of husbands and wives agreed in party identification significantly more than could be expected by chance; therefore, married couples were more likely than random pairs of people to have similar partisan backgrounds. But the initial party identification of husbands and wives (when they were 21 years old) was much more in agreement than that reported for their parents. Hence we have support for selective mating.

A third explanation accounts for even more of the partisan agreement in married couples—*conjugal socialization,* that is, the influence of marriage partners on each other's ideas.[59] All the old jokes about problems with in-laws attest to the degree to which bride and groom, in establishing a new family unit, disturb their relationships with their parents. And much of the tension no doubt stems from the fact that the new husband and wife begin to modify their behavior and preferences as they adjust to, and influence, each other. Their changes may be seen by parents as a rejection of original family values. The hackneyed question at weddings as to whether the bride's parents have "gained a son or lost a daughter" attests to the concern about the direction that the expected change will take.

Whatever the results for other practices and beliefs, in politics the bride's parents more often "lose" a daughter than "gain" a son. Politics has been traditionally viewed as a masculine arena.[60] Just as society expects husbands

---

[57] Richard G. Niemi, Roman Hedges, and M. Kent Jennings, "The Similarity of Husbands' and Wives' Political Views," *American Politics Quarterly,* 5 (April 1977), 136.

[58] Terry S. Weiner, "Homogeneity of Political Party Preferences between Spouses," *Journal of Politics,* 40 (February 1978), 208–11.

[59] The correlations of the party identifications were: husband's parents and wife's parents, .21; husband at age 21 and wife at age 21, .40; husband currently and wife currently, .64. See *ibid.,* p. 210.

[60] Support for this point and the possibility that the situation may be changing can be found in Marjorie Random Hershey, "The Politics of Androgyny? Sex Roles and Attitudes Toward Women in Politics," *American Politics Quarterly,* 5 (July 1977), 261–85.

118

PART 2
inputs of the
political
system: who
wants and needs
what?

to defer to their wives' judgment in matters of religious training, so has it encouraged wives to accept their husbands' influence in politics. The 15-year study we have been citing found that wives were much more likely than husbands to change their partisanship to agree with that of their marriage partners. Nevertheless, the process works both ways, and wives now appear to have somewhat more influence on their husbands' politics than was formerly thought to be the case.[61] The struggle for the Equal Rights Amendment signals women's growing dissatisfaction with a second-class status in politics.

Although agreement among friends and fellow workers is not as great as in the immediate family, the tendency toward like-mindedness is still present. The same factors that encourage agreement between husbands and wives—similar backgrounds, selectiveness in choosing associates, and mutual influence—are all no doubt also at work, though less intensely, in other primary-group contacts. From the very first election studies, citizens have been found to live mostly in homogeneous political environments.[62] When we talk about politics with our friends, we are not typically debating but reinforcing one another's opinions. Although young people more often find themselves with at least one friend of a different political persuasion, with advancing years one's immediate friends tend to be increasingly unified in their political outlook.

The degree of consensus among co-workers is not as great as among friends, because individuals cannot ordinarily choose the people with whom they work. But the more homogeneous the political environment of the workplace, the firmer the employees' attitudes will be. Conversely, those in a personal environment that is politically divided are more likely to be swayed by the dominant attitudes in the larger community. In the 1968 presidential election, people who preferred the third party candidate, George Wallace, were vulnerable to the argument that they should not vote for him because he had no real chance of winning. Wallace fans whose friends and co-workers were also for Wallace were not swayed by this argument as easily as were Wallace fans whose friends included Nixon or Humphrey supporters.[63]

THE EXPRESSION OF POLITICAL OPINIONS

When we defined *public opinion* as *"the expression of attitudes on a social issue,"* we left open the question of just *how* opinions are expressed. Americans express their political opinions most obviously on election day, but voting is only one of many ways in which popular preferences are revealed.

[61] Weiner, "Homogeneity . . . ," pp. 210–11. Also see Paul Beck and M. Kent Jennings, "Parents as Middle-persons in Political Socialization," *Journal of Politics,* 37 (February 1975), 87–93.

[62] See particularly chapter 6, "Social Process: Small Groups and Political Discussion," in Bernard R. Berelson, Paul F. Lazarsfeld, and William N. McPhee, *Voting: A Study of Opinion Formation in a Presidential Campaign* (Chicago: University of Chicago Press, 1954), pp. 88–117.

[63] David M. Kovenock, James W. Prothro et al., *Explaining the Vote: Presidential Choices in the Nation and the States* (Chapel Hill, N.C.: Institute for Research in Social Science, 1973), Part III.

Forms of political participation

Political participation is many things. A street-corner gang beefing about the lack of a public swimming pool, housewives planning over morning coffee how to confront the superintendent of schools with a problem, a farm family attending a campaign barbecue, a union member contributing money to one of labor's political committees—all are taking part in the daily round of democratic government. Political participation includes all these activities and many more; it can perhaps be best described as *all behavior through which people directly express their political opinions.*

Various kinds of political participation are so closely related that they can be viewed as different dimensions of the same activity. When a successful candidate is formally sworn into office and when a disappointed voter informally swears to a friend that the new officeholder will never be reelected, both are taking part in politics. But running for public office is a much more demanding and costly activity than merely talking with friends about the candidates. Hence different kinds of participation can be ranked from the cheapest (least demanding of time, energy, and ability) to the most costly (those which require an application of almost all one's resources).

The number of people who claim to engage in different forms of political participation varies greatly, as Fig. 4 · 4 indicates. Perhaps the easiest form of participation is talk; one of the hardest or most demanding is openly demonstrating to protest public policies. As the figure indicates, only 2 percent say that they have demonstrated in recent years, while 68 percent claim to vote in most elections. Because all these actions represent different aspects of the same general kind of activity—political participation—the individual activities are *cumulative;* that is, people who engage in the more demanding forms of activity, such as seeking political funds, will almost certainly engage in all the less demanding forms. And a person who fails to express opinions in the least costly ways, such as merely talking about politics, will rarely express them in any of the more demanding ways.

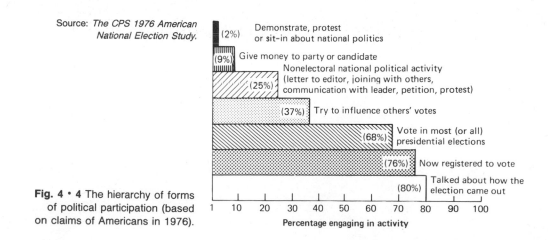

Source: *The CPS 1976 American National Election Study.*

(2%) Demonstrate, protest or sit-in about national politics

(9%) Give money to party or candidate

(25%) Nonelectoral national political activity (letter to editor, joining with others, communication with leader, petition, protest)

(37%) Try to influence others' votes

(68%) Vote in most (or all) presidential elections

(76%) Now registered to vote

(80%) Talked about how the election came out

Fig. 4 · 4 The hierarchy of forms of political participation (based on claims of Americans in 1976).

Percentage engaging in activity

120

PART 2
inputs of the
political
system: who
wants and needs
what?

The cumulative nature of political participation is tremendously fortunate for students of the problem because it simplifies their task of explanation. Suppose each form of political behavior were unrelated to other forms; that even if we knew someone was a campaign fund raiser, for example, we would not be able to assume that the same person probably wore a campaign button and voted. In such a chaotic situation we would have to develop a separate explanation for each discrete political act. Luckily, this is not the case, as

UPI

United Press International photo.

The perceived threat of a "melt down" at the Three Mile Island nuclear power plant intensified opposition to nuclear power, but supporters of nuclear power dramatized their lack of fear by jogging with a nuclear fuel rod.

far as we can judge from survey data.[64] But more exotic forms of political participation—such as lying down in the path of a bulldozer at a nuclear construction plant or taking part in a protest march—show up in general surveys too rarely to be studied in any detail. And clearly illegal activities—bribery, assassination—are, fortunately, even more rare. Without enough cases of such behavior to study it at the individual level, we must shift to a broader, system-wide level of analysis.

[64] Sidney Verba and Norman Nie do argue that political participation is not cumulative, that it is made up of different "modes" of activity that cannot be scaled along a single dimension. But their two "modes" of activity may not fit with others because their modes are not truly forms of political participation. Their two modes are: (1) Contacting anyone in local, state, or national government about a particular, i.e., nonsocial problem. (We think this is no more political than complaining to one's automobile mechanic.) (2) Being involved in community organizations, such as the PTA or Scouts. (We think this "mode" could sometimes overlap with political activity but is mislabeled as a whole.) See *Participation in America*. Despite their conceptual position, Verba and Nie treat participation as unidimensional in much of their book, suggesting that they find their conception of political participation difficult to use consistently. Lester W. Milbrath and M. L. Goel accept Verba and Nie's argument in *Political Participation: How and Why Do People Get Involved in Politics?* 2nd ed. (Chicago: Rand McNally, 1977), chap. 1. In the rest of the book, however, they, too, ignore the strained conception they have accepted.

122

PART 2
inputs of the
political
system: who
wants and needs
what?

Structural factors and conventional participation

Each citizen does not "decide" to attend party meetings, ring doorbells in a political campaign, vote, or run for office. The possibility of such activity is so completely foreign to the way many people live that the idea of active participation never comes up. The overall social system defines some people in, and some out of, the political system.

The socialization process systematically *trains* some people for a leading role in politics and others for apathy. The degree of activity—seeking governorships, congressional seats, posts on international bodies, the presidency— that is more or less taken as an obligation in the Rockefeller and Kennedy families, for example, is beyond the wildest dreams of most Americans. Indeed, what is remarkable about the preceding sentence is that it seems almost demeaning to speak of Rockefellers and Kennedys seeking "congressional seats" in general—the Senate seems unquestionably more appropriate for them than the House of Representatives.

In compiling all the propositions on political participation they could find in the vast literature, Lester Milbrath and M. L. Goel find that a pattern emerges if one moves from social to personal to immediate factors. First, using findings from all the Western democracies, they report that a *social position* toward the center of society rather than toward its outer edges contributes to a politically active role:

Persons close to the center occupy an environmental position which naturally links them into the communications network involved in policy decisions for the society. They become identified with the body politic. They receive from and send more communications to other persons near the center. They have a higher rate of social interaction, and they are active in more groups than persons on the periphery. This central position increases the likelihood that they will develop personality traits, beliefs, and attitudes which facilitate participation in politics. There are many more political stimuli in their environment, and this increases the number of opportunities for them to participate.[65]

This concept of "centrality" is vague, and deliberately so, since it is designed to include more factors than social class. But clearly every advantage listed for "centrality" is more common among those in higher than in lower status positions. The next body of findings Milbrath and Goel cite supports the crucial point that participation is consistently more likely among higher-class than among lower-class persons. Shifting to *personal factors* they report that participation is a function of psychological involvement, feelings of political efficacy, sense of civic duty, political sophistication, lack of absorption with personal problems, self-confidence, and lack of cynicism toward politics. For *every one* of these attitudinal or personality traits, persons of higher socioeconomic position (as measured by income, occupation, and especially education) are more likely to have the trait favoring participation. The *immediate factors*—political stimuli—follow the familiar pattern. The more political stim-

[65] Milbrath, *Political Participation*, p. 89.

uli people have, the more likely they are to participate. People who are attracted to politics have higher media exposure. Political information-seeking is cumulative, and so on.

This group of findings, all related to class position, suggests that lower-status children somehow learn that their role in society does not require active participation. Indeed, they might expect only discomfort from trying to understand, much less get involved in, the abstract, middle-class world of politics that their parents ignore. The better restaurants in the United States, for example, do not actually exclude lower-status people. Formal exclusion is not necessary; lower-status people stay away from such places not only because they cannot afford the high prices but also because they would feel uncomfortable in such an atmosphere. Politics is somewhat similar. "Central" in the United States means middle class.

Violence as a form of political participation

The United States has always been marked by a high level of violence. This is something we kept pretty well brushed under the rug until the urban and campus violence of the 1960s became so acute that a presidential commission was appointed to study the problem. Its findings offered facts and interpretations new to most Americans. To begin with, the nation was established by a violent revolution. This fact was, of course, a celebrated one, but less well-known were the accompanying attacks on loyalists in the colonies. The American tradition of tarring and feathering was established in what an American historian, Richard Brown, calls "the patriotic campaign to root out Toryism,"[66] a campaign that must have seemed highly *un*patriotic to the tarred, feathered, and loyal Tories. The longest, most brutal and most unnecessary war in American history was that against the Indians, which began in Tidewater, Virginia, in 1607 and formally ended with the final white massacre of Indians in 1890 at Wounded Knee, South Dakota.

The black version of racial violence in America began when the first slave was brought to this country and has continued ever since. The blacks have always fought back—the first slave uprising occurred in 1812 in New York City—but the whites have enjoyed overwhelmingly superior resources and have crushed every black effort at counterviolence. But ethnic violence has not been restricted to reds and blacks. Before the Civil War, anti-Catholic riots and convent burnings scarred the Northeast. Urban riots have been so common that "the fact is that our cities have been in a state of more or less continuous turmoil since the colonial period." Slum conditions and ethnic and religious conflict between immigrants and native Americans made the period from the 1830s to the 1850s "the era of the greatest urban violence America has ever experienced." The modern urban police system was estab-

[66] Richard M. Brown, "Historical Patterns of Violence in America," in Hugh D. Graham and Ted R. Gurr, *Violence in America, Historical and Comparative Perspectives* (New York: New American Library, 1969), p. 58. This volume is the Report to the National Commission on the Causes and Prevention of Violence, June 1969. Other historical facts in this and the following paragraph are also from Brown's article unless otherwise noted. The second direct quotation is from p. 50.

124

PART 2
inputs of the
political
system: who
wants and needs
what?

lished in response to these riots. The Civil War came shortly thereafter as the most extreme and bloody outbreak of domestic violence in American history.

Labor-management conflict replaced racial differences as the prime source of violence in the 1909–1938 period.[67] As early as 1877 a nationwide railroad strike led to riots that left large areas of Baltimore and Pittsburgh in smoking ruins. The present National Guard system was established in response to the 1877 uprisings, but employers also hired private armed forces to break organizing efforts and strikes by labor.

Violence is clearly nothing new to the United States. Why, then, the great shock in the 1960s when a black leader of the time (H. Rap Brown) called violence "as American as cherry pie"? Until the 1960s most of the violence had been by people in positions of power against those who were disadvantaged. But now the disadvantaged were threatening to turn the tables. It was not the idea of violence but the idea of *blacks* violently attacking *whites* that was new and shocking in the black leader's statement. In fact, however, the racial riots of the 1960s differed from earlier ones not only in the aggressive role of blacks but also in the fact that they entailed few deaths. Attacks were concentrated on property rather than on people, and the casualties (mostly black) came from black confrontations with police rather than with white civilians.

How does the rate of violence in the United States compare with that in other countries? The most recent data are from the 1960s, but they are not very reassuring. In the total magnitude of strife, as Table 4 · 6 indicates, the United States ranks first in comparison with 17 democratic European nations. In comparison with 113 other nations—democratic and undemocratic, developed and underdeveloped—it ranks 24th. Out of all these nations, 90 have less civil strife than the United States, whereas only 23 have more civil strife. The American system is not uniquely characterized by violence, then, unless the comparison is restricted to developed democracies. But even when the comparison includes all countries, it ranks toward the more violent extreme. With few exceptions, the countries ranking as more strife-torn are those that went through internal wars during the period of study—such as Algeria, Vietnam, and Venezuela.

Table 4 · 6 deserves careful scrutiny. It is based on Professor Gurr's comprehensive study of civil strife in 114 nations and colonies from 1961 through 1965. Gurr defines "civil strife" as "all collective nongovernmental attacks on persons or property that occur within a political system, but not individual crimes."[68] At least 100 people must take part in an attack before it is counted as a case of civil strife, and the attack may be either symbolic, as in political demonstrations, or physical, as in guerrilla war. The "total magnitude" of strife is derived from the first three measures of strife in the table. The first,

[67] Sheldon G. Levy, "A 150-Year Study of Political Violence in the United States," in Graham and Gurr, *Violence in America*, p. 91.

[68] Gurr, "A Comparative Study of Civil Strife," *ibid.,* p. 545. The next two quotations are from the same page, the third from p. 593.

TABLE 4·6 | **Some general characteristics of strife in the United States, 1963–1968, compared with strife in other nations, 1961–1965**

	U.S.	17 democratic European nations	113 polities
Proportion of population that participated (pervasiveness)	1,116 per 100,000	676 per 100,000	683 per 100,000
Casualties from strife as proportion of population (intensity)	477 per 10 million	121 per 10 million	20,100 per 10 million
Rank of U.S. compared with other nations:			
Pervasiveness		7	27
Intensity		3	53
Duration		1	6
Total magnitude of strife		1	24
Magnitude of turmoil		1	6
Magnitude of conspiracy		2	38

Source: Gurr, "A Comparative Study of Civil Strife," in Graham and Gurr, *Violence in America* (New York: New American Library, 1969), p. 549.

pervasiveness, refers to the proportion of the population taking part in civil strife. On this measure, the United States is seventh in comparison with 17 other democracies and twenty-seventh in comparison with 113 other countries. *Intensity* refers to the proportion of casualties (deaths or injuries) resulting from civil strife. On this the United States ranks third among the democracies and fifty third among all countries. *Duration* refers to the number of days during which strife occurred in the 5-year period under study. Here the United States is first among democracies and sixth among all countries. The *total magnitude* of strife is derived from the three preceding measures, with the United States ranking first among democracies and twenty-fourth among all countries.

The last two items in the table refer to different forms of strife. *Turmoil* is "relatively spontaneous, unorganized strife . . . , including political demonstrations and strikes, riots, political and ethnic clashes, and local rebellions." The United States is first and sixth, respectively, in turmoil. *Conspiracy* is "highly organized political assassinations, small-scale terrorism, small-scale guerrilla wars, coups d'etat, mutinies, and antigovernment plots." The American system is second and thirty-eighth in producing conspiratorial strife.

Why does the United States rank so high in its level of strife? Professor Gurr finds that most of the variation in levels of civil strife among all these countries can be statistically accounted for or "explained" by three sets of variables. First and most important is "deprivation-induced discontent": the greater the gap between what people believe they deserve and what they think they can get, the unhappier they are. The great emphasis on equality in the American tradition coupled with extreme inequalities in practice thus is the main cause of civil strife.

126

PART 2
inputs of the
political
system: who
wants and needs
what?

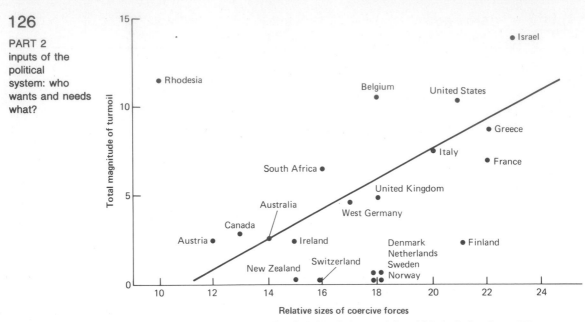

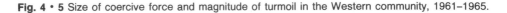

Source: Gurr, "A Comparative Study of Civil Strife," in Graham and Gurr, *Violence in America,* p. 585.

Fig. 4 · 5 Size of coercive force and magnitude of turmoil in the Western community, 1961–1965.

Second, people are more apt to be violent if such behavior is viewed as justifiable or if the political system is viewed as illegitimate. The American system is widely regarded as legitimate, but its history of violence tends, in an unofficial or "underground" fashion, to sanction violence as a political technique.

Third, the structures of national political systems are related to their levels of strife. Three such characteristics are important: (1) the size of coercive (military and police) forces; (2) strength of political and economic institutions; (3) presence of social conditions that could lead to strife.

Surprisingly, the amount of strife does not decrease as the size of armed forces increases. This is a complex relationship, but for the 21 countries of the Western community, at least, Fig. 4 · 5 shows that the amount of strife is higher in countries with relatively large armed forces. Whether violence leads to a system's enlargement of its armed forces or vice versa, we don't really know.

The second structural feature, the strength of political and economic institutions, is measured by: large trade unions, the important role of government, and stable political party systems. American trade unions and the role of government are relatively restricted by our emphasis on individualism and private enterprise. Compared with other developed democracies, the United States ranks high only in having stable political parties. Even on this item, the increasing proportion of Independents has led some scholars to conclude that the current party system is disintegrating.

Finally, social conditions that could lead to violence include extremist political organizations and outside support for rebels. Neither of these social conditions is important in the United States or, for that matter, in other countries in the Western community.

The United States is not characterized by all the conditions that lead to high levels of turmoil in other countries, but it does have enough of those characteristics to place it first among the Western democracies in its rate of civil strife. And little change has occurred in what Professor Gurr identified as the sources of our high rate of violence—persisting deprivation, the inflated size of the nation's coercive forces, and the restricted role of the system's political and economic institutions. Indeed, the marked decrease in public trust in government and further signs of weakness in the political party system underscore the seriousness of his warning that the United States is ripe for a major upheaval unless it deals with the causes rather than the symptoms of discontent.

POLITICAL OPINIONS IN THE POLITICAL SYSTEM

Public opinion affects two kinds of decision making: day-to-day decisions on the specifics of policy, and long-lasting decisions on the broad direction of policy.

The policy functions of political opinions

On particular policy decisions, unorganized public opinion plays little direct role. Even in Congress, which is the area of decision making most exposed to the public, the pressures on decision makers come mostly from special and limited groups, usually with professional lobbyists to push their interests. Decision makers try to anticipate possible reactions to their policies, but the fact that the details of public policy are largely unknown to the general public gives officials considerable leeway in making decisions.

When we turn to the general goals of public policy, however, we find that general public opinion is more influential. Public attitudes set some general limits on public policy. Government control of the press, for example, has been ruled out because the public is against it.

In addition to this restrictive influence, mass political opinions play a more positive role through the election system. The broad goals of public policy are usually set on election day. If American elections do not establish policy goals, the fault lies less with the voters than with the failure of parties and candidates to make their positions clear or to carry through on positions they have taken. In the 1964 presidential election, Lyndon Johnson was elected as a "peace candidate" and Barry Goldwater was rejected as a dangerously "trigger-happy" candidate. Public opinion failed to set the broad goals of national policy in that election because Johnson reversed himself and stepped

128

PART 2
inputs of the
political
system: who
wants and needs
what?

up the war in Vietnam. But such drastic departures from campaign commitments are the exception. American political parties fail to present a coherent set of policies that voters can confidently expect to be carried out, but they do normally offer at least vaguely meaningful alternatives. Even if the typical election carries no clear mandate for a particular set of policies, it at least empowers the winners to act as if it did.

The system level functions of political opinions

Three functions of public opinion in the political system can be roughly sketched. First, political opinions perform a *permissive function*. Public indifference or ignorance about many public questions is so widespread that officials enjoy a wide range of discretion in making decisions. Even though the public favors government action on an issue, it may be a long time before the government acts, often because mass sentiment is not strongly expressed. On the admission of Hawaii to the Union and on the right of the residents of the District of Columbia to vote in presidential elections, a vast majority of the public expressed approval 10 to 15 years before Congress took favorable action.[69] The people did not feel *strongly* on either subject, however, and they gave no evidence of voting against members of Congress who did not support their opinion. Such a situation permits decision makers to act as they see fit without fear of angering the public.

Second, political opinions perform a *supportive function,* giving existing policies and actions a general sense of legitimacy and approval. However intense the opposition to a measure, it tends to receive widespread support once it becomes the "law of the land." The Social Security Act of 1935, for example, was bitterly opposed by Republicans, but its provisions were approved by about 90 percent of the voters as soon as it was enacted. It is especially easy to see the importance of the supportive function when it is missing. Consider the difficulties that result from attempts to enforce laws against the use of marijuana and other drugs.

Third, political opinions sometimes perform a *demand function.* At all times, of course, small segments of the public intensely support particular measures. And permissive support often enables a small but intense group to block legislation wanted, but without overriding intensity, by a vast majority of the general public. (The American Medical Association's long success in opposing government aid for medical care is perhaps the prime recent example.) But the general public occasionally makes such clear demands that officials would not dare ignore them. Although opinion survey data do not go back to the early 1930s, the voters of that era seem to have been in a mood that demanded some government response to the country's economic depression. If their demands had not produced a major response of some kind (such as the New Deal), violence might well have reached major proportions. More recently, the intense dissatisfaction of America's blacks with the stigma

[69] V. O. Key, Jr., *Public Opinion and American Democracy* (New York: Knopf, 1961), pp. 32–33. The data on the two following functions of political opinions are also from Key, pp. 29–39.

Farmers attempt to win broader support for their demands.

of "second-class citizenship," coupled with the supportive or permissive attitudes of most other Americans, required (and achieved) some kind of positive response from the government.

The permissive and supportive functions of political opinions apply to all political systems. The demand function is constitutionally supported only in procedural democracies, those emphasizing the *way* people are governed, rather than the *results* of governing. In the next three chapters, we shall consider the principal institutions—political parties, pressure groups, the mass media, and the electoral system—through which the American political system achieves or fails to achieve these functions.

SUMMARY

Public opinion is the expression of attitudes on a social issue. It is part of the "input" activities of the political system. The basic political functions of public opinion are the choice of leaders and the communication of public interests to official decision makers.

130

PART 2
inputs of the
political
system: who
wants and needs
what?

Political socialization transmits both facts and opinions about politics. Most young people inherit their partisan position from their parents, but the correspondence is not as close as people once believed, and parent-child opinions on specific political questions are still farther apart. In school, where education is expected to produce loyal, supportive, law-abiding citizens, the opinions, even of children, respond meaningfully to political realities.

Class position greatly affects attitudes on issues and voting choices. America is the only industrialized democracy in which strong class differences in participation combine with weak expression of class differences in organized politics. Lower-status people are not encouraged to participate, because they have no party that speaks directly to their needs. Other factors that influence people's early political socialization are the size and location of the town in which they live, the ethnic group to which they belong, their religion, national origin, and race.

Political socialization continues into adulthood, when other factors strongly influence adult political opinions, for example, college attendance and the personal environment (spouse, friends, co-workers).

Political participation includes all the ways in which people directly express their political opinions. Voting, campaigning, and running for office are the more obvious forms of political behavior, but violence and riots (racial, labor, civil strife) are also forms of political behavior. Compared with other industrial democracies, the United States ranks low in the former and high in the latter forms of participation.

political
parties

132

PART 2
inputs of the
political
system: who
wants and needs
what?

Democracy is impossible without political parties. They organize opposition against those in control of the government and try to build majority support for taking over the government. These are activities that no dictatorship but every democracy permits: majority rule (or choice of rulers) and minority rights. Students of political parties have therefore concluded "that the political parties created democracy and that modern democracy is unthinkable save in terms of the parties."[1]

Knowing the importance of political parties for democracy, we might expect them to be among the most respected groups in America; however, when Americans are asked which institution they are most confident "will do what is right," political parties are ranked *last*. Given a choice among the Supreme Court, the President, Congress, the national political parties, "the people who vote in national elections," and "the nationally organized interest groups," only one percent choose political parties.[2]

This low level of respect has led some observers to question the survival of the American party system.[3] If parties are as essential to democracy as they appear to be, to question their strength is to question the strength of democracy itself in the United States.

PARTIES AND PARTY SYSTEMS

Power as the purpose of political parties

What is a political party? Certainly, it is different from other political groups in terms of its purpose and methods.[4] The *purpose* of a party is to win and exercise political power—specifically, to gain control of the government. It is this aim that sets political parties apart from other institutions that struggle for political power. Pressure groups, for example, try to influence public policy, but they are concerned with *specific* policies rather than with control of the government *as a whole*. The American Rifle Association tries to prevent regulation of firearms, but it is uninterested in controlling taxation and foreign affairs. If this or any other group were to move beyond the attempt to influence specific policies and seek to win general control of the government, then that group would, by definition, become a political party.

[1] E. E. Schattschneider, *Party Government* (New York: Rinehart, 1942), p. 1. This and other views of political parties are nicely summarized in Jack Dennis, "Trends in Public Support for the American Political Party System," *British Journal of Political Science,* 5 (April 1975), 187–230.

[2] Dennis, "Trends in Public Support . . . ," p. 228.

[3] See, for example, Walter Dean Burnham, *Critical Elections and the Mainsprings of American Politics* (New York: Norton, 1970); David S. Broder, *The Party's Over: The Failure of Politics in America* (New York: Harper, 1971); Everett C. Ladd, Jr., *Where Have All the Voters Gone?* (New York: Norton, 1978); and Jeane J. Kirkpatrick, *Dismantling the Parties: Reflections on Party Reform and Party Decomposition* (Washington, D.C.: American Enterprise Institute, 1978).

[4] On the distinctive characteristics of political parties and for an excellent general treatment of American parties, see Frank J. Sorauf, *Party Politics in America,* 3rd ed. (Boston: Little, Brown, 1976), especially pp. 17–21.

Senator Edward Kennedy's campaign for the Democratic presidential nomination in 1980 highlighted differences between his and President Carter's views on issues.

To be an authentic party, a political group must either enjoy power now or have a fair prospect of gaining power in the future. Organizations such as the Socialist, Prohibitionist, Greenback, and Vegetarian parties, which neither gain nor lose power in American elections, are better understood as educational movements or interest groups, rather than political parties. Many state laws recognize this distinction and require that an organization receive a specified percentage of the vote in the preceding election before it can be classed a "political party" and appear on the official ballot.

Some minor parties do have short-term impact. A recent example was the American Independent (George Wallace) party. Although a minor party has no real chance for victory, it has some impact on the major parties, because it could create a constitutional crisis by preventing either major party candidate from winning a majority of the electoral votes. Even so, these "parties" remain more akin to pressure groups than to political parties in that they try to influence rather than to take control of the government.

134

PART 2
inputs of the
political
system: who
wants and needs
what?

If we try to define political parties in terms of more specific purposes, rather than simply in terms of the attempt to gain control of the government, the definition doesn't fit even the major parties. Perhaps the most famous concept of party is that advanced by Edmund Burke, a British statesman of the eighteenth century: "Party is a body of men united, for promoting by their joint endeavours the national interest, upon some particular principle in which they are all agreed." But what "particular principle" serves to "unite" Democrats such as Senators Edward Kennedy of Massachusetts and Robert Morgan of North Carolina, or Republicans such as Senators J. Strom Thurmond of South Carolina and Charles Percy of Illinois? Their disagreement on principles is exceeded only by their lack of unity in Senate voting. Clearly, principles vary from one member to another within the same party, but *all* the members are united in their desire to win control of the government. A definition broad enough to apply to all parties must therefore stop short with the statement that their objective is to acquire political power.

Winning votes as a party's route to power

The method by which a political party tries to gain power is to win votes. Nonparty organizations like the mass media and pressure groups may also try to mobilize votes, but they do not themselves offer candidates for office. All kinds of groups may try to influence elections, but only political parties try to win them with their own candidates.

Political parties are combative. We use the language of warfare when we talk about political "battles" and "campaigns"; but party combat is in the appeal for votes, which replaces armed conflict with peaceful competition. In a democracy, ballots eliminate the necessity to use bullets. We are reminded of the incalculable importance of this distinction when we see the difficulties of people who must still rely on bullets. When young activists representing what seemed to be a majority of the people in South Korea tried to oust their rulers in 1980, they could not win by merely counting their supporters. South Korean leaders promptly and ruthlessly demonstrated that modern weapons in the hands of a few render mere numbers ineffectual if the numbers do not have votes that will be recognized.

Competition is as essential among political parties as is the peaceable nature of that competition. It is the competitive route to power that distinguishes parties in a democracy from the "parties" of totalitarian or dictatorial regimes like the People's Republic of China. To "become a party" to something means to identify oneself with one group rather than with another—to make a *choice*. Because totalitarian regimes deny individuals this right to choose one party instead of another, they never permit multiple parties to function.

For parties to operate in a meaningful way, they must be respected by the government. Conversely, they must respect the government as a distinct institution once they have achieved power; that is, they must not transform the government into an arm of one party. Richard Nixon's use of the Internal Revenue Service, the FBI (Federal Bureau of Investigation), and the CIA (Central Intelligence Agency) to harass people on his "political enemies list" was accordingly one of the most shocking revelations to come from the Watergate scandal.

Democracies differ from totalitarian regimes in that critics of the party in power are treated as "opponents" rather than "enemies." Indeed, in Great Britain the government pays a salary to the leader of "Her Majesty's Loyal Opposition." The idea of a government paying someone to oppose it represents democracy in its purest form. It is based on the belief that opposition is not only lawful but desirable. And the opponents are loyal in the sense that they, too, would respect the right of opposition were they to achieve power. A one-party regime is thus contrary to democratic principles.

Different types of political parties

By our definition, all political parties offer candidates in competitive elections. Beyond this common feature, however, parties differ greatly. Two of their differences important to the way the parties perform are: (1) the characteristics of *party members,* and (2) the characteristics of *party supporters.*

The most widely accepted classification of political parties was offered by a French scholar, Maurice Duverger, whose identification of two types of parties was based on their membership: *clique-oriented* and *mass-membership* parties.[5] A clique-oriented party has many supporters, but they are more comparable to the fans of, say, the Pittsburgh Steelers football team than to the *members* of the British Labour party. These fans identify with "their" team or party, sometimes with such intensity that the word *fan* is a short form of *fanatic.* But they do not pay dues or take part in the affairs of the organization beyond general support (voting or cheering; perhaps attending a rally or game, or displaying a bumper sticker). A mass-membership party, as the term suggests, has many actual members in addition to fans. Members pay dues, attend meetings, and sometimes even center their social lives around their party organization.

This classification is helpful because it is derived from a basic characteristic of parties—their membership—which is a clue to their other features. Table 5 · 1 summarizes the differences between the two types of parties, differences that stem from the nature of their membership. The table indicates that both American parties qualify as clique-oriented in every respect: first, they fit the basic definition by having lots of fans or supporters but few members and no dues-paying requirement. Both have all the other characteristics that seem to derive from such a limited membership:

1. They concentrate on electing candidates but are not concerned with educating members on party doctrine.

2. They are active during elections but lapse into quiescence the rest of the time.

[5] Duverger used the term *cadre* for what we think is better understood as *clique-oriented.* See *Political Parties: Their Organization and Activity in the Modern State* (New York: Wiley, 1955), pp. 5–16, 63–71.

136

PART 2
inputs of the
political
system: who
wants and needs
what?

3. Party leaders are mostly officeholders or "notables," not full-time party personnel.

4. Candidates are chosen in primary elections or by temporary coalitions put together by the candidates, not by the party itself.

5. The candidate, not the party itself, puts together a staff, directs it, and directs the campaign.

6. Instead of the party directing the officeholders, it is the other way around: the members who hold important offices direct the party.

TABLE 5·1

Comparison of clique-oriented and mass-membership political parties

Membership	Clique-oriented parties *Generally few members, lots of fans*	Mass-membership parties *Many dues-paying members as well as fans*
1. Activities	Mainly electoral	Ideological and educational as well as electoral
2 Organizational continuity	Active chiefly at elections	Continuous activity
3. Leadership	Few full-time workers or leaders (avocational)	Permanent staff and full-time leaders (vocational)
4. Selection of candidates	By primary elections, or temporary coalitions	By leaders of party organizations
5. Campaign leadership	Candidate-directed	Directed by continuing party leaders
6. Relation to officeholders	Usually subordinate to party members in government	Usually some influence over party members in government

Source: Five of the above characteristics are adapted from Sorauf, *Party Politics in America*, p. 63.

The characteristics of their supporters offer a second criterion for classifying political parties. Researchers at the University of Strathclyde in Scotland developed such a classification by looking at the social composition of all the political parties (totaling 76) in 17 Western nations that have competitive party systems.[6] They conclude that a party can be called *socially cohesive* if over two-thirds of its votes come from people with a common social characteristic—religion, class, region, "communal nationalism" (which they define as a minority linguistic or ethnic identity), age, or sex. Parties in which none of these social characteristics is predominant are called *socially heterogeneous*. Among the parties examined, 19 turned out to be heterogeneous, 57 cohesive.

Religion and class are the most common sources of socially cohesive parties, with region or "communal nationalism" entering in as a second shared feature in some cases. Neither age nor sex was a basis of cohesion for any party.

[6] Richard Rose and Derek Urwin, "Social Cohesion, Political Parties and Strains in Regimes," *Comparative Political Studies*, 2 (April 1969), 7–44.

The details are shown in the accompanying table.

Heterogeneous parties	19
Cohesive parties (single source of cohesion)	
Religion	18
Class	20
Cohesive parties (plural sources of cohesion)	19
Total	76

Both American parties are of the heterogeneous type. Indeed, the United States is virtually unique in this regard. It is the only industrialized democracy without a socialist or labor party,[7] and it is one of only two countries with a substantial number of Catholics but no party made up mostly of Catholics.

Just as the clique-oriented or mass-membership character of a party reveals a clue to its other characteristics, so does the heterogeneous or cohesive nature of a party imply other things about it. One obvious implication is for the party's principles: heterogeneous parties are much less likely to develop a coherent ideology than are socially cohesive parties. An ideology that appeals to the needs of all the varied supporters of a heterogeneous party would be hard to develop. The survey of 17 countries confirms this prediction from the classification. Among the 19 heterogeneous parties, 14 have no formal ideological positions, and America's "Republicans and Democrats are prototypes of this group." Although we shall see that they consistently differ on policies, "they do not do so in the name of a consciously articulated ideology."[8] A second implication is that the interests of particular groups will be less intensely represented by heterogeneous parties. Working-class interests, the most conspicuous example, are less openly and strongly championed in the United States, where there are only heterogeneous parties, than in other democracies where some parties are based principally on the working class.

Types of party systems

In classifying parties, we dealt with the characteristics of each party as a separate unit, disregarding the other parties with which it competes. In classifying party systems, on the other hand, we are concerned with all the parties in a country and how they relate to one another.

The most common way to classify party systems is also the most obvious: according to the number of parties in the system. We generally distinguish among one-party, two party, and multiparty systems.[9] Professor Harry Eckstein, an authority on comparative politics, suggests that the term *one-party system* be applied to any system in which one party regularly gets 60 percent or more of the votes and in which its votes outnumber those of the next

[7] Ireland also lacks a class-based party, but it is not highly industrialized.

[8] *Ibid.,* pp. 29–30.

[9] For a thoughtful approach to this problem, see Giovanni Sartori, *Parties and Party Systems: A Framework for Analysis* (London: Cambridge University Press, 1976), chap. 5.

138

PART 2
inputs of the
political
system: who
wants and needs
what?

party by more than two-to-one.[10] "One-party" does not literally mean only one party exists, then, but only that one party dominates.

If the notion of simply counting parties is taken literally, with every organization calling itself a party to be counted, then no case of a two-party system can be found. We have tried to take care of this problem by counting only those organizations with *some prospect of victory* as political parties. Admittedly, "some prospect of victory" is a loose criterion, but it can be expressed with mathematical precision. Professor Eckstein offers this formula: A two-party system is one in which two parties usually get 75 percent or more of the votes and legislative seats, with the first party outnumbering the second party by less than two-to-one, and with the second party outnumbering the third party more than two-to-one.

With its ambiguities thus reduced, we shall employ the numerical typology of party systems in our more detailed look at American parties.

FUNCTIONS OF POLITICAL PARTIES

In chapter 4 we said that for the political system, public opinion functions to choose leaders and to communicate public interests to official decision makers. We also pointed out that political parties are necessary for democratic achievement of these results. In the broadest terms, then, political parties are needed for the public choice of leaders and the open and organized expression of public interests.

Functions for the individual

In view of the low esteem Americans have for political parties, it is not surprising that only about one fourth of all adults strongly identify with any party.[11] The others are probably not greatly influenced by political parties. The small segment of strong supporters, however, tell us the party functions for that minority and potentially, at least, for everybody.

For those who strongly identify with them, parties become reference groups that help citizens organize their opinions. They thus perform the function we called "object appraisal" when we were talking about public opinion. Once citizens have decided which party they prefer, they have a cue for reacting to new issues and personalities. They can assume that their party will take more appealing positions on issues and nominate better candidates than the other party. Second, party identification increases voting turnout and work for the party. Third, exposure to party activity results in greater

[10] "Party Systems," in David L. Sills, ed., *International Encyclopedia of the Social Sciences,* Vol. 11 (New York: Macmillan, 1968), p. 489.

[11] More data on party identification will be presented later in this chapter; see especially Table 5 · 4.

interest in, and information about, public affairs. The competition for votes can make people more politically oriented, more active, more interested in politics, and better informed about public affairs.

One way of getting insight into the functions or consequences of a political institution is to imagine life without that institution. Looking at functions at the individual level, we need not resort entirely to imagination. For people with no strong party identification, parties, in effect, do not exist; at least they do not exist in the sense of having a positive influence. If we have correctly recognized how parties function for the individual, then, the consequences we have noted should not be present in people for whom parties are not important.[12] They should therefore be less likely to have consistent opinions on issues; they should be less likely to vote or otherwise take part in politics; they should be less interested in, and informed about, public affairs. By and large, these expected differences do exist, a fact that gives us greater confidence in our analysis of party functions for the individual. But two developments warn that American political parties are in trouble: (1) far fewer people strongly identify with parties today than they did a generation ago; (2) the contrast between those who so identify and those who do not has decreased.

The rest of this chapter will help explain why political parties appeal to fewer Americans today and why they are less important to those to whom they do appeal.

Functions for the political system

In the preceding edition of this book, our discussion of party functions for the political system began with these words:

At the level of the political system, political parties serve many functions in addition to their basic role in leadership selection and interest identification. If you can imagine what our political life would be like without political parties, you will be able to identify these additional functions. With no political parties, the struggle for power would certainly be less open, less predictable in its outcome, more apt to be influenced by minorities. . . . Without parties, groups would pursue many different policies, and so many choices would be available it would be difficult to choose among them. Each election . . . would present so many candidates that voters could hardly know what policies they were supporting. Finally, with no party program to help organize their work, official decision makers would rely much more heavily on groups organized to promote special interests.

That description sounds remarkably close to what our political life has actually come to be. This suggests that American parties have ceased to exist, or at least that they have ceased to perform the basic functions of parties in other democratic societies. Anthony King, a British scholar accustomed to the better organized parties of his country, adopts the more extreme of these conclusions:

[12] To the extent that some other institution has replaced political parties for those citizens to whom parties are not important, our expectation will not be correct. We note in chap. 6 the tendency of the mass media to take over some functions of political parties.

140

PART 2
inputs of the
political
system: who
wants and needs
what?

"With regard to the parties," he says, "it is open to ask whether the United States any longer possesses such things, at least for the purposes of nominating and electing Presidents."[13]

Professor King may be premature in announcing the disappearance of American parties, but he is certainly correct in saying they have ceased to perform basic functions that they once more nearly achieved. He relies on the 1962 edition of this book for the functions of America's two major parties at that time:

1. to give the people a chance, through group action, to influence the direction of policy;

2. to organize public opinion, so that different policy options could be classified and interested citizens enlightened on the policy choices of the day;

3. to moderate the differences that exist between the various interests that make up the electorate ("In order to win majority support, they must avoid taking any extremist position.");

4. to serve as agencies for the selection of public officials (since the parties controlled nominations); and

5. to help overcome the obstacles to government action thrown up in the United States by checks and balances and the separation of powers.[14]

As we pointed out in that early edition, the American parties of the 1950s and 1960s did not perform all of these functions satisfactorily or all of the time. Nevertheless, they certainly came closer than they do today. King describes the current performance of parties perceptively:

1. Insofar as the people at large are capable of influencing public policy, it would appear to be much more through individual candidates, and interest and issue groups, than through the parties.

2. The parties would appear in the late 1970s to do virtually nothing to enlighten citizens on the policy options currently facing the United States.

3. Whether they moderate the differences between the clashing interests that make up the electorate is, we now know, a matter of contingent fact: usually they do; sometimes [as with the Republican nomination of Barry Goldwater in 1964 and the Democratic nomination of George McGovern in 1972] they do not.

4. As agencies for the selection of public officials, the parties are evidently in a state of . . . decline.

5. They were, moreover, never very good at building bridges between the executive and legislative branches; since the presidency of Lyndon Johnson they have hardly performed this function at all.[15]

---

[13] "The American Polity in the Late 1970s: Building Coalitions in the Sand," in Anthony King, ed., *The New American Political System* (Washington, D.C.: American Enterprise Institute, 1978), p. 375.

[14] Here we are indirectly quoting ourselves (the 1962 edition of *The Politics of American Democracy*, p. 294), but we adopt King's summary of our statement for easier comparison with his description of changes since the 1960s, which follows.

[15] King, "The American Polity in the Late 1970s," pp. 384–85.

Although we agree with this assessment of the performance of American parties, we think it portrays parties that have weakened rather than parties that have disappeared. Scholars may differ on whether American parties are dead or merely sick. What is clear beyond doubt is whose interests are helped and whose are hurt by political parties. This consideration need not be speculative. In the early days of the Republic, before political parties developed, future members of Jefferson's Republican party complained about the advantages enjoyed by "the Weight of Talent, Wealth, and personal and family interest." Melancton Smith argued that the influence of

. . . the well-to-do and eminent will generally enable them to succeed in elections. [Those of] conspicuous military, popular, civil, or legal talents . . . easily form associations; the poor and middling classes form them with difficulty. . . . A substantial yeoman, of sense and discernment, will hardly ever be chosen. From these remarks, it appears that the government will fall into the hands of the few and the great. This will be a government of oppression.[16]

The "poor and middling classes" still have less clout than the well-to-do in decision making, but they have a weight they could not possibly have achieved without political parties. Some kind of organized effort is essential if large numbers are to count in politics. In Western democracies, this effort has been through the vehicle of political parties.

In recognition of this essential role of parties, the gradual decline of old-style party organizations led us to observe in 1962:

If developments of this sort tend to broaden and nationalize the political concerns of Americans, they are probably a wholesome influence. But if they mean simply that the organizational continuity and responsibility of the old party machine are to be replaced by the confusion of recurrent popularity contests, they may well create a new, less easily identifiable "machine" of professional public relations men and their employers.

Professor King submits, "Two decades after Irish and Prothro wrote, American electoral politics has largely become what they feared it might: a 'confusion of recurrent popularity contests.' "[17]

THE AMERICAN PARTY SYSTEM

To this point we have noted that each American political party is clique-oriented and heterogeneous and that each has declined drastically in strength. But how important is it that we have two such parties rather than more or one? This question turns attention from the qualities of each party to the relationships between (or among) parties, that is, from *parties* to *party system*.

[16] Quoted in William Chambers, *Political Parties in a New Nation* (New York: Oxford University Press, 1963), p. 13.
[17] *The New American Political System,* p. 386.

PART 2
inputs of the
political
system: who
wants and needs
what?

The two-party system

The American party system is an example of the two-party type. The country has many "minor parties," but whatever power political parties have in the United States is really controlled by the Republican and Democratic parties. In 1978, for example, minor parties failed to win a single seat in Congress or the governorship of any state. Quite clearly, this cannot be described as a multiparty system. Nor can it be called a one-party system. The trend is toward a more competitive party balance in all states.[18]

How does the two-party system compare with the single-party and multiparty systems? A country with a single-party system at the national level cannot be democratic, because it has no organized opposition. Although one-party systems were once dominant in most southern states, the recent trend has been strongly toward a competitive party balance throughout the United States, including the South. The original function of Democratic one-party dominance in the South was the disfranchisement of blacks, who could not vote in primaries because they were not admitted to the party. This function was eventually overruled by the larger national system.[19] But in the absence of such democratizing pressure from a larger system, one-party politics at the national level is typically the politics of repression and dictatorship.

A multiparty system, on the other hand, is not only compatible with democracy but is also the normal democratic arrangement; it is much more frequent than the two-party system. A multiparty system claims several advantages:

- Minority groups have a chance to win some seats in the legislature and perhaps some power in the cabinet of the executive branch.
- More groups win representation, bring more issues into view, and protect the disadvantaged minorities from being ignored.
- Parties take clear positions rather than equivocate, thereby making party membership more meaningful.
- Political participation increases.

And yet, to most American observers, the two-party system seems more satisfactory. Four advantages are claimed for the two-party system.

First, *it guarantees that both parties will have a wide appeal to the electorate.* Wide appeal, however, sometimes makes the parties so similar that any choice between them means little or nothing; it also decreases radical or divisive appeals. Since both parties must seek majority support in order to acquire power, both must please substantially the same people, a requirement generally viewed as a virtue. The fact that the two parties resemble each other so closely, then, may simply mean that both are doing a good job of interpreting "mainstream" opinion.

[18] Austin Ranney, "Parties in State Politics" in Herbert Jacob and Kenneth N. Vines eds., *Politics in the American States,* 3rd ed. (Boston: Little, Brown, 1976); Malcolm E. Jewell and David M. Olson, *American State Political Parties and Elections* (Homewood, Ill.: Dorsey, 1978), chap. 2.

[19] See Donald R. Matthews and James W. Prothro, *Negroes and the New Southern Politics* (New York: Harcourt, 1966).

Second, *the two-party system encourages compromise within each party before the election, rather than compromise among several parties after the election.* This situation results in the voters electing the group that will control the legislature. If many parties were elected, some of those parties would have to form a coalition to gain control of the legislature. (In the United States, the winning party often cannot be held responsible, however, because it does not remain strongly united in Congress.)

Third, *by making certain that someone will win a majority in every elected body, the two-party system increases the chances of coherence and stability in government.* Under an ideal two-party system, control of the government is fixed by the voters for the entire period between elections, rather than being subject to change if the coalition of ruling parties breaks up. The second part of that ideal view fits the American system: with only two parties, postelection maneuvers do not determine which party will control the government. But the reference to "the government" is too neat to fit the American system. An American election may bring victory to nonpartisan city officials, a Republican governor and state senate, a Democratic state house, a Republican President, and a Democratic Congress. Which party then controls "the government" or, for that matter, any level of government?

The President and both houses of Congress have been of the same party only slightly over half the time (16 of 28 years) from 1952 to 1980. In contrast, from 1900 to 1952, the same party controlled the presidency and both houses of Congress for 36 years, and party control was split for only 16 years. At the state level, too, split control has increased. In the 1970s, about half the states had governors who faced majorities of the other party in their state legislatures. The result of split control is to decrease further the meaning of party and to dilute the claim that the two-party system produces coherence and stability by putting the government under the control of one party.

Fourth, *the two-party system gives the chief executive the claim to represent the wishes of a majority of the citizens.* Because of the central importance of majority rule in the ideals of democracy, this claim greatly enhances the power and prestige of those who can make it. A President chosen by the voters in a two-party system thus enjoys a mandate greater than that of a chief executive who comes to office as the representative of one of the minority parties in a governing coalition. Whether the elevated power that comes with the claim to such a mandate is healthy or unhealthy is a matter of dispute. (Since the Watergate scandals of the early 1970s, Americans have been more inclined to doubt the desirability of enhancing presidential power.) Whatever one might prefer, the American situation poorly fits the two-party ideal once again: voter turnout is so low that a President may be elected by about 27 percent of the eligible electorate. This actually occurred in 1976, when 54 percent voted, of whom 50.1 percent voted for Jimmy Carter.

On balance, the advantages of an ideal type of the two-party system look impressive—assurance of a wide appeal to the electorate, a continuing and recognizable group on which the voters can fix responsibility, greater coherence and stability because one of the parties is ensured a majority, and a chief executive who must have a broad national mandate. But in the United

144

PART 2
inputs of the
political
system: who
wants and needs
what?

States, except for the first advantage, each of the claimed advantages of a two-party system is greatly reduced or carries with it a danger. And even the one "advantage"—a wide appeal by each party—is a disadvantage from some points of view. The fact that *both* parties in the United States are of the heterogeneous type greatly influences their appeals to voters. Unencumbered by ideology, both American parties strive for the middle-of-the-road position, where most of the votes are. This maximizes the likelihood of freezing out candidates with innovative ideas and of neglecting significant minority interests. Jockeying for the "moderate middle" position is not conducive to an imaginative response to neglected needs. Hence the alienation and hostility among those who are neglected.

Why two parties?

All democracies have more than one party. But why do some countries stop at just *two* while most establish more?[20] Let us look at a few of the explanations. Duverger says that "the two-party system seems to correspond to the nature of things," because "political choice usually takes the form of a choice between two alternatives."[21] Thomas Jefferson pointed to the nature of man rather than to the nature of things: "The sickly, weakly, timid man fears the people and is a Tory by nature. The healthy, strong, and bold, cherishes them and is formed a Whig by nature. . . ."[22] Alexander Hamilton found the explanation in economic factors: "All communities divide themselves into the few and the many," he argued before the Constitutional Convention. "The first are the rich and the well born, the other the mass of the people."[23] Some observers cite the historical fact that the United States divided into two parties early in its history, but this throws no light on the reasons *behind* the division. Others emphasize the lack of religious, racial, or class cleavages among the American people. But that seems inadequate—America has all these cleavages; they are simply not the basis of socially cohesive parties.

These explanations are so broad and vague that they would be hard to prove or disprove. But one general technical factor—the officially prescribed electoral system—is a clue to the party system in *every* country. The *single-member district system with plurality election* correlates almost perfectly with the two-party system. The "single-member district system" is the system under which only one representative, rather than several, is elected to a given office from any one district. "Plurality election" means that the candidate with the largest vote is elected even if the votes do not constitute a majority, so that there is never any need for a second balloting to produce a majority

---

[20] Only 8 out of 30 countries with recognized opposition parties in 1964 had two-party systems. See Robert A. Dahl, *Political Oppositions in Western Democracies* (New Haven, Conn.: Yale University Press, 1966), p. 333.

[21] Duverger, *Political Parties,* p. 215.

[22] See Charles A. Beard, *Economic Origins of Jeffersonian Democracy* (New York: Macmillan, 1936), pp. 420–21*n,* for letter to Lafayette (November 4, 1823).

[23] Max Farrand, ed., *The Records of the Federal Convention of 1787* (New Haven, Conn.: Yale University Press, 1911), p. 299.

vote. Because parties always try to win elections, the election procedures that are prescribed by law cannot help but mold the character of party politics. A country that has a two-party system almost always uses this electoral scheme; and if it uses this electoral scheme, it will almost certainly have a two-party system.[24]

The way in which the single-member district system freezes out minor parties is fairly obvious. Only one victor is possible in each race, whether for the presidency or for the legislature. Because the minor parties have no chance at all of capturing the presidency, and little chance of ever enjoying any legislative power, they quickly die out.

The influence of plurality election is also important. In countries where a majority vote is required for victory, a second balloting between the candidates who led on the first ballot is necessary. This system encourages minor parties to offer candidates in the first election in the hope of slipping into the runoff election. (The second ballot was one of the causes of the multiparty system in France's Third Republic.) But in countries where only a simple plurality is needed for victory, minor parties are encouraged to join forces with one of the major parties, in the hope that they may become identified with the winner. Understandably, the major parties tend to make concessions to the minor parties in order to broaden their base of support. Where there is only one election, then, coalitions must be formed before the election rather than in the interval between the first and second balloting.

Although these technical features of the electoral system seem particularly well adapted to two-party politics, we still cannot say that the party system of a country is a direct result of its electoral system. From data on 5 European countries, John Grumm concludes that the party system shapes the electoral system, rather than the other way around.[25] Denmark and some other countries once had the single-member district and the plurality system of elections but maintained a multiparty system. The parties then changed the electoral system to help themselves. Without attempting to unravel cause and effect, we can say that single-member districts and plurality elections are found together with two-party systems, just as proportional representation from multi-member districts and majority elections (calling for runoff elections) are associated with multiparty systems.

So many factors work to shape both the electoral and the party system of a country that the question of *why* a particular system develops cannot be answered exactly. But any pattern of behavior, once established, tends to perpetuate itself. Generations of Americans have been taught the superiority of the two-party system, and it has been elevated from mere habit to

---

[24] As Duverger explains, the exceptions to this rule are rare (Canada offers the only current exception) and result from special conditions. He accordingly finds the limits of this system's influence to be as follows: "It tends to the creation of a two-party system inside the individual constituency; but the parties opposed may be different in different areas of the country." Duverger, *Political Parties,* p. 223. For insight into this problem, the authors are particularly indebted to Duverger's discussion on pp. 216–28, and to Schattschneider, *Party Government,* chap. 5.

[25] "Theories of Electoral Systems," *Midwest Journal of Political Science,* 2 (November 1958), 345–76.

the level of a celebrated tradition. Despite Americans' distrust of both their political parties, a large majority of Americans nevertheless endorse the idea of the two-party system.[26]

THE STRUCTURE OF AMERICAN PARTIES

Like the overall party system, the internal organization of each party is structured by the country's official electoral practices. Because the purpose of each party is to gain control of the government by winning elections, party organization is built around the electoral system. And the way elections are won as we enter the 1980s has vastly changed the organization of political parties.

Formal party organization

The first formal constitution for a major American political party was adopted by the Democrats in 1974. It lays out the formal organization that characterizes both major parties.

The Democrats' national charter says: "The *national convention* shall be the highest authority of the Democratic Party. . . ."[27] As the highest authority in both parties, the national presidential conventions choose candidates for President and Vice-President and adopt platforms. Meeting only a few days once every four years, several thousand delegates at national conventions can ratify or modify the work of their platform committee and nominate candidates, but they obviously cannot conduct or direct the on-going activities of a political party.

The authority to direct the affairs of each party between national conventions is vested in a *national committee.* Both parties long had national committees made up of one man and one woman from each state, but they have recently enlarged the committees to give additional representation to larger states and to states supporting the party in the last election. The image of the national committee as a confederation of equal state organizations thus no longer holds.

The most authoritative study of the national committees, published in 1964, was entitled *Politics without Power,*[28] for national committees then did little beyond making detailed arrangements for the next nominating convention. The choice of delegates was entirely at the discretion of the state party organizations. After 1968, however, the Democratic National Committee be-

[26] Dennis, "Trends in Public Support for the American Political Party System."

[27] Article Two, Section 2. The text of the Democratic party's charter can be found in *Congressional Quarterly Weekly Report,* 32 (Dec. 14, 1974), 3334–36 (emphasis added).

[28] Cornelius P. Cotter and Bernard C. Hennessy, *Politics without Power: The National Party Committees* (New York: Atherton, 1964), pp. 10–11.

UPI

Chicago Mayor Jane Byrne has struggled to maintain a role in national politics comparable to that of former Mayor Richard Daley.

gan to take control of the entire delegate selection process; with somewhat less clout, the Republican National Committee has followed suit.[29] Although the overall functions of political parties have waned, then, the focus of authority within the party has shifted to the national level.

The *national chairperson* officially speaks for the party and is charged with carrying out the programs and policies of the national convention and the national committee. Other party leaders disagree with the national chairperson often and loudly enough, however, to demonstrate that the party has no single voice. The national chairperson is officially chosen by the national committee but is in fact named by the party's presidential nominee. The chairperson's primary task is to manage the presidential campaign. If the

[29] Charles Longley, "Party Reform and Party Nationalization: The Case of the Democrats" and "Party Reform and the Republican Party," papers presented at the annual meetings of the Midwest Political Science Association, Chicago, 1976, and of the American Political Science Association, New York, 1978, respectively.

148

PART 2
inputs of the
political
system: who
wants and needs
what?

campaign is successful, chances are the chairperson will be allowed to continue as party administrator, fund raiser, and spokesperson. After a losing campaign, however, the national committee may choose a new chairperson who reflects the dominant forces on the committee. The national chairperson thus *reflects* rather than *exercises* the power of the party.

At the next level are the *state committees,* which have various functions, methods of selection, and titles. All these committees are concerned with conducting state campaigns, but some of them also exercise control over state party activities in general. Unlike the "higher" levels of the party structure, controlled mainly by the rules of the party, the organization of these committees is generally governed by state law.

County and *city committees* are organized around townships, precincts, and wards. The chairpersons of these committees often possess real power in local politics. Old-style bosses like Mayor Richard Daley of Chicago also enjoyed tremendous influence over the choice of candidates for national office; but as they lost control over the selection of delegates, their power in national politics suffered severely. The change was dramatically demonstrated when Mayor Daley and his entire delegation were denied seats at the 1972 Democratic convention because they violated national party rules.

The pattern of power

For decades, American political parties have been correctly described as both weak and decentralized—"loose confederation[s] of state and local bosses for limited purposes."[30] The limited purposes of American parties— their failure to develop mass support or to achieve solidarity behind a party program once in office—were and still are the marks of their weakness. Indeed, these weaknesses have become even more extreme. But almost unnoticed, the feature of decentralization has changed: *the parties have become more centralized even while they were becoming weaker.* The power to set rules and procedures for choosing delegates to the national conventions was completely changed in the 1970s, shifting from state to national party organizations. Moreover, the courts have declared national party rules to be superior not merely to state party rules but even to state laws.[31]

Leading students of political parties still described American parties as totally decentralized—"local, parochial interests without any control by the national party"—as late as 1976.[32] Difficulty in seeing the trend toward central-

---

[30] The quotation is from Schattschneider's classic, *Party Government,* pp. 132–33. More recent expressions of this view are in Joyce Gelb and Marion Palley, *Tradition and Change in American Party Politics* (New York: Crowell, 1975), p. 211, and Frank B. Feigert and M. Margaret Conway, *Parties and Politics in America* (Boston: Allyn and Bacon, 1976), p. 141.

[31] We shall look at these developments in more detail in Chapter 7, "The Electoral System." See Austin Ranney, "The Political Parties: Reform and Decline," in King, ed., *The New American Political System,* pp. 222–30; and for a more comprehensive analysis, Charles Longley, "Party Nationalization in America," in William Crotty, ed., *Paths to Political Reform* (Lexington, Mass.: D. C. Heath, 1979).

[32] Sorauf, *Party Politics in America,* p. 114.

ization—even though it began between 1968 and 1972—stems, no doubt, from the tendency to assume that weakness and decentralization go together. With so much attention on the declining strength of American parties, we failed to notice that they were nevertheless becoming more centralized. Party organization and party experience mean less in choosing candidates, in conducting campaigns, and in running the government than at any other time in the history of political parties. Nevertheless, these weakened organizations are more centralized than at any time since the early 1820s! As we shall see when we consider the electoral system (in chapter 7), the national nominating conventions—the one great activity of parties that they still carry out—are now truly "national" for the first time.

Although such power as American parties exercise is now found more at the national level, the fact remains that the centrally important powers of political parties throughout the world are not found in American parties at all. To locate the controlling power of a party, one normally asks two questions: Who controls the nominations? Who controls the government when the party is in power? What is baffling to foreigners about American political parties is that the parties have almost no organizational control over either nominations or the government, whether through their national, state, or local committees and officers.

So far as nominations are concerned, the mass media play an increasingly important part in identifying, screening, and evaluating candidates. Individual candidates' organizations and public relations firms plan campaign strategy and raise funds. The political action committees ("PACs") of corporations, unions, and special interest groups educate citizens on issues and get out the vote. All of these are activities that were once handled mostly by party organizations. But today neither the party label nor the party organization has the importance it once did in the United States (and still does, for the most part, in other democracies).

For the electorate to choose a President of one party and a Congress of the other would be unthinkable in most countries. But the increasing tendency of American voters to cast "split tickets" appears to be a realistic response to the weakness of American political parties. Who controls the government when a party is in power? For most democracies the answer would be obvious: the winning party. But winning control of the government probably means less in the United States than in any other democracy. Because election to the presidency requires national support, the President usually stands for the policies of his party as a national organization. After all, the organization is so weak that anyone with enough support to win the party's nomination will also have enough strength to say what its policies are. Members of the same party in Congress are even more independent of the national party. They win nomination and election by local efforts and, once elected, the advantage of name recognition that goes with incumbency gives them a tremendous advantage in subsequent elections. Consequently, senators and representatives are free to disregard the national platform of their party, with little fear that it will damage their chances of reelection.

PART 2
inputs of the
political
system: who
wants and needs
what?

Party personnel: "members" and leaders

Duverger notes that the expression "party member" has different meanings in different parties and countries, and he adds in fascination, "For American parties, it even has no meaning at all. . . ."[33] What he has in mind is the lack of party members in the sense that Boy Scout troops, for example, or Rotary Clubs, or college fraternities, or mass political parties in Europe may be said to have members. "Republicans" and "Democrats" undergo no official initiation (except, in some states, when they indicate their party affiliation in registering to vote). They need not meet standards of fitness for membership or pay dues. Nor are they required to show any obligation to the party or to attend regular mass meetings.

The passive attitude of most Americans toward party organizations is hardly surprising. Historically, the mass political parties of Europe, which actively try to organize the electorate, appeared after the industrial revolution had created a distinctive—and disadvantaged—class of industrial laborers. Typical of these parties were the socialists, who sought both to educate the workers and to reform the existing order. In order to avoid becoming dependent on the "moneyed interests" that opposed reform, they were obliged to finance their campaigns by levying membership dues.

The major American parties, on the other hand, were formed before the industrial revolution and therefore before laborers began to organize against corporate power. As a result, both are of the clique-oriented rather than the mass-membership type. American workers already had a party identification before the labor movement developed. Hence, American labor organizations have concentrated primarily on economic objectives rather than organizing any socialist or other specifically class-based party. The lack of a class-based political party and the middle-class orientation of the two major parties make lower-status Americans feel left out. One result, as we saw in chapter 4, is that the difference in participation between the "haves" and "have nots" is greater in the United States than in any other democracy.[34]

The activists who choose presidential nominees have been called "the presidential elite,"[35] and as the term suggests, they are far from typical voters. In 1972, as before and after, "The delegates to both conventions were an overwhelmingly middle to upper middle-class group, and they knew it."[36] What was different in 1972 was that the delegates were less overwhelmingly male, middle-aged, and white. Both parties have responded to demands for greater recognition of women, youth, and blacks. Nevertheless, the percentage of delegates with high incomes, in professional employment, and with graduate degrees has increased. More young people, blacks, and women are participat-

[33] Duverger, *Political Parties*, p. 61.

[34] Sidney Verba and Norman H. Nie, *Participation in America: Political Democracy and Social Equality* (New York: Harper, 1972), pp. 340–41.

[35] See Jeane J. Kirkpatrick, *The New Presidential Elite* (New York: Russell Sage Foundation and Twentieth Century Fund, 1976).

[36] In addition to the above source, see Jeane J. Kirkpatrick, "Representation in the American National Conventions: The Case of 1972," *British Journal of Political Science*, 5 (July 1975), 285.

ing than ever before, but they do not often represent a different social status from that of the older white men who have so long controlled the parties.

Party activists also differ from rank-and-file party members in policy orientations. An early study of party leaders and regular party identifiers found the leaders (defined as delegates to national conventions) to be considerably more committed than the rank and file to their party's positions.[37] This difference is exactly what one would expect from the greater exposure of convention delegates to party doctrine. Jeane Kirkpatrick's recent study found similar differences between leaders and followers, but with a new twist. The Republican delegates' conservatism on the social welfare issues of the 1950s was so extreme that the Republicans they were supposed to represent were closer to the position of Democratic delegates. But on the new social issues of the 1970s—crime, school busing, rights of political demonstrators—the Democratic delegates' liberalism was so great that the Democrats they were supposedly representing were closer to the position of Republican delegates![38]

THE DOCTRINAL AND SOCIAL BASE OF AMERICAN PARTIES

The doctrines—the principles and policies—of a party reflect the needs of the groups and interests with which it tries to win elections. Those who think parties should always stick to the same principles are doomed to disappointment, because it is precisely through the effort to win elections by meeting the changing needs of popular interests—not through dedication to fixed principles—that American parties "make sense." Doctrines are created simply to serve human interests.

Shifting doctrines

Comparing the positions of America's major parties today with the positions of earlier parties, we can suggest how changing economic and social conditions have led parties to modify their doctrines. Originally, the Jeffersonian Republicans (later to become known as the Democratic party) were on one side, and the Federalists (the grandfathers of the present Republican party) were on the other. The Jeffersonians stood for the needs of a farming society—"least government" as the best government, states' rights, decentralization, laissez-faire, legislative rather than executive power, and economy in government. The Federalists, on the other hand, favored the needs of an industrial, urban society—energetic government, nationalism, centralization, government intervention in the economy, executive rather than legislative power, and a managed public debt.

[37] Herbert McClosky, Paul J. Hoffmann, and Rosemary O'Hara, "Issue Conflict and Consensus Among Party Leaders and Followers," *American Political Science Review,* 54 (June 1960), 406–27.

[38] Kirkpatrick, *The New Presidential Elite,* chap. 10. Also see Frederick Lee, *Presidential Elite Support for the American Presidency,* Ph.D. dissertation, University of Michigan, 1978.

152

PART 2
inputs of the
political
system: who
wants and needs
what?

The two present-day parties have neatly changed positions on every one of these issues. Does this mean that they have abandoned their principles? Did the Democrats reject Jeffersonian values for Hamiltonian values, while the Republicans did the reverse? Not necessarily. Jefferson had faith in the masses and was suspicious of power in almost any form; at the time, the government was the only national organization that might wield enough power to threaten popular interests. Hamilton was more impressed with the superiority of the "rich, well-born, and able," and he wanted to create a strong government, to reflect that superiority and control the "unthinking majority." By now the Jeffersonian view of the people has triumphed to such an extent that no politician would reject majority rule as such. But the Democratic party is still more concerned with the needs of the "underprivileged," and the Republicans, like the Federalists, are more interested in greater rewards for the "deserving."

The first great shift in party doctrines occurred in the 1820s and 1830s, when Jacksonian Democracy established the President as the chief spokesman for the voters. The Federalist party had died out and was succeeded by the Whigs. Unlike Federalists, Whigs rejected the idea of a strong executive, but supported a strong legislature, in which minority interests might block the majority. At the same time, the Democrats began to prefer strong executive power, rather than strong congressional power.

A second change in doctrines took place after the Civil War, when rapid industrialization concentrated private power in the hands of corporations strong enough to threaten majority interests. The Democratic party came to look on this concentration of private power as the chief danger to fulfillment of popular needs. It began to view government as not merely a necessary evil but as a means of coping with this dangerous force. Republicans, on the other hand, adopted the old Jeffersonian fear of government when, late in the nineteenth century, government began turning to such "socialistic" schemes as income taxes and business regulation.

The Great Depression that fell on the country in 1929 revealed these new orientations in a naked light and sharpened the contrast between the parties. Since the New Deal era of the 1930s the Democrats have pushed for social welfare programs, an active governmental role in creating jobs and promoting economic growth, regulation of "big business," and tax measures designed to reduce, at least mildly, the great disparities in income. Republican leaders have tended to oppose these programs as unnecessary and as dangerously increasing the power of government. They have championed reliance on private enterprise, although they have not regarded the "private" emphasis as inconsistent with government's aids to business as a means to economic growth.[39]

The extent of this switch in party doctrines is indicated by roll call votes in Congress. Despite the loose nature of American parties and the lack of party discipline in Congress, the contrast in the voting records of the parties

[39] For an examination of party platforms, see Gerald M. Pomper, *Elections in America* (New York: Dodd, Mead, 1971). Henry Fairlie, *The Parties: Republicans and Democrats in This Century* (New York: St. Martin's Press, 1978) is a stimulating analysis of both major parties in this century.

President Franklin Roosevelt described the social reforms of the New Deal as an Economic Bill of Rights.

is clear. Table 5 · 2 presents the proportion of Democrats and Republicans supporting various measures in the House of Representatives since World War II. Although one could select other proposals on which party differences would

TABLE 5·2 | **Democratic and Republican support for selected proposals in the House of Representatives**

Year	Proposal	Democrats for	Republicans for
1945	Full Employment Act	90%	36%
1950	Exempt independent gas producers from price regulation	46	60
1954	Increase unemployment compensation	54	9
1958	Recommit (kill) National Defense Education Act	23	52
1961	Against increase in minimum wage	34	86
1963	Accelerated public works program	86	12
1964	Antipoverty program (Equal Opportunity Act)	84	13
1968	Housing assistance for low-income families	78	44
1970	Overriding veto of bill for aid to hospital construction	99	44
1974	Regulation of strip mining	78	34
1975	Emergency employment appropriations	99	30
1978	Extension of time for ERA ratification	69	28

154

PART 2
inputs of the
political
system: who
wants and needs
what?

not look so stark, this list shows that Democrats are far more apt to support proposals for the government to help the unemployed find jobs, regulate business, increase wages and unemployment compensation, and extend aid to a variety of programs on which the "have-nots" depend more than the "haves" (such as hospital construction, housing, and educational benefits). These are all measures that call for an active government, the very "principle" to which Jeffersonians objected. But they are also measures designed with a concern for the disadvantaged, the very groups Jeffersonian principles were to serve. Republican opposition to these measures is in similar contrast to the Hamiltonian commitment to an activist government but consistent with the concern for protecting the advantages of the "haves," both as an appropriate reward for their accomplishments and as an incentive for the less accomplished. To understand these changes in party policies, we turn to the enduring social base of the parties.

Persisting bases of support

The concern of Democrats for the disadvantaged and of Republicans for the advantaged is illustrated by a comment on the Democratic-Whig division of the nineteenth century:

Jacksonian Democracy originated as the personal following of one who symbolized the idea of justice for the masses. He was represented as a champion of the underdog and the Democratic Party has always relied for its voting strength primarily upon the counties with poorer soils and the crowded wards of the great cities largely populated with recent immigrant stock. . . .

To the well-to-do, however, Jackson was a demagogue, a preacher of social discontent, and the prosperous became the backbone of the opposition to Jackson. The dominant elements of the Whig party consisted of the great financial, commercial, and emerging industrial interests of the East, the more prosperous agrarians of the North and the great slaveholding planters of the South.[40]

"Great slave-holding planters" no longer exist, but this statement otherwise describes the bases of strength on which Democrats and Republicans rely to this day. Although the contending political groups in America require programs far different from those in Jackson's day, each group is fairly consistent in the party it looks to for the realization of its needs.

After the Civil War, several factors greatly modified the appeal of the two major parties to different social groups:

1. The regional splits produced by the war.
2. Eagerness of both parties to please corporate interests during late nineteenth-century industrialization.

---

[40] Wilfred Binkley, *President and Congress* (New York: Knopf, 1947), pp. 86–87.

3. Failure of the Democrats to capture eastern labor and urban votes when those groups "went radical" in the 1890s.[41]

As a result, the Republican party dominated the national scene from the Civil War until 1932. Grover Cleveland and Woodrow Wilson were the only two Democratic presidents during that 72-year period. But the Great Depression that began in 1929 produced the current party system, which, in popular support, is remarkably similar to the Democratic-Whig era before the Civil War.

The Depression suddenly made the business community unpopular, and the Democrats took advantage of the chance to label the Republicans the party of big business. In addition to antibusiness feelings, long-run trends helped the Democrats and hurt the Republicans in 1932. These influences were: the increased voting strength of immigrants and their children, the high birthrate of lower-income groups, the shift of people from farms to cities, and the increasing political awareness of ethnic minorities. Al Smith, the Democratic presidential nominee in 1928, had been an effective governor of New York; but more important, he was a Catholic who had an East Side New York City accent and occasional grammatical difficulties. Although he lost the election, he created for many an image of the Democrats as the party of the underprivileged. The Depression gave the Democrats a perfect opportunity to capitalize on this image just when it had the most appeal. Vestiges of their success can still be seen; many voters still view Republicans as sympathizing with big business and Democrats as favoring the "little man."

Party support today

The coalition supporting each of the major parties in presidential elections for the 24-year period from 1952 to 1976 shows both stability and change. As Table 5 · 3 indicates, the core of the Democratic coalition during the contemporary era has been the poor, blacks, union members, and Catholics. Geographically, the Democrats have relied on the South and the central cities. The bottom line of Table 5 · 3, the percentage of the national vote for Democratic presidential candidates, shows wild fluctuation, all the way from Lyndon Johnson's 61 percent in 1964 to George McGovern's 37 percent in 1972. Such extreme variations show that the Democratic party has a weak hold on those who call themselves Democrats.

The first six lines in the table show what percentage of each group voted for Democratic candidates. Comparing these percentages with the percentages of the national vote for Democratic candidates (bottom), one can see the relative deviation of each group toward the Democrats. These deviations are noted in parentheses in each group. At the beginning of this period, for example, every element of the coalition voted more heavily Democratic than did

[41] Most scholars identify 5 different "party systems," a system being defined in terms of organizational structures or electoral coalitions. See Burnham, *Critical Elections and the Mainsprings of American Politics,* and W. N. Chambers and W. D. Burnham, eds., *The American Party Systems: Stages of Political Development,* 2nd ed. (New York: Oxford University Press, 1975).

TABLE 5·3

Percent voting for Democrats (% deviation from national average in parentheses)

	1952	1956	1960	1964	1968	1972	1976
Poor	47 (+2)%	47 (+5)%	48 (−2)%	69 (+8)%	44 (+1)%	45 (+8)%	67 (+17)%
Blacks	83 (+38)	68 (+26)	72 (+22)	99 (+38)	92 (+49)	86 (+49)	88 (+38)
Union families	59 (+14)	55 (+13)	66 (+16)	80 (+19)	51 (+8)	45 (+8)	63 (+13)
Catholics	57 (+12)	53 (+11)	82 (+32)	75 (+14)	61 (+18)	36 (−2)	57 (+7)
South	55 (+10)	52 (+10)	52 (+2)	58 (−3)	39 (−4)	36 (−2)	53 (+3)
Central cities	51 (+6)	55 (+13)	65 (+15)	74 (+13)	58 (+15)	61 (+24)	61 (+10)
National	44.4	42.0	49.7	61.1	42.7	37.5	50.1

Source: Robert Axelrod, "Communications," *American Political Science Review,* 72 (June 1978), 623.

the nation as a whole. The greatest deviation in 1952 was among black voters, 83 percent of whom voted Democratic compared with 44 percent of all voters. The smallest pro-Democratic deviation in 1952 was among the poor. In *relative* terms, however, even though only 47 percent of the poor voted Democratic in 1952, they were still more Democratic than the nation as a whole. And every other group in the Democratic coalition deviated far enough to give the Democratic candidate a majority of their votes. If these groups had been the only voters in 1952, Adlai Stevenson rather than Dwight Eisenhower would have become President.

Despite the fact that the groups shown in Table 5 · 3 are relatively more Democratic than the rest of the voters, the basic fact that Democrats have won only 3 of the last 7 elections remains. This is far from a dependable coalition of supporters. Moreover, in three successive elections from 1964 to 1972, the formerly "Solid South" actually deviated in a Republican direction. It returned to the Democratic fold in 1976 only because black voters in the South overcame the majority support that white southerners gave to Gerald Ford. Even with a southerner leading the Democratic ticket, the party's appeal in the region was probably only temporarily revived, and not very impressively at that.

Because Democrats have outnumbered Republicans since 1932, we have concentrated on the overlapping groups that made up the New Deal coalition. If we examined the Republican coalition in the same manner, we would discover it to be the reverse of the Democratic coalition, with relatively greater support from nonpoor, whites, nonunion families, Protestants, and geographically, from outside the South and outside the central cities. Two developments are encouraging for the Republicans. First, they can win the presidency despite the Democrats' advantage in party identification. Second, the South has shown a willingness to desert the Democrats.[42]

[42] Excellent treatments of developments during the fifth party system beginning with the New Deal are: Everett C. Ladd, Jr., *Transformations of the American Party System,* 2d ed. (New York: Norton, 1978); Herbert B. Asher, *Presidential Elections and American Politics,* rev. ed. (Homewood, Ill.: Dorsey, 1980); Warren Miller and Teresa Levitin, *Leadership and Change: Presidential Elections from 1952 to 1976* (Cambridge, Mass.: Winthrop, 1976).

Has the New Deal era come to an end? Certainly the nature of the issues and even the nature of the party organizations will make the politics of the 1980s vastly different from that of the early New Deal period. In terms of Democrats outnumbering Republicans, however, the dominance that began with the New Deal is still with us. As Table 5 · 4 indicates, Democrats outnumber Republicans almost 2 to 1, an even greater superiority than they enjoyed three decades ago.

TABLE 5·4

Distribution of party identification in the United States, 1952 to 1976

	1952	1954	1956	1958	1960	1962	1964	1966	1968	1970	1972	1974	1976
Democrat	47%	47%	44%	47%	46%	46%	51%	45%	49%	43%	41%	38%	40%
Independent	22	22	24	19	23	22	23	28	27	31	34	36	36
Republican	27	27	29	29	27	28	24	25	23	24	23	22	23
Apolitical "Don't know"	4	4	3	5	4	4	2	2	1	2	2	4	1
	100%	100%	100%	100%	100%	100%	100%	100%	100%	100%	100%	100%	100%

Source: Center for Political Studies, Institute for Social Research, University of Michigan.

Findings such as those in Table 5 · 4 have led many analysts to emphasize the stability of party identification.[43] But the percentages in the table are for the total adult population. Millions of people could have changed their party identification without any change at all appearing in the overall figures; changes in one direction might simply be matched by changes in a different direction and thus produce no difference in the overall figures. In fact, this has happened.

For two of the years in the table (1956 and 1958) the surveys included the same people, revealing individual switches, rather than changes within the population as a whole. That period showed very little overall shift in partisanship; but in fact, *20 percent of all adults made a major shift* (among the Democrat—Independent—Republican categories) *during the two-year interval.*[44] When we turn from overall distributions to individual changes, then, what once looked highly stable is revealed to contain a surprising amount of instability. And remember that the 20 percent rate of change is for a two-year period only. A careful estimate of the long-term rate of change holds that 40 percent of the voters have at some time altered their partisan position

[43] The classic works that developed the concept of party identification are Angus Campbell, Gerald Gurin, and Warren E. Miller, *The Voter Decides* (Evanston: Row, Peterson, 1954); A. Campbell, P. E. Converse, W. E. Miller, and D. E. Stokes, *The American Voter* (New York: Wiley, 1960); and by the same four authors, *Elections and the Political Order* (New York: Wiley, 1966).

[44] John C. Pierce and Douglas D. Rose, "Nonattitudes and American Public Opinion: The Examination of a Thesis," *American Political Science Review,* 68 (June 1974), 631, note 35.

Drawing by John Ruge.

"Roger and I have stayed
in the Republican party
because of the children."

from one to another of the three basic positions—Democrat, Independent, or Republican.[45]

Even in terms of overall party losses and gains, the degree of stability has been overstated. Millions of voters have abandoned both parties and now call themselves Independents. In 1966, the proportion of Americans identifying as Independents emerged as greater than the proportion identifying as Republicans. For the first time since data had been collected, the second of America's "major" parties dropped to a point at which its followers were outnumbered by Independents. The numerical supremacy of Independents over Republicans steadily grew to reach a nearly 2-to-1 ratio. The Democrats have also lost party identifiers to the ranks of Independents. Today the Democrats and Republicans can claim a smaller proportion of adult Americans as supporters than at any time in recent history.

The dramatic increase in the proportion of Independents is the more threatening to the major parties because it comes disproportionately from young people and from the college educated. As education levels continue to increase and as more new voters enter the electorate, the hold of the parties on American politics may slip even more. In the first presidential election survey carried out by social scientists (in 1940), Independents were found to be more politically apathetic, ignorant, and uninvolved than those with a party commitment.[46] By the 1970s these old-style Independents were being joined by well-educated, well-informed, and interested citizens who thoughtfully re-

[45] David M. Kovenock, James W. Prothro, et al., *Explaining the Vote: Presidential Choices in the Nation and the States* (Chapel Hill, N.C.: Institute for Research in Social Science, 1973).

[46] Paul F. Lazarsfeld, Bernard Berelson, and Hazel Gaudet, *The People's Choice,* 2nd ed. (New York: Columbia University Press, 1948).

jected both parties.[47] Not only is partisan identification less stable than once believed, then, but the characteristics of people within a given category are also changing. What does this mean for the American party system?

IS THE AMERICAN PARTY SYSTEM COLLAPSING?

In 1974 the Democratic National Committee retained a top-flight New York direct mail firm, Rapp and Collins, to plan a fund-raising campaign. "We tried six or seven different approaches in test marketings," said Thomas Collins, the director of the firm. "Nothing worked. Response didn't compare to the response we get for individual candidates; the candidates did 3 to 10 times better. The response was, 'Why should someone give to the Democratic party?' or 'What does the party stand for?' And the questions were coming not from the general public, not from registered Democrats, but *from the 1 percent of Democrats on hot liberal lists.*"[48]

If even the small proportion of Democrats with a record of contributions to liberal causes and candidates have such a sour view of their party, how must it look to the general public? Jack Dennis explored this question. His research includes data on general ("diffuse") support for parties, evaluation of the performance of the party system, and feelings about system reform.[49] Dennis first measured diffuse support for the party system in 1964 by asking people to agree or disagree with the following statements:

1. It would be better if, in all elections, we put no party labels on the ballot.
2. The parties do more to confuse the issues than to provide a clear choice on issues.
3. More often than not, the political parties create conflicts where none really exists.

Each of the above statements corresponds to one of the functions we described as contributions of political parties to democracy—providing voters a cue for evaluating candidates and issues, clarifying issues, and peaceably organizing conflicts that would otherwise be violent. Dennis's sample of Wisconsin adults showed a fairly high level of support for the parties only in their disagreement with the first statement. As Fig. 5 · 1 indicates, 67 percent of the respondents were in favor of keeping party labels on the ballot in 1964. On the other two statements, however, the parties enjoyed little support: only 21 percent denied that parties confuse the issues, and only 15 percent

---

[47] Norman H. Nie, Sidney Verba, and John R. Petrocik, *The Changing American Voter* (Cambridge, Mass.: Harvard University Press, 1976), chap. 4.

[48] Quoted in Richard Reeves, "Nationally, the Democrats Are a Fiction," *New York Times,* June 1, 1975 (emphasis added).

[49] Unless otherwise indicated, the data in this subsection are from Jack Dennis, "Trends in Public Support for the American Political Party System."

The declining appeal of both political parties encouraged Representative John Anderson to run for President as an Independent in 1980.

denied that parties create conflicts where none really exists. In 1964, then, the results on general support for parties were mixed.

The change over the 10-year period covered by Fig. 5 · 1 produces negative rather than mixed results. The proportion of adults agreeing that party labels should be kept on the ballot dropped steadily through the decade to reach a low of 38 percent in 1974. On the other two indicators, the proportions denying that parties confuse issues and create unnecessary conflict remain very low. General support for political parties was not impressive in the 1960s; it dropped even lower in the 1970s.

The same pattern holds for what Dennis calls the "partisanship norm"— voting for the party rather than the individual. In the 1950s, almost 75 percent of American adults said it is better to vote for the candidate rather than the party; by 1968, the proportion with that view had risen to over 80 percent. Some of the people who say they vote for the candidate rather than the party are no doubt influenced by their party preference when they evaluate candidates. Nevertheless, Americans adhere to an antiparty norm on this question, and the proportion who do so has been increasing.

The performance of the party system is also viewed negatively. Only decreasing minorities say that parties help make the government pay attention to what the people want, that parties are interested in people's opinions rather than only in their votes, and that parties "pretty much keep their promises." In comparison with the three official branches of the government, political parties come out a miserable last when Americans are asked which "has done the *best job* in the past couple of years." Table 5 · 5 shows that less than 4 percent of American adults rated political parties first in either 1972 or 1973.

TABLE 5·5 | Perception of party system performance in general: comparisons among four institutions, U.S., 1972, 1973

Question: 'Which of the parts of the government on this list has done the best job in the past couple of years?'

	Congress	Supreme Court	President	Political parties
1972	33.1%	16.1%	47.0%	3.8%
1973	45.1	26.2	25.2	3.6

Source: Dennis, "Trends in Public Support for the American Party System," p. 207.

The low esteem of political parties cannot be attributed to the Watergate scandal, which had not really broken open in 1972, but it had become an issue at the time of the 1973 survey. Its impact is indicated by the fact that the President dropped from the highest rating (47 percent) in 1972 to third place (25 percent) in 1973. But the shift in confidence from the President went entirely to Congress and the Supreme Court. Political parties remained at the bottom of the heap.

When asked if various institutions—Congress, Supreme Court, Office of the President, national parties, national elections, national interest groups—should be abolished, reformed, or "kept as is," few Wisconsin adults were in

SOURCE: Jack Dennis, "Trends in Public Support for the American Party System," *British Journal of Political Science,* 5 (April 1975), 200.

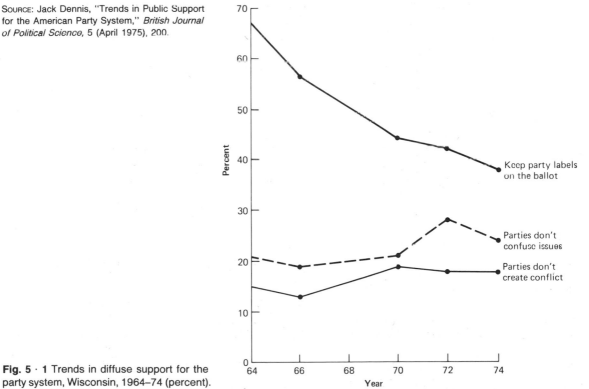

Fig. 5 · 1 Trends in diffuse support for the party system, Wisconsin, 1964–74 (percent).

162

PART 2
inputs of the
political
system: who
wants and needs
what?

TABLE 5·6

Wisconsin data on party system reform, 1970

We sometimes hear these days that parts of the American political system ought to be abolished or reformed. What I want to ask next is how you feel about each of the things listed on this card. First, in your opinion, should the U.S. Congress be abolished, reformed, or kept as it is? Do you feel the U.S. Supreme Court should be abolished, reformed, or kept as it is? . . . the Office of the President? . . . the national political parties? . . . national elections? . . . national interest groups?

	Congress	Supreme Court	Office of President	National parties	National elections	National interest groups
Abolished	—%	1%	1%	4%	1%	7%
Reformed	28	33	19	41	40	26
Kept as it is	66	60	77	47	56	56
Don't know	5	5	3	7	3	13
Not ascertained	1	1	1	1	1	1

Source: Dennis, "Trends in Public Support for the American Party System," p. 213.

favor of abolishing any of them. But as Table 5·6 shows, their principal target for reform is political parties. Even so, almost half the respondents say that the institution of political parties should be "kept as is." What this probably means is that although people are indeed unhappy with the performance of political parties, they have difficulty in thinking how they should be changed.

The focus on parties' need for reform may also mean that people realize how important they are for democracy. This is supported by the fact that in the need for reform, national elections rank a close second to political parties—and hardly anyone can doubt the importance of elections to a democratic society. People have not been happy with the choices given to them in recent elections, however, so both parties and election procedures are under suspicion. In their concern for improving both, an increasing majority of Americans are ready to eliminate the one important function that keeps the parties meaningful as national organizations: nomination of presidential candidates by the national conventions. The proportion of Americans who believe presidential candidates should be chosen by national primary elections rather than by party conventions has risen from a small majority in the 1950s to an overwhelming majority today. With the disappearance of the nominating function, American parties would lose much of their meaning, so the willingness to strip it away is a serious threat to the party system.

The progressive attack on parties and partisanship

Decomposition, disaggregation, delegitimation, atrophy, rigidification, degeneration—these are some of the unflattering, awkward terms recently used to describe what is happening to American political parties. What evidence in addition to increasing public disrespect for political parties leads to such a dismal diagnosis? Before we look for signs of decay in our present-day parties, we need some historical perspective to see what parties have decayed from.

Most Americans today have no idea of what party competition was like in the late nineteenth century. For one thing, there wasn't much else available in the way of public entertainment—no movies, television, radio, stereo systems, comics, professional sports, beauty pageants, dog shows, Disneyland, Little League baseball, or even shopping centers. When a political figure came to town, it was an important event. Or for that matter, people would travel far under difficult conditions to see a political figure. The estimate is that 750,000 people from all over the country went to McKinley's Ohio home during his "Front Porch" campaign for President in 1896, a number that amounted to 5 percent of the total vote. That is equivalent to approximately 4,077,600 people from the 1976 electorate. Imagine that much travel without airplanes or interstate highways—indeed, without automobiles—to see a political candidate.

Ronald Reagan's long career as a movie actor developed skills easily transferable to political campaigns.

164

PART 2
inputs of the
political
system: who
wants and needs
what?

The interest Americans showed in politics in the 1890s is unimaginable today. Movies, professional sports, *Playboy,* and television did not divert public interest away from politics. Except for traveling carnivals and vaudeville, a visiting politician had little competition for public attention. In the entertainment market today, political parties cannot compete. Their best chance to get a mass audience is to insert a 5-minute "spot" into the television time between programs, time normally given to advertisements of beer or cosmetics. In pure entertainment terms, however, when one has Farrah Fawcett and Robert Redford, who needs politicians?

Losing entertainment value, political parties also lost socializing value. Party campaigns, speeches, and volunteer work were means through which people could socialize and interact. Religion performed a similar role, with the summer tent meeting often a highlight of the community's social calendar. But the tents have come down, in both religion and politics, as the people have found other means for social interaction. Walter Dean Burnham, one of the most thorough and imaginative students of political parties, lists the following features of party politics during the nineteenth century:

1. highly active parties with control by party activists of nominations and platforms through the convention;

2. printing and distribution of ballots or party tickets by the political parties;

3. a large number of elective offices at all levels, plus party control of most appointive positions;

4. a partisan, mobilized electorate;

5. virtually full mobilization of the eligible voters;

6. straight-ticket voting as the norm with the few independents called "traitors," "turncoats," or corrupt sellers of their votes;

7. a highly partisan press, with newspapers openly championing one party and decrying the evils of the opposition.[50]

As Professor Burnham has brilliantly demonstrated, "progressive" reforms that began in the 1890s and peaked in the early twentieth century were aimed at reducing the power of political parties, and the influence of "mere numbers," especially the increasing numbers of immigrants. These reforms began with adoption of the "Australian ballot," a ballot printed by the government rather than the parties. Rather than using their own party's ballot, which ensured straight-ticket voting, voters were faced with an official ballot. Many leaders correctly felt that loss of the function of printing and distributing ballots would undermine political parties.

A second reform that often accompanied adoption of the Australian ballot was a separate listing of candidates for each office (called the "office-block ballot") rather than grouping candidates for all offices by political party. The new ballot form made it difficult and confusing to vote a straight party ticket, especially among people with little education.

[50] These features are taken, for the most part verbatim, from Burnham, *Critical Elections,* pp. 72–76.

"HOW BINDING ARE CAMPAIGN PROMISES MADE ONLY IN PRIMARIES?"

A third reform took the nominating function away from party organizations by establishing direct primary elections. So many states were under one party control during the early twentieth century that the direct primary was very appealing as a means of ensuring some public influence over who should take public office. But primary elections deprive the minority party of its place as a haven for those who are dissatisfied with officeholders. Since the direct primary permits some opposition within the major party of a state, voters can voice their objections within their party; they do not have to switch to the minority party in order to express their dissatisfaction. The direct primary thus reinforced one-party control. It also spotlighted the candidate. The candidate's personal appeal became more important than the support of the party, a situation that further weakened political organizations.[51]

A fourth set of reforms was more openly aimed at weakening parties. Taking the business corporation as a model of efficiency and the urban political machine as a model of corruption, the upper-status leaders of "progressivism" tried to wipe out political parties in city politics. Not satisfied with bypassing the party organization in nominations through the direct primary, they eliminated parties entirely through nonpartisan elections. Voters were offered a choice of candidates who did not indicate their party affiliation. This kind of race tended to give the advantage to local "notables" whose names were

[51] The classic analysis of this effect is by V. O. Key, Jr., *American State Politics* (New York: Knopf, 1956).

166

PART 2
inputs of the
political
system: who
wants and needs
what?

well known. At-large election of city council members was another weakening factor, this one being felt by ethnic minorities concentrated in poorer neighborhoods. In a district election, they could put one of their own on the city council; but if the candidate had to draw votes at large, from the whole city, the minority group had less chance. Finally, the movement toward the city-manager plan was designed to produce efficient, businesslike local government free from party influence.

All of these reforms had wide appeal to the well-educated, refined leaders of the "progressive" movement in both political parties. They were championed as ways of reducing the crudeness, vulgarity, and occasional corruption of party politics. But what was overlooked is that democracy itself is to some degree by definition crude and vulgar—and especially early in the century when a majority of the population had less than a high school education. In weakening political parties, the reformers were—in some cases no doubt without realizing it—weakening majority influence over public policy.

Another set of reforms modified voting requirements to the disadvantage of lower-status people. Aliens (immigrants) who had declared their intention to become citizens had been allowed to vote in many states in the nineteenth century. By 1920 only Arkansas and Indiana still permitted such voting, and they eliminated it in the 1920s. When women were given the right to vote, the change was a clearly democratic reform. But it had the immediate effect of further weakening the influence of lower-status citizens, especially the newer immigrants, because female participation in politics was contrary to their cultural traditions. Indeed, support for female suffrage came heavily from middle-class Protestants who were highly suspicious of big cities and their immigrant populations. The most obvious moves to restrict voting were made in the South, where long residence requirements, the poll tax, and difficult literacy tests were added to outright intimidation to exclude blacks from voting.

All of these legal requirements also decreased voting by lower-status whites. "Good government" meant government by upper-status whites. Finally, the requirement of personal registration long before the date of an election did much to reduce voting. In most democracies, citizens are automatically eligible to vote. The requirement of personal registration clearly helps to depress voting in the United States.[52]

In addition to all these reforms designed to bypass or purify political parties and the mass electorate, another development early in the twentieth century had a profound impact: the rise of mass journalism and the disappearance of a partisan-oriented press. As newspapers (and later radio and television) began to appeal to a mass audience and to stand above "mere partisan politics," voters' party loyalty was not reinforced by partisan reporting of news events. This situation "required the development of entirely new party and candidate strategies for winning elections."[53] These new strategies emphasized an adver-

---

[52] See the excellent study of William J. Crotty, *Political Reform and the American Experiment* (New York: Crowell, 1977), especially chaps. 1–3.

[53] Burnham, *Critical Elections*, p. 76.

tising approach in which name recognition and the "selling" of individual candidates took precedence over the party as an organization.[54]

167

CHAPTER 5
political parties

Signs of party decay today

All of these changes had the effect of weakening political parties and of reducing the degree of partisanship in the public during the early twentieth century. The emergence of the New Deal coalition in response to the Depression of 1929 put new life into the parties and a renewed spirit of partisanship into the voters. But the evidence suggests that this was a temporary revival. Signs of party decay since 1952 are overwhelming.

First, the national vote in presidential elections has flip-flopped at a wild rate. The Republicans have varied from a low of 38.5 percent of the vote in 1964 to a high of 60.7 percent in 1972. The Democrats, although claiming many more identifiers than the Republicans, have managed a majority vote for President only twice during this quarter century (in 1964 and 1976). But one of those margins went all the way up to 61.1 percent! Such swings, especially in the absence of accompanying shifts in votes for Congress, suggest that parties have lost their hold on voters.

Second, direct measures of partisan commitment also indicate party decay. In Table 5 · 4 we saw a continuing decrease in the proportion of Americans who call themselves Republicans or Democrats, accompanied by corresponding increases in the proportion of Independents. Of those who *do* identify with parties, a smaller fraction feel strong in that identification. The percentages for 1952 and 1976 are shown in Table 5 · 7. The total number of strong party identifiers thus decreased from 35 percent to 25 percent of the electorate.

TABLE 5·7

Strength of party identification

	1952	1976	Gain or loss
Strong Republican	13%	10%	−3
Weak Republican	14	13	−1
Independent	22	34	+12
Weak Democrat	25	26	+1
Strong Democrat	22	15	−7
Apolitical, "Don't Know"	4	2	−2
	100%	100%	

Source: Center for Political Studies, Institute for Social Research, University of Michigan.

[54] For a general treatment of political communication, see Dan Nimmo, *Political Communication and Public Opinion in America* (Santa Monica, Calif.: Goodyear Publishing Company, 1978). On the specific question of campaigns within a thoughtful general study of political parties, see Ruth K. Scott and Ronald J. Hrebenar, *Parties in Crisis: Party Politics in America* (New York: Wiley, 1979), chap. 6.

168

PART 2
inputs of the
political
system: who
wants and needs
what?

Third, voter turnout has declined. In the last half of the nineteenth century, turnout ranged from a low of 75 percent (in 1872) to a high of 86 percent (in 1876). In 1896, the last election of the nineteenth century, 79 percent of the electorate voted, a level that has never been achieved since then.[55] After falling to 49 percent in the 1920s, turnout increased again during the New Deal era, although it never reached the level of the nineteenth century. In 1952, 64 percent of the electorate voted. As Fig. 5 · 2 indicates, turnout in presidential elections declined by 9 percentage points between 1952 and 1976, and the vote in congressional elections has similarly declined. Voting or not voting hinges on many things besides the strength of political parties,[56] so the decline in turnout is not direct proof of party decay. Nevertheless, the contrast with nineteenth-century America and with contemporary democracies elsewhere is striking.

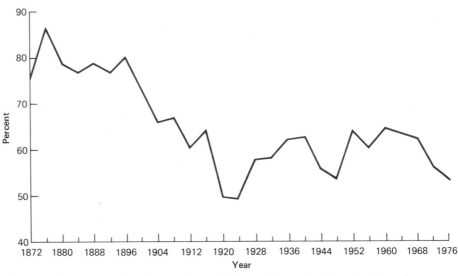

Source: Adapted from Robert E. Lane, *Political Life* (New York: Free Press, 1959), p. 21, and
U.S. Bureau of the Census, *Statistical Abstract of the United States: 1977* (Washington, D.C.), p. 508.

Fig. 5 · 2 Voting turnout in presidential elections, 1872–1976.

Fourth, split-ticket voting has increased. A voter "splits" a ticket by voting for candidates of different parties on the same ballot, thus ignoring party affiliation. In the days of active parties and a mobilized electorate, you could be pretty certain that if a district went Republican in its presidential vote, it would also go Republican in its congressional vote. In 1900, as Fig. 5 · 3 shows, only 3 percent of all districts split their tickets. Except for 1912 (when Theodore Roosevelt ran on a third-party ticket) and 1928 (when southerners tempo-

[55] Robert E. Lane, *Political Life: Why People Get Involved in Politics* (Glencoe, Ill.: Free Press, 1959), p. 21.

[56] See Jack Dennis, "Support for the Institution of Elections by the Mass Public," *American Political Science Review,* 64 (September 1970), 819–35.

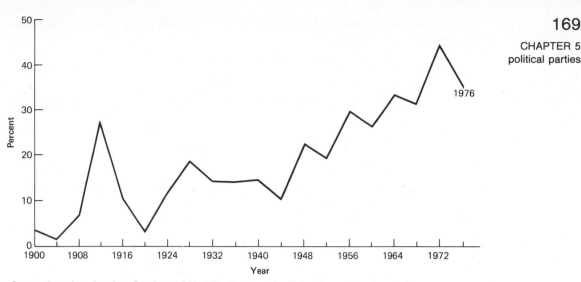

ource: Based on data from Burnham, *Critical Elections and the Mainsprings of American Politics,*
p. 109, and Burnham, "American Politics in the 1970's: Beyond Party?" in Chambers and Burnham, eds.,
The American Party Systems, p. 321. The 1976 figure is from the authors' own analysis of election returns.

Fig. 5 · 3 Proportion of districts with split results in vote for Congress and President, 1900–1976.

rarily deserted the Democrats at the presidential level to vote against Al Smith and the Pope), the proportion of districts with split results remained below 15 percent until the late 1940s. Since then, however, split results have grown more and more common, 44.1 percent of all districts having split their tickets in 1972. This approaches the point at which party loses all meaning.

Taking all of these trends together—the volatility in presidential voting, the decline in party identification, the decline in voting, and the increase in split-ticket voting—American political parties appear to be decaying at an accelerating rate.

Can we do without political parties?

We may be excessively alarmist in our interpretation of the signs of party decay. One authority on political parties, James Sundquist, offers a more optimistic view.

In the long run, the prospect may well be for a further gradual decomposition of the two-party system. But there is at least as much reason to believe that in the shorter run the headlong march toward decomposition that marked the late 1960s will be checked and even reversed, the New Deal party system will be reinvigorated, and most of those who ceased identifying with one or the other major party in the recent turmoil will reidentify.[57]

This cautiously optimistic view is based on the expectation that the basic issues of the 1980s will be economic and that they will again divide the voters into

[57] *Dynamics of the Party System,* p. 373.

170

PART 2
inputs of the
political
system: who
wants and needs
what?

those championing an active domestic program versus those taking a conservative stance.

But what if party decay continues? Even in that event, our guess is that some vestiges of party organizations will remain.[58] Someone has to nominate candidates, even if we reach the point at which party identification is unimportant to most candidates no less than to most voters. If primary elections completely replaced party conventions as a nominating procedure, some form of party organization would be necessary to organize the primary elections. If the primaries were conducted in an open fashion with no party labels, those who won office would probably still look for common ground with other officeholders in order to organize the Congress. And presidents, governors, and mayors would still seek out some friendly and more or less organized members of legislative bodies to help them carry out their policies.

Such weakened political parties would not be very effective, however, in what parties are all about—organizing votes to obtain majority control of the government. In such a weakened party system, pressure groups and the mass media would become much more important. As we shall see in the next chapter, they have already achieved a chilling degree of influence on American politics. That they have done so underscores the extent of decay that is already evident in the American party system.

SUMMARY

Democracy is impossible without political parties, for they alone permit majority rule (or choice of leaders) and minority rights (organized opposition to those in power). The objective of a party is to win political power, and power comes with winning votes. Only those organizations that try, with some prospect of victory, to take over the government by winning elections can be considered political parties.

American political parties are, in terms of party members, clique-oriented; in terms of party supporters, they are heterogeneous, having no predominant religion, class, or other social characteristic (as distinct from mass-membership—dues paying—and homogeneous parties).

Political parties function in the public choice of leaders and the open and organized expression of public interests. Traditionally, they have helped citizens to influence policy and have organized public opinion behind opposing policies. They have moderated differences of opposing groups, recruited and nominated candidates, and provided overall control of government. American parties fall far short of performing these functions today, which decreases the influence of middle- and lower-status people in politics.

America has a two-party system. Although there are many minor parties, almost all offices are held by Democrats and Republicans. Theoretically, this

[58] On the flexibility and likely persistence of parties, see James F. Ward, "Toward a Sixth Party System? Partisanship and Political Development," *Western Political Quarterly,* 26 (September 1973), 385–413.

gives each party a wide appeal and gives the President a wide base of support. The electoral system (single-member district with plurality elections) has shaped the two-party system. Because minor parties have no chance of capturing the presidency, they quickly die out.

The parties themselves are organized into national, state, and local committees. The national committees have taken control of procedures for selecting delegates to the national conventions. The leaders tend to come from upper socioeconomic classes. Party doctrines change to meet changing needs in society. The Democrats tend to look to the needs of the disadvantaged; the Republicans, to the needs of the advantaged. Democrats since the 1930s have been mainly supported by the poor, blacks, union members, Catholics, southerners, and residents of central cities. Republican support is the reverse. (Before 1976, however, the South began to desert the Democrats and lean in a pro-Republican direction.)

Early in the twentieth century, a number of factors began to weaken political parties. Their decay seems to be continuing today, as indicated by wild swings in support from one presidential election to the next, increasing numbers of Independents, decline in voter turnout, and increased split-ticket voting.

pressure groups and the mass media

6

John Gardner, the founder of Common Cause, "the citizens' lobby," compared "the paralysis of government under the Special Interest State" to a checkers game.

Two urgent matters before the nation are the energy crisis and the economy. On both fronts policy-making has been gravely complicated by the underground struggle of powerful interests.

One might liken any top policy-maker today to a person who is trying to win a game of checkers when someone leans over his shoulder, puts a thumb on one checker, and says, "Go ahead and play. Just don't move this checker." Someone else leans over the other shoulder and puts a thumb on another checker. A third person covers still another. Pretty soon—all thumbs, no moves.

The thumbs are, of course, the special interests. The owners of the thumbs don't really wish to paralyze the nation's policy-solving efforts. Each just wants to immobilize one checker. But collectively they prevent a solution.[1]

Gardner's analogy illustrates the immobility of American politics since the Vietnam War. If the gloomy picture is inaccurate at all, it probably understates the severity of the problems faced by those striving for effective national policies. Some of the special interests, particularly the multinational corporations, are not content merely to put their thumbs on checkers. They prefer to pick up the checkers and put them in their pockets! To attack problems coherently without being able to command all one's pieces is hard enough; to do so when powerful interests pick them off is well-nigh impossible.

THE IMPORTANCE OF PRESSURE GROUPS IN AMERICAN POLITICS

Although Americans remain committed to their general system of government, they are skeptical about most of its institutions: Congress, the executive branch, and political parties. Only a very small number—around 5 percent—think the overall system is working extremely well (see Fig. 6 · 1). Those who think the system is working less than extremely well put the blame first on "too much influence on government by special interest groups and lobbies." Admittedly, none of the other choices in the survey included terms with such negative connotations as "special interest groups" or "lobbies." But the essential point remains: if these are "buzz words" to most Americans, why do the groups they describe have so much power? We don't pretend that we can answer this question fully, but we can have a shot at it.

Is America the "special interest state"?

Four reasons seem to stand out in Common Cause's view of the United States as the Special Interest State.

[1] "Thumbs on the Checkerboard," *In Common: The Common Cause Report from Washington*, 9 (Fall 1978), 5.

HOW WELL DOES GOVERNMENT WORK?

Question: How well do you think our system of government is working these days—extremely well, fairly well, not very well, or not at all well?

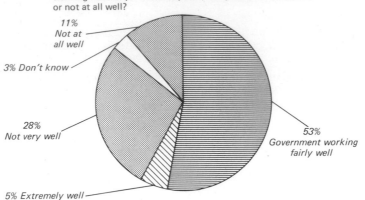

*11%
Not at
all well*

3% Don't know

*28%
Not very well*

*53%
Government working
fairly well*

5% Extremely well

AND WHAT CAUSES PROBLEMS

Question: Which of these reasons, if any, do you think is the main reason our system of government doesn't work better than it does? (Hand respondent card) (Asked only of the respondents who think government system working less than extremely well = 92%.)

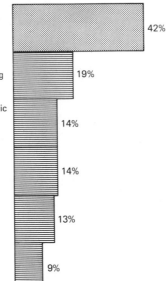

There is too much influence on government by special interest groups and lobbies — 42%

Too many people vote without thinking — 19%

Our two political parties, the Democratic party and the Republican party, don't really give us a workable two-party system any more — 14%

Not enough people vote — 14%

The people who run for office aren't a good choice to vote for — 13%

There's something the matter with our system of government itself — 9%

Note: Categories not shown include none (volunteered) 1% and don't know 3%. Multiple responses per respondent.

Fig. 6 · 1 Appraisals of how well the American political system works and of why it does not work better

1. The *number* of pressure groups. Countless organizations speak for economic, ideological, humanitarian, religious, medical, cultural, recreational, ethnic, educational, and aesthetic interests.

2. *Narrow interests,* usually economic, seem to have the most influence, whatever the cost to everybody else.

3. Because of their restricted membership and special interests, these groups are both *unaccountable* to, and *unrepresentative* of, the general public.

4. Even though no one group dominates policy making, the influence of each group in its own area of special interest is enough to *keep the broad public interest from being served*—to produce the Special Interest State.

This line of argument does not claim that America is ruled by any single elite group. And it seems to leave open the possibility that, for reasons we shall note later in this chapter, broad public interests can occasionally win out in the struggle to control policy. After all, Common Cause itself is given some of the credit (or blame) for reforms such as public financing of presidential campaigns, U.S. House and Senate committee reform, "sunshine" rules (open committee meetings) in Congress, and Civil Service reform.[2] Common Cause's argument is simply that the interests of those with economic power and privilege tend to be over-represented in policy making and that the interests of the less fortunate tend to be under-represented or ignored.

Careful readers of preceding chapters might have predicted an increase in the power of pressure groups in the United States. From what we know about political systems, what would we expect in a system when its political parties decline in public respect, organizational strength, and political clout? We learned in the first chapter that certain basic functions must be carried out in any system and that two of these universal functions are the selection of leaders and the identification of citizens' interests. We also learned that the elements of a system are so interrelated that a change in one element will affect others. And we said in the chapter on political parties that they are the one unofficial agency that tries to organize and speak for a majority of the people. If parties carry out that task less effectively, then other organizations speaking for more special interests can be expected to pick up the slack. Both in election campaigns and in influencing the decisions of officeholders after they are elected, pressure groups (and as we shall shortly see, the mass media) have accordingly become more and more important. This means, to use the language of Jefferson's time, that the "poor and middling classes," for whom the primary weapon is the political party, have been hurt. The "well-to-do and eminent" (a category that now includes spokespersons for the better organized labor unions), for whom the primary weapon is the pressure group, have been helped.

The role of pressure groups in Congress aptly illustrates the point. In the last two congressional elections held in nonpresidential election years, contributions of pressure groups to congressional candidates tripled: from $12.5

[2] Godfrey Sperling, Jr., "Common Cause Taking on Energy Department," *Christian Science Monitor,* March 1, 1979.

176

PART 2
inputs of the
political
system: who
wants and needs
what?

million in 1974 to $35.1 in 1978.[3] So many corporations, labor unions, business and financial associations, and professional organizations have formed political action committees that the acronym "PAC" has come into common usage. The PACs of business corporations grew most rapidly, from 89 in 1974 to 954 in 1980. The total number of PACs went from 516 in 1974 to 2,010 in 1980, and the number is still climbing, especially among corporations, which have been chartering new PACs at the rate of 10 a week.[4] Although contributions to candidates made up less than half of the PACs' 1978 expenditures ($77.8 million), they were still at a record high. The biggest donor of all was the American Medical Association's PAC, which reported contributions of $1,644,795. If one adds the American Dental Association's $510,050, the medical profession's contributions to candidates went well over $2 million before adding in donations from more specialized groups. The top 5 contributors were rounded out by the PACs of the National Association of Realtors ($1,-122,378), the National Automobile Dealers Association ($975,675), the United Auto Workers ($964,465), and the AFL-CIO ($920,841).

PAC contributions to candidates seem to be well directed. In the first place, incumbents are favored over challengers. In 1978, for example, incumbents got $19.9 million; challengers, $7.7 million (with the remaining $7.4 million going to candidates for open seats). With Democrats outnumbering Republicans in Congress by 2 to 1, they also enjoyed an advantage, though much smaller, in PAC donations: $19.7 million to $15.3 million. Committee heads were particularly favored. In the House of Representatives, for example, the average amount of PAC money received by committee heads was $45,000. New members of the House were also targeted for generous treatment: the 77 House freshmen received an average of $43,000 each in PAC funds. Granted that each PAC is limited to $5,000 in contributions to a single candidate, the newly emerging PACs of corporations exerted exceptional influence because of their sheer numbers. By 1978 the number of corporate PACs in the campaign was almost twice that of PACs representing either labor or professional, business, and trade associations. As Common Cause says, "the money that interest group PACs disperse is frankly labeled an 'investment' by the givers." The chairman of Dart Industries, whose PAC was the third leading corporate giver in 1978, with $119,300, seems to justify that interpretation. Dialogue with politicans, he observes, "is a fine thing, but with a little money, they hear you better."[5]

Confidence that "they hear you better" after financial support was strengthened in 1979 when the House Administration Committee voted 17 to 8 against reporting to the floor a bill to provide public financing for congressional candidates—challengers no less than incumbents. The bill would have shifted the emphasis to smaller contributions by providing matching funds

[3] See "Political Action Committee Spending Soared in 1978," *Congressional Quarterly Weekly Report,* 37 (June 2, 1979), 1043–45.

[4] Jonathan Tumin, "The Conservative Money Offensive: How to Bury Liberals," *The New Republic,* 182 (May 24, 1980), p. 13.

[5] "Special Interests at Center Stage," *In Common: The Common Cause Report from Washington,* 10 (Spring 1979), 3.

for individual contributions of $100 or less. Even though the House leadership had given the reform measure the highest priority—the coveted designation H.R. 1—PAC opposition carried the day, as it had against similar bills in 1974, 1976, and 1978. On the 1979 failure, a *New York Times* editorial, after noting the tremendous increase in PAC spending, added: "And the big growth lies ahead, as corporations discover the art form. In four years, the number of corporate PACs has jumped from 89 to 821. Unless campaign financing is changed by 1980, it may be too late. Congress may already be sold."[6]

Despite such dire statements in the press about the dominance of pressure groups, they have not been the subject of burgeoning attention by political scientists. Most studies of pressure groups today rely for their approach on works published in the 1960s or even the 1950s. Even the best of studies illustrate this point. Michael Hayes offers a penetrating analysis in a 1978 article, "The Semi-Sovereign Pressure Groups: A Critique of Current Theory and an Alternative Typology."[7] The average publication date of books and dissertations cited in his article is between 1968 and 1969. A 1977 book on public interest groups, in citing the works whose approaches are to be employed, has citations with an average publication date between 1964 and 1965.[8]

How does one account for the paucity of current work on pressure groups? Professor Hayes offers an explanation that is surprising in view of the developments presented above. "In recent years, a new conventional wisdom has arisen concerning the role of interest groups in the legislative process, one that minimizes their importance, regarding them as little more than service bureaus to be used or ignored by Congressmen at will. As a consequence," he continues, "research on interest groups, at least among political scientists, has come to a virtual halt."[9] Hayes's conclusion seems to apply more to students of Congress than of politics in general, for he notes that studies of particular policies run contrary to the conventional widom.[10] And the importance of pressure groups in bureaucratic decision making has often been noted.[11] This may simply be a case in which events have moved faster than our ability to interpret them. But Hayes's thoughtful study suggests that pressure groups probably always had more influence than the conventional wisdom of the 1960s and '70s recognized. His term "The Semi-Sovereign Pressure Groups" seems to capture the qualified acceptance we gave above to the idea of "The Special Interest State."

[6] *The New York Times,* June 7, 1979.

[7] *Journal of Politics,* 40 (February 1978), 134–61.

[8] Jeffrey M. Berry, *Lobbying for the People: The Political Behavior of Public Interest Groups* (Princeton, N.J.: Princeton University Press, 1977), chap. 1.

[9] "The Semi-Sovereign Pressure Groups," p. 134. His prime example of the conventional wisdom is Raymond A. Bauer, Ithiel de Sola Pool, and Lewis A. Dexter, *American Business and Public Policy* (New York: Atherton, 1963).

[10] See, for excellent examples, Francis Fox Piven and Richard A. Cloward, *Regulating the Poor* (New York: Random House, Vintage Books, 1971), John Ferejohn, *Pork Barrel Politics: Rivers and Harbors Legislation, 1947–68* (Palo Alto, Calif.: Stanford University Press, 1974), Mark V. Nadel, *The Politics of Consumer Protection* (Indianapolis: Bobbs-Merrill, 1971), and Bruce Ian Oppenheimer, *Oil and the Congressional Process* (Lexington: Heath, Lexington Books, 1974).

[11] One of the most popular examples of this genre is Theodore J. Lowi, *The End of Liberalism: Ideology, Policy, and the Crisis of Public Authority* (New York: Norton, 1969).

PART 2
inputs of the
political
system: who
wants and needs
what?

The nature and functions of pressure groups

Pressure groups have much in common with political parties and even with official decision-making agencies such as the United States Congress. All fall within the general meaning of "political interest group" if we accept David Truman's definition of that concept as "a shared-attitude group that makes certain claims upon other groups in the society" by acting "through or upon any of the institutions of government. . . ."[12] The official status of decision-making agencies such as the House of Representatives or the Supreme Court clearly distinguishes them from political parties and pressure groups. Nevertheless, all of them make claims on other groups by acting through or on government institutions. Political parties and pressure groups are both unofficial agencies, but their purposes and methods differ.

The *purpose* of the pressure group is to influence specific policies, rather than to achieve control over the government as a whole. Another difference is in the *method* of acquiring power. The political party concentrates on winning elections, whereas the pressure group never offers voters candidates in its own name. The pressure group may be vitally concerned with every stage of the election process, but it does not campaign under its own banner; and it is just as interested in other means of influencing policy as it is in elections themselves. We can define a *pressure group*, then, as *an organized attempt to influence government policy decisions without officially entering election contests.*

Pressure groups are based on the constitutionally guaranteed freedoms of assembly and petition. Consequently, they are no less characteristic of democracy than are political parties. Freedom of speech and freedom of the press would mean little if various interests could not organize to gain recognition. Just as political parties try to mobilize a majority of the voters, pressure groups give special representation to minorities. For the political system as a whole, then, they play an indispensable part in identifying the various interests in society and in establishing the national agenda of issues.

Pressure groups also add a different dimension to the official system of representation. In our single-member district system of election, each legislator is supposed to represent everybody in his or her district. But, of course, political opponents are found within the same district, and political allies are found in different districts, for shared interests cut across district lines. Some group—building contractors or carpenters, let's say—may be a minority in one district; but if it combines forces with others of the same interest in other districts, they have a better chance of being heard. By speaking for interests without regard to geography, pressure groups therefore supplement the official system of representation.

Taking part in pressure groups greatly enriches the lives of many people who are members, stimulating political interest, knowledge, and participa-

---

[12] David B. Truman, *The Governmental Process* (New York: Knopf, 1951), p. 37. Although he offers this broadly inclusive concept of political interest groups, Truman then uses it in reference only to what we call pressure groups. See, for example, his chapter on "Interest Groups and Political Parties," which suggests that political parties are not political interest groups.

tion.[13] Especially when we have an official representative in Congress who almost always votes the wrong way from our point of view, many of us find great satisfaction in being able to contribute money or time to some group that "represents" our views in a truer sense. The familiar pressure groups that represent economic interests, such as the American Medical Association, the AFL–CIO, or the National Association of Manufacturers, serve to promote material interests in this way. But noneconomic groups such as the League of Women Voters or the American Civil Liberties Union and single issue groups such as the Sierra Club may have even greater impact on their members' lives. Participation in such groups undoubtedly reduces alienation from American society, because such activity gives a sense of contributing to something one believes in, even when one's official representative works for opposite causes.

The activities of lobbyists

What is the principal activity of the people who speak for pressure groups (lobbyists)? The first classic study of the subject, which dealt with the tariff of 1930, found lobbyists to be tough, aggressive, and successful in getting benefits for their clients.[14] But the findings of the 1960s presented a different picture, an interpretation we referred to above as the new conventional wisdom. The most influential source of these findings and interpretations was a new study of business lobbying on the tariff issue, this time from 1953 to 1962.[15] This landmark study presented a quite different view, one of diffident, ill-organized, underfinanced lobbyists who mostly provided information to members of Congress already known to agree with their group. The basic view we received from this study was that "the lobbyist becomes in effect a service bureau for those congressmen already agreeing with him, rather than an agent of direct persuasion."[16]

According to the "service bureau" interpretation, the task of the lobbyist is not to influence Congress or bureaucrats so much as to interpret the group's point of view to officials who are friendly toward the group. Indeed, the conclusion was that the lobbyists taught their groups more about views and problems of government officials than they taught those officials about the views and problems of the groups. Lobbyists' efforts to interpret, therefore, were more

[13] L. Harmon Zeigler and G. Wayne Peak, *Interest Groups in American Politics,* 2d ed. (Englewood Cliffs, N.J.: Prentice-Hall, 1972).

[14] E. E. Schattschneider, *Politics, Pressures, and the Tariff* (Hamden, Conn.: Archon Books, 1963, first published by Prentice-Hall in 1935). Two other early studies that deserve to be called classics are Peter H. Odegard, *Pressure Politics: The Study of the Anti-Saloon League* (New York: Columbia University Press, 1928) and E. Pendleton Herring, *Group Representation Before Congress* (Baltimore: The Johns Hopkins Press, 1929).

[15] Bauer, Pool, and Dexter, *American Business and Public Policy.* In their careful examinations of this literature, both Hayes ("The Semi-Sovereign Pressure Groups," p. 135) and Berry (*Lobbying for the People,* p. 217) conclude that this study was the principal source of political scientists' view of interest groups. But see also Lester Milbrath, *The Washington Lobbyists* (Chicago: Rand McNally, 1963).

[16] Bauer, Pool, and Dexter, *American Business and Public Policy,* p. 353 (emphasis omitted).

180

PART 2
inputs of the
political
system: who
wants and needs
what?

effective on their own group than on governmental decision makers.[17] The information that lobbyists feed their employers was felt to make the employers understand problems of governmental decision makers and of other interests that must be taken into account. An unintended result of pressure group activity was thus held to be the tempering of demands from any particular group. James Q. Wilson summed up this view nicely: "It is now well understood," he concludes, "that what an organizational representative does in furthering his group's interests before government has more to do with his management of a communications system than with his exercise of influence. 'Pressure groups' rarely 'press.' "[18]

Pressure groups with little pressure, service bureaus for their friends in government—that pretty well sums up the view of pressure groups that came to be accepted. Note that one could accept this view—as the authors of this book did—and still recognize the strong bias of public policy in favor of powerful interests. It was just that the "facts" reported by specialists in this area required us to explain the influence of these interests in terms other than lobbying, such as their influence on nominations and elections, their impact on public opinion, and the upper-status biases they share with their friends in government. In retrospect, we feel that we were naïve in accepting the idea that pressure groups don't also exert pressure; but an argument that begins "contrary to popular impression," or "unlike what you read in the newspapers" has a seductive appeal to scholars, for their commitment is to look beyond the "apparent" to the "real." After all, who wants to do research on a problem only to report that everything is exactly as it has appeared to be?

In this case, however, we might better have trusted popular impressions and newspaper reports that Congress and other decision-making agencies are under great pressure from special interests. Recent research has brought us full circle, back to this earlier view. In part, the revisionist view results simply from new developments in the real political world since the conventional wisdom was developed. The proliferation of PACs and the accompanying rise of single-issue groups has vastly changed the political landscape. When political columnist David Broder described the plight of Senator Wendell Anderson (D-Minn.) in 1978, he was portraying a problem that is painfully real. Senator Anderson, former governor, had long been a leading figure in Minnesota politics, but he found himself under intense pressure in the Senate from a variety of uncompromising groups. "The single-interest constituencies," Anderson complained, "have just about destroyed politics as I knew it. They've made it miserable to be in office—or to run for office—and left me feeling it's hardly worth the struggle to survive."[19] Broder reported that similar complaints are "heard everywhere from Capitol Hill to California as officeholders

---

[17] L. A. Dexter, *How Organizations Are Represented in Washington* (New York: Bobbs-Merrill, 1969), p. 153.

[18] *Political Organizations* (New York: Basic Books, 1973), p. 316.

[19] Quoted in David S. Broder, "One-Issue Groups Becoming an Issue," *Washington Post,* September 14, 1978.

and office-seekers find themselves whipsawed by interest groups who judge them solely on the basis of a single issue."

This is a new kind of no-compromise competition between groups. Single-issue groups often focus on ideological matters of principle that cannot be compromised and on which the member of Congress must take a clear-cut position. In supporting one side, an official incurs the enmity of the other; and the official who avoids taking a position incurs the hostility of both sides. On matters of high principle, "if you're not with us, you're against us." Senator Anderson was bedeviled by lobbyists for organizations such as right-to-life advocates and abortion supporters, gun-owners and gun-registration advocates, environmentalists trying to ban motorboats from the entire Boundary Waters Canoe Area and resort owners and putt-putt operators insisting that motorboats be permitted in the area. Lobbyists for these groups certainly did not devote themselves to explaining Anderson's problems to their members, nor did they fail to produce all the pressure they could. Anderson lost. As Rudy Boschwitz, his Republican successor, hears demands from these and other groups, no one could reasonably claim that he is not being pressured, for Senator Boschwitz surely remembers his predecessor's fate.

The growth of single-issue groups is not the only reason for adopting a new view of the role of lobbyists. Michael Hayes convincingly argues that the conventional wisdom never was quite correct. The peculiar characteristics of the tariff issue examined by Bauer, Pool, and Dexter in their seminal study of the 1960s led them astray: they understandably but wrongly assumed that what was true of that issue at that time would apply to issues in general throughout the modern period. Their portrayal of timid lobbyists of the service bureau type was thus based on two false assumptions: "that one-sided pressures are the exception rather than the rule; and that the typical outcome of the legislative process is not to resolve conflicts but rather to determine the ground rules for the continuation of the group struggle."[20] Let's look at the implications of these assumptions, one at a time.

First, it goes almost without saying that if Congress were beseiged by many interest groups taking the same position, the pressure on its members would be intense. Bauer, Pool, and Dexter did find "large numbers of pressure groups" active in the making of tariff policy, but they also found competition among these groups.[21] And at least in the case of the tariff, they found that this competition permitted members of Congress to play one group against the other and thereby escape much pressure from any group. They recognized that the outcome would have been different in the absence of active competition among the organized groups, but they denied such a possibility: "it is in the nature of the democratic struggle that that does not happen."[22]

As is so often the case, the particular fact (a large number of opposed groups) was correctly observed, but the grand assumption (about "the nature

[20] Hayes, "The Semi-Sovereign Pressure Groups," p. 139. As indicated above, our broader critique owes much to this article.

[21] *American Business and Public Policy,* p. 324.

[22] *Ibid.*

182

PART 2
inputs of the
political
system: who
wants and needs
what?

of the democratic struggle") was in error. Subsequent research has shown that *on many issues the pressure is lopsided,* with no meaningful competition among pressure groups. We have become more aware, for example, that the overall bias of the pressure system on some issues—public as opposed to private enterprise, the most obvious case—is so great that opposing voices are not raised.[23] In more specific terms, one study of interest group blocs in Congress over a 16-year period found that a majority of congressional hearings (55 percent) were noncompetitive.[24] And John Kingdon reports that pressure groups actively supported different sides in only 12 percent of the cases included in his study of *Congressmen's Voting Decisions.*[25] We must thus reject the general assumption that so many interests will appear on both sides of an issue that they will render lobbyists ineffective.

Even when competition among pressure groups is present, we still have no guarantee that this competition will reduce the pressure on members of Congress. Former Senator Anderson painfully learned that a member of Congress cannot always play one group off against another and nullify the power of both.

This brings us to the second false assumption of the conventional wisdom—that congressional decisions are generally confined to setting general ground rules, delegating to bureaucrats the power to make specific decisions.[26] The argument is that members of Congress thus avoid the hard choices between different groups and are therefore able to keep both sides reasonably happy. This is true for some issues, such as the setting of specific tariff rates, an authority Congress delegated to the executive branch in the Reciprocal Trade Agreements Act of 1934. But it was not true for the tariff before 1934, and it is still not true for many issues, such as the availability of Medicaid funds to pay for abortions.

On three counts, then, we reject the conception of the lobbyist as Mr. Milquetoast or Ms. Jellyfish. First, newly demanding and unforgiving pressure groups have appeared. The intensity of their ideological commitment to a single issue and their willingness to punish even former friends for a single incorrect vote make them much harder to deal with than the "service bureau" lobbyist. Second, the number of issues on which really powerful groups take opposite sides has been exaggerated. Absence of conflict, however, does not mean absence of pressure. On the contrary, it means that all pressures are in the same direction. Third, even when competition among pressure groups is present, it does not always relieve the pressure on members of Congress—

[23] Peter Bachrach and Morton S. Baratz, *Power and Poverty: Theory and Practice* (New York: Oxford University Press, 1970).

[24] Robert L. Ross, *Dimensions and Patterns of Relations Among Interest Groups at the Congressional Level of Government* (unpublished Ph.D. dissertation, Michigan State University, 1962), p. 281. Also see his "Relations Among National Interest Groups," *Journal of Politics,* 32 (February 1970), 96–114. These and the following two studies are cited in Hayes, "The Semi-Sovereign Pressure Groups."

[25] John W. Kingdon, *Congressmen's Voting Decisions* (New York: Harper, 1973), p. 142. This point is also supported by the case studies cited in fn. 10.

[26] This is a central theme of Theodore J. Lowi, *The Politics of Disorder* (New York: Basic Books, 1971).

certainly not in the case of ideologically committed single-interest groups. Even among more traditional groups, their competition relieves Congress only when issues are handled by delegating rule-making authority. In many areas of foreign and domestic policy—such as the Panama Canal treaties in 1978 or the windfall profits tax on oil in 1979—members of Congress themselves make the significant decisions.

We feel compelled to introduce a fourth reason for rejecting the conventional view: lobbyists can sometimes play an active and demanding role because they or the groups they represent have bribed, blackmailed, or bought off decision makers. Their ways are perhaps legal but nevertheless immoral (such as the mention of future jobs for people who do not expect to stay in public office until retirement age). This is the sleazy side of public life that political scientists have largely ignored. Instead of acting like detectives or muckraking journalists who feel free to look through keyholes, tap telephones, and otherwise snoop into people's private affairs, political scientists have tended to rely on publicly recorded acts and on interviews. Needless to say, a public "servant" like former Vice-President Spiro Agnew did not make it an official event when he accepted bribes. Similarly, when scholars ask lobbyists about their tactics, they recognize that it would be pointless to ask if they have engaged in illegal or unethical activity. ("Have you ever put a hit on a committee member who opposed your group's position? If 'yes,' how often? If 'no,' why not?")

Lester Milbrath did include bribery in asking lobbyists about the effectiveness of various tactics, but he did not ask if they themselves had bribed anyone.[27] His respondents gave bribery a 0.1 rating on a 10-point scale (10 being most effective), compared with a rating of 8.4 for personal presentation of the group's viewpoint and 7.4 for presentation of research results! These are nice things to say, but one would assume that a bribe, however rare, would actually be 100 percent effective for every case in which it was employed. On the other hand, one would not expect those who give bribes to admit their success.

The Watergate scandal, Korean interests' bribery of some congressmen, and other cases of corruption, large and small, suggest that evidence made public understates the actual influence of pressure groups. One of the authors of this book, having helped to raise funds in $5 and $10 amounts for the campaign of a member of Congress, knows from personal experience that those who contribute even small sums have a sense of access, although this author always failed when it came to exercising real influence on the congressman's vote, just as the conventional wisdom said. This congressman was subsequently indicted for lying before a congressional committee when he denied knowledge of a $10,000 campaign contribution from the Korean lobbyist Tungson Park. (Conviction was avoided through a technicality: a quorum of the committee was not present when the congressman lied before it.) We cannot help but feel that on issues in which they were interested, the Korean "constituents" of this congressman had more direct influence than did most constituents in his home district, even those who had given $5 or $10 to his campaign.

[27] *The Washington Lobbyists.*

184

PART 2
inputs of the
political
system: who
wants and needs
what?

Without succumbing to *The National Enquirer* mentality, we must recognize that *some* things do happen behind the scenes and under cover. Although public scrutiny no doubt renders the level of morality in government higher than in private business, commercial practices sometimes invade the public sphere. As E. E. Schattschneider argued, the more conflict is "privatized," the better off the special interests and the worse off the general public will be.[28]

Politics as a struggle among groups

James Madison saw the origin of the group struggle as "sown in the nature of man." As Madison wrote in *Federalist* essay No. 10,

. . . the most common and durable source of factions has been the various and unequal distribution of property. Those who hold and those who are without property have ever formed distinct interests in society. Those who are creditors, and those who are debtors, fall under a like discrimination. A landed interest, a manufacturing interest, a mercantile interest, a moneyed interest, with many lesser interests, grow up of necessity in civilized nations, and divide them into different classes, actuated by different sentiments and views.

Although many noneconomic organizations, from the American Civil Liberties Union to Zero Population Growth, are active in politics, economic differences are just as predominant in the activities of pressure groups now as they were in Madison's day. Indeed, the specialization of our industrial economy has created so many pressure groups that we can only guess at their total number. The number of groups active at the national level of government alone numbers in the thousands. Primitive societies in which there is little division of labor have few pressure groups, but complex industrial societies tend to produce them in ever-increasing numbers.

Bankers in Florida have more in common with bankers in New England than they have with fruit pickers in their own counties. Moreover, organizations like the American Bankers' Association keep banks aware of these common interests and provide an organization to represent them before the government. The fruit pickers who are not organized with other farm laborers seldom discover that their interests are shared by others scattered across the country. Therefore, they have little political influence. The legislator who is supposed to represent both the banker and the fruit picker is more aware of the interests of the organized group. Only if the fruit picker's interests happen to become part of some political interest group (either a pressure group or a political party, or both) will they carry any real weight.

The success of Cesar Chavez in winning economic concessions for grape workers in California stemmed partly from his ability to overcome the formidable barriers to effective organization. But it stemmed also from his ability to broaden the scope of the conflict by involving consumers. The nature of a conflict changes as new participants become involved. And pressure groups

---

[28] *The Semi-Sovereign People* (New York: Holt, 1960).

involve others, including the government, precisely when they don't like the results of the struggle between private groups. The new participants broaden the struggle to include interests far beyond the narrow concerns of the original contenders.

E. E. Schattschneider classified interest groups as *public* or *special interests* according to the basis of membership: open or exclusive.[29] Only manufacturers are eligible to join the National Association of Manufacturers (NAM), for example, so it is a *special interest group*. One would not expect an organization restricted to manufacturers to attract people who want to promote religious, cultural, or philanthropic interests. The exclusive basis of membership implies concern for the exclusive interests of manufacturers. Any interested person may, on the other hand, join the American League to Abolish Capital Punishment, so it is a *public interest group*. Its membership is certainly not restricted to people indicted for murder. Indeed, probably none of the ALACP members expects to be hanged or electrocuted. This is a publicly oriented group, then, with members who do not expect to benefit personally from the policy they favor.

Although Schattschneider stressed open membership in distinguishing public from private interest groups, what he actually had in mind seems to have been the group's concern for nonmembers no less than for its members. In practice, the openness or collective nature of the "good" sought by the group replaces the openness of membership as a criterion. Open membership generally goes along with the pursuit of some "collective good," of course, but it does not necessarily do so. The Lawyers' Committee for Civil Rights Under Law, for example, is presumably open only to lawyers, but its concern is for the civil rights of everyone, not just lawyers. Hence, it is classified in Jeffrey Berry's recent study as a public interest group.[30] Under any definition, public interest groups are not very numerous. Professor Berry could find only 83 organizations in Washington that could be called public interest groups. Of these, about half cannot openly lobby before Congress because they are tax-exempt as educational organizations.[31] The resources of these organizations are minuscule compared with those of private interest groups. Only 16 of the public interest groups reported assets over $1 million.[32] In contrast, the PACs officially registered with the Federal Election Commission—which are the tip of the iceberg so far as private interest groups are concerned—*spent* $77.8 million in 1977–78.[33]

Schattschneider's second basis for classifying interest groups was a distinction between *organized* and *unorganized* groups. Obviously, any group has some degree of organization. But Schattschneider reserves the term *organized group* for those with enough interest in politics to have established a formal organization with officers, bylaws, and memberships. These are the pressure

[29] *The Semi-Sovereign People,* chap. 2.
[30] *Lobbying for the People,* p. 299.
[31] *Ibid.,* p. 51.
[32] *Ibid.,* p. 60.
[33] *Congressional Quarterly Weekly Report,* 37 (June 2, 1979), 1044.

186

PART 2
inputs of the
political
system: who
wants and needs
what?

groups actively trying to influence public policy at every stage. Schattschneider accordingly defines the *pressure system* as made up of organized special-interest groups (such as the NAM). The unorganized groups (the fruit pickers) and the organized public interest groups (the ALACP) play a role in the broader political system, but he regards the narrower pressure system as restricted to the activities of organized, special interest groups.

Organization represents "a mobilization of bias," in Schattschneider's felicitous phrase, "in preparation for action."[34] Business organizations dominate the pressure system both numerically and in expenditures, and even nonbusiness organizations tend to be biased in an upper-class direction. Conversely, most of the population is completely outside the pressure system, dependent on the political parties or formal representation in Congress to support their interests. Schattschneider concludes, "The flaw in the pluralist heaven is that the heavenly chorus sings with a strong upper-class accent. Probably about 90 percent of the people cannot get into the pressure system. . . . *Pressure politics is a selective process* ill-designed to serve diffuse interests. The system is skewed, loaded and unbalanced in favor of a fraction of a minority."[35]

BASES OF PRESSURE GROUP STRENGTH

What makes some pressure groups so much stronger than others in their influence on policy? And before we get to individual groups, how did pressure groups as a whole come to be so influential?

Political environment as a source of strength

First, the strength of all pressure groups is affected by the *political environment* in which they operate. In dictatorships, for example, an organized effort to influence policy might get the organizers jailed or killed. In a democracy, on the other hand, different interests are free to advance their claims before the government without fear of punishment. And people are contentious enough to take advantage of this right wherever they have it. "Liberty is to faction what air is to fire," Madison observed. The techniques employed and the degree of influence achieved by pressure groups vary greatly from society to society, but in every democracy these groups are at least given an opportunity to seek power.

Second, the *formal organization of the government* affects the strength of pressure groups. In the United States, there are three levels of government: national, state, and local. There is also separation of powers at each level among the legislative, executive, and judicial branches. This separation produces many points at which government policy may be influenced. These

[34] *The Semi-Sovereign People*, p. 30.
[35] *Ibid.*, p. 35.

many points are openings for agencies (pressure groups) that seek to influence specific policies. But the separation of power in the system hurts agencies (political parties) that seek to control the entire government.

When a pressure group is trying to *block* government action that it regards as detrimental, for instance, it finds that opportunity knocks not just once but over and over again. If a group cannot prevent an issue from being raised, its cause is not necessarily lost, for if it fails in one house of Congress, it can try the other. Indeed, as we shall see in chapter 8, "The Legislators," the manner in which Congress is organized provides pressure groups with a number of points of access in each house. Power is so scattered in Congress that a group can sometimes block a bill by influencing just one key member. If a member sits on a committee that is considering an objectionable measure— or better still, chairs the committee—the one member may kill the measure before the entire house ever has a chance to vote on it.

If the pressure group fails to win the backing of any member of Congress, it may still strive for a presidential veto. But the end of the trail does not come even there. Once a law has been passed, it is still subject to challenge in the courts, where, even if it is held constitutional, the group may succeed in having it interpreted to the group's advantage in specific cases. And when a law is put into operation, the group can continue to communicate with those who interpret and administer the law day by day.

The federal system offers still more opportunities for interest groups at the state level. If a group cannot muster effective power at any point in national politics, it may still realize its ambitions in at least some of the states. The old saw, "If at first you don't succeed, try, try again," is taken very seriously by American pressure groups. If none of these efforts to influence the government is successful, the group may finally attempt to influence nominations and elections to state or national office.

Third, the *weakness of political parties* strengthens pressure groups in the United States. Government power is spread out and allows pressure groups to *block* policy decisions they oppose; and weak political parties permit strong efforts of these groups to *promote* policy decisions they favor. The failure of the majority party to organize Congress effectively and to act with cohesion on policy matters produces a power vacuum that tends to be filled by organized interest groups.

Group characteristics as sources of strength

Although specialists on the study of pressure groups say "there is nowhere in the existing literature any systematic attempt to specify the conditions for group influence,"[36] we must make the effort if we are to understand the place of such groups in today's politics. Some of the group characteristics that appear to be important are status, organization, leadership, social base, and doctrines.

Status is probably the most important of all characteristics in determining the strength of a pressure group. If the group has a position of high prestige,

[36] Hayes, "The Semi-Sovereign Pressure Groups," p. 136, fn. 3.

188

PART 2
inputs of the
political
system: who
wants and needs
what?

its leaders will enjoy easy access to key points of decision, access denied to low-status groups. Junior legislators or administrators may actually be flattered to have a leader of a group like the American Bar Association or the American Legion come to them for help. But an organization of the far left (like the National Council of American-Soviet Friendship) or the far right (like the John Birch Society) may find it difficult even to get a hearing.

High-status pressure groups talk the same language as officeholders. Since they have similar class backgrounds, similar experiences, and similar contacts, they quickly discover similar interests. Moreover, a high-status group is able to develop common interests with other pressure groups and enlist their support. Finally, in the United States, the groups with greater status will almost automatically be able to command greater financial resources, a necessary commodity in pressure politics, as our discussion of PACs has already demonstrated.

Organization is another characteristic that helps determine the power of pressure groups. The closer and more frequent the interaction among members, the more cohesive—that is, the more effectively organized—the group will be. And organization means power. Tight organization allows a pressure group to keep in constant contact with the government. The good lobbyist works hard to gain the respect of members of Congress and bureaucrats by offering material for speeches, data on impending legislation, detailed information on the needs of the lobbyist's clients, and other services. Conversely, the officeholders can keep the lobbyist informed on new developments and on their own and their colleagues' inclinations. This kind of relationship demands time no less than skill. One lobbyist for a business group explained that he concentrated on a few strategic members of Congress because he could not maintain a sufficiently close relationship with a larger number. "To keep these friendships alive and genuine, I have to stop around to see them quite often, just to say hello. For example, if I don't see _____ at least once a week, he'll say, 'Where the hell have you been? You only stop around when you want something from us.' Even a few contacts on the Hill demand a good deal of time and attention."[37] Only a group well enough organized to have lobbyists constantly on the job can hope to build this kind of mutually rewarding relationship.

Leadership is a third characteristic that affects the strength of a pressure group. To be effective, a group needs spokesmen or spokeswomen with official contacts and with knowledge of the political process. Many administrators and legislative assistants become lobbyists for various groups after leaving government service—an indication of both the experience and the contacts that lobbyists need. One study of Washington lobbyists disclosed that "over half of the lobbyists had worked for the federal government either in a staff position on the 'Hill' or in one of the agencies or as an appointive or elective officeholder."[38] Contrary to popular assumption, only a few former members of Congress are lobbyists in Washington.

[37] Quoted in Donald R. Matthews, *U.S. Senators and Their World* (Chapel Hill: University of North Carolina Press, 1960), p. 181.

[38] Lester W. Milbrath, "The Political Party Activity of Washington Lobbyists," *Journal of Politics,* 20 (May 1958), 346.

The wide geographical distribution of teachers lends strength to their Washington lobbies, but poor organization hurts local efforts.

Unless leaders maintain cohesion within their own organization, they will have little impact in Washington, even if they employ the best of lobbyists. Cohesion, moreover, is threatened by indifference and overlapping membership in various groups. Since few people are totally identified with a single group, members may be alienated or even lost if an organization demands great commitment or conflicts with too many other loyalties. A member of the American Legion, for example, may also be a Baptist, a fisherman, a pipefitter, a father, a union member, and a Mets fan. The effective leader must somehow keep that member interested in the American Legion and minimize the cross pressures of other loyalties. To this end, skillful leaders use devices such as internal propaganda, services to members, and the maintenance of at least the appearance of membership control.

The *social base* of a pressure group is a fourth characteristic that affects its strength. Although a broad social base with many members is important, numbers do not always signify strength. In fact, the larger a group grows, and the more diffuse the social base, the more likely it is to become disunited. If the AFL–CIO could maintain the cohesion in politics that it does in collective bargaining, it would have more political power. Its millions of members have

190

PART 2
inputs of the
political
system: who
wants and needs
what?

so many other loyalties, however, that its power does not match its size. *Cohesion* is a key determinant in *every* element of group strength.

The geographical distribution of the members is another important factor in the social base of a group. If members are widely scattered, the group will probably be less unified than it would be if they could frequently meet face-to-face. On the other hand, if almost all the members live in a *single* area, as importers tend to be concentrated in New York, their effectiveness before Congress may suffer. Since the importer is not a vital force in most congressional districts, when tariff increases are under consideration "his opposition is taken for granted, discounted in advance, and if he is heard it is with irritation."[39] If the members of a group are fairly well concentrated in urban areas, as the members of labor unions are, the group will enjoy greater influence in the Office of the President (who depends on national majorities) than in Congress (where rural areas are more heavily represented). The strong influence of farm groups on Congress, conversely, springs in part from the wide geographical distribution of their members—every state has farmers.

Finally, the *doctrines* or policy objectives of a pressure group directly influence its strength. If the aims of a group fit the dominant values in the country at large, the group will enjoy easy access to the government, and cross pressures (conflicting loyalties) among the members will be kept at a minimum. Everyone is in favor of good health, for example, so the American Cancer Society has the advantage of almost no opposition. On the other hand, it may not be able to count on very *strong* commitment; mild approval may lead to an absence of opposition, but not necessarily to active support. If the doctrines of a group are different from the prevailing values, however, its chances of effectiveness will be slight, and its status will suffer accordingly.

The more goals a group tries to achieve, the weaker it becomes in the pursuit of any one of them. If it can concentrate on a single, overriding aim, as the Anti-Saloon League did in battling for prohibition, its chances of maintaining cohesion and winning success are increased. Both the AFL–CIO and the League of Women Voters, on the other hand, pursue complete programs rather than only a few issues, and they are reported to be among the most unpopular lobbying groups on Capitol Hill. As one member of Congress put it, "They just cover so damn much; and they tell you all about it."[40] The pressure group, unlike the political party, is not concerned with winning general control of the government, however, so it need not develop an overall political program for the country at large.

Collaboration among groups as a source of strength

We have tried to understand the strength of American pressure groups by looking at characteristics of our political system and at resources of individual pressure groups. Further insight may be gained by considering the degree of competition or agreement among all the groups active on an issue.

[39] Schattschneider, *Politics, Pressures, and the Tariff*, p. 162.
[40] Dexter, *How Organizations Are Represented in Washington*, p. 70.

In studying the passage of some particular statute, there is a strong temptation to assume that what one sees would apply to all statutes. Comparing the results of different studies permits a better perspective. Take Schattschneider's classic study of the tariff: he found pressure groups playing a dominant role in congressional decisions.[41] A generation later, Bauer, Pool, and Dexter looked at tariff legislation again and found that members of Congress could vote pretty much as they pleased.[42] Instead of deciding that Schattschneider's findings were no longer valid or that the more recent results were wrong, we might seek a broader interpretation that integrates the apparently contradictory findings. We can do this by looking for the conditions under which each set of results would occur. Michael Hayes has done just this with the suggestion that *different patterns of demands by pressure groups produced these different policy processes.*[43] In the passage of the tariff of 1930, virtually all of the pressures came from pro-tariff groups, with each manufacturing interest seeking tariff protection for itself and willing to see others get protective tariff rates as well. By the 1950s, business groups were active on both sides of the issue, so they cancelled out each other's influence and reduced the pressure on members of Congress.

The proposition we can draw from this contrast seems to be that when the organized groups in the pressure system collaborate, the pressure on official decision makers is intense. (As we saw earlier, even when pressure groups disagree among themselves, officials do not always enjoy wide discretion in making decisions.) This is not a very profound proposition, but at least it helps reduce the confusion about the strength of pressure groups. The people who are outside the pressure system—90 percent by Schattschneider's estimate—may rarely control policy, but they have a better chance when interests within the pressure system are divided among themselves. If those who are organized in the pressure system disagree, then greater attention may be given to broader public interests represented by public interest groups, political parties, or even unrepresented in any organized way except by their representatives in Congress.[44] The fact that many policies in the United States reflect collaborative efforts of pressure groups is thus another reason for pressure group strength.

PRESSURE GROUP TACTICS

Pressure group efforts are felt at every stage of the political process. Day after day, they work to create a favorable public opinion, to influence nominations and elections, and to sway governmental decisions.

---

[41] *Politics, Pressures, and the Tariff.*

[42] *American Business and Public Policy.*

[43] "The Semi-Sovereign Pressure Groups," pp. 142–43.

[44] The contrast between conflictive and collaborative efforts by pressure groups also helps explain the outcomes of public policy, as we shall see in chapter 8, on Congress.

192

PART 2
inputs of the
political
system: who
wants and needs
what?

Influencing the general public

When most people consider pressure groups at all, they tend to think of efforts to influence public officials. Actually, though, pressure groups have become aware that their causes need the support of public opinion; and to enlist it, they spend millions of dollars every year on *mass advertising* political ideas. Many businesses sell "correct" ideas on general political questions along with favorable attitudes toward the company and its product. If the company's definition of the American Way becomes the public's definition, also, then the company will be able to count on public support whenever a critical issue arises.

The rights of a corporation to promote general ideas to its liking has long been recognized. As far back as the 1950s General Mills decided it was not satisfied simply to sell Wheaties, "The Breakfast of Champions." The company went into teaching economics. General Mills made aids available to high school teachers. Without charge (they didn't even have to send in a Wheaties box top), teachers received fully planned teaching units, complete with color comic books and examinations on economic questions accompanied by answers. Children are consumers not only of cereals but of ideas; and if they absorb the proper beliefs along with the proper foods, they will one day grow into sturdy supporters of sound public policies. In recent years, the most conspicuous example of corporate editorializing has been Mobil Oil, which buys newspaper space for chatty editorials on all sorts of subjects, mostly emphasizing the devotion of oil companies to the public interest. This "public interest" is presumably that of the United States, for the ads do not mention the multinational nature of the oil companies.

Influencing elections

Another tactic used by pressure groups is *electioneering*. By definition, a pressure group does not run candidates under its own name; to do so would transform it into a political party. But such groups play a mighty role, as we saw earlier, in who is nominated and elected by both political parties. Abuses by such groups in the presidential election of 1972 helped bring passage of the Federal Election Campaign Act of 1974, which we shall consider in detail when we get to the electoral system in the next chapter. Congressional investigation of the Watergate scandal of 1972 revealed, among other things, that the Associated Milk Producers had promised a $2 million contribution to President Nixon's reelection campaign just prior to a presidential decision to raise price supports for milk. This decision brought a $60 million increase in revenue to the milk producers. Just to play safe, the Milk Producers also contributed to Democratic candidates; indeed, one of the late Senator Hubert Humphrey's campaign aides was found guilty of accepting an illegal contribution from the Milk Producers. Whoever wins, the well-heeled pressure group that supports both sides will not lose. The more flagrant of these abuses are now prohibited in presidential campaigns, but we saw above the degree to which PACs now dominate the financing of congressional elections.

A Supreme Court decision in 1978 may have opened the door to even more direct and open corporate participation in elections.[45] The courts have always recognized the right of corporations to lobby on issues that affect them materially, and companies have even been free to advertise their political ideology. But the decision in *First National Bank v. Bellotti* permitted corporations to move farther and more fully into elections than ever before. In a 5-to-4 decision, the Court declared unconstitutional a Massachusetts law prohibiting corporations from spending stockholders' funds on ballot issues in which the corporation had no material interest. The First National Bank of Boston and other companies that challenged the law were thus allowed, as an exercise in free speech, to spend money campaigning against a referendum to raise the state's personal income tax.

This close decision raised more issues than it settled, and both the American Bar Association and business groups responded with conferences to consider the issues. A corporation is not really a person but a legal entity, an "artificial person" that (or who?) typically brings together the funds of thousands of investors and the work of thousands of employees under centralized management. A number of major corporations now have total assets greater than those of state governments. Hence the argument that because corporations can muster so much more financial and therefore political weight than any real person can, corporations should not have the same right to unrestricted political speech as a real person does. In addition, corporations are chartered, and their stockholders invest in them, to engage in a profit-making enterprise. Should the managers of such an enterprise be allowed to use its resources for political purposes that are unrelated to the charter and possibly opposed by investors?

Business finds such arguments unimpressive. "A corporation is more than a legal entity; it is an adaptive learning group," Edward Littlejohn, public affairs chief for Pfizer Corporation, submitted to one conference on the new legal situation. He added, in massive understatement, "Corporations quite evidently have a role in the political process as it exists today."[46] Others argued that too much fuss was being made over the decision. They hold that corporations will not start speaking out on a great number of issues, whatever the court says, because some are too far removed from their concerns as a company. Others are so divisive that by taking a position, the company might lose customers. Business corporations exist to make profits, and that can be trusted to take precedence over other concerns.

Influencing public officials

Although mass advertising campaigns and electioneering are increasingly important, the tactic most often associated with pressure politics is *lobbying*—directly attempting to influence public officials. As we saw earlier, lobbying

[45] First National Bank v. Bellotti, 98 S. Ct. 1407 (1978).
[46] These conferences are reported in Bradley Graham, "The Corporate Voice," *The Washington Post,* March 25, 1979.

194

PART 2
inputs of the
political
system: who
wants and needs
what?

techniques range all the way from infrequent instances of bribery to polite willingness to answer questions about a group's needs and views. We also saw that many more lobbyists exert much more pressure than was thought to be the case in the 1960s.

People think mostly of Congress when they hear about lobbying, but pressure groups focus even more on the executive branch. For example, the International Telephone and Telegraph Corporation wanted to prevent the election of Salvador Allende as President of Chile, then to prevent his taking office, and finally to have his regime overthrown. To do this, ITT worked through the State Department, the CIA (Central Intelligence Agency), and the White House. The Associated Milk Producers went to the White House because the President has the authority to raise the price support for milk. To be sure, lobbyists for these interests do not neglect Congress; but bureaucrats make more decisions affecting lobbyists than members of Congress do, so lobbyists go where the action is. This focus on the executive branch is encouraged also by the fact that the more publicity an issue gets, the less influence pressure groups have. They have more influence on decisions made deep in the recesses of the bureaucracy—decisions made with no public debate and little publicity—than on decisions made in Congress.

UPI

Ralph Nader's success as a consumer advocate came in part from his ability to win publicity for his causes.

In contrast, public interest groups often seek maximum publicity for their various causes. Their best chance of influencing policy is to broaden the scope of conflict beyond the narrow pressure system. Whereas private interest groups are often concerned with keeping their lobbying activities inconspicuous, public interest groups typically have the opposite problem of trying to attract public attention to their causes. As the best-known crusader for consumer interests, attorney Ralph Nader is among the few spokesmen for a public interest group who can be assured of media attention when he attacks a problem. After Nader won fame and respect for his criticisms of the safety of Chevrolet's Corvair, he recruited a staff of dedicated young assistants who became known as Nader's Raiders.[47] Their investigations of private and public agencies made the Nader Study Group Report a very useful instrument of reform politics. Jeffrey Berry concludes that one of the first of these investigations, *The Nader Report on the Federal Trade Commission*, was at least partly responsible for the "eventual rejuvenation of the FTC into a much more consumer-oriented agency."[48]

The techniques used by a pressure group will thus vary with its objectives. If it needs to bring more participants into the controversy, as public interests often do, it may seek maximum publicity. Groups that enjoy advantages under the status quo, on the other hand, will try to avoid publicity, for it might bring in more participants and lead to change.

CHECKS ON PRESSURE GROUP POWER

We noted at the beginning of this chapter that Americans blame special interest groups and lobbies, above all else, for the failure of their government to work well. This is in keeping with a tradition even older than the Republic. In arguing for adoption of the Constitution, James Madison said, "The regulation of these various and interfering interests forms the principal task of modern legislation. . . ."[49] The "interfering interests" Madison had in mind, which he generally called "factions," were very similar to what we call special interest groups.[50] Before we get to the problem of their regulation by government, we need to note two other statements of Madison on factions: that they are "adverse to the . . . interests of the community" and that their influence is reduced by a "variety of parties and interests."[51]

---

[47] See Charles McCarry, *Citizen Nader* (New York: Saturday Review Press, 1972), especially pp. 3–29.

[48] *Lobbying for the People,* p. 247.

[49] *The Federalist,* Number 10.

[50] The principal difference is that we have focussed on pressure groups as representing minorities, whereas Madison included majority factions (which we treated as political parties).

[51] *The Federalist,* Number 10.

196

PART 2
inputs of the
political
system: who
wants and needs
what?

Pressure groups as "adverse to the . . . interests of the community"

By definition, pressure groups represent minority instead of majority interests. We saw in the preceding chapter that the have-nots are under-represented even by political parties. Since pressure groups exist to promote special interests with enough resources to demand attention, the have-nots are even more severely under-represented in the pressure system. A relatively small number of public interest groups try to speak for the underprivileged, because the poor cannot or will not speak for themselves. Although the upper-status members and the poor do not really have the same perspective, the better educated, more articulate champions of the underprivileged are responsible for initiating many social reforms.

In considering the functions of pressure groups, we noted positive contributions to the political system and to individuals. Nevertheless, pressure groups appear less satisfactory than political parties as agencies for expressing broad public interests.

1. Pressure groups do not represent all interests equally—the underprivileged and noneconomic interests especially are underrepresented.

2. The complexity of current domestic and international problems demands a coherent and stable overall policy, and this kind of policy cannot be achieved if every problem is tackled by a different coalition of special interests.

3. Because every person, no less than every district, has a variety of interests, the pressure group leader can speak no more accurately for all the members of the group than elected representatives can speak for all their constituents.

4. Pressure groups cannot be held accountable by the general public for the manner in which they use their power, because they do not win it through popular election.

The deep-rooted public suspicion of pressure groups is probably based mostly on the first and last problems on our list. If all interests were equally represented by pressure groups, they would add a marvelous richness to the expression of public needs and demands that we get so crudely through political parties. But, of course, such groups are highly unrepresentative. If pressure groups, however elitist in their makeup, were somehow accountable to the general public, we could feel comfortable in the knowledge that they could be made to pay for any wrongdoing. But, of course, pressure groups—however much they may influence elections—do not depend exclusively on elections for their power.

Pressure groups play a negative more often than a positive role, even though they have a significant part in all major actions of government. Truly major policy accomplishments—social security, Medicare, civil rights laws, the Tennessee Valley Authority, national aid to education—may depend in part on the work of pressure groups, but they come more from political parties and such "nonorganizational" factors as actual events, political leaders, and the mass media.[52] Pressure groups are at their best in blocking action,

[52] Wilson, *Political Organizations*, p. 330.

as the American Medical Association and its allies have blocked national health insurance for over 30 years. If adaptation and change are positively valued, then, pressure groups are viewed as playing a negative role.

Their negative stance and their persistent behind-the-scenes effort, no less than their unaccountability and unrepresentativeness, round out the picture of pressure groups as a source of problems. Even when a new policy is enacted, the interests most closely affected often manage to "capture" the administrative agency charged with carrying it out. The defeats suffered by special interests thus turn out frequently to be more apparent than real. Murray Edelman, the leading authority on the use of symbols in politics, points out that many laws that seem to solve some problem actually give the appearance of victory merely to "cool off" public concern.[53] When public opinion is mobilized, Congress may strike a symbolic blow for consumer protection, for example, but the industry being regulated retains high interest in the law after it is passed and helps shape its implementation long after the public clamor has died down.

Informal checks from a "variety of parties and interests"

The idea that *competition among a large number of varied interests* reduces the possibility of dominance by any one interest has been advanced as forcefully in the twentieth century as it was in the eighteenth. E. E. Schattschneider thus talks about the importance of broadening the scope of conflict and bringing in more participants.[54] Grant McConnell similarly finds that the larger the constituency, the less chance of control by narrow elite interests.[55]

Just as the structure of government includes a system of formal checks and balances, which handicaps majority interests, so do the variety of interests outside government produce a system of informal checks and balances, which reduces the power of special interests.[56] In considering the role of lobbyists, we found that their influence on broad-gauged or general policy enactments was reduced when a large number of groups took different positions.

The rise of single-issue groups represents a development that is simply outside the theory that competition among a variety of groups decreases their power. For one thing, the competition here is usually *between two groups*, not *among many groups*. What happens in a two-group process is not covered by a proposition that assumes a multiple-group process. Moreover, the issues here are matters of principle (yes or no), not matters of degree (how much), and the demands are quite specific. Thus one side wins, the other loses, and

[53] *The Symbolic Uses of Politics* (Urbana: University of Illinois Press, 1964), and *Politics as Symbolic Action* (Chicago: Markham, 1971).

[54] *The Semi-Sovereign People.*

[55] *Private Power and American Democracy* (New York: Knopf, 1966).

[56] We need to remember that Madison was particularly fearful of majority factions. As our discussion of the adoption of the Constitution in chap. 2 indicated, separation of powers and checks and balances reflected this concern.

198

PART 2
inputs of the
political
system: who
wants and needs
what?

neither will accept a compromise. The theory that a variety of interests reduces group power breaks down completely when collaboration among special interests produces such lopsided pressure that it suppresses threatening issues (such as nationalization of oil companies) or shapes legislation helpful to such interests (such as special tax advantages).

In addition to competition as a check on pressure group power, the existence of a variety of interests leads to *overlapping memberships* (members belonging to two or more groups). This is a second source of informal restraint on pressure groups. Overlapping membership means that all the members of a pressure group cannot be mobilized completely on any question of general importance, for they are also involved in other groups. Consequently, group leaders must sometimes modify their own demands in order to accommodate the demands of other groups. Moreover, loyalty of members to any group varies—as in a college club where involvement ranges from complete indifference to active, creative participation.

The latent power of *unorganized interests* constitutes a third natural check on pressure group power. Unorganized interests are potential groups that may be stimulated to organize if they are flagrantly neglected.[57] This is not a very effective check, to be sure, because basic interests that are unorganized can be assumed to lack the resources—money, time, training, strategic position in the economy, or what have you—necessary for organization. Nevertheless, even those seriously lacking in resources can be driven to organize if they are too shabbily treated. The ability of the suppressed people of Nicaragua to drive the dictator Somoza into exile, despite his U.S.-trained and equipped national guard, attests to the possibility of organization in the face of extreme provocation. During the early days of industrialization in the United States, corporate leaders like Andrew Carnegie hired private armed forces to suppress strikes, but such flagrant actions have passed from the scene. Mass advertising of ideology may represent a sublimation of those earlier rude efforts to "teach them a lesson."

Political parties are a fourth informal check on the power of special interests. If any unofficial agency is going to mobilize the broad majority, the political party is the agency to do it. Only the party has a real stake in organizing underlying majority interests and in stimulating potential groups to action. Political parties thus may restrain organized power with greater organized power. As we noted at the beginning of this chapter, the power of American pressure groups has increased in direct response to the decline in the power of political parties. As the political party has been replaced by *ad hoc,* candidate-centered organizations that raise campaign funds and run campaigns, officeholders are left with no buffer organization to protect them from single-issue groups. And these groups have also learned to raise their own campaign funds and to reach voters directly through targeted mailing lists. To expect leaders of such groups to look at the general program of one's party or even at one's own overall voting record is, as former Senator Anderson discovered, unrealistic. These developments led David Broder to predict,

[57] Truman, *The Governmental Process,* p. 514.

"Eventually, the American voters may rediscover the truth that without strong political parties, Congress and the president will be unable to come to grips responsibly with serious national problems. But until that happens, the single-interest groups will ride rampant through the system. . . ."[58]

Formal checks: "regulation of these . . . interfering interests"

In looking at the power of pressure groups, we pay so much attention to unofficial groups that we may forget the most obvious and authoritative check on their power: the *official decision-making agencies* themselves. After all, Madison saw the capacity to cure the "mischiefs of faction" as one of the chief virtues of the government set up under the Constitution. Official decision makers are far from being passive pawns moved at will by pressure groups; they are active participants in the determination of policy. However badgered, beleaguered, pressured, and criticized they may be, public officials are still the only people whose decisions have the force of law. This is not to deny the strong influence of pressure groups, but to remind ourselves that they still fall far short of being in control. When the Associated Milk Producers (AMP) send lobbyists to the White House or to a congressional office, they can be reasonably confident of being heard, but they cannot be certain that their request will be granted. The AMP needs a favorable decision from the officeholder, perhaps even more than the officeholder needs AMP support.

When decision makers take office, they bring along with them their beliefs and the commitments they made during their campaigns for election. Their long-held beliefs and newly made commitments do more to mold their decisions in office than do all the postelection activities of pressure groups. The group's advice and wishes, in fact, may be so similar to the decision maker's thinking that pressure is unnecessary. The pressure group is only reinforcing the congressman's predispositions and is likely to do little more than that. Moreover, insofar as officeholders view their task as the representation of a general public interest, they may look on special interests with at least some skepticism.

The most direct way for Congress to demonstrate the authority of official agencies over pressure groups is by passing legislation regulating the practices of the pressure groups themselves. But we said above that pressure groups are at their best in a defensive stance; that is, they can block major policy changes more easily than they can produce them. Efforts of Congress to regulate pressure groups certainly show the groups' defensive strength. Despite repeated efforts since 1946, Congress has failed to pass significant legislation regulating pressure group activity.

The Federal Regulation of Lobbying Act of 1946 was a weak measure when it was passed, and it is now hopelessly out of date. The act imposes no restrictions on lobbying; it merely requires professional lobbyists before

[58] "One-Issue Groups Becoming an Issue," *Washington Post*, September 14, 1978.

200

PART 2
inputs of the
political
system: who
wants and needs
what?

Congress to register their names, file information about themselves and their employers, and submit quarterly reports of receipts and expenditures. The weakness of the Lobbying Act was clear from the outset. It was designed to expose the top of the iceberg—direct lobbying of members of Congress— but it left submerged the larger part of the iceberg—lobbying contacts with the administrative agencies and the White House. Moreover, the reports required of congressional lobbyists mean little, because no enforcement agency was provided. The meaningless, unsensational reports do not attract the mass media, and the lack of publicity also reduces the effect of the law. The Supreme Court further diminished the force of the act by narrowly interpreting it to apply only to expenditures in direct contacts with members of Congress, thus excluding the modern technique of lobbying through publicity beamed at the general public.[59] A second loophole left by the Supreme Court is the law's application only to organizations such as the American Conservative Union, Common Cause, and the National Rifle Association, whose "principal purpose" is to influence legislation. A corporation can send any of its officers to lobby without bothering to register.

In view of these weaknesses, most students of politics would agree with John Gardner that the lobbying act is "almost totally useless." A lobbyist for the American Nurses Association frankly states, "I just have to laugh every time I see these [annual] lobby spending totals."[60] Common Cause managed to get realistic regulation of lobbying on the public agenda when it placed a tough measure on lobbying on the 1974 ballot in California and won approval by a 2-to-1 margin. Public support for such regulation clearly exists. A new Lobby Disclosure Act has accordingly been proposed in every Congress since 1975. The bill got farther in the Ninety-Sixth Congress than ever before, but when the Ninety-Seventh Congress convened in 1981, the task of significant change in the old 1946 act remained. Pressure groups have great staying power and defensive strength.

THE MASS MEDIA AS A POLITICAL INSTITUTION

Journalists like to view themselves as tough and dedicated, doggedly pursuing the "news" and presenting it instantly. They also tend to deny that they do anything else—such as making news themselves or influencing the events or institutions they cover.[61] Political scientists have, we think, too readily accepted the journalists' modest view of their importance in shaping the events and institutions on which they report. At least this seems indicated by the fact that only two articles about television have appeared in the *American Political Science Review* in the 30 years from 1950 to 1980.

[59] United States v. Harris, 347 U.S. 612 (1954).

[60] *Congressional Quarterly Weekly Report,* 32 (July 27, 1974), 1949.

[61] William Gormley, *The Effects of Cross-Media Ownership on News Homogeneity* (unpublished Ph.D. dissertation, University of North Carolina, Chapel Hill, 1976).

People talk about "the mass media" without bothering to define the term, which is a tribute to the importance of whatever the term stands for. To be more certain of clarity, let us specify the meaning we have in mind. First, *mass* is used to refer to the great body of ordinary people, in contrast to any presumably superior minority (elite). Second, *media* is the plural of medium, a channel or means of communication. Hence the mass media are all the means through which communication to the great bulk of the population occurs. Newspapers are the oldest such medium in the United States. Magazines, radio, and television emerged later to help make up the general system of mass communication. Because newspapers came first, "the press" is the term now used to mean all the mass media.

The role of the mass media in presenting political information and influencing opinions has long been recognized. Today, however, the mass media have developed beyond these traditional tasks to the point at which they also deserve examination as a political institution in their own right. Political parties and pressure groups are recognized as unofficial political agencies, and we analyze them the way we do Congress, the presidency, and the courts. We propose to look at the mass media as an unofficial political institution comparable in significance to parties and pressure groups.

Spokespersons for two important political institutions meet.

Paul Conklin, Monkmeyer.

PART 2
inputs of the
political
system: who
wants and needs
what?

In a country as large as the United States, we cannot possibly have direct experience with all the events and personalities that dominate politics. Even Presidents and members of Congress depend on the mass media for most of their information about American politics. National political leaders read an average of 2.8 newspapers a day,[62] and almost everything we ourselves know about current political events comes from the mass media.[63] The primary political function of the mass media is, then, as obvious as it is important: *communication of information about politics.* But the media also perform four important functions for the political system.

1. Gatekeeper, regulating the flow of demands into the political system.
2. Watchdog over public officials.
3. Loyal opposition to the administration of the government.
4. Selector and screener, when candidates emerge.

Gatekeeper. Reporters and news managers decide what will or will not be publicized, thereby determining which demands will become issues. To decide which issues will be raised and which will be suppressed is to decide what politics is all about, and the media are not free to exercise such awesome power in total independence of other political institutions. Political parties, pressure groups, and churches are among the other institutions that also serve as gatekeepers. Even individual political figures, especially the President, may stress some issue so heavily that the media could not ignore it completely. Nevertheless, the mass media play the central role in deciding which issues will receive attention. Some commentators have even gone so far as to say that the media "set the agenda" for political debate; although this may overstate the power of the media, they undoubtedly *shape the agenda* by spotlighting particular issues.[64]

Watchdog. As H. L. Mencken put it, the mission of the press is to "comfort the afflicted and afflict the comfortable." Although the media have frequently neglected the afflicted, they have worked hard at afflicting government officials. The most impressive demonstration that investigative reporters can unearth wrongdoing at even the highest level was the *Washington Post's* relentless pursuit of President Nixon's guilt in the Watergate scandals.[65] Even though some people argue that the federal prosecutors, Judge Sirica, the FBI, and the Senate Watergate Committee deserve most of the credit

---

[62] Carol Weiss, "What America's Leaders Read," *Public Opinion Quarterly,* 38 (Spring 1974), 1–22.

[63] Doris A. Graber, *Mass Media and American Politics* (Washington, D.C.: Congressional Quarterly Press, 1980).

[64] Maxwell McCombs and Donald Shaw, *The Emergence of American Political Issues: The Agenda-Setting Function of the Press* (St. Paul, Minn.: West, 1978); for an earlier study see Bernard Cohen, *The Press and Foreign Policy* (Princeton: Princeton University Press, 1963), p. 13.

[65] Bob Woodward and Carl Bernstein, *All The President's Men* (New York: Simon & Shuster, 1974).

Washington Post reporters Woodward and Bernstein were instrumental in exposing President Nixon's role in the Watergate scandal.

for unraveling the Watergate story,[66] all of these others might have been less vigorous without the constant prodding and support of the mass media. If the media did not uncover Watergate, they at least stimulated others to do so.

In marked contrast to the Watergate story was the media's superficial treatment of the Korean lobby case, in which a Korean lobbyist appears to have used cash gifts and lavish entertainment to "win friends and influence people" in Congress and the State Department. The implication was that this technique of lobbying had crossed the line of legality, that the agent of a foreign government was improperly winning financial aid and other favors for his country, and that some of the aid was being siphoned off—in an endless cycle—to finance his influence on American policy. Had reporters pursued these allegations with the endless persistence of the *Washington Post's* Woodward and Bernstein, we might have learned much more about the Korean connection. As it was, neither the Justice Department nor Congress carried through to full disclosure. Perhaps more strongly than Watergate, even though less positively, the Korean case attests to the value of the media's watchdog function.

[66] Edward Epstein, "Did the Press Uncover Watergate?" *Commentary* (July 1974), pp. 21–24. Also see his *News From Nowhere* (New York: Random House, 1973).

UPI

Senator Thomas Eagleton discusses how his medical problems affected his viability as a Democratic vice-presidential nominee in 1972.

Loyal opposition. A third function of the media is *loyal opposition* to the administration of the government. The old-style *muckraker*—exposer of wrongdoing—dug up particular cases but left it largely to the opposition party to disagree publicly with the administration. In recent years, however, as political parties have become less meaningful to Americans, the mass media have begun to assume the role of critic of the administration, in a more general sense. Theodore H. White, the author of *The Making of the President* series of books, observes, "The national media have put themselves into the role of permanent critical opposition to any government which does not instantly clean up the unfinished business of our time." As a result, "no government will satisfy them."[67] Samuel Huntington, an expert on comparative politics, describes the adversary relationship between media and the presidency and the bureaucracy as a new conflict comparable to the old cleavages between the major political parties, between state and national government, and among executive, legislative, and judicial branches of government.

At stake [are] not merely conflicting personalities and differing political viewpoints, but also fairly fundamental institutional interests. The media have an interest in exposure, criticism, highlighting and encouraging disagreement and disaffection within the executive branch. The leaders of the executive branch have an interest in secrecy,

[67] "America's Two Cultures," *Columbia Journalism Review,* 8 (Winter 1969–70), 8.

hierarchy, discipline, and the suppression of criticism. The function of the press is to expand political debate and involvement; the natural instinct of the bureaucracy is to limit it.[68]

Regardless of which party is in power, then, the media tend to become part of the opposition.

Candidate screening and selection. Finally, a fourth political function of the mass media is that of *candidate screening and selection.* Here the media have moved into an activity that was once controlled by political parties. But American political parties have not kept pace with other developments in American society. With their decline in importance and respect,[69] the mass media have taken over the function of screening candidates.[70] George Romney, former governor of Michigan, was the leading candidate for the Republican nomination for President in 1968, for example, but the press eliminated him from the race. Subject to constant evaluation by the mass media, Mr. Romney was found wanting when he slipped and said the American military had "brainwashed" him on policy toward the Vietnam war. He withdrew from the race *before* the first state primary; in fact, he was eliminated by the mass media. Similarly, the mass media can be said to have forced the replacement of Senator Thomas Eagleton as the Democratic nominee for Vice-President in 1972. They did this by unearthing information about—and then dwelling incessantly on—his mental health. Press treatment of prospective candidates has always carried weight; but that weight has increased enormously, in part because of the decrease in vitality of party organizations, in part because of the great impact of television.

In addition to assessing the abilities and personalities of candidates, the media set the standard by which each candidate's effort is judged. As we shall see in the following chapter on elections, the media rely on public opinion polls not only to report on each candidate's popularity but also to set the media's standards by which to judge the candidate's success or failure. (Golfers may be reminded of handicap golf.) Eugene McCarthy thus "won" the Democrats' 1968 presidential primary in New Hampshire with 42.0 percent of the votes, Edmund Muskie "lost" the same state's primary in 1972 with 47.8 percent, and Jimmy Carter "won" in 1976 with 29.4 percent. Why? Because journalists had decided what they expected these candidates to get, but they had guessed too low for McCarthy and Carter and too high for Muskie. Now, no one is interested in a news story about how wrong journalists were in their analyses (nor do journalists like to write such stories), so the "news" became these media-defined "victories" and "defeats" of the candidates. This approach has the advantage of drumming up interest in the horse-race

---

[68] Samuel P. Huntington, "Postindustrial Politics: How Benign Will It Be?" *Comparative Politics,* 6 (January 1974), 184–85.

[69] Jack Dennis, "Trends in Public Support for the American Political Party System," *British Journal of Political Science,* 5 (April 1975), 187.

[70] M. J. Robinson, "TV's Newest Program: The 'Presidential Nominating Game'," *Public Opinion,* 1 (May–June, 1978), 41–46. Also see Timothy Crouse, *The Boys on the Bus* (New York: Random House, 1973), p. 37.

206

PART 2
inputs of the
political
system: who
wants and needs
what?

aspect of an election but never letting the mass media lose! The disadvantage of the practice is that it diverts attention from political issues to the daily racing form on who is winning various primaries. A disadvantage for candidates is that they are put in the awkward position of trying to look like winners, without creating such expectations that the mass media can define a victory as defeat.

The relationship of the media to other political institutions

In considering the functions of the media, we have just seen how they have helped to diminish the role of political parties as vehicles for screening candidates and winning elections. The media have had less dramatic effects on other political institutions.

Americans' unusual interest in the President, his family, and every detail of life in the White House is, at least in part, the work of the media, whose complete coverage of the presidency turns any occupant of the office into a larger-than-life figure. Journalists, tending to deal with personalities rather than institutions or issues, contribute to the elevation of the presidency and to the inclination of voters to credit or blame the President for national fortunes and misfortunes.

Journalists' search for news has complicated the lives of almost all public officials, but it has not really changed the functions of most political institutions. The presence of the media poses special problems for the courts, for example, with sensational coverage of some cases making it extremely difficult to select an unbiased jury.[71] To cope with the problem, most courts ban photographers and cameras from the courtroom and sequester members of the jury, to prevent their exposure to prejudicial publicity.

Congress has been more open to publicity. Because senators are fewer and better known than are representatives, the media focus on the Senate. Senators crave publicity no less than reporters crave stories, so they have a good relationship. After televised coverage of Senate committee hearings brought instant fame for senators such as Joseph McCarthy, Richard Nixon, J. William Fulbright, and Sam Ervin, senators developed a preference for committees that most often have televised hearings. One result of media attention is that the Senate has become chief "incubator of Presidential hopefuls."[72]

With 435 members, the House of Representatives is not a good base on which to build individual name recognition. Perhaps to overcome their relative obscurity, members of the House voted to allow TV cameras to cover floor debates with gavel-to-gavel telecasts for the first time in 1979. Carried by cable television systems serving 5 million to 6 million households, and reaching all 50 states, these telecasts proved surprisingly popular. An explanation of their appeal was offered by House Speaker Thomas P. ("Tip") O'Neill

[71] Herbert Jacob, *Justice in America* (Boston: Little, Brown, 1972), p. 137.
[72] Nelson Polsby, "Goodbye to the Inner Club," in Polsby, ed., *Congressional Behavior* (New York: Random House, 1971), pp. 108–9.

Senator Joseph McCarthy (R-Wis.) was one of the first to exploit television as a route to political power.

(D-Mass.). Though not especially flattering to his colleagues, it reflects the realism of a seasoned politician: "There's not much else to watch in the daytime except soap operas," he said. "And a lot of people don't like soap operas. And it's incredible how many people out there are turning on the House debate." But the new-found attention quickly led to exploitation. Eager to impress the home folks, some representatives began to notify constituents of the time they planned to give a "special order" speech (the House term for a speech having little to do with the chamber's legislative business). These speeches are often made when no other members are present and even the galleries are empty, but the cameras are required to focus only on the speaker. This gives the representative maximum time "on camera" and almost equally important, prevents a view of the vacant chamber. Thus, with most of his colleagues already gone for the August 1979 recess, Representative Larry Winn (R-Kan.) told a virtually deserted floor—but many home viewers—about the benefits of "moving the capitol to Kansas."[73]

The impact of the media on political institutions is thus not unwelcome. Representative Winn may never be as well recognized as Erica, the scheming temptress of "All My Children," but every exposure helps. Like all political developments, the impact of the media will help some and hurt others; office-holders will vary in the ways they try to ensure that they are among the helped.

In addition to these specific effects on political institutions, the media may have had a more general effect on the political system as a whole.

[73] *Raleigh* (North Carolina) *News and Observer*, August 4, 1979.

208

PART 2
inputs of the
political
system: who
wants and needs
what?

By highlighting the weaknesses of public officials at all levels, the media may have contributed to the erosion of trust in government, a characteristic of the last decade. Whether decline in trust is warranted by actual events is a matter on which readers will no doubt differ. But news people do seem to harbor a special contempt for politicians and to look upon politics as "essentially a game played by individual politicians for personal advancement, gain, or power."[74]

In assuming the worst about politicians, journalists may not be wrong, but they may also create a stereotype that could discourage talented, principled people from entering public life. If the media were less interested in spectacular events and more concerned with significant trends, they might examine their own influence on the political system. And if they were equally unrelenting in calling attention to abuses of power in the private sphere, they might create a more balanced impression. But as part of the private sphere, they are less likely to be negative about it.

Few public agencies have as many tasks as the media, and none has less public accountability. Who are these spokespersons of the fourth branch of government, these private people with public responsibility? How are they organized, how uniform is their voice, what influences their message? Three features of contemporary American media help answer these questions: (1) the media are private, free organizations with only limited governmental controls; (2) the media are increasingly less competitive, with more power coming into fewer hands; (3) despite this concentration, there continues to be conflict within the media between professional and business norms.

The media as free private organizations

In some countries, such as the Soviet Union, the mass media are government owned and operated. Other countries, such as Chile, have both government and private mass media, but the military government exercises control over privately operated media. Some nations, such as Great Britain, have primarily private ownership and operation; but a government agency, which is carefully screened from partisan political control, competes with the privately conducted media (in Britain, the British Broadcasting Corporation). Still other countries have privately owned and operated media (as in the U.S.) with very little competition from, or control by, the government.

The mass media in the United States claim explicit recognition of their right to be free from government control. The First Amendment of the Constitution states: "Congress shall make no law . . . abridging the freedom . . . of the press. . . ." The framers of the Constitution regarded freedom of the press as important to any kind of popular government. History has proved them correct. Just as every democracy has competing political parties and active pressure groups, so does every democracy have mass media that are free of direct government control. Conversely, in every dictatorship the government controls the media, either directly or indirectly.

---

[74] Paul Weaver, "Is Television News Biased?" *The Public Interest,* 26 (Winter 1972), 69.

Although direct governmental interference is rare in the United States, the news staffs of television and radio stations are subject to at least some governmental regulation. A license must be secured from the Federal Communications Commission (FCC) in order to operate a radio or television station, and the licensee is legally bound to use the public airways in the public interest. The FCC can refuse to renew licenses of stations that disregard the public interest.

The media: many voices or few?

Although media voices are everywhere, coaxing, selling, and informing, they are not as diverse as they used to be. In 1979 the United States had 1,756 English language daily newspapers with the following circulations: morning, 27,656,739; evening, 34,333,258; Sunday, 53,990,033.[75] In addition, 4,497 AM radio stations, 3,743 FM stations, and 984 television stations supply entertainment and news to almost all Americans.[76] (In 1978, 98+ percent of all U.S. households had radios, and 98 percent had at least one television set.)

With so many newspapers and broadcasting stations, America's free press appears to be in good condition, giving citizens access to news from many competing sources. In fact, however, the trend has been a dramatic decline in competition. The percentage of American cities with competing newspapers has decreased from roughly 60 percent in 1910 to 21 percent in 1930, to 15 percent in 1950, to below 4 percent in 1972. To make things worse, more and more of the remaining newspapers are under "chain" or "group" control. Television and radio are controlled by three major networks. A testimony to their position in America is that they are among the few organizations a textbook can mention merely by initials with assurance that readers will know what is meant. In 1979, NBC had 212 affiliates, ABC had 200, and CBS had 198.[77]

Newspapers and TV stations both are thus organized into larger chains or groups. Some facts highlight this development: (1) The share of daily newspaper circulation held by chain or group newspapers rose from 43 percent in 1950 to 60 percent in 1972. (2) The 10 largest groups of daily newspapers have a yearly revenue of approximately $2.2 billion, roughly a fourth of the total revenue for the entire industry. The three national television networks went from $2.5 million in sales of advertising time in 1948 to more than $3.4 billion by 1977.

The trend toward concentration of ownership is defended on the ground that large-scale organization can provide money, talent, and management to keep a local newspaper or broadcasting station in competition with other advertising media—all of which could lead to improved quality of news coverage. In addition, the tax system encourages this type of growth.

[75] *Editor and Publisher International Yearbook 1979.*

[76] See Edwin Emery and Michael Emery, *The Press and America: An Interpretative History of the Mass Media,* 4th ed. (Englewood Cliffs, N.J.: Prentice-Hall, 1978), p. 404.

[77] *Broadcasting Yearbook 1979,* pp. D–25, 34, 40.

The trend toward nationalization through giant corporations is characteristic of the entire economy. If we get much the same reports and interpretations of the news wherever we live, and a few companies make the profits, this is consistent with other aspects of our lives. We can travel across the entire United States with no change in the quick-service foods we eat—Big Mac, Whopper, Colonel Sanders' Kentucky-Fried Chicken—and we can spend every night in an identical room at a Holiday Inn or Ramada Inn. If a man needs a new shirt on the trip, or a woman needs cosmetics, they can buy brands identical to those sold in their home towns. Little wonder, then, that when we read a newspaper, we see the same wire-service news we would have read at home; and when we turn on the TV, we have the familiar choice among Dan Rather, John Chancellor, and a less traditional ABC team headed by Frank Reynolds. People who have accepted nationalization and standardization of food, clothing, and shelter can hardly be surprised to see it also in the treatment of the news.

But several dangers exist in the concentration resulting from the "rush to chain ownership."[78] First is the concentration of power in a few hands. Such power can be used for good as well as evil, but democratic norms encourage wide distribution of power, especially when such power is in private hands. Second, the large news organizations are big businesses that are typically more concerned with their profit and loss than with social problems. Third, simply in terms of social costs, advertising rates go up as competition is eliminated, and these costs are passed on to the public. All of these dangers lead to concern on the part of students of journalism for "the First Amendment protection of those readers and listeners whose right to know is subordinated to the right to make a financial killing."[79]

Conflict between professional and profit norms

As business organizations producing something for sale and profit, the mass media sell advertisements, entertainment, and news. But some of the people employed to produce these saleable items develop norms of their own, which are occasionally different from the money-making objectives of the corporation, and therein lies a source of tension between working journalists and owners and directors of mass media.

For the working newsperson, journalism is a profession. *Professionalism* means that journalists are trained, educated, and committed to their trade. For example, a reporter who threatens to quit unless a certain story is made public is responding to the norms of journalism rather than to profit-making norms. The first norm of journalists is the public's *right to know*. They will let the public know as much as possible, regardless of who is helped and who is hurt. Ethical journalists try to be objective, to report all sides and positions, and to be the first to communicate an event. There is much competition to scoop, or beat, another network, even by seconds. Being first with the news is regarded as a major achievement. Journalists today also attempt to explain events rather than simply report them. The public's *right to understand* appears to be an emerging norm.

Some owners and directors of mass media are also professionals—trained, educated, and committed to their trade—whereas some journalists are interested primarily in making a name and money for themselves. With this self-interest on both sides, commercial considerations usually win out. A newspaper locked in a circulation battle will increase the amount of attention to "immediate-reward news," such as scandals, crimes, fires, and accidents.[80] Because of the greater expense of moving personnel and equipment and of transmitting stories by special cables whenever they report from remote places, TV net-

---

[78] Robert Bishop, "The Rush to Chain Ownership," *Columbia Journalism Review,* 11 (November–December 1972), 10, 14–15.

[79] *Ibid.,* p. 19.

[80] Galen Rarick and Barrie Hartman, "The Effects of Competition on One Daily Newspaper's Content," *Journalism Quarterly,* 43 (Autumn 1966), 459–63.

212

PART 2
inputs of the
political
system: who
wants and needs
what?

works give a disproportionate amount of attention to news that originates in a few large cities.

The tension between business and profession, between informing and entertaining the public, is most clearly revealed in the television industry. The news departments of the networks are operated by people who seem to be real journalists. They even take pride in monetary *losses* suffered by their department; the higher the losses, the greater the proof that the news departments are engaged in real journalism rather than selling and advertising. In effect, then, the money-making programs pay for the news departments.

When professional standards come into direct conflict with commercial considerations, one is reminded that the mass media are, after all, huge corporate enterprises. The most dramatic example of such a confrontation occurred in 1966 when Fred W. Friendly resigned as president of the CBS News Division. He resigned because higher officials insisted on carrying a fifth rerun of "I Love Lucy" and an eighth rerun of "The Real McCoys" instead of permitting him to present live television coverage of Senate hearings on the Vietnam war. Mr. Friendly's letter of resignation, which presents the role of the journalist in the mass media much better than we could, read in part:

I am resigning because CBS News did not carry the Senate Foreign Relations Committee hearings last Thursday, when former Ambassador George Kennan testified on Vietnam. It was the considered news judgment of every executive in CND [Columbia News Division] that we carry these Vietnam hearings. . . . I am convinced that the decision not to carry them was a business, not a news, judgment.

. . . What happens to [the] sense of fairness and balance . . . when one day's hearings, and perhaps the most comprehensive, are omitted? How can we return on Thursday and Friday of this week without denying [the] argument that "the housewife isn't interested"? Why were NBC's housewives interested? . . .

The concept of an autonomous news organization responsible only to the chairman and the president was not a creation of mine. It is a concept almost as old as CBS News, and is a tradition. . . . The dramatic change in the concept is, to my mind and that of my colleagues, a form of emasculation. . . .

My departure is a matter of conscience. At the end of the day it is the viewer and the listener who have the biggest stake in all this. Perhaps my action will be understood by them. I know it will be understood by my colleagues in news and I know Ed Murrow would have understood. A speech he delivered . . . in 1958 spelled it all out:

"One of the basic troubles with radio and television news is that both instruments have grown up as an incompatible combination of show business, advertising, and news. Each of the three is a rather bizarre and demanding profession. And when you get all three under one roof, the dust never settles. The top management of the networks, with a few notable exceptions, has been trained in advertising, research, sales, or show business. But, by the nature of the corporate structure, they also make the final and crucial decisions having to do with the news and public affairs. . . .

"There is no suggestion here that networks or individual stations should operate as philanthropies. I can find nothing in the Bill of Rights or the Communications Act which says that they must increase their net profits every year, lest the republic collapse."[81]

---

[81] *The New York Times,* February 16, 1966. For further elaboration of this theme see Newton Minnow, *Equal Time: The Private Broadcasters and the Public Interest* (New York: Atheneum, 1964).

However difficult the task may be for journalists, their struggle to be "professionals" may help stop the decline in media competition. As journalists compete with each other for scoops, exclusives, and in-depth reports, news reporting maintains some of its diversity. And in their frequent conflicts with their corporate paymasters, they help maintain some balance of power in an otherwise concentrated industry. The sameness and blandness, though not the political power, of the mass media are easy to overestimate. Single voices do speak out against the tide of national opinion, occasionally with great impact. For example, individual reporters challenged the wisdom of our Indochina policies early and persistently. With courage and conviction, some welcomed desegregation of public schools and helped bring ecology and pollution problems to the fore of national attention. For the time being, at least, in the marketplace of political ideas, there are some competing brands.

SUMMARY

As pressure groups have become more powerful, political parties have weakened, until we now have pressure groups over-representing the powerful, and political parties under-representing those without power. Pressure groups differ from political parties in that the pressure groups try to influence specific policies rather than gain control of the government as a whole. Nor do pressure groups offer candidates of their own for election, but they supplement the official system of representation by giving special representation to minorities.

The aggressiveness and pressure of lobbyists before Congress vary with: (1) the nature of the group (single-issue groups are tough and uncompromising); (2) the presence or absence of competition among groups (on many issues powerful groups collaborate to produce lopsided pressure); (3) the nature of the policy decision (only when specific decision making is delegated to bureaucrats can Congress play competing groups off against each other); and (4) the ethics of the group (some resort to unethical or even illegal pressure, e.g., bribery).

Pressure groups derive strength from the American political environment, with its rights of free speech and petition, its decentralized governmental structure, and its weak political parties. Each group's own status, organization, leadership, social base, and doctrines further influence its strength. The strength of pressure groups as a whole is increased by collaboration among groups.

Besides lobbying, pressure group tactics include mass advertising to influence public opinion, and helping cooperative candidates get elected. Informal checks on these groups come from their own intergroup competition, the inability of groups to mobilize all their members, the threat of potential groups, and political parties. The formal government is the most authoritative check on the power of private groups.

The mass media have come to be as significant as parties and pressure groups in the political system. The mass media regulate the flow of demands into the political system (by deciding what will or will not be publicized);

214

PART 2
inputs of the
political
system: who
wants and needs
what?

they are "loyal opposition" to the administration, and they screen candidates.

The media bias their presentation of politicians by focusing mainly on those of national interest (such as senators) and by highlighting the weaknesses of public officials at all levels (thus contributing to the lack of trust in government).

Television stations all over the country are affiliated with the three major networks: the American, Columbia, and National broadcasting companies. This concentration of power has turned the mass media into a big business that is more concerned with profit than with social issues. Journalists concerned with objectivity and the public's "right to know" tend to clash with the business-minded owners and directors of the media.

the
electoral
system

216

PART 2
inputs of the
political
system: who
wants and needs
what?

As the 1980 campaign for President got under way, the *Los Angeles Times* poll asked a sample of Americans, "Do you think our system of nominating a President is basically sound or not too sound?" The newspaper's analysts were surprised to find 70 percent of the respondents saying the system is basically sound. Their surprise stemmed from the contrasting evaluation of presumed experts: "Professors, pundits, and politicians often complain that America's system of nominating its presidential candidates is too drawn out, too awkward, too exhausting, too costly and unfair."[1]

Why do the experts and the general public judge the electoral system so differently? The most obvious answer is that students of any social institution are almost always critical of what they see, for they know of other arrangements that might be better. Average citizens, on the other hand, are more willing to accept whatever exists, for most are not acquainted with any alternatives. As Thomas Jefferson said in the Declaration of Independence, "mankind are more disposed to suffer, while evils are sufferable, than to right themselves by abolishing the forms to which they are accustomed." But another explanation may be that the reformist generation of the late 1960s *did* find the "evils" of the old system insufferable and achieved a greater role for the general public in presidential nominations. Whether this greater role is good or bad is, like everything in politics, debatable.[2]

THE ELECTORAL SYSTEM AS AN OFFICIAL AGENCY OF GOVERNMENT

Only about one fourth of the nations of the world hold elections in which the adult population freely chooses among competing candidates. Heredity is the route to public office on the island monarchy of Tonga. The military coup is most common in Argentina. The Communist party's choice is followed by ratification (without opposition) at the polls in the Soviet Union. Although Americans regard competitive elections as the "natural" way to decide who will manage public affairs, the system is really a relatively recent innovation.

The U.S. Constitution only roughly outlines the leadership selection process, but it does set forth the essential features of any election system: who is eligible for public office and a way of choosing among those who are eligible.

---

[1] George Skelton, "U.S. Political Process—The Voters Like It," *Los Angeles Times,* January 27, 1980.

[2] For expert analyses sympathetic to the opening up of the electoral system, see William J. Crotty, *Political Reform and the American Experiment* (New York: Thomas Y. Crowell, 1977); *Decision for the Democrats* (Baltimore: Johns Hopkins University Press, 1978); and (with Crotty as editor) *Paths to Political Reform* (Lexington, Mass.: Heath, 1980). Less sympathetic interpretations are in Austin Ranney, *Curing the Mischiefs of Faction: Party Reform in America* (Berkeley: University of California Press, 1975) and *The Federalization of Presidential Primaries* (Washington, D.C.: American Enterprise Institute, 1978); also Nelson W. Polsby and Aaron Wildavsky, *Presidential Elections: Strategies of American Electoral Politics,* 5th ed. (New York: Charles Scribner's Sons, 1980).

Constitutional provisions on political recruitment

The constitutional provisions on eligibility for national office are quite simple. Representatives must be at least 25 years old; they must have been U.S. citizens for at least 7 years, and must live in the states in which they are elected. Senators must be 30 years old, must have been citizens for 9 years, and also must live in the states in which they are elected. The President must be at least 35 and a natural-born citizen who has resided in the United States for at least 14 years. No eligibility requirements are provided for judges and other national officials appointed by the President.

Such minor restrictions on eligibility represent an opposite extreme from the restrictions of some systems. Where no one is eligible for an office except a single person—the eldest male in a particular family, for example—the office may be said to be officially *assigned*. Where many people are eligible, as in the United States, official status is based on *achievement* rather than official assignment.[3]

If eligibility requirements are simple, the manner in which we choose national officials from the many who are eligible is extremely complicated. The Constitution does not include detailed procedures: the system for choosing members of Congress is left to the states, subject to alteration by Congress. Election of the President must be by electors, again selected as the state legislature may provide. Judges and other officers of the United States are appointed by the President with the advice and consent of the Senate. These procedures ensure a different constituency for every branch of the government. The Constitution also provides different terms of office for members of each branch: 2 years for representatives, 6 for senators, 4 for the President, and during "good behavior" for judges.

Nominating procedures are not mentioned in the Constitution, except for the provision that the President "shall *nominate*, and by and with the advice and consent of the Senate, shall appoint" Supreme Court justices and certain other national officials. With the Constitution silent on the subject, nominating procedures for presidential and congressional candidates were developed by political parties. These procedures go so far in determining who governs that they are clearly an important part of our constitutional system, despite their neglect in the written Constitution. Moreover, as we shall see below, decisions by both the Supreme Court and Congress have taken the nominating process out of the exclusive control of political parties. Nominations are thus a part of the official constitutional system.

Authoritative election decisions

The crucial decisions of an election concern: (1) Who will be the candidates for each party's nomination? (2) Who will be nominated? (3) Who will be

---

[3] As we shall see below, informal requirements add considerably to the restrictions on eligibility. Women, for example, have been effectively if informally banned from the presidency.

218

PART 2
inputs of the
political
system: who
wants and needs
what?

elected? As we go from the first to the third decision, the number of partici-pants increases from hundreds to thousands to millions. Authoritative decision making on the choice of rulers in the United States eventually involves all its many millions of voters.

Each voter has, of course, only a minuscule fraction of the decision-making authority. But on election day, the normally small circle of authoritative deci-sion making is expanded to include every voter. In this chapter we shall accordingly focus first on the voters, second on nominations, third on the election process, and finally on the general place of elections in the political system.

FORMAL VOTING REQUIREMENTS

Americans must personally take the initiative to register if they want to vote. In many states they must register far in advance of the election, at a time before interest in the election has developed. Elections are held on working days. These features of elections in the United States seem simple, but they help account for the fact that over half of the eligible citizens fail to vote in congressional elections, and almost half fail to vote in presidential elections. In Italy and Germany, where registration is automatic and elections are held on Sunday, voter turnout has been much higher since World War II: over 92 percent in Italy and from 78 percent to 88 percent in West Germany.[4] Clearly, we cannot understand voting behavior without taking into account official controls over elections.

The extension of voting rights

The original Constitution let the states decide who could vote. Presidential electors are chosen in whatever manner the state legislatures provide; repre-sentatives (and, through the Seventeenth Amendment, senators) are chosen by voters in each state who are qualified to vote for "the most numerous branch of the State legislature." The question of how far to go toward democ-racy was too divisive an issue to be handled by the framers of the Constitution. As good politicians, they evaded direct action by leaving the matter in the hands of the states. For those favoring popular control, this was probably fortunate, for the Constitutional Convention was less in favor of majority rule than were the first state constitutions. Even so, by modern standards of democ-racy the varying state requirements for eligibility to vote in the early years

[4] In Italy, for example, the polls are open not only on Sunday but also on Monday until noon. On the U.S. requirements, see Steven J. Rosenstone and Raymond E. Wolfinger, "The Effect of Registration Laws on Voter Turnout," *American Political Science Review*, 72 (March 1978), 22–48. A more comprehensive study is their volume, *Who Votes?* (New Haven: Yale University Press, 1980).

of the Republic were highly restrictive. Although popular suffrage (the right to vote) came to the United States earlier than to other countries, and although the trend has been toward extension of the right to vote, even today the requirements for voting in the United States are stricter than in many other democracies.

Religious qualifications for voting were the first general restrictions to be eliminated. These restrictions prevailed in the original New England colonies but were being eliminated by the time of the Revolution. Somewhat slower to fall were a second set of restrictions: property-holding and taxpaying barriers. But by the time of the Civil War, most free men could vote. Around the turn of the century, the southern states adopted a new type of taxpaying requirement, an annual "poll tax" of one or two dollars that had to be paid before a citizen could vote. The desire to prevent black citizens from voting united southern whites in support of the poll tax. Many upper-status whites were pleased that the tax also decreased voting by poor whites, who would nevertheless accept the poll tax because of their racial prejudice. The idea of a government making it harder rather than easier to vote seemed so undemocratic that the poll tax fell into disfavor even in the South. The adoption of the Twenty-fourth Amendment in 1964 made the poll tax unconstitutional for national elections. Two years later the Supreme Court found it unconstitutional for state elections as well.

Race has been a third ground for denial of the vote. Although the Fifteenth Amendment, adopted shortly after the Civil War, provides that states cannot deny the vote "on account of race, color, or previous condition of servitude," southern states found a variety of devices, legal and illegal, to nullify this prohibition effectively until well into the twentieth century. The poll tax and literacy tests were among these devices, but the basic barrier for about the first 40 years of this century was the "white primary." The Democratic party restricted its membership—and thus participation in its primaries—to white voters. Blacks, unable to vote in the primary election, could not influence the choice of candidates in areas where the Democratic nominee always won the general election. The Fifteenth Amendment prohibited any *state* from denying the vote, but the Supreme Court viewed the Democratic party as a private association to which state election regulations did not apply. Consequently, the white primary seemed a perfect weapon for the guardians of "white supremacy."

In 1944, however, the Supreme Court took a closer, more realistic look at the situation and decided that the white primary was part of a continuous process for choosing public officials.[5] Since the primary was endorsed and enforced by the state—for example, the state certified party nominees for inclusion on the general election ballot—the Court ruled that the denial of the ballot to blacks by the Democratic party constituted state action in violation of the Fifteenth Amendment. The result was an increase in black voter regis-

[5] *Smith v. Allwright,* 321 U.S. 649 (1944). In *U.S. v. Classic,* 313 U.S. 299 (1941), the Supreme Court had already determined that "where the primary is by law made an integral part of the election machinery," Congress has constitutional power to regulate primary as well as general elections.

220

PART 2
inputs of the
political
system: who
wants and needs
what?

tration. The estimated number of black voters in the South was 250,000 in 1940. The number had doubled within 2 years after the Supreme Court decision. In 1960 it had reached almost 1.5 million; in 1964 it skimmed past 2 million; and by the mid-seventies, it reached 3.5 million.[6] Since 1945, blacks have been elected to over 1,300 offices in the South, from city commissioner to state legislator, and every southern state has blacks in elective office.[7]

Much of this progress has been due to the Civil Rights Acts of 1957, 1960, 1964, and 1965, which all had as their major goal the elimination of racial discrimination in voter registration in the southern states. These laws demonstrate that if legislation cannot eliminate prejudice, it can greatly reduce prejudicial behavior. The Voting Rights Act of 1965, generally regarded as the most effective civil rights legislation ever enacted, made four important changes:

1. Directed the Attorney General to challenge the constitutionality of state poll taxes (this led to the Supreme Court decision noted above, declaring such taxes unconstitutional).

2. Suspended literacy tests and similar devices in all states or counties in which less than 50 percent of voting age citizens were registered to vote in 1964.

3. Provided for the appointment of federal examiners to register voters in these areas and to oversee the election process.

4. Required officials in the areas covered to submit any changes in election laws to the Attorney General for preclearance, with the changes subject to veto if they are found discriminatory.

In the year after passage of the act, federal examiners went into 60 counties, and black voter registration in the states principally affected—Alabama, Georgia, Louisiana, Mississippi, and South Carolina—increased by 78 percent. In 1975 the Voting Rights Act of 1965 was extended to 1982, with these additional provisions:

1. Preclearance and federal observer protections were extended to "language minorities" in areas where

   a) over 5 percent of voting age citizens are of a single language minority

   b) election materials were printed only in English for the 1972 presidential election

   c) less than 50 percent of voting age citizens were registered or voted in the 1972 presidential election

---

[6] These estimates are only rough approximations because of the decentralized character of registration records. They are based on: Henry Lee Moon, "The Negro Vote in the South: 1952," *The Nation* (Sept. 27, 1952), 245–48; Margaret Price, *The Negro and the Ballot in the South* (Atlanta: Southern Regional Council, 1959); *Report of the United States Commission on Civil Rights: 1959* (Washington, D.C.: Government Printing Office, 1959); *1961 Commission on Civil Rights Report: Voting,* Book 1 (Washington, D.C.: Government Printing Office, 1961); Voter Education Project, *Voter Registration in the South, Summer, 1968* (Atlanta: Southern Regional Council, Inc., 1968). An excellent overview has been written by David J. Garrow, *Protest at Selma: Martin Luther King, Jr., and the Voting Rights Act of 1965* (New Haven: Yale University Press, 1978), chap. 1.

[7] David Campbell and Joe R. Reagin, "Black Politics in the South: A Descriptive Analysis," *Journal of Politics,* 37 (February 1975), 129–62.

DIRECTIONS FOR VOTING ON THE VOTING MACHINE

PULL the red handle of the curtain lever (lower left side of the machine) from the left to right as far as it will go and **leave it there** (this will close the curtain around you and unlock the machine for voting).

The Voter about to Close the Curtain   The Voter Closing the Curtain   The Curtain Closed the Voter Inside, Voting

On the ballot shown at the right you will find title of public office or party positions. The names of the candidates or group of candidates will follow under each title. Turn down the pointer at the right of the candidate or candidates you wish to vote for until an ☒ mark appears at the right of each candidate's name for whom you intend to vote, and leave the ☒ mark showing, from

this

John Doe

to this

John Doe ☒

Leaving the pointer or pointers down in their voting position, pull the red handle of the curtain lever to the left as far as it will go and leave it there (this will register your vote and return the pointers to their first position, after which the curtain will open).

DIRECCIONES PARA USAR LA MÁQUINA DE VOTAR

AL entrar en la cabina Ud. verá en la esquina izquierda de la máquina una palanca roja, muévala hasta el extremo derecho y la cortina quedará cerrada. La máquina está ya lista para votar.

Votante moviendo la palanca   Votante cerrando la cortina   Cerrado la cortina, el votante hace su votación.

En las listas de la derecha, Ud. tiene los títulos y nombres de los candidatos para los diferentes puestos de cada partido. Debajo de los títulos se hallan los nombres de cada candidato o grupo de candidatos. Vire Ud. hacia la izquierda el pequeño indicador negro que se encuentra a la derecha del candidato o candidatos por quienes Ud. quiere votar hasta que aparezca una ☒ al lado del nombre. Haga Ud. lo mismo con todos sus candidatos preferidos dejando los indicadores hacia abajo enseñando la ☒.

Bilingual ballots are required in areas with significant numbers of language minorities.

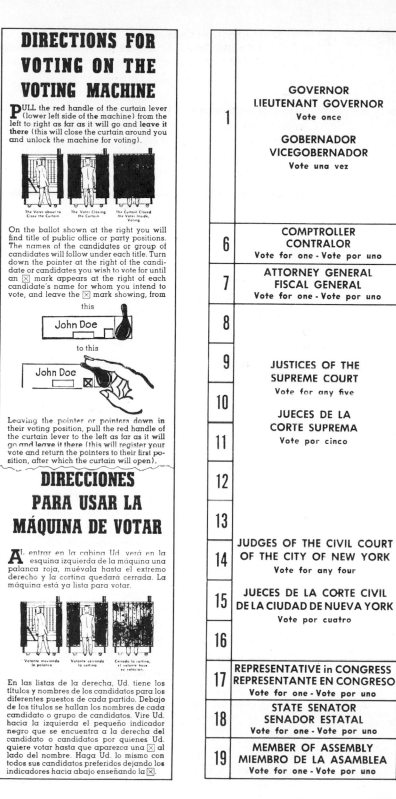

1	**GOVERNOR** **LIEUTENANT GOVERNOR** Vote once **GOBERNADOR** **VICEGOBERNADOR** Vote una vez
6	**COMPTROLLER** **CONTRALOR** Vote for one - Vote por uno
7	**ATTORNEY GENERAL** **FISCAL GENERAL** Vote for one - Vote por uno
8	
9	**JUSTICES OF THE** **SUPREME COURT** Vote for any five **JUECES DE LA** **CORTE SUPREMA** Vote por cinco
10	
11	
12	
13	
14	**JUDGES OF THE CIVIL COURT** **OF THE CITY OF NEW YORK** Vote for any four **JUECES DE LA CORTE CIVIL** **DE LA CIUDAD DE NUEVA YORK** Vote por cuatro
15	
16	
17	**REPRESENTATIVE in CONGRESS** **REPRESENTANTE EN CONGRESO** Vote for one - Vote por uno
18	**STATE SENATOR** **SENADOR ESTATAL** Vote for one - Vote por uno
19	**MEMBER OF ASSEMBLY** **MIEMBRO DE LA ASAMBLEA** Vote for one - Vote por uno

222

PART 2
inputs of the
political
system: who
wants and needs
what?

2. Bilingual elections were required for the language minority areas specified above and also for areas with significant numbers of language minorities whose illiteracy rate was above the national average (all of Alaska and parts of 24 other states).

3. The temporary ban on literacy tests became permanent.

These provisions finally put the national government in the position of actively promoting the *right* to vote, rather than merely preventing the states from being excessively restrictive on the *privilege* of voting.

A fourth general barrier to voting—the denial of the vote to women— was not broken down completely until the Nineteenth Amendment was adopted in 1920. The struggle for female suffrage began before the Civil War and was closely linked to the movement to abolish slavery. Success had been achieved in 15 states before the federal amendment was adopted. The extremist arguments on both sides now appear highly "sexist," for women have neither been "unsexed" and degraded by political participation, nor have they purified politics by their "loftier" morals. According to one historian of the crusade:

[two] supreme influences were implacably opposed to suffrage for women: the corporations because it would vastly increase the votes of the working classes, the liquor interests because they were fully aware of the hostility of women to their business and everything connected with it.[8]

As things turned out, the first of these groups need not have worried: not many women, especially working class women, turned out to vote for several decades after the achievement of women's suffrage.[9] The liquor interests, on the other hand, did have reason to worry, for in all countries where votes can be compared in terms of sex, women favor more strict regulation or curtailment of the liquor industry than do men.

The fifth and last general obstacle to voting—disqualification by age— still exists, but the required age was set at 18 by the Twenty-sixth Amendment in 1971. As far back as 1954, President Eisenhower had recommended a constitutional amendment to fix 18 as a uniform voting age, but support for the proposal was not intense enough to carry it through the cumbersome amendment process. Until 1970, the required age for voting in most states was 21, but a few states had lower voting ages (Georgia and Kentucky, 18; Alaska, 19; Hawaii, 20). Because of these variations and because 18-year-olds are subject to the same military duty and other legal obligations as 21-year-olds, many people felt that most states denied 18-, 19-, and 20-year-olds their constitutional right to equal protection of the laws. Indeed, this was precisely the argument used by Senator Edward M. Kennedy (D.-Mass.) in pushing through a congressional requirement of the vote for 18-year-olds in 1970.

[8] Ida Husted Harper, *The History of Woman Suffrage* (New York: National American Woman Suffrage Association, 1922), Vol. 5, p. xviii. Quoted in V. O. Key, Jr., *Politics, Parties, and Pressure Groups*, 5th ed. (New York: Thomas Y. Crowell, 1964), p. 614.

[9] On the early gap in participation, see Angus Campbell et al., *The American Voter* (New York: Wiley, 1960), chap. 5. On recent turnout trends, see David B. Hill and Norman R. Luttbeg, *Trends in American Electoral Behavior* (Itasca, Ill.: F. E. Peacock Publishers, 1980), chap. 3.

Most proponents of a lower voting age had long conceded that the change depended on a constitutional amendment. But after years of bitter protests by American youth against America's military intervention in Vietnam, and with evidence of increasing feelings of alienation toward government among the young citizens forced to fight in that war, only "strict constructionists" such as President Nixon argued that Congress lacked the constitutional authority to set 18 as the maximum age for voting. To the surprise of such strict constructionists, who insisted that the Constitution gave the states discretion in establishing voting standards, the Supreme Court upheld the right of Congress to grant the vote to 18-year-olds in national elections. The Court declined to extend its decision to cover state and local elections, but the momentum behind the change was so great that the Twenty-sixth Amendment extended the provision to all elections the following year. Under this Amendment, neither the national government nor the states may deny the right to vote to any citizen who is 18 or older.

Voting as a right, not a privilege

Is voting a right or a privilege? Is the task of government to encourage voting or to keep the ballot out of unworthy hands? Official policy throughout most of American history suggests the restrictive answer to both of these questions, but recent signs of change have appeared.

As we have seen, the framers of the Constitution doubted the ability of the people to vote responsibly. In opposing popular election of the President, one of the Virginia delegates argued that it would be "as unnatural to refer the choice of a proper character for chief magistrate to the people as it would to refer a trial of colours to a blind man." From its highly restricted beginning, the American electorate has greatly expanded. Old barriers based on religion, property ownership, tax payments, race, sex, and age have been removed or (in the case of age) reduced. But until very recently the government has done nothing positively to encourage voting. Until the 1960s, the most the national government did was to eliminate the state-imposed barriers to voting, listed above. Finally, however, the Civil Rights Act of 1960 provided for the appointment of federal "referees" to register potential voters when the courts found a "pattern or practice" of depriving blacks of their vote in a specified area. This began a program of active government support of the right to vote, which was extended by later acts. In 1970 all voting residence requirements of longer than 30 days for national elections were abolished. In 1975 government support was extended, as we saw, to language minorities. The government requirement that election materials be printed in minority languages in specified areas is much more than a formal protection; it is active encouragement to vote.

Overall, the changes of the last decade have moved the United States far toward a nationally defined electorate. Most of the barriers to voting have now fallen. In 1970, Representative Morris Udall (D.-Ariz.) began pushing a Universal Enrollment Plan under which the national government would play

23

CHAPTER 7
the
electoral
system

224

PART 2
inputs of the
political
system: who
wants and needs
what?

an active role in a door-to-door effort to enroll all eligible citizens as voters. The country has finally moved a long way from the day in which politics was thought to be the exclusive preserve of "gentlemen of principle and property." The greatest remaining barrier is that the voter must register in person before the election. Existing registration restrictions are estimated to have decreased turnout in national elections by about 9 percent.[10] When the United States moves toward some form of government enrollment of citizens, we can more accurately call voting a right rather than a privilege.

NOMINATING THE CANDIDATES

Over 90 million American citizens were legally eligible for election as President in 1980. But in the election, the voters had an effective choice among only three people. What happened to the other 90 million or more possibilities? They were eliminated by the nominating process. If nominations take care of 99.9 percent of the political recruitment function, they are quite evidently a major part of the electoral system.

Caucuses and conventions

The first stage in the official election process in the United States is the nomination of candidates to represent each party (or independent group) that is seeking public office.[11] In other democracies, nominations are made informally by party organizations or caucuses. But in the United States the nomination has taken on an official and elaborate form. The basic reason for this difference is probably that American political parties are less responsible as a group for the conduct of government than are the parties in other democratic regimes. Where voters are certain that the platform of a party will be supported by all its members in the legislature, they need not be especially concerned about which member gets the party nomination. Americans do not enjoy that certainty; consequently, the person who seeks office under the party label takes on greater importance as an individual.

The first nominating device used by American political parties, for both national and state office, was the legislative *caucus*. The caucus was composed of party members in Congress (or in the legislature for state elections). But the Jacksonian Democrats denounced the caucus as an undemocratic device and advocated the party convention as a means of ensuring at least indirect nomination by the party rank and file. Although the convention came into universal use during the nineteenth century as the means of choosing nominees

---

[10] Rosenstone and Wolfinger, "The Effects of Registration Laws . . . ," p. 41. Also see Polsby and Wildavsky, *Presidential Elections,* pp. 240–44.

[11] Although most states permit independent candidates to secure nomination, generally by a petition signed by a given percentage of the voters, party nominees dominate.

to state offices, it came to be associated with boss rule and domination by special interests during the Progressive Era in the twentieth century. Like the caucus before it, the convention was discarded for a more popular method of nomination. Today, representatives, senators, and most state officers are nominated by direct primary elections, and party conventions persist only in nominations for the presidency.

Direct primary elections

The direct primary really serves as a preliminary official election. It is usually conducted under state laws, just as the subsequent general election is, and it provides the members of each party with an opportunity to take part in choosing the party's nominees. Aspirants to the United States Senate, the House of Representatives, and to various state offices secure a place on the primary ballot either by simply announcing their candidacy and paying a fee or by presenting a petition signed by a required number of voters. Candidates for nomination may enter only their own party's primary, and in most states they must be able to demonstrate that they are actually members of the party—by attesting that they supported its nominees in the last general election, for example.

Direct primary elections are either "closed" or "open." In the closed primary, voters must be able to demonstrate that they are party members, and they may vote only in the primary of their own party. The tests of party allegiance are often quite simple, involving merely an assertion of past, present, or future identification with the party—that one voted for the party nominees in the last general election, is a member of the party, or plans to vote for the candidates nominated by the party. In about half the states, however, party affiliation is recorded at registration, and one is not permitted to vote in the primary of any other party without changing registration. In the open primary, on the other hand, any qualified citizen may vote in the primary of any party. Party regulars resent the idea that nonmembers can affect the choice of party nominees and condemn the open primary as destructive of party responsibility.

To what extent has the direct primary succeeded in "democratizing" party nominations? Nomination by direct primaries has decreased the extent to which a statewide organization can control nominations, but it has not brought about the selection of candidates by a broad cross section of party members. In the first place, participation in primaries has been disappointingly low. The turnout in presidential primaries has averaged about 28 percent of the eligible electorate, roughly half the turnout in presidential elections.[12]

In the second place, the small number who do vote in primaries do not

[12] See Austin Ranney, *Participation in American Presidential Nominations, 1976* (Washington, D.C.: American Enterprise Institute, 1977), p. 20. On earlier years, see his "Turnout and Representation in Presidential Primary Elections," *American Political Science Review,* 68 (March 1972), 21–37. V. O. Key, Jr., *American State Politics* (New York: Knopf, 1956) is an earlier work on the same problem at the state level.

226

PART 2
inputs of the
political
system: who
wants and needs
what?

accurately represent the entire party following. In Massachusetts, for example, the Boston area has supplied about half the Democratic party's primary election votes but only a third of the party's general election votes. As a result, Boston—which supplied only one out of four Democratic nominees for state office under the convention system—came to supply over 80 percent of the Democratic nominees under the primary system.

Functions of the national convention

Although the party convention has been replaced by the direct primary in nominations for Congress and most state offices, it remains alive in the nomination of presidential candidates. Indeed, the national nominating conventions of the political parties are as American as baseball, violence, and hotdogs. Spectators at national conventions are usually awed, shocked, or repulsed by the noise, numbers, and hard bargaining that characterize this quadrennial political pageant. Many observers regard the circus atmosphere as inappropriate to the choice of a candidate for one of the world's most powerful positions. Like war veterans, businesspeople, and other nonpolitical conventioneers, American politicians do make a holiday of the convention, but they also manage to accomplish serious and generally successful work.[13]

Intended consequences. The principal function of the national convention is to nominate candidates who will serve as the party's standard-bearers in the quest for America's most prized political plum—the presidency of the United States. A second function is to create enthusiasm, both inside and outside the convention, for the party and its presidential and vice-presidential candidates. Third, the convention serves to suggest the party's position on the key issues of the day, perhaps more by the candidates it selects than by the platform it adopts.

The selection of candidates, the creation of support, and the adoption of positions on issues are the intended consequences or purposes of the convention. But the convention system also has unintended consequences that are frequently overlooked.

Unintended consequences. For the parties themselves, the most important of these unintended results is the creation or ratification of party consensus. Through bargains and compromises, the convention unites 50 state parties into a single national party, at least for the duration of the campaign. Occasionally, the convention fails to bring about this unity, and such failures show the importance of this latent function. The Republican convention of 1964 could be called dysfunctional (destructive) so far as party unity is con-

---

[13] For a detailed treatment of the history of party conventions, see Paul T. David, Ralph M. Goldman, and Richard C. Bain, *The Politics of National Party Conventions* (Washington, D.C.: Brookings, 1960); also Richard C. Bain and Judith H. Parris, *Convention Decisions and Voting Records*, 2nd ed. (Washington, D.C.: Brookings, 1973) and Denis G. Sullivan et al., *Explorations in Convention Decision Making: The Democratic Party in the 1970s* (San Francisco: Freeman, 1976).

cerned. Even so, none of the major Republican leaders left the party to support the Democrats, and most went through at least the motions of supporting Senator Goldwater. The 1972 Democratic convention perhaps best illustrates the fact that conventions can be highly dysfunctional. The bitter divisions in the party over the Vietnam war were worsened rather than healed by the convention. The party was in a state of shambles rather than unity at the end of the convention. The resulting loss of morale and contributions spelled defeat.

The convention's second unintended function is that of a ceremony or ritual in which the democratic nature of parties is celebrated. For a few days every 4 years, hundreds of minor figures enjoy the official right to decide on the destiny of their party. Although the candidate who has emerged as frontrunner in the presidential primaries typically wins nomination on the first convention ballot, formal nomination occurs at the convention. Moreover, in addition to voting for a presidential nominee, the delegates settle disputes over credentials, adopt rules of procedure, and produce a party platform. In all the decisions, any delegate may challenge the vote as reported by the delegation's chairperson. The exercise of this right and the subsequent poll of the delegation reaffirm the dependence of the leaders on their followers.

Third, the national convention, by doing away with the intent of the electoral college procedures prescribed in the Constitution, has become one of the key devices through which political parties have democratized the choice of the President. Here we see an unexpected development of great importance for the political system as a whole rather than simply for the parties themselves. The expectation of the Constitutional Convention that members of the electoral college would exercise independent judgment in voting for a President and Vice-president was quickly dashed by the development of political parties. And the convention has succeeded better than the party caucus in turning the electoral college into a recording device for its choices as endorsed by the electorate. Conventions as noisy gatherings of the party faithful, representing members in all the states and territories, give the party rank and file an influence that would have horrified the more genteel among the Founding Fathers, who recoiled at the thought of such turbulent "mob action."

A fourth indirect consequence is the basic nature of our national party system. V. O. Key went so far as to imply that our national system of party government itself is a direct function of the national convention: "When the national convention was contrived to designate presidential nominees, viable national party came into existence."[14] This is probably too strong a statement, as another comment by Key himself suggests. "Without [the national convention] or some equivalent institution, party government for the nation as a whole could scarcely exist." The crucial phrase here is "or some equivalent institution." Other nations without national nominating conventions have national party systems. Without this particular nominating device, we would probably also have developed something else, such as a national presidential primary election.

[14] Key, *Politics, Parties, and Pressure Groups*, p. 431.

228

PART 2
inputs of the
political
system: who
wants and needs
what?

National conventions in action

The national conventions are held in the summer of the election year. The preliminary work is done by 4 committees. The committee on *credentials* judges the qualifications of delegates and recommends solutions of disputes to the convention as a whole. In the convention, the "temporary roll," compiled by the national committee, determines which of the contending delegates will be seated. Bitter disputes occasionally produce an early indication of which faction controls the convention. In the Democratic convention of 1972, the delegations from California, where Senator George McGovern had won in a winner-take-all primary, and from Illinois, where Chicago Mayor Richard Daley had put together an anti-McGovern slate, were both challenged. When the McGovern delegation from California was seated and the Daley delegates from Chicago were ousted, it was clear that McGovern supporters were in control of the convention.

The committee on *permanent organization* nominates a permanent chairperson and standing committees to replace the temporary officers who were appointed by the national committee. The chief function of the temporary chairperson is to deliver a keynote address praising the party and condemning the opposition. The permanent chairperson presides over the convention. Both are key officers, and their selection is another indication of which faction holds control. The President usually controls these choices for his party, but they may be hotly disputed in the opposition party.

The committee on *rules* recommends a set of rules to govern the convention. Generally, it recommends that the rules of the House of Representatives be adopted insofar as they are applicable.

The committee on *resolutions* draws up the party platform—a statement of the policies the party will follow if its candidates are elected. Although party platforms are often said to be meaningless, one study of platforms found that three-fourths of the policy pledges are fulfilled.[15] The platform committee conducts hearings at which interested persons may appear, but the basic platform is settled in advance by the group in control of the convention.

The chief business of the convention—the nomination of a candidate for President—begins with an alphabetic roll call of the states. This is an occasion for nominating and seconding speeches in behalf of those seeking the nomination. Then the voting begins, again by the states in alphabetical order, and is continued until one of the candidates receives a majority. If no candidate captures a majority on the first ballot—a rarity since World War II—bargaining among factions increases. During such contests, a losing candidate can gain influence—or even the vice-presidency—by shifting to the apparent winner at the right moment. By means of such bargaining, the convention performs its function of uniting the party behind a single candidate. The symbol of this achievement is the common practice of making the vote unanimous once the outcome has become clear.

[15] Gerald Pomper, *Elections in America: Control and Influence in Democratic Politics* (New York: Dodd, Mead, 1968), chaps. 7 and 8.

"You don't have to vote, Sam. The networks predicted the winner three hours ago."

The nomination of the vice-presidential candidate has traditionally been a much less dramatic matter. The presidential nominee has a strong voice in the selection of his runningmate, and his nod frequently goes to an opponent whose supporters helped the winner gain his majority. This is especially true if the opponent can "balance the ticket" by representing a different area of the country, policy position, or faction of the party. Ironically, then, the vice-presidential candidate has often been one of the party figures *least* likely to ensure continuity should the President die in office. This irony is increased by the fact that 9 of the 38 men who have served as President moved into the office from the vice-presidency.

The degree to which the mass media have come to dominate American politics is seen in the staged-for-television quality of today's party conventions. Since the first telecast of national conventions in 1952, television coverage has come to be a prime (as in *prime time*) concern in the location, staging, and scheduling of conventions. The leisurely, nontheatrical style of the past can no longer be permitted. As Stephen Wayne points out, "timing is perhaps the most critical element."[16] The managers of the convention try to schedule major unifying events to get maximum national attention. The presidential nominee's acceptance speech, for example, will ideally be at 10:30 P.M. Eastern Daylight Savings Time. Delaying McGovern's 1972 acceptance of the Democratic nomination until 2:48 A.M. was thus a portent of a disastrous campaign.

The television networks, even more than convention leaders, are committed to a maximum audience, for that is their overriding concern. Thus television, seeking drama, emphasizes conflict, disunity, and turmoil whenever they can be found. Party leaders, in contrast, want an audience only for the positive, unifying events of the convention. The inevitable result is tension between media and parties.

---

[16] Stephen J. Wayne, *The Road to the White House: The Politics of Presidential Elections* (New York: St. Martin's Press, 1980), p. 126.

Americans have the most elaborate procedure in the world for picking candidates for their highest office. Nevertheless, the number of Americans with any chance of becoming President is minuscule. In the first 36 years of Gallup polling on the subject, only 109 people (62 Democrats, 47 Republicans) were named by as many as one percent of their fellow party members as presidential possibilities.[17] The number of people with any real chance of being nominated for President is thus very small. How do these presidential possibilities emerge? The two key factors appear to be *favorable attention from the mass media* and *availability* in the sense of occupying a political office regarded as good preparation for the presidency.

In analyzing the mass media (in chapter 6) we discovered that it has gone far toward taking over from political parties the task of screening and selecting candidates. The kind of media attention needed for one to emerge as a presidential possibility is, for the most part, not for sale. Just any publicity won't do; it must be publicity that is seen in a political, preferably a presidential, context.[18] Otherwise, Robert Redford and Bo Derek would probably have been viewed as presidential possibilities. As former governors, Jimmy Carter (in 1976) and Ronald Reagan (in 1980) had to be taken seriously as soon as they began to win delegate support.

The second factor, availability, refers to occupying an office regarded as a training ground for Presidents. Among the 109 people regarded as presidential possibilities in Gallup polls from 1936 to 1972, 90 percent held some public office, and most of the others had some close link to public affairs; for example, prominent generals (Douglas MacArthur, Dwight Eisenhower) or close relatives of Presidents (Milton Eisenhower, Theodore Roosevelt, Jr., James Roosevelt). Cabinet officers, U.S. representatives, mayors, and Supreme Court justices are among the sources of presidential possibilities. But three public offices stood out: the vice-presidency, the United States Senate, and state governorships furnished 60 percent of all people who surfaced in the polls as presidential possibilities.

Putting it the other way around, *all* Vice-Presidents, 10 percent of all senators, and 6 percent of all state governors emerged as possibilities. *Every* nominee who had held any public office came from one of these three offices. Two nominees (Willkie in 1940 and Eisenhower in 1952) had not held any public office at the time of their nominations. If you are not a governor, senator, or Vice-President, then, you have scant chance of nomination for the presidency. If you are the Vice-President, you are automatically under consideration. If you are a senator, especially if you're not too old you have a good chance—if not for the presidency by a direct route, at least for the vice presidency as another stepping stone. As Fig. 7·1 shows, 7 of

[17] Donald R. Matthews, "Presidential Nominations: Process and Outcomes," in James David Barber, ed., *Choosing the President* (Englewood Cliffs, N.J.: Prentice-Hall, 1974), pp. 39–40.

[18] William R. Keech and Donald R. Matthews, *The Party's Choice* (Washington: Brookings, 1976).

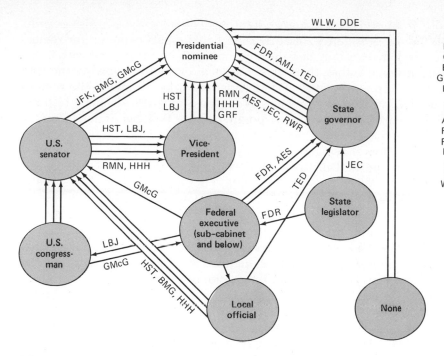

FIG. 7 · 1 Pattern of public office-holding by presidential nominees, 1937–1980.

JEC: Jimmy E. Carter
TED: Thomas E. Dewey
DDE: Dwight D. Eisenhower
GRF: Gerald R. Ford
BMG: Barry M. Goldwater
GMcG: George McGovern
HHH: Hubert H. Humphrey
LBJ: Lyndon B. Johnson
JFK: John F. Kennedy
AML: Alfred M. Landon
RMN: Richard M. Nixon
RWR: Ronald W. Reagan
FDR: Franklin D. Roosevelt
AES: Adlai E. Stevenson
HST: Harry S. Truman
WLW: Wendell L. Wilkie

the 16 nominees from 1936 to 1980 came from the Senate (3 directly, 4 via the vice-presidency). Governors are the next most prominent source, having supplied 6 nominees. Why do Vice-Presidents, senators, and governors dominate the field so completely?

The Vice-President, whatever the shortcomings of real power in the office, is guaranteed frequent publicity in a presidential context. He stands in for the President at various functions; he has usually proved his ability as a vote-getter; and next to the President, he becomes his party's best-known leader. The degree to which a Vice-President can demonstrate leadership qualities depends, of course, on the attitude of the President under whom he serves. The conspicuous roles of Walter Mondale and George Bush suggest that the vice-presidency will remain a principal source of presidential candidates. Even Hubert Humphrey, though often humiliated by Lyndon Johnson as his Vice-President, was able to win his party's nomination in 1968 after Johnson withdrew from the contest.[19] Whatever their liabilities, then, Vice-Presidents are invariably near the top of the polls as presidential possibilities.

Although not automatically thrust into consideration, a senator who wants to run for President can take advantage of a number of assets that come with the office. The mass media focus heavily on Washington, and the individualistic tradition of the Senate permits a senator to become an independent national figure. Senators have demonstrated their vote-getting ability at a statewide level; their six-year terms give them more time than governors have,

[19] Matthews, "Presidential Nominations," in Barber, ed., *Choosing the President*, p. 58.

232

PART 2
inputs of the
political
system: who
wants and needs
what?

for example, to emerge as well-known figures. The six-year term also permits "free shots" at the presidency, because their Senate seats come up for reelection in presidential years only one-third of the time. Senators deal with international and national rather than state and local problems, allowing them to develop expertise on problems of a presidential type. Finally, their votes on issues of concern to every pressure group give senators a chance to build up financial support from powerful corporate or labor Political Action Committees.

The six governors shown in Fig. 7·1 as presidential nominees are bunched at the beginning and end of the 1936–1980 period. Franklin D. Roosevelt (1936, 1940, 1944), Alfred M. Landon (1936), Thomas E. Dewey (1944, 1948), and Adlai E. Stevenson (1952, 1956) were all nominated within the first 5 elections of that 12-election span. Jimmy E. Carter (1976, 1980) and Ronald W. Reagan (1980) came in the last two elections after a 20-year period in which no governor had won either major party's nomination. During that hiatus, political scientists came to the premature conclusion that state governorships, once a chief recruiting ground for presidents, would not again produce availability. Governors were submerged, so the argument went, in unappealing provincial issues; they were far removed from everyday coverage by national television; they were often no longer the leaders of a state political machine and, even if they were, the party apparatus was of decreasing importance. These explanations for the decline in selection of governors as presidential nominees were valid for the 1956–1972 period (at least we hope so, for we were among those who offered them). But by 1976, *availability* had come to have a more literal meaning: changes in the nomination process gave a great advantage to candidates who were *available to work full time for the nomination* from one election to the next. New and complicated caucus, convention, and primary election procedures at precinct, county, district, and state levels suddenly gave a tremendous advantage to candidates who could spend several years in a full-time effort to build local support in state after state.

This change in the contest for nomination explains not only the reappearance of governors as presidential nominees but also a characteristic shared by Carter and Reagan among all the gubernatorial nominees for President: both Carter and Reagan had been out of office for several years when they won nomination. In the earlier period, every governor first won nomination as an incumbent who could take advantage of his state and party leadership. As those resources declined in importance, governors disappeared as nominees. As free time for painstaking effort to establish a personal following and organization became important, people out of office suddenly had a great advantage. The lack of office once meant the lack of a base of power for strengthening a party organization or addressing national issues. Now it means opportunity to build a personal following.

Despite the elaborate and drawn out presidential nominating process, almost all presidential possibilities since 1936 have emerged before the formal nominating process began. The pool of possible candidates is first recruited through senatorial and gubernatorial elections. From this pool of available prospects, a more select group wins the necessary attention of the mass media, to become front runners. Today nobody is surprised to hear that the national nominating conventions merely ratify decisions already made by state caucuses, conventions, and primaries. Perhaps more surprising is the finding that, for the most part, all these state-by-state nominating procedures themselves merely ratify the results of the Gallup and Harris polls at the beginning of each election year. In fact, as Table 7 · 1 shows, of the 24 major-party nominations from 1936 through 1980, 18 went to a front runner at the beginning of the election year; in 2 cases (1940 and 1964 for the Republicans) no candidate held a lead in January; only 4 clear exceptions appear.

Incumbent Presidents dominate their parties so much that we must take separate looks at the party in control and that out of control of the White

TABLE 7 · 1 | **Continuity and change in presidential nominating politics, 1936 to 1980**

Year	Leading candidate at beginning of election year	Nominee
Party in power		
1936 (D)	Roosevelt	Roosevelt
1940 (D)	Roosevelt	Roosevelt
1944 (D)	Roosevelt	Roosevelt
1948 (D)	Truman	Truman
1952 (D)	Truman	Stevenson
1956 (R)	Eisenhower	Eisenhower
1960 (R)	Nixon	Nixon
1964 (D)	Johnson	Johnson
1968 (D)	Johnson	Humphrey
1972 (R)	Nixon	Nixon
1976 (R)	Ford	Ford
1980 (D)	Carter	Carter
Party out of power		
1936 (R)	Landon	Landon
1940 (R)	?	Willkie
1944 (R)	Dewey	Dewey
1948 (R)	Dewey-Taft	Dewey
1952 (R)	Eisenhower-Taft	Eisenhower
1956 (D)	Stevenson	Stevenson
1960 (D)	Kennedy	Kennedy
1964 (R)	?	Goldwater
1968 (R)	Nixon	Nixon
1972 (D)	Muskie	McGovern
1976 (D)	Humphrey	Carter
1980 (R)	Reagan	Reagan

Source: Matthews, "Presidential Nominations," in Barber (ed.), *Choosing the President.*

234

PART 2
inputs of the
political
system: who
wants and needs
what?

House. Table 7·1 therefore shows separately the outcome of nominating politics for the in-party and the out-party. Looking first at the party in control of the White House, we see that in every case in which he was eligible for reelection, the President was the leading candidate in the polls for his party at the beginning of the election year. (In 1960, Eisenhower was ineligible under the Twenty-second Amendment.) Moreover, every President who sought nomination for another term received the nomination even when, as in 1948 and 1980, his chances of being reelected looked bad.

In two of the ten cases, the President—Truman in 1952, Johnson in 1968—withdrew from the nomination contest after faring poorly in the early primaries. Even though both could probably have won renomination, the humiliation of poor showings in the early primaries led to their withdrawals. Had the Iranian seizure of American embassy personnel in late 1979 not produced a temporary surge of support for President Carter, the primaries might have forced another withdrawal. Primaries can have an impact, then, even though an obstinate President can secure renomination. For the in-party, Matthews finds the "significant result of the primaries" in the fact that "they can raise the costs and reduce the value of renomination to a point where a deeply troubled President may decide to withdraw."

For the out-party, primaries have had an even greater impact, despite the apparent tedium of having the January front runner emerge finally as the nominee. The "rule" that the original front runner wins has been violated in 2 of the last 3 elections for the out-party. Moreover, these exceptions began as soon as the primary became the principal means of delegate selection: it was in 1972 that delegates chosen in primaries first began to make up a majority of the delegates at party conventions. Accordingly, the rule has been broken by the out-party 2-out-of-3 times since the emergence of a new mode of delegate selection. For all we know, then, the apparent exceptions may be on the way to becoming the new rule.

A new style of presidential nominations

How well does the American nominating process work? Let's consider the recent record:

1. Both parties have nominated candidates who were almost certain losers (the Republicans in 1964, the Democrats in 1972).

2. The Democratic convention of 1968 was accompanied by bloody confrontations between Chicago police and antiwar protestors, with the activity inside the hall only slightly more civil than that outside.

3. Assassins killed a leading presidential candidate in 1968 and crippled another in 1972.

4. A Vice-President resigned from office and pled no contest to charges of income tax evasion in order to avoid charges of extortion and bribery.

5. A President of the United States resigned from office to avoid impeachment for complicity in illegal activities aimed at, among other things, ensuring his reelection and influencing the opposition party's nomination.

6. The President who resigned was granted a full pardon by his successor, the man whom he had appointed to replace the tax-evading Vice-President.

7. A President with the lowest approval rating of all time (Carter) won another nomination.

8. Both parties have, in the same year (1980), nominated candidates widely regarded as unqualified by temperament or capacity for the presidency.

9. Voter turnout has steadily declined.

This record hardly qualifies as civilized, let alone satisfactory.

Each event in this miserable list produced, not surprisingly, a great wringing of hands and viewing with alarm by political experts. The Republican debacle under Barry Goldwater, who carried only five states in 1964, led to the conclusion that the Grand Old Party was less grand than it was old. Indeed, many commentators were ready to pronounce it dead or near death, only to see a suddenly revived GOP win the presidency four years later. Similarly, when George McGovern lost every state except Massachusetts (and the District of Columbia) in 1972, the pundits found the Democratic party near extinction, its coalition of supporters totally destroyed. The Democrats' victory four years later proved the pundits wrong again. Both parties may be weak, and they are viewed with great distrust, but some semblance of party is essential in elections, and these are the only ones we have. Representative John Anderson, a spurned candidate for the Republican nomination in 1980, discovered that the parties, however reviled, still dominate American elections. Running as an independent, Anderson got only 7 percent of the vote, only about half the votes George Wallace won as a third-party candidate in 1968. Much is no doubt wrong with America's electoral system, but its two major parties refuse to die.

In addition to general lamentations, the sorry record of the electoral system has produced two kinds of reform—one by the parties themselves, the other by Congress. First, in response to the fiasco that was their 1968 convention, the Democrats reformed their delegate selection and convention procedures. Second, in response to the Watergate scandals, Congress enacted the Campaign Reform Act of 1974. (We consider party reforms here and campaign financing in the following section.)

From a long-run perspective, the most drastic change in the rules governing Democratic party nominations after 1968 was the demonstration by the party's national organization that it, and not the state organizations, would henceforth control delegate selection. For over 100 years the state parties and legislatures had determined how delegates to the national convention would be chosen, while the party's national agencies—the convention and the national committee—confined their role on delegate matters to deciding how many votes each state and territory would be alloted.[20] As a reaction

---

[20] Austin Ranney, "Changing the Rules of the Nominating Game," in Barber, ed., *Choosing the President,* p. 83. On rules changes from the 1790s to the 1970s, see the comprehensive study by Austin Ranney, *Curing the Mischiefs of Faction: Party Reform in America* (Berkeley: University of California Press, 1974).

236

PART 2
inputs of the
political
system: who
wants and needs
what?

to the defiant racism of southern Democratic organizations, however, the national organization began to assert control over the states' delegate selection procedures in the 1960s.

By 1968 the Democratic party was divided not only on civil rights but even more on the Vietnam war, urban violence, and student protests. And that year Eugene J. McCarthy (Minn.) and Robert F. Kennedy (N.Y.) won almost 70 percent of the votes in Democratic primaries by challenging the party leadership and championing the dissident views on these issues. But the party leadership easily won the nomination for Vice-President Hubert Humphrey, who had not entered the campaign for nomination until after the filing dates for the state primaries. The Humphrey victory was helped by the fact that 59 percent of the delegates in 1968 came from states using the convention and appointment methods of delegate selection. The bitterness of the losers was directed largely at the party's delegate selection process, which they denounced as unfair and unrepresentative of party preferences. After all, the *losers* in the convention had won the support of a large majority of all party members who had voted in the primaries. With even some Humphrey delegates joining in the call for reform, the convention provided for a Commission on Party Structure and Delegate Selection to revamp delegate selection procedures. This commission set out to take the control of nominations from party leaders and vest it in the rank-and-file members.[21] The shift of control from the state to the national level was consummated almost incidentally, but it was a historic shift nevertheless.

The Democrats' reform commission adopted guidelines "designed to open the door to all Democrats who seek a voice in their Party's . . . choice of its presidential nominee."[22] The Democratic National Committee adopted the recommended guidelines; for the first time, state party organizations were required to follow specific rules and procedures laid down by the National Committee. State parties were required to

- schedule the entire process of selecting delegates during the calendar year of the convention
- limit the number of delegates selected by the state committee to no more than 10 percent of the delegation
- prohibit the "unit rule," under which all delegates from a precinct or district to a higher level meeting, such as the state convention, were required to vote together as a unit
- take affirmative action to achieve proportionate representation of minority groups, youth, and women

The effects of these reforms in making the delegate selection process more democratic are difficult to assess, but they certainly did open up the process and involve more people in it. So far as the composition of conventions is concerned, the Democratic national convention of 1972 was vastly different

---

[21] See Commission on Party Structure and Delegate Selection, *Mandate for Reform* (Washington, D.C.: Democratic National Committee, 1970).

[22] *Mandate for Reform,* p. 10.

from that of 1968: the proportion of women delegates increased from 13 percent to 40 percent; of people under 30, from 4 percent to 21 percent; of blacks, from 5.5 percent to 15 percent. Many of the young delegates inside the Miami convention hall in 1972 looked like the protestors who were being clubbed by police outside the Chicago convention hall in 1968. Only 10 percent of the delegates in 1972 were classified as "politicians," whereas in 1964 a majority (55 percent) were party officials, and 37 percent were public officials.[23] Few could doubt that the reforms had accomplished their intent of creating a more open party with broader opportunities for participation. By 1980, television viewers had grown accustomed to seeing as many women as men at Democratic conventions; they could also take for granted a proportionate number of young people, blacks, and Hispanics.

While national party organizations were imposing reforms, several states also responded to demands for more public participation in presidential nominations. The number of states with presidential primaries increased from 17 in 1968 to 23 in 1972, to 32 in 1976, and 36 in 1980. Some observors interpret this growth in primaries as an unintended result of the new rules. One argument is that state parties saw the primaries as a means of delegate selection less subject to challenge for failure to meet the new guidelines than were conventions or caucuses.[24] Another is that state party leaders thought they could maintain their control of *state* party decisions by splitting off the choice of *national* convention delegates as a separate procedure.[25] The assumption here is that old-style politicians resented any intrusion of amateurs and that they were willing to give the public complete control of their state's presidential politics in order to preserve unquestioned professional control of purely state concerns.

These arguments probably overstate the effect of reforms at the national level by the Democratic party. In the first place, they neglect the presence of the same forces for reform in state as in national party organizations. Second, they neglect the adoption of similar, if less stringent or binding, reforms by the Republican party. The greater number of primaries and the resultant increase in the proportion of amateur delegates at national conventions came, we believe, from broader influences than the reforms of the Democratic National Committee.

We started this section with a list of nine horrors recently produced by the presidential nominating system, then considered reforms made in response to those horrors. Have the reforms helped? The virtually unanimous judgment of political scientists is that the reforms have not helped. Indeed, the conventional wisdom is that the new rules are the source of most ills of the system. By now the reader probably knows that all authors regard "the conventional wisdom" as wrong (we say "expert assessment" when we agree).

[23] The 1972 figure is from a study by the Democratic National Committee; the 1964 figures are from a survey by the Citizens' Research Foundation. Both are quoted in a comprehensive report by F. Rhodes Cook, "Delegate Selection: Change Goes on for 1976," *Congressional Quarterly Weekly Report*, 33 (August 6, 1975), 1807–17.

[24] Cook, "Delegate Selection," *Congressional Quarterly Weekly Report*, 1810.

[25] Ranney, "Changing the Rules," in Barber, ed., *Choosing the President*, p. 73.

238

PART 2
inputs of the
political
system: who
wants and needs
what?

What is the argument of the conventional wisdom? Why is it merely conventional instead of wise?

Readers of almost any political columnist, ranging from James Kilpatrick to Anthony Lewis, have been exposed to the conventional view. It is probably advanced most cogently and persistently by David Broder of the *Washington Post*, for Broder attends meetings of the American Political Science Association and reads the research reports of its members. The argument goes like this: Presidential primary elections were an acceptable way to choose convention delegates as long as only a few states used them. As exotic sideshows, they stimulated interest and permitted candidates to demonstrate their appeal if they needed to, at the same time permitting others to bypass any primary that did not promise to help the cause. With professional politicians making up a majority of convention delegates—having been selected by themselves or by less experienced party figures—amateurs could never gain control of convention proceedings. Long-term party goals, not issues or candidates, were the guiding concern of these experienced leaders. The result was the nomination of seasoned party figures who had demonstrated the ability to appeal to a wide coalition of interests through artful compromise. As soon as the rank and file came to make up a majority of the convention, amateur concern for ideological goals and for the nomination of some popular hero came to dominate the proceedings. Primary elections as the way of selecting most delegates further turned control over to amateurs. The result was the emergence of candidates without a solid record of party experience or leadership.[26] The result was Carter and Reagan. As James David Barber puts it, the result was "politics as theater."[27]

This line of argument is not only conventional but also convincing. And it surely contains some truth. Nevertheless, we think it places too much weight on the effect of recent party reforms. The principal weakness of the argument is that it celebrates a golden age of party government that never existed in the United States. If we reexamine the list of nine disasters with which we began this look at the new style of presidential nominations, the first six turn out to have preceded, in whole or in part, the reforms alleged to be the source of our troubles. The reforms cannot have caused that which they were designed to correct. The nomination of a certain loser, a bloody and divisive convention, armed assaults on candidates, nomination and election of a venal Vice-President, nomination and election of a dishonest and corrupt President, succession to the presidency by an appointee of the disgraced (but quickly pardoned) President—these horrors led to reform rather than resulted from it. One can say that party reform failed to slow the decay, or even that it accelerated the process; but one cannot say that party reform caused the decay.

The real explanation for the miserable record of the American electoral system is more basic than mere party reform. As we indicated in analyzing political parties (in chapter 5), American political parties are less strongly orga-

---

[26] An academic treatment reflecting these views is Nelson W. Polsby and Aaron Wildavsky, *Presidential Elections: Strategies of American Electoral Politics,* 5th ed. (New York: Scribner's, 1980).
[27] See *The Pulse of Politics* (New York: Norton, 1980).

nized, less rooted in a mass membership, less expressive of the needs of the underprivileged, and less capable of organizing the government than are parties elsewhere. Moreover, the American electoral system is less designed to encourage citizen participation than are the systems of most democracies. The difficulty is in the system, not the citizens.

CAMPAIGNS AND ELECTIONS

A successful political campaign must achieve three objectives: (1) get the party's message to the voter; (2) raise and utilize campaign funds to produce attitudes favorable to the candidates; (3) stimulate people to come out and vote for the party's candidates.

Getting the message heard and believed

Thousands of messages compete for our attention each day. We must cope with decisions about our jobs, our families, and the hassles of life in technological America. In addition, we are implored to make the right decisions about our armpits, our breakfast cereals, and ugly brown spots on our hands. Constantly we are advised to listen, believe, join, follow, support, and buy.

The chief obstacle to getting a campaign message heard is the tendency of voters to ignore political appeals. Those who do pay attention, moreover, typically listen to their preferred candidate and tune out the opposition. The best way to overcome these obstacles is to get the candidates together for a face-to-face debate. To begin with, the debate itself becomes a campaign event, and the drama of personal confrontation vastly increases the audience over what it would be for any appeal by a single candidate. Second, the appearance of both candidates guarantees each a chance to appeal to undecided voters and those leaning to the opposition. To watch and hear your favorite, you are virtually forced to watch and hear his opponent. Three such debates have been staged in presidential elections since 1960. Although their impact on voting is not precisely known, at a minimum they affected the morale of partisans, campaign workers, and candidates. In each case, the candidate seen as winning the critical debate also won the election. The apparent debating victory may have had little to do with later victory in the election, but no campaign can afford to discount the possibility that it was decisive.

The Kennedy-Nixon debates of 1960 established the point that clear front runners should not debate their challengers. Nixon was an incumbent Vice-President with the advantage of name recognition and reputation for achievement. He had no need for exposure or for any new basis of comparison with his less-known opponent. Moreover, public opinion polls early in the race showed Nixon in the lead. In addition to being little known nationally, Kennedy was less experienced, his maturity was suspect, and his ability to

perform under fire was doubted. In the debate, however, Kennedy appeared forceful; Nixon seemed fatigued and furtive. The public thought, by a 2-to-1 margin, that Kennedy won the debate. Nixon lost his lead and Kennedy captured the presidency by the narrow margin of 50.1 percent to 49.9 percent. It is unlikely that he would have won his thin victory without his success on television. Indeed, Nixon blamed much of his loss on his appearance in the first debate.

Because the better-known candidate is usually unwilling to debate and give his opponent exposure, sitting Presidents (Johnson and Nixon) often will not agree to television debates. Thus, a second set of presidential debates did not occur until 1976, when Gerald Ford became the first sitting President to agree to debate his opponent. Because he was in the unusual position of being an unelected incumbent and an underdog, he felt he had more to gain than lose. Trailing Jimmy Carter by 18 points in the public opinion polls when the campaign began in September, Ford had made a dramatic comeback, pulling even with Carter in October. In the first debate, Carter seemed intimidated by being in a forum with the President of the United States, and he failed to do as well as expected. In a second debate on foreign policy, however, Carter won a decisive advantage in the minds of the electorate, and the Ford comeback was halted. Carter won in another breathtakingly close election, 51.1 percent to 48.9 percent. Carter's whole national political career had been made possible by media exposure: he rode television into the presidency.

As President, however, Jimmy Carter did not want to debate in 1980. His strategy of using incumbency to create favorable publicity while appearing to stay above the campaign seemed to work: Carter won the nomination of his party for a second term even though he refused to debate his major challenger, Senator Edward Kennedy. He hoped to extend his strategy of being "presidential" and above debate into the general election campaign. But it was unfortunate for his game plan when public opinion polls showed him running behind Reagan in every section of the country except the South. Carter decided he needed to debate Reagan, but he continued to refuse so long as independent candidate John Anderson was included. The League of Women Voters nevertheless scheduled a debate in late September, and Reagan and Anderson appeared without their chief opponent, Carter, present. Although this debate was widely regarded as a stand-off or as an Anderson victory, Anderson's support in the polls slipped from 15 percent to 8 percent; the League declared him no longer a viable candidate and scheduled a Carter-Reagan debate for one week before the election.

Both Carter and Reagan viewed the debate as critical. George Gallup observed: ". . . never in the 45-year history of presidential election surveys

has the Gallup poll found such volatility and uncertainty in voter preference as it has in the current election year."[28]   The lead had changed three times since January, and the debate was seen as crucial in helping undecided voters make up their minds. Just as Nixon suffered in 1960 from the contrast between expectation and performance, so did Carter in 1980. His presumed advantage in knowledge and mental quickness was of little help. In the effort to look presidential and responsible, he appeared wooden and tense; in the effort to show his knowledge, he appeared to be criticizing a Reagan who wasn't there— someone who had taken extreme positions, which Reagan simply rejected as his. The veteran actor appeared, if not especially quick, at least reassuringly moderate, with an avuncular tolerance for Carter's attacks. The mobility of his facial expressions permitted him to communicate amused disbelief, stern concern, or strength under pressure even while Carter was talking. Most of all, Reagan had the advantage of being able to cite Carter's record in the White House.

A CBS News Poll reported that 44 percent of the viewers thought Reagan won the contest, with 36 percent choosing Carter and 20 percent calling it a tie. More important, the debate helped dispel the belief that Reagan was a warmonger, stupid, or too old at 69 to be President. Nor did Reagan seem intimidated by the President. "After all," he observed, "I've been on stage with John Wayne." Reagan picked up support at the average rate of 1.2 percent *each day* after the debate until the election. Although many other factors contributed to the Reagan victory, he was certainly helped by the impact of his television performance.

The professional public relations people who direct American campaigns shape every aspect of the party's message. They prepare it, package it, and sell it. In careful and elaborate ways, they use the message to build images that fit the voters' aspirations and fears. Despite the high level of sophistication reflected in current campaigns, the reality of life as experienced by voters

[28] George Gallup release, "Reagan Regains Edge" (November 3, 1980).

242

PART 2
inputs of the
political
system: who
wants and needs
what?

sets limits on the PR people's capacity for influence. Nor can they ever forget that election results are determined by who votes, no less than by how they vote.

Getting out the vote

After the campaign strategists have caught the citizen's attention and have created a favorable attitude toward their candidates, their final task is to get the voters to the polls. At this stage, party organization at the precinct level becomes vitally important. Street by street, house by house, local party workers try to register new voters and encourage voting by those who lean their way. On election day, hundreds of thousands of phone calls are made to party supporters to remind them to vote. Volunteers ring doorbells, serve as baby-sitters, and furnish transportation to the polls. Parties are joined by interest groups that actively promote participation by their members.

For all of the efforts by parties, candidates, and independent groups to "get out the vote," American voter turnout remains the lowest of any industrial democracy, and nonvoters increase with each presidential election. Although Ronald Reagan was elected with a clear majority of those who participated in the 1980 election, he moved into the White House with the votes of barely 25 percent of the eligible electorate in America. Since the election of 1960, when 64 percent participated, voter turnout has steadily declined, reaching its lowest level in 1980 with 52.5 percent. This unbroken decline for five presidential elections is unprecedented in American history.[29] What are the reasons for the low voter turnout in the U.S.?

As Fig. 7 · 2 shows, part of the problem can be attributed to the expansion of the electorate when the voting age was lowered from 21 to 18. The 11 million new voters made eligible by this constitutional amendment could participate in their first election in 1972. In that election and in every subsequent election, participation by the 18- to 21-year-olds has been lower than by the population at large. In this, the younger citizens share voting habits of other groups that have been added to the eligible electorate. The percentage of participation also dropped overall when blacks and women first became eligible to vote. Thus, the expansion of the electorate, making government less elite and participation more universal, has resulted in a decline in overall turnout. But this cannot explain why American turnout is so much lower than in other countries with equally broad electorates.

The American electoral system reduces turnout by complex registration requirements. In contrast to the universal and automatic registration systems of many countries, the United States has a maze of registration rules, all determined by the individual states. Some states require registration almost two months before the election; only five states permit registration on election day. The evidence is strong that rigid registration laws reduce participation in every level of government.[30]

[29] Rhodes Cook, "Just Over Half the Electorate," *Congressional Quarterly Weekly Report,* 38 (October 25, 1980), 3193–95.

[30] See William Crotty, *Political Reform and the American Experiment* (New York: Crowell, 1977), pp. 81ff.

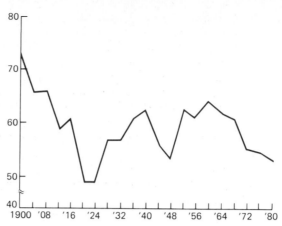

Source: *Historical Statistics of the United States: Colonial Times to 1980* (1975) for elections through 1968. Census Bureau publicaton, "Population Estimates and Projections" (March 1980) for 1972 and 1976 elections. For 1980, wire service reports. Adapted from *Congressional Quarterly Weekly Reports*, 38 (October 25, 1980), 3195.

FIG. 7 · 2 Voter turnout in presidential elections, 1900–1980 (percent of voting age population casting ballots).

These specific, campaign-related efforts help keep the American record of voter turnout from being even worse than it is. But for the United States to approach the level of voting in other countries, helpful policies and more attractive choices would be necessary. Among the changes that might significantly raise voter turnout, we have already suggested several: mass-based political parties, especially one with a direct appeal to the underprivileged; a system of universal enrollment to make every citizen eligible to vote; scheduling of elections on holidays or over a weekend; clarity in choices offered by parties; and better records of carrying out platform and campaign promises.

Money in elections

The Federal Election Campaign Act of 1974 (also known as the Campaign Reform Act) was a result of Watergate. The act was a direct attempt to rid American politics of the corruption exposed during two years of inquiry into the Nixon presidency. It set up a system of public financing for presidential elections and laid down strict limits on contributions and expenditures for both presidential and congressional elections. Specific provisions included:

1. Spending limits of $10 million for each presidential nomination campaign and $20 million for each major-party nominee's general election campaign. Lower limits were set for congressional candidates.

2. Matching federal funds for candidates for a major-party presidential nomination, with a maximum of $5 million for candidates who qualify.

3. For the two major-party nominees, $20 million apiece is available from the Treasury.

4. Limits on individual contributions were set at $1,000 per candidate for presidential and congressional primaries, $1,000 more in the general election, and $25,000 in all in any year. Organizations other than political parties are limited to $5,000 per candidate per election. A presidential candidate and his family are limited to a total of $50,000.

5. Limits were set on the amounts that may be spent by presidential candidates in each state ($200,000 for the New Hampshire primary, for example) with any unspent quota nontransferable to another state.

243

244

PART 2
inputs of the
political
system: who
wants and needs
what?

6. Accounting of funds must be by a single committee for each candidate, with regular reports on receipts and expenditures, with every donor of $100 or more identified, and with no cash contributions in excess of $100 permitted.

7. A Federal Elections Commission of six members was established to enforce the new campaign financing provisions.

The 1974 Campaign Reform Act attempted to reduce the dominance of "fat cats"—contributors of $50,000 or $100,000—in American campaigns. Its detailed accounting and reporting procedures are designed to prevent the illegal use of "laundered" money or large sums of cash from major business interests. The act has had both expected and unexpected effects on campaigns. The limitation on the amount that may be spent in each state discourages the "blitz," a technique of throwing a large part of one's resources into a single crucial state. Unintended consequences for campaign tactics include the discouragement of late-breaking candidates, for prior planning and early effort are necessary to raise the required funds in small donations. Similarly, the old technique of gambling on an early state primary to serve as a spur to donations becomes less feasible. A third unintended effect on tactics is to increase the importance of the direct-mail technique in fund-raising. Close connections with well-heeled interests are now less important than access to computerized mailing lists of "hot" prospects in the general public.

In the middle of the 1976 campaign, the Supreme Court ruled on the constitutionality of the Campaign Reform Act.[31] The Court required a restructuring of the Federal Election Commission; but of more lasting consequence, it also declared unconstitutional the act's limit on expenditures by candidates or their supporters. Such limits were held to violate the right of free speech (giving official status to the old maxim, "money talks"). The Court did uphold spending limits for those presidential candidates who accept the matching funds offered under the act: in voluntarily agreeing to accept the funds, a candidate also agrees to accept the spending limits. The absence of matching funds for congressional candidates means the absence of any legal limits on expenditures in those races. By the same token, any candidate for President who declines to accept government matching funds is also free from any limit on expenditures. As the 1980 favorite of top executives in the largest corporations, for example, John Connally of Texas declined to accept matching funds and their accompanying restrictions, confident that his corporate friends would supply all the money he needed to win the Republican nomination. Although completely legal, this exclusively big-business approach yielded only one delegate at a cost of $12,000,000. With the smallest and most expensive per-delegate bloc of support in all history, Big John withdrew from the race and threw his not-so-weighty support to Reagan.

In addition to being exempt from spending restrictions by Supreme Court decree, well-heeled candidates for Congress enjoy another advantage under the Campaign Reform Act that completely nullifies the goal of equalizing expenditures in such races. The 1974 law allows national party committees to contribute much more to congressional candidates than can individuals or PACs. Every national party committee, for example, can spend up to

[31] Buckley v. Valeo, 424 U.S. 1 (1976).

$34,720 for a House seat and $987,548 for a Senate seat.[32] Both national parties have a number of committees collecting funds and making contributions to congressional races. But the three major committees for each party— the National Committee, the Senatorial Campaign Committee, and the Congressional Campaign Committee—have varied greatly in their abilities to raise the funds allowed under the law. In 1979–80, the Republicans were far more successful than the Democrats: the three main Republican committees contributed $5.8 million to legislative races, while their Democratic counterparts raised slightly more than $1 million. This 5-to-1 Republican advantage ended the speculation that the Campaign Reform Act would benefit the Democrats, who have traditionally found fund-raising harder than have the Republicans. Although the act has benefited Democrats in presidential races, it has not done so in congressional contests.

Even at the presidential level, loopholes in the law gave Reagan a great advantage over Carter in 1980 expenditures. Although the Court upheld expenditure limitations on federally aided presidential campaigns, it permitted "independent groups" to spend unlimited amounts. The result was a surge of independent spending, the overwhelming majority of which was for the candidacy of Ronald Reagan.[33] The right-wing Congressional Club, for example—the political organization of only one senator, Jesse Helms (R-North Carolina)—reported spending $2.73 million on Reagan's behalf through the middle of October during the 1980 campaign. Common Cause and the Carter-Mondale campaign challenged these expenditures as not truly independent efforts and as violating both the spirit and the letter of the Campaign Reform Act. The Federal Elections Commission ruled that such groups were technically independent of the candidate's own campaign and that they could therefore spend without restriction on his behalf.

The independent groups appear to have had significant impact in the election, for both President and Congress. Five conservative, "new-right" groups spent nearly $15 million for the Reagan campaign and for conservative congressional candidates. In addition, conservative religious groups such as the Moral Majority targeted liberal senators and House members for elimination and poured campaign funds into support of their opponents. Although such religious politicos were accused of being "more excited about missiles than about the Messiah," most of the targeted liberals were defeated in the Reagan sweep.

Lavish campaign spending does not always pay off. Indeed, one study of congressional contests concluded that heavy campaign expenses were often a sign of weakness and that incumbents who spend the most often lose.[34] Even so, gross imbalances in available funds for transmitting one's political message seem unfair. The Campaign Reform Act has made significant improvements over the corrupt practices of the 1972 campaign. Continued improvements are necessary to limit expenditures in congressional races or

[32] Larry Light, "Republican Groups Dominate in Party Campaign Spending," *Congressional Quarterly Weekly Report,* 38 (November 1, 1980), 3234.

[33] Larry Light, "Independent Reagan Groups," *Congressional Quarterly Weekly Report,* 38 (October 18, 1980), 3152–53.

[34] Gary Jacobson, "The Effects of Campaign Spending on Congressional Elections," *American Political Science Review,* 17 (June 1978), 469.

Although President Reagan and Vice-President Bush are from different wings
of the Republican party, Bush eagerly accepted the chance to be Reagan's
running mate and to serve the conservative goals of the administration.

to give challengers access to matching funds, to decrease the advantages of
incumbency in raising campaign funds, to reduce the financial dominance
of corporate PACs, and to eliminate loopholes in the application of the Campaign Reform Act to presidential campaigns.

The 1980 election in the trend toward no-party politics

Political parties, issues, candidates, PACs, polls, money, the mass media—
these are the key elements in American elections. Among them, only one
has recently declined in importance: political parties. Their decline has been
accompanied by growing distrust of government and its leaders and by continuing increases in the number of nonpartisan or unattached voters. The result
is a fragmented, disorganized politics—what some call a "mass society"—without effective mediating organizations (such as political parties) between leaders
and followers. For interpretations of presidential acts, for example, journalists
consult public opinion polls, not party leaders. The President-public relationship is one-to-many, direct, vastly impersonal, with no softening or interpreting
mediation through party leaders. Evaluations are instant, in terms of this
one President's personal achievements, not long run or in terms of an overall
party record.

The lack of control over the nominating process by party leaders and
the weakening of party ties both for voters and candidates decreases stability
and predictability in nominations and elections, in the electorate, and in the
conduct of government. If the key to nomination, were service to party and

demonstrated ability to unite its various wings and factions, an experienced party leader like former Senator Edmund Muskie (D-Maine) instead of a self-proclaimed outsider like Jimmy Carter might have been the Democrats' candidate; similarly, a moderate leader like Senator Howard Baker (R-Tenn.) instead of a symbol of extreme conservatism like Ronald Reagan might have been the Republicans' candidate. But Jimmy Carter was able to take advantage of discontent with parties and with the government to build a personal organization in early caucus and primary states, to win media attention, and to ride his "outsider" status to victory in 1976. Four years later, Vice-President George Bush—then known as a former congressman, chairman of the Republican party, and Richard Nixon's Director of the CIA—copied Carter's tactics down to the last detail. Coming out of the Iowa precinct caucuses with a victory, he gleefully announced that "Big Mo" (by which he meant momentum) was on his side. But Ronald Reagan proved that a single loss need not eliminate a candidate with 12 years of organizational effort and lots of money undergirding his campaign. In a televised New Hampshire debate, paid for by Reagan, he completely upstaged a querulous Bush, chastising the debate's moderator with the sincere, tight-lipped look that was exhibited in 55 feature-length films between 1937 and 1964. With television more important than ever before, Americans finally nominated and elected a professional actor to become their President.

The talents developed in Reagan's early career, combined with the increasing impact of the mass media, suggest that he was the first, not the last, actor to become President. In the only movie in which President Reagan ever played a politician, *That Hagen Girl* (1947), his political ambitions were sublimated to his growing love for Shirley Temple, playing a high school Lolita. Although the President regards this as his worst film—even it helped. There, as in other films, he practiced the familiar "aw shucks" shrug and the shy downward glance with which he apologizes for a factual error. Also to serve him well were the pregnant pause and the quick, emphatic nod that added poignancy to his first love scene with Jane Wyman in *Brother Rat* (1938). His "Gee, Claire, you're really . . . [pause, nod] swell" includes the same pause and nod that added emotion to his campaign statements about the economy: "The culprits for inflation are not business and labor. The cause of inflation is . . . [pause, nod] government." Earnestness was the key to his advertising pitch for Chesterfield cigarettes in 1948, for Van Heusen shirts in 1953, and for the General Electric Company from 1954 to 1962. As long as party amounts to less, projection of personal qualities will amount to more. Such projection carried Ronald Reagan to the White House.

What are the implications of an electoral system in which parties play a diminishing part? If they were completely banned, we know (from Chapter 5) that a nondemocratic regime would follow. But what can we expect when parties, though not banned, become largely irrelevant, when politics is organized by ad hoc coalitions built around particular candidates? Neither scholars nor journalistic pundits seem to have recognized that the politics of the old one-party South offers the best available answer. As, V. O. Key explained in his classic analysis of southern politics in the 1940s, a one-party system

248

PART 2
inputs of the
political
system: who
wants and needs
what?

really amounts to a no-party system, for the notion of party implies opposition. Political competition without opposing parties is a struggle among ad hoc, candidate-centered coalitions. The causes of the old no-party system of the South were vastly different from the influences we have cited as diminishing the importance of national parties today. Even if the causes are different, however, the results of no-party politics will be similar. As the United States approaches the eclipse of parties, then, Key's comments on the effects of a regional no-party politics suggest where national politics may be going.

At the individual level, Key says a no-party system fails in several ways:

- it does not give citizens stable or reliable clues for evaluating issues or candidates;
- it thereby discourages voter turnout, especially among less educated and poorer people;
- it similarly fails, through lack of clarity and continuity, to stimulate interest in, and information about, public affairs.

At the system level, Professor Key found the discontinuities of no-party politics similarly injurious:

- with the emphasis on individual candidates, political strife is so unstructured that the "outs" and the "ins" cannot even attack each other as groups with any collective spirit or responsibility
- the individualistic emphasis of no-party politics places a premium on demagogy and appeals of personality
- in its fluidity and discontinuity, government under no-party politics eludes the control of ordinary citizens.

Little-known and complicated politics is obviously more nearly mastered by people who have the training to unravel its complexities or the money to hire lawyers, lobbyists, and public relations experts. Just as a healthy party system has a bias in favor of the majority, a no-party system has an anti-majoritarian bias. What Key said about a few states over 30 years ago comes chillingly close to describing national politics today:

The significant question is, who benefits from political disorganization? . . . Politics generally comes down, over the long run, to a conflict between those who have and those who have less. In state politics the crucial issues tend to turn around taxation and expenditure. What level of . . . public services shall be maintained? How shall the burden of taxation for their support be distributed? . . .

It follows that the grand objective of the haves is obstruction, at least of the haves who take only a short-term view. Organization is not always necessary to obstruct; it is essential, however, for the promotion of a sustained program in behalf of the have-nots. . . . It follows, if these propositions are correct, that over the long run the have-nots lose in a disorganized politics. They have no mechanism through which to act and their wishes find expression in fitful rebellions led by transient demagogues who gain their confidence but often have neither the technical competence nor the necessary stable base of political power to effectuate a program.[35]

---

[35] V. O. Key, Jr., *Southern Politics in State and Nation* (New York: Knopf, 1949), p. 307.

ELECTIONS AND THE POLITICAL SYSTEM

249
CHAPTER 7
the
electoral
system

Aside from their direct significance, elections are important for what they tell us about how choices are made and how power is distributed among individuals and groups, in and out of government. They may also be viewed in historical perspective, each election regarded as a single political event, as one unit in a continuing series of electoral decisions with consequences for the total political system.

Types of elections

Elections may be classified according to two criteria. The first and most obvious is in terms of *which party wins.* If it is the incumbent party, the election results in *party continuity;* if it is the party out of office, a *party change* is the result. Since the question of who will control the government is the central concern of any election, this first factor tends to dominate popular discussion. In 1928, then, the Republicans were happy because they retained control of the presidency by a handy margin.

Professional horse players differ from amateurs, however, in that their concerns go beyond the simple question of which horse won a particular race. They are also alert to the promise of strength in a loser and to signs of future weakness in the winner. And so it is with careful observers of elections. They are concerned with the second and less obvious criterion: whether the election reflects change or continuity in the party *preferences of significant groups* in the electorate. If deviations from the usual party preferences of major voting groups are not very great or enduring, the election may be called one of *electoral continuity.* If significant and enduring deviations occur, the election is one of *electoral change.* Viewing the 1928 election from this perspective, the Republicans seem to have won a battle while they were losing a war.

The Herbert Hoover-Al Smith presidential contest of 1928 has been called a critical election because, viewed as one in a series of electoral decisions, it formed a realignment of significant groups within the electorate. Specifically, the candidacy of Al Smith intensified and solidified the movement of low-income, Catholic, urban voters of immigrant stock into the Democratic party.[36] We often forget that the long-run consequences of an election may be in terms of shifts in the electorate that do not show up in the win column. Franklin Roosevelt's victory in 1932 was not the only critical election, then, for Democratic dominance during the last generation. The identification of low-income and minority groups with the Democrats was carried further in 1932, but—because almost all groups showed some shift to the Democrats

---

[36] See V. O. Key, Jr., "A Theory of Critical Elections," *Journal of Politics,* 17 (February 1955), 3–18.

250

PART 2
inputs of the
political
system: who
wants and needs
what?

in 1932—the contrast between low- and high-status groups may actually have been greater in 1928.

In chapters 4 and 5 we stressed the supporting function of political opinions and the moderating function of political parties for the political system. We also emphasized the impressive stability of party identification, which permitted us to divide the nation's political history into only 3 periods in terms of basic majority coalitions—the Democratic majority, 1800–1860; the Republican majority, 1860–1932; the Democratic majority, 1932 to the present.

If recent elections are viewed in the light of these stable factors, they can be understood as deviating more or less from a "standing decision" rather than as unique events. The most stable feature of the current political era has been control of Congress by the Democratic party. What makes the present era different from earlier ones is that the majority party's dominance is confined to Congress. Presidential election outcomes have varied widely, with the Republicans winning more often than the Democrats since 1952. "Other things being equal," the majority party should win presidential elections, but "other things" have not often been equal in recent elections. The declining ability to predict presidential voting from congressional voting has, as we observed in chapter 6, serious implications for the party system—and, in turn, for the meaning of the electoral system.

Functions of the electoral system

From the point of view of the political system as a whole, the electoral system selects, as intended, the official decision makers. It contributes less clearly to the identification of citizen interests. When Americans elect a Republican President and a Democratic Congress, for example, what policies are they trying to say they want? If one agrees that the electoral system operates as a great "echo chamber," then public opinion can give back no more intelligent or meaningful a message than it receives from the parties and their candidates.[37] These split results seem to be saying that the messages lack clarity, meaning, and conviction. If neither party is really trusted, then it makes sense to allow neither control of the entire government. But the winners of elections do not take this negative view. They tend to interpret the results as approval for whatever they want to do, regardless of the overall pattern of outcomes.

The electoral system also has several consequences that might be unanticipated. First, the entire process of popular elections serves to celebrate and to reinforce the concept of self-rule. The result is to legitimize governmental power, to convince everyone of the right of the elected officials to make general policy. The losers of American elections are expected to show their good sportsmanship by rallying around the winner.

---

[37] The seminal statement redirecting researchers to this view is by V. O. Key, Jr., *The Responsible Electorate* (Cambridge, Mass.: Harvard University Press, 1966). We have extended this view to the study of public opinion for insights into the political system as a whole, particularly in chaps. 1 and 4.

A second unplanned result of a system of popular elections is to extend the amount of popular participation. Early in American history, the right to vote was restricted to groups such as property owners and taxpayers. But once it is argued that *some* people deserve the right to vote, it is hard to deny the same right to others. Equally important, party competition for votes leads to the search for new supporters. One of the parties is thus likely to urge extension of the vote to any excluded groups.

Third, a popular electoral system changes the context within which public decisions are made. As we have seen, some elements in the population have a greater opportunity for leadership than others have. But decisions on public policy in a system without popular elections are vastly different from similar decisions in a democracy. Even if elections cannot positively direct policy, decision makers must always anticipate public reactions to their decisions. In V. O. Key's words, the suffrage means that "the wishes and probable actions of a vast number of people at the polls must be taken into consideration in the exercise of public power."[38]

To this point, we have talked about broad functions of popular elections for political systems in general. But just how do American elections serve to link public preferences (and indifference) to the policy outputs of government? Political opinions, political parties, pressure groups, and the mass media all converge in the electoral process. Democratic theory assumes that out of this convergence the elected official will somehow represent the interests or views of constituents.

At least three concepts of the relationship between constituents and decision makers have been presented as describing either the actual or the desired model. The *instructed delegate* model holds that officials act (or should act) to carry out the preferences of constituents, following their mandate in official decisions. The view traditionally opposed to that of the instructed delegate sees representatives performing as *independent statesmen*, acting in the interest of constituents as the representative sees it, even though this may be contrary to their preferences. The *responsible party* model sees representatives as agents of a national rather than a local constituency. The independent statesmen and responsible party concepts both view the official as free to act contrary to constituency preferences, but they differ in that independent statesmen act in terms of their own views of constituency. Which relationship holds true in America?

Constituency control over the voting behavior of a member of Congress is possible in two ways: (1) the constituency may elect representatives who share the views of a majority in the area, so that they will automatically vote the constituency's preferences in voting their own; (2) representatives may have a reasonably accurate idea of constituency preferences, which they follow regardless of their personal views. The possibility of either form of constituency control over a representative's behavior depends on three requirements.[39]

---

[38] *Politics, Parties, and Pressure Groups*, p. 622.

[39] Our discussion here is based on Warren Miller and Donald Stokes, "Constituency Influence in Congress," *American Political Science Review*, 57 (March 1963), 45–56.

252

PART 2
inputs of the
political
system: who
wants and needs
what?

First, officeholders' votes must agree either with their own views or with their perception of constituency views. At first glance, this requirement might appear to be obviously met, but on reflection one recognizes that a member of Congress might instead follow the advice of the President, of party leaders in or out of office, or of lobbyists. Examining the votes of members of Congress in three areas of legislation—social welfare, foreign policy, and civil rights— scholars find this first condition to be realized in all three issue areas. Even so, a minority of representatives were found to follow the lead of the administration, regardless of their own preferences or their perception of constituency preferences.

Second, the representative's own attitudes or perceptions of constituency attitudes must correspond with the actual opinions held in the district. This second requirement is not as well fulfilled as is the first. Representatives most accurately perceive their constituents' preferences on the civil rights issue, but neither their own attitudes nor their beliefs about constituent attitudes are strongly related to actual constituency opinions on issues of foreign policy or social welfare. But these are severe tests. Popular opinions on questions of foreign policy are so unstable and so poorly supported by information that the representative could hardly be expected to have a highly accurate impression of them. On social welfare issues, if we compare the representatives' perceptions and attitudes with those of the majority who supported the representatives, rather than with the entire constituency, a stronger relationship is found.

Third, in deciding how to vote, the constituency must consider the candidate's position on issues. This information is necessary if the constituency is to be in control, but it is the least fulfilled requirement. Most researchers have tended to blame the voters for their failure to consider issues more seriously in deciding how to vote. But voters cannot consider anything that is not presented in the campaign. Given a chance to make a choice based on issues, Americans appear as competent to do so as are the voters in other countries. Similarly, when policy differences between political parties are clear, party identification plays a dominant role. People must focus on personalities when that is all they are given a chance to evaluate. Political choices, like political opinions in general, thus suggest more about the characteristics and limitations of our political system than they do about the characteristics and limitations of our citizens. Even in the poorly organized American party system, issues count. We shall see in examining Congress (in the next chapter) that Democratic and Republican members do oppose each other, even if less predictably than do party members in most legislatures. And four-fifths of the representatives opposed for reelection felt that the outcome was strongly influenced by their voting records in Congress.

In varying degrees, then, the requirements of constituency influence through popular elections seem to be realized. The model of constituency-representative relationship that is actually adopted varies from one issue to another. The instructed delegate model appears predominant in the area of civil rights. On this issue, the representatives' perceptions of district attitudes are twice as influential as their own attitudes in determining variations in their roll-call votes. The responsible party model more nearly explains the relationship on social welfare issues, where party differences have been clear enough to enable the voter to rely on party label as a way of communicating preferences. Finally, the independent statesman model finds some support in congressional behavior on foreign policy questions, in that members do not look to their districts in making up their minds. But even here the member of Congress does not make an independent decision: ". . . the reliance he puts on the President and the Administration suggests that the calculation of where the public interest lies is often passed to the Executive on matters of foreign policy."[40]

SUMMARY

The Constitution sets forth eligibility requirements for candidates for national office but does not give detailed procedures on how to choose officials from those who are eligible. Nominating procedures have been developed by the political parties.

The original Constitution let the states decide who could vote. Restrictions based on religion, property ownership, tax payments, race, and sex have been eliminated over the years. Recently, the government actively began to enroll all eligible citizens as voters. These changes have moved the U.S. toward a nationally defined electorate.

The first stage in the official election process is the nomination of candidates to represent each party. Today, most national and state officials are nominated by direct primary elections; party conventions are used only to nominate candidates for the presidency. (Nominations for President are often determined by the state primaries, the convention merely ratifying decisions made earlier.) Two key factors influencing success in becoming a candidate appear to be favorable attention from the mass media and "availability," having occupied a political office regarded as good preparation for the presidency.

In response to the 1968 Democratic convention and to the Watergate scandals, reforms have been made in delegate selection, convention procedures, and campaign financing. The broad objective of the Campaign Reform Act was to prevent one presidential candidate from simply overwhelming the others by using his own money or large donations. State primaries have begun to be more important with increased demands for openness, fairness, and popular participation in party affairs.

In campaigns and elections following the nominations, a successful campaign strategy must get the party's message to the voter (through all channels of the media), produce favorable attitudes toward the candidate, and stimulate people to vote for the right candidate.

[40] *Ibid.*, p. 56.

DECISION-MAKING AGENCIES AND ACTIVITIES: WHO DECIDES WHAT AND HOW?

part 3

the
legislators

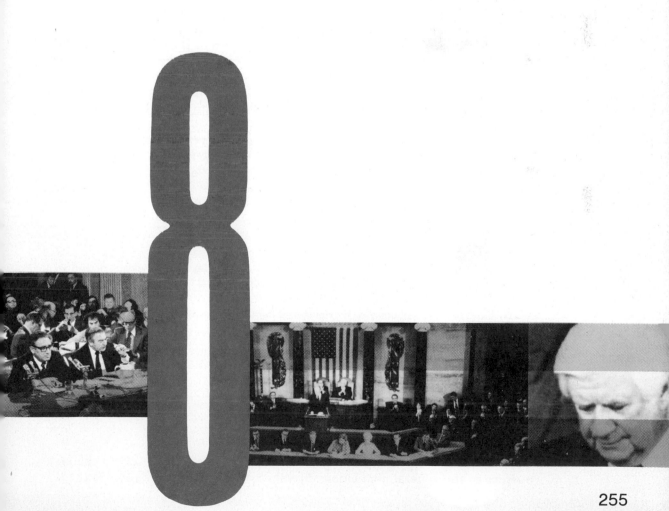

256

PART 3
decision-making
agencies:
who decides
what and how?

The Constitution of the United States begins with this declaration: "All legislative powers herein granted shall be vested in a Congress of the United States which shall consist of a Senate and House of Representatives." This statement has an appealing simplicity; we prefer to picture government as being neat rather than confusing. Generations of schoolchildren have been taught that government is the business of three branches: Congress enacts laws, the President executes them, and the courts settle disputes under the law. This partitioning tells part of the story, and it correctly emphasizes a principal function of each branch of our government; but if taken too literally, it can be misleading.

The Constitution itself assigns powers that result in different branches of government performing similar functions. A secretary of defense makes rules when he declares certain areas off limits to service personnel because real estate agents try to discourage black tenants. The President makes rules when he asks Congress to pass a foreign aid bill. The Supreme Court makes rules when it declares that election districts must be drawn so that each vote will have roughly equal weight in choosing legislators.

If *legislation* is defined as "all acts passed by Congress," then Congress is our only legislative agency. But if legislation is viewed as those activities that result in the establishment of general and authoritative rules for society, all the official decision-making agencies of government play some part in the process. And although they cannot make officially binding decisions, unofficial agencies such as political parties, pressure groups, and the mass media express most of the inputs that shape public policies. Despite the Constitution's reference to "all legislative powers," then, we can hope to understand Congress only as one part of a complex rule-making system.

Although members of Congress, the President, bureaucrats, and judges differ greatly in their responsibilities and in the way they work, they share one central characteristic: all are involved in making official decisions in the name of the government. To understand the place of each agency in the American political system, we need answers to the following questions:

1. What kind of people does the system recruit for positions in the decision-making agency?
2. How is the role (of a member of Congress, President, bureaucrat, or judge) defined? That is, what behavior do other people expect of anyone who occupies the position, and what behavior does the occupant think the position calls for?
3. How are roles structured by the performance of people in these positions?
4. What are the relationships among different structures or agencies of authoritative decision making?
5. What functions does the agency perform for the broader political system?

THE RECRUITMENT OF LEGISLATORS

The United States Congress has never been "representative" of the characteristics of the general population. Members of Congress may represent the wishes of people quite unlike themselves, of course, but those who are not literally represented naturally suspect that those who are represented are also getting preferred treatment.

What kind of people become legislators?

Perhaps the most noticeable characteristic of members of Congress is that they are, by and large, middle-aged men. The average age of the members of the 96th Congress (1979–1981) was 49.5 years. The average senator was almost 53; the average representative, about 49. Clearly, the official policies of the United States are not made by inexperienced youngsters or by many women. In the 96th Congress there were only 17 women representatives and one woman senator. Blacks are as rare as women in Congress; the total of 16 blacks in 1979–1981 was the largest number since Reconstruction.

Most people come to Congress, as we would expect, from occupations of at least upper-middle-class standing. Lawyers account for more than half the membership of Congress, and business people and bankers fill almost a third of the seats. A third of the senators are millionaires, and two-thirds have outside incomes of over $20,000 a year to supplement their $57,500 congressional salaries. The House is only a little less rich a body: 30 or more representatives are millionaires, and nearly 100 have outside incomes in excess of $20,000 a year in addition to their $57,500 salaries. The 96th Congress had no one from a blue-collar occupation and only 4 people from labor union leadership ranks. Legislators are similarly unrepresentative of the family backgrounds, ethnic origins, education, and religion of their constituents. The proportion of officeholders who have a high social status exceeds the proportion of high social status groups in the total population. Low-status people tend to be virtually excluded from office.

The constitutional qualifications for election to Congress are quite simple. A representative must be at least 25 years of age, a citizen for 7 years, and an inhabitant of the state from which he or she is elected. A senator must be 30 years old, a citizen for 9 years, and an inhabitant of the state from which he or she is elected. Any citizen can meet these requirements simply by staying alive, but various informal requirements narrow the field sharply. If one plans to serve in Congress, it will normally be advantageous to arrange to be the following: a middle-aged male lawyer whose father was of the professional or managerial class; a native-born white, or—if he cannot avoid being an immigrant—a product of northwestern or central Europe or Canada, rather than of eastern or southern Europe, Latin America, Africa, or Asia; a college graduate and a Protestant, preferably a Methodist, Presbyterian, Episcopalian, or Baptist.

The most extreme bias is directed toward gender: women make up 52 percent of the adult population but only 3 percent of Congress. Some bias, however, may be more apparent than real; Congress may not be unrepresentative at all. A large majority of the members are Protestants, for example, but the size of their majority in Congress is no larger than in the general population. Indeed, discrimination against Catholics and Jews in election to

Congress in session. Predominantly rich, white, male, and middle-aged, the members try to represent the needs of all the people without representing their other characteristics.

Congress, though still evident in the 1960s, had disappeared by the 1980s. Catholics, 22 percent of the population, comprised 24 percent of the 96th Congress (1979–1981); Jews, 3 percent of the population, accounted for 5 percent of Congress. The specific denominations most overrepresented were Episcopalians and Presbyterians, each accounting for less than 2 percent of the population but over 12 percent of the 1979–1981 Congress. Discrimination along religious lines now seems to apply in greatest extreme to nonbelievers: about 9 percent of the adult population say they have no religion, but less than 1 percent of the members of Congress express no religious connection. Members of Congress thus overrepresent attributes of power, status, and conventional values.[1]

[1] *Congressional Quarterly Weekly Report,* 37 (January 20, 1979), 533; 37 (September 1, 1979), 1823. The datum on the percent of the general public with no religion is from *The CPS 1978 American National Election Study.*

TABLE 8·1

259

CHAPTER 8
the legislators

| Congress | Dates | Elected more than once | |
		To House	To Senate
42nd	1871–73	53%	32%
50th	1887–89	63	45
64th	1915–17	74	47
74th	1935–37	77	54
87th	1961–63	87	66
91st	1969–71	91	72
94th	1975–77	80	65
96th	1979–81	83	52

Percentage of veteran members in Congresses from 1871 to 1981

Although we expect congressional leaders to be different from the rank and file, how do they compare with other top-level leaders? Comparing the Senate's 100 members with the presidents of America's 100 largest industrial corporations, Andrew Hacker found important contrasts. First, the median tenure (length of time in office) of the senators (7 years) was almost twice that of the corporation presidents (4 years).[2] Legislators, then, have been at their jobs a relatively long while. This has not always been the case, as the figures in Table 8·1 demonstrate. In the Congresses of the late nineteenth century, almost half the members of the House and over half the members of the Senate were serving in their first elective term. But the length of tenure steadily increased to the point where 91 percent of those elected to the House in the 1969 1971 term had been elected more than once; for the 1979–1981 session, the figure was 83 percent. The tendency is more extreme in the House than in the Senate because contests for house seats receive much less attention than Senate races. The result is that, with party affiliation meaning less and less, the advantage that incumbents enjoy in name recognition may be enough to return them to the House. Even landslide presidential elections no longer help members of the winning presidential candidate's party to ride in on his "coattails." When Republican Warren G. Harding won his landslide victory in 1920, some 50 Democratic incumbents were unseated; Richard M. Nixon's equivalent landslide victory in 1972 saw only 8 Democratic incumbents defeated.[3]

Legislators are thus largely immune to the tides of political change, but they are not totally immune. In 1974, the publicity resulting from impeachment hearings gave them a new visibility. An unusual number took advantage of a change in retirement provisions and decided not to seek reelection, and a larger minority of incumbents than usual were defeated. The losers included

[2] Andrew Hacker, "The Elected and the Anointed: Two American Elites," *American Political Science Review,* 55 (September 1961), 539.

[3] Walter Dean Burnham, "American Politics in the 1970s: Beyond Party?" in W. N. Chambers and W. D. Burnham, eds., *The American Party Systems: Stages of Political Development,* 2nd ed. (New York: Oxford University Press, 1975), p. 320.

260

PART 3
decision-making
agencies:
who decides
what and how?

a number who had defended Nixon until the bitter end. Even so, 80 percent of the representatives and 65 percent of the senators in the first post-Watergate Congress had been elected at least once before. These proportions are far above those for normal elections of the nineteenth or early twentieth century, so the trend toward stability remains.

A second difference between members of Congress and other national leaders is that a smaller proportion of them come from the metropolitan centers that otherwise dominate American life: 52 percent of the corporation presidents but only 19 percent of the senators grew up in areas with a population over 100,000. And the proportion of senators (32 percent) whose fathers were farmers was more than twice as high as it was for corporation presidents. Congressional representatives not only come from a more rural background but, more important, they seem to prefer a rural environment. The average senator traveled a bit farther than the average corporation president from home to college, but the senators' early identification with the section of the country where they grew up is demonstrated by their greater tendency to return to the home environment after college. The median distance between the childhood home and the current residence of senators is 22 miles; for corporation presidents, 342 miles. Members of Congress are thus "home town" types, and their homes have a distinctly rural and small-town quality.

These social characteristics do not, of course, determine the legislator's complete behavior. Recognizing that members of Congress are "drawn disproportionately from the elite sectors of the social structure," William Keefe, an expert Congress-watcher, says, "Nonetheless, it is far from obvious that their backgrounds shape their outlook on public policy questions, leading them to use their positions to confer unusual benefits on the upper-class interests in society."[4] From all the evidence we examined in chapter 4 on political opinions, we know that experts on public opinion would disagree: people's backgrounds do shape their outlooks. But the student of public opinion can also say that the resultant "benefits [to] the upper-class interests" are not "unusual"; we saw in chapter 6 on pressure groups that upper-class benefits are unmistakably "usual" in American policy making.

Forget for the moment that we are talking about Congress and imagine that someone had just told you about the members of a wholly unknown political group. You discover that this group is almost entirely male, that its members are mostly middle-aged or older, that a large majority are WASPs (white Anglo-Saxon Protestants), that many are millionaires and all are affluent, that the members tend to remain in office for increasingly long periods, and that—despite their high education and high status—they tend to come from rural and small-town backgrounds and continue to live near where they grew up. With no more information than this, you could safely predict that such an organization would have a conservative outlook. In fact, it is remarkable that the voting record of Congress is not more conservative than it is. The influence of constituency and party helps make the record more understandable and less remarkable.

[4] William J. Keefe, *Congress and the American People* (Englewood Cliffs, N.J.: Prentice-Hall, 1980), p. 57.

Members of Congress all start out as representatives of a particular constituency, and the problem of being reelected never permits them to forget the folks back home. However else they may differ, virtually all members of Congress share a common goal: reelection. Reelection is not merely their common goal, it is also their first priority. "Nothing else matters so much, so preoccupies their attention, or so firmly shapes their behavior."[5]

The constituencies that members of Congress worry about differ enormously. In some, as in South Dakota's Second District, the voters are all rural or small-town residents; in this instance, 8 percent of the constituents are native Americans (Indians) and 15 percent are of foreign stock (born abroad or with parents from abroad). In New York's Eighth District, in contrast, voters are piled up in high-rise apartments in the central part of a single borough, Queens, in New York City; few Indians live here, and 59 percent of the voters are of foreign stock. The voters in the First District of Illinois, on Chicago's South Side, are 89 percent black. In the Fifteenth District of Texas, which includes one ranch (the King Ranch) with more acreage than the state of Rhode Island, 75 percent are of Mexican origin or descent. Four percent of Utah's First District are of Mexican birth or descent, but blacks are too few to make up a percentage. Half the eligible voters in Florida's Sixth District (St. Petersburg) are over 58 years old; 39 percent are 65 or older. Over half the potential voters in Michigan's Second District, which includes the University of Michigan and Eastern Michigan University, are under 37 years old, and 15 percent are college students. In the Cumberland Plateau, Kentucky's Fifth District is distinctively poor, 33 percent of its families falling below the poverty level of income and over half its people having less than 9 years of education. In Maryland's Eighth District, only 3 percent of the families are below the poverty level and over half the people have at least some college education. Representatives are required to adopt quite different styles in appealing to such diverse constituencies.[6]

The one factor common to all these congressional districts is the size of their population. Thanks to the Supreme Court's one-person-one vote ruling (discussed in the preceding chapter), each congressional district is required to include roughly the same number of people—now about half a million. In the Senate, on the other hand, constituencies vary as much in population as in other characteristics. Because the framers of the Constitution designed the Senate to represent states rather than people, each state is awarded two senators, regardless of its population. What would be denounced as malappor-

[5] William J. Keefe and Morris S. Ogul, *The American Legislative Process: Congress and the States*, 4th ed. (Englewood Cliffs, N.J.: Prentice-Hall, 1977), p. 106. The interpretation of congressional behavior in terms of the pursuit of reelection is most authoritatively developed in David R. Mayhew, *Congress: The Electoral Connection* (New Haven: Yale University Press, 1974).

[6] For a fascinating account of how representatives adjust their style to the nature of their constituency, see Richard F. Fenno, Jr., *Home Style: House Members in Their Districts* (Boston: Little, Brown, 1978). For data on congressional districts, see *Congressional Districts in the 1970s* (Washington, D.C.: Congressional Quarterly, 1974), 2nd ed., and Michael Barone, Grant Ujifusa, and Douglas Matthews, *The Almanac of American Politics 1980* (New York: Dutton, 1979).

262

PART 3
decision-making
agencies:
who decides
what and how?

tionment in the House is thus constitutionally protected for the Senate: at the extremes, California senators represent 66 times as many people as do their Alaskan colleagues.

Distinctive characteristics of a constituency would hardly be worth noting if they did not influence congressional voting. One school of thought indeed implies that they are not very important, that representatives may vote as they please because it is difficult for them to find out the prevailing view in their districts.[7] But the most convincing evidence suggests that constituency characteristics do have a direct and important impact. After all, the kind of person who has a chance of being elected in the First District of Illinois will not have the same views as a person recruited in Utah's First District. "Before the congressman casts a single vote, the broad pattern of his voting has already been determined by this [recruitment] process."[8]

More Democrats than Republicans vote on the liberal side of social welfare questions, not just because of their party or ideology but also because they come from different kinds of districts.[9] Outside the south, Democratic districts are more urban, more liberal-minded, have smaller proportions of home owners, and have more people per square mile than are in Republican districts. Constituencies with these characteristics are generally expected to be on the liberal side of social welfare questions. The discovery that they tend to elect Democrats is therefore not surprising. More surprising is the fact that even when the comparison is between representatives in the same party, constituency characteristics still make a difference—Democrats from lower-status districts vote even more often for liberal measures than do Democrats whose constituents are of higher status.

The party affiliation of members of Congress

Important as they are, constituency characteristics by themselves can't explain congressional behavior. The most important fact of all about congressional representatives is that they are all members of either the Republican or Democratic political party.

Despite the weakened state of American political parties, the basic differences in Congress are between Democrats and Republicans. If you could ask for only one fact about members of Congress in order to predict their voting behavior, you should ask for party identification. Democrats and Republicans from the same constituencies in different Congresses differ drastically in their votes on issues important for those constituencies. For example, a comparison of Republicans and Democrats who occupied the same congres-

---

[7] Lewis A. Dexter, "The Representative and His District," in Robert L. Peabody and Nelson W. Polsby, eds., *New Perspectives on the House of Representatives* (Chicago: Rand McNally, 1977), pp. 3–25.

[8] John W. Kingdon, *Congressmen's Voting Decisions* (New York: Harper, 1973), p. 46.

[9] Lewis A. Froman, Jr., *Congressmen and Their Constituencies* (Skokie, Ill.: Rand McNally, 1963), chap. 7. A comprehensive study of constituency influence is Morris P. Fiorina, *Representatives, Roll Calls, and Constituencies* (Lexington, Mass.: Lexington Books, 1974).

TABLE 8·2

Congressional votes on roll calls that produced party division, 1979

	House		Senate		Both Houses	
	Democrats	*Republicans*	*Democrats*	*Republicans*	*Democrats*	*Republicans*
With party	69%	73%	68%	66%	69%	72%
Against party	23	19	22	25	23	20
Not voting	8	8	10	9	8	8
	100%	100%	100%	100%	100%	100%

Source: Recomputation of data from the *Congressional Quarterly Weekly Report,* 38 (January 19, 1980), 145–46.

sional seats found that in every district the Democrat exceeded the Republican predecessor or follower in supporting a larger role for the national government in the social welfare area.[10] Although constituency characteristics have some influence of their own, then, party affiliation has a far greater influence. Generally, of course, both forces work together: "liberal" districts elect Democrats and "conservative" districts elect Republicans. This normal match of constituency characteristics and party affiliation leads to great differences in party performance in Congress.

Party unity in the United States Congress does not approach that of either the Conservative or Labour parties in the British Parliament,[11] but it is much greater than most people realize. In 1979, for example, a majority of Democrats opposed a majority of Republicans on 47 percent of the roll call votes. The average Democrat voted against his party on 23 percent of these roll calls; the average Republican voted against his party on 20 percent (see Table 8·2). If we recalculate the figures ignoring failures to vote, about 76 percent of both the Democratic and Republican votes are found to be in support of their party majorities. This is far from perfect party unity, but it is even farther from perfect disunity.

The greatest departure from party unity in the United States comes from southern Democrats. In 1979, southern Democrats in the House supported their party on 55 percent of the roll calls in which Democratic and Republican majorities were in opposition. In the Senate, the figure was 56 percent.[12] (The average *opposition* to their party was 37 percent in the House and 34 percent in the Senate.) As a result of southern defections, the Democrats

[10] Clarence N. Stone, "Inter-Party Differences and Congressional Voting Behavior: A Partial Dissent," *American Political Science Review,* 57 (September 1963), 665–66. Also see John L. Sullivan and Robert E. O'Connor, "Electoral Choice and Popular Control of Public Policy: The Case of the 1966 House Elections," *American Political Science Review,* 66 (December 1972), 1256–68; Morris Fiorina, "Electoral Margins, Constituency Influence, and Policy Moderation: A Critical Assessment," *American Politics Quarterly,* 1 (October 1973), 479–98; and David W. Brady and Naomi B. Lynn, "Switched-Seat Congressional Districts: Their Effect on Party Voting and Public Policy," *American Journal of Political Science,* 17 (August 1973), 528–43.

[11] For a thoughtful analysis that includes comparisons of Congress with British, French, and West German legislatures, see John E. Schwarz and L. Earl Shaw, *The United States Congress in Comparative Perspective* (Hinsdale, Ill.: Dryden, 1976).

[12] *Congressional Quarterly Weekly Report,* 38 (January 19, 1980), 145–46.

264

PART 3
decision-making
agencies:
who decides
what and how?

need more than a bare majority to push through legislation. As Figure 8 · 1 shows, such large majorities were achieved in the 1965–1966 and 1975–1976 terms of Congress. What happened in each of those terms demonstrates that, although a large majority may be *necessary* for an active legislative program, it is not *sufficient* to produce such results *unless the same party holds the presidency*. With a Democrat (Lyndon B. Johnson) as President in the 1965–1966 term, the large Democratic majority in Congress adopted reforms such as Medicare that had been blocked for an entire generation. But with a Republican (Gerald Ford) as President in the 1975–1976 term, an equally large Democratic majority accomplished little. Here we see a basic fact about Congress: in the absence of party control, it has not been able to develop effective leadership or to introduce and see through its own legislative program.

FIG. 8 · 1 Percentage of House and Senate seats held by Democrats, 1953–1980.

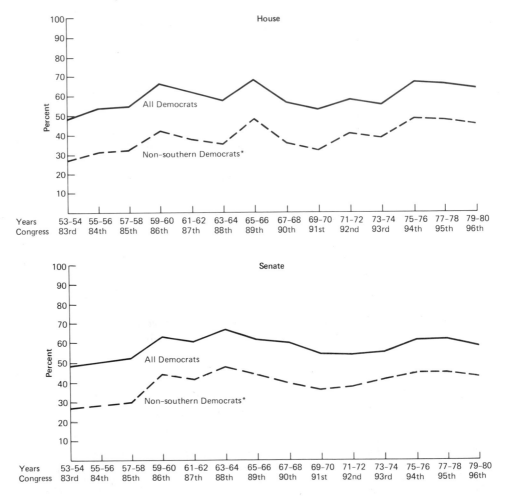

*Democrats from states other than the eleven that formed the Confederacy.

The record of Congress under Jimmy Carter demonstrates that the above statement needs further qualification. The decline of American political parties has now reached the point that even when the President has a large majority of his own party in Congress, he *still* has no assurance of getting his overall legislative program enacted. Carter ran as an outsider, relying on his own organization rather than on the Democratic party. Fellow Democrats in Congress then proceeded to treat him as an outsider to a much greater extent than they would have dared during Johnson's presidency.

THE ROLE OF MEMBERS OF CONGRESS

A role is a combination of "will" and "ought" expectations (predictions and norms) about the behavior of people in particular positions. These expectations are supported by sanctions—rewards and deprivations—of varying degrees of generosity or severity. How do they apply to congressmen?

External expectations

Although the Constitution does not stipulate the role of legislators, it clearly implies certain expectations. Underlying the formal phrases from the eighteenth century is the obvious expectation that the members of Congress would play a major role in the new government. Not only are they granted "all legislative Powers," but they are expected to determine how to exercise those powers. Congress is expected to manage its own affairs, determine its own rules of procedure, judge "the Qualifications of its own Members," and select its leaders (except that the Vice-president is designated as president of the Senate). In addition, it has the power to expel a member by a two-thirds vote. The belief that Congress should be free from harassment in carrying out these responsibilities is manifest in this protection: "They shall in all cases, except Treason, Felony and Breach of the Peace, be privileged from Arrest during their Attendance at the Session of the respective Houses, and in going to and returning from the same; and for any Speech or Debate in either House, they shall not be questioned in any other Place."

The great power and independence given to Congress is not given without restraints. And the restraints are also based on official expectations about congressional behavior. The new legislators need to read beyond the first sentence of Article I, with its grandiose reference to "all legislative Powers herein granted"; when they get to Section 9, and later to the Bill of Rights, they discover that some powers (primarily those that could be used for legislative punishment of individuals or denial of basic rights) not only are not "herein granted" but are specifically denied. They will also discover that the apparent congressional control of those legislative powers which *are* granted is not complete. The President, for example, has the right to veto legislation and the

266

PART 3
decision-making
agencies:
who decides
what and how?

duty to recommend legislation. In addition, the Constitution clearly intended Congress to be under public control. The provision for popular choice of its members (for senators, this dates from the adoption of Amendment 17 in 1913) is supplemented by two requirements: each house must publish a "Journal of its Proceedings" and "the Yeas and Nays of the Members on any questions shall, at the desire of one fifth of those Present, be entered on the Journal."

Officially, then, the role of members of Congress calls for the exercise of great (but not unlimited) rule-making power in a relationship of responsibility to the public. And the general public regards Congress as having even more responsibility than the President for dealing with national problems. Congress is said to have "the most say" by a margin of 53 to 13 percent (with 34 percent saying Congress and the President have an equal say).[13] When it comes to writing their representatives to influence the way they carry out that responsibility, however, those who must write for themselves are far behind those who can dictate letters to a secretary. Among the general public, only about 16 percent say they have written their representative or any other national leader in the last two or three years. Among the heads of business firms employing 100 or more employees, the contrast is striking: almost 80 percent say they have communicated directly with Congress.[14] Frequently they ask their representatives to perform some service—furnish information or clarify a problem with an administrator, for example—that has nothing to do with their constitutionally defined role of lawmaker. These requests imply that the legislator is expected to represent the constituency not just as legislator but as "go-between" and agent of constituents in relation to other agencies of government.

The local and national leaders of the legislator's party, all the people who invested time and money in the campaign for offfice, the President (especially when both belong to the same party), organized interest groups in his or her constituency—all of these expect the congressional representative to give at least a sympathetic hearing to their demands. The more knowledgeable among them know that members of Congress are the objects of such a welter of expectations that no simple stimulus-response model will predict their behavior, whether the stimulus comes from constituents, party, President, or pressure groups.

Life in Congress: internal demands

Congress has a group life of its own. Just as being a member of a Boy Scout troop, a neighborhood gang, or a college sorority influences a person's behavior and habits, so does being a member of Congress. Like any other functioning group, Congress has certain norms to which the new members must adjust. The members must show respect for Congress as an institution

---

[13] The CPS 1978 National Election Study.
[14] Raymond A. Bauer, Ithiel de Sola Pool, and Lewis Anthony Dexter, American Business and Public Policy (New York: Atherton, 1963), p. 201.

For many people, the Capitol symbolizes the power of the national government.

and must adjust their behavior to the needs of the group. They will act, in other words, not merely as particular kinds of persons with a given party identification and constituency background, but also as members of Congress who are involved in its needs as an organization. The "club atmosphere" of the Senate demonstrates the respect members show one another, even those who disagree on everything except the Senate's importance.

What unwritten norms do the Senate and House impose on new members?[15] First, the freshmen members are expected to be "seen and not heard," to serve (without complaining to the "upperclassmen") a decent period of apprenticeship, during which they perform routine chores without glory.

[15] Material in this and the next paragraph comes largely from Donald R. Matthews, *U.S. Senators and Their World* (Chapel Hill: University of North Carolina Press, 1960). Richard F. Fenno, Jr., finds a strikingly similar set of norms to be functional for the integration of some House committees but not for others. See *Congressmen in Committees* (Boston: Little, Brown, 1973).

268

PART 3
decision-making
agencies:
who decides
what and how?

Second, they are expected to devote themselves primarily to routine legislative tasks rather than to seek publicity by proposing major policies or by trying to dominate public committee hearings or congressional debate. Third, they are expected to specialize in the area of legislation in which their committee or constituency has a particular stake; to try to take the lead in other legislative areas would be to challenge the leadership and the special rights of their colleagues. Fourth, they are expected to cooperate with their colleagues, show themselves willing to "give and take" rather than insist on their own principles without compromise. Their ideology may be firmly fixed in their own minds, but they must be willing to compromise. Finally, and especially in the Senate, they are expected to show great respect for their colleagues as individuals and deep attachment to their branch of Congress as an institution. It is because of these unofficial rules of behavior that we hear very little from new members of the Senate or House during their first years in office.

Why do the norms take the particular form we have described? Donald Matthews suggests that they are highly "functional." That is, they are necessary if Congress is to survive without major change. His remarks about the Senate may be applied with almost equal force to the House:

These folkways . . . are highly functional to the Senate social system since they provide motivation for the performance of vital duties and essential modes of behavior which, otherwise, would go unrewarded. They discourage frequent and lengthy speech-making in a chamber without any other effective limitation on debate, encourage the development of expertness and a division of labor in a group of overworked laymen facing unbelievably complex problems, soften the inevitable personal conflicts of a

UPI

Outspoken ideologists such as
Senator Barry Goldwater (R.-Ariz.)
must be willing to compromise in
the Senate in order to win the
respect of their colleagues.

problem-solving body, and encourage bargaining and the cautious use of awesome formal powers. Without these folkways, the Senate could hardly operate with its present organization and rules.[16]

Other pressures on a member of Congress—such as ambition for the presidency, a fixed ideology, or the special demands of his constituency—are sometimes strong enough to outweigh congressional norms in governing his behavior. Behavior that is functional for Congress as a group may not be functional for an individual's career or, for that matter, for society at large.[17] Nevertheless, a majority conform.

Getting Reelected: unsafe at any margin[18]

New members of Congress begin to worry about reelection even before they take their seats. Both political parties, in orientation seminars for their newly elected colleagues, primarily emphasize ways to stay in office. Some critics think the focus should be on how to enact the policies in the party's platform, but that is not the emphasis of current American politics. Representatives and senators win office mostly through their own campaign organizations, not through any district or state party organization. This means they cannot look to the party organization for protection against future challengers—hence the feeling of vulnerability, the need to "run scared" and to run at all times.

Despite—or perhaps because of—their fear of defeat, incumbents who seek reelection to Congress are successful over 90 percent of the time.[19] Moreover, the margin of victory for incumbents has increased so much over the last 20 years that fewer and fewer challengers come even close to an upset.[20] What accounts for the remarkable success of incumbents? The traditional explanation of congressional elections was in terms of voters' feelings about the political parties, the President, and the condition of the economy.[21] But none of these factors can explain the success of incumbents of both parties. The answer seems to be found in the increasing atomization or personalizing of American politics. With parties less important as institutions, feelings about members of Congress are not necessarily tied in with feelings about national

[16] *U.S. Senators and Their World,* p. 116.

[17] See Ralph K. Huitt, "The Outsider in the Senate: An Alternative Role," *American Political Science Review,* 60 (September 1961), 566–75, and Professor Matthew's letter in the following issue of the *Review.*

[18] This section relies heavily on Thomas E. Mann, *Unsafe at Any Margin: Interpreting Congressional Elections* (Washington, D.C.: American Enterprise Institute for Public Policy and Research, 1978).

[19] *Ibid.,* p. 2. The House record is more impressive than that of the Senate.

[20] David R. Mayhew, "Congressional Elections: The Case of the Vanishing Marginals," *Polity,* 6 (Spring 1974), 295–317; John A. Ferejohn, "On the Decline of Competition in Congressional Elections," *American Political Science Review,* 71 (March 1977), 166–76; Albert Cover and David Mayhew, "Congressional Dynamics and the Decline of Competitive Congressional Elections," in L. C. Dodd and B. I. Oppenheimer, eds., *Congress Reconsidered* (New York: Praeger, 1977), pp. 54–72.

[21] See, for example, Edward Tufte, *Political Control of the Economy* (Princeton: Princeton University Press, 1978).

270

PART 3
decision-making
agencies:
who decides
what and how?

leaders or institutions. Candidates become more important as individuals. The result is that "modern publicity-conscious, service-oriented incumbents"[22] have an enormous advantage. Members of Congress are keenly aware that their greatest campaign resource is Congress itself. William Keefe makes the point with admirable clarity:

> . . . members, supported by their staffs, search steadily for ways to win the next election. Congress is there to help them. They use public business to distribute private and local side benefits. And they do it with exceptional skill. By imaginatively using their institutional position, the vast majority of members have insulated themselves from the risks and vicissitudes of elections.[23]

The advantage of incumbency began to increase during the 1960s because members of Congress came to concentrate more on nonpartisan, noncontroversial, errand-boy activities and less on partisan and controversial legislation and national policies.[24] David R. Mayhew specifies three kinds of activities that solidify "the electoral connection" of incumbents: advertising, credit claiming, and position taking.[25] Note that none of these requires the member to achieve any legislative goal. On the contrary, members serve their reelection goal better by less controversial activity. They need to achieve name recognition by appearing in the district as often and with as much favorable publicity as possible *(advertising)*. They can create good will by winning federal projects for their district or by helping constituents who have dealings with the bureaucracy, such as trying to get one voter's child into a service academy or another's relative out of the army *(credit claiming)*. And they can take positions in opposition to inflation, in favor of national security, or on whatever issue seems helpful *(position taking)*. The necessity is not to solve problems but to take sound positions on them, for the legislator "as a position taker is a speaker rather than a doer." As Mayhew says, "the electoral requirement is not that he make pleasing things happen but that he make pleasing judgmental statements."[26]

With all these appeals helping them, why are members of Congress so fearful about reelection? Are they merely paranoid? Not at all. Despite the overall success of incumbents, *congressional seats really are unsafe at any margin.* Thomas Mann demonstrates that during the very period when the winning margins of incumbents were increasing, the range of variation in votes was also increasing.[27] Most incumbents were winning by large margins, but some were losing in equally spectacular fashion. The individualistic tone of congressional campaigns thus works both ways: *once a challenger is able*

---

[22] The phrase is from David Broder, "November Mystery: Incumbents' Chances," *Washington Post,* June 18, 1978.

[23] *Congress and the American People,* p. 46.

[24] Morris P. Fiorina, *Congress: Keystone of the Washington Establishment* (New Haven: Yale University Press, 1977).

[25] *Congress: The Electoral Connection* (New Haven: Yale University Press, 1974), especially pp. 49–77.

[26] *Ibid.,* p. 62.

[27] *Unsafe at Any Margin,* p. 85.

to raise substantial funds, he or she can offer a serious threat to the incumbent.[28] And the name recognition that incumbents work so hard to achieve can prove disastrous if the image turns negative. In 1974, this helped seal the fate of Republican members of the House Judiciary Committee who had most stoutly defended Richard Nixon against impeachment.[29]

Because opinion polls found a majority of people unable to name the candidates, researchers long underestimated the influence of individual candidates on congressional election outcomes.[30] But in the polling booth the voter's task is merely to recognize names, not to recall them without help. Any student who has ever failed to recall the answer to an exam question that could have been recognized in a multiple-choice format can appreciate the difference. Voters face a multiple-choice ballot, not an essay exam. Recognition of candidates' names is actually quite high, averaging well over 90 percent for incumbents, over 70 percent for challengers, and 76 percent for opponents seeking open seats.[31] But the important point for our argument here is the *difference from one district to another in candidate recognition.* The range for incumbents was from 74 to 100 percent; for challengers, from 47 to 96 percent; for opponents seeking open seats, from 46 to 97 percent. Overall election results may be a product of broad national forces, but these variations strongly support Thomas Mann's argument: "Increasingly, congressmen are responsible for their own margins of victory or defeat, and the electoral constraints they face are defined largely in their individual districts." These district forces "include the reputation of the candidates, the campaign effort, and volatile local issues—all of which are to some extent within the control of the candidates themselves." Thus, "as a corrective to a large body of literature arguing that party and incumbency explain congressional elections," he redirects attention to what might appear to be obvious: the importance of "the voters' reactions to the candidates in their districts."[32]

The importance of a candidate's reputation and the difference between name recall and recognition were both illustrated in the 1976 reelection campaign of Utah's Representative Alan Howe. During the summer doldrums of the campaign, Congressman Howe was arrested for seeking to buy sexual favors from a Salt Lake City policewoman who was disguised as a prostitute. Needless to say, interest in the hapless Congressman increased dramatically.

[28] Gary C. Jacobson, "The Effects of Campaign Spending in Congressional Elections," *American Political Science Review,* 72 (June 1978), 469.

[29] Gerald C. Wright, Jr., "Constituency Response to Congressional Behavior: The Impact of the House Judiciary Committee Impeachment Votes," *Western Political Quarterly,* 30 (September 1977), 401–10. Also see Robert S. Erikson, "Is There Such a Thing as a Safe Seat?" *Polity,* 8 (Summer 1976), 623–32.

[30] Donald E. Stokes and Warren E. Miller, "Party Government and the Saliency of Congress," in A. Campbell et al., *Elections and the Political Order* (New York: Wiley, 1966), pp. 194–211. The same point of view was expressed more recently in Warren E. Miller and Teresa E. Levitin, *Leadership and Change: Presidential Elections from 1952 to 1976* (Cambridge, Mass.: Winthrop, 1976), p. 33.

[31] Mann, *Unsafe at Any Margin,* p. 32. The data are from a sample of districts in 1974 and 1976. The surveys were conducted 2 to 6 weeks before election day, so the results probably understate recognition of the candidates, especially nonincumbents, on election day.

[32] *Ibid.,* pp. 3, 22–23, 99.

"To close on an upbeat note, I'm happy to report we received twenty-two per cent more in kickbacks than we paid out in bribes."

Drawing by Dana Fradon; © 1976. The New Yorker Magazine, Inc.

Nevertheless, a survey in the district later in the summer found only 41 percent of his constituents able to *recall* his name. Nothing could better have demonstrated the inappropriateness of name recall as a measure of public awareness of a candidate. In fact, 99 percent of the respondents in the same survey *recognized* his name and 61 percent reported negative feelings about him (only 12 percent reported positive feelings). This was an increase from an 89 percent recognition rate in a survey conducted the preceding year and, most significantly, an increase from only 6 percent expressing negative feelings in the earlier survey. The Utah story was repeated on a larger scale and with even more serious misconduct in 1980 when a number of congressmen were charged with accepting bribes from FBI agents posing as representatives of foreign interests. All these former members of Congress could attest to the invalidity of the old axiom that unfavorable publicity is better than none at all.

These illustrations are, of course, as unusual as they are dramatic. Most members of Congress become favorably known to their constituents through advertising, credit claiming, and position taking. But all are subject to a form of accountability, lest they become unfavorably known. This negative accountability extends to policy issues, also. Incumbents must avoid taking positions that could lead their districts to challenge their policies no less than their personal rectitude or sincerity.[33]

ROLE PERFORMANCE: STRUCTURE OF CONGRESSIONAL ACTIVITY

Role performance does not always conform to role expectations: an occasional minister takes off with the church treasury and organist. Some failures to conform violate internal rather than external expectations: an occasional doctor tells a patient that another doctor's treatment was incompetent. Deviations from external expectations are likely to bring judgment from society as a whole (the erring minister would be jailed). Deviations from internal expectations are likely to bring judgment from one's fellow group members (the erring doctor would receive few referrals of patients from colleagues).

The organization of Congress is well adapted to meet internal expectations. Some critics argue, however, that Congress is *not* structured to fulfill the principal external expectation: authoritative rule making. We will be in a better position to assess this charge later.

Congress as a separate system of power

The chief difference between the United States Congress and most other national legislatures is its relative independence from the executive branch. In most western democracies the chief executive and other cabinet officials are chosen from, and retain membership in, the legislature. The United States Congress is in a quite different position. Members of Congress and the President are separately elected, they have different constituencies, and Congress chooses its own leaders. Members of Congress may not hold an office in the executive branch; this reinforces the status of Congress as a separate system of power.

With Congress separated from the executive, it had to develop its own sources of information and its own agencies for considering legislation. This need led to the committee system. If most parliamentary government is really government by cabinets, congressional government is, as Woodrow Wilson observed, government by committees. As we shall see below, these committees are not only free from any direct control by the executive but also largely free from control by the internal leaders of Congress itself. Power in Congress is thus widely dispersed in contrast to the concentration of power in parliamentary governments.

A second peculiarity in the organization of Congress is that it is truly bicameral (divided into two houses). Most other national legislatures also have

[33] Kingdon, *Congressmen's Voting Decisions*, chap. 2.

274

PART 3
decision-making
agencies:
who decides
what and how?

two houses, but the lower house has generally acquired the exclusive power to legislate, with the upper house reduced to the point where it can delay but not block the enactments of the lower house. The necessity for positive action by both houses of the United States Congress further spreads power and adds more points at which legislation may be blocked.

The House of Representatives was originally conceived as the "popular" branch of Congress, with members elected directly by the people for two-year terms. Each state was guaranteed at least one representative; beyond that provision, representation in the House was to be apportioned among the states according to population. Accordingly, the House was planned as the only popular agency of the national government—popular both in the manner in which its members were elected and in the scheme of apportioning representation. The Senate, by contrast, was planned as the "nonpopular," or federal, branch of Congress. Its members were to be elected for six-year terms by the state legislatures, and each state was guaranteed two senators regardless of its population.

Some ironic twists have radically altered the intention of the founding fathers that the Senate be a conservative body checking the more liberal House members, all freshly elected every two years and brimming with new ideas. Two things went wrong with these plans. First was the *democratization of the Senate* in the twentieth century as a result of the adoption of popular election of senators and the spread of two-party competition to a majority of the states. The greater variety in the senators' statewide electorates may actually encourage a more liberal stance than is permitted in smaller congressional districts often dominated by a single interest. By 1970, urban residents made up a majority of the population in 41 states. Thus, few senators can afford to champion the virtues of a simple and conservative rural way of life. They face active competition to keep them attuned to the needs of their urban constituents.

The second twentieth-century change that has reversed the expectations of the founding fathers is the *professionalization of the House career*. In the nineteenth century, the House was a place where an ambitious young man (no women were eligible) could quickly make a name for himself and move on to greater things.[34] But while the Senate has become more competitive and more responsive to change than the framers of the Constitution intended, the House has confounded their expectations in an opposite manner. The advantage of incumbency applies more to the House than the Senate: among incumbents seeking reelection in 1978, the victory rate was 94 percent for representatives, 60 percent for senators. Instead of returning a fresh group of popular spokesmen every two years, House districts regularly return the incumbent. Only the retirement of an unusual number of representatives

---

[34] Samuel Kernell, "Toward Understanding 19th Century Congressional Careers: Ambition, Competition, and Rotation," *American Journal of Political Science,* 21 (November 1977), 669–93. Also see Charles S. Bullock III, "House Careerists: Changing Patterns of Longevity and Attrition," *American Political Science Review,* 66 (December 1972), 1295–1300; Morris P. Fiorina, David W. Rohde, and Peter Wissel, "Historical Change in House Turnover," in Norman J. Ornstein, ed., *Congress in Change: Evolution and Reform* (New York: Praeger, 1975), pp. 24–57.

in the 1970s, after Congress voted greatly improved retirement benefits for itself, kept the House from approaching gerontocracy (rule by the elders) in the 1980s. This is certainly contrary to the hopes of liberals and the fears of conservatives among the framers.

Richard Fenno highlights these points in his comparison of the Committee on Interior and Insular Affairs of the House with that of the Senate. The most recurrent battle confronting these committees is waged between conservationists and commercial users of public lands and other natural resources. In the House, the basic slant of the committee is toward "protection for the commercial users of land and water resources"; in the Senate, it is toward "adequate preservation of land and water resources." Part of Fenno's explanation is the greater liberalism of the Senate committee: "Although we cannot equate liberals with conservationists (or vice versa), it does seem likely that the more liberally inclined a political group, the less sympathetic it will be to the economic interests of commercial users." Differences in the constituencies of House and Senate round out the explanation: "Senators have larger, more diverse constituencies, less easily dominated by a few economic interests. A Senator must do more balancing of interests, and conservationists will loom larger in these calculations." A Senate committee member sums the point up nicely (albeit with some exaggeration of rural representation in the House):

Senators represent entire states. Since the popular election of Senators, they have been responsive to all the people of the state. House members represent more of the rural areas; but Senators are concerned about city people as well. These people are the ones who feel the need for outdoor recreation. And the sportsmen—they are becoming increasingly numerous and they tend to gather in the cities. That's why the Senate Committee is more in favor of conservation than the House Committee.[35]

Rules of congressional procedure

Groups must have recognized leaders and rules of procedure if they are to function. Just how complex their organization needs to be depends on the size of the group and the purpose it sets for itself. The House, for example, is larger and therefore more highly organized than the Senate. The executive branch, by the same token, is even more highly organized than the House. Administration calls for more unified and rapid action than does legislation, and the size of the executive establishment is too vast for any coherent action to be taken without a much more structured organization.

Table 8·3 compares the characteristics of the House and Senate. The larger size of the House and its smaller constituencies lead to much greater specialization there than in the Senate. These differences in the degree of specialization are a key to understanding how each house contributes to policy making. The committees in which the specialized work is done are much

[35] Richard F. Fenno, Jr., *Congressmen in Committees* (Boston: Little, Brown, 1973), pp. 59, 168 (emphases removed).

276

PART 3
decision-making
agencies:
who decides
what and how?

TABLE 8·3

Major differences between House and Senate

House	Senate
Larger (435 members)	Smaller (100 members)
More formal	Less formal
More hierarchically organized	Less hierarchically organized
Acts more quickly	Acts more slowly
Rules more rigid	Rules more flexible
Power less evenly distributed	Power more evenly distributed
Longer apprentice period	Shorter apprentice period
More impersonal	More personal
Less "important" constituencies	More "important" constituencies
Less prestige	More prestige
More "conservative"	More "liberal"

Source: Lewis A. Froman, *The Congressional Process: Strategies, Rules, and Procedures* (Boston: Little, Brown, 1967), p. 7.

more important in the House, and the individual is much more important in the Senate. With almost an equal number of "standing" (permanent) committees (22 in the House, 17 in the Senate) and over 4 times as many representatives as senators, each senator will serve on 3 or 4 committees, while each representative concentrates on 1 or 2.

In view of the large number of representatives, then, the House must be more tightly organized if it is to act. It is a complicated job for 435 representatives to act on any matter, even one on which a majority is in strong agreement. During the early years of the House, when its membership was small, the only important function of the Rules Committee was to report a system of rules at the beginning of each Congress. As the House increased in size, however, the power of the Rules Committee increased to make it the key coordinating committee of the entire body. If the Rules Committee opposes a bill, it may simply refuse to recommend a rule under which it can be scheduled for consideration. When it does propose a rule for the consideration of a measure, the rule may drastically limit debate, or it may limit the amendments that may be offered. The members of the House may reject the Rules Committee's resolution (it is not subject to amendment), but to do so is to lose the chance to consider the measure at all and to incur the disfavor of a powerful committee. Affirmative action on the committee's proposed rule is thus almost always assured.[36]

Although the rules of the House show far less respect than those of the Senate for the right of individual members to debate, they do show special respect for the power of the standing committees. When a committee unfriendly to a measure refuses to report that measure to the floor for consideration, the only way the bill can be pried loose is by means of a "discharge

---

[36] For a good overview of Congress, see Randall B. Ripley, *Congress: Process and Policy,* 2nd ed. (New York: Norton, 1978); on the committee system, see chap. 5.

petition" signed by a majority of the total House membership. Although this is not so extreme as the requirements for cloture in the Senate (discussed below), respect for the committee system is so great—and absenteeism so regular—that the discharge petition is not used often. A majority cannot be permanently frustrated in the House, but if it is to make its will prevail it may have to mobilize its strength completely and show real determination.

In contrast to the House, the Senate—which likes to call itself "the greatest deliberative body in the world"—operates under a rule of unlimited debate. A "previous question" motion enables a House majority to bring a measure to a vote, but the Senate has no previous question rule. By permitting full debate, Senate rules also permit the "filibuster," a practice that enables a minority to prevent the passage of a law by talking it to death, never letting it come to a vote. Minorities also use the filibuster to get the majority to give in on certain points.

The process of closing off debate so that a question can be voted on (called "cloture") has long been difficult in the Senate. From 1949 to 1959, the rule was that debate could be ended only with the approval of two-thirds of the *entire membership* of the Senate. In 1959, the Senate restored a 1917 rule which required a favorable vote by two-thirds of the senators *present and voting*. But northern and western liberals argued that the change did not go far enough, and in 1975 they won another concession. Since 1975, cloture has been adopted by a vote of *three-fifths of the entire membership* (60 senators if there are no vacancies). The present rule still limits the majority to a degree that would have seemed severe to the founding fathers; for the first 20 years of Senate history, debate could be ended by a simple majority vote!

Respect for the individual member is so great in the Senate that cloture is difficult to apply. Liberals and conservatives both employ the filibuster, as they did when liberals opposed a loan to Lockheed Aircraft in 1971 and conservatives opposed establishment of a consumer agency in 1974. But the filibuster was most conspicuously employed by southerners, to oppose legislation benefiting blacks. From 1917 to 1964, eleven bills to help blacks—from anti-lynching laws to civil rights acts—were opposed by filibuster. None of them won passage. In 1964 for the first time, a filibuster was broken to pass a civil rights act. From 1917 through 1970, a total of 49 cloture votes were taken, only 8 being successful. Beginning in 1971, however, the frequency of both cloture votes and the imposition of cloture increased. This change, little noticed by most observers of Congress, indicated a significant weakening of the filibuster as a weapon even before the 1975 change in Senate rules. With the change, the power of a minority to frustrate a majority in the Senate has been further weakened.

Elected party leaders

As these key rules and norms suggest, Congress is not dominated by strong leaders. If there is any overall leadership, it comes from outside, from the President. Within the Congress itself, the bicameral system combined with

278

PART 3
decision-making
agencies:
who decides
what and how?

the weakness of American political parties makes unified leadership out of the question. The Constitution permits each house to determine the power of its own leaders. As we would expect from the tighter organization of the House, the leaders there have more influence on their colleagues than do leaders in the Senate.

Before Congress convenes, the Republican and Democratic members of each house meet in party conference or caucus to select slates of candidates for the offices of their respective houses. Electing these officers in merely a formality, however; voting as a bloc, the members of the majority party in each chamber always elect their slate.

In the House the principal officer is the *speaker.* He is the leading member of the majority party in the House and is frequently described as "the second most powerful man in Washington." Before the powers of the speaker were curtailed early in this century, his influence was even greater than it is today. At one time he exercised life-and-death control over legislation. Even today he is the strongest figure in Congress. The speaker plays several roles: he is the presiding officer and a highly respected member of the House; he acts as contact man with the President when they are of the same party; and he serves as the leader of his party in the House. As presiding officer, the speaker announces the order of business, puts questions to a vote and reports the vote, recognizes members who want the floor, interprets the rules, squelches delaying tactics, refers bills to committees, and appoints the members of select and conference committees. Although a decision of the speaker may occasionally be overruled by the House itself, as in referring a controversial bill to a committee, his normal control over these functions gives him so much influence that even the House Rules Committee can ill afford to buck the speaker. In 1975 the House Democratic caucus increased the speaker's power by allowing him to nominate all Democratic members of the Rules Committee, subject to ratification by the caucus. (The Republicans still employ a Committee on Committees to make all their committee assignments.)

As a member of Congress, the speaker is entitled to participate in debate and to vote. On the rare occasions when the speaker descends from the rostrum to take a direct part in the debate, other members recognize that the issue must be an important one, and his fellow party members realize that a "wrong" vote may put them and their future projects in danger of the speaker's disapproval. His close contact with the President, particularly when the speaker and the President are of the same party, lends further weight to his views. The elevation of a representative to the speakership, though it does not give him a national constituency, does cause him to behave more as a national and less as a local figure.

The speaker is assisted by the *majority leader* (or floor leader) and the majority whip.[37] These three are general leaders who, together with commit-

---

[37] The minority party strives for a coherent opposition under a minority leader and a minority whip. The title "whip" is derived from a British fox-hunting term, the "whipperin," applied to the man responsible for keeping hounds from leaving the pack. The term came to be used in the British Parliament in the late eighteenth century. See Robert Luce, *Legislative Procedure* (Boston: Houghton Mifflin, 1922), pp. 501–2.

tee and subcommittee chairpersons and perhaps other senior committee members, manage specific pieces of legislation. The last nine speakers all served previously as floor leaders. This career line underscores the importance of the floor leader's position and reveals the similarity of personal qualifications needed for the two roles. These attributes are mainly the skills of a *negotiator*, a person who can bargain with fellow House members on a personal basis of trust, and who is more devoted to the House than to any broader cause. If these sound like strange qualifications for a party leader, remember that the parties in Congress are a reflection of the kinds of parties we have outside Congress. The lack of strong party leadership in Congress was once explained by the fact that American political parties are merely loose coalitions of local party organizations. Now that the local party organizations in House districts have been so largely replaced by temporary, candidate-based organizations, the parties are even more nebulous as institutions. Accordingly, the speaker and majority leader must rely on personal negotiation and persuasion. Nevertheless, whatever chance the House has for centralized leadership comes from its speaker and majority leader.[38]

The majority leader's task is to lead the party's efforts on the floor and to arrange the day-to-day House schedule. The majority whip, who helps in this task, has lots of assistants—4 deputy whips and 20 assistant whips for the Democrats, 4 regional whips and 12 assistant whips for the Republicans. What both parties try to accomplish through this organization is to: (1) ensure that a maximum number of their party's members are present when critical votes are taken; (2) give information to party members on pending measures; (3) find out how members of their party will vote on important legislation; (4) induce wavering members to vote with their party.

The success of these efforts by the party leadership is difficult to assess. When the majority party's whip organization is active, however, attendance for voting is greater than when the whip is inactive. Despite the relative weakness of political parties, then, party leaders in the House can succeed when they apply their *bargaining resources* and their *control over events and information*. In bargaining, they are dealing with members who know that their cooperation may be rewarded by favorable consideration of their own pet projects. Controls may be as subtle as transportation arrangements. A subcommittee, about to leave on a foreign trip, may be informed that takeoff on its air force plane has been delayed so that cooperative members of the subcommittee will have time to remain on the floor for a crucial vote. Nevertheless, the chances of success in these efforts decrease as the issue becomes more visible and more important to particular constituencies.

Power is even more dispersed in the Senate than in the House. Because each member of the smaller body is relatively more powerful, the possibility for centralized leadership is reduced. The Vice-President is the presiding officer but not a leader. He presides over the Senate as Vice-President, not as a product of the Senate itself. The majority and minority floor leaders are the key party leaders of the Senate, but their positions are even more

[38] See Ripley, *Congress: Process and Policy,* chap. 6.

280

PART 3
decision-making
agencies:
who decides
what and how?

personal and less institutional than those of their counterparts in the House.

Students of Congress generally agree that Lyndon B. Johnson was the most skillful and successful Senate floor leader in recent history. Johnson himself described the position in terms of persuasion, observing that "the only real power available to the leader is the power of persuasion. There is no patronage; no power to discipline; no authority to fire Senators like a President can fire his members of Cabinet." One can argue that *all* power is ultimately based on persuasion, but the Senate floor leader enjoys few of the resources that assist in persuasion. As the center of the legislative party's network of communication, he can help keep a cooperating senator informed on crucial questions of timing, and he can help a member secure an assignment to a special committee or even get that member's pet legislation before the Senate for a vote. But the potential of the position is much more dependent on the personality of the occupant than is, say, the potential of the presidency. When Senator Mike Mansfield (D.-Mont.) succeeded Johnson as floor leader, his easygoing personal qualities produced radically different role expectations and role performance. General party leadership was reduced to the point where other senators complained that they were not being sufficiently led! When Senator Robert Byrd (D.-W. Va.) became majority leader in 1977, the office took on still a different role, falling between those of Johnson and Mansfield in assertiveness.

Party conferences (Democrats in the House call them caucuses) do more than choose the official leaders in their respective houses. They are the governing bodies of the political parties in Congress. The conference is to the party in each house what the national convention is to the party in the nation, and it is almost equally ineffective as a real governing body. In addition to selecting the party leaders in each house, the conference sets up committees to make assignments to legislative committees and tries to create party consensus on policy and procedure. In 1975 the House Democratic caucus created a flurry of excitement by flexing its muscle enough to show signs of actually behaving as a governing body for House Democrats. The 1974 election, in the wake of Watergate, brought in 75 new Democratic representatives, most of them liberals. This freshman class dared to challenge the seniority system by joining with other liberal Democrats in the caucus to oust three chairmen of important standing committees. (The ousted chairmen were all southerners, and all were replaced by non-southerners.)

Having demonstrated that a party's caucus could exercise enough power to dent the seniority system, the House Democratic caucus of 1975 went on to make procedural reforms, the first significant changes for the House since 1946. The Democratic members of the Ways and Means Committee had previously held the power to make Democratic committee assignments. The caucus took that power away and gave it to the caucus's Steering and Policy Committee, with the exception that the speaker—if a Democrat—was allowed to nominate Democratic members of the Rules Committee. The caucus further required that nominees to chair the appropriations subcommittees be approved by the caucus itself. These and other changes were designed to enhance the power of the caucus at the expense of old-time seniority leaders.

Flushed with their success in defying the seniority system and in making procedural changes, liberal Democrats moved in early 1975 to employ the caucus as a means of influencing legislation. The caucus instructed Democrats on the House Rules Committee to bring to the floor two amendments to legislation on oil depletion, and it adopted a resolution opposing more military aid to Indochina. This is precisely the sort of influence that the governing body of a party would be expected to exercise if the party were committed to a unified, disciplined approach to policy. But many Democratic representatives viewed such efforts by the caucus to influence their votes as a threat to the power of standing committees. The Democrats failed in a series of efforts to override President Ford's vetoes of their legislation despite the fact that—with a 291 to 144 majority—all they needed was solid support from their own party to override a veto. The freshmen representatives who had helped push through reforms became bitter toward their elders and blamed their party's leaders in large part for the legislative defeats. The leaders found the freshmen "politically naive and accuse[d] them of seeking instant solutions to complex problems. Congress changes, but at glacial speed. Congressional government continues to be government by committees.

Seniority leaders and the committee system

The basic organizational units through which Congress works are the *standing committees.* Every bill that reaches the floor of Congress has first been considered by a committee. In contrast to the practice in most state legislatures, no bill is reported out for the consideration of all the members until it has first won a majority vote in the committee.[39] The House has 22, the Senate 17, of these virtually independent centers of power, each dealing with a different policy area—agriculture, appropriations, banking and currency, veterans' affairs. These roughly correspond to the major policy areas of the national government. Although the committees do not correspond exactly to departments in the administrative structure, they provide regular channels for communication about policy between the executive and legislative branches. They also provide a means through which Congress can exercise control over the administration of policy. In policy making, Congress and the Administration function as parts of a single system, sharing rather than dividing powers. Hence, each committee sets up its subcommittees to work closely with counterparts in the bureaucracy.

As the bureaucracy grows more complex, Congress tends to create new subcommittees. In the last major reorganization of Congress in 1946, the number of subcommittees was reduced to 148 (89 in the House, 59 in the Senate). By 1980 the standing committees had 257 subcommittees (156 in the House, 101 in the Senate). Their specialized knowledge of a narrow policy area permits members of these little-known subcommittees to exercise much influence in standing committee decisions and hence in Congress as a whole.

· [39] A measure may be discharged from a committee by vote of the House or Senate, but this is a rare and difficult procedure.

282

PART 3
decision-making
agencies:
who decides
what and how?

How is the membership of standing committees determined? The majority party in each house fixes the ratio of seats on the committees, giving itself a majority in most committees roughly corresponding to its majority in the house as a whole. No fixed guidelines are used in deciding which party member gets what committee assignment. Seniority is the most important qualification, although other factors also can be taken into account: reputation as a "responsible" legislator (one who is moderate in approach, politically flexible but not without conviction) and the desire of members of Congress to be on committees handling legislation of particular interest to their constituents.[40]

Party leaders are thus not so powerless as they are generally thought to be. Committee appointments are the chief weapons of party leaders in affecting the output of the standing committees. In 1975, for example, conservative Senator James B. Allen of Alabama wanted appointment to a Democratic vacancy on the Judiciary Committee. Because the Judiciary Committee handles civil rights legislation and was soon to consider an extension of the Voting Rights Act of 1965, the liberal majority on the Senate's Democratic Steering Committee filled the vacancy instead with a liberal, Senator James Abourezk of South Dakota. And the frustrations of 75 Democratic freshmen representatives in the 94th Congress perhaps began when they looked at their committee assignments. They made up 26 percent of all Democratic representatives and found themselves with over half the Democratic seats on some committees. But the three most powerful House committees—Rules, Appropriations, and Ways and Means—had only 7 freshmen among 73 Democratic members. No freshman representative was assigned to the Rules Committee. With a view toward getting their policies produced, leaders had appropriately molded the committees.

Just as Congress functions through its standing committees, so each committee functions through its chairperson. But although the general power of Congress is scattered, committee power is concentrated in the hands of the chairperson. Because he or she possesses the authority to call committee meetings, determine the agenda, appoint subcommittees, and refer bills to subcommittees, the chairperson has almost unlimited power in every standing committee. In 1885, Woodrow Wilson said the United States government could be described as "government by the chairmen of the Standing Committees of Congress." Ninety years after Wilson's comment, the Interstate and Foreign Commerce Committee became the first committee in the House to provide for the election of subcommittee chairpersons by secret ballot. Although this change was heralded as a move toward "democratizing" the committee system, the rate of change is hardly breathtaking. The chairpersons retain great power over congressional committees, including the Commerce Committee of the House.

How does a legislator reach this height of power? This is one question about Congress that can be answered very simply: by staying alive and getting reelected. Complicated questions about service to party, commitment to party platform, and competence in the subject matter of the committee have little

[40] Ripley, *Congress: Process and Policy*, pp. 161–66.

to do with seniority; therefore, they do not enter into the choice of a chairperson. Once a representative or senator takes a seat on a committee, he or she need only keep the seat in order someday to move to the head of the class. A rare exception to this rule (the first since 1925) occurred in 1965. Democrats in the House deprived two Democratic representatives (from Mississippi and South Carolina) of their committee seniority because they had openly supported Republican Senator Barry Goldwater (Ariz.), for President. Even though these representatives were not denied their claim to committee assignments as Democrats, they were deprived of their chairmanships. The removal of three chairmen in 1975 by the Democratic caucus was another exception to the rule that seniority alone matters. Again, some modest trend toward requiring at least minimal support of one's party gives hope to opponents of the seniority system.

Despite the many critics of the seniority system—and more are found outside than inside Congress—it dominates the organization of both houses. If new members object to it, they find themselves left with the most minor committee assignments and cut off from the necessary support of the old hands in carrying out their plans. So long as they do not blatantly challenge the seniority system, newcomers with ability and dedication can begin to exercise great influence after they have served in Congress for as few as two terms. By then they will begin to say that seniority at least assures that the top positions are held by men and women who know the ways of Congress and who have acquired specialized knowledge in the policy area of their committee.

The process of policy making

In order to pass a bill, Congress must complete eight not-so-easy steps.

1. Introduction
2. Referral to committee
3. Floor debate
4. Voting
5. Completion of the first 4 steps in the other house
6. Change by the second house; referral to conference committee; compromise, and a return to both houses
7. Presidential action
8. Passage over President's veto

As we trace these steps, we will see that getting an important measure through Congress is no routine matter. Policy making always involves the tense drama of power in conflict and compromise.

1. Introduction. First, *the bill must be introduced.* This is the easiest part of all. A representative simply hands the bill to the clerk of the House

"JUST BETWEEN US, FORBES — HOW _DOES_
A BILL BECOME A LAW?"

or tosses it into the "hopper," a box on the clerk's desk. A senator must be recognized by the presiding officer in order to announce the introduction of a bill; then he or she gives it to the secretary of the Senate. Of the 10,000 or so bills introduced in every Congress, each has little better than one chance in ten of becoming a law. Most of these bills are relatively trivial. Many, despite efforts to reduce their number, are "private" bills dealing with things such as individual claims against the government. Although bills are actually introduced by members of Congress, most of them are probably the ideas of others. Major legislation usually represents the joint efforts of many people who have been called upon by a legislator for advice or support.

2. **Referral to committee.** The second step begins when the parliamentarian of the House (under the speaker's direction) or the president of the Senate _refers the bill to an appropriate committee for consideration._ This is as far as most bills get. The committee, which has life and death power over the proposals that come its way, may pigeonhole a bill, disapprove it, rewrite it completely, amend it, or approve it as presented. But only if a bill wins the approval of a majority of the committee does it normally reach the floor of either house. An unfriendly chairperson may bury a bill so that it never comes up or—if it is too important to ignore completely—may appoint an unfriendly subcommittee to consider it.

Measures that are found worthy of consideration are generally given open hearings at which interested government officials, lobbyists, and other experts are permitted to testify. Next, the committee members assess the technical and political implications of the bill on the bases of the hearings, their own knowledge or convictions on the subject, the results of staff research, and their individual contacts with fellow legislators, party leaders, lobbyists, and constituents. Because Congress usually goes along with what the committees recommend,[41] the work they perform is the real heart of legislation. Aware of this fact, the sponsor of a bill tries to stimulate publicity and support from influential groups outside as well as inside Congress. The chances of passing the bill are better, of course, if the sponsor is a senior member or the chairperson of the committee.

In the Senate, the committee phase comes to an end when a majority of the committee votes to report the bill for consideration on the Senate floor. But in the House there is a second committee hurdle for all measures except money bills.[42] Before a nonmoney bill reaches the floor of the House, the Committee on Rules must rule whether, when, and under what conditions the bill may come up for floor debate. The Rules Committee may block a measure, report it to the floor with suggested amendments, recommend a substitute bill, or set up special rules to speed its passage.

3. Floor debate. When one of the standing committees reports a bill back to the chamber in which it was introduced, it is placed on a calendar a list of pending bills—where it awaits the third big step, *floor debate.* If the bill is important enough, however, its sponsor may not have to wait for it to take its turn on the calendar. In the Senate, the Policy Committee of the majority party serves as chief traffic manager. It establishes the order in which the bills are to be brought up, often (thanks to the cooperation of the minority leader) by unanimous consent of the Senate. In the absence of unanimity, the scheduling of bills is by majority vote. Debate in the Senate is unlimited unless it is cut off by unanimous consent or a vote of cloture.

In the House, departures from the calendar are made at the direction of the Rules Committee, which also provides for limitations on debate. The Rules Committee may even provide a "closed rule," which permits only members of the reporting committee to offer amendments. If a representative objects to these rules, they are referred to the entire House for a vote, but

---

[41] See Anne L. Lewis, "Floor Success as a Measure of Committee Performance in the House," *Journal of Politics,* 40 (May 1978), 460–67.

[42] In addition to bills from the committees on Appropriations and Ways and Means, certain bills from three other committees—Public Works, Veterans' Affairs, and Interior and Insular Affairs—may be brought to the floor at any time. Only the Appropriations Committee takes routine advantage of this privilege. Other committees prefer to go through the Rules Committee because this leads to consideration of their bills under favorable rules.

286

PART 3
decision-making
agencies:
who decides
what and how?

in practice such appeals are hardly ever successful. When the House sits as the "Committee of the Whole," as it does in considering appropriation bills, for example, it transforms itself into one committee so that it can operate more informally. No record is kept of the votes, the time for debate is divided equally between those for and against, and debate on each amendment is limited to five minutes.

4. Voting. By the time a bill is ready for the fourth step—*voting*—its sponsor has a fairly good idea of what its chances for passage are. In the House, a vote may already have been taken on the rules governing debate (especially if a "closed rule" was involved), and in both chambers the votes on various amendments will have shown the alignment of the forces for and against. Indeed, the votes on amendments crippling the bill and on the motion to recommit the bill to committee are usually more revealing of sentiment than the final vote on passage. If opponents of the bill have failed in their efforts to weaken it or send it back to committee, they know they cannot block final passage. Accordingly, if the bill has wide popular appeal but is opposed by a strong pressure group, some of the members who have tried to defeat it at first may swing over to its support once its final passage is assured. The politics-wise pressure group will appreciate the fact that these representatives opposed the bill as long as they had any chance of defeating it. By pointing to their "aye" votes on final passage, however, they can also claim credit from the voters for supporting the bill.

5. Completion of the first 4 steps in the other house. Even after a bill has passed one house, it is still less than halfway through the process of becoming a law. We may lump together all the steps described so far as a fifth giant step—namely, *the successful completion of the same steps in the other chamber.* If the bill is rejected or ignored in this chamber, of course, it is dead. But if it manages to clear all the hurdles a second time, it need only be signed by the President to become a law. If it passes in slightly altered form, the house of origin must agree to the revisions before it goes to the President.

6. Conference committee. When a bill is greatly changed by the second house, it usually enters a sixth stage, in which it is sent to a *conference committee* made up of senators and representatives who try to iron out the differences. The members of the conference committee are appointed by the presiding officer in each house from among the senior members of the committee that originally considered the bill. Again the cards are stacked in favor of the older members. Neither the Senate nor the House members of these committees can consistently dominate. The results are usually closer to the original Senate version of appropriations bills and to the House version of social security legislation, but they mostly reflect compromise.[43] If a majority of the members

[43] See Keefe, *Congress and the American People,* p. 69, and John Ferejohn, "Who Wins in Conference Committee?" *Journal of Politics,* 37 (November 1975), 1033–46.

of the conference from each house agree on a compromise version, the bill is reported back to both houses in its new and final form.

7. Presidential action. If the compromise version is now approved by both houses, the bill is ready for its seventh step, *presidential action.* The President may allow the bill to become law (which is automatic after ten working days) without his signature. He may indicate his approval by signing it; or if he disapproves of the bill, he may refuse to sign it and return it to Congress with a message explaining the reasons for his veto.

8. Passage over President's veto. In the case of a veto, the bill is probably doomed to failure, although it can still become law if both houses take it through the eighth step—*passing it by a two-thirds vote over the President's veto.* But the chances that this will happen are not good. Original passage requires a simple majority vote, but a two-thirds majority is necessary to override a veto. Instead of putting together a majority, all the opponents have to muster is one-third plus one of the votes in either house in order to sustain a veto. The Constitution thus stacks the cards in favor of the status quo. Supporters of a vetoed bill not only face the handicap of winning an extraordinary majority, they are also handicapped by the ability of the White House to influence members of Congress who want government contracts placed in their districts, appointments to federal jobs for constituents, and other favors.

Even when a bill is originally passed in both houses by majorities greater than two-thirds, passage over the President's veto cannot be taken for granted. In 1975, for example, a bill to regulate strip mining of coal passed both houses with majorities far in excess of two-thirds (333–86 in the House, 84–13 in the Senate). But President Ford's veto was sustained after an intense lobbying campaign in which coal companies were joined by utility companies in the threat of higher utility prices if the bill were passed. In this case the Democrats in the House had enough votes within their own party ranks to override the veto. But the lack of party discipline and the intense interest of coal and utility companies in the measure permitted them to convert enough Democrats from support to opposition to kill the bill. Although the vote in the House was 278 to 143 in favor of overriding the veto, the majority fell 3 votes short of the necessary two-thirds. This case illustrates the continuing effect of the founding fathers' bias against majority rule. The requirement of a two-thirds majority does not mean merely a dampening of majority control over policy; it often means, as in this instance, minority control over policy. In combination with the President, slightly over one-third of the members of Congress permitted strip mining to continue, free of requirements to reclaim the wasted land.

How do legislators decide how to vote?

The performance of Congress comes down finally to "aye" and "nay" votes on specific measures. Since every act of Congress helps some interests and hurts others, and since Congress must deal with a bewildering variety

288

PART 3
decision-making
agencies:
who decides
what and how?

of issues, the legislators' decision-making task is not easy. How do they decide?

We have already seen that the most important determinant of congressional voting is party identification. We have also seen that other influences, such as constituency characteristics, pressure groups, and the legislators' personal preferences, reinforce or disrupt the impact of party. These are underlying influences, but they are not much immediate help to the legislators as they rush from a committee meeting to cast their votes on some complicated question they have not had time to study. Nor can they solve the problem by saying, "Oh, well, I'll just vote the way my constituents want me to."

Donald Matthews and James Stimson have pointed out the impossibility of legislators making day-to-day decisions on the basis of constituents' demands. In the first place, there are far too many issues upon which voters have no position or knowledge. Second, members of Congress often do not know what the constituents' preferences are, for the communications they receive are rarely representative of all their constituents. Finally, the sheer volume of business with which legislators must deal makes it impossible for them to seek out citizen opinion on more than a handful of issues. This being the case, Matthews and Stimson suggest that much legislative decision making is done by personal cues taken from fellow legislators. Given the fact that the issues upon which legislators must make decisions are both numerous and complex, and that the cues they receive from outside Congress are neither numerous nor clear, it seems reasonable that legislators pick up cues from colleagues who are trusted and better informed on the issues at hand. As Matthews and Stimson observe,

When a member is confronted with the necessity of casting a roll call vote on a complex issue about which he knows very little, he searches for cues provided by trusted colleagues who—because of their formal position in the legislature or policy specialization—have more information than he does and with whom he would probably agree if he had time and information to make an independent decision.[44]

Faced with having to make judgments on many issues, legislators often simply ask, "Who is supporting this bill, and who opposes it?" Given the answer to this question, they are able to shortcut the painful decision-making process and arrive at their own vote. Possible cue givers for members of Congress are the state party delegation, the President, party leaders, committee heads, the ranking party member on a committee, and groups such as the Conservation Coalition. By isolating predominant positive and negative cues for each member of Congress, Matthews and Stimson were able to forecast votes with a high degree of accuracy. They found, for example, that the typical legislator votes with (or against) at least one of these cue givers over 95 percent of the time. Twenty percent of the members voted with, or against, their principal cue giver on every roll call in the year studied. Indeed, only 2 percent of the representatives failed to vote with one of the cue givers at least 80 percent of the time.

[44] Donald R. Matthews and James A. Stimson, *Yeas and Nays: Normal Decision Making in the U.S. House of Representatives* (New York: Wiley, 1975).

Although Congress is the most visible site of authoritative rule making, it is only the center of a policy-making system that includes local constituencies, pressure groups, and political parties. The other official agencies of government are even more obviously a part of the system, as we saw in the case of presidential vetoes. The overall decision-making system is made up of a set of policy "systems" in which all of the groups concerned with particular policies share in making, modifying, and carrying out decisions. Specialization is thus characteristic not just of Congress but of other participants in the legislative system as well.

A particular policy is made by the people in the agencies, public and private, who are interested in and know about that policy area. There is an almost continuous interchange among committee members, their staffs, the executive (that is, agency personnel, White House staff, and private persons appointed to "task forces," and the like) and representatives of private associations at almost every stage of the process, from the first glimmer of an idea to compromise in conference and to administration of the act.[45]

Judges and policy making

Although judges are never seen on the floor of Congress or scurrying about the corridors, they also participate in policy making. Despite the myth that they are neutral in political wars, judges help to make policy in several ways. First, every time they interpret an act of Congress they are deciding policy. Legislators usually write statutes in general terms that leave room for detailed policy making by the courts.

A second, more negative, means by which judges influence policy stems from their power to declare state or congressional enactments unconstitutional. When a court blocks a statute, it continues current policy unless (and until) Congress comes up with another modification that it approves. The Supreme Court has exercised considerable restraint in negating national laws, but the variety of state laws and practices has led to a much more active role for the Court in invalidating state actions. As has been so clearly demonstrated in the area of civil rights, the Court's review of state actions may almost single-handedly create new national policy.

Third, the possibility that the Court may declare an act unconstitutional leads members of Congress themselves to think in legalistic terms. Because

---

[45] This statement is by a political scientist who also served as a Senate staff member and as Assistant Secretary for Legislative Affairs of the Department of Health, Education, and Welfare: Ralph K. Huitt, "Congress, the Durable Partner," in Elke Frank, ed., *Lawmakers in a Changing World* (Englewood Cliffs, N.J.: Prentice-Hall, 1966), p. 19. For a more recent analysis, see Hugh Heclo, "Issue Networks and the Executive Establishment," and Samuel C. Patterson, "The Semi-Sovereign Congress," in Anthony King, ed., *The New American Political System* (Washington, D.C.: American Enterprise Institute, 1978), pp. 87–124; 125–78.

290

PART 3
decision-making
agencies:
who decides
what and how?

the courts have the power of judicial review, legislators must worry about the constitutionality as well as the political wisdom of every statute, and this alone makes the judges a constant factor in policy making. Senator Barry Goldwater (R-Ariz.) justified his highly publicized vote against the Civil Rights Act of 1964 on the ground that it was unconstitutional, leaving in abeyance the question of its wisdom as policy. Arguments about constitutionality can thus replace arguments about the desirability of a policy even in Congress.

The President and policy making

The President's contribution to congressional activity is much more direct than that of the judges. Both the formal Constitution and the informal pattern of American politics make the President our chief executive. The Constitution underwrites the President's policy-making role in several ways. First, it says that the President shall initiate policy in the annual "state of the union" address and in other speeches and messages to Congress. Preparation of the congressional agenda is thus the work of the executive, not of Congress itself. Second, the Constitution gives the President the power to veto any legislation of which he disapproves. Although Congress can override a veto, the veto and the threat of a veto are powerful weapons. The clear intent of the founding fathers that the President should serve as a legislative leader is seen in a third constitutional provision: the President has the authority to convene either or both houses of Congress in special session. Regular sessions of Congress are now so extended that the convening power hardly needs to be used, but it was important in originally establishing the President as the leader of Congress. Fourth, the Constitution specifies that the President "take care that the laws be faithfully executed." We have seen that laws are simply broad declarations of policy when they come from Congress and that the courts continue the policy-making function as they interpret laws. But the executive branch plays an even greater role than the courts in filling in details and interpreting laws. Laws are not self-enforcing; the President decides how vigorously particular policies such as civil rights guarantees and antitrust legislation will be pursued.

The division of Congress into two houses and the decentralization of power in each house mean that the presidency is the only source of general leadership. Even members of Congress who regularly disagree with a President depend on him to furnish a general program they can attack. His followers look to him for a coherent set of objectives they can support. We have seen that party leaders in Congress are the principal source of coordination and that party affiliation is the principal influence on a legislator's vote. The President's status as head of his party therefore increases his legislative leadership. His party's leaders in Congress normally follow his lead and manage to rally most of the party faithful behind them. But as we have seen, party discipline is not tight.

The weakening of parties in the United States puts more emphasis on the individual, and it has given Americans a national government with split

The President's State of the Union message is his most conspicuous exercise of legislative leadership.

party control—a President and Congress of different parties—for most of the last quarter century. This has worked greatly to the advantage of the President as the central figure in American policy making. The attention given the President by the mass media outweighs that given to Congress as a whole, let alone that given to individual leaders in Congress. The President's influence on Congress is increased by his daily command of the media and his ability to appeal directly to the people for support.

Bureaucrats and policy making

Bureaucrats furnish the detailed information and the expert knowledge necessary for congressional action. These career officials are vitally important parts of the different policy systems through which public policies are decided. Although they cannot openly oppose presidential recommendations, they may develop ties with private interests and with members of Congress through which they covertly support policies opposed to the President's program.

292

PART 3
decision-making
agencies:
who decides
what and how?

Every executive agency and operating division develops interests of its own, and all subordinate officials are eager to preserve or extend their agency's role, even when they are advising the President or interpreting his orders. Government agencies recommend legislation to Congress directly and through allied interests inside and outside government. Although each executive department is legally subordinate to the President, it does not always support his policy. When President Carter recommended creation of a new Department of Education in 1978, for example, the proposal failed in part because lobbyists for the old Department of Health, Education, and Welfare failed to give the proposal active support. The new department was established in 1979 only after appointment of a new Secretary of HEW and an all-out effort by the President to get the support of "his" administration.[46]

Policy systems are made up of coalitions that include elements of a divided bureaucracy no less than of Congress and private groups. Congress has a total of almost 300 subcommittees, a number that permits a high degree of specialization, so that legislators come to know quite well the key personnel and activities of executive agencies dealing with policies within their subcommittee jurisdictions. Members of Congress and bureaucrats thus become part of common policy systems, some as opponents, others working together. The bureaucrats in these systems continue to shape policies in the process of administering them. Moreover, in their contacts with legislators they offer feedback that is considered in the drafting of new legislation in Congress.

Reciprocity in legislators' relations with other decision makers

The congressional investigating committee is one of the most familiar examples of Congress and the executive agencies sharing one another's functions. Legislation deals with issues about which members of Congress are no more automatically informed than are college students and professors. In order to legislate wisely, lawmakers must be able to acquire the information they need, even if it means subpoenaing witnesses and compelling them to testify on pain of punishment for contempt of Congress. Many vital legislative reforms would never have been made if Congress had been unable to investigate problems in this manner. The Securities and Exchange Commission, for example, which offers what is now regarded as minimum protection to investors, could hardly have been created in the early 1930s without the technical information and political impact produced by the Senate Banking and Currency Committee's probe into Wall Street practices.

This power of inquiry also gives life and meaning to congressional supervision of the administration. Under the separation of powers spelled out by the Constitution, Congress would be hopelessly overshadowed by the executive if it had no power to call administrators to account. A law acquires meaning only as it is administered, and legislators would have little power if they were

---

[46] See "Education Department Wins Final Approval," in *CQ Guide to Current American Government: Spring 1980* (Washington, D.C.: Congressional Quarterly, 1979), pp. 87–91.

denied the right to inquire into whether administrative practices and rulings are in keeping with the broad policy directives of Congress. Although Congress can expel executive officers only through the laborious process of impeachment, its power of investigation, coupled with its control over appropriations, assures it the power to supervise the work of even the most powerful executive officers.

The impact of Congress on the other branches of government was most dramatically demonstrated in 1974, when Richard Nixon, on threat of impeachment (the equivalent of indictment) by the House and conviction by the Senate, became the first President of the United States to resign from that office. As President, Nixon had been acutely conscious of actions that set historical "firsts"; the only satisfaction he could have taken from the first presidential resignation was that it avoided another and worse precedent—that of being the first President to be convicted of impeachable crimes. After the Senate Watergate committee spent 18 months investigating presidential corruption, and the House Judiciary Committee made another investigation, Nixon resigned. The Senate committee avoided any statement on presidential guilt because of the House Judiciary Committee's impeachment inquiry, but the unanimous findings held that

The Watergate affair reflects an alarming indifference displayed by some in high places to concepts of morality and public responsibility and trust. Indeed, the conduct of many Watergate participants seems grounded on the belief that the ends justified the means, that the laws could be flaunted to maintain the present administration in office.

The Senate's Watergate investigation was conducted for the formal purpose of getting information as a basis of corrective legislation. Its informal purpose was to uncover hidden information for the public. The House Judiciary Committee's inquiry, on the other hand, was to determine if the President's possible guilt in "high crimes and misdemeanors" appeared sufficiently probable to warrant impeachment and trial. The 38 members of the Judiciary Committee, with a sense of care, solemnity, and reluctance that gave many viewers of the proceedings on television a new respect for their representatives, found that impeachment was warranted on three counts: obstruction of justice, abuse of powers, and contempt of Congress (by votes of 27 to 11, 28 to 10, and 21 to 17, respectively). Less than a week after these formal charges were adopted, Nixon was required by a Supreme Court decision to release previously withheld tapes of conversations that demonstrated his guilt so clearly that the dissenters on the Committee joined their colleagues in calling for impeachment. Nixon's resignation saved him from formal impeachment; but Congress had demonstrated that, however cumbersome, the ultimate power of impeachment is a mighty weapon.

The Congress alone did not remove Richard Milhous Nixon from office. The mass media, a federal grand jury, Judge John J. Sirica, the Supreme Court, and the special prosecutor also played key roles. (Significantly, efforts of the opposition political party had been ineffectual. In the 1972 campaign, candidate George McGovern's charges of immorality and abuse of power were dismissed as partisan moralizing.) Whoever was most responsible, however,

While Henry Kissinger was Secretary of State, senators frequently used their powers of inquiry to discover the facts about American foreign commitments.

removal would not have occurred without the congressional powers of investigation and impeachment. This achievement was so impressive that some observers concluded that the "imperial presidency" was at an end and that a new era of "congressional government" was upon us. As we have seen above, however, these illusions ignored the scattering of power and lack of leadership in Congress. Less than a year after dethroning Nixon, a Congress with an overwhelming majority of Democrats could not muster enough votes to override vetoes by the Republican whom Nixon had selected as his successor. Inquiry and, ultimately, impeachment are critically important for responsible government, but they apply to the extreme case. The Congress still lacks internal leadership for the continuing task of policy making.

THE FUNCTIONS OF CONGRESS

Evaluations of Congress depend on how much the evaluators like or dislike its policy output. The response to practices like the filibuster, for example, seems to depend on the critic's attitude toward the measures being talked to death rather than on general beliefs about majority rule or minority rights. Thus in the 1920s, when the presidency and the Senate were dominated by antilabor conservatives, the American Federation of Labor praised the filibuster for making the Senate "the only forum in the world where cloture does not exist and where members can prevent the passage of reactionary legislation." By the 1940s, the political tides had changed; labor and other liberal groups were frequently in favor of measures supported by a majority of senators. The AFL accordingly reversed its position on filibusters and joined in a campaign with other liberal groups to establish majority rule in the Senate. The stand of the AFL is typical: the way most of us evaluate congressional procedures depends on who gets helped and who gets hurt by the laws being passed, not on any fixed principles about the "right" way of organizing Congress.

Protection of organized minorities

By asking what the system would be like without Congress, we can hope to get some reasonably objective insight into the consequences of congressional activity for American politics. Imagine that we have no Congress. Without congressional input in the 1920s, the policies would have been more conservative than those adopted. (Remember that the AFL regarded the filibuster as essential in protecting the public against reactionary dominance, for Presidents were then so conservative that the filibuster was an asset to liberals.) If we consider the policies advocated by Presidents, bureaucrats, and judges from the 1930s until 1968, the United States would undoubtedly have had a more liberal set of social and economic policies than were possible in view of the more conservative stance of congressional leaders. On the other hand, without the participation of Congress after Nixon's election as President in 1968, the mildly progressive programs pushed through Congress in the preceding generation might have been dismantled. In general terms, then, a basic policy consequence of congressional activity is to protect organized minorities in various policy systems from total eclipse by organized majorities.

Authoritative rule making

The principal intended function of Congress is legislation, the enactment of the laws that govern our lives. To conclude that Congress legislates may appear a redundancy. But legislation is not really the function of the Supreme Soviet in the USSR or even of the British Parliament. And critics of the U.S. Congress charge that it, too, has lost the capacity to legislate. Has it? We conclude that it has not.

To understand the role of Congress, we need to distinguish between originating legislation and shaping legislation. Although most bills are drafted in the executive branch of our government, Congress does not simply give them a rubber stamp of approval. In fact, the President's success in winning adoption

296

PART 3
decision-making
agencies:
who decides
what and how?

of his proposals in recent years has varied greatly, with proposals frequently never even coming to a vote. For all measures on which Congress acted, the highest support score was Lyndon Johnson's 93.0 percent in 1965; the lowest was Richard Nixon's 50.6 percent in 1973. Carter's 76.8 percent rate of support in 1979 was higher than that of Ford or Nixon, but below that of his Democratic predecessors. Presidential success is thus far from complete, and many of the proposals that are adopted are significantly changed in the process. Nor does Congress always simply react to presidential initiatives. In 1966, after President Johnson's great success in winning congressional support for a massive domestic program in 1965, he decided to hold the line on spending. But Congress, with a large Democratic majority including 70 liberal freshmen, seized the initiative. "The committees in both houses, legislative and appropriations alike, . . . set about expanding the programs of the year before and inventing new ones. This bit of legislative history may require a simple explanation: that elections do count and representation does work."[47]

On balance, then, Congress does appear to perform its prescribed constitutional function of authoritative rule making. Despite the fragmentation of power in Congress, it is stronger in relation to the executive, more truly "at the heart of public policy making," than is the legislative body of any other country we know about.[48]

Representation of popular interests

In rule making, legislators act in the name of their constituents: they stand for, or represent, the people. As we saw earlier in this chapter, constituency interests tend to coincide with party interests often enough to make party affiliation the key factor for understanding congressional performance. Many constituencies are sufficiently varied, so that a Democrat's view of the needs of a given district will be quite different from a Republican's view of the same district. Where constituency opinions are clear, as on civil rights, the representatives' relationship to their constituents tends to be that of the instructed delegate.[49] Where party differences are clear and voters tend to react to party label, as on social welfare questions, the relationship is closer to the responsible party model. Where constituency preferences are least clear, as on foreign policy questions, legislators must look elsewhere for cues. For members of the majority party, this means largely to the President and his administration. The member of Congress thus reflects constituent attitudes in an uneven manner, with the accuracy of the reflection on each issue depending on the extent of public information and interest.

[47] Huitt, "Congress, the Durable Partner," in Frank, ed., *Lawmakers in a Changing World,* p. 18.

[48] Ripley, *Congress: Process and Policy,* p. 3.

[49] The original observations on this subject were reported in a study by Warren E. Miller and Donald E. Stokes, "Constituency Influence in Congress," in Campbell et al., *Elections and the Political Order,* pp. 351–72. Also see Charles F. Cnudde and Donald J. McCrone, "The Linkage Between Constituency Attitudes and Congressional Voting Behavior," *American Political Science Review,* 60 (March 1966), 66–72; Kingdon, *Congressmen's Voting Decisions,* p. 20.

Most members of Congress want to vote with their party, and they feel more comfortable when they can. Party and constituency pressures are such that they can usually represent both interests. Even at the roll-call stage, however, a vote may be so highly publicized that constituency pressures require them to vote against their party's majority. Whether voting with or against party leaders, however, they feel that they are performing the function of representing popular interests.

Unanticipated functions

Protection of minority interests, authoritative rule making, and representation of popular interests are clearly intended in the organization and procedures of Congress. Members of Congress have always appeared to share the intent of the original framers of the Constitution that Congress should perform these functions. What additional and less clearly intended functions does Congress perform? Several additional functions appear particularly important to the maintenance of the political system: *special representation, communication,* and *legitimization.*

Special representation. We say *special* to distinguish this function from the expected kind of representation that occurs as part of rule making. What we have in mind here is the importance of Congress in overseeing and controlling the vast bureaucracy. Some students of Congress believe that control of administration is replacing legislation as the primary function of the modern Congress. In fact, critics of Congress probably overstate its effectiveness in general control of administration, as much as they understate its effectiveness in legislation.[50] But representation of particular interests of individual citizens in relation to the bureaucracy is an undeniably important function of Congress. In the special representation of particular interests, members of Congress are not so much concerned with general problems of administration as with helping a local businessperson, farmer, social security applicant, or draftee as an individual dealing with the bureaucracy.

Bureaucrats occupy a position that requires them to operate in a framework of abstract and general policies. Congressional representatives also want to act in terms of a broad national interest, but their roles make them particularly sensitive to individual problems in their constituencies. Even if they have trouble trying to oversee the bureaucracy in general, they can effectively intervene to influence how a policy will be applied to a particular individual or business in their district.

Communication. Like all official decision-making agencies in the American political system, Congress performs an important function in *communication* of political information to the public. Woodrow Wilson felt that investiga-

---

[50] Huitt, "Congress, the Durable Partner," in Frank, ed., *Lawmakers in a Changing World,* pp. 19–20.

298

PART 3
decision-making
agencies:
who decides
what and how?

tions of the administration were important primarily for their effect on public opinion. "The informing function of Congress should be preferred even to its legislative function," he observed. "The argument is not only that discussed and interrogated administration is the only pure and efficient administration, but, more than that, that the only really self-governing people is that people which discusses and interrogates its administration." Wilson's comment about an "interrogated administration" being the "only pure" one may overstate the degree of purity that is possible, but the Watergate investigation verifies the importance of the need for interrogation. The informing function has been extended far beyond administrative matters, as Congress has pushed its investigations into areas such as civil liberties, concentration of economic power, labor and business practices, lobbying, and campaign expenditures. The hearings of the Senate Foreign Relations Committee on the war in Vietnam were primarily designed as an educational enterprise. With the help of the mass media, they helped to change American opinion about the wisdom of the country's military involvement in Indochina.

Legitimization. In the process of realizing its other functions, Congress lends the mark of *legitimacy* to the policies of the national government. Richard Fenno submits that "the resolution of conflict and the building of consensus are among the major functions which Congress performs for American society."[51] Conflict is never resolved in any complete sense, of course, but the decision-making activities of Congress bring conflict into the open, permit it to find peaceable expression, and reduce its intensity by responding to citizen demands. Congressional compromise, in which the minority and majority have equal time for debate, is a reassuring process. The policy that emerges never pleases everybody, but the way in which it was enacted creates a consensus at least on the legitimacy of the policy. After a law has been enforced for some time, acceptance often shifts into what we termed, in our discussion of political opinions, *supportive consensus.* Congress thus serves to unify the public behind the government by giving expression to differences of opinion as well as by turning the dominant opinions into legislation that is generally accepted as legitimate.

SUMMARY

The United States Congress is a representative rule-making body, but it is not literally representative of the population. Most its members are rich, older, upper-middle-class, white men. There are few women and few blacks. Most come from rural areas, and most are Protestant. Congressional voting is not as conservative, however, as these characteristics might indicate. The makeup of constituencies and party affiliations have a direct effect on

[51] "The House of Representatives and Federal Aid to Education," in Peabody and Polsby, eds., *New Perspectives on the House of Representatives,* p. 195.

members' voting behavior. Hopes and fears about reelection dominate congressional life. Despite the overwhelming rate of success for incumbents in general, the individual member is vulnerable to a well-financed opponent.

Congress functions independently of the executive branch. Its members are elected separately, it chooses its own leaders, and it has its own distinctive norms. It is divided into two houses: the House of Representatives and the Senate. The House, because of its larger membership, is more tightly organized than the Senate.

Congress works through its standing committees, which consider all bills that reach the floor. Membership of the committees, which specialize in different policy areas, is determined by the ratio of Democrats and Republicans in Congress. The seniority system dominates the organization of both houses and determines who will chair each committee.

The other branches of the government also contribute to policy making. Judges make policy by their interpretations of congressional acts and by their power to declare laws unconstitutional. The President initiates policy, can veto legislation, call special sessions of Congress, and decide how forcefully to pursue various policies. Bureaucrats supply detailed information and expert knowledge necessary for congressional action. In turn, congressional committees have the power to investigate the other branches of the government, as they did when the Senate Watergate Committee and the House Judiciary Committee investigated President Nixon's administration.

The intended functions of Congress are the protection of organized minorities, authoritative rule making, and representation of popular interests. The unintended consequences include the special representation of individual interests against the bureaucracy, communication of political information to the public, and the legitimization of government policies.

the
President

In July, 1976, a politically obscure, southern peanut farmer who had served one term as governor of Georgia captured the Democratic party nomination for President of the United States. Jimmy Carter claimed the nomination as a Washington "outsider" and proclaimed, "We've been a nation adrift too long. We've been without leadership too long. We've had divided and dead-locked government too long." As he sought a second term, Carter was often reminded of those phrases. The most frequent criticisms leveled against his presidency were indecisive and ineffective leadership, public policies adrift, and responsibility for a bitterly divided legislature and executive. As difficult and improbable as winning the presidency had been, Carter found the exercise of presidential powers even more elusive. The proud "outsider" struggled to get inside the political machinery of national governance and watched his popularity fall with each failure. Only the nationalistic reaction of Americans to the unprecedented seizure of embassy personnel in Iran and the Soviet invasion of Afghanistan reversed this downward spiral.

Many reasons were cited for the President's failures. The authority of the presidential office was diminished in the post-Watergate era. Congress tried to be assertive in foreign policy and to exercise greater control over the budget. Congress's own power, however, had been fragmented by dozens of new subcommittee chairpersons and weak party leadership. Finally, because Carter raised basic and long-neglected issues, lobbyists for special interests increased their activities and expenditures.[1]

Some of the problems, however, were of the President's own making. His anti-Congress attitude during and after the campaign made cooperation difficult. The parochial and inexperienced White House staff did not know how to deal with, nor did it understand, a hostile bureaucracy. Above all, the disenchantment probably came from the high expectations raised by the promises of candidate Carter.

In promising much and delivering much less, Jimmy Carter was in a com-mon tradition of American presidential candidates. Although the office of President brings with it many potential powers, incumbents often find it frus-trating, if not impossible, to use the office's authority in achieving a program.

VIEWS OF THE AMERICAN PRESIDENT

Inflated expectations

We began this book with a few misconceptions about American politics, but we didn't include any about the American President. Thomas Cronin, political scientist and former White House Fellow, would view this as a serious oversight. In his study of the "textbook" President, Cronin charges that Ameri-can government textbooks have not only failed to expose the myths surround-

---

[1] Terence Smith, "Presidential Courtship," *New York Times News Service* (August, 1978).

302

PART 3
decision-making
agencies:
who decides
what and how?

ing the office of President but also have been largely responsible for creating them.² From his study of texts, he concludes that the President has been falsely portrayed as (1) the unifying element in the American political system; (2) the genuine architect of United States public policy; (3) the nation's personal and moral leader, the only one who can guide us to the fulfillment of the American dream; and (4) the only leader capable of making things go well for the society, providing that he is the right man.

Cronin feels that there are many reasons for these exaggerated and misguided ideas of presidential power. And he believes we pay a high price for the way we have overidealized the presidency. High expectations have forced Presidents to make claims about what they will accomplish, claims that are nearly impossible to achieve. Idealization has made opposition to the President weak and ineffective. Finally, and most importantly, it has affected the way Presidents conceive of themselves and their job. "Superstar" status reduces the amount and quality of critical advice Presidents receive from their staffs. It allows them to believe in the textbook image. When a President (Johnson) fends off critics of his Vietnam policy by claiming that "I am the leader of the free world," or when a President (Nixon) sees himself as "The President vs. the Enemies," the textbook President and presidential behavior become one. Both are illusions. Both are dangerous.

In seeking to correct the view of the presidential office, Cronin probably carries his critique too far. Presidential power has probably been no more misunderstood than many other features of American political life: free enterprise, the classless society, equal opportunity for all, popular control over decisions, aggressive warfare as protective defense. Much of what we believe is a comforting mixture of myth and reality. Nor should textbooks be the scapegoats for our distorted views. Citizens believe what they want to believe and need to believe, regardless of textbooks. Insofar as they do have an influence, textbooks have brought more realism than error to political socialization and learning.

Necessary leadership

Although the people's view of the presidency is distorted, we should not let this drive us into thinking that the President is powerless. Presidents *are* powerful. We do not think that they are superstars, but we do believe that they have the constitutional, legal, and historic capacities for exercising vast power. In addition, we believe that Presidents *should* be powerful and that the constitutional system was designed to encourage extensive presidential leadership. We will seek to show that the powers are not only the result of presidential roles, but the way in which these roles are played and the psychological makeup of the people who play them.

Former President Harry Truman was asked about his firing of General Douglas MacArthur: "Mr. President, when you discharged General MacArthur,

---

² Thomas Cronin, "Superman, Our Textbook President," *Washington Monthly* (October 1970).

weren't you afraid that he might become a martyr, that in fact you might be helping him become President of the United States?" Mr. Truman's reply was simple and direct: "I didn't give a damn what became of him. He disobeyed orders, and I was commander in chief, and either I was or I wasn't. So I acted as commander in chief and called him home."[3]

This is the exercise of power. We will try to explain where it comes from and how it is used. We will also try to examine why the powers are often not used or misused.

RECRUITMENT OF THE PRESIDENT

The United States' electoral system of selecting a chief of state is unique among modern governments. Most democratic national governments are governed by parliamentary systems, which means that the head of government is chosen out of the dominant party in parliament. Normally, this person has moved up the political ladder by long service to the party in parliament and in executive offices responsible to the parliament. But no such regular route leads to the American presidency.

Background and qualifications

The constitutional requirements for the nation's highest office are very modest: a President must be a native-born citizen, must have resided in the United States for 14 years, and must be at least 35 years old. All our Presidents, of course, have met the constitutional specifications; the practical rules that determined their ultimate "availability" as candidates have changed considerably, however, since 1789.

Despite American folklore that Presidents proceed "from log cabin to White House," less than half a dozen Presidents have risen from the ranks of the very poor. Most Presidents have grown up in the upper middle class; a few, like George Washington, Franklin Roosevelt, and John Kennedy, have been very wealthy. We saw in chapter 7 that the Campaign Reform Act of 1974 tries to reduce the advantage of personal wealth by making it possible for presidential candidates to receive federal matching funds. Even so, before candidates have a chance to wage a campaign on a national scale, they must secure outside financial backing.

Other factors, more or less personal, also condition the people's choice. The need to secure a majority vote in a very large and mixed electorate has prevented the candidacy of any overt representatives of special interests such as business or labor. Many of our Presidents have been military leaders, ten have been army generals. Most Presidents have been college or university

---

[3] Merle Miller, *Plain Speaking: An Oral Biography of Harry S Truman* (New York: Berkley, 1973), p. 335.

Occupants of the White House are expected to stand as symbols for the entire nation.

graduates, and a majority of them have been lawyers. Nearly all of our Presidents have been professional politicians. They have served as Cabinet officers, members of Congress, and governors of states. In recent years, the U.S Senate has furnished many candidates for both parties: John Kennedy, Richard Nixon, Barry Goldwater, Lyndon Johnson, Hubert Humphrey, and George McGovern.

Religion and sex also enter into presidential politics. Up to 1960, the Protestant tradition was strong enough to prevent a Roman Catholic from becoming President. In 1928, when New York's Governor Alfred Smith unsuccessfully ran for the office, his defeat was widely attributed to his Roman Catholic faith, although he was also hurt by other issues. But Kennedy's 1960 victory, however close, dispelled the myth that a Roman Catholic cannot be elected to the country's highest post. After 200 years, however, no Jew or other non-Christian has won the nomination of a major party. Prejudice against women in politics has excluded them from many policy positions in American government, and it will probably continue to exclude them from the office of chief executive for some time to come. A black candidate has been similarly inconceivable because of racial prejudice.

If the President is to represent "the essence of the nation's personality," he—and his family—must appear as one of us. Though well over half the American people now live in cities, the notion persists that city men are "slickers" and "wicked," whereas rural folks are "decent and respectable." Only two of our Presidents, William Taft and John Kennedy, were born and raised in large cities. Harry Truman from Independence, Missouri; Dwight Eisenhower from Abilene, Kansas; Lyndon Johnson from Stonewall, Texas; Richard Nixon from Yorba Linda, California; Jimmy Carter from Plains, Georgia—all typify American small-town talent.

Although American Presidents have had many background characteristics in common, each administration inevitably bears the unique stamp of the individual President's personality and particular experience. That a President is a small-town lawyer from the Midwest may tell us something about the way he will behave; but if we are really to understand how he will use presidential power, we must seek to understand his personality and his view of himself and the office.

Filtering the people's choice: the electoral college

The authors of *The Federalist* observed that the only part of the Constitution to escape strong disapproval during the fight for ratification was the provision for an electoral college to choose the chief magistrate. The electoral college system of which they were so proud gives each state as many electors as it has senators and representatives in Congress. Each state legislature is authorized to decide how the electors for its state will be chosen. In the first elections under the Constitution, presidential electors in most states were simply appointed by the state legislature. By 1836, however, South Carolina was the only state in which the members of the legislature kept the choice of electors to themselves instead of allowing ordinary citizens to vote for electors. (South Carolina held to choice by its legislature until it adopted a new constitution in order to be readmitted to the Union after the Civil War.) To become President, a candidate must receive a majority of the electoral votes. If no one receives a majority, the choice of a President is made by the House of Representatives, with each state having a single vote.

The election system sketched in the preceding paragraph is in the original Constitution and applies to this day. Ironically, however, some features of the much admired electoral system had to be changed after only a decade of experience with it. The system originally provided that each elector should "vote by Ballot for two Persons," with no distinction between the presidential and vice-presidential preferences. Accordingly, whoever came in first would become President and who ever came in second in presidential votes would become Vice-President. In case of a tie for first place, the House would select the President; in case of a tie for second place, the Senate would choose one of those in the tie as Vice-President. The founding fathers anticipated that the electors would be free agents, each of whom would decide for himself (women were ineligible) for whom to vote. The assumption was that after the universally popular George Washington left the scene, no one would normally win a majority of the electors' votes. In that event, the choice of a President by the House of Representatives would be from *the top five vote getters in the electoral college*. The early development of political parties required that these provisions be changed.

306

PART 3
decision-making
agencies:
who decides
what and how?

Political parties began to organize support for electors who were committed to vote for their party's candidates. Through that commitment, the people began to have a direct say in the choice of Presidents, despite the founding fathers' efforts to prevent them from doing so. Instead of being free agents who could vote as they pleased, electors came to be chosen precisely because they were committed to vote for their party's nominees for both President and Vice-President. Parties thus greatly decreased the possibility of scattered votes for numerous candidates. Indeed, since the emergence of political parties in the election of 1800, the typical election has produced electoral college votes for only two candidates, the nominees of the two major parties. Only twice have as many as five candidates received votes (in 1836, when Van Buren was elected, and in 1872, when Grant won). The original provision for the House of Representatives to choose among the top five vote getters was clearly based on the expectation of a system drastically different from the one the parties helped create.

With electors pledged to vote for their party's nominee for President and for Vice-President, the idea of counting both votes as if cast for two presidential candidates became unrealistic and dangerous. The electors who voted for Jimmy Carter and Walter Mondale in 1976 submitted separate ballots listing the former as their choice for President, the latter for Vice-President. In 1800, the supporters of Thomas Jefferson and Aaron Burr were equally clear that they wanted Jefferson for President and Burr for Vice-President. But with no distinction provided on the ballot, the two winning candidates came out technically in a tie vote for President. The result was to throw the election into the House of Representatives, despite the clear intent of the voters and the electors to make Jefferson President.

To prevent such confusion, the Constitution had to be changed to separate the votes for the two offices. Thus the Twelfth Amendment now requires separate balloting for President and Vice-President. It also reduces to three the number of vote getters from whom the House of Representatives chooses if no one wins a majority. As the system now works, the voters in each state do not vote directly for President and Vice-President. Instead, they elect a group of presidential electors designated by the party organizations in their states. The slate of electors that wins the popular vote in the state casts all the electoral votes of that state for their party's candidates for President and Vice-President. In reality, the electoral college never meets as an electoral unit. The winning electors of each state meet in their state's capital and perform the ceremonial function of "voting" for President and Vice-President. In fact, they simply record who got the most popular votes at the polls.

Under the electoral college system, 15 Presidents, including Nixon in 1968, have been chosen without getting a majority of popular votes.[4] Three received fewer popular votes than their major opponents. In two of these three elections, the House of Representatives had to choose the President after the electoral college failed to cast a majority vote for any candidate. In 1824,

---

[4] Only Abraham Lincoln won with less than 40 percent of the popular vote (39.8 percent). In the 1860 election, his name did not appear on the ballot in the seceding states.

the House chose John Quincy Adams over Andrew Jackson, despite Jackson's lead in popular votes. In 1876, the Democratic candidate Samuel J. Tilden won a clear majority of the popular vote, but there was a dispute about which electors should be certified from 4 of the Confederate states. Congress established a bipartisan Electoral Commission to resolve the issue, but its vote was strictly partisan: 8 Republicans won over 7 Democrats to certify Republican electors in each state and elect Rutherford B. Hayes as President. In 1888, Benjamin Harrison was the third candidate to become President even though fewer people voted for him than for his opponent, the incumbent Grover Cleveland.

Congress has entertained various proposals for reform in the method of selecting a President. In 1969, the House passed a proposed constitutional amendment that would abolish the electoral college, authorize Congress to establish uniform national residence requirements for voting in presidential elections, set a minimum of 40 percent of the popular vote as sufficient to elect a President and Vice-President, and provide for a runoff election between the two top candidates if no candidate obtained the requisite 40 percent. The Senate, however, filibustered the measure until it was withdrawn from consideration.

Politicians and political scientists disagree as to whether popular elections would swing the balance of power to the right or to the left. The electoral college system, which favors the big pivotal states with large urban populations, is said to have a built-in liberal bias. On the other hand, these same big pivotal states have large suburban populations, which are inclined to be conservative. Urban blacks in big states have a special interest in the existing unit vote system, since the urban vote is apt to carry the state for the Democrats. But traditionally Democratic blacks in Mississippi and Alabama might be more influential in a national popular vote. If a state is carried by one party (say the Republicans in this example), the other votes are lost to the national total. A popular vote accumulation, in that case, might be a Democratic advantage. Blacks in Mississippi and Alabama, traditionally Democratic, might have more influence in a popular vote when they add their votes to the national count and perhaps turn the tide of an election. By the same token, so might other interest groups: Mexican-Americans, public school teachers, business people, and retirees. Opponents of popular election fear the development of splinter parties and argue that the requirement of a majority vote in the electoral college has supported the two-party system. On the other hand, it can be pointed out that popular election of governors has not brought about a multiple party system in any state. Some fear that the abolition of the electoral college would jeopardize the whole federal system. Their opponents argue that the President is not an agent of the states but is the representative of all the people, for "it is people who have preferences, not states."[5]

A presidential nominee chooses his own candidate for Vice-President.

---

[5] For a full spectrum of the argument, see *Electoral College Reform,* Hearings before the Committee on the Judiciary, House of Representatives, 91st Congress, First Session, February 5 to March 13, 1969 (Washington, D.C.: Government Printing Office, 1969).

308

PART 3
decision-making
agencies:
who decides
what and how?

In 1968, and again in 1972, Richard Nixon chose Spiro Agnew, Governor of Maryland, an unfortunate choice. Later forced to resign his office because of bribery, Agnew created additional problems for the already enfeebled Nixon administration. The importance of the nominee for Vice-President was shown also in George McGovern's selection of Senator Tom Eagleton of Missouri in 1972. When reporters discovered that Senator Eagleton had received medical treatment for emotional depression, McGovern asked Eagleton to resign from the ticket, for fear that the entire campaign would be spent defending Eagleton's mental health. The long effort to find a vice-presidential replacement was an embarrassment to the McGovern campaign, and the hostility engendered by the Eagleton affair hurt an already weak candidacy. In the close election of 1976 between Gerald Ford and Jimmy Carter, the candidates for Vice-President were critical. A number of voters who had no strong preference for Carter or Ford found Republican Robert Dole offensive and went for the more attractive Democrat, Walter Mondale.

ROLES OF THE PRESIDENT

The powers of the President are defined in the Constitution. On this foundation, multiple layers of presidential authority have been added by statutes, historic precedents, and informal practices.

The constitutional specification of presidential roles

Article II of the Constitution defines presidential power in broad terms: "The executive Power shall be vested in a President of the United States of America." When the authors of *The Federalist* tried to explain to their contemporaries the meaning of "executive power," they declared that "the dim light of historical research" and the experience of other nations offered little instruction. As they viewed it, the office of "Chief Magistrate" in the new federal republic had no counterpart in any other country. A good part of their argument in defense of Article II was designed to show that a vigorous executive is not inconsistent with republican government.

Article II also briefly outlines the President's duties and responsibilities.

1. He is commander in chief of the armed forces.
2. He may require the opinion in writing from his principal officers in the executive departments.
3. He may grant reprieves and pardons for offenses against the United States.
4. He may make treaties, with the advice and consent of two-thirds of the Senate.
5. He appoints ambassadors, judges, and other officers of the national government with the advice and consent of a majority of the senators.

6. He informs the Congress from time to time on the State of the Union and recommends to them measures which he considers necessary and expedient.

7. He may on extraordinary occasions convene either or both houses of Congress; and if they disagree on the time of adjournment, he may adjourn them.

8. He receives representatives of foreign governments.

9. He commissions all officers of the United States armed forces.

10. He takes care that the laws be faithfully executed.

Added to this outline of constitutional powers is a broad array of powers which are implied, have grown up informally, or have been given to the President by Congress or the courts. Some also have simply been assumed. In any case, when a President swears to "preserve, protect, and defend the Constitution of the United States," he does so with an awareness that there is much more to "preserving and protecting" than those powers outlined in Article II. It is only after he has been in office that he becomes aware of the limitations upon the exercise of his presidential powers. When John Kennedy announced his candidacy for the presidency in 1960, he offered his concept of the office:

The times . . . and the people demand . . . a vigorous proponent of the national interest . . . , the head of a responsible party . . . , a man who will formulate and fight for legislative policies. . . . He must above all be the Chief Executive in every sense of the word. He must be prepared to exercise the fullest powers of his office—all that are specified and some that are not. . . . He must originate actions as well as study groups. He must reopen the channels of communication between the world of thought and the seat of power.[6]

But after President Kennedy had been in the office two years he was much more restrained in his notions of what the chief executive could do:

In the first place, the problems are more difficult than I had imagined they were. Secondly, there is a limitation upon the ability of the United States to solve these problems.

The responsibilities placed on the United States are greater than I imagined them to be, and there are greater limitations upon our ability to bring about a favorable result than I had imagined them to be . . . because there is such a difference between those who advise or speak or legislate and between the man who must select from the various alternatives proposed and say that this shall be the policy of the United States.[7]

The change in role perception notable in the views of candidate Kennedy and President Kennedy reminds us that Presidents are but actors in an environment. The President is Chief of State but cannot say, "I am the United States" or "I run this government." He is part of the political system. He cannot ignore the Constitution without running serious risks to his political career. He must live with commitments established by former Presidents and the

---

[6] *The Congressional Record,* January 18, 1960, pp. A–353–54.

[7] Radio-television interview, December 16, 1962. Reprinted in Donald Bruce Johnson and Jack L. Walker, *The Dynamics of the American Presidency* (New York: Wiley, 1964), p. 142.

310

PART 3
decision-making
agencies:
who decides
what and how?

Congress. He is often a captive of the opinion of experts, interest group policies, and events outside his control. Later we shall discuss more of the formal and informal limitations on presidential powers; let us now look at the way in which these constitutional powers have expanded.

The President plays many roles, and in each he exercises many kinds of formal and informal power. Of course, he does not play only one role at a time; but it is useful to look at the many facets of his job, in order to sense the magnitude of his tasks. We shall look at the President as head of state, director of foreign policy, commander in chief, chief executive, legislative director, and head of the economic program. Each role brings with it power; each has limitations; some can be performed more easily and effectively than others. In many instances the President does not play these roles personally: they are performed for him by his cabinet members, aides, and advisers. In this sense they are "office" roles that go beyond the personality of one man, but they are basic to understanding presidential power.

Head of state

As head of state, the President entertains visiting royalty and heads of other governments, receives foreign ambassadors and ministers, addresses Congress on the state of the union, and speaks to the people on crises in world affairs. Mr. President is not a private person, and his time is not his own. Wherever he goes, he is under guard; much of what he does officially or informally is reported in press, radio, and TV. A steady stream of callers at the White House symbolizes that a democratic leader is accessible directly to the people.

A typical presidential calendar in any week will include scheduled and sometimes special meetings with the Cabinet, the National Security Council, and the congressional leadership. The President will also have individual appointments with members of Congress, administrative assistants, and various heads of departments. He may meet with the press in formal conference or informally as he walks about the White House grounds. He will brief American ambassadors before their departure and be briefed by them on their return from posts abroad. He will receive foreign ministers and ambassadors on their arrival and as they leave the country. He will meet with governors, mayors, bankers, defense contractors, labor leaders, military leaders, scientists, astronauts, leaders of minority groups, religious leaders, educational leaders—in short, all manner of representatives from special interest groups.

The President has endless tasks to perform: monuments to unveil, medals to bestow, public works to dedicate. He has speeches to make—to the Sons of St. Patrick and the Daughters of the American Revolution, to the Veterans of Foreign Wars and the United Cookie Cutters of America, to the members of Congress and the families of America assembled in front of their television sets. He serves as honorary president of the American Red Cross; he tosses out the first ball of the baseball season; he pays tribute to Washington, Lincoln, Jackson, and Jefferson on their birthdays; he joins the children hunting Easter eggs on the White House lawn; he chats with Indian chiefs, movie actresses, and America's Mother of the Year; he proclaims the Fourth of July, Labor Day, and Thanksgiving; he buys the first Christmas seals. And he struggles with a mountain of paper work, much of it before television and news cameras. There are treaties to sign, bills to approve, bills to veto, commissions to grant, appointments to make, diplomatic reports to study, gifts to acknowledge, letters to write, budgets to revise, economic reports to digest, military reports to review, more speeches to prepare. All these are routine matters in the President's daily round of activities.

Those who have studied presidential days at close hand, who have spent a day or a week following the president around have been struck by the tightness of his daily schedule. Governed by 10- and 15-minute time frames, the President is moved by his aides from the oval office to the East Room to the Rose Garden in an unending succession of symbolic acts. John Hersey's week with President Ford brought forth a picture of a man who slept 5 hours a night, worked 12 hours a day in the West Wing of the White House, arose at 5:30 A.M., and was seldom in bed until after midnight.

It is understandable why Presidents complain about these clearly time-consuming and exhausting functions, and why a "private" person such as Richard Nixon would have a palace guard of presidential aides to protect him from such exposure. Valuable time is consumed on head of state role performance, which leaves a President less time to participate significantly in policy decisions of greater importance. Five minutes with Miss America may not be a long interruption, but thousands of others also want five minutes with the President, and his minutes are never equal to the demand.

Whether or not a baseball fan, an American President (here, Herbert Hoover) is expected to include baseball pitching among his presidential acts.

UPI

Director of foreign policy

Half a century ago, Supreme Court Justice Sutherland referred to the President as "the sole organ of the federal government in the field of international relations."[8] This seems historically accurate, for most of our foreign policies are named after Presidents: the Monroe Doctrine, Wilson's Fourteen Points, Roosevelt's Good Neighbor Policy, the Truman Doctrine, the Eisenhower Doctrine for the Middle East. In recent years, however, largely because of the Vietnam war, the totality of presidential authority in foreign policy has been frequently challenged. Such challenges appear to be grounded in sound constitutional principles.

The Constitution contains few details on how foreign policy will be made, but John Jay argued in *The Federalist* that the President would have certain advantages because of the unity of his office, his capacity for secrecy and speed, and his sources of information. Both the Constitution and those who defended it were clear, however, that Congress was to be active in foreign policy decisions. Edward Corwin concluded that "the substantive content of American foreign policy is a *divided* power, with the lion's share falling usually to the President, though by no means always."[9] This division is reflected in the fact that the Constitution does *not* make the President the "sole organ" in foreign affairs. Article II of the Constitution specifically authorizes the President: (1) to make treaties, by and with the consent of the Senate; (2) to receive foreign ambassadors and ministers; (3) to nominate and appoint ambassadors, ministers, and consuls, with the advice and consent of the Senate; (4) to report to Congress on the state of the union and to recommend whatever measures he deems expedient; (5) to act as commander in chief (but Congress is given the power to declare war). Clearly, the Constitution requires the President to share his foreign policy powers and domestic powers. However, in practical terms, the President has primary responsibility for foreign affairs.

The research of Aaron Wildavsky reveals how dominant the President has been in foreign policy. Wildavsky believes that the presidency has two sides—one for domestic affairs and one for defense and foreign policy. The foreign policy side of the President has enjoyed much greater success than the domestic side. In fact, Wildavsky claims that since 1930, "In the realm of foreign policy there has not been a single major issue on which Presidents, when they were serious and determined, have failed."[10] President Ford suffered congressional rebuffs when he sought funds first to prevent the collapse of the government of South Vietnam and second to underwrite military activities in Angola, but these were exceptions. Wildavsky estimates that, from 1948 to 1964, only 40 percent of all presidential proposals of domestic

[8] United States v. Curtiss-Wright Export Corp., 299 U.S. 304 (1936).

[9] *The President: Office and Powers* (New York: New York University Press, 1940).

[10] Aaron Wildavsky, "The Two Presidencies," in Wildavsky, ed., *Perspectives on the Presidency* (Boston: Little, Brown, 1975), pp. 448–61. For review and revision of the Wildavsky thesis, see Donald Peppers, " 'The Two Presidencies': Eight Years Later," in Wildavsky, ed., *Perspectives*, pp. 462–71.

The President's role in foreign policy has required
increasing contact with leaders of the Middle East.

policies were enacted by Congress. In contrast, Congress passed 73 percent
of all proposals dealing with defense and 58 percent of those on foreign relations. When one adds to this the multitude of foreign policy decisions that
are never referred to Congress, the record of presidential success is even
more impressive.

For a number of reasons, Presidents exercise greater authority in foreign
than in domestic matters. Except in time of war or of other provocative acts
against American interests, most people are only dimly aware of foreign policies. They normally have far greater interest in, and awareness of, domestic
policies. Members of Congress reflect this interest, for they are usually much
more involved in the concerns of their constituents and in their own reelection
than in matters outside the United States. Few strong interest groups exist
to influence foreign policy. These factors support a President when he asserts
that he alone has the information, time, and expert talent to protect the national
security in foreign affairs.

The President has the sole power to initiate and negotiate treaties.
All the Senate can do is to approve or disapprove what the President has in
effect already promised in the name of the United States. Actually, the Senate

314

PART 3
decision-making
agencies:
who decides
what and how?

has rejected only about 1 percent of the treaties sent to it by the President, has amended or made specific reservations in about 15 percent, and has approved all the rest without change. The approval of the Panama Canal treaties in 1978, despite a well-financed effort by conservative groups to defeat them, demonstrated the President's leadership in this area once again.

The Constitution says nothing about the House of Representatives in defining the President's treaty-making powers. But Washington's second administration was nearly wrecked on this very point. Because Washington failed to inform the House on the negotiations that led to the unpopular Jay Treaty (1795), the representatives decided not to appropriate the funds he had requested to put it into operation. Washington insisted on the importance of preserving secrecy in diplomatic matters, and refused to send the House any papers or documents on the treaty. Thereupon the House threatened to impeach him. Although the House finally passed the appropriations, Presidents ever since Washington's time have profited by his unhappy experience. Because the House initiates the appropriations necessary to implement foreign policy, the President finds it advisable to consult with House leaders as well as with Senate leaders in his conduct of foreign affairs.

Presidents have simply assumed the authority to make agreements with the chief executives of other countries. These executive agreements are actually used more often than treaties in the conduct of foreign affairs. Although the Constitution does not even mention executive agreements, the Supreme Court has declared that the President may enter into agreements with foreign governments as "a modest implied power" under his treaty-making authority.[11] Thus treaties—which must have the approval of the Senate—and executive agreements—which are made solely under the authority of the President— both have the force of law in the courts.

In recent years, presidential commitments have loomed large in the conduct of foreign affairs. We were told that "commitments" made by four Presidents required us to fight in Vietnam. Outraged by secret understandings, letters of presidential commitment, and other executive arrangements, Congress has tried to reduce the President's exclusive power over executive agreements. Members of Congress have introduced legislation that would give Congress a 60-day period in which it could block any new executive agreement. Such legislation is designed to prevent a President from making secret pledges that obligate the country to undesirable action. (One such secret pledge occurred when President Nixon sent a letter to President Thieu of South Vietnam pledging that the United States would use "full force" if North Vietnam violated a cease-fire accord. Congress was not informed of this or other pledges until months later, after violations of the cease fire had occurred.)

In 1972 (in the Case Act) Congress provided that a copy of all executive agreements be filed with Congress. It is clear, however, that all such agreements have not been put in the record—partly because no one is sure what an executive agreement really is. In addition, the executive departments have failed to send some agreements to Congress because they claim that their

[11] United States v. Pink, 315 U.S. 203 (1942).

release would injure national security. This struggle between President and Congress is an example of several modest efforts by the legislature to regain its share of foreign policy powers.

As the Congress begins to reassert its foreign affairs authority, some analysts argue that there is a danger of congressional government encroaching on the functions of the executive office in foreign policy and national security. They contend that such limitations weaken the executive and make a coherent policy impossible.[12] Typical of such limitations was Congress's refusal to permit President Carter to provide military supplies to one group among the various revolutionary factions in Africa in 1978.

In assigning the President authority to receive foreign ministers and ambassadors, the Constitution implies that he also has authority to recognize foreign governments and new states. During most of our history, the President has followed the customary international practice of recognizing a new foreign government if it can fulfill international obligations. Recognition does not depend on whether Americans approve of its principles. Under President Woodrow Wilson, however, the American policy of recognition took a new turn when he refused in 1913 to recognize the government of President Victoriano Huerta in Mexico. Wilson refused because Huerta had risen to power by force and did not rule by "consent of the governed." No doubt this withholding of American recognition contributed to the downfall of the Huerta regime. Wilson followed the same policy with respect to the communist government that was established in Russia in 1917, but this time the United States' lack of recognition did not break the new regime. Since Wilson's time, every American President has used recognition as an instrument of American foreign policy. The decision to recognize or not to recognize a foreign government is a political decision that belongs to the President alone. Neither Congress nor the courts can legally force or forestall the President's decision.

The Constitution gives the President power to appoint ambassadors and other diplomats, but only with the consent of the Senate. He also selects the Secretary of State and other key figures concerned with foreign affairs. These officials constitute the President's team in making foreign policy. Just how the President uses his team members, or whether he uses them at all, depends mostly on his personal inclinations and his capacity for statesmanship.

When we assess the President as director of foreign policy, it is important to note at least three constraints upon his powers, aside from those exercised by Congress. First, most foreign policy is a response to actions taken by others elsewhere in the world. An embassy is seized, and a President tries to respond. The Organization of Petroleum Exporting Countries reduces production, and a responsive policy is required. A revolution begins, and we become involved. Grand designs are put aside as a President deals with the crisis of the moment. Second, Presidents are restricted by treaties, rules, and understandings developed over the last 200 years. Presidents normally follow these understandings.

[12] This argument is represented in Robert Novak, "Washington's Two Governments," in John C. Hoy and Melvin H. Bernstein, eds., *The Effective President* (Pacific Palisades: Palisades Publishers, 1976), pp. 95–104.

President Carter invites media attention to his foreign policy
leadership as he signs a nuclear nonproliferation treaty.

In exceptional cases, as President Carter's abrogation of defense treaties with
Taiwan, the President may have to defend his action before the Supreme
Court. The fact that the Court upheld Carter's action is less significant than
the Court's right to rule on the matter. Finally, the President is often only
a broker of interests in the State Department, Foreign Service, and Defense
Department. With expertise, time in service, and vested interests on their
side, these forces often try to influence rather than assist Presidents. Every
modern President has complained about the poor quality of information he
receives and about the failure of the bureaucracy to respond to his dictates.
For all of his powers, the President is not a man on a white horse. Political
and practical considerations prevent him from being so.[13]

[13] For discussion of the contemporary foreign affairs role of the President, see Marian D. Irish, "The
President's Foreign Policy Machine" and Norman A. Graebner, "Presidential Power and Foreign
Affairs," in Charles Dunn, ed., *The Future of the American Presidency* (Morristown, N.J.: General
Learning Press, 1975), pp. 130–77 and 179–203.

Commander in chief

The Constitution designates the President as commander in chief of the armed services of the United States and also of the state militia when it is called into the service of the United States. But the Constitution does not give the President complete power over the military. Rather, it specifies that Congress shall have power to

1. Tax for the common defense
2. Declare war
3. Make rules concerning captures on land and water
4. Raise and support armies
5. Provide and maintain a navy
6. Make rules governing the armed forces
7. Call out the state militia and provide for its training and discipline

The Federalist is quite frank in explaining the President's military power: "Of all the cares or concerns of government, the direction of war most peculiarly demands those qualities which distinguish the exercise of power by a single hand." The founding fathers, who elected General George Washington as the first President, expected the President to assume direct command in time of war. In fact, President Washington personally headed the U.S. troops for a short period during the Whisky Rebellion of 1792. Abraham Lincoln frequently took part in the operation of the Army of the Potomac until General Ulysses S. Grant finally insisted on sole field command. President Wilson was more interested in "organizing for peace" than in supervising the military strategy of World War I; but President Roosevelt, along with Prime Minister Churchill, participated in all the top-level military decisions of World War II. President Truman made the most momentous decision of any commander in chief in history when he gave the order to drop the first atomic bomb on Hiroshima in 1945. President Nixon personally ordered the invasion of Cambodia in 1970.

Although the Constitution specifically gives Congress power to declare war, Congress has never done so except at the urgent request of the President. Indeed as commander in chief, the President may use the armed forces in such a way that Congress has no alternative but to issue a declaration of war. Congress has five times declared war—the War of 1812, the Mexican War, the Spanish-American War, World War I, and World War II—but the President has entered this country into many more major military operations (to protect American citizens or American property abroad and to support his view of American interests in many parts of the world) without any formal declaration or authorization from Congress. Lincoln, Wilson, Roosevelt, and Truman are all remembered as "warriors" who expanded presidential war powers.[14]

[14] Louis W. Koenig, "The Awesome Power: The President as Commander-in-Chief," in Philip C. Dolce and George H. Skau, eds., *Power and the Presidency* (New York: Scribner's, 1976), pp. 187–98.

318

PART 3
decision-making
agencies:
who decides
what and how?

The war in Vietnam brought agonizing reappraisal of many questions about the role of the President as commander in chief:

1. Does the President have constitutional authority to conduct a major war on foreign soil without a declaration of war by Congress?

2. If Congress authorizes the President to take what steps he deems necessary to repel attacks on U.S. armed forces, is that "the functional equivalent with respect to declaring war"?[15]

3. Can the President make and carry out commitments to foreign nations involving the use of American armed forces without seeking the advice and consent of the Senate?

4. Must the Senate deliberate and offer its advice even, or especially, if it is not asked for by the President?

5. Are members of Congress bound to support the military operations of the commander in chief and to make a show of national unity, despite their personal views?

6. Do individual citizens have the right not only to protest the decisions but to disobey the orders of the commander in chief when they believe them to be unconstitutional or immoral or unwise?

If the war in Indochina brought forth serious questions about the President's powers as commander in chief, it also confused and clouded the answers. Critics of that war saw in presidential decisions such extravagance of purpose, arrogance, and blindness that severe reforms were demanded.[16] Respected leaders such as Senator J. William Fulbright, who had once championed presidential power, were turned into critics by the Vietnam experience. The Vietnam war was long, unpopular, unwon, and unnecessary. Had it been short, popular, victorious, and perceived as truly in the national interest, our view today of presidential power would undoubtedly be different. Such a claim was made by Adolph Berle, in defending presidential war powers, when he offered the candid but unfashionable conclusion that:

The rumpus kicked up was not because the Presidents in question misused their powers. It was because they used their powers legitimately to act and to achieve objectives that their critics did not want.[17]

We do not have to accept the Berle view to recognize that many deceptions, many losses, and many false "lights at the end of the tunnel" led to demands that the war be stopped and legislative authority over foreign affairs be reasserted.

American Presidents have historically used three main doctrines to justify their discretionary authority in waging war: (1) self-defense, used repeatedly

[15] The quotation, referring to the 1964 Gulf of Tonkin Resolution, is from the testimony of Undersecretary of State Nicholas Katzenbach, before the Senate Foreign Relations Committee, reported in *The New York Times,* August 18, 1967.

[16] John Emmet Hughes, *The Living Presidency* (New York: Coward, 1973).

[17] "Power in Foreign Relations," in Rexford G. Tugwell and Thomas E. Cronin, eds., *The Presidency Reappraised* (New York: Praeger, 1974), p. 80.

by President Johnson in escalating the Vietnam conflict; (2) protection of American lives and property, used to justify interventions since World War II in Lebanon, Dominican Republic, Cambodia, and Laos; and (3) "hot pursuit," used in Korea and again in Laos in what the Pentagon called "protective reaction."[18] Historian Henry Steele Commager is unimpressed with the way Presidents have used these doctrines.

. . . we can say with some confidence that with the exception of the Civil War—a special case—and perhaps of the Korean War where the President acted in conformity to the decision of the UN Security Council—there are no instances in our history where the use of war-making powers by the Executive without authority of Congress was clearly and incontrovertibly required by the nature of the emergency that the nation faced.[19]

Although Congress tried in the 1970s to regain its share of war powers, the most significant effort came in 1973 with passage of the War Powers Act. The act states that a president can continue to undertake emergency military action without a declaration of war, but that 48 hours after he sends armed forces abroad he must report to Congress. If Congress does not agree to the mission, the President must discontinue it within 60 days, but the deadline can be extended for another month if necessary for the safe withdrawal of troops. Any time during the engagement, however, Congress can demand immediate withdrawal by passing a concurrent resolution. President Ford responded to the letter of the new law when he ordered rescue of the American vessel Mayaguez, captured by Cambodians after the collapse of the American effort in Indochina. Ford reported to Congress on the bombing and invasion of the land area and the rescue of the ship. But because this effort was short, successful, and highly popular with the American public, the incident was not a good test of the War Powers Act.

Louis Koenig argues that the act is a mistake and "bears seeds of future constitutional crisis."[20] He contends that the act's constitutionality is doubtful and that it is unclear how the courts could settle a crisis conflict between the Congress and the President. "Precisely how Congress, as a practical matter, could reverse Presidential commitment of the armed forces strains one's imagination." More importantly, he argues, the act could have the effect of expanding presidential war power, giving the executive a free hand to fight anywhere so long as the conflict lasts no longer than 90 days.

Most analysts conclude their evaluations of presidential war powers with the observation that things are not likely to change significantly until we redefine America's role in world affairs. They contend that so long as we operate with the "Cold War vision" as guardians of the world, we can expect no decline in presidential authority. As Donald Robinson concludes, "There is no way to restore the classical constitutional balance in American government without

[18] Louis Fischer, "War Powers: A Need for Legislative Reassertion," in Tugwell and Cronin, *ibid.,* pp. 62–65.

[19] Henry Steele Commager, "The Misuse of Power," *The New Republic* (April 17, 1971).

[20] Louis W. Koenig, *The Chief Executive* (New York: Harcourt, 1975). p. 220.

320

PART 3
decision-making
agencies:
who decides
what and how?

reconceiving our foreign policy and its national security requirements."[21] Although few Americans would support unlimited war authority in the hands of the President, many feel forced to agree with the conclusion of Clinton Rossiter: "We have placed a shocking amount of military power in the President's keeping, but where else, we may ask, could it possibly have been placed?"[22]

Chief Executive

Although the Constitution does not even outline how the executive branch should be organized, it does empower the President to "require the opinion, in writing, of the principal officer in each of the executive departments, upon any subject relating to the duties of their respective offices." Apparently the founding fathers anticipated the establishment of executive departments to assist the President, but they could not have imagined the tremendous super-structure of administrative organization which today almost dwarfs the legislative and judicial branches.[23]

The Constitution charges the President to "take care that the laws be faithfully executed." Obviously he cannot carry out this task without help. He must have assistants; and to ensure their responsibility to him, he must have the power to appoint and remove them. The Constitution accordingly provides that with the advice and consent of the Senate, the President shall appoint "ambassadors, and other public ministers and consuls, judges of the Supreme Court, and all other officers of the United States" whose appointment is not otherwise provided for by law. But Congress may empower the President alone or the heads of executive departments to appoint "inferior officers" without obtaining Senate consent. The Constitution leaves it up to Congress to draw the line between "superior" and "inferior" officers.

"Superior officers" seem to include diplomatic officers, justices of the Supreme Court, members of the Cabinet, commissioners of the independent regulatory agencies, and under-secretaries and assistant-secretaries in the executive departments. Whenever the President names someone to fill one of these posts, the nominee must be confirmed by the Senate. The Senate usually goes along without much debate on the President's choice of ambassadors and members of his own Cabinet. The fact that President Nixon had to work through a Congress controlled by the opposition party explains in part his difficulties in clearing some nominations. (For example, the Senate refused to confirm two nominees to the Supreme Court.) In other appointments, especially those federal officials located in regional offices or states, the President is expected to consult with the senators of the state in which a position is to

---

[21] "The President as Commander in Chief," in Stanley Bach and George T. Sulzner, eds., *Perspectives on the Presidency* (Lexington, Mass.: Heath, 1974), p. 381.

[22] *The American Presidency* (New York: Harcourt, 1960).

[23] Edward S. Corwin, "The President as Administrative Chief" in Richard Loss, ed., *Presidential Power and the Constitution* (Ithaca: Cornell University Press, 1976), pp. 72–112.

be filled. If these senators are of the opposition party, the President consults with the state leaders of his own party before making a nomination. Whenever a President fails to observe this rule of party politics, he is likely to encounter "senatorial courtesy"—a polite way of saying that, in courtesy to their slighted colleagues, the senators will refuse to confirm the President's nominee, no matter how qualified the nominee may be for the post.

Although the President's power of appointment is now curtailed by civil service regulations, thousands of presidential appointments are still made on the basis of party politics. Key offices in the administration are filled by leaders of the party faithful, preferably those who backed the President during his campaign. Some ambassadorships and certain other positions of power and prestige customarily go to generous financial supporters. Most presidential backers, however, prefer to take their rewards in the form of personal access to the White House or influence on administrative policies after the election has been won. Since the national parties are made up of local blocs, the President is in a unique position to pull local strings through his power to appoint thousands of tax collectors, federal marshals, district attorneys, and judges throughout the country. And yet these same local strings are also pulling on the President, seeking favors for their areas.

To supervise and control the national administration, the President relies on many high-level political executives, who fall into several categories: (1) those whose personal loyalties will center on the Chief Executive; (2) people who were promised appointments as part of party bargaining during the campaign; (3) program executives with the special knowledge and technological background needed in the modern business of government; (4) career administrators who come up through the ranks of the civil service or foreign service.

Although the Constitution is fairly specific on the President's power of appointment, it is silent on the power of removal. In *Myers v. United States*

Carter and Ford discuss common problems of a Chief Executive.

UPI

322

PART 3
decision-making
agencies:
who decides
what and how?

(1926), the Supreme Court held that Congress cannot restrict the President's power to remove executive officers whom he has appointed with the consent of the Senate.[24] In a lengthy opinion, Chief Justice Taft took the position that since the President alone is responsible for the actions of his executive subordinates, he must have the sole power to dismiss them. The legal power to dismiss may be curtailed, however, by political considerations. Note how long J. Edgar Hoover was in office. He was appointed as Director of the FBI by President Coolidge and stayed in that post unitl his death during the Nixon administration. Despite growing criticism of his performance, Hoover had acquired so much power that several Presidents were apparently fearful of removing him.

Although they are responsible for the actions of their subordinates, Presidents often do *not* know what is going on. If they do know, they do not move to prevent illegal activities. Such was shown, beginning in 1974, in revelations of activities of the CIA and FBI. *The New York Times* published reports that the Central Intelligence Agency had conducted a "massive illegal domestic intelligence operation." This was confirmed the next year by the report of the Rockefeller Commission, which President Ford appointed to investigate the charge. The commission documented CIA activities that "unlawfully exceeded the CIA's statutory authority" and revealed that the agency had "piled up large quantities of information on the domestic activities of American citizens." These adventures included wire tapping, opening mail, and infiltrating domestic organizations. Later, the Intelligence Subcommittee of the Senate added to the list of CIA infractions by exploring intelligence operations abroad. There was evidence of the CIA's involvement in assassination attempts on foreign leaders and transfers of large sums of money into foreign political movements. While these activities were not directly linked to presidential knowledge or instructions, there were charges that Presidents and Congress both had failed in their responsibilities to supervise intelligence agencies.

Equally serious abuses by the FBI were revealed. In addition to running a continuous campaign against civil rights leader Martin Luther King and civil rights organizations, Director Hoover maintained extensive files on the political and sexual activities of public and private citizens, making such information available to Presidents for their "entertainment." Few Americans expect Presidents to know everything that goes on in the massive bureaucracy, but most do not expect them to participate in, or condone, illegal activities by subordinates. These revelations accordingly contributed to the decline of trust Americans placed in their leaders and political institutions.

As Chief Executive, the President acts in the role of general manager of his administration. To play this role effectively and efficiently, he needs authority to control the entire national administration. Since 1939, Congress has periodically authorized the President to submit plans for reorganization, reserving to itself, however, the right to veto any proposed plan.

[24] Myers v. United States, 272 U.S. 52 (1926).

The assumption that the Chief Executive is a "general manager" or "reorganizer" may be misleading. Jimmy Carter became the first President since Herbert Hoover to show much interest in administrative management. The constitutional responsibility of the President is to see that the laws are faithfully executed, but this is a problem that calls for political leadership far more than skill in administrative management. This point is illustrated in the President's role as chief legislator.

The Chief Legislator

The Constitution itself gives the President legislative powers, requiring him from time to time to "give to the Congress information of the State of the Union and recommend to their consideration such measures as he shall judge necessary and expedient." The President, then, has the constitutional right to assume legislative leadership. But Congress is under no obligation to accept what the President thinks is "necessary and expedient." Political circumstances, as well as the character of the President himself, determine how much influence the Chief Executive actually exerts as legislative leader. Lyndon Johnson's rating as a legislative leader, rounding out the unfinished term of President Kennedy, is probably unmatched by any other President. His rapport with Congress, his own legislative skill, and (after the trauma of Kennedy's assassination) a groundswell of popular support brought about landmark legislation. But gradually his controversial performance as Commander in Chief overshadowed his legislative role.

Party fortunes also have a lot to do with the check and balance between President and Congress. A President is usually "weak" when both houses of Congress are controlled by the opposing party. This has been the typical plight of Republican Presidents in the current era of Democratic dominance of Congress. Conversely, Presidents have traditionally had a chance to appear "strong" when their own party has controlled both houses of Congress. But the declining importance of American parties in both presidential and congressional nominations and elections decreases the chance for party ties to unite members of Congress behind a President of their party. Party is simply less significant today in every aspect of government. The constitutional separation of powers can thus prevent a party platform or any other coherent program from being adopted. Ironically, the founding fathers seem to be winning out in the long run. Political parties emerged as a democratic device to enable a majority of the voters to put their party leaders in control of the government. Parties thus ran counter to the founding fathers' effort to prevent unified popular control of the government. The weakening of parties today tilts the scales back against unified popular control. With the President and members of Congress all less dependent on party organization for their offices, special interest groups tend to win out over political parties.[25]

[25] On the president as legislator, see Neil MacNeil, "The Chief Legislator," in Sidney Wise and Richard F. Schier, eds., *The Presidential Office* (New York: Crowell, 1970), pp. 209–47.

324

PART 3
decision-making
agencies:
who decides
what and how?

Perhaps the most distinctive feature of the American presidential system is that the President's term of office is established by the Constitution and except for impeachment is not dependent on the will of Congress. Congress similarly enjoys considerable independence of the President: for example, it assembles at least once a year and may stay in session as long as it pleases. The President has no power to dissolve it, no matter how disagreeable it may be with respect to the "administrative program." The Constitution permits the President to convene Congress in extraordinary session; in case of disagreement between the two houses on whether or not they should adjourn, he may adjourn them to such time as he thinks proper. So far, however, no President has ever adjourned Congress.

The veto power gives the President great influence over legislation. The mere threat that a President might veto a measure serves to influence the way Congress draws up the bill in the first place. On the other hand, Congress sometimes passes a bill knowing that the President will veto it. This practice allows members of Congress to fulfill their local commitments without jeopardizing national interests. Later on, when they are talking to their constituents back home, they can say, "I voted for the bill. The *President* vetoed it." Historically, Congress has rarely asserted its constitutional authority to override a presidential veto. In 1960 Congress overrode President Eisenhower's veto of a federal pay raise, but it failed to override a single veto by Kennedy or Johnson. After 1970, however, Nixon and Ford faced Congresses both willing and able to override their vetoes. Repeatedly arguing for fiscal conservatism and restraint, these Presidents vetoed expenditures for domestic programs deemed important by the Democratic majorities in Congress. Overriding a number of these vetoes, Congress demonstrated to the Chief Legislator that it, in the end, is the Final Legislator. President Carter's vetoes fared better; even with weakening party loyalty, mustering a two-thirds vote against a Democratic President is difficult in a Congress dominated by Democrats.

Presidents have sometimes tried to "legislate" by refusing to spend funds appropriated by Congress. Thus, both Nixon and Ford impounded funds for programs they did not like. To prevent such action, Congress adopted the Budget and Impoundment Control Act of 1974. It provides that either chamber of Congress can force release of funds withheld by the President by a resolution disapproving the impoundment. Such a resolution was adopted in 1975 by the Senate, forcing President Ford to release $9.1 billion in federal highway funds. Clearly, then, the "imperial presidency" of the Nixon era stimulated a more jealous attitude in Congress about presidential usurpation of legislative powers.

Despite these efforts by Congress, the President still has far more flexibility in the expenditure of funds than is commonly recognized. The growth of presidential spending power through executive and departmental commitments, lump-sum appropriations, reprogramming, transfer of funds, and hidden costs of some programs, has been largely unchecked by Congress.[26]

---

[26] Louis Fisher, *Presidential Spending Power* (Princeton: Princeton University Press, 1975).

How effectively the President helps in shaping the nation's economy depends on the economic setting, constitutional provisions, how Congress plays its part, and how well members of the President's cast support him. The Constitution does not expressly grant any economic powers to the President. The founding fathers believed that the authority to raise revenue by taxation, to borrow money on the credit of the United States, and to appropriate money for government functions belonged to the people's representatives in the legislature. For more than one hundred years, Congress carried out its fiscal assignment unaided. But as the functions of the federal government expanded, there was increasing waste and incompetence. Long after the need for more unified direction and more professional management was apparent, the President still had little influence and no supervision over the requests for appropriations or the spending practices of the various agencies of which he was "Chief Executive." Not until 1921 did Congress finally concede that it was unable to control the chaotic finances of the sprawling and disorganized national government. In that year of "fiscal revolution," Congress passed a Budget and Accounting Act, which provided that the President prepare and transmit an annual budget of the United States to guide Congress in making decisions on taxation and appropriations.

The intent was to give the President an effective tool for planning and programming the overall activities of the government and also to give him specific controls over the national fiscal accounts. In his budget message to Congress at the beginning of each session, the President specifies the major items on which he expects Congress to take legislative action. Since the President releases his legislative recommendations through the mass media, Congress is put at a disadvantage. If Congress cuts the budget for national defense or human resources, its members have to do some difficult explaining to their constituents. If they add to the budget, the President can charge them with fiscal irresponsibility or pork-barrel legislation. The easiest, and the usual, course is for Congress to adopt the President's budget, with minor tinkering.

The Office of Management and Budget, reorganized in 1970, is the President's agency; it is loyal to his values, responsive to his directives. But as we shall see later, the budget process is not wholly satisfactory as a tool for executive management. Congress does have final say in the matter of appropriations, and it can change the priorities or add new programs. Moreover, expenditures are only one side of fiscal management. Congress controls the tax policies. The President, encouraged by his Council of Economic Advisers, may recommend tax cuts or tax increases. Tax cuts, of course, are politically much more appealing than tax increases. A President can more easily obtain an increase in governmental expenditures to ward off recession than he can obtain an increase in taxes to deal with inflation. The President's role as leader in economic policies may also be upstaged by the Federal Reserve Board, to which Congress has given wide powers over monetary policy to be exercised independently of the President's judgment.

326

PART 3
decision-making
agencies:
who decides
what and how?

In the final analysis, however, it is the economic setting which confounds the President's effort to influence the nation's economy. In an economic system committed to the principle of private enterprise, the President has great difficulty winning support for wage and price controls. Except for wartime, Presidents do not have the political clout to direct firmly or control America's economic life.

ROLE PERFORMANCE: STRUCTURE OF PRESIDENTIAL DECISION MAKING

In discussing presidential roles, we have outlined many executive powers. We have suggested that some are more effectively used than others and that all have formal and informal constraints. How effectively these powers are used is not determined by the Constitution. Rather, the use of presidential power is determined by the individual—his personality, intelligence, ambition, and skill.

Presidential power and presidential personality

Richard Neustadt, former White House aide and political scientist, has suggested that the most meaningful way to view presidential power is in terms of the behavior of the holders of that office.[27] Studying how Roosevelt, Truman, and Eisenhower performed in office, Neustadt concludes that presidential power stems mostly from the President's personal influence on the behavior of those who hold policy positions in government. Whether history rates him "strong" or "weak," "leader" or "clerk," depends most of all on the President's own character and capabilities.

In Neustadt's view, presidential power is the *power to persuade*. The authority and status of the President's office give him great advantage in bargaining, which is one aspect of persuading. The bargaining power of the President is enhanced by his professional reputation and his popular prestige. These involve more than the image created by public relations experts. They include the opinions of others about his skill and determination. The presidency is no place for an amateur in politics; use of presidential power calls for extraordinary expertise. The way a President sees his advantages and uses his influence to get what he wants done—"his sense of power and of purpose and his own sense of self-confidence"—these are "politics of leadership."

The Neustadt thesis offers insight into why Presidents are weak or strong in the performance of their presidential roles. That understanding is enhanced by the work of James David Barber.[28] Barber examines presidential perfor-

---

[27] *Presidential Power* (New York: Wiley, 1960).

[28] James David Barber, *The Presidential Character,* 2nd ed. (Englewood Cliffs, N.J.: Prentice-Hall, 1977).

mance by looking at the President's *style* (the political habits he brings to office) and his *character* (his basic orientation toward his own life). From close examination of style and character, Barber believes that one can predict the strength and weakness of Presidents. Presidential style is revealed in the way a President relates to national audiences, advisers, subordinates, and enemies, and in the way he manages policy making. This style is either active or passive. Presidential character is either positive (happy and optimistic) or negative (sad, irritable, and pessimistic). Combinations of style and character give us 4 types of Presidents with distinctive "personality packages."

The "active-positive" type tends to show confidence, flexibility, and a focus on producing results through rational mastery. The "active-negative" tends to emphasize ambitious striving, aggressiveness, and the focus on the struggle of power against a hostile environment. "Passive-positive" types come through as receptive, compliant, other-directed persons whose superficial hopefulness masks much inner doubt. The "passive-negative" character tends to withdraw from conflict and uncertainty, to think in terms of vague principles of duty and regular procedure.[29]

This style-character model admittedly simplifies vast complexities by sorting everyone into one of 4 pigeonholes. But it suggests some of the differences among occupants of the nation's highest office. All had similar constitutional powers. Each used the powers in ways reflecting his individual life view and personality style. Harry Truman (active-positive), Dwight Eisenhower (passive-negative), Lyndon Johnson (active-negative), Richard Nixon (active-negative), Gerald Ford (active-positive), and Jimmy Carter (active-positive) were all dealt similar hands of cards. They played their presidential cards of power differently because their political environments were different and because their styles and characters were different. Thus, the man and the political conditions under which he operates must be added to the Constitution in explaining presidential power.

Institutionalization of the presidency

We have been talking primarily about the President as a person, what *he* (someday, *she*) is empowered to do, *his* use of power, *his* personality strengths and weaknesses. We have cautioned that all presidential roles require the assistance of others. The nature and tasks of "the White House" cannot be understood without considering these "others," for the White House is no longer one man. It is an institution.

Dorothy James, in her study of the institutionalized presidency, notes 5 major twentieth-century trends that have contributed to the growth of presidential power:[30]

---

[29] James David Barber, "Passive-Positive to Active-Negative: The Style and Character of Presidents," in Charles Peters and Timothy Adams, eds., *Inside the System* (New York: Praeger, 1970), p. 61.

[30] "The Future of the Institutionalized Presidency," in Charles Dunn, ed., *The Future of the American Presidency* (Morristown, N.J.: General Learning Press, 1975), pp. 95–96.

328

PART 3
decision-making
agencies:
who decides
what and how?

1. Impact of the Great Depression and support for economic intervention by the government
2. Increased significance of military policy during two world wars and the Cold War
3. Public demand for greater social intervention by government, such as in Social Security, with an attendant growth of the bureaucracy
4. Expanded need for national response to social problems such as civil rights, crime, and poverty
5. Technological developments in transportation and communication that have helped make the President the central figure in America's political life.

In order to assist the President in meeting the demands made upon him, Congress has institutionalized the presidency with thousands of individuals and scores of institutions to assist him in carrying out his increased responsibilities.

The Executive Office of the President

When we hear the word *Pentagon,* we instantly think of bigness. Our first impressions of almost any national agency—State Department, FBI, HEW—are of size. Before World War II, however, the terms *presidential aides* and *Executive Office of the President* suggested a few close intimates, a former campaign manager, a press secretary, a telephone operator, a few people to type letters, someone to write speeches. This vision of the Office of the President was not valid much beyond the term of John Adams.

Today, within the presidency, there is a sizeable bureaucracy. It is not housed in cozy offices next to the Oval Office. Rather, it fills two wings of the White House and nearby office buildings with well over a thousand people. From the early 1950s to the early 1970s the White House Office staff grew from under 300 to almost 600, and the entire Executive Office of the President from roughly 1,000 to well over 5,000. The "presidential establishment," as it has been labeled, is anything but cozy. It is big. It is powerful. And most observers of the Washington scene have long assumed it must grow with every new administration.

Cynical about promises to reduce the trappings of power, most journalists and political scientists regarded as empty rhetoric Jimmy Carter's 1976 campaign commitment to reduce the Executive Office staff. Indeed, early in his administration, as Carter tried to cut back what he had called "the imperial presidency," White House reporters predicted failure to go beyond cosmetic changes, giving the false appearance of a reduction. By the middle of Carter's term, however, it turned out that he had actually made a significant staff reduction. Carter's White House office staff in 1978 had 370 members, compared with 575 under Nixon 7 years earlier, a reduction of 36 percent. The total Executive Office staff had dropped from 4,796 to 1,573, an apparent reduction of 67 percent. We call this an apparent reduction because much of it reflects the transfer of activities from the Executive Office to other agencies. The most accurate comparison is of staff size in those agencies, found in the Executive Office under *both* Nixon and Carter:[31]

Agencies in the Executive Office of the President	Employees	
	Nixon	Carter
White House Office	575	370
Office of Management and Budget	700	589
Office of the Vice-President	39	23
Council of Economic Advisers	53	30
Council on Environmental Quality	57	56
Domestic Council	49	53
Executive Mansion and Grounds	74	88
Office of Special Representatives for Trade Negotiations	32	46
Office of Science and Technology Policy	82	27
National Security Council	78	69
Subtotal	1,739	1,351
"Other" agencies	3,057	222
TOTAL	4,796	1,573

The subtotals above represent a decrease of 22 percent in staff size for all agencies included in both Presidents' Executive Offices. Contrary to the denials of "expert" observers of the White House, then, staff reductions can be achieved. But a bureaucracy of some size is essential in view of the President's responsibilities.

Because the *White House Office* works most directly with the President, it enjoys the special aura and the prestige that come from proximity to power. Although all employees in the executive branch serve under the President through an elaborate chain of command, the people in the White House Office serve him directly. Their task is to assist him in carrying out all the detailed activities that are his responsibility. Much of their effort is devoted to serving as a communications link between the President and members of Congress, policy makers in the executive departments and independent agencies, political party leaders, special interest groups, the mass media, and the general public. Essentially they are supposed to do three things: (1) give the President the information and advice he needs to make decisions; (2) give him the technical support he needs to carry out his daily routine; and (3) represent his views and needs to the world outside the White House.

These are heady responsibilities. Although serving on a President's staff can be demeaning, as some who were subjected to Lyndon Johnson's heavy-handed humor discovered, most staff people get a special sort of high from their identity with the White House, whoever the chief occupant may be.

[31] Data are from "Federal Civilian Workforce Statistics," *Monthly Release: Employment and Trends as of May 1978 and October 1971,* U.S. Civil Service Commission, Bureau of Personnel Management Information Systems. The other agencies in the Carter executive office were Office of Administration (179 employees) and Council on Wage and Price Stability (43 employees).

The staff of the Office of Management and Budget struggled
to produce a balanced budget during the election year of 1980.

Sometimes their confidential relationship to the President imbues them with
a confidence that exceeds their competence. As Theodore Sorensen, a former
White House aide, points out, White House advisers may see a problem in a
wider context than a Cabinet officer, but they may also be less knowledgeable
about actual operations, about Congress, and about interest groups.[32]

The Office of Management and Budget (OMB) was designed to help the
President control, coordinate, and evaluate government programs. In its impact on the government, the OMB is more powerful than any other agency
in the Executive Office. Its main task is to prepare the budget for the President
to submit to Congress. No agency can request congressional appropriations
without clearance by the OMB. If an agency's requests do not conform to
the President's overall guidelines, the OMB can refuse to approve them.
In addition, OMB closely watches the operations of all agencies to promote
economy and efficiency.

The Council of Economic Advisers has a small professional staff, mostly
economists and statisticians, whose collective job is to analyze the nation's
economy, appraise the economic programs and policies of the national government, and assist the President in his annual Economic Report to Congress.

[32] *Decision-Making in the White House,* (New York: Columbia University Press, 1963), especially
chap. 5.

The Council consists of three members appointed by the President with the consent of the Senate. Because its recommendations tend to be general, it has fairly good relations with the operating agencies. Although it has sometimes been accused of tempering its economics with political expediency, the Council offers the President substantial assistance in economic planning and is important to his effort to control the economy.

The National Security Council is the primary policy-developing agency in preparing the United States for any possible war. Its function is to advise the President on the best way to integrate the domestic, foreign, and military policies that relate to national security. Each President is free to use the National Security Council in the manner he finds most suitable and helpful. He alone is responsible for determining what policy matters will be brought before the council and how they will be handled. The council's statutory members are the President, Vice-President, Secretary of State, Secretary of Defense, and Director of the Office of Emergency Preparedness. The President may, and frequently does, invite other advisers to attend the council meetings. The Central Intelligence Agency, which coordinates all the intelligence activities of the departments concerned with security matters, reports to the council through its director.

These and the other units in the Executive Office are designed to provide the President with an advisory system that will give him expert advice. The intent is to enlarge the President's base of knowledge, to make him aware of the full range of options beyond those offered by his Cabinet, and to give him the resources needed to do his job. But the scope and size of the presidential establishment raises the danger that it may isolate him from the outside world rather than keep him in better touch with it.

The powers enjoyed by the Executive Office are now much more than advisory. The Executive Office has put a new layer of bureaucrats between the President and his Cabinet. But this alone is not the problem, for the President cannot even deal directly with all the units of the Executive Office. So still another layer emerges—the White House staff—to provide a tighter net around the Chief Executive. They become the ones through whom the President sees the world. If his aides are wise and open, the President's world is realistic and balanced. But as gatekeepers who control the people and ideas that reach the President, "all the President's men"[33] exercise vast powers for which no article of the Constitution speaks.

The Vice-President

The role of the Vice-President has always been rather unusual in American politics, his principal responsibility being to wait on the sidelines for the President to be disabled or impeached, to resign or die. Because Vice-Presidents may become Presidents, they must meet the constitutional qualifications for

[33] See Carl Bernstein and Bob Woodward, *All the President's Men* (New York: Simon and Schuster, 1974).

332

PART 3
decision-making
agencies:
who decides
what and how?

the presidential office: a native-born citizen, at least 35 years old, and a resident of the United States for 14 years.[34]

In the process of nominating candidates, each national convention concentrates on the presidential candidate. Choosing a vice-presidential candidate is a troublesome afterthought. The convention seldom debates the choice; it waits instead for the presidential candidate to make his recommendation and then confirms it. Since the presidential candidate and his staff are usually exhausted from preconvention and convention politics, they are in poor shape to choose a vice-presidential running mate in the 24 hours left for a recommendation to the waiting delegates. If they have not investigated in advance, they do not have time to do so after the nomination. Thus, George McGovern chose Tom Eagleton in 1972 as his running mate, only to find out later about Eagleton's mental health history. Richard Nixon's choice of Spiro Agnew was not only surprising but avoidable, had more preconvention investigative work been done. In 1976, Jimmy Carter's early assurance of nomination permitted more careful screening of prospects before Walter Mondale was chosen.

In seeking support from senators, governors, mayors, and representatives, presidential candidates use the chance of a vice-presidential nomination as bait. Campaign aides for John Kennedy were reported to have told dozens of would-be Kennedy supporters, "I know Senator Kennedy has narrowed the vice-presidential choice down to you and one other man." Because no one knew who the "other man" was, it was a safe story. But when the "chickens come home to roost" on the night of nomination, the candidate has to look at the twenty or thirty "other men" who are waiting for the phone call and choose the candidate who best meets his and the party's political needs.

The vice-presidential candidate is usually chosen to "balance" the presidential ticket. This means that whatever the political qualifications of the presidential candidate, the Vice-President's are often the opposite. If the President comes from the liberal, urban East, it is good politics to choose his running mate from the conservative, rural South: Kennedy and Johnson. If the President is a senior statesman, his Vice-President should be a rising young politician: Eisenhower and Nixon. If the President is an anti-Washington outsider and moderate, his Vice-President may well be a liberal with established credentials in Washington: Carter and Mondale. Although the balanced ticket is demanded by campaign strategy, it can have serious and even tragic consequences if the Vice-President is called on to fill out the President's term (as when Andrew Johnson succeeded Abraham Lincoln). Eight presidents have died in office.

Richard Nixon's choice of Spiro Agnew for Vice-President in 1968 was in part dictated by the "southern strategy" at the Republican Convention. When Nixon was pressed to detail his reasons for singling out the Governor of Maryland, he explained, "There can be a mystique about a man. This guy has got it. People say he's not known. That's nonsense in this day and age. He's known now and as the campaign goes on he'll become better and better

---

[34] See Irving G. Williams, "Waiting in the Wings: The Vice-Presidency," in Dolce and Skau, eds., *Power and the Presidency,* pp. 175–84.

Vice-President Mondale tirelessly defended
Carter's policies during the 1980 campaign.

known."[35] In truth, the outspoken Spiro Agnew became probably the best-
known Vice-President in the history of the office. If his controversial activities
as Vice-President were not enough to ensure him a place in history, his resignation from the office was. "This guy has got it" took on new meaning and
became a cruel joke when bribery and income tax evasion charges forced
the Vice-President from office.

With the resignation of Agnew, President Nixon became the first President
to make use of the Twenty-fifth Amendment, permitting him to nominate a
Vice-President subject to majority confirmation by both houses of Congress.
After seeking suggestions from all members of the House and Senate, he chose
a favorite of the House of Representatives, Minority Leader Gerald Ford.
Ford moved to the vice-presidency only to find President Nixon achieving
another first in constitutional history—the first President to resign. Ford's
own promotion and his selection of Nelson Rockefeller as Vice-President gave
the country its final first in this rapid series of events. The Ford-Rockefeller
team was the first in American history to come to office with no participation
by the voters in the selection process.

In earlier years, the position of the Vice-President was mostly symbolic.
The Constitution provides that he shall preside over the Senate but allows
him to vote only to break a tie. As moderator in the Senate, he merely keeps
parliamentary order. In recent years, however, the office of Vice-President
has begun to acquire political status. President Eisenhower deliberately built
up the political stature of his Vice-President. More conscious of the possibility
of succession than his predecessors had been, probably because of his advancing
age and severe illnesses, he took every opportunity to point to Richard Nixon
as "the most valuable man on my team." Under Kennedy, Vice-President

[35] Reported in the *Congressional Quarterly Weekly Report,* August 16, 1968, p. 2171.

334

PART 3
decision-making
agencies:
who decides
what and how?

Johnson attended the Cabinet and National Security Council meetings and was a presidential adviser.

Under President Carter, Walter Mondale was given really important responsibilities. He was assigned the "second in command" position in the administration, acting in the roles of deputy chief of state, deputy party leader, emissary for the President in foreign affairs, trouble-shooter for the President in various legislative and administrative assignments, and spokesman on many issues. Still, the most important task of any Vice-President is to wait and be ready. If he does not move up through misfortune to the President, the Vice-President can hope that his service and preparation will enable him to capture for himself the party nomination for President.

FUNCTIONS OF THE PRESIDENT

If we ask what American society would be like without the President, we can begin to see some of the consequences of his constitutional powers, roles, and performances.[36] These functions have impact on the broader political system and are of considerable importance to society as a whole.[37]

Symbol and personalization of government

Although the government is viewed as vast and impersonal, the President is a human being in whom we have great interest, about whom we have great knowledge, and for whom we have great concern. He is, in the words of Clinton Rossiter, a "one-man distillation of the American people."[38] As a symbol of the society and a personalization of the abstract values we respect, the President meets important psychological and emotional needs of the citizens. This role is revealed in psychiatric case histories of patients' attitudes toward authority figures. From an examination of such cases, Fred Greenstein directed his research toward public attitudes and behavior caused by presidential deaths—behavior that included weeping, loss of appetite, insomnia, nervousness, and tension. Greenstein concluded that the American President has symbolic and psychological meaning for citizens on a number of fronts. The President:

1. *Simplifies the perception of government* for the people and gives them a focus for understanding what government is doing

---

[36] For a recent bibliography on 3,000 presidential studies since the 1930s, see Fred I. Greenstein, Larry Berman, and Alvin S. Felzenberg, *Evolution of the Modern Presidency: A Bibliographical Survey* (Washington: American Enterprise Institute for Public Policy, 1977). Also see Hugh Heclo, *Studying the Presidency* (New York: Ford Foundation, 1977).

[37] For these and other functions see Thomas E. Cronin, *The State of the Presidency* (Boston: Little, Brown, 1975), pp. 250–58.

[38] *The American Presidency,* p. 16.

Despite record lows in voter approval, Jimmy Carter won renomination in 1980—in part because international crises rallied voters around him as a symbol of the nation.

2. Provides citizens with an *outlet for emotional expression;* a figure who is publicized and does exciting things with which citizens can identify

3. Serves as a *symbol of unity* for the people, especially in times of national crisis

4. Gives the citizens a sense of involvement, a *vicarious means of taking political action*

5. Gives people a sense of *social stability* [39]

James David Barber would agree that emotional needs are met by the presidential image. He argues that we look to the President to satisfy three needs: reassurance that all is well, a sense of progress and action, and a sense of legitimacy. "Given the centrality of the presidency to our political emotions, the chances that these feelings will fasten themselves to the president and presidential candidates are great. These are even greater after a period of emotional disappointment, of accumulating frustration." [40]

Because Presidents have such important symbolic meaning for the society, poor performance or abuse of power is heavily criticized by the public, whose high expectations are rarely fulfilled or sustained.

[39] Fred I. Greenstein, "The Best-Known American," in Walter Dean Burnham, ed., *Politics-American* (New York: Van Nostrand, 1973), p. 143.

[40] James D. Barber, "The Presidency: What Americans Want," *The Center Magazine* (January–February 1971), p. 6.

336

PART 3
decision-making
agencies:
who decides
what and how?

Definition of national priorities

Once elected, the President should be in a unique position to exercise political leadership for the society as a whole. He is the only elected representative who can claim a national constituency and is thus seen as spokesman for the nation—defining the problems, proposing the solutions, and representing the "general will." Even when he is unsuccessful in obtaining support for his list of priorities or achieving agreement with his solutions, it is, by and large, *his* list to which we relate and which we debate. It is *his* leadership we view as critical in the success or failure of governmental policies. Although a host of individuals and groups had well-developed opinions and proposals on public issues at the outset of the Carter administration, serious debate on the Panama Canal, on the sale of aircraft to the Arab States and Israel, or on reorganization of the executive branch did not begin until the President announced his position. In American politics there is much standing and waiting for the President to move.

At the center of attention and respect, the President is in the best position for setting an agenda through which legislation is proposed. In part this is because of the imagined presidency with its lofty powers and expectations. But in fact the President's power is no greater than his ability to persuade others to share his goals.

If the President seeks to define priorities without consultation with Congress or is insensitive to the political needs of legislators, he can find them inattentive, hostile, and unresponsive. As a Washington outsider, President Carter experienced great difficulty with Congress, even though it was controlled by his party. As a result, his priorities were modified and often abandoned in the first two years of his presidency.

Even under favorable conditions, presidential proclamations of national priorities are often a long way from actual national priorities. On TV, in press conferences, and before Congress, President Carter repeatedly proclaimed reduction in oil consumption as one of our national priorities. The real priorities of Congress, special interests, and the American people, however, led us to expand our consumption of oil, continue to waste energy, and worsen our unprecedented deficit in foreign trade. The priority of the balanced budget, proclaimed by most Presidents, is always an early victim to unemployment, inflation, military expenditures, and new social programs. Racial justice, another priority of President Carter, was low on the priority list of many of his fellow citizens.

For all of the failures and partial successes, Presidents do give some direction to government actions. Without Presidents, governments would be more aimless than at present. Imagining what national policies would have been in recent years without Presidents, we conclude that they would have been less bold and creative, more socially conservative, and more often a reflection of the influence of special economic interests. Presidents have often fought for priorities that addressed major social problems; they often proclaim national dreams and goals. Sometimes they win.

Americans like to believe that someone is in charge of their government and is coordinating and supervising the bureaucracy. As Greenstein observes,

It is a caricature of the complex, sprawling, uncoordinated nature of the American political system to see it as a great ship of state, sailing on with the President firmly at the helm. But a great many people find comfort in this simplified image.[41]

The sign on President Truman's desk, "The Buck Stops Here," is an oft-repeated example of the fact that the man in charge sits in the White House. In fact, the President often does not have the slightest notion of where "the buck" even is. The very bureaucratic hierarchy that is designed to create presidential control often creates confusion, infighting, duplication of effort, and lack of coordination. The bureaucracy can also offer severe resistance to presidential direction. The growth of government in complexity and size makes it physically impossible for one person to supervise and coordinate it. With a variety of political subsystems operating within the bureaucracy and Congress, Presidents must accept great limitations on their powers. These limitations have led one student of the presidency to conclude

The really persistent, and frightening, fact about the modern presidency is that while the office has increasingly become a primary medium for responsible government in the United States, the president does not control the government in either the making or the administering of policy.[42]

The popular belief that such coordination should and does exist in the presidential office probably contributes to the failure to reorganize the presidential tasks in any reasonable fashion. Only recently has defining and managing presidential objectives become a serious concern to public administrators and social scientists.[43] If the President is to give real direction to the bureaucracy, major structural and legal revisions are required.

Management of crisis

Much of the growth in presidential power over the last forty years is a direct result of crises in American society—economic depression, world wars, social unrest, natural disasters, communist expansion, inflation, and shortage of natural resources. Americans believe that the President should solve crises when they arise, and they often cite President Franklin Roosevelt's dramatic response to the Depression as a classic example of how Presidents should act.

Yet many crises, both short- and long-term cannot be removed by presidential action. Events may be beyond the President's control. He may not have

[41] Greenstein, "The Best-Known American," p. 143.

[42] Grant McConnell, *The Modern Presidency* (New York: St. Martin's Press, 1976), p. 108.

[43] See Richard Rose, *Managing Presidential Objectives* (New York: Free Press, 1976) and Stephen Hess, *Organizing the Presidency* (Washington: The Brookings Institution, 1976).

338

PART 3
decision-making
agencies:
who decides
what and how?

sufficient resources or authority to make our major problems disappear. Indeed, some crisis situations are generated by presidential decisions made with inadequate information or poor judgment. John Kennedy's Bay of Pigs invasion of Cuba and Nixon's expansion of the Vietnam war into Cambodia were both presidential choices that placed the country into temporary and potentially dangerous crises. Even if a President does not lead the country into danger, he will certainly be faced with averting relatively minor confrontations or difficulties. A poor President will stand by and make noises while the country muddles through until the next election. A good President will find the right people to institute solutions to the problems. A great President will create situations that gain momentum and turn the tide for the country.

SUMMARY

For most Americans, the President *is* the national government, a symbol of unity and social stability. The President plays many roles. As head of state, he entertains representatives of other nations, addresses Congress, presents the nation's annual budget, and keeps the public informed. As director of foreign policy, he can develop treaties and make agreements with other countries (although all such agreements are to be filed with Congress).

Presidents have generally exercised greater power in foreign than in domestic affairs. Congress has the power to declare war, for example, but has never done so except at the request of the President.

As Chief Executive, the President appoints cabinet officers, ambassadors, and the many other officials who make up the vast bureaucracy of government. The people who surround the President—the White House staff—are able to exert extreme influence on their chief, but all units of the Executive Office are designed to provide the President with expert advice. Because the Constitution gives the President legislative powers, he may assume legislative leadership. Success in that leadership of Congress, however, depends partly on his own party having a majority in office.

Presidential power has been described as the influence the President has over policy makers—his ability to persuade. Style, character, and the way he relates to others also help explain the degree of power a President has. Abuse of power is ultimately controlled by the threat of impeachment.

Most Presidents have come from the upper middle class. Many have been military leaders; most have been college or university graduates, and a majority have been lawyers. Nearly all have served in some other branch of government before becoming President.

The President is elected by the electoral college system, which allows a President to be elected even if he does not receive a majority of the popular vote. The Vice-President is usually chosen by the President, often to "balance" the ticket geographically or ideologically. The position is mostly symbolic, but there have been efforts to promote a higher "second in command" status. The Vice-President's most important task, however, is to be ready to assume office should anything happen to the President.

the
bureaucrats

340

PART 3
decision-making
agencies:
who decides
what and how?

The 1976 presidential campaign was somewhat unusual in that both the incumbent (Ford) and the challenger (Carter) ran against big government and the Washington bureaucracy. Ford, a moderate Republican, was such a newcomer to the presidency that he could get away with attacking the administrative structure which he headed. And Carter, outside a Washington power base, treated the bureaucracy as though it were a foreign, occupying force. Pledging to reduce the 1900 federal agencies to some 200, Carter assailed the "horrible bureaucratic mess" with its "incomprehensible policies."

It was not surprising that both presidential candidates—and most of their opponents along the way—decided to take on the bureaucracy. It is a common target of political candidates, journalists, and the average citizen. In this chapter we shall see who these bureaucrats are, what they do, and why they are under attack.

BUREAUCRACY IN THE POLITICAL SYSTEM

Bureaucracy is a result of bigness and complexity in modern society. Any large organization, whether it is a big business, a big church, or a big government, is bureaucratic. If bureaucracy is a common feature of our daily lives, why do many of us view it as something bad? The answers usually include the words *impersonal, confusing, awesome,* and *inefficient.* Government bureaucracy does not have many vocal friends. As James Q. Wilson recently observed,

The federal bureaucracy, whose growth and problems were once only the concern of the Right, has now become a major concern of the Left, the Center, and almost all points in between. Conservatives once feared that a powerful bureaucracy would work a social revolution. The Left now fears that this same bureaucracy is working a conservative reaction. And the Center fears that the bureaucracy isn't working at all.[1]

Federal bureaucracy's desertion by many of its former supporters cannot be easily explained. One expects conservatives to attack the federal bureaucracy. They have long opposed active government, preferring to keep power in corporate ("private") hands or to deal with local bureaucrats whose behavior can be anticipated and influenced. But liberals and nationalists have, in the past, been strong supporters of federal bureaucrats, for they preferred public to private control. They believed the federal government was the means by which public policy could be lifted from local control and shaped instead with a national focus. We will try to explain this change in attitude in more detail as we explore the organization and role of federal bureaucrats in the United States.

[1] James Q. Wilson. "The Rise of the Bureaucratic State," *The Public Interest,* 41 (Fall 1975). 77–103.

Bureaucracy in its ideal form

Whatever their differences from one country to another, bureaucrats are those people who carry out public policies. And despite the tendency to associate bureaucracy only with governmental agencies, bureaucrats are equally common in private organizations, where they carry out private rather than public policies. Public or private, bureaucratic structure usually includes four features: (1) *hierarchical organization;* (2) *differentiation* or *specialization* in the tasks assigned; (3) *qualifications* and *competence* as the basis for recruitment and promotion; (4) *institutionalization* of procedures.

American bureaucracy has all four organizational features. It is hierarchical—the thousands of departments, bureaus, and subdivisions are organized from the top to the bottom, with each lower office under some kind of supervision from a higher office. It operates by specialization—each department functions with a division of labor, and each bureaucrat has assigned tasks. Through civil service requirements, the federal bureaucracy seeks to recruit by qualification and promote by merit. Finally, a highly complex network of rules and procedures guides the bureaucrat's decisions and behavior.

In addition to these organizational features, the ideal bureaucracy is supposed to be *politically neutral,* so that it can carry on the day-to-day activities of government, regardless of which party happens to be in power. No matter how drastic the shift in policy leadership, bureaucrats are expected to remain at their posts, follow their institutionalized routine, and provide continuity for the government.[2]

Being politically neutral, a democratic bureaucracy is expected to be *responsible to elected leaders,* not to have a stubborn will of its own. It is not elected by the people and therefore cannot be held accountable to them for its actions. Rather, it should be responsible to elected officials who, in turn, are accountable to the people. If "higher law" or moral conscience requires the bureaucrat to refuse an order, he has no choice but to resign. Thus, when President Nixon ordered Attorney General Elliot Richardson to fire Special Prosecutor Cox during the investigation of the Watergate scandal, the Attorney General resigned, refusing to carry out the order because it would have violated his moral convictions.

Finally, in a democratic society, bureaucracy is supposed to be *open and representative.* Not only should public service jobs be open to all classes, but bureaucrats should be supportive of democratic norms and institutions. Bureaucrats are to be no less committed to the "general will" and to the rights of citizens than are Congress and the President. Although they may have special training, intelligence, and expertise, bureaucrats are, above all else, servants of the public. They are supposed to do the public's bidding.

[2] Elke Frank, "The Role of Bureaucracy in Transition," *Journal of Politics,* 27 (November 1966), 725–53. Also see Lewis Manzer, *Political Bureaucracy* (Glenview: Scott, Foresman, 1973).

The American bureaucracy in fact

When we shift from the ideal bureaucracy to actual bureaucratic behavior in the American federal system, we find a great contrast. American bureaucrats do not perform perfectly with a model script. On the other hand, they are not the monsters that their sharpest critics claim.

Among those critics is Matthew Dumont, who contends that although there are many written rules for proper behavior of federal civil servants, all are less important than the unwritten rules. Dumont claims that the real, unwritten rules of bureaucracy are:

1. Maintain your tenure through inconspicuous, noncreative, noncontroversial behavior.
2. Keep the boss from getting embarrassed, by protecting his tenure even if it means not fulfilling your responsibility.
3. Make sure all funds are spent at the end of the year, even if wasteful and unrelated to the agency's purpose.
4. Keep the program without questioning whether its purpose has been met or even if it is serving any useful purpose at all.
5. Maintain a stable constituency with friendly relationships with those you are obligated to regulate.[3]

There is certainly some truth in Dumont's characterization of the federal bureaucracy. One can cite *examples* of all his bureaucratic principles. Many programs have continued after their purpose has been served. For example, the National Screw Thread Commission was created during World War I to try to standardize the threads of screws. In 1939 it was reorganized into the Inter-departmental Screw Thread Committee and continued right on into the last decade, still trying to put the screws on, to little effect.

Or we think of "bureaucratic procedures" and remember the bureaucratic memo issued by the National Labor Relations Board in 1969. It instructed its employees on their behavior in the event that the government is under military attack, and they cannot report to work. According to the memo, one is to report to the nearest Post Office and fill out a special registration card and mail it in. This is important because "it will enable us to keep you on the roster of active employees and enable us to forward your pay." (The memo does not state whether checks will be delivered by the enemy's army or the postal officers.)

Senator William Proxmire (D-Wisc.) has established a "Golden Fleece Award" for the bureaucratic decision or project that most flagrantly fleeces the public. He has given the award for such federally funded projects as the study of "Why Rats, Monkeys, and Humans Clinch Their Teeth." Each of these announcements brings the senator a flurry of publicity, and the threat of the award is no doubt designed to keep public servants on their toes.

[3] "Down the Bureaucracy," in Walter Dean Burnham, ed., *Politics-America* (New York: Van Nostrand, 1973), pp. 166–69.

These cases are examples of a reality, but are they representative examples? Do they paint an accurate picture of the federal bureaucracy? We think not. And some, we think, are cheap shots. After all, a weird-sounding study called *The Monograph of the Sub-Class Cirripedia, with Figures of All the Species. The Lepadidae; or Pedunculated Cirripedes* might well have received the Golden Fleece award in 1851. This was one of the studies of Charles Darwin that led finally to the theory of human evolution.

Public administration in the United States has always been touched by personal and partisan considerations. The model of an objective and politically neutral body of administrators has not been part of American culture. (Even though never completely realized, the model at least describes aspirations in some Scandanavian countries.) An administrative class with professional management and special competence was slow to develop in the American civil service. Moreover, careers in public service have never been as prestigious in the United States as in European democracies.

When de Tocqueville visited America in the 1830s he was struck by the fact that "public officers in the United States are not separate from the mass of citizens. . . . No public officer in the United States has an official costume but every one of them receives a salary." It is still true that American officials wear no uniforms, form no separate class, move freely into, and out of, public employment, and are usually paid for their services.

Yvonne Freund, Rapho/Photo Researchers, Inc.

Taxpayers resent the special treatment given to bureaucrats. They see it as contrary to the bureaucrats' role as public servant.

The Internal Revenue Service's misuse of its powers in the 1970s
was an example of excessive responsiveness to political direction.

The growing bureaucracy of the United States is a response to the demands
of powerful groups emerging from the industrial revolution and from the
increasing complexities of a postindustrial economy. Every bureaucratic
agency was created in response to pressures from outside the government
itself, from citizens who hate bureaucracy in general but want something
done for them. Although bureaucrats develop interests of their own, they
can never forget that their fate is tied to the public—or that portion of the
public—whom they are supposed to serve.

In a thoughtful analysis of American bureaucracy, Francis Rourke makes
this point: "Basic to any agency's political standing in the American system
of government is the support of public opinion. If it has that, an agency can
ordinarily expect to be strong in the legislative and the executive branch as
well"[4]

An administrative agency seeks the favor of the general public and builds
alliances with the interest groups that have special stakes in its activities.
With external support, the agency is in a better position to pressure Congress
for new policies or more funds. Rapport with lawmakers and overt public
support give one agency advantages over others when all are making competing claims on the President's budget and policy agenda.

The concept of a democratic and responsible bureaucracy calls for bureaucrats to be under the control of elected officials to ensure that they serve
the public interest. But if the elected leaders themselves attempt to misuse
their power, the concept breaks down. In fact, there is frequent tension be-

[4] *Bureaucracy, Politics, and Public Policy* (Boston: Little, Brown, 1969), p. 13.

tween being responsible to elected leaders and at the same time being professional and ethical. Consider the charges in 1974 that the Internal Revenue Service was giving special treatment to White House friends such as Billy Graham and John Wayne but "hunting down" White House enemies. In a memo to H. R. Haldeman, White House aide Tom Huston wrote, "Nearly eighteen months ago, the President indicated a desire for IRS to move against leftist organizations taking advantage of tax shelters. I have been pressing the IRS since that time to no avail. . . . What we cannot do in a courtroom via criminal proceedings to curtail the activities of some of these groups, IRS could do by administrative action."[5] An investigation of the IRS by a Senate subcommittee showed that the IRS had tried to follow the President's order. In its audit of a million tax returns, the IRS had used its powers to assist the President's friends and harass his enemies. In this instance, the bureaucracy was indeed being responsive to popularly chosen officials. But was it professional and ethical? Clearly not. The struggle between the two is a problem for many public servants.

Finally, when one considers efficiency and work performance, many bureaucrats seem to fall short. Because of the demands of hierarchy and responsibility, there *is* an enormous amount of red tape and delay. But when we evaluate efficiency, it is important to ask, "Efficiency compared to what?" If we are using some ideal standard, bureaucrats come off pretty badly. But compare them to big business or big educational organizations or big labor unions. It is also necessary to recognize that the problems the federal bureaucrats are asked to solve are extremely complex. In many cases, problems are given to bureaucracy because no one in the private sector could solve them, and we have turned to government for a remedy. Who would seek to "abolish poverty" except a government? Who would try to integrate minorities into the whole social fabric except a bureaucracy? That it is done at all, however poorly, is a remarkable achievement.

As we consider the policy-making functions of the bureaucracy later in this chapter, we shall see other differences between the ideal and the reality of bureaucratic behavior. Even at this point, however, we can conclude that the federal bureaucracy is an imperfect instrument of government faced with many conflicting demands that it cannot possibly fulfill. If we are to consume government services at the level we now demand and expect, this imperfect instrument is necessary.

RECRUITMENT AND BACKGROUND OF BUREAUCRATS

When President Washington made his several hundred appointments to the federal service, he declared that he had chosen from among the best qualified persons for each job. As his administration became increasingly pro-

---

[5] As quoted in Louise Brown, "The IRS: Taxation with Misrepresentation," *Readings in American Government* (Guilford: Dushkin, 1975), p. 106.

346

PART 3
decision-making
agencies:
who decides
what and how?

Federalist, however, it turned out that the "best qualified" were usually Federalists. When Thomas Jefferson became President in 1800, he more openly dispensed what patronage he could to friends in his own party who had worked for "the great victory." Citing the need for due participation by both political parties, he immediately removed a great many Federalists to make room for Democratic-Republicans.

"The spoils system"

When Andrew Jackson became President in 1829, he at once threw out of office about 10 percent of the 10,000 employees in the civil service. His enemies charged him with introducing a "spoils system," although Jackson chose to call it "rotation in office." Jackson feared the bureaucracy, convinced that no man could long hold public office without being corrupted. He insisted that no appointee should be allowed to claim a vested interest in his office (that is, that holding the office is a legally defensible property right).

There is still something to be said for "due participation" of the parties and "rotation in office." It is a democratic approach to self-government based on faith in the ability of the common people. It is also a practical way of strengthening the party in power and of achieving more direct political responsibility to the people.

But as the federal government grew bigger over the years, and as its activities became more technical and specialized, due participation of the parties and rotation in office were no longer enough to ensure an effective public service. Job seekers converged on Washington with every change of party fortunes (in 1881 President Garfield was shot by a disappointed applicant). A movement for civil service reform was begun by the National Civil Service Reform League, and in 1883 the Pendleton Act established a classified civil service under a Civil Service Commission.

The civil service

The Pendleton Act originally affected about 10 percent of the federal service. Today 80 percent of federal employees fall under the rules and regulations of the United States Civil Service Commission. Most of the few agencies that do not come under the commission have established their own merit systems, as in the Tennessee Valley Authority.

The purpose of the merit system was to take politics out of the public employment. Appointments and promotions were to be based on relative fitness for positions, without regard to political affiliation. People were to be fired only for incompetence, inefficiency, or illegal behavior. Over the years, civil service rules and congressional legislation have increasingly restricted the political activities of public employees. The Hatch Act of 1939 forbids any officer or employee in the federal civil service to take an active part in party politics or political campaigns. In 1940, a second Hatch Act extended this prohibition to state employees whose salaries are paid wholly or in part by federal loans or grants.

These restrictions were designed to protect federal employees from political coercion and to protect the public from the spoils system. But it is ironic that the very people who are most familiar with the operation of our government should be prohibited from participating freely in the political activities that give it shape and substance.[6] In 1975, revisions in the Hatch Act reduced the restrictions on civil servants' involvement in anything "political." While there is little demand that public servants be allowed to return to the political activism of the "spoils system" some organizations representing civil servants are demanding that their members be allowed a more realistic and normal participation in the political life of the society.

Although the merit system has eliminated many of the abuses of patronage, it, too, has come under increasing attack. Critics have argued that it protects incompetents, promotes on the basis of seniority rather than performance, and makes it too difficult to remove employees in order to restructure agencies. Jimmy Carter was such a critic in his campaign for President. He argued that reform of the civil service was the cornerstone of his reorganization plans for the federal government.

Based on a report prepared by a team of 110 civil servants, business leaders, and academicians, Carter proposed in 1978 a major reorganization into two agencies, one responsible for personnel management, the other for handling complaints about agencies' employment practices. He proposed that performance bonuses replace automatic pay increases and some job security for top federal bureaucrats. He strongly supported a streamlined appeal process to make it easier for managers to dismiss incompetent employees. Finally, he asked that preference for hiring veterans be reduced in order to increase opportunities for minorities and women.[7] With modifications, Congress adopted the revisions. Whether the changes will create a major modification in the merit system remains to be seen. Vested interests in the bureaucracy are stronger and larger now than in Jackson's era, so Carter's reforms seem unlikely to produce great change.

Federal civil servants come from every level of American society and perform jobs similar to almost every job in the private sector. Although the number of national government employees increased rapidly in this century, it has remained fairly constant in recent years.[8] Currently the national government has 2.9 million civilian employees and 2.1 million members of the armed services. Fortunately, such a band of bureaucrats is not concentrated around

[6] How effective the restrictions are is a matter of controversy. Quantitative data collected by the Commission on Political Activity of Government Personnel indicate that federal employees generally are pretty much confused as to what is permitted and what is forbidden. See James W. Davis, Jr., *The National Executive Branch* (New York: Free Press, 1970) for a brief discussion on the political activity of public employees.

[7] *Congressional Quarterly Weekly Reports,* 36 (July 15, 1978), 1777.

[8] For the most complete study of the civil service, see Franklin P. Kilpatrick, Milton Cummings, Jr., and M. Kent Jennings, *The Image of the Federal Service* (Washington: The Brookings Institution, 1964).

348

PART 3
decision-making
agencies:
who decides
what and how?

the nation's capital. Only about 12 percent work in the Washington area; the rest are flung all over the world (and occasionally into space). Because of the magnitude and complexity of governmental activities, the civil service has a high proportion of managerial, technical, and scientific personnel—a much higher proportion than in private employment. With the creation of a retirement program in 1920 and increased fringe benefits over the last 20 years, civil servants now earn incomes comparable to those in private enterprise, except at the very top. Their benefits, in part, explain the lower turnover of career administrators than of politically appointed executives.[9]

The U.S. civil service is open to all, without regard to sex, marital status, race, creed, or political affiliation. At least, that is what the laws say. In actual practice, certain preferences and discriminations do exist. Black employees and women workers have been concentrated at the low-level grades. In the 1960s, strong political pressure was exerted to give minority groups more visible representation in administrative and professional positions. As a result of special recruiting efforts, the proportion of blacks employed in the civil service is actually higher than in the overall work force in the United States. But at the higher levels, underrepresentation is still obvious in all but a few agencies. A 1975 study concluded that "bureaucratic policy-making is taking place in an environment which is racially and ethnically different from that of the nation as a whole."[10] Although much attention was given to employment rights of women in the 1970s, slow progress is the most optimistic claim one can make for the federal service. About two-thirds of the subprofessional white-collar workers are women, but only a handful of women hold top jobs.

The politically appointed bureaucrat

Candidates talk a lot in political campaigns about "new blood" and "throwing the rascals out." However, most new appointees in any administration have not only extensive government experience but also close ties with corporate, legal, and educational establishments. Jimmy Carter, campaigning for President, spoke often of "insiders" too long in control of government and of his desire to "turn the government of this country inside out." Yet, in selecting his cabinet, he opted for little new blood, going instead for experience over inexperience and for familiar blood lines over unknown ones. His 11 cabinet heads had about 70 total years in public service, held 30 corporate directorships, and had average annual incomes of $211,000. This collection led one critic to conclude that "what distinguishes Jimmy Carter 'outsiders' from that GOP regime of privilege and power is that the present Cabinet members are individually and collectively far wealthier."[11]

Students of politics were not surprised that President Carter chose experi-

[9] For a discussion of turnover rates, see Eugene B. McGregor, Jr., "Politics and the Career Mobility of Bureaucrats," *American Political Science Review,* 68 (March, 1974), 24.

[10] Peter N. Grabosky and David H. Rosenbloom, "Racial and Ethnic Integration in the Federal Service," *Social Science Quarterly,* 56 (June 1975), 71–84.

[11] Roger Morris, "Jimmy Carter's Ruling Class," *Harper's Magazine* (October 1977).

enced cabinet leaders as opposed to the maverick "outsiders" anticipated by some voters. Because he had run as an outsider against the Washington establishment, Carter needed to create early credibility with that very establishment in the bureaucracy and the legislature if he were to have any hope of seeing his program adopted. Although the effort was not successful, he tried to allay fears by naming Democrats with proper backgrounds to major governmental posts. He could exercise more freedom, of course, in appointing unfamiliar campaign aides to the White House staff. Freedom in that area was more willingly granted to him because he had stayed with the conventional and familiar in his major appointees.[12]

Cabinet members and heads of other agencies select political appointees below the Cabinet level, although sometimes they allow a member of Congress or of the President's staff to make the selection. Occasionally, a President will choose subordinates before he chooses the agency head, but this is unusual. Over two-thirds of all agency heads conduct personal searches among friends and associates for their top-ranking assistants.[13]

With average incomes of over $200,000 a year, Cabinet members are unlikely to be acquainted with very many poor but competent prospects for appointment. In fact, the skills needed by a high-level administrator are unlikely to have been developed by ordinary citizens. Hence, the higher status levels are vastly overrepresented in major political appointments. Nevertheless, variation in the degree of elitist bias among different agencies has been reported:

Political executives in most of the major domestic departments appear to come from a broad spectrum of American politics, with . . . a great deal of political, especially administrative experience and there is a strong tendency to choose them from the President's party. In contrast, the political executives who have served in the military departments, in the Department of State, and the Treasury Department have tended to come from considerably more restricted backgrounds. . . . Northeastern, Ivy-League, and high church.[14]

If some agencies are more "representative" at the top than others, it is largely because their clienteles are different. The Department of Agriculture, for example, is linked to a broad clientele across the nation and draws its leadership from a variety of educational institutions, private agricultural businesses, and interest groups. In contrast, Departments of State and Treasury emphasize the business and professional world of the eastern seaboard. Even in the most parochial departments, however, executives tend to be more urban and mobile than their counterparts in the United States Congress. Although they share the upper-status bias of Congress, they may in their mobility and urban backgrounds be more "representative" of the American citizenry than are the "representative" institutions of the legislature.

---

[12] For fuller analysis of ruling elites, see Thomas R. Dye, *Who's Running America: The Carter Years*, 2nd ed. (Englewood Cliffs: Prentice-Hall, 1979).

[13] Dean E. Mann, "The Selection of Federal Political Executives," *American Political Science Review*, 58 (March 1964), 81–99.

[14] *Ibid.*, p. 98.

To define the roles of bureaucrats is somewhat more complicated than to discuss the roles of legislators or the President. There are a number of bureaucratic roles, with differing expectations. Someone in the Executive Office of the President quite clearly has a different role from that of someone in an agricultural extension station in Montana. Although the label of "bureaucracy" probably covers as many differences as similarities in the federal service, it is useful to consider some major bureaucratic roles and role conflicts.

Different role expectations

The role of the politically appointed bureaucrat is defined differently from that of the civil servant or career bureaucrat. In addition, there are role differences among the politically appointed as well. Appointees to the Executive Office of the President, for example, are official representatives of the administration. They are appointed by the President, often come from his campaign staff, serve at the pleasure of the President, and give their whole loyalty to the administration of which they are an integral part. Speaking for the President and representing his point of view, the Executive Office and White House staff bureaucrat is expected to play the role of a presidential "hired gun" in the bureaucracy, in congressional committees, with legislative leaders, and with media representatives. Because of single-minded loyalty to the President, executive office bureaucrats often distrust even politically appointed bureaucrats at the departmental levels, whom they see as having divided loyalties and multiple roles.

A department head may play several roles at once. Like their counterparts in industry, government department heads are answerable to those above them—up to the President—and to those below them in their own departments. Department heads are expected to implement the broad policy views of the President and of Congress within their departments. They are expected to provide a direct line of communication from the White House to all the various offices in their departments and to see to it that the views of the people in those offices reach the President.

The chief executive of a department must direct and coordinate the activities of an immense organization. Most department heads come to identify themselves with their organizations and support the points of view and special interests of their own departments. But in any case, department heads are responsible for seeing to it that the expertise of the people under them reaches the right places at the right time to count in decision making.

Some department heads play still another role: they represent their clientele's interests in the policy process. Indeed, they may have been chosen because they represent an important constituency such as labor, agriculture, or minorities, but this factor may become a source of tension between a President and his own appointees. The more a President tries to include different interests in his administration, the more likely are the chances that he will have to face conflict within his community of policy makers.

Finally, each department head is expected to act as "the President's principal adviser" in the area covered by his or her department. The *Organization Manual* describes the Secretary of State as "head of the Department of State and the principal adviser to the President in the formulation and execution of the foreign policy of the United States." The President must make his own decision when, as sometimes happens, his principal advisers represent competing interests or recommend conflicting policies.

In theory, at least, the sharpest role differences are found among the political executives who make policy and career administrators who carry out and apply policy. The political executives help make the policies with the Chief Executive and with him assume responsibility for the government. They come and go with the President in power. The career administrators, on the other hand, provide knowledge and managerial competence and serve through successive party or presidential changes. Their role is to provide the methods and organization to do what politically responsible bureaucrats determine should be done. In fact, because public administration is seldom divided into clear policy-making and policy-applying tasks, the career civil servant is often heavily involved in making critical decisions that distribute resources in the society. Their mixed roles lead the career bureaucrats into conflicts—sometimes unavoidable, sometimes deliberate—with the "President's men and women."

Political executives and professional bureaucrats

The policy makers, top members of the President's team, are his most important political appointees. Sharing his responsibility for administering the affairs of the country, they are expected to make public policy in response to whatever mandate the last election presumably gave them, to represent the people to the government and the government to the people. Below the policy makers is the permanent bureaucracy in the civil service. Incoming political executives, eager to make policy changes, are likely to be dismayed by the massive and seemingly immovable bureaucracy. Nor is their apprehension without justification. All Presidents echo the sentiment of Harry Truman when he observed that he could not "make the bureaucracies do a damn thing." Cabinet secretaries and White House staff, whether Democratic or Republican, complain that the "professionals" do not respond to their directives. Struggling to make or change public policy, political representatives often charge that policy making really goes on within the permanent bureaucracy without regard to either legislative or executive will.

Such claims are, no doubt, often exaggerated. But career administrators can define their roles so that they are able to undermine political programs with which they disagree. The problem is most acute when there is a party change in control of the White House. It is especially severe when the change is from a Democratic to a Republican administration, because the career bu-

352

PART 3
decision-making
agencies:
who decides
what and how?

reaucracy is dominated by "closet" Democrats. In a study of career executives in 18 federal agencies in 1970, Aberbach and Rockman concluded that Nixon's suspicion that the career bureaucracy would be disinclined to support the new Republican administration, "has substantial grounding in fact." They found a bureaucracy with little Republican representation but, more importantly, "a social service bureaucracy dominated by administrators ideologically hostile to many of the directions pursued by the Nixon administration."[15] As we shall note later, President Nixon sought to control the bureaucracy by creating the Office of Management and Budget. In addition, he encouraged crude and illegal attempts by the White House staff to dominate the career service.

Even in the absence of partisan conflict, differences develop as a result of the policy-making role of the career service. The policy-making of federal bureaucrats is shown best in the activities of the former HEW (Health, Education, and Welfare) over the last decade. In an effort to eliminate discrimination in federally assisted education, Congress outlined this general objective in Title IX of the Educational Amendments of 1972. But the specific policies by which this objective was to be achieved were left largely to the bureaucracy, subject to congressional veto. In 1975, HEW announced regulations banning sex discrimination in the nation's schools and colleges. The agency announced that women could not be subject to stricter curfew laws than men are or denied admission to certain classes. It called for integrated physical education courses and demanded equal athletic opportunity for both sexes. Such rules, representative of thousands created each year by federal bureaucrats, refute the myth that bureaucracy is uninvolved in policy decisions and rule making.

Professional bureaucrats play a significant role at every stage in the policy process. When the principal officers of a government agency go before congressional committees to obtain legislative authorizations and appropriations, they are usually accompanied by their career officers, to back up their presentation, to interpret the supporting documents, and to answer the difficult and technical questions. When a new policy is authorized, bureaucrats work out the personnel and fiscal requirements and the operating procedures. In addition to developing the rules and regulations for the implementation of policy, bureaucrats interpret and apply the rules in specific cases. At the center of policy making and application, bureaucrats play a variety of roles. Sometimes their own roles are in conflict with one another; often they are in conflict with roles played by others.

EXECUTIVE OFFICE OF THE PRESIDENT

The Executive Office of the President became visible and controversial during the Nixon administration. It was here that the "Palace Guard" of the

---

[15] Joel D. Aberbach and Bert A. Rockman, "Clashing Beliefs Within the Executive Branch: The Nixon Administration Bureaucracy," *American Political Science Review,* 70 (June 1976), 458.

White House staff achieved extraordinary power in the policy making of the government. Both the power and its abuse became campaign concerns of Jimmy Carter; and in 1977 he reorganized the Executive Office, abolished some units, and returned other functions to Cabinet-level departments. Retaining a White House staff of press secretary, counsels, political aides, and assistants, he reduced and streamlined other units.

The Office of Management and Budget maintains a central position in the Executive Office.[16] Other important staff include the National Security Council, Council of Economic Advisers, Council on Wage and Price Stability, and Council on Environmental Quality. Because members of the Executive Office staff are concerned with many policies that overlap Cabinet-level concerns, there is inevitable conflict among these presidential appointees. Although President Carter was able to reduce the size of the Executive Office, it is still viewed with concern and often fear, both by departmental level executives and congressional leaders. Its collective powers are still vast, despite efforts at decentralization, and critics of the Carter presidency argue that ineptitude by the White House staff and other Executive Office agents (including former OMB Director Burt Lance) was the major reason for failure of early Carter proposals in Congress.

The executive departments

The government now has 13 executive departments. For purposes of protocol and of succession to the presidency, they rank as follows: State, Treasury, Defense, Justice, Interior, Agriculture, Commerce, Labor, Health and Human Services, Housing and Urban Development, Transportation, Energy and Education. Each executive department is headed by a secretary appointed by the President with the consent of the Senate. The 13 secretaries are among the top political figures in the national administration, in the so-called line of succession to the presidency. They sit in the President's Cabinet; each heads a large and important operating agency; and next to the President and Vice-President, they earn the highest salaries in the administrative hierarchy.

The typical pattern of departmental organization is hierarchical, with levels of authority clearly established, from the secretary as the chief executive of the department, to the lowest units in the bureaucracy. Most departments carry on activities that are more or less related to a single major function, such as conduct of foreign affairs, administration of justice, finance, or national security. The Department of Health and Human Services obviously performs two functions. Four of the departments—Agriculture, Commerce, Labor, and Housing and Urban Development—serve particular segments of the population rather than the country in general. Also, a good many of the bureaus in the departments tend to be independent; e.g., the Federal Bureau of Investigation in the Justice Department, the Corps of Engineers in the Defense De-

[16] On the work of the OMB, see Richard Rose, *Managing Presidential Objectives* (New York: Free Press, 1976).

354

PART 3
decision-making
agencies:
who decides
what and how?

partment, and the Agency for International Development in the State Department. These units gain their independence because they have their own supporters outside the department. The Corps of Engineers, for example, is a favorite agency of many members of Congress because the Corps provides jobs and contracts in so many constituencies.

The Cabinet

The Constitution makes no provision for a body to advise the President in his role of Chief Executive. In the first administration, President George Washington was snubbed when he tried to use the Senate as an advisory council and rebuffed when he went to the Supreme Court for an advisory opinion. So he turned for collective advice to his principal administrative officers (the Secretary of State, the Secretary of Treasury, the Secretary of War, and the Attorney General). This was the informal beginning of the President's Cabinet. Today the Cabinet comprises the heads of the 13 major executive departments. Appointment to Cabinet positions is usually dictated by party, geographic, and socioeconomic factors as well as special capabilities. The Senate unhesitatingly confirms most presidential nominations to the Cabinet, although occasionally questions may be asked about possible "conflicts of interest."

President Carter relied on his Cabinet as a group,
rather than singling out one member as a special confidant.

Paul Conklin, Monkmeyer.

Just how important the Cabinet is depends upon the personality and work style of the President. Indeed, the prestige enjoyed by the American Cabinet seems to spring more from political tradition and protocol than from actual power in the government. Individual secretaries may be very important to the President, as Attorney General Robert Kennedy was to his brother, as Attorney General John Mitchell was to Nixon, and Secretary of State Henry Kissinger was to Ford. Carter, on the other hand, did not rely especially on one member but used his Cabinet as a group. Unlike the cabinet in a parliamentary government (as in Britain, Germany, or Japan), the members of the U.S. Cabinet have no official responsibility for furnishing broad political leadership. Cabinet decisions are not binding even on its own members, and neither the President nor Congress is bound to heed its views.

Other regulatory agencies

The *United States Government Organization Manual* lists more than 40 independent agencies that are not under the executive departments. Some are small and obscure; others are large and powerful. In the powerful category are the *regulatory boards and commissions,* whose services and activities affect vital areas in our national economy: Interstate Commerce Commission (created 1887), Federal Reserve Board (1913), Federal Trade Commission (1934), Securities and Exchange Commission (1934), National Labor Relations Board (1935), Civil Aeronautics Board (1938). All are headed by boards or commissions with multiple membership. All are free from direct responsibility to the President. All engage in policy making and regulatory activities, mostly in the economic sphere. All have some legislative and judicial powers.

Taken together, these commissions exercise tremendous authority over transportation by railroad, bus, truck, pipeline, merchant ships, and planes; communication by telephone, telegraphy, radio, and television; hydroelectric development, interstate electric power, water resources, flood control, and interstate transportation of natural gas; unfair practices in labor-management relations; banking practices, credit policies, issuance of securities, and trading in the national stock markets.

The independent regulatory commissions were set up outside the cabinet departments for several reasons. Because the commissions have semi-judicial duties—an NLRB ruling on charges of unfair labor practices, for example—their work can best be performed by independent and impartial persons. Also, because regulatory tasks often include rule making—semi-legislative power such as a CAB ruling on air traffic patterns—it is argued that such rule-making powers should be handled by a body with enough members for several points of view to find expression, rather than by a single administrator. A more philosophical justification stems from the concept of separation of powers; because the regulatory commission exercises judicial and legislative as well as executive powers, it ought not to be put wholly under the President.

356

PART 3
decision-making
agencies:
who decides
what and how?

Regulatory boards and commissions are, in practice, seldom "independent" or "free from politics." Their political life is not highly visible; but in the day-to-day decisions of who gets helped and who gets hurt, regulatory agencies are big-time operators. The powers they exercise are vast, and their deliberations are crucial to the well-being of major economic enterprises. The interests affected seek to control the decisions of the commissions and to staff them with sympathetic personnel.

Regulatory agencies are required by law to be bipartisan, but Presidents do their best to find appointees whose policy orientation is similar to their own. Once appointed, however, the member is free of presidential control. The result is that commissioners with differing party backgrounds often vote differently in disputes before the agency. For example, split votes along party lines in the NLRB are as typical as split decisions made by the Supreme Court. Both "independent" commissioners and "independent" Supreme Court justices cling to political values and vote their convictions. When one adds to partisanship the fact that many commissioners gained their expertise by prior service in the very industries they are trying to regulate, it is easy to conclude that independent regulatory commissions do not always measure up to the standards of impartiality claimed for them.

Critics of every political orientation, from the consumers' advocate Ralph Nader to the economist Milton Friedman, have called for revision of federal regulatory activity. Much of their attack has centered around the charge that the regulatory agencies have been captured by industry-dominated advisory committees. They contend that the agencies, designed to protect the public interest, are in fact used to suppress competitive behavior. Thus, the ICC, created in 1887 in response to Western farmers' cries that they were being abused by railroads, now has control over rail, truck, and water transportation and has reduced competition among them.

In spite of these attacks, government regulation of economic activities will hardly diminish in the years ahead. On the contrary, as economic enterprises become more complex and interdependent, one can forecast greater involvement of government in supervision and coordination of our economic life. As this occurs, we can expect that regulatory agencies will become much more visible and controversial. Moving them out of the shadows and into the political light will reveal how important and political they really are.

Administrative management

Every President from Franklin Roosevelt to Jimmy Carter has tackled the job of reorganizing the national administration, but none has been entirely successful. In 1949, the Hoover Commission, appointed by President Truman, made many recommendations for improving the general management of the executive branch. The commission reported that the executive branch was "a chaos of bureaus and subdivisions," and it made nearly 300 specific recommendations for change. The response was the Reorganization Act of 1949, in which Congress authorized President Truman to submit reorganization plans that would go into effect unless vetoed by either House within 60 days. This act has been many times amended, renewed, and revived, but Congress always imposes a time limit, so that reorganization authority will not extend beyond the term of the President in office.

When Richard Nixon became President in 1969, the overall picture of the national administration was still one of immense chaos and clutter.[17] His immediate concern was to sharpen the tools of management and policy analysis in the Executive Office. He tried to do this by a reorganization plan, which restructured the old Bureau of the Budget into a supermanager agency known as the Office of Management and Budget (OMB). This elite presidential agency was to become so powerful that it was referred to as "World Headquarters" by some, and by *The New York Times* writer John Herbers as "the other presidency."[18]

In creating OMB, President Nixon wanted to strengthen central control of the bureaucracy. As is the case with most Presidents, he was frustrated by internal bureaucratic fighting, and he wished to coordinate the bureaucracy for the achievement of presidential programs and goals. In addition, he was motivated by extraordinary concern that bureaucrats would destroy his program and his presidential effectiveness. Post-Watergate revelations showed his distrust of all but a few advisers, and OMB appealed to his instincts for tightly coordinated, elite control of potential "enemies from within."

Under director Roy Ash (former president of Litton Industries) and deputy director Frederic Malek (friend of H. R. Haldeman and former deputy director of the Committee for the Reelection of the President) OMB grew into an agency of 660 staff members. Its functions swiftly developed to include approving how much to spend on each government program, overseeing how each program was being carried out, reviewing all legislation submitted by agencies to Congress, and recommending presidential vetoes or approvals of legislation. It became heavily involved in the day-to-day operations of government departments to a degree unexperienced under the old Office of Budget.

During the Watergate scandal, presidential advisers were dismissed, the Cabinet played even less of an advisory role, and most of the President's attention was focused on staying in office. During the collapse of Nixon's administration, according to one observer, OMB "played a stronger role than usual in keeping the Government from flying apart or grinding to a halt. In many respects it has become a surrogate President, administering the Nixon policies as its top officials see them."[19]

If reorganization and control were concerns of Richard Nixon, they were almost obsessions for candidate Jimmy Carter. Presenting himself to the electorate as a businessman and tough manager, he repeatedly promised to eliminate waste, reorganize the bureaucracy, and use business management principles to achieve efficiency. These pledges were strengthened by the claim

---

[17] See Stephen K. Bailey, "Managing the Federal Government," in Kermit Gordon, ed., *Agenda for the Nation* (Washington, D.C.: The Brookings Institution, 1963), pp. 301–34.

[18] John Herbers, "The Other Presidency," *The New York Times Magazine* (March 3, 1974).

[19] *Ibid.*

"This could be trouble — get those desks into a circle...!"

that, as governor of Georgia, he had abolished 278 of the 300 state agencies. He also hoped to follow his gubernatorial achievements of zero-based budgeting (every expenditure having to be justified anew every year) and sunset legislation (fixed dates for the termination of programs) at the national level. After difficult compromises with Congress, he won approval to begin reorganization efforts in 1979. Two years into his presidency, study groups were investigating alternative reorganization plans. Even at those early stages, agency bureaucrats and their allies in Congress were preparing strategies to offset substantial reorganization plans when they were offered. Carter's determination to establish a bold record in reorganization thus turned restructuring the federal government into a major battle.

INTERACTIONS OF BUREAUCRATS WITH OTHER BRANCHES OF GOVERNMENT

Presidential controls

The bureaucracy is, of course, directly under the President as the chief executive officer. The one person officially authorized to give an order through the chain of command right down to the lowliest clerk or soldier is the President. Or for shock value, he could call and give the command directly.

Franklin Roosevelt occasionally showed his intimate involvement in every facet of government by ignoring the chain of command.

We recognize the President's role as general manager of the government when we speak of the Ford administration or the Carter administration. Because the President appoints most of the important officials in the executive branch—many of them his close friends, all of them presumably his supporters—he puts a personal stamp on his administration at the very outset. This personal relationship is institutionalized in the meetings of the Cabinet and the National Security Council, over which the President presides. In practice, many of these officials deal more frequently with the White House Office than with the President himself, but the administrative responsibility is still the President's. Since nearly all presidential appointees serve at his pleasure, he is able to influence their attitudes and to dismiss them when their views differ too sharply from his own.

Congressional controls

Congress has never been willing to give the President complete control over the administration of its policies. Congress determines the functions of the government and, accordingly, the tasks of the bureaucracy. Congress can create or abolish any administrative unit or require the President to do so. It can decide whether a new unit will be established as a department, independent agency, regulatory commission, board, or corporation. Both Roosevelt and Truman tried without success to induce Congress to establish a new Department of Public Welfare in the President's Cabinet. The Congress accepted Eisenhower's Reorganization Plan of 1953 and created a larger Department of Health, Education, *and* Welfare. Congressional authority to create, destroy, or divide an agency is a powerful political weapon.

Congress maintains the General Accounting Office (GAO) as a congressional watchdog over the Treasury. The Comptroller General, who heads the GAO, is principally responsible to Congress, appointed with the consent of the Senate, and can be removed only with the consent of both houses of Congress. The GAO has broad authority over government expenditures. Every government warrant must be countersigned by the Comptroller General. No money can be paid out of the Treasury unless the Comptroller General's countersignature certifies the legality of the expenditure.

Some political scientists and many people on the staffs of Presidents have argued that the GAO should not play such a decisive role in administration and yet be independent of the Executive Office. The fact remains, however, that Congress holds the purse strings, and the bureaucrats are as conscious of congressional control through the General Accounting Office as they are of presidential management through the Office of Management and Budget.

The committee system gives Congress another way of controlling the administration. Department heads may not appear on the floor of Congress to defend or promote pending legislation, but they are regularly called into the committee rooms of Congress to explain and justify their administrative pro-

360

PART 3
decision-making
agencies:
who decides
what and how?

grams. When, for example, the Senate Committee on Foreign Relations chooses to consider some current problem in foreign policy, it may summon the Secretary of State, the Secretary of Defense, the Chairman of the Joint Chiefs of Staff, and sometimes a whole crew of special assistants, assistant secretaries, office directors, bureau directors, and division chiefs to explain or defend their policies.

The most effective point of congressional control over the bureaucracy is in the appropriations process. The President's budget, as he submits it to Congress, is a single document. It is not only a complete financial report but also a planned program of activities for the entire executive branch. Congress, however, never debates the budget as such. In practice, each house accepts the recommendations of its appropriations committee, paying very little attention to general policy. Moreover, each appropriations committee normally accepts the bills proposed by its respective subcommittees. In effect, this piecemeal consideration of the budget vests the power of the purse in a score of small, relatively independent subcommittees.

Congress also makes frequent use of its power to investigate administrative agencies. How far Congress can go in compelling officials to give testimony or produce documents is not clear. The courts have generally upheld the congressional power of investigation as essential to the legislative function. They have never recognized any inherent right of federal officials to withhold information from Congress (or the courts). Nevertheless, officials in certain departments, notably State, Defense, and Justice, have successfully claimed the "privilege" of refusing to give information on the ground that disclosure might endanger national security.

Normally, of course officials cannot afford to appear unfriendly to Congress, for the consequences might be drastic. Although Congress has no effective authority to remove officials from office or to single them out for discipline, it does have the power to abolish any agency, to eliminate specific programs, and to "reduce force." Understandably, then, most administrators are eager and cooperative when they appear at committee hearings. In fact, some departments, such as State and Defense, employ special staffs to keep in touch with Congress.

The importance of congressional and presidential investigations of bureaucratic activities was shown in the 1970s in the joint investigations of CIA activities in the United States. A presidential commission headed by Vice-President Rockefeller was joined by a Senate investigation chaired by Senator Frank Church. After almost three thousand pages of sworn testimony, the presidential commission concluded that some of the CIA activities at home were "plainly unlawful and constituted improper invasions upon the rights of Americans." These activities included intercepting 2.3 million pieces of mail, installing wiretaps on newspeople and subjecting them to physical surveillance, and administering LSD to an unsuspecting victim who died "apparently as a result." The Church committee focused on foreign activities of the CIA and found charges of assassination attempts on foreign leaders, bribery, and counterfeit activities.

Among the more amusing "intelligence" plans uncovered by congressional investigation was a CIA plot to destroy Fidel Castro's image as "The Beard." When agents learned that Castro was planning to leave Cuba on a trip, they assumed that he would leave his shoes outside his hotel room to be shined. The plan was to pour thallium salts on his shoes, in hopes that the powerful depilatory would cause his beard to fall out. By chance, Castro canceled the trip and kept his beard.

Judicial controls

If we wanted to find the bulk of federal "law" that governs the country today, we would go not to the *Statutes at Large* passed by Congress, but rather to the *Federal Register*, which contains the executive orders, directives, rules, and regulations adopted by the national administration. Congress enacts general policies, but more and more it leaves the details of regulation to administrative agencies. Not only the independent regulatory commissions but also the executive departments issue regulations with the force of law. Just as the Interstate Commerce Commission fixes maximum rates in interstate transportation, so does the Secretary of Agriculture regulate the marketing of agricultural products. Today a hundred or more federal agencies make rules that are legally binding.

The bureaucrats who make these rules are subject to control by the courts no less than by the President and Congress. The Administrative Procedures Act of 1946 authorizes judicial review of administrative decisions. The courts, to protect themselves against a flood of litigation, normally refuse to review questions of fact, in order to focus on questions of law or constitutional authority.

In practice, administrative agencies enjoy a large measure of independence from judicial review. Because administrators know that their actions may be subject to judicial review, however, they consult continuously with the attorneys in their agency, to be sure they are acting in a legal manner. This very fact often discourages the private citizen from taking legal action.

Moreover, judicial restraint tends to favor the administration. The same reason that made the legislature delegate rule-making authority makes the courts reluctant to review administrative decisions: the subject matter is often so technical that it is beyond the understanding of the judges. Even when the courts do attempt review, they must listen to expert versus expert and then decide. Yet, when President Nixon and his bureaucratic staff attempted to dismantle the Office of Economic Opportunity and impound funds appropriated by Congress for water pollution and highways, the courts stepped in and stayed his hand. There is comfort in the democratic theory that no official is above the law, that all must operate within the law, and that any private citizen has the right to take court action against arbitrary or excessive bureaucracy.

If we ask ourselves what the system would be like without a bureaucracy, we can begin to see the consequences of bureaucratic activities in the American system. Without bureaucrats, public policies would be announced but never carried out, legislators and Presidents would have to act on the basis of their own knowledge, each administration would start off without established procedures, and decisions would be made in each case without uniform guidelines.

Policy administrators

The primary function of the bureaucracy is to administer the policies of the government, "to apply the rules" that have been worked out by the President and Congress. As we have seen, the neat statement that bureaucrats apply policy is as much a simplification as the statement that Congress makes policy, or that the President supervises the application of policy, or that courts settle disputes. All of these statements are true in the sense that they point to the primary function of the official decision-making agencies in American politics. With no bureaucracy, the entire machinery of government would collapse, for laws do not carry themselves out; they require a vast number of people to do all the chores entailed in carrying out any program. But in its unqualified form, the description overstates in one sense and understates in another sense. As we have just seen, the bureaucrats are controlled and directed in a variety of ways in their application of policy. On the other hand, the bureaucrats play a part themselves in shaping policy rather than merely applying the rules.

Expert knowledge in rule making

A basic function of the bureaucracy is to introduce specialized knowledge and expertise into the policy-making process. We could describe this as an unintended consequence, because bureaucratic agencies are set up to carry out policies made by others (the first function we identified above). But in the very act of performing this intended function, bureaucrats develop greater familiarity with the working details of policy in actual practice. The feedback from those who carry out policies is of great help in making better informed policy decisions. Bureaucrats are thus doubly equipped to add specialized knowledge to policy making: they are often recruited in the first place for some professional skill; their work makes them better informed than anyone else about what it is like out in "the field" where individuals come into contact with government. This specialized knowledge may lead to overenthusiasm about one's specialty, to the point that advice becomes biased. But the wise political leader knows that experts in the navy are addicted to ships; in the air force, to bombs; in the army, to ground forces.

Continuity in policy

A third function of the bureaucracy is to lend continuity to the work of government. An incoming political executive, while still learning, may be much relieved to have a supporting cast of qualified advisers who can carry on. On the other hand, it can often be difficult to change from old ways of doing things to new. The permanence of bureaucracy is both an advantage and a disadvantage; it offers continuity in the periods of transition between one set of principal actors and the next, but it also establishes a routine that tends to resist innovation.

Rule by objective standards

A fourth consequence of bureaucracy is decision making on the basis of rules and objective standards. This, of course, is the source of much criticism of bureaucracy. Each of us wants to be treated as an individual, a rational human being, not simply one case in a certain category. Nevertheless, we can understand that bureaucrats dealing with hundreds of cases could not possibly come to know each one personally. Even if they did, we would like protection against the possibility that their biases would lead them to treat us unfairly. Objective procedures are introduced as a safeguard against favoritism or poor judgment, but so-called objectivity has its perils, too. It may prohibit or at least discourage the use of good judgment.

Problems in using the bureaucracy

If the President is to act like a Chief Executive and to see to it that the laws are faithfully executed, then he must master the bureaucracy at the outset. In the phrasing of Richard Neustadt, the classic problem of the man on top in any political system is how to be on top in fact as well as in name. The lines of authority from the President's office must be clear and positive; all the books in public administration tell him so. Hence, Presidents from Franklin D. Roosevelt to Jimmy Carter have struggled to reorganize the national administration so that the President is unquestionably at the top of the organization. But study commissions are always appalled to discover that our national administration is actually a confused structure of departments, bureaus, divisions, boards, commissions, corporations, and other independent establishments in which the lines of authority and responsibility appear hopelessly scrambled.

Cries for improvement will continue in the future. As James Q. Wilson has suggested, improvements will be directed along 5 lines.[20] (1) There will be increased demands that elected officials exercise *more control* over bureaucrats and hold them *more accountable,* so that we can use acceptable methods

---

[20] "The Rise of the Bureaucratic State." *The Public Interest,* 41 (Fall 1975), 77–103.

President Nixon's fear of the bureaucracy led him to misuse it, as revealed in the Watergate tapes.

to achieve goals. The investigation of the CIA clearly pointed to the dangers of an unsupervised bureaucratic enterprise. (2) We should continue to explore ways by which *equality* can be achieved in dispensing public services, so that similar cases are treated alike, according to prescribed rules known in advance. (3) At the same time, we should improve the bureaucrats' *responsiveness*, so that they may use compassion and common sense in dealing with cases that do not fall into neat categories. (4) We should establish more direct procedures to guarantee *fiscal integrity* (honest handling of money), reduce conflict of interests, and watch expenditures of public monies more carefully. (5) Finally, we will continue to pursue the age-old goal of *efficiency*. This may require, in the future, greater decentralization of bureaucracy and smaller units of government, although there is no assurance that decentralization will be more efficient or acceptable.

SUMMARY

The federal bureaucracy is the hundreds of thousands of civil servants who make up the government at work. The ideal bureaucracy is politically neutral, so that the government keeps running no matter which party is in power. Bureaucrats are supposed to be open and representative; above all else, they are servants to do the public's will. To ensure that they serve the public interest, bureaucrats are, to a certain extent, under the control of elected officials. Conflicts can develop when elected leaders try to misuse bureaucratic services to achieve their own ends.

Within the bureaucracy, levels of authority are clearly established from the Chief Executive on down. Most departments carry out functions related to one specific area; the President's Cabinet is made up of heads of the 13 major executive departments.

Civil service jobs used to be given to friends and party favorites. In 1883, a merit system was introduced to take the politics out of public employment. Most civil servants take examinations to get their jobs, but the top political appointments are made by the President.

The roles of bureaucrats vary with their jobs. They are expected to carry out public policy, and department heads must make their department's views known to the President. Department heads also advise the President in their areas of specialization. Federal bureaucrats often have policy-making roles; since they are appointed by the President, he can influence their attitudes and dismiss them if their views differ sharply from his.

The President is not the only one with control over the bureaucracy. Congress can create or abolish any administrative unit, and it controls the funds necessary to carry out bureaucratic programs. In addition, all bureaucratic agencies are subject to judicial review. The bureaucracy is never perfectly responsive to presidential leadership, but that leadership is more effective when the President asserts control very soon after he takes office.

the
judges

11

In *The Brethren,* a best-selling exposé of the Supreme Court, Watergate reporters Bob Woodward and Scott Armstrong sought to tear the veil of secrecy and respectability from the high court. With gossipy revelations from 170 former law clerks, the writers paint the justices as a maneuvering, warring, petty group with great power. Chief Justice Burger is seen as pompous, vain, and incompetent; Justice Marshall, lazy and frivolous; Justice Blackmun, indecisive. Profiles of the justices reveal a blind and ill Harlan signing a bed sheet instead of a court order, a petulant and senile Douglas demanding that a tenth chair for him be put back on the bench long after his retirement, and a breezy Marshall asking the chief justice, "How's it shaking, chiefy baby?"

Although tales of high power are interesting to a public with an insatiable curiosity about its leaders, *The Brethren* does not greatly advance our political knowledge about the judiciary. It simply tells us again that law in our society is not revealed from on high but fashioned by human hands. It confirms that the process of judicial decision making is a flawed, human enterprise in which the personal values and imperfections of the justices are blended in an output that is both legal and fallible.

THE JUDICIAL SYSTEM

Although most Americans see the federal courts as part of the government, many do not recognize that this means the judiciary is part of the political process. Courts are seen as powerful but somehow removed from the political tug-of-war. Courts do perform their political roles somewhat differently from other agencies of government, but this does not make their activities any less political. Courts are neither separated from, nor irrelevant to, the political system. Their activities involve many of the same social issues and clashes of interests that are present in Congress and the bureaucracy. Thus, we can examine judges in the same fashion as we examined legislators and bureaucrats—as actors in a political setting, responding to demands and pressures, allocating rewards and punishments through their decisions.

To appreciate the unique role of judges in the American political system, it is useful to consider the influence that two groups, or subcultures, have on American courts. These subcultures—the legal subculture and popular subculture—help define the special nature of our judiciary.[1]

The legal subculture

Americans are fond of saying that we have "a government of laws and not of men." But the fact is that all laws are made by men (and women) to

[1] For discussion of these subculture influences on federal court development, see Richard J. Richardson and Kenneth N. Vines, "The Politics of Federal Court Development," in Ronald Wheeler and Howard Whitcomb, eds., *Judicial Administration* (Englewood Cliffs, N.J.: Prentice-Hall, 1977). Also, Richardson and Vines, *The Politics of Federal Courts* (Boston: Little, Brown, 1970), pp. 7–11.

368

PART 3
decision-making
agencies:
who decides
what and how?

rule other men (and women). And the group in society that has an extraordinary influence on the judiciary is the group of men and women who are lawyers.

When Tocqueville visited the United States in the early nineteenth century, he was impressed by the leadership of lawyers in American society. Everywhere he went, he found the legal profession to be a sort of privileged body, a political aristocracy that was used to check the excesses of democracy or popular rule. The greatest collective influence of this legal subculture has been on the courts. Lawyers view the judiciary as their special domain and have struggled to control its personnel and procedures. They have been extremely successful. For example, they have shaped the rules and procedures that govern the judicial function, determined what qualifications persons must have before becoming judges, helped determine what kinds of conflicts can be brought before the federal courts and where they are to be decided, told us how judges ought to behave, and specified what kinds of guidelines should be used in making decisions. Among the groups and institutions that express legal values and seek to influence the judicial function are the law schools, the bar associations, the judicial councils, and other bodies that spring up from "the bench and the bar." These primary advocates of the legal subculture have established codes of behavior for judges, lawyers, and the clientele they serve. The American Bar Association's Codes of Professional Responsibility and Judicial Conduct is the bible of the profession, and those who violate its commandments may be punished. On the surface, lawyers appear to have captured the American judiciary, to exercise exclusive control over its policies. But other influences are also at work in the judiciary, seeking to make it responsive to American popular values.

The popular subculture

Of all the federal political institutions, the courts appear to have been least affected by democratic control and popular values. Other remote and removed institutions that were included in the original Constitution, and praised by Madison for filtering out popular passions, have one by one become more responsive to an expanded electorate. Even courts at the state level have been touched by democratic control, and many state judges stand for election. The federal courts alone seem untouched.

We can consider explicitly the extent to which the federal judiciary has lagged behind Congress in providing for democratic controls:

1. All of the legislators are now elected directly by the voters, but all federal judges are appointed by the President.
2. Members of Congress stand for office at regular intervals and must compete for reelection, but federal judges are appointed for life.
3. Judges are shielded from the *direct operation* of popular forces such as political parties and pressure groups that are a fundamental part of congressional politics.
4. Judges do not interact regularly or directly with other political officials, but members of Congress do so with little restraint.

5. Legislators have strong constituency ties and shifting self-defined clienteles.

Given the apparent lack of popular influence on the judicial system, it is remarkable that the courts have continued to operate in the American system, as sensitive as we have become to the values of popular responsibility.

The courts have survived in democratic society because representatives of the popular subculture have also struggled for influence over the courts. In addition to the influences of the legal subculture, the representatives of political parties, social and economic groups, and local and state political elites have influenced what our courts do and how they do it. In staffing the courts, determining their structure and organization, and fixing their jurisdiction, as well as in implementing their decisions, these populist forces have been significant. Because the federal courts are located throughout the states and regions, they are unusually susceptible to local and regional values.

The interactions and conflicts between the two subcultures—legal and popular—result in a judicial system in the United States that is accommodating to both. The imprint of both subcultures can be found throughout judicial institutions. As we look at judicial selection, backgrounds of judges, roles of courts, and the structure of their activities, as well as at their interactions with other actors in the political process, we will take into account the legal and popular influences on the courts.

SELECTION OF JUDGES

Recruitment of judges is the major way political values are implanted in the federal courts. Arguments over the method by which judges are selected and over the choice of a particular judge indicate the importance of, and concern about, those who do the judging in American courts. Although recruitment is important for all political institutions, it is especially important for the judiciary; because once judges are appointed, they serve for life and are shielded from direct pressures, except for those admitted under the controlled channels of the legal process.

The Constitution provides that the President shall appoint judges of the Supreme Court with the advice and consent of the Senate, but it does not spell out how judges of the inferior (lower) courts are to be selected. As a matter of law, the President appoints all federal judges with approval of a majority of the Senate, but the role and powers of the President and Senate vary greatly, depending upon the level of the appointment. Although the formal process of selection seems to have changed little since the creation of the lower federal courts in 1789, the number of those doing the selection has actually increased greatly; and power has shifted both within and between the groups of legal and popular representatives.

Historians of judicial recruitment agree that the writers of the Constitution and early statutes intended to give the President the initiative for making

370

PART 3
decision-making
agencies:
who decides
what and how?

appointments and to give the Senate only a negative check through its power to advise and consent. The arrangement was to guard against any exceptionally bad appointments that a President might try to make.[2] Despite Hamilton's confident statement that, "there will be, of course, no exertion of choice on the part of the Senate," the power shifted over time from the President to the Senate in the selection of district court judges.

District judge selection

Two features of American politics have led to the crucial power of the senators in selection of district court judges. One feature is the organization of the district courts. State and local political elites have demanded from the beginning that every district court be set up within the boundaries of a single state, creating the likelihood that district courts would be linked to the state political organization and therefore to senators from the state. The second feature is senatorial courtesy, which requires senators to support other senators who object to a federal appointment in their state, so long as the objecting senator is of the same party as the President. When senators talk about courtesy, they have reference to other senators, not to the President or his judicial nominees.

Senatorial courtesy gave rise to the "blue slip" device. The Senate Judiciary Committee reviews all judicial nominees of the President and makes a recommendation to the full Senate. Before making its recommendation, the committee sends to the senators of the state in which a judicial vacancy exists a request to approve or disapprove the nomination. The request is printed on a standard blue form, the "blue slip." In practice, the senator or senators who are from the nominee's home state and also in the President's party must approve the nominee, or no hearing will be scheduled. The nomination dies for the lack of approval or veto of the home state senator(s). If there is no senator of the President's party from a state, the committee receives advice from the state party organization of the President's party. When the President and home senators agree on a nominee for the lower courts, the nomination usually goes through "advice and consent" without delay. In fact, the Senate has rejected less than one percent of the candidates nominated by the President with the support of home senators or party leaders. Appointment has traditionally been routine in such cases with perfunctory hearings conducted by the Senate Judiciary Committee. This has not meant that a home senator can demand a particular appointment. It does mean that the nominee must come from a group of candidates acceptable to the home senators and the state party organizations.

Presidential candidate Jimmy Carter was determined to change the recruitment system for lower court judges. During the campaign he frequently promised that he would promote a "merit system" for selection of federal judges, its dual objectives being the appointment of more "qualified" judges

---

[2] For the evidence, see Joel Grossman, *Lawyers and Judges* (New York: Wiley, 1965), pp. 24ff.

and of more women and minorities. Soon after his election, he issued an Executive Order establishing a United States Circuit Judge Nominating Commission for the selection of judges for the United States Courts of Appeals. Because of strong opposition in the Senate, however, and especially strong opposition by the Chairman of the Senate Judiciary Committee, Mississippi Democrat James Eastland, he was unable to establish nominating commissions for all district judgeships. Rather, Senator Eastland agreed to encourage senators voluntarily to create nominating commissions in the states for their district judge nominees. Senators from 26 states followed the President's suggestion and established nominating commissions for district judgeships. The Attorney General was charged with the responsibility of ensuring that affirmative action procedures had been followed in district judge nominations and that the process had been fair.

The decision by President Carter to introduce a new recruitment process into the federal judiciary was especially significant because he was to appoint more federal judges than any other President in American history. The Omnibus Judgeship Act created 152 *new* judgeships for him to fill (117 at the District Court level and 35 at the Circuit level). Together with retirements and deaths on the bench, this meant that Carter would appoint one-third of the federal judiciary in 4 years. The inability of the President to require nominating commissions for all district court nominations was a serious blow to his visions of merit selection. But the retirement of James Eastland as Chairman of the Senate Judiciary Committee and the promotion of Senator Edward Kennedy to the chairmanship was a great advantage for the President's plan. It is ironic that Senator Kennedy, President Carter's chief rival for the Democratic presidential nomination in 1980, was the instrument through which Carter hoped to implement his judicial reforms. Senator Kennedy came to the chairmanship "absolutely committed to ensuring that qualified women and minorities are appointed to those judgeships." He pledged to modify the blue slip process by conducting hearings even when home senators' slips were not returned. In addition, the committee developed its own questionnaire for nominees requiring disclosure of their financial status and of potential conflicts of interest. The committee also created its own investigative staff.[3]

It is too early to determine if the revisions in judicial recruitment will have lasting impact on district judgeships.[4] But a study of the backgrounds of Carter's first 45 nominees found striking differences between them and the appointees of Presidents Ford, Nixon, and Johnson.

- *Experience.* Almost half of the Carter nominees had experience on state courts, compared with only one-third of the Johnson and Nixon appointees. This suggests that merit nominating commissions may have identified more well-regarded state court judges than were selected in the past.

[3] Elliot E. Slotnick, "The Changing Role of the Senate Judiciary Committee in Judicial Selection," *Judicature,* Vol. 62 (May 1979), pp. 502–10.

[4] Timothy Schellhardt, "Reshaping the Federal Judiciary," *The Wall Street Journal,* 26 (February 23, 1978).

372

PART 3
decision-making
agencies:
who decides
what and how?

- *Minorities.* A much larger proportion of blacks and women came to the bench under Carter. Women accounted for 13 percent of Carter's district court nominations—seven times the rate of the Ford Administration. Black nominations were 9 percent, compared with 5.8 (Ford), 2.8 (Nixon), and 3.3 (Johnson).

- *Government posts.* Carter nominated fewer judges holding governmental posts at the time of appointment than did any of his three predecessors.[5]

Although these differences are noteworthy, Carter followed the pattern set by all other Presidents in selecting members of his own party for district judgeships. Ninety-one percent of his appointees were Democrats, confirming that even in a "merit" system, few members of the opposition party are found to have enough merit.

Appeals judges

In the selection of appeals court judges, the President and his advisers (the Deputy Attorney General or Attorney General) have always had greater discretion than they have had in selecting district judges. Their authority is greater because the circuits are composed of a number of states, and no single senator can claim the federal appointment as being within the home state. Justice Department officials do, however, consult with the senators from the state in which a potential nominee resides, and they also clear nominations with state party organizations. In general, the President is less bound by the wishes of home senators than in the case of district judges.

The Circuit Judge Nominating Commission created by President Carter is not a single commission, but rather 13 individual panels for the Washington, D.C., circuit and the 10 other circuits, with dual panels for the Fifth Circuit and the Ninth Circuit. Each panel of 11 members is appointed by the President and is supposed to include women, minorities, laymen, and members of the bar. The panels are obligated to have an open, publicly advertised search for potential nominees. After questioning all finalists, the panels must recommend 3 to 5 names to the President for each vacancy in the circuit courts.[6]

Although the nominating panels have been put forth as a merit system, the actual operation of the panels indicates that politics has not been removed from the selection process for circuit judges. Clearly, the panels are political in their makeup. In the Eighth Circuit panel, for example, every member was a Democrat, and the panel chairman was a former adviser to Walter Mondale. A comprehensive study of all panels revealed that 62.5 percent of the members were attorneys, 87.5 percent were white, and 86 percent were Democrats. More importantly, the panels were manned by Carter activists:

[5] Sheldon Goldman, "A Profile of Carter's Judicial Nominees," *Judicature,* Vol. 62 (November 1978), pp. 247–54. For material on the early appointing process, see Harold W. Chase, *Federal Judges: The Appointing Process* (Minneapolis: University of Minnesota Press, 1972).

[6] For discussion of the commission's operation see Elliot E. Slotnick, "The U.S. Circuit Judge Nominating Commission," *Law and Policy Quarterly* Vol. 1 (October, 1979), pp. 465–487. Also Susan Carbon, "The U.S. Circuit Judge Nominating Commission: A Comparison of Two of Its Panels," *Judicature* Vol. 62 (November 1978), pp. 233–245.

44.1 percent of the panelists confirmed that they participated in President Carter's election campaign, and 67.8 percent of these said they supported the President before he received the Democratic party nomination.[7]

Given the makeup of the panels, no one was surprised that 11 of President Carter's first 12 appointments to the circuit courts went to Democrats, some with long service and activity in the party. Although only 3 of the first Carter appointees were black (25 percent), this was an infinite increase over the rate of black appointments to appeals courts by Presidents Ford and Nixon, for they appointed none. Thus, while the nominating commissions appear to be using the recruitment process for a more representative bench in ethnic terms, it is certainly not using it for equally balanced political party representation. Nor is there evidence that home state senators have been displaced in their role. Although they are limited by the three to five names sent to the President by the nominating panels, they have a great deal to say about which of the five will receive the actual nomination to the circuit court. The nominating commissions appear to be a new vehicle for the old interplay between legal interests, home state concerns, and party politics.

Selection of Supreme Court justices

John Schmidhauser has drawn a collective portrait of the Supreme Court justices from 1789 to 1979.[8] He finds that Presidents have overwhelmingly chosen nominees from socially advantaged families. Every justice has been male, and the typical justice has been a WASP (white, Anglo-Saxon Protestant) with high-church status. Only a handful of the justices were of humble origin. Two-thirds of the justices came from politically active families, and a third came from families with careers in the judiciary. All of the justices have had legal training, all have practiced law at some time, and most made law their major occupation. Schmidhauser concludes his review of Supreme Court backgrounds with the observation that "very few sons of families outside the upper or upper-middle social economic classes have been able to acquire the particular type of education and the subsequent professional and especially political associations which appear to be unwritten prerequisites for appointment to the nation's highest tribunal." He might have added that *none* of the daughters of these or other families has been able to win nomination.

Politics is usually paramount in the selection of Supreme Court justices. Although other factors are important—including age, geographic, religious, and ethnic representation on the bench, professional reputation, and personal friendships—Presidents are most attentive to the political values of potential justices.[9] When we speak of the political nature of appointments, we do not mean that justices will be slavishly favorable to interests of the party faithful or that an appointment is always a political plum for an active party supporter

[7] Slotnick, pp. 479–80.

[8] *Judges and Justices: The Federal Appellate Judiciary* (Boston: Little, Brown, 1979), p. 96.

[9] See Henry Abraham, *The Judicial Process,* 4th ed. (New York: Oxford, 1980), pp. 65–76, for discussion of selection criteria.

"QUOTAS IN SCHOOLS DON'T BOTHER ME, QUOTAS IN UNIONS DON'T BOTHER ME, QUOTAS IN INDUSTRY DON'T BOTHER ME. BUT A QUOTA HERE ON THE BENCH—— THAT WOULD BOTHER ME."

of the President. Rather, we mean that Presidents want to place on the high court people who share common political viewpoints and hold common political values. Long after a President is out of office, his judicial appointments will continue as his political legacy for the nation. He hopes to ensure that his programs both during and after his tenure will have sympatic hearing before the Supreme Court.

To ensure a common political view on the Court, Presidents usually appoint members of their own party to the Supreme Court. Only about 15 percent of appointments have gone to members of the opposition. Even in some of these "cross-over" appointments, Presidents have chosen nominees whose "real" political views were closer to those of the President than to those of members of their own party. President Theodore Roosevelt, discussing a possible appointment of Horace Lurton, a Democrat, with fellow Republican Henry Cabot Lodge, observed:

The nominal politics of the man has nothing to do with his actions on the bench. His real politics are all important. . . . He is right on the Negro question; he is right on the power of the federal government; he is right on the Insular business; he is right about corporations, and he is right about labor.[10]

Although Senator Lodge agreed, he urged the President to find a Republican who was also "right" on the major questions. Roosevelt agreed and appointed William Moody, who had the correct views *and* the correct (Republican) party affiliation. A review of the personnel on the current Supreme Court reveals the mixture of personal and political factors that lead to judicial appointments.

Warren Earl Burger (born 1907). It may appear that being named Earl Warren or Warren Earl is a good beginning for a young man aspiring to become Chief Justice of the United States. But the name was not the reason Richard Nixon appointed Warren Burger as the fifteenth Chief Justice of the United States. During the 1968 presidential campaign, the Republicans had capitalized on the "law and order" issue, and Nixon pledged that if elected he would appoint strict constructionists to the Supreme Court. Nixon defined "strict constructionist" as someone who would apply the Constitution by the "letter of the law." His definition implied that loose constructionists had bent the Constitution for liberal rather than conservative political purposes. With the retirement of Chief Justice Earl Warren, Nixon selected Warren Burger to fulfill his campaign pledge. Little known outside legal circles, the Minnesota Republican had been appointed to the United States Court of Appeals for the District of Columbia by President Eisenhower. While on the appeals bench, he was best known for his critical reactions to Supreme Court decisions restricting the discretion of law enforcement officials and expanding rights of the accused.[11] Although not a personal friend of Nixon, he was known in party politics for the key role he played in swinging the Minnesota delegation to Eisenhower in the 1952 national Republican convention. This role had earned him appointment to the Department of Justice as Assistant Attorney General and later to the Court of Appeals. With a judicial philosophy that called for restraint on human rights and a tough attitude toward crime, Burger seemed a good Nixon choice to assume the position as chief and lead the court away from the Warren Court's activism.

Harry Andrew Blackmun (born 1908). A close personal friend of Chief Justice Burger, Harry Blackmun attended grade school with him and was best man in his wedding. Another Minnesota Republican, he was serving on the United States Court of Appeals for the Eighth Circuit when he was selected as President Nixon's second appointment to the Supreme Court. Although a Republican conservative, he was not active in politics, and his appointment to the Court was not a reward for party service. Rather, he was chosen because of the intercession of his friend the Chief and because his judicial views appeared to correspond to those of the President. In fact, his voting behavior on the bench has not been a mirror of Burger's, as he

---

[10] *Ibid.,* p. 78.

[11] Charles Lamb, "The Making of a Chief Justice: Warren Burger on Criminal Procedure, 1956–1969," *Cornell Law Review,* Vol. 60 (June 1975), pp. 743–88. Also see Lamb, "Warren Burger's Lower Court Experience," (Ph.D. dissertation, University of Alabama, 1974).

376

PART 3
decision-making
agencies:
who decides
what and how?

has been moderate-to-liberal on civil rights questions and moderate-to-conservative on issues of law and order.

Blackmun was not the President's first choice for the Court vacancy. President Nixon first nominated Clement Haynsworth of South Carolina, Chief Judge of the Fourth Circuit Court of Appeals, to fill the vacancy. But the Senate refused to give its advice and consent by a 45 to 55 vote in the first Senate rejection of a presidential nominee to the Supreme Court since 1930. President Nixon tried once more to place a conservative southerner on the Court. His inexplicable choice was Harold Carswell of Florida, from the Fifth Circuit Court of Appeals.[12] After heated debate, the Senate also turned down the Carswell nomination, 45 to 51.

The Senate's rejection of two presidential nominations in succession was unprecedented and certainly atypical of the usual Senate approval of presidential appointments to the Supreme Court. Angry that he was unable to make a conservative southern appointment but eager to find someone acceptable, Nixon turned to Blackmun, whom the Senate Judiciary Committee described as a "man of learning and humility." His appointment was unanimously confirmed by the Senate.

Lewis F. Powell, Jr. (born 1907). Stung by the Haynsworth and Carswell defeats, Nixon recognized that if a conservative southern appointment was to succeed in the Senate, he would have to select a person with strong legal credentials and reputation. A prominent Virginia attorney, Powell had served as President of the American College of Trial Lawyers. Although a Democrat, he had impressive conservative credentials, including several sharp attacks on the Supreme Court for decisions favoring rights of defendants in the Warren era. Lewis Powell had served on the President's Commission on Law Enforcement and Administration of Justice, and his record was pleasing to conservative Republicans. He was older (64) at the time of his appointment than Nixon desired and had been passed over once because of his age. But because he was a strong law and order conservative and would receive the approval of southern Democrats as well as Republicans in the Senate, Powell was chosen as Nixon's third appointment to the Court.

William H. Rehnquist (born 1924). In 1971, Nixon balanced the appointment of elder Powell with the selection of William Rehnquist, the youngest member of the Court. A doctrinaire conservative, the Arizona Republican had served as lawyer for the party in Phoenix. He joined the Nixon administration as Assistant Attorney General in the Department of Justice and represented the President in dozens of hearings before Senate and House committees. He was the most outspoken of all of the Nixon appointees prior to his

---

[12] Although the ABA had found Carswell qualified for appointment to the Court, this evaluation was widely challenged by lawyers, judges, law school deans, and law professors. The liberal Republican Ripon Society called the nomination "an insult to southern jurisprudence." On the other hand, Senator Roman Hruska of Nebraska, ranking Republican on the Judiciary Committee, who managed the floor fight on behalf of the President's nominee, countered the charge that Carswell was a judicial mediocrity: "Even if he was mediocre, there are a lot of mediocre judges and people and lawyers. They are entitled to a little representation, aren't they, and a little chance? We can't have all Brandeises and Cardozos and Frankfurters and stuff like that."

selection. He supported with vigor a long list of conservative causes, including wiretapping, *de facto* segregation, and mass arrests of demonstrators. Like Burger, he was a critic of the Supreme Court's earlier decisions on defendant rights. His nomination was opposed by the Leadership Conference on Civil Rights and the American Civil Liberties Union, but the opposition was unable to derail his confirmation as justice, the Senate approving 68 to 26. Rehnquist has been the Court's most consistently conservative member, often aligned with the Chief Justice in his opinions.

John Paul Stevens (born 1920). The most publicity that Gerald Ford ever got as a congressman from Michigan came in his efforts to impeach Justice William Douglas from the Supreme Court. Ironically, Congressman Ford's failure to get Justice Douglas impeached gave him later, during his brief presidency, his only chance to name a Supreme Court justice. Douglas resigned in 1975, having served longer on the Court than any other justice in the history of the country. President Ford nominated Seventh Circuit Judge John Paul Stevens from Chicago. A former law clerk in the Supreme Court, Stevens had the enthusiastic backing of Ford's Attorney General, Edward Levi, former Dean of the University of Chicago Law School. With no partisan political

The formality of the Supreme Court's portrait helps explain the surprise when people discover that justices bicker and otherwise behave as normal people.

378

PART 3
decision-making
agencies:
who decides
what and how?

ties, modest and intellectual, Stevens seemed an ideal choice for the Ford presidency. A highly respected circuit judge, he was often referred to as a "judge's judge" because of the thoroughness of his opinions and his fairness. Because of Ford's political conservatism, Stevens was expected to be a judicial conservative. His voting record on the bench has been remarkably moderate, however, following closely his circuit court performance.

Thurgood Marshall (born 1908). President Johnson's one remaining appointee on the Supreme Court is Thurgood Marshall, great-grandson of a slave and the only black ever to serve on the high court. A Democrat, he earned his reputation as legal counsel for the National Association for the Advancement of Colored People (NAACP), arguing over thirty cases before the Supreme Court, including *Brown v. Board of Education.* After his remarkable successes as a civil rights lawyer, he was appointed to the Second Circuit Court of Appeals by President Kennedy. Later, President Johnson appointed him solicitor general of the U.S., to argue the government's cases. A consistent liberal on the court, his opinions often lack technical merit, but his personality sometimes enables him to win concessions from opponents. Influential during the Warren era, he has become less important as a member of the diminishing liberal minority on the current Court.

Byron R. White (born 1917). A close personal friend of John F. Kennedy, Justice White came to the Court after a distinguished academic and athletic record. A Rhodes Scholar and selected to the Football Hall of Fame, the Colorado Democrat had not been an active participant in politics until the 1960 presidential campaign. Because of his friendship with John Kennedy, he became involved in party politics and was instrumental in delivering Colorado's delegation to Kennedy at the Democratic Convention. During the campaign he led the Citizens for Kennedy and worked in the Department of Justice after the election. His judicial philosophy was largely unknown when Kennedy appointed him to the Court in 1962. In practice, he has been a member of the Court's conservative bloc, a disappointment and surprise to many Kennedy supporters.

William J. Brennan, Jr. (born 1906). When Dwight Eisenhower was elected President in 1952 as the Republican party's candidate, he had no political track record or known political philosophy. Thus, it was difficult to forecast what kind of judicial appointments he would make to the federal courts. His selection of Earl Warren as Chief Justice was followed by his appointment of William Brennan as justice. Brennan, a New Jersey Democrat, was not an active partisan. As a member of the New Jersey Supreme Court, he had established a reputation as an innovative and progressive jurist who solved problems in backlog in caseloads and inefficiency in the state system. The son of an immigrant family, Brennan grew up in a working-class home and held many judicial values of a liberal-activist bent. On the Court, he became identified as a member of the Warren bloc and has been a liberal jurist in the minority under the Burger administration.

Potter Stewart (born 1915). An early supporter of Senator Robert Taft for the Republican party nomination, Potter Stewart worked in 1952 for the election of Dwight Eisenhower. He served as mayor of Cincinnati and was appointed by Eisenhower to the Sixth Circuit Court of Appeals. Later he was promoted to the Supreme Court as Eisenhower's last appointment in 1959. A moderate, Stewart has allied himself with both conservative and liberal blocs. His influence on the Court has often come from his swing vote position.[13]

In selecting justices, the President plays a dominant role. But representatives of the legal subculture play a part in all appointments to the federal judiciary. Since 1945, the American Bar Association, acting through a Standing Committee on the Federal Judiciary, has rated the qualifications of nominees. It offers the Department of Justice an informal report on any person being seriously considered for nomination. After investigating the potential nominees, the committee rates them: "Exceptionally well qualified," "Well qualified," "Qualified," or "Not qualified."

A President need not be bound by ABA ratings. President Kennedy made a number of appointments in the face of a committee rating of "not qualified." Understandably, there is room for honest disagreement concerning the qualifications of a "good" judge. The ABA committee has shown a distinct bias toward corporate trial lawyers, but a law professor or a labor lawyer or a lawyer-politician may have more understanding of the problems that people take into courts. Moreover, as we have shown, factors such as personal friendship, ethnic or religious considerations, group affiliations, as well as service to the party may enter into the nomination.

When President Nixon, twice rebuffed on his Supreme Court nominations, announced that he would give the ABA a screening role in future appointments to the high bench (and then later changed his mind), immediate reactions were mixed. The ABA President thought the idea was "an extremely wise one and clearly in the public interest." A spokesman for Americans for Democratic Action viewed the new procedure as "a weak-kneed capitulation to one of the most reactionary forces in America, a move in the wrong direction."[14] But the *Washington Post* observed that the ABA's committee was at least a better source of information on professional qualifications than the FBI was, even though it characterized the ABA as "a trade association of lawyers that tends to be conservative in its outlook, nearsighted in many of its concerns, and a bit stuffy in its hierarchy."[15]

STRUCTURE OF JUDICIAL ACTIVITIES

Under the Constitution, the judicial power of the United States extends broadly to two kinds of cases:

---

[13] For fuller discussion of justices see Congressional Quarterly Guide, *Current American Government* (Washington: Congressional Quarterly, 1980). For an excellent analysis of the Court, see Stephen Wasby, *The Supreme Court in the Federal Judicial System* (New York: Holt, 1978), pp. 83–108.

[14] *Washington Star,* July 28, 1970.

[15] *Washington Post,* July 31, 1970.

380

PART 3
decision-making
agencies:
who decides
what and how?

1. According to the *nature of the controversy*
   a) Cases arising under the Constitution, laws, and treaties of the United States
   b) Cases under admiralty and maritime law
2. According to the *nature of the parties*
   a) Cases affecting ambassadors and other foreign diplomats
   b) Controversies to which the United States is a party
   c) Controversies between two or more states
   d) Controversies between citizens of different states

The Constitution defines the *original jurisdiction* of the Supreme Court as "All cases affecting Ambassadors, other public ministers and Consuls, and those in which a State shall be a Party." Otherwise, the Constitution leaves it up to Congress to determine the jurisdiction of federal courts.

Trial judges and courts

The only national court the Constitution mentions by name is the Supreme Court. The Constitution did, however, give Congress power to create any other courts that may be needed. Under this provision, Congress has established a complete set of courts:

1. District courts of the United States
2. United States courts of appeals (sometimes also called circuit courts)
3. The Supreme Court of the United States.
4. Other courts, such as the courts of the District of Columbia and various special courts.

The *district courts of the United States* are courts of original jurisdiction where most federal cases begin. The most common exceptions are cases that begin in the independent regulatory agencies and bypass the district courts to go on appeal to the courts of appeals. There are one or more district courts in each state, with the number of judges assigned to each court depending on how congested the docket is. In 1980 there were 91 district courts with a total of 507 judges. Note that each district court is staffed by a judge and company; the "company" in each district includes a clerk's office, a marshal's office, one or more referees in bankruptcy, probation officers, court reporters, and one or more commissioners or magistrates. The district judge is expected to act as the administrative manager for the court. In addition, each district has a U.S. district attorney who acts as the representative of the United States, whether it is prosecutor, plaintiff (the party bringing the complaint), or defendant.

District court judges hear both civil and criminal cases. In civil cases the U.S. government may appear as plaintiff or defendant in a wide range of controversies. For example, it may bring suit in land condemnation proceedings or appear as defendant in tax suits or personal injury claims. Most frequently it is a party to disputes involving "federal questions" under national antitrust laws, labor laws, and consumer protection laws.

Federal District Courts are found in territorities and trusts,
such as Micronesia, as well as in all of the states.

Civil cases

About a third of the *civil cases* begun in court are settled out of court,
and only 10 percent ever reach the trial stage. If the case is tried in court,
the lawyers for plaintiff and defendant explain to the judge and jury what
the dispute is all about. They examine witnesses and explain why their client
should win. The judge instructs the jury on the facts that have been brought
out by the lawyers in court and on the rules of law that are applicable.
The jury then deliberates and returns to the courtroom with a verdict in
favor of either the plaintiff or the defendant. The judge hands down a decision
in accordance with the jury's verdict.

This model of civil procedure is, of course, much simpler than the actual
procedure. The dual system of state and national courts presents complicated
questions of jurisdiction at the outset. Plaintiffs may choose to sue in either
a state or national court; but if the defendants are sued in the court of a
state of which they are not a citizen, they are permitted to have the case
removed to a national court. Increasingly complex conflicts in modern society

382

PART 3
decision-making
agencies:
who decides
what and how?

may often mean that a jury will not understand the problem before the court, so that most disputants may prefer not to have their case tried by jury.

District courts are trial courts in both criminal and civil law and the same judges try both types of cases. All crimes against the United States are specified in statutes passed by Congress, and all such crimes are prosecuted only in the national courts. Whether a case will be prosecuted depends on the U.S. District Attorney, who follows guidelines from the Department of Justice.

Criminal cases

In the assembly line of justice, the trial judge occupies a key position, but not necessarily the crucial one. The administration of justice in *criminal cases* begins with detection and investigation, and many crimes are never reported, never detected, and never investigated. Judges have no part in proceedings until after an arrest is made; then, they may be asked to issue a writ of habeas corpus (an order that a person be brought to court so that he or she can find out what the charge is), or to fix bail for the temporary release of the accused. Either before or after a preliminary hearing, the U.S. Attorney may decide to drop charges; if so, that is the end of the case. If the U.S. Attorney decides to prosecute, the Constitution requires that charges and preliminary evidence be carried to a national grand jury. (A defendant may waive the right to a grand jury and take a chance instead on charges prepared by the U.S. Attorney.) The grand jury may refuse to indict (charge the accused with an offense); if it does, *that* is the end of the case. If the grand jury does indict, and if the accused pleads "not guilty," then the district attorney must be prepared to prosecute the case in court. At this point, however, bargaining is likely to take place between the U.S. Attorney and the defendant's lawyer to obtain a plea of "guilty" and so to avoid a court trial. Defendants who choose, or are persuaded, to plead "guilty" are brought before the judge, who immediately imposes sentence. Defendants who plead "not guilty" are entitled to trial by judge and jury. The trial proceeds in much the same manner that we outlined for civil cases except that the U.S. Attorney has the role which the plaintiff's lawyer plays in a civil case. At the close of the lawyers' summations to the judge and jury, the judge instructs the jury both as to the admissible evidence and the applicable law. The jury returns a verdict of "guilty" or "not guilty"; if the verdict is "guilty," the judge imposes sentence.

The constitutional rights of defendants in national criminal cases include

1. Guarantee against unreasonable search and seizure
2. The right to indictment by grand jury
3. The writ of habeas corpus
4. Protection against double jeopardy (trial more than once for the same offense)
5. Security against self-incrimination
6. A speedy and public trial by an impartial jury
7. The right to be informed of the nature and cause of the accusation

8. The right to have witnesses subpoenaed (compelled to appear in court)

9. Assistance of counsel at all stages from the preliminary hearing to release or conviction, at public expense if the defendant is poor

10. Protection against high bail, high fines, and cruel and unusual punishments.

Yet, despite all these rights, most defendants plead guilty, and few elect to stand trial by jury.

Many reasons are offered to explain why court trials are the exception and guilty pleas the normal procedure in criminal cases. U.S. Attorneys confronted with many more cases than they can prosecute in a court term pick the cases they want to try—perhaps for the publicity value, if they have political ambitions. Naturally they choose the best cases, those they are most likely to win. They may simply drop from the list the ones they think they will probably lose; they may try to negotiate others with the defendants for pleas of guilty. The prosecutor's interest is in maintaining a public image of effective law enforcement and successful prosecution. The defendant's interest is in receiving the lowest penalty, the most mercy, and the least severe charges. These interests converge in a steady flow of guilty pleas and convictions. Judges, from their elevated position on the bench, may be uncomfortably aware of what goes on in the bargain basement of justice, but their job is to judge only the cases that reach their courts. If the defendant elects to stand trial, the judge is expected to see to it that all the rules of procedure are correctly followed. But with national courts full and the resultant delays of justice causing public annoyance, the trial judge is not likely to question guilty pleas too sharply, especially since all such pleas come into court with the consent of the defendants' lawyers.

The appellate judges and courts

Nine out of ten cases never go beyond the trial courts, but Congress has set up courts of appeals to consider cases that have for one reason or another not been satisfactorily resolved in the courts of original jurisdiction.

The United States is divided into 11 judicial circuits. In each circuit, there is a *United States court of appeals.* The District of Columbia constitutes one circuit; the states and the territories are grouped in the 10 remaining circuits. The 11 circuits include 132 judges. From 3 to 9 circuit judges are assigned to each court of appeals, depending on how much work has to be done. The chief judge of each circuit summons all the circuit and district judges to an annual conference to discuss and plan the year's business in the circuit. The chief judge also represents the circuit in the Judicial Conference of the United States, an annual meeting of the chief judges of the judicial circuits summoned by the Chief Justice of the United States. The conference keeps an eye on the volume of business in the national courts, assigns judges to district and circuit courts according to the amount of judicial business anticipated, and suggests to the various courts how they might better manage their business.

384

PART 3
decision-making
agencies:
who decides
what and how?

The courts of appeals have *appellate* jurisdiction only. They hear cases *on appeal* from the district courts and also from various administrative agencies such as the Federal Communications Commission and the Securities Exchange Commission.

Examining judicial behavior on appeals courts is difficult because not all of the judges in a court of appeals sit on every case. Usually a 3-panel bench makes the decision, and membership on the panels varies from case to case. When an appeals court takes a case on appeal from the lower court, it may affirm or reverse the judgment of the lower court, unanimously or by 2-to-1 vote.

The Supreme Court

The *Supreme Court of the United States* is the highest tribunal in the land. Congress fixes the number of Supreme Court justices. Since 1869, there have been 9 justices on the Court at any given time, but the number has changed half a dozen times in the Court's history, ranging from as few as 5 to as many as 10. Under the Constitution, the Supreme Court has both original and appellate jurisdiction. Its original jurisdiction extends to (1) all cases affecting ambassadors, other public ministers, and consuls; (2) all cases in which a state is a party. In *Marbury v. Madison* (1803), Justice Marshall held that Congress does not have the power to extend this original jurisdiction, and the decision still stands. The Court hears perhaps one or two cases in original jurisdiction during each term.

Congress fixes the appellate jurisdiction of the Supreme Court. Under present law, the Supreme Court may review cases both from state courts and from lower national courts. The Court must hear appeals from any lower court decision that invalidates an act of Congress. It must also hear appeals from final judgments of the highest courts in the states if (1) the question involves the validity of a national law or treaty and the decision has been against its validity; (2) the state court has upheld the validity of a state law alleged to be in violation of national law or contrary to the Constitution. The Supreme Court will not review any cases from state courts, however, unless national law or constitutional rights are involved.

Most cases reach the Supreme Court by means of the writ of certiorari, a court order calling a case up for review. Under certiorari, the Supreme Court may call up any case involving a federal question that at least four of the justices feel is of sufficient national importance to warrant the Court's attention. The writ is entirely discretionary, which means that the Court is free to deny most petitions for review.

Most cases do not begin in the Supreme Court; by the same token, most of them do not end there. Many decisions go back to the lower courts for further judicial proceedings. In *Brown v. Board of Education*, the school desegregation cases of 1954, the Supreme Court did not make a final judgment on the issue. After stating the "fundamental principle that racial discrimination in public education is unconstitutional," the Supreme Court remanded the

The Supreme Court building is the principal symbol of justice under law in the United States.

386

PART 3
decision-making
agencies:
who decides
what and how?

cases to the district courts "because of their proximity to local conditions."[16] (In 1980, Linda Brown, who was a Kansas schoolgirl when the 1954 decision was made in response to her plea, reopened the case—never officially closed—with the plea that her son in junior high school was deprived of equal protection by the Kansas school system!) When the Supreme Court declared that the New York State prayer program in the public schools violated the First Amendment, and therefore the Fourteenth Amendment, it remanded the case to the New York court in which the case originated.[17] In 1962, when the Supreme Court held that a state's failure to reapportion its legislature may constitute denial of equal protection of the laws, it did not require all state legislatures immediately to reapportion. It simply found that the issue of reapportionment could be ruled on and that, in this case, the complainants from Tennessee—which had failed to reapportion its legislature since 1901—were entitled to a trial and decision in the federal district court in Tennessee.[18] In all these cases, although the Supreme Court stirred the whole country to action—and reaction—it simply stated the constitutional principle and then left the problems of policy implementation to the local authorities.

We do not have much firm information on how the justices act in their conference sessions; such meetings take place behind closed doors, and there are no reports to the press. We know that the chief justice presides, that he summarizes each case and indicates how he thinks it should be decided. Each of the judges, usually in order of seniority, expresses his separate view. During this presentation, however, some agreement is likely to emerge. When the members are ready to vote—the order is now reversed, with the junior justice voting first and the chief justice last—a majority of judges decides who wins (enjoys rewards) and who loses (suffers deprivations).

If the chief justice has voted with the majority in a case, he assigns the writing of the opinion to one of the judges in the majority or chooses to write it himself. If the chief justice has voted with the minority, the senior justice in the majority decides who will write the opinion. Opinions are important documents. Not only do they announce the winners and the reasons for the victory, but they set examples for future cases. They also serve as messages to a variety of constituencies. They may warn or inform the bar association, lower court judges, the President, Congress, or bureaucrats. Thus, opinion assignment is taken seriously, and the contents of opinions are carefully studied.

A decision requires a majority vote of the justices. If the justices disagree—as they frequently do—those who differ from the majority may prepare a dissenting opinion. The frequency with which the justices of the highest Court disagree has caused complaint and uncertainty. Many people feel that the Court should develop a greater corporate spirit and should function institutionally to provide us with a firm statement of what the law says with reference to a specific case. But to hope for unanimous agreement on the law is idealistic. Justices hold differing political and legal views, which they show in frequent dissents.

[16] Brown v. Board of Education, 349 U.S. 294 (1955).
[17] Engel v. Vitale, 370 U.S. 421 (1962).
[18] Baker v. Carr, 369 U.S. 186 (1962).

As we look at judicial roles, we will be concerned with legal expectations and requirements of judicial behavior, as well as judges' views of themselves. These images of judges will be compared to their actual behavior. Judicial role behavior is made up of activities of a judge that reveal what he or she ought to do and can do as a judge.[19]

Legal prescriptions

The Constitution does not prescribe judicial behavior. It simply specifies that judicial power shall be exercised by one Supreme Court and in such lower courts as Congress chooses to establish. It does not tell us what kind of people shall staff the courts or how they should behave once they are on the court.

One aspect of the judicial role does seem implicit in the Constitution. The framers wanted to help ensure judicial independence. For example, Article III provides that the salary of judges shall not be decreased. It also specifies that they will hold office for life during good behavior. Removal of judges was made difficult in order to protect their independence. They may be impeached by the House of Representatives, tried in the Senate, convicted by a two-thirds vote. If convicted of "treason, bribery, or other high crimes and misdemeanors," they are removed from office.

As we have shown earlier, the framers' concern for independence of the judiciary led them to make the selection three steps from direct election. Judges were appointed by the President (who was indirectly chosen by an electoral college) and were confirmed by the Senate (appointed by the state legislatures). Hamilton feared that the legislature might be too responsive to the majority will and be persuaded into "dangerous innovations in government." Therefore, he and others put their faith in the "independency of the judiciary"—independence, that is, from direct popular control.

Thus, if you were trying out for the role of judge in the script designed by the Constitution, you would know that you should be somewhat independent of popular pressures and stay clear of "treason, bribery and other high crimes." Beyond that, your part would be ill-defined by the basic instrument of government. But the Constitution is not the only legal document to address the judicial role. Thousands of statutes, judicial codes, and standards offered by professional organizations draw elaborate role requirements for federal judges. In these we find multiple and complex standards for behavior, including how a judge should be trained, receive evidence, conduct a trial, and relate to all of the participants in the judicial proceeding. These rules define "conflict of interest," instruct on how the judge is to use precedent in arriving

[19] Joel Grossman, "Dissenting Blocs on the Warren Court: A Study in Judicial Role Behavior," *Journal of Politics,* Vol. 30 (1968), pp. 1071. For role analysis, see Sheldon Goldman and Thomas Jahnige, *The Federal Courts as a Political System* (New York: Harper, 1976), pp. 199–210.

388

PART 3
decision-making
agencies:
who decides
what and how?

at judgments, and describe proper behavior both on and off the bench. From these tomes, judges learn that they are to be impartial, fair-minded to all participants, protective of the rights of defendants, and possessive of "judicial temperment." Able to rise above their own prejudice, they are to administer justice and the law as it is written.

Judges, of course, are not independent. Nor are they free from personal values and political preferences. All of them are conditioned by the social and political environments within which they work; their values and experiences constitute a screen through which they filter facts and impressions of cases. Although judges are perhaps less free than legislators to inject their personal opinions into their decision making, judicial behavior is still human behavior. Because of this, judges must adapt the legal role expectations to the realities of judging.

How judges see their role

Felix Frankfurter, a distinguished Supreme Court justice, was asked, "Does a man cease to be himself when he becomes a justice? Does he change his character by putting on a gown?" Frankfurter answered, "No, he does not change his character. He brings his whole experience, his training, his outlook, his social, intellectual, and moral environment with him when he takes a seat on the Supreme bench. . . ."[20]

In acknowledging the continued "humanity" of judges, Frankfurter was quick to point out that "The outlook of a lawyer fit to be a justice regarding the role of a judge cuts across all his personal preferences for this or that social arrangement." From this role definition, Frankfurter argued that judges should show judicial restraint and support whenever possible the decisions of legislatures and executives. In addition, justices should be restrained in the sense of keeping their personal preferences in abeyance when interpreting law or writing public policy.

Although professing to restrain their own values, most judges recognize that this ideal is never perfectly achieved. Federal Judge John Minor Wisdom, acknowledging that "the district judge is personally accountable to the local community and to the local bar,"[21] had no illusions about the political nature of the role he was playing. He concluded that "federal judges . . . perform firmly and fully their friction-making, exacerbating political role." Solving political questions and imbued with their own political values, judges cannot escape placing their values into the decisions.

Judges who see their role as "activist" are less concerned about the mix between their values and their decisions. They believe that their task is to adapt the Constitution and its interpretations to contemporary needs and to lead the society in correcting its ills. Certainly activist Justice William Douglas

[20] "The Judicial Process and the Supreme Court," in Philip Elman, ed., *Of Law and Men* (New York: Harcourt, 1956).

[21] John Minor Wisdom, "The Friction-Making Exacerbating Political Role of Federal Courts," *Southwestern Law Journal*, Vol. 21 (1967), pp. 419ff.

was not fearful of his beliefs nor reluctant to incorporate them into his decisions. To have failed to have done so would have denied his view of his role on the high court.

From this brief treatment of self-perceptions, we conclude that judges do not agree on the nature of the judicial role. Some view judging as marked by restraint, others by activism. Some are liberal, others conservative. All carry values that define their tasks of decision making.

These variations among judges are not erased by the certainty of law or precedents in arriving at decisions. One can choose among precedents when arriving at a decision, and the law does not provide a clear road map to a verdict. Joseph Hutcheson, Chief Judge of the Fifth Circuit, candidly discussed how he arrived at decisions. As a young lawyer, he had believed that the law would provide clear direction to the right decision. But as a judge, he confessed to making his decisions by "judicial hunch" and by what he termed a "roll of the little mental dice." His values, his personal view of what was just and right ensured that the hunch and the role of the dice would give him a decision that he viewed as proper. Given the difference in role views, judges behave in very different ways as they do their jobs.

Role performance

Because the justices of the Supreme Court have great control over their docket, they decide what conflicts they want to hear and are guided in their decisions by which cases have the greatest policy impact on society. Most appeals to the Court are denied, for the Court is not primarily in the business of correcting errors made in the lower courts or ensuring justice for everyone in society. The Court has neither the time nor inclination to try to correct all of the procedural problems in appealed cases. Rather, it uses cases as the backboard off which it bounces larger public policies.

Obviously, the Court disagrees on which cases will have the greatest policy importance. The substance of some conflicts seems so important that justices feel obligated to consider the cases. But in large measure, a justice is free to choose a case by his own values. An appeal or petition to the Court is a stimulus to the justices' values. If at least four justices are stimulated positively by the brief for review, the case will be brought to the Court for argument on its merit. Although the Court will be aware of precedents and numerous regulations governing and limiting its behavior, the justices will still have great freedom in choosing how to act. As Howard Ball notes, "whenever the justice chooses to act in a certain way, he does so in large measure upon the values he has developed."[22]

Because of differing role perceptions and values, intense conflict often develops among the justices during conference sessions as a final judgment is reached. These differing values produce voting blocs within the Court. The voting blocs of justices can be clearly identified, and future voting behavior

---

[22] Howard Ball, *Courts and Politics* (Englewood Cliffs, N.J.: Prentice-Hall, 1980), p. 264.

390

PART 3
decision-making
agencies:
who decides
what and how?

Yoichi R. Okamoto, Photo Researchers, Inc.

The importance of the Chief Justice is suggested by the practice of
identifying Court periods with their names, as today's "Burger Court."

can often be predicted in cases involving political freedom, economic liberalism, and political equality. The evidence is now conclusive that courts with
several members characteristically partition themselves into blocs of liberal,
moderate, or conservative subsets.[23]

External and institutional forces modify the personal proclivities of justices
and reduce the visibility of their conflicts. They are not always able to ignore
the restraints placed on them from outside the court system, but differences
on judicial roles do force the justices into a continuing battle with one another
over who should win and who should lose in the high stake game of judicial
politics.

INTERACTIONS OF JUDGES WITH OTHER ACTORS IN THE POLITICAL PROCESS

Although we speak often of an independent judiciary, clearly the judiciary
is independent of neither the political process nor other actors in the political
system. Interests make demands on the courts, and court decisions are responses to these demands. Sometimes the court output is in conflict with
decisions made by executives and legislatures, sometimes it is supportive.
It almost always requires interaction with other decision makers, for justices
act within a contemporary political environment. Their decision making is

[23] John Sprague, *Voting Patterns of the U.S. Supreme Court* (Indianapolis: Bobbs-Merrill, 1968), p. 11.

influenced by this environment and, in turn, affects it. Two avenues through which the judiciary interacts are (1) judicial review of other actors' decisions and (2) interpretation of statutory and constitutional law.

Judicial review and interpretation: the avenues of interaction

All laws passed by Congress must be "in pursuance of the Constitution." The President, sworn to uphold the Constitution, may veto any act he considers beyond the constitutional powers of Congress. All administrative rules and regulations are governed by constitutional limitations. In short, every public act—national, state, or local—must conform to constitutional requirements. Because the Constitution is "the supreme law of the land," it is binding on all parts of the American political system and must be enforced in all the courts of the country. The legal character of the Constitution has given rise to the practice of *judicial review.*

Judicial review gives courts the power to declare "null and void" (do away with) any act of the national government or of the states which they see as contrary to the Constitution. Any court, national or state, may exercise judicial review; but because the Supreme Court is at the top of the judicial hierarchy, its judgment in constitutional law is final in any given case. The judges undertake such review only if someone takes the trouble to challenge in the courts the constitutionality of a particular act.

In the American system, judges rather than legislators have the final word in deciding what is constitutional law. An act that has been passed by both houses of Congress and approved by the President may still be declared null and void by the judges. And an act passed by a state legislature under the state's own constitution may be invalidated by the United States Supreme Court if a majority of the justices agree that the act conflicts with national law or the national Constitution. When the President and the 50 governors issue executive orders, their orders may similarly be invalidated.

Thus in law the Constitution becomes "what the judges say it is"—for the time being. The Court may later reverse its own decisions; or the legislators may discover a way to do the same thing by slightly different means that the judges will find constitutional; or the people may overrule the Court's judgment by constitutional amendment. The Eleventh and the Sixteenth Amendments attest to this ultimate power retained by the people.

The great precedent for judicial review is the case of *Marbury v. Madison* (1803), in which the United States Supreme Court declared invalid a part of the Federal Judiciary Act of 1789.[24] Before President Adams left office in 1801, he had appointed some 60 Federalists to newly created judicial positions. Among them was William Marbury, who had been appointed as a justice of the peace for the District of Columbia. Marbury's appointment had been approved by the Senate and his commission to office had been signed and sealed. But Madison, Secretary of State for President Jefferson, refused to deliver this commission and others, for he recognized them as a last-minute

[24] Marbury v. Madison, 1 Cranch 137 (1803).

392

PART 3
decision-making
agencies:
who decides
what and how?

"court-packing" effort on the part of the Federalist party. Marbury went directly to the Supreme Court for a writ of mandamus (an order from a court requiring a government official to perform his duty) to compel Madison to deliver his commission. Chief Justice Marshall—himself a leading Federalist politician—declared that Marbury had a lawful right to his commission and that it was quite proper for Marbury to bring suit. After so scolding the administration, however, Marshall's opinion took a surprise twist and announced that the Judiciary Act of 1789 was in part unconstitutional. This act had authorized the Supreme Court to issue writs of mandamus in cases of original jurisdiction (original jurisdiction refers to cases brought to a court in the first instance). Since the original jurisdiction of the Supreme Court is clearly defined in the Constitution, however, Marshall ruled that Congress has no power to enlarge this jurisdiction to include mandamus cases. The justices held that the act was repugnant to the Constitution and dismissed Marbury's petition because the Court did not have jurisdiction.

Yet we must not assume that in *Marbury v. Madison* Chief Justice Marshall simply seized for the national judiciary supreme power over interpreting the Constitution. His argument for judicial review is entirely reasonable. If the Constitution is the supreme law of the land and the Court's function is to settle all controversies in law, the Court has a duty to decide in favor of the Constitution when any conflict arises between the Constitution and ordinary law. Marshall felt that this principle is essential to all written constitutions; namely, that any law contrary to the Constitution is void.

This argument was not original with Marshall; it shows striking similarity to Hamilton's words in *The Federalist* (Numbers 78 and 80). Although the founding fathers did not spell out the power of judicial review in the Constitution, they probably intended the judiciary to have such power. Back in the colonial period, the British Privy Council had established the precedent of judicial review over acts passed by the colonial legislatures. More influential perhaps was the fact that the courts in 10 states prior to 1803 had already exercised the same power. Lower national courts had also "reviewed" both state and national laws. But *Marbury v. Madison* was the first case in which a national court actually decided that an act of Congress was unconstitutional.

The power of judicial review has been used sparingly except during the 1930s. After *Marbury v. Madison*, Chief Justice Marshall never declared an act of Congress unconstitutional again. No other act of Congress was ruled invalid until the eve of the Civil War, when Chief Justice Taney, in the *Dred Scott Case*, held the Missouri Compromise unconstitutional after it had been in operation more than 30 years.[25] The Supreme Court has more frequently declared state laws unconstitutional. Because the states enact thousands and thousands of laws every year, this is to be expected.

Justice Owen Roberts, an arch conservative, once explained that when the United States Supreme Court considers a constitutional question, it "has only one duty, to lay the article of the Constitution which is involved beside the statute which is challenged and to decide whether the latter squares with

---

[25] Dred Scott v. Sandford, 19 How. 393 (1857).

the former."[26] But this explanation is much too simple. Every case that goes to the Supreme Court involves a controversy of national importance. Probably every case in constitutional law that has been decided by the Supreme Court could reasonably have been decided otherwise. How else can we explain that the state legislatures or Congress—whose members are all sworn to observe and uphold the Constitution—have already passed the laws which the courts are asked to review? How else can we account for the frequent disagreements among the justices themselves and the Court's not infrequent departure from its own previous decisions? The idea that the Constitution clearly dictates the Court's decision in each case is a myth, and "strict construction" is simply a political cliché.

Quite obviously, when the court engages in judicial review, it is engaged in a very substantial—and perhaps hostile—interaction with other decision makers. But as we have suggested, it does not do this very often. Far more often, it interacts by interpreting the specific meaning or intent of the thousands of decisions made by other actors.

Laws are not self-executing. Statutes and constitutional phrases are broadly written. Legislatures and executives use broad language for a variety of reasons, two of the most important being to ensure flexibility in the law and, by accommodating conflicting interests, to ensure compromise and agreement. Courts must deal daily with this broad, often vague language in very specific and concrete cases. When individuals or groups are brought before them with a charge of violating a law, the judges must determine what the wording means in this specific instance, with this specific set of facts. In so doing, they interpret the law, often expanding, modifying, or completely changing the meaning of the words from the original intent.

In constitutional interpretation, the power of the courts is especially important. Making old and very broad language relevant to contemporary problems is a powerful and important responsibility of the courts. For example, while the Bill of Rights forbids "cruel and unusual" punishment, courts must determine what the words "cruel and unusual" mean in today's society. Should the Court at some future date decide that these words mean capital punishment should be outlawed, it would simply be giving old words a new interpretation guided by contemporary values. Thus, interpretation of the language of others is the way the Court interacts most frequently with other political agents.

Congress and the judges

Collisions between Congress and the judges have occurred at frequent intervals in American history. Immediately after the Civil War, Congress kept its Reconstruction Acts from reaching the Supreme Court by taking advantage of the Constitution's provision that the Supreme Court's appellate jurisdiction is subject to "such Exceptions, and . . . such Regulations as the Congress shall make." Congress simply passed a law removing the Reconstruction Acts from the Supreme Court's jurisdiction. In the first third of this century, the judges

---

[26] United States v. Butler, 297 U.S. 1 (1936).

394

PART 3
decision-making
agencies:
who decides
what and how?

persistently blocked progressive economic and social legislation by strictly construing the powers of Congress over taxation and commerce.

The bitterest battles between Congress and the judges were fought over Franklin Roosevelt's New Deal in the 1930s. Within 2 years, national district judges signed some 1,600 injunctions against enforcement of New Deal legislation and administrative regulations, and the Supreme Court declared one major act after another beyond the power of Congress. But in 1937, when President Roosevelt asked Congress for authority to increase the number of judges on the Supreme Court to 15 or to make an additional appointment for every justice on the Court who refused to retire at age 70, the Judiciary Committee of the Senate recoiled in horror at the thought of "court-packing." (The storm over Roosevelt's proposals gradually died down as a succession of retirements and funerals made it possible for the President to fashion a new Court of his own choosing.)

In the late 1950s, the Senate Judiciary Committee, which in the 1930s had looked upon an independent judiciary as "the only shield of individual rights," went back to the Reconstruction Era for tips on how to curb the jurisdiction of the Supreme Court, especially in the area of civil rights. Some members of Congress, particularly from the South, angrily protested the Court's outlawing racial segregation in public schools and other public places. Others were outraged by the way the Court was chipping away internal security legislation designed to meet the "Communist Conspiracy." A rash of bills was introduced to check judicial activism. In 1959, the Jenner-Butler bill, which would have limited the jurisdiction of the Court in specified areas, was shelved by a close margin. Similar bills were introduced in the 1970s to prevent the Court from placing restrictions on prayer and Bible reading in public schools.

Court-curbing legislation is difficult to pass, although Congress does have a major arsenal of weapons it can use against the Court. It can, of course, begin the amending process to change a Court decision, as was the case in the Sixteenth Amendment. It can rewrite laws to overcome effects of a decision or reduce the Court's jurisdiction. And in most extreme cases, it could restructure the entire federal judicial system.

Efforts to curb the Court have appeared during certain specific periods of American history; they seem to be stimulated by special kinds of conditions between Congress and the Supreme Court. When the Court has exercised judicial review over federal statutes, usually a rash of Court-curbing bills are introduced.[27] In addition, legislation seems to be introduced when a political party difference characterizes the congressional and Court majorities, when Court decisions are frequently based on divided opinions, and when separation of powers and federal-state relations are the subject of cases. Because the courts are aware of power in the hands of Congress, few court-curbing bills have to be approved to bring the judiciary into line. The courts do not obstruct the will of the Congress or the President for very long.

[27] Stuart Nagel, "Court-Curbing Periods in American History," in Theodore Becker and Malcolm Feeley, eds., *The Impact of Supreme Court Decisions* (New York: Oxford, 1973), pp. 9–21.

The executive and the judges

In earlier chapters we have discussed the relationship between the executive branch and the courts, and in this chapter we have given special attention to interactions at the recruitment and appointment stage. Clearly, the interdependence of courts and executive is great, especially if public policies are to have any stability and coherence.

The most provocative question remaining is the degree to which the Supreme Court can obstruct the President or Congress. In its protection of minority rights, for example, can the Court prevent the majority leader, the President, from leading the majority?

The question is not answered easily. Robert Dahl has provided interesting suggestions through an examination of actual cases in which federal laws were declared unconstitutional.[28] Dahl believes that the Court has rarely been able to prevent a President who has a supportive Congress from achieving major policies to which he is committed. Although one can find many examples of courts delaying public policies, as in the New Deal, the Supreme Court can delay them for only a relatively short time if a President can find a majority in Congress to support his position. From these data, Dahl concludes that minorities have not received and cannot expect protection from a national majority if a President is determined to work his will. Although minorities can be comforted by the Court's protecting them from state and local policies, they have no such guarantee against national measures that some regard as violations of their rights.

Dahl supports his basic thesis by reference to the appointing powers of the President. He notes that Presidents appoint a new Supreme Court justice on an average of every 23 months and that most Presidents could tip the ideological balance on the Court in two terms. Because, as we have shown, Presidents select justices with a primary interest in their political values, the Chief Executive can gain the upper hand over the Court (with the cooperation of the Senate) in a comparatively brief time. Thus, "the policy views dominant on the Court will never be out of line for very long with the policy views dominant among the law-making majorities of the United States." Knowing this, the Court tends to adjust its policies according to the current coalition in the President-Congress majority and to legitimize the policies of this coalition.

The Dahl view that the Court is almost powerless to affect national policy without support from the President has not been accepted by all students of the judiciary.[29] Critics point out that to limit the study to statutes declared unconstitutional ignores a great deal of what the Court does. In addition, evidence that the Court may prevent some majority policies from being implemented for as long as 25 years suggests that Dahl underestimates the importance of delay as a foil to presidential action. Finally, because the Court cannot

[28] Robert A. Dahl, "The Supreme Court's Role in National Policy-Making," in Sheldon Goldman and Austin Sarat, eds., *American Court Systems* (San Francisco: Freeman, 1978), pp. 616–21.

[29] See Jonathan Casper, "The Supreme Court and National Policy Making," in Goldman and Sarat, pp. 622–37.

396

PART 3
decision-making
agencies:
who decides
what and how?

easily stop a majority President from acting, this does not mean that it does not influence the final policy and modify it when it is approved and implemented.

Certainly the federal judiciary is not powerless against the executive branch. At the same time, it does seem that the balance of power in the American system is, even in periods of judicial activism and involvement, in the hands of presidents, bureaucrats, and legislators.

THE JUDICIAL FUNCTIONS

When we consider the functions of the judiciary, we will be concerned with those things that would be missed in the American political system were the judiciary to disappear. Of course, the functions would not be completely missed, because some other decision makers would probably begin to do them. Even so, it helps us identify major functions of the courts if we think what would be absent without them.[30]

Peaceful settlement of disputes

To a great degree, all of politics involves settlement of disputes and conflicts, but it is a primary function of the courts. Operating within an elaborate system of legal norms, judges administer the processes through which a peaceful settlement of disputes can be affected. Courts do not search for disputes. Problems are brought by individuals or agents of the state. Judges do not deal in advisory opinions or hypothetical disputes. The judges consider only controversies in which the legal rights of individuals are actually at stake. And they try to give both a final and peaceful resolution to the thousands of battles, large and small, brought before them.

We speak of courts as the final authority, the last place one can go in the system. When we talk of "carrying our case all the way to the highest court in the land," we are acknowledging the finality of much court action in settling disputes. But realism requires us to confess that much dispute settling by courts is neither peaceful nor final. Although the Supreme Court declared segregation illegal in 1954, the dispute was hardly settled. It was transferred to many new forums, including lower courts, state houses, and school districts; and new battles broke out. In many public policy areas, one dispute follows another, as one battle follows another in a major war. The courts are present at each conflict as the policy is developed and unfolds. Although many disputes are settled by courts with one decision, a large number require multiple resolutions with the participation of many actors in the political process.

[30] For excellent discussion of functions see Howard Ball, *Courts and Politics, op. cit.,* pp. 21–53.

Umpiring federalism

Within the American Constitution, political power is divided, cross-checked, balanced, and limited.[31] Federalism, as we have seen, was a unique plan of constitutional framers by which two sets of governments could operate at the same time over a common territory. Each had special categories of power and, for these powers, different sets of decision makers were given primary responsibilities.

The courts operate as umpire over the struggles that develop between and among these units of power. Someone has to have final authority in a federal system for saying, "It is your right under the rules to act." Although not the only umpires in the system, courts are primary ones. Courts have to settle power claims between the states and the national government, between states, between governments and the people, and between agents of rule-making, application, and adjudication. When a President claims powers because of national security and a Congress claims that he abuses his powers, it is a court that decides. Throughout history, when states have claimed intrusion on their reserved powers by the national government, the cases have gone to court. And when an individual claims that no government has the legal power to act in violation of his Bill of Rights, courts determine who wins and who loses. Umpiring the federal game is a major function of the American judiciary.

Special protection of minority rights

Although all decision makers are obligated to protect minority rights in a democracy, courts perform a special function in this regard. Less obligated to popular will and majority demands, courts have the responsibility of sometimes saying to the majority, "Even you do not have the authority to do this." Because of this function, minority interests often turn to courts for protection, when representative institutions have ignored their claims. A history of the judiciary can be written by following the two centuries of minority claims made before it. As we have noted earlier, courts may be able only to delay or warn against violations of minority rights by the majority. A determined majority will have its way, ultimately, regardless of constitutional restrictions. Usually, however, once the minority wins its rights in court, other institutions will move in time to conform to the court's judgment. As courts function to administer justice in American society, they are obligated to be especially attentive to the needs of those who are disadvantaged by being in the minority, whether because of race, age, sex, or belief. However imperfectly the courts may perform this function, it is a task that would be greatly missed without the courts' participation.

---

[31] For this role, see *The Courts: The Pendulum of Federalism,* Final Report (Washington: The Roscoe-Pound-American Trial Lawyers Foundation, 1980).

398

PART 3
decision-making
agencies:
who decides
what and how?

Legitimizing political values and policy

Whether courts have any more legitimacy-conferring capacity than other constitutionally established branches of government is questionable, but courts do seem to have a special function in declaring what is "right," "proper," or legitimate among American political values and policies. Candidates may support particular policies, but the policies have no special status until the candidates are elected to office and can find others to agree that the policies should be given the status of law. At that point, these values are lifted to a special status as binding rules in the society. But before they can be truly acceptable, they must pass the test of the judiciary and be deemed properly within the framework of the constitutional value system. As Dahl suggests, courts have an important function of validating the national ruling coalition. With the blessing of the judiciary, decision makers are able to receive the support necessary for ruling in the society.

The judge, an important symbol in American society, personifies both the law and the conscience of the people. When we dress our judges in black robes and place them on thronelike platforms, we are honoring the rule of law and saying that a function is being performed that is greater than the desires of an individual judge. We want the decisions to be impartial, reasonable, and just. Courts are supposed to serve as supports for the basic values and interests of the society and to the degree that they achieve this function, the political system is more stable and responsive to the people. Although we have overdone the "cult of the robe" and pretended that judges were all wise and apolitical, the judicial symbol remains an important function in the country.

The federal judiciary embodies many divisions, individuals, and policies. Numerous as the various participants and courts may seem, the judiciary does work as an important part of the American political system. The conflicts between legalists and populists for control of the judicial task appear to have built a system that benefits both. The distinctive idea of the federal court system—a diffusion of national power throughout the states by means of federal judicial agents—has provided us with institutions and practices that support America's democratic ideals.

SUMMARY

The federal judicial system has been influenced by two groups or subcultures—legal and popular. Judicial selection is heavily influenced by both.

The President, with consent of the Senate, appoints all federal judges; judicial appointments to lower courts are recommended by home state senators. Efforts by President Carter to create merit nominating commissions for lower courts have resulted in some changes in the racial, sexual, and occupational backgrounds of lower court judges. Political values are important in presidential selection of justices to the Supreme Court.

District courts (where most federal cases begin) hear both civil and criminal cases. The courts of appeals hear cases on review that have not been resolved in the courts of original jurisdiction. Most of the cases in the Supreme Court come on appeal, and justices choose which ones to hear because of their policy consequences.

Judicial roles and behavior are not defined by the Constitution but are somewhat prescribed by laws and professional norms. Even so, judges see their roles differently, and their divergent views result in conflicts in arriving at decisions.

Judicial review and interpretation of laws are ways by which the courts relate to other decision makers. Although courts have great power, they usually can only delay decisions made by the President and Congress.

Judicial functions include peaceful settlement of disputes, umpiring, federalism, special protection of minority rights, legitimizing political values and policy, and symbolizing the rule of law.

OUTPUTS OF THE POLITICAL SYSTEM: WHO GETS HELPED. WHO GETS HURT?

government
impact
on the
rights
and liberties
of
Americans

12

ABOLISH CAPITAL PUNISHMENT

ERA YES!

ERA YES!

NATIONAL COMMITTEE OVERTURN THE BAKKE DECISION

402

PART 4
outputs of the
political system:
who gets helped,
who gets hurt?

We have looked at the institutions and processes of American politics and have attempted to show the interactions of the people and their decision makers. That analysis should help us understand the outputs of the system.

In a representative democracy, outputs should represent the public will; the rewards and deprivations of government policies should reflect the public's intentions and desires. That describes the relationship in a model political system. What actually happens, however, is not easy to demonstrate. We *should*, perhaps, be able to predict outputs, but outputs of public policy are often not what we expect or desire. Even more often, *outcomes* of public policies, their impact upon society, are not what policy makers had in mind when they formulated the policy. Why aren't they?

First, we do not completely understand the complicated interrelationships in the American political system. In our discussions thus far, we have examined the most significant of these interrelationships, but there is much we do not know about the processes of politics. Second, unforeseen inputs may enter the policy processes and greatly transform expected outputs. Some racial minorities reacted negatively to desegregation in the 1960s. They protested the loss of black schools and destruction of black symbols. This unforeseen reaction gave rise to black pride movements and efforts to preserve black identity, which had an unexpected, dramatic impact on the policies of desegregation in the 1970s. Third, decision makers seldom know what policies to adopt in order to solve our problems. When the country faced soaring energy costs, recession, and inflation in 1980, President Carter certainly recognized, along with everyone else, that we had serious economic problems. But hardly anyone agreed on what policies could or should be adopted to solve the problems. As a result, proposal after proposal was picked to pieces by opponents, and the few policies that were approved offered only the dimmest hope that they would achieve the desired outcomes. Fourth, forces in the world at large affect the nation's political environment to such an extent that they have sometimes been the crucial determinants of major policy decisions. For example, our energy, ecological, and economic policies have been deeply affected by the external input of price-fixing by the oil-producing foreign states.

THE FOUNDATION OF AMERICAN LIBERTIES AND RIGHTS

Because it is impossible to investigate all the policies that have affected the public, rewarding some and depriving others, we have chosen to discuss the outputs and outcomes of civil liberties and civil rights. We shall take a more general look at policy in the next chapter. But because liberty was what the system was about in the beginning, policies affecting the public's rights and liberties seem most deserving of a close look. We shall see how the ideals were translated into public norms in the Bill of Rights and Civil Rights Amendments, investigate what they mean and how they have been applied as public policies, and evaluate their impact and outcome in American society.

The ideology

403

CHAPTER 12
government
impact on the
rights and
liberties of
Americans

The Declaration of Independence holds that all men are "endowed by their Creator with certain unalienable rights, that among these are Life, Liberty and the pursuit of Happiness . . . to secure these rights, Governments are instituted among men. . . ." This is the American ideology—that all people possess basic rights and liberties simply because they are human beings entitled to decent respect from their fellows.

Life, liberty, and pursuit of happiness are grand words, but their meaning and the public policies necessary to make them real were disputed even among the people who adopted the Declaration. Liberty was the ideology reaffirmed in the Constitution, but its specifications continued to be vague.

"To secure the blessings of Liberty for ourselves and our Posterity" is one of the goals proclaimed by the Preamble to the Constitution of the new republic. But some thought that the Constitution did not go far enough in securing these blessings. Thomas Jefferson, writing to James Madison, expressed his concern about "the omission of a Bill of Rights. . . . A bill of rights is what the people are entitled to against every government on earth, general or particular, and what no just government should refuse or rest on inference." Jefferson's concern was shared by others, and a listing of rights became the first mission of the new government.

The Bill of Rights

After the American colonists had broken away from the British Crown, the Continental Congress advised them to organize "conventions of the people" that would provide permanent constitutional government in each of the new states. Virginia was the first state to draft a constitution, a constitution prefaced by a Declaration of Rights that became the model for lawmakers in the other states.[1] The delegates to the Constitutional Convention in Philadelphia felt that these new state constitutions adequately protected the fundamental rights of the individual; they decided it was not necessary to attach a detailed bill of rights to the federal Constitution.

They did put a few restrictions on the national and state governments, but their failure to mention basic rights such as free speech strengthened the popular demand for a true bill of rights as part of the national Constitution. If promises had not been made in the state conventions that such a bill of rights would immediately be added to the original text, the Constitution would certainly not have been ratified.

During the fight for ratification, more than 100 civil rights amendments were proposed to the various states. In the first Congress, James Madison intro-

---

[1] See Allen Rutland, *The Birth of the Bill of Rights, 1776–1791* (Chapel Hill: University of North Carolina Press, 1955) for a historical account of the background of the Bill of Rights. Authorship of the Virginia Declaration of Rights is attributed principally to George Mason and Patrick Henry— the same Colonel Mason who refused to sign the Constitution drafted in Philadelphia at the Constitutional Convention of 1787 because it did not include a similar Bill of Rights for the whole people, and the same Patrick Henry who refused to attend that convention because he "smelt a rat."

404

PART 4
outputs of the
political system:
who gets helped,
who gets hurt?

duced a series of amendments to reassure the people that the new government had no intention of denying or disregarding "those rights of persons and property which by the Declaration of Independence were affirmed to be unalienable." The House actually passed 17 of these amendments, although 2 of them were rejected by the Senate. The remaining 15 were consolidated into 12 and then submitted to the state legislatures. Ten were ratified. These first 10 amendments constitute the "American Bill of Rights," though only the first 8 amendments actually specify the rights of individuals.

In brief, these amendments are:

I. Free exercise of religion, freedom of speech and press, rights of assembly and petition.

II. The right of the people to keep and bear arms.

III. Protection against quartering of soldiers in private homes.

IV. Protection against unreasonable searches and seizures of persons, houses, papers, and effects.

V. Procedural rights of persons accused of crime and guarantees of due process of law with respect to life, liberty, and property.

VI. Further rights of the accused, including trial by jury and the right to assistance of counsel.

VII. Provisions for trial by jury in civil cases.

VIII. Prohibition of excessive bails or fines and of cruel or unusual punishment.

Among the amendments that Madison originally proposed as part of the national bill of rights, one provided: "No State shall infringe the right of trial by Jury in criminal cases nor the rights of conscience, nor the freedom of speech, or of the press." This proposal was rejected by the Senate. The rejection is one clue that Congress intended the first 8 amendments to restrict only the national government. More direct evidence is that the First Amendment begins, "Congress shall pass no law . . ." with no reference to restrictions on the states. Chief Justice Marshall in the case of *Barron v. Baltimore* (1833) accordingly rejected the proposition that the Bill of Rights applied to the states as well as to the national government. If Congress had so intended, he held, "they would have declared this purpose in plain and intelligible language."[2]

The civil rights amendments

The Bill of Rights is concerned principally with individual rights and personal liberties. The Thirteenth, Fourteenth, and Fifteenth Amendments, written into the Constitution immediately after the Civil War, add new dimensions: the privileges and immunities of citizens and the civil rights of minority groups. These amendments were specifically concerned with the rights of blacks who had recently been freed in the southern states. The Thirteenth Amendment

[2] 7 Peters 243 (1883).

405

CHAPTER 12
government
impact on the
rights and
liberties of
Americans

prohibited slavery, finally ending—at least in its official form—the nation's most conspicuous violation of the principle of human equality. The Fourteenth Amendment defined citizenship to include former slaves, prohibited the states from violating the privileges and immunities of United States citizens, and further prohibited the states from depriving any person (whether a citizen or not) of "life, liberty, or property without due process of law." The Fifteenth guaranteed the right to vote regardless of race, color, or previous condition of servitude. In contrast to the Bill of Rights, with its concern for abuse of power by the national government, these amendments utilized the power of the federal Constitution to protect people against the state governments.

Congressional debates on the Fourteenth Amendment show the intent, at least on the part of those who spoke out, to make the entire Bill of Rights applicable to the states. Immediately following the adoption of the Thirteenth Amendment, Congress had enacted the Civil Rights Act of 1866, which gave citizenship to the newly freed blacks and provided that they should have "full and equal benefit of all laws and proceedings for the security of person and property as is enjoyed by white citizens." President Andrew Johnson vetoed the bill on the ground that Congress did not have the constitutional power to "repeal all state laws discriminating between whites and blacks. . . ." Congress not only passed the Civil Rights Act over the President's veto, but it also introduced the Fourteenth Amendment to ensure the constitutionality of national legislation on civil rights. Unquestionably, the framers of the Fourteenth Amendment hoped to overrule the decision of *Barron v. Baltimore* and to bring the states under the same limitations as the national government with respect to individual rights and liberties. The opponents of the Amendment were equally clear in viewing it as shifting responsibility for civil rights from the states to the national government.

No sooner was the Fourteenth Amendment ratified than the Supreme Court began to interpret its meaning without reference to the pertinent congressional debates. Within a decade the expressed intentions of Congress were ignored in a series of judicial decisions that denied Congress the power to pass general legislation on civil rights. In effect, the Supreme Court acted in the last quarter of the nineteenth century as if the South had won the Civil War. The Court's role in interpreting the Fourteenth Amendment was not, as it turned out, a unique display of its power in civil rights policies. The Court has continued to exert extraordinary power over the meaning of each of the "rights amendments."

THE COURTS: DEFINERS OF RIGHTS

In the American political system, no single set of decision makers has the responsibility for defining and protecting individual rights and liberties. All are equally committed to "protect and defend" the Constitution, and each has some involvement in establishing public policies that enhance or restrict

406

PART 4
outputs of the
political system:
who gets helped,
who gets hurt?

the rights of citizens. Citizens themselves are involved significantly in the "real world" meaning of the Bill of Rights. By demanding certain interpretations of rights or refusing to support the interpretations offered by courts or legislatures, they can effectively modify or destroy the implementation of public policies designed to protect one interest from another. Thus, although certain rights are guaranteed in the Constitution, the quality of the warranty is everyone's responsibility, for rights are subject to constant interpretation and change, conflict, expansion, and reduction.

Throughout much of our history, the federal courts have assumed a major responsibility for determining the winners and losers in the battles for liberties. Constantly faced with cases that pit one claimed liberty against another, the courts have been required to state which rights are superior to others and in what kinds of claims. The broad and often vague language of the Constitution and statutes has to be interpreted and applied to contemporary problems and conflicting demands. Although the words of the Constitution may be static, the problems and needs of the society are not. Less sensitive to the majority's will, more insulated from direct political pressures, and especially obligated to protect minority interests, courts—particularly the Supreme Court—have been major architects of our public policies on rights and liberties. As we discuss these important outputs, it is appropriate that we focus on the activities of the courts.

The Burger Court: ambiguity and conflict

For over a decade Warren E. Burger has presided over the Supreme Court as Chief Justice of the United States. Appointed by Richard Nixon to replace the retired and controversial Earl Warren, Burger was selected for his "strict constructionist" philosophy, ideological conservatism, and experience in lower courts. Conservatives hoped that Burger could lead the Court to reverse the liberal and activist record of the Warren years. That has not occurred. Rather, under his leadership, the court has created a patchwork of conflicting rulings, some of which amend, some of which support, most of which confuse existing policies on civil liberties. Unable to command unanimity or even strong majorities, the Chief Justice has watched a fragmented Court move erratically along the path of civil rights law. At times, members of the Court have been in almost open warfare, attacking each other in their opinions, from the bench, and in public forums. With its zigs and zags, multiple opinions, and shifting majorities, the Court has given uncertain guidelines to the lower courts and established no solid philosophical character of its own. In arriving at its positions on civil liberties policies, it has

- upheld a woman's rights to abortion, but upheld a company's benefit plan that excludes temporary disabilities related to pregnancy.
- upheld the rights of journalists to report the news, but sanctioned the exclusion of the public and newspaper reporters from a pretrial hearing in which two men sought to withdraw their confessions to a second degree murder.

- struck down a racial quota on medical school admissions, but acknowledged that race could be "considered" in admissions. Then the Court upheld affirmative action plans in the private industrial sector, which sought to promote unskilled workers to craft positions with a quota for minorities.
- upheld laws that give preference to veterans in hiring for state positions (a clear advantage to males), but otherwise seemed to oppose sex biases, as in supporting the right of a female to sue a congressman when she was dismissed because she was a woman.
- extended a defendant's right to a lawyer. Previously, that right belonged to those accused of a felony (a major crime); the Court extended it to misdemeanors (minor offenses) if the defendant faces the possibility of a jail sentence. But the Court declined to prohibit overcrowding in a federal jail or to stop body cavity searches in a federal facility.
- supported busing to achieve racial integration and racial balance, but declined to extend it beyond city boundary lines.

The result of the Court's uncertain grappling with civil liberty issues has been, according to Court specialist Bruce Fein, "a growing inability to provide principled, long-term guidelines—a jurisprudence designed to guide judges and the citizenry beyond the confining factual circumstances of particular cases."[3]

To be sure, the broad outlines of the Court's direction are sometimes visible. On these occasions, the drift seems clearly away from the positions of the Warren Court majority. Whereas the Warren Court greatly expanded the guarantees of the Bill of Rights by making more of them applicable to the states, the Burger Court has often limited and reduced this protection. The Warren Court gave extraordinary preference to First Amendment rights; the Burger Court has modified this emphasis and has been more restrictive. In elevating individual rights over community rights and national rights over states' rights, the Warren Court stimulated an outcry of opposition from losing litigants. The new Court has given increased support to states' rights, in efforts to shift the imbalance. But as soon as one tries to locate a clear new direction on the Burger Court, divergent decisions will emerge and becloud the picture. One can best characterize the civil liberties record as one of some continuity, some change, and a great deal of fluidity.[4]

Sources of the Court's ambiguity

What explains the hesitant "one step forward, two steps backward" approach of the Burger Court? In part, the explanation lies in the nature of the larger problems facing American society. Contemporary problems are complex, and an acceptable balancing of interests is often impossible in seeking

[3] As quoted in *Washington Post*, July 8, 1979.

[4] For this transition, see Stephen L. Wasby, *Continuity and Change: From the Warren Court to the Burger Court* (Pacific Palisades: Goodyear, 1976) and Richard Funston, *Constitutional Counter Revolution?* (New York: Schenkman, 1977). Also see Darlene Walker, "Moving the Law Backward," in Theodore Lowi and Alan Stone, eds., *Nationalizing Government: Public Policies in America* (Beverly Hills: Sage, 1978), pp. 359–90.

408

PART 4
outputs of the
political system:
who gets helped,
who gets hurt?

solutions. If the Burger Court seems directionless and contradictory, it is hardly more so than the Congress or the President. One can list a dozen pressing national problems over the last decade that have escaped solution by American decision makers at all levels. Like the other official decision-making agencies, the judiciary has limped along with imperfect leadership, dubious vision, and inadequate solutions.

A second explanation of this ambiguous record is that although Warren Burger heads the Court, he does not run it. The Court has no clear ideological majority that will accept Burger's leadership on civil liberties questions. Two Warren Court members, Justices William Brennan and Thurgood Marshall, vote a solid liberal position on most civil liberty issues. Chief Justice Burger and Justice William Rehnquist are allied on the conservative side of these questions. In the middle is the majority of the Court, five justices who shift between the conservative and liberal positions to make or break liberal or conservative majorities: Justices White and Stewart from the Warren Court "center" share the middle position with Justices Powell, Blackmun, and Stevens. Although the general position of these swing voters is often conservative, it is not consistently so. Thus, Burger and Rehnquist cannot count on any of the swing judges as firm allies. For example, Blackmun and Powell, both Nixon appointees, have shown far more independence from the Chief Justice and Rehnquist, two other Nixon appointees, than was originally expected. Justice Stevens has played a classical middle position since his appointment to the Court by President Ford. Since neither liberals nor conservatives hold a firm majority, civil liberties policy moves back and forth between the poles. When a position is finally taken by the Court majority, it is often with multiple opinions that agree on the outcome of the case but disagree on the reasons for the verdict.

A third reason for the ambiguity in the current state of the law is found in the special problems faced by conservative justices when they are forced to deal with liberal precedents. A "restrained" or "conservative" judge has a strong commitment to prior opinions and rulings of the Court. Such judges often profess to base their judgments on the principle of *stare decisis* ("let the decision stand"), relying on the sum of prior rulings on the question at hand. But in the current Court, conservative justices find that the most recent relevant rulings are those created by the liberal Warren Court majority. Thus the problem: how to make a conservative judgment on the case at hand without violating the precedent and thus becoming "unrestrained"? The Warren Court record therefore becomes a great roadblock to conservatives. As conservative justices try to distinguish between the civil liberty claim they are considering and the claim granted in a former liberal decision, they often create conflicting precedents for lower courts and for themselves.

Finally, some explanation for the Court's divisiveness may be found in the personality and style of the Chief Justice. Earlier in this text we noted the importance of the "task" and "social" roles of the Chief. We observed that a primary function of the Court's head is to ensure that the justices operate with minimum conflict and maximum cooperation, and that the flow of work is such that the judiciary can complete its tasks. Although Chief Justice Burger has shown great managerial interest in the workloads of the judiciary and has constantly campaigned for reforms, he does not appear to have been effective in guiding his associates or serving to unify them. His open hostility to the press has sometimes been turned upon his judicial colleagues. In one decision he publicly attacked his five colleagues in the majority as "intellectually dishonest," strong language for someone who must provide leadership for the body.

Fortunately, civil liberties policies are not the products of one Court, one time, or one Chief Justice and his majority. Although the Burger Court will have substantial impact on our rights and liberties as citizens, we should not underestimate the long history and many compromises that have brought us to our present positions. As we look at these policies, we shall be aware of current developments and changes, but we cannot understand the policies without awareness of prior struggles that in large measure define our contemporary notion of rights.

409

CHAPTER 12
government
impact on the
rights and
liberties of
Americans

PRIVILEGES AND IMMUNITIES OF CITIZENS AND IMMIGRANTS

The Articles of Confederation mention "the free inhabitants of these States," "free citizens in the several states," and "the people of each State." The Constitution of 1787 speaks of "citizens of each State" and "citizens in the several States," but it adds a new phrase and a new concept: "citizens of the United States." Not until the adoption of the Fourteenth Amendment in 1868, however, do we find a constitutional definition of United States citizenship.

Citizens of the United States

Until the Fourteenth Amendment, United States citizenship was widely viewed as derived from state citizenship. Thus, after the Declaration of Independence, all persons born or naturalized (given citizenship by legal process) in one of the Colonies, say Georgia or Massachusetts, became citizens of the new state of Georgia or Massachusetts. Under the Constitution of 1787, the citizens of each state also became citizens of the United States. In the famous *Dred Scott* case (1857), Chief Justice Taney argued that "citizens of each state" meant citizens of the United States as understood at the time the Constitution was adopted and that blacks were not then considered capable of citizenship.[5] The Dred Scott decision was reversed by the Civil War. When the war was over, Congress faced the problem of defining the status of the freed black.

---

[5] Scott v. Sandford, 19 How. 393 (1857). Justice Curtis disagreed with Taney, asserting that as a matter of fact there were free black citizens in 1789 and that it was then understood that a state was free to extend citizenship to new classes of persons within its borders. The Court ruled, also, that a slave did not become free even when taken into a free state; nor could Congress prohibit slavery in a territory.

Under the Dred Scott decision, even slaves who escaped to
free states were not considered citizens of the United States.

Through the Fourteenth Amendment, it deliberately overturned Taney's judgment in the *Dred Scott* case.

The Fourteenth Amendment means just what it says: "All persons born
or naturalized in the United States and subject to the jurisdiction thereof,
are citizens of the United States and of the state wherein they reside."
When Congress, responding to the pressure of racial prejudice on the West
Coast, passed a law that prohibited the naturalization of persons of the yellow
race (Orientals) and then excluded from citizenship the children of aliens
ineligible to become citizens, the Supreme Court held that all persons born
in this country are citizens regardless of the race or nationality of their parents.[6]

Nations establish citizenship under two general principles of international
law: (1) *jus soli* (law of the land) and (2) *jus sanguinis* (law of blood). Under
jus soli the country in which a person is born determines citizenship; under

[6] United States v. Wong Kim Ark, 1969 U.S. 649 (1898).

jus sanguinis, the citizenship of the parent is passed on to the child. The Fourteenth Amendment adopts the policy of *jus soli.* Congress has by statute also adopted the policy of *jus sanguinis.* Thus a person born abroad of American parents may be an American citizen. Since other countries also define citizenship on the basis of *jus soli* or *jus sanguinis* or both, many people may actually have two citizenships.

411

CHAPTER 12
government
impact on the
rights and
liberties of
Americans

The Fourteenth Amendment prohibits the states from abridging the privileges and immunities of citizens of the United States. But nowhere in the Constitution is there any complete listing of these "privileges and immunities." From time to time, however, the Supreme Court has specified some of them. In *Crandall v. Nevada* (1868), a case decided while the Fourteenth Amendment was before the states for ratification, the Court identified various "citizen rights": to have access to the government, to transact business with it, to seek its protection, to share its offices, to engage in administering its functions, to have entrance into its courts of justice, and to travel from state to state without restriction or payment of a tax.[7]

The first Supreme Court ruling on the meaning of the "privileges and immunities" mentioned in the Fourteenth Amendment was handed down in the *Slaughter House Cases* (1873).[8] These cases, which involved the validity of a Louisiana statute, offer an excellent example of how vague and confused Supreme Court decisions can sometimes be. Under the state's power to protect public health, the Louisiana legislature authorized a slaughterhouse monopoly in New Orleans. The independent butchers of New Orleans protested that the monopoly deprived them of one of their privileges as United States citizens—the right to earn a living, in this case by operating a slaughter house. The Court decided 5 to 4 in favor of the monopoly. Justice Samuel Miller, speaking for the majority, held (in shocking violation of the historical record) that when Congress framed the Fourteenth Amendment it had no intention of making any radical change in the relations between the state governments and the national government, or in the relations of either of these governments to the people. With this restrictive view, the Court concluded that the Louisiana legislature did not violate the privileges and immunities of national citizenship in granting the monopoly to a single slaughterhouse.

The decision in the *Slaughter House Cases* was hailed by the proponents of states' rights, especially in the South. According to the Court's interpretation, the Fourteenth Amendment gave the national government *no additional positive power over civil rights.*

If no change had been intended, the amendment would hardly have been introduced. Hence, many students of constitutional law feel that the Court's decision in the *Slaughter House Cases* virtually nullified the privileges and immunities clause of the Fourteenth Amendment. The decision severely limited the privileges and immunities of national citizenship and permitted various forms of discrimination from state to state. Justice Stephen Field, who dis-

[7] Nevada had levied a head tax on every person leaving the state by public transportation. The Court held that because it is the right of the citizen to move freely from one state to another, a state tax restricting such movement was unconstitutional. 6 Wall. 35 (1868).

[8] Slaughter House Cases, 16 Wall. 36 (1873).

412

PART 4
outputs of the
political system:
who gets helped,
who gets hurt?

sented in the *Slaughter House Cases*, could not convince his colleagues to join him in the view that the Fourteenth Amendment meant "The fundamental rights, privileges, and immunities which belong to [an American, former slave or not] as a free man and a free citizen, now belong to him as a citizen of the United States, and are not dependent upon his citizenship of any state. . . ."

The right to pass freely from state to state is one of the rights of national citizenship that had to be reaffirmed in the twentieth century. In the depression years of the 1930s, some states tried to bar the entrance of poor migrants. In 1941, the Supreme Court considered a California statute aimed against the entrance of "Okies," poverty-stricken refugees from the Oklahoma dust bowl. The Court unanimously found the California statute unconstitutional: five of the justices said the prohibition imposed an unconstitutional burden upon interstate commerce; four thought the prohibition violated *the privileges and immunities of citizenship*. Justice Douglas was especially keen on this latter point:

> The right of persons to move freely from state to state occupies a more protected position in our constitutional system than does the movement of cattle, fruit, steel, and coal across state lines. . . . The right to move freely from State to State is an incident of *national* citizenship, protected by the privileges and immunities clause of the Fourteenth Amendment against state interference.[9]

Whether one argues from the position of the majority or of the concurring four in the case, it seems clear that constitutional law protects personal freedom of movement from state to state both under the commerce clause and under rights of national citizenship.

The Court has been less clear on the right of American citizens to travel abroad without restrictions. The Department of State has placed certain countries of the world "off limits" for travel when the department holds that such travel would not be in the interests of the United States. (These restrictions usually apply to countries with new communist regimes.) Although the Court has not announced if such restrictions are legal, it has decided that citizens who go to such countries, although not committing a crime, cannot expect full protection from the United States government.[10]

Most of the individual liberties and rights that Americans can claim under constitutional law belong to all persons, not just citizens. In every state, however, the right to vote is extended only to citizens of the United States. Moreover, after a long struggle, the citizen's right to vote is recognized and enforced as national public policy. The Voting Rights Act of 1965, extended in 1970 and legitimized by Supreme Court decision and constitutional amendment, turned the talk of universal suffrage and constitutional democracy into reality for all citizens 18 years of age and older. No longer could poll taxes or literacy tests or other requirements act as a deterrent to voting. However gradually, the privileges and immunities of citizenship do grow.

[9] Edwards v. California, 314 U.S. 160 (1941).
[10] United States v. Laub. 385 U.S. 475 (1967).

Immigrants

413

CHAPTER 12
government
impact on the
rights and
liberties of
Americans

Not until the end of the nineteenth century did this land of immigrants begin to close its gates to certain classes of foreigners. Congress passed its first major immigration act in 1882, barring the entrance of idiots, lunatics, convicts, and paupers. In the same year it enacted the first Chinese Exclusion Law, a controversial statute that was not repealed until World War II, when China was an American ally.

A big increase in immigration from 1900 to 1920—more than a million immigrants in a single year—caused great concern in many quarters. Congress took no action until 1917, however, when it established a literacy test for all immigrants and excluded virtually all immigration from most of Asia and the Pacific Islands. The racist biases in these early immigration laws did not seem shocking to the WASP-dominated society that enacted them.

After World War I, when immigration from Europe was reaching new highs, Congress imposed its first numerical limits. In 1924, Congress limited the total annual immigration to approximately 150,000, a mere fraction of the hundreds of thousands of pioneers and settlers who once came to the United States every year. This total was broken down into quotas based on "national origins." The national origins policy was designed to admit the largest number of immigrants from northern and western Europe, the smallest number from southern and eastern Europe. (The combined quotas for the British Isles and Germany accounted for nearly three-fourths of the legal total.)

In 1952, The McCarran-Walters Act, which was supposed to revise American immigration policies, eliminated all racial barriers as such but retained both numerical restrictions and the national-origins quotas. (Immigration from the Western Hemisphere was not placed under the quota system.) President Truman vetoed the Immigration Act of 1952, declaring that its provisions were "insulting to large numbers of our finest citizens, irritating to our allies abroad, and foreign to our purposes and ideals." Nevertheless, Congress passed the bill over his veto.

The Immigration and Nationality Act of 1965, amended in 1976, finally made major changes in American immigration policy. This act fixes an overall annual limit of 170,000 immigrants, with a maximum of 20,000 allowed to any one country. Preference is given to: (1) children, spouses, and other relatives of citizens in the United States; (2) professionals with exceptional ability in sciences and arts; (3) skilled or unskilled labor, not of a temporary or seasonal nature, for which there is a shortage of willing and employable persons in the United States; (4) political refugees, especially from communist countries, up to 6 percent of the total number in any one year. Immigrants from within the Western Hemisphere are limited to a total of 120,000 a year.

Although the 1965 Immigration Act has a strong bias in favor of talented and educated immigrants, it does permit the immigration of some "huddled masses" fleeing from persecution of one form or another. In 1979, for example, President Carter pledged to accept more refugees who were fleeing Vietnam and ordered the American fleet to rescue all of the "boat people" who sought assistance. The Hanoi government's abuse of its Chinese ethnic minority, la-

414

PART 4
outputs of the
political system:
who gets helped,
who gets hurt?

beled by U.S. Representative Robert Drinan as "one of the most fundamental violations of human rights in this century," had caused 110,000 citizens to escape, often in flimsy rafts and fishing boats, during only two months of 1979. Over a four-year period, the exodus from Vietnam was close to a million. With the assistance of an emergency United Nations conference, the United States took leadership in the Vietnamese relocation. Although such efforts have not been universally applauded in all American communities, the influx of the new immigrants is in the tradition of the immigrant origins that Americans share.

Aliens and naturalized citizens

Although the Constitution does not mention immigration, it does specify that Congress shall have power to establish uniform rules of *naturalization* (the process by which a person becomes a citizen). In his first annual message, President Washington urged Congress to determine by law "the terms on which foreigners may be admitted to the rights of citizens." Congress passed the first Naturalization Act in 1790, making naturalization an activity of the national and state courts.

With little central control, standards were not uniform and procedures were often lax. To correct abuses, in 1906 Congress provided for special examiners to assist the courts with naturalization.

An alien (citizen of another country) applying for naturalization must be "attached to the principles of the Constitution of the United States and well disposed to the good order and happiness of the United States." When the court grants a petition for naturalization, the applicant gives up allegiance to the foreign country of which he or she has been a citizen and promises to be loyal to the United States. *Allegiance* is the legal crux of differentiation between the citizen and the alien. The citizen is required to defend this country and to support its constitutional principles.

In 1952, racial barriers to naturalization in the United States were finally removed. The law now requires that the candidate be able to speak, read, and write simple English and have some knowledge of the history, principles, and form of our government. In most countries, a married woman takes the citizenship of her husband. Under American law, however, an American woman who marries an alien does not lose her American citizenship even though under the laws of her husband's country she may acquire his citizenship. Similarly, an alien who marries an American citizen does not acquire American citizenship, though the process of naturalization is shortened and simplified for the alien spouse.

Naturalized citizens enjoy the same constitutional privileges and immunities as native-born citizens. There is only one exception: a naturalized citizen is not eligible to be elected President or Vice-President of the United States. Whatever civil rights are implied as part of national citizenship—such as the right to participate in elections or to move without restriction from state to state—belong equally to those who acquired citizenship at birth and to those who acquired it by choice through naturalization.

415

CHAPTER 12
government
impact on the
rights and
liberties of
Americans

The basic civil rights guaranteed by the American Constitution belong to all *persons,* not just to *citizens.* This policy is expressed in the Fifth and Fourteenth Amendments. In everyday affairs, then, the status of aliens is not very different from that of the citizen. They must obey the laws, pay taxes, and send their children to school. They have access to the courts and if prosecuted or sued, they are entitled to the same rights as a citizen. Increasingly, the courts have declared state laws unconstitutional if they restrict the rights of aliens. For example, states cannot prevent aliens from practicing engineering or being admitted to the bar. They cannot exclude aliens from all forms of state financial assistance or exclude them from all jobs in state government.[11] In the future, aliens may well enjoy all of the rights of citizenship with the exceptions of voting and holding public office.

In one respect, however, the status of the alien in this country is totally different from that of the citizen. Upholding the government's right to deport Iranians in the United States without proper papers, the Supreme Court reaffirmed in 1980 that the alien has no *right* to stay in the United States. Aliens may be sent back to their own country if they: (1) entered the country unlawfully; (2) were admitted for a specific time or purpose and subsequently violated the conditions of their admission; (3) prove to be undesirable residents through criminal, immoral, or subversive acts.

THE GREAT RIGHTS

Members of the First Congress spelled out in the First Amendment the rights they regarded as most basic. These First Amendment freedoms have been given a "preferred position" by the courts and were among the first provisions of the Bill of Rights to be interpreted (under the Fourteenth Amendment's restriction on the states) to apply against the state no less than against the national government.

These freedoms are not public policies. They are guidelines within which decision makers are expected to operate when making or carrying out specific policies. They must be applied in specific instances of conflict, must often be placed in relative balance against one another, and must constantly be interpreted in the light of new circumstances. In all of these tasks—application, balancing, and interpretation—the courts of the United States have played central roles.

Freedom of speech and press

The authors of the Bill of Rights believed that republican government must be grounded in full and free discussion. To this end, the First Amendment

---

[11] See Graham v. Richardson, 403 U.S. 365 (1971); *in re* Griffiths, 413 U.S. 717 (1973); Examining Board v. Flores de Otero, 426 U.S. 572 (1976).

416

PART 4
outputs of the
political system:
who gets helped,
who gets hurt?

guarantees freedom of speech and of the press, with no law permitted to "abridge" either of these freedoms.

But no freedom is absolute. Common law has always held, for example, that neither free press nor speech may offend public morals or public decency. Thus, the government may forbid the publication of whatever is "obscene," "lewd," or "lascivious." The difficulty in regulating obscenity is in arriving at a formula that does not improperly impinge upon free speech and press. This problem is especially acute in a society such as ours, with great variety in moral values and sexual behavior. It is made more difficult by the fact that even these differences are not stable but are undergoing constant and rapid change.

The Supreme Court has frequently been asked to act as a "supercensor"—to uphold or strike down community standards for regulating pornographic materials. By 1957, the majority of the Court had concluded that obscenity was that which was "utterly without redeeming social importance." The test of obscenity was "whether to the average person applying contemporary community standards the dominant theme of the material taken as a whole appeals to prurient [lustful] interest."[12] Seven years later, the Court sought to clarify its position by contending that such standards could not be determined by local communities alone, but "that the constitutional status of an alleged obscene work must be determined on the basis of a national standard."[13] Therein lay the problem, for no true and explicit national standard could be defined by the Court. Thus people could not be certain whether or not what they were printing, filming, or viewing was legally obscene. The situation became even more uncertain when the Court unanimously concluded that, while laws regulating obscenity might be justified, the state could not enter the privacy of a person's home and confiscate obscene materials. "If the First Amendment means anything, it means that the State has no business telling a man, sitting alone in his own house, what books he may read or what films he may watch."[14] Although this was a liberal ruling, it contributed nothing to the clarification of what is or is not obscene. Confusion grew as to what was permissible under Warren Court standards. Actually, the members of the Warren Court were never able to agree on what was obscene. Even in the decision that had announced the necessity to follow a "national standard," no more than two justices were in agreement on the specifics. The division sometimes became so sharp that local enforcement officials could not discern effective guidelines. As a result, the Warren Court had little impact on the increasing flow of sexually explicit materials.

One could expect the Burger Court to seek to remedy the widespread distribution of alleged pornography. President Nixon, who appointed four members of the Burger Court, had himself attacked the report of the President's Commission on Pornography and Obscenity in 1970, because it tended

---

[12] Roth v. U.S., 354 U.S. 476 (1957).

[13] Jacobellis v. Ohio, 378 U.S. 184 (1964).

[14] Stanley v. Georgia, 394 U.S. 557 (1969).

toward a permissive view. As a principal Nixon appointee, Chief Justice Burger shared his view.

417

CHAPTER 12
government
impact on the
rights and
liberties of
Americans

In a 5-to-4 decision of the Court, Burger brought forth the "new game plan" on obscenity. Arguing that the Court should not view the First Amendment freedoms as absolute, simply because it could not find an easy way to regulate objectionable material, the Chief Justice abandoned the idea of "national standards" and stated the new view that local communities could use their own standards to detemine if material should be censored. "It is neither realistic nor constitutionally sound to read the First Amendment as requiring that the people of Maine or Mississippi accept public depiction of conduct found tolerable in Las Vegas or New York City."[15]

The Court's new position favoring local standards appears, on the surface, to be easier to administer. But who or what groups in a community determine local standards? What is to prevent small vocal groups from rising up within a community and claiming that their minority judgments are "the local community standards," without regard to, or knowledge of, majority attitudes? Although the Court hoped to shift the burden of obscenity regulation back into the local communities, this ruling did not have that effect. As soon as prosecutors and police began to enforce local pornography regulations, defendants challenged the action in the federal courts as not representing the sense of the community. The first case of this kind that the Court received was an appeal of a decision in Atlanta, Georgia to stop the showing of the film *Carnal Knowledge.*[16] The Court ruled that the film was not obscene and thus brought itself back into the mad, mad world of pornography standards. In a companion case on the same day, the Court found that an *advertisement* for an illustrated version of the *Report of the Presidential Commission on Obscenity and Pornography* was hard core pornography.[17]

Both these cases illustrated that the Court was in trouble with its "community standards" doctrine. The Court had already begun to undermine its own guiding principles of local standards, the moment it agreed to hear the cases. When it overturned the community standard of Atlanta, it confirmed the division and uncertainty of the justices. They compounded the problem in 1975 by ruling that a list of books found to be obscene in Mobile, Alabama could not be used to arrest a bookseller in Birmingham.[18] Thus, even a community standard in one city in a state could not be applied in another. In 1976, the Court gave Detroit a 5-to-4 approval of its plan to zone one area of the city for adult theaters. Unfortunately, that act of helpfulness created new doubt about what local communities could do to contain or regulate offensive material.[19]

Although the Court could entirely abandon its efforts to regulate pornography and adopt a libertarian position, it does not seem inclined to do so.

[15] Miller v. California, 413 U.S. 15 (1973).

[16] Jenkins v. Georgia, 418 U.S. 153 (1974).

[17] Hamling v. U.S., 418 U.S. 87 (1974).

[18] McKinney v. Alabama, 424 U.S. 669 (1975).

[19] Young v. American Mini Theatres, 427 U.S. 50 (1976).

418

PART 4
outputs of the
political system:
who gets helped,
who gets hurt?

Not only would such a posture violate the ideology of some of the justices, it would certainly offend popular values in many American communities.[20] Although some would argue that this area of civil liberties is no more confused now than it was under the Warren Court,[21] no one can deny that it is highly confused.

Compared to pornography, however, much weightier problems develop in applying the First Amendment. Should information on social and political issues flow freely through the media? How much secret or classified information can be withheld from news sources? How staunchly may news people protect their sources of information?

In a stormy and controversial case involving publication of the Pentagon Papers (documents revealing misstatements and malpractices by U.S. military leaders), the Court held in a 6-to-3 vote with 9 separate opinions that the government did not have sufficient justification for stopping the *Washington Post* and *The New York Times* from publishing classified material on the U.S. role in Indochina. The material had been obtained and released by a Defense Department employee, Daniel Ellsberg. For his role in releasing the documents, Ellsberg became the subject of a smear campaign by Nixon aides and an "investigation," including a break-in at the office of his psychiatrist, to obtain Ellsberg's medical files. Holding that a free press was necessary for an enlightened people, the majority of the Court ruled that the *Post* and *Times* were within their rights to publish the material. In the view of Black, joined by Douglas, "The press was to serve the governed, not the governors. The government's power to censor the press was abolished so that the press would remain forever free to censure the government."[22]

Although "free to censure the government," the press has become increasingly concerned about the direction of the Burger Court in issues concerning its freedom. As in other areas of civil liberties, significant victories have been won, but these have been diluted by losses. One blow came to the press in the Court's split decision on the right of reporters to protect informants and to refuse to reveal secret information to grand juries. Investigative reporters had witnessed and written of people involved in the illegal manufacture and sale of drugs, but the reporters would not give the names of their sources or of the alleged criminals to grand jurors also investigating such crimes. Although the Court recognized that the First Amendment protects news gathering, it declared that "reporters, like other citizens [must] respond to relevant questions put to them in the course of a valid grand jury investigation or criminal trial."[23]

On the other hand, reporters had reason to be encouraged in 1976 when the Court ruled that a gag order was an unconstitutional prior restraint. The order had been issued by a judge in Nebraska, limiting what the press

---

[20] See Richard S. Randall, "Erotica and Community Standards: The Conflict of Elite and Democratic Values," in Stephen Wasby, ed., *Civil Liberties* (Lexington: Lexington Books, 1976), pp. 169–77.

[21] For this view see Lane Sunderland, *Obscenity* (Washington: American Enterprise Institute, 1975).

[22] *The New York Times* Company v. U.S., 403 U.S. 713 (1971).

[23] Branzburg v. Hayes, 408 U.S. 665 (1972).

419

CHAPTER 12
government
impact on the
rights and
liberties of
Americans

could say about pre-trial proceedings in a mass murder case.[24] Some members of the Court felt, however, that gag orders in limited or special circumstances might be constitutional. This caveat left news people concerned about future decisions involving gag orders.

The decision of the Burger Court most heavily criticized by the press came in 1979, when a majority of the justices decided that the Sixth Amendment's guarantee of a public trial does not apply to pretrial hearings.[25] The Court therefore rejected the plea that the press had a right to attend and report on a pretrial hearing. The case arose when a New York judge closed a hearing in which two defendants tried to "suppress" (have withheld as evidence) confessions they had made to a charge of second-degree murder. The Supreme Court upheld this decision on the ground that hearings on suppression of evidence present "special risks of unfairness" to defendants. In response to this decision, and to avoid prejudicial publicity, a number of other judges issued orders to exclude the press from hearings. As a result, an American Civil Liberties spokesman labeled it "one of the worst decisions of the Burger Court."

Before the Nixon appointees began their interpretations of the First Amendment, the law did not offer commercial speech the same protection given to expression of noncommercial beliefs. The Burger Court has changed precedents in this area to include some commercial speech within the First Amendment. In 1974 it overturned the conviction of a Virginia newspaper editor who printed an advertisement for an abortion referral agency,[26] but the Court did not directly say what kind of commercial speech was now to be protected. Its most important decision on this subject declared the unconstitutionality of a Virginia law prohibiting the advertisement of prescription drug prices. Advertising that is not misleading or false is thus protected.[27] This line of interpretation led to a 1977 decision striking down a law in Arizona that prevented advertising by lawyers.[28] Clearly the notion of unprotected commercial speech has passed from the legal scene; but because it still has not been given the same status as ordinary speech, how future cases may be adjudicated remains uncertain.

Freedom to differ

Periods of social anxiety and economic stress, especially following wars, have sometimes caused collective hysteria and political repression in the United States. During these times the great rights of freedom of speech, press, association, and dissent have suffered. The principle of free discussion was put to a severe test in the first decade of the Republic when the Federalists attempted

[24] Nebraska Press Association v. Stuart, 427 U.S. 539 (1976); also see Oklahoma Publishing Company v. District Court, 51 L. Ed. 355 (1977).

[25] Gannett Company v. DePasquale, 61 L. Ed. 608 (1979).

[26] Bigelow v. Virginia, 419 U.S. 1017 (1974).

[27] Virginia State Board of Pharmacy v. Virginia Citizens Consumer Council, Inc., 425 U.S. 748 (1976).

[28] Bates v. State Bar of Arizona, 433 U.S. 350 (1977).

420

PART 4
outputs of the
political system:
who gets helped,
who gets hurt?

to squelch the rising opposition of the Jeffersonian Republicans through the Alien and Sedition Acts of 1798. The victory of the Jeffersonian Republicans and the election of Thomas Jefferson in 1800 put a quick end to these acts. Not until World War I would Congress again try to control freedom of political expression. (In 1917, Congress passed an espionage act that was intended to restrict political dissent while the nation was at war.) In 1940, Congress passed the Smith Act, the first peace-time sedition act to be put on the books since the Alien and Sedition Acts of 1798. The act forbids verbal support of the violent overthrow of the government and conspiracies designed to cause this overthrow. The Smith Act was but a legislative expression of a growing illness in American society during and after the war. Irrational fears about enemy subversion from "within and without" created a witch hunting atmosphere, which was to blossom in the 1950s.

Although known to TV viewers as "The Happy Days," the 1950s are known to historians as the era of McCarthyism, when Senator Joseph McCarthy (R-Wisc.) led many members of Congress in a campaign against communism. At one point, at least half a dozen congressional committees were investigating un-American activities and subversives in all sectors of American society—university professors and public school teachers, Hollywood actors, writers and directors, news reporters and editors, clergymen, and especially former New Dealers. Informers and witnesses, many of them ex-Communists, appeared before congressional committees to give testimony about Communists, Communist sympathizers, fellow travelers, and "liberals." Those who refused to cooperate with the committees were liable to be held in contempt of Congress, and those who failed to tell the whole truth about their past or present political associations could be tried for perjury. For many, the "pitiless publicity" became harsh punishment involving loss of job, impairment of professional reputation, and strong disapproval in their communities.[29]

In 1950, Congress passed a comprehensive Internal Security Act. This act set up a Subversive Activities Control Board charged with determining, at the request of the Attorney General, whether a particular organization is Communist "action," Communist "front," or Communist "infiltrated." It required every Communist organization to register each year with the Attorney General, report the names of its officers and members, identify the sources of all its funds, and label Communist propaganda all its publications sent through the mails or across state lines. Also according to this act, members of Communist organizations could not obtain passports, hold elective national positions, serve as officers or employees of a labor union, or work in a defense plant.

Over the years, the Supreme Court pursued a somewhat irregular course in its review of the Communist cases, reflecting changes in the makeup of the Court as well as changes in the political environment. The Supreme Court upheld the Smith Act in the highly dramatic *Dennis* case (1951), which sprang

---

[29] For an account of "the extraordinary career of the House Committee on Un-American Activities" from the 1930s to the 1960s, see Walter Goodman, *The Committee* (New York: Farrar, 1969).

from the conviction of 11 top U.S. Communists who had violated the act.[30]
The majority of the Court viewed the role of the Communist party in the
United States as "a well organized nationwide conspiracy."

Justices Douglas and Black dissented vigorously in the *Dennis* case.
Douglas could see no "clear and present danger" in the Communist party:

Some nations less resilient than the United States, where illiteracy is high and where
democratic traditions are only budding, might have to take drastic steps and jail these
men for merely speaking this creed. But in America they are miserable merchants
of unwanted ideas: their wares remain unsold.

The majority of the Court were unconvinced. The Smith Act was allowed
to stand. In 1957, however, the Court adopted the "clear and present danger"
standard to decide if a speech was seditious. It held that "advocacy and teaching of forcible overthrow as an abstract principle, divorced from any effort
to investigate action to that end" was not sedition and was protected by the
First Amendment.[31] Later it held that one's advocacy to overthrow would
have to incite "imminent lawless action" before punishment for such advocacy
could be confirmed.[32]

In 1961, the Court considered the membership clause of the Smith Act.
In a lengthy and complicated opinion, Justice Harlan upheld the conviction
of an *active* member of the Communist party, who had *knowledge* of the
party's illegal purpose and specific intent to overthrow the government of
the United States. In the same term, the Court also upheld the registration
requirements of the Internal Security Act of 1950.[33] Justice Frankfurter, speaking for a majority of five, found that the act neither violated the First Amendment freedoms nor constituted a bill of attainder. Justice Black argued in
dissent that "freedom of speech, petition, and assembly guaranteed by the
First Amendment must be accorded to the ideas we hate, or sooner or later
they will be denied to the ideas we cherish."

Later in the 1960s, the judges became less inclined to accept restrictions
on the rights of Communists. In 1964, the Supreme Court struck down the
section of the Internal Security Act that prohibited the issuance of U.S. passports to American Communists: "[The section] sweeps too widely and too
indiscriminately across the liberty guaranteed by the Fifth Amendment."[34]

In 1965, the Court invalidated a statute that made it a crime for a member
of the Communist party to serve as an officer or employee of a labor union.[35]
Chief Justice Warren declared that the statute was, in effect, a bill of attainder
inflicting punishment without trial. The Court next ruled that the requirement
of registration as Communists imposed upon individual members was a viola-

---

[30] Dennis v. United States, 341 U.S. 494 (1951).

[31] Yates v. United States, 354 U.S. 298 (1957).

[32] Brandenburgh v. Ohio, 395 U.S. 444 (1969).

[33] Communist Party of U.S. v. Subversive Activities Board, 367 U.S. 1 (1961).

[34] Aptheker v. Secretary of State, 378 U.S. 500 (1964).

[35] United States v. Brown, 381 U.S. 437 (1965).

421

CHAPTER 12
government
impact on the
rights and
liberties of
Americans

422

PART 4
outputs of the
political system:
who gets helped,
who gets hurt?

tion of the constitutional guarantee against self-incrimination.[36] This decision ended compulsory registration of *individual* Communists, so long as the Smith Act (or other legislation) retains criminal penalties for membership in the Communist party. Finally, in 1967, when the Circuit Court of the District of Columbia held that the registration requirement for Communist *organizations* was also a violation of the Fifth Amendment, the Justice Department, worn out by 15 years of litigation, gave up on efforts to enforce the registration requirement.

The Burger Court has handled very little freedom of association litigation of the kind faced by the Warren Court. It has upheld the right of the Attorney General to refuse to permit a Marxist professor to enter this country to give lectures[37] but has prohibited state bar associations from requiring applicants to give lists of their organizational memberships before admission to the bar.[38] Although the Burger Court has been more conservative on national security questions than was the Warren Court, it has certainly not returned to a supportive position for Smith Act advocates. In this respect, the Nixon appointees have been a disappointment to ultraconservative interests in American society.

In the late 1960s and early '70s, discontent in America moved to university and college campuses and thousands of students expressed their differences with a society they viewed as war-mongering, fat, racist, technocratic, middle-class, and polluted. Their protests were action oriented, intended to change policy, not gradually but immediately.

Data from 1969 show that 292 major student protests occurred on U.S. campuses, over half of which involved black students' demands and a fourth of which involved violence.[39] The most frequent demands were for black recognition and an increase in student power in university decision making. In the early period of student protests, only 2 percent of the protests called for an end to the Vietnam war and an end to the draft. War issues became more central in the spring of 1970, when the United States invaded Cambodia. Initially, however, the issues were overwhelmingly academic and racial, transferring to educational institutions many of the frustrations of blacks that showed up earlier in urban protests and confrontations.

Legislatures and courts were generally slow in responding to campus unrest. However, the increased disruptions and violence brought state legislatures into the role of spokesman for the electorate and active participant in the conflict. With only one exception, all legislation passed in this period was negative toward students; it was often repressive toward disruptive faculty and administrators as well. State legislatures came down solidly against disruptive "freedom of expression" and in support of traditional definitions of the role of the university and the normal power structure by which university policies are determined. In so doing, in many instances they redefined the

---

[36] Albertson v. Subversive Activities Control Board, 382 U.S. 70 (1965).

[37] Kleindeinst v. Mandel, 408 U.S. 753 (1972).

[38] Baird v. Arizona, 401 U.S. 1 (1971).

[39] Material for this section is taken from *Student Protests 1969* (Chicago: Urban Research Corporation, 1970) and *Legislative Response to Student Protest* (Chicago: Urban Research Corporation, 1970).

legislature's role in the politics of education, to make them instruments of state power against violent or disruptive dissent.

423

CHAPTER 12
government
impact on the
rights and
liberties of
Americans

Revolution, however celebrated in the American past, is not a right guaranteed by the First Amendment. Accordingly, "symbolic" expressions of dissent, such as throwing rocks, destroying academic records, blowing up military research centers, and "trashing" campuses have not been protected by the courts. As Justice Black observed, "The Constitution does not confer upon any group the right to substitute rule by force for rule by law. Force leads to violence, violence to mob conflicts, and these to rule by the strongest groups with control of the most deadly weapons." Although the court upheld a federal law prohibiting the destruction of draft cards,[40] it did hold that pupils in public schools had the right to wear black armbands during school to protest the Vietnam war.[41] In addition, it has held that a state law making it a crime to cast contempt on the American flag was unconstitutional and that wearing a flag on the seat of one's pants was acceptable symbolic protest behavior, as was displaying the flag with a peace symbol taped on top of it.[42]

If American history is any guide, we can be certain that protests will emerge in the future, as strongly and as violently as they did in the 1960s, to disappear as quietly and unexpectedly as they did in the fall of 1970. We cannot predict what form the right to differ will take; but we can expect that if economic, political, and social rights are not transformed from talk to reality, one right—that of dissent and protest—will be an ever present feature of our political system.

Religious freedom and liberty of conscience

The only reference to religion in the original Constitution is in Article VI, which prohibits religious tests for offices in the national government. But the First Amendment, which has been called "the First Article of our Faith," says, "Congress shall make no law respecting an establishment of religion, or prohibiting the free exercise thereof." The primary purpose of this amendment was to prohibit the establishment of a favored national church such as the Anglican Church in England. Since several states had tax-supported religious institutions, however, it was generally understood that the First Amendment restricted only the national government and not the states on religious matters. The Anglican Church had been separated from the government in Maryland, the Carolinas, Georgia, and Virginia during the Revolution. But all the New England states except Rhode Island continued to give preferred status to the Congregational Church. Not until 1833 did Massachusetts amend its constitution to place all religious denominations on an equal footing. For many years, New Hampshire, New Jersey, Massachusetts, and North Caro-

---

[40] U.S. v. O'Brien, 391 U.S. 367 (1968).

[41] Tinker v. Des Moines Independent Community School District, 393 U.S. 503 (1969).

[42] Street v. New York, 394 U.S. 576 (1969) and Smith v. Goguen, 415 U.S. 566 (1974); Spence v. Washington, 418 U.S. 405 (1974).

424

PART 4
outputs of the
political system:
who gets helped,
who gets hurt?

lina required that officeholders be Protestants. Delaware and even Pennsylvania (which had a Bill of Rights affirming the unalienable right of all men to worship God according to the dictates of their own conscience) disqualified Jews and other non-Christians for public office.

Because "liberty" under the Fourteenth Amendment has been interpreted by the Supreme Court to include all the basic freedoms specified in the First Amendment, the basic relationship between church and state as defined for the national government in the First Amendment now also applies to state governments. In other words, neither Congress nor the states may establish a church or prohibit the free exercise of religion. This does not mean, however, that government cannot regulate religious practices that may offend public morals, jeopardize public health, or in other ways endanger the public welfare. In such cases, the police power of the state is paramount to the dictates of individual conscience.

In the first 150 years after the adoption of the First Amendment, the Supreme Court decided only one important case on freedom of religion. Congress had passed a law making polygamy (the practice of having more than one wife) a crime in the Territory of Utah. Under this law a Mormon who had two wives, in conformity with the doctrine of his church, was tried and convicted. The Supreme Court upheld the statute, ruling that although laws may not interfere with religious beliefs and opinions, they may control religious practices which are "in violation of social duties or subversive of good order."[43]

Most of the constitutional law on both the free exercise of religion and the separation of church and state dates from the 1940s, and nearly all of the cases concern state laws rather than acts of Congress. In 1972, for example, the Court overturned a Wisconsin education law requiring school attendance until age 16, because it violated religious beliefs of the Amish.[44] The famous *Flag Salute* case, decided when the nation was at war in 1943, indicates the high priority that we officially accord to an individual's religious beliefs, even when these run counter to prevailing patriotic sentiments. When children brought up in the faith of Jehovah's Witnesses refused to salute the flag as part of the daily exercises in Americanism prescribed for the public schools in West Virginia, the Supreme Court upheld the right of the children to follow the dictates of their religion.[45] In a still memorable opinion, reversing an earlier decision, Justice Jackson spoke for the majority of the Court:

If there is any fixed star in our constitutional constellation, it is that no official, high or petty, can prescribe what shall be orthodox in politics, nationalism, religion or other matters of opinion or force citizens to confess by word or act their faith therein. If there are any circumstances which permit an exception they do not now occur to us.

[43] Reynolds v. U.S., 98 U.S. 145 (1878).
[44] Wisconsin v. Yoder, 406 U.S. 205 (1972).
[45] West Virginia State Board of Education v. Barnette, 319 U.S. 624 (1943).

A flag salute ceremony is common in American schoolrooms, as shown by these Eskimo children, but cannot be required if it violates religious convictions.

The number of church-state questions that go into court attest to the variety of opinions that Americans hold on the meaning of religious freedom. In 1962, the Supreme Court declared that it was unconstitutional for the New York State Board of Regents to prescribe a prayer as part of the daily exercise in the New York public schools. Even though the Board of Regents claimed that the prayer was "nondenominational" and even though students who did not wish to participate in the exercise were permitted to remain silent or be excused from the schoolroom, the Court held that such an officially established prayer program violated the "establishment," prohibition, and the "free exercise" guarantee of the First Amendment.[46]

[46] The prayer in question read, "Almighty God, we acknowledge our dependence upon Thee, and we beg Thy blessings upon us, on our parents, our teachers, and our country." Engel v. Vitale, 370 U.S. 42 (1962).

426

PART 4
outputs of the
political system:
who gets helped,
who gets hurt?

In 1963, the Court struck down a Pennsylvania statute that called for "at least ten verses from the Holy Bible to be read without comment at the opening of each public school on each school day." (Any child was excused from the exercise upon written request of his parent or guardian.) For a non-Christian, the phrase "the Holy Bible" would no doubt be enough to demonstrate that the law approved a particular religion. The Court declared the Pennsylvania law unconstitutional, holding that the "establishment" and "free exercise" stipulations in the First Amendment require the government to be strictly neutral in matters of religion, "protecting all, preferring none, disparaging none."[47]

The Court's decisions in the prayer cases—"taking God out of the schools"—outraged many people and stirred heated controversy in press and pulpit, in Congress and in state legislatures. Some groups advocated passing a constitutional amendment to prohibit the Court from interfering with state educational policies, so that school children would not be deprived of moral instruction. On the other hand, leaders of the major denominational groups generally supported the Court's doctrine of governmental neutrality with respect to religious activities. As a matter of practice, many public schools still require the flag salute and include prayers in their daily exercises. Supreme Court decisions are not self-enforcing and few parents, even within the non-Christian minority, resent the many biases in favor of Christianity enough to sue their local school board. Both the financial costs of litigation and the psychological costs that must be paid by the children of such parents are enough to keep most parents silent.

To the intense dissatisfaction of the tiny minority who want strict separation of church and state, the American government has always officially encouraged religious practices and offered special concessions to churches. By act of Congress, the pledge of allegiance to the United States is made to "one nation under God." The currency of the country carries the national motto, "In God We Trust." The Supreme Court of the United States opens each session with the intonement, "God save the United States and this Honorable Court." Each house of Congress appoints a chaplain who invokes divine blessings and prays for God's guidance in the daily proceedings. Chaplains are attached to all the armed forces of the United States. Thanksgiving, Christmas, and Easter are observed in every community in the country. The Bible is commonly used in taking court oaths, usually ending in "so help me God."

The official "wall of separation" between church and state appears easy to penetrate when it comes to property rights, tax exemptions, and public assistance to churches. Back in the 1920s, Oregon passed a law requiring that all children attend the Oregon public schools; in effect, this law would have eliminated all private and parochial schools. Without referring directly to any religious rights involved, the United States Supreme Court held the law invalid under the Fourteenth Amendment, on the grounds that it was a seizure of private property without due process of law. More recently, on

---

[47] School District of Abington Township v. Schempp, 374 U.S. 203 (1963), and Murray v. Curlett (1963).

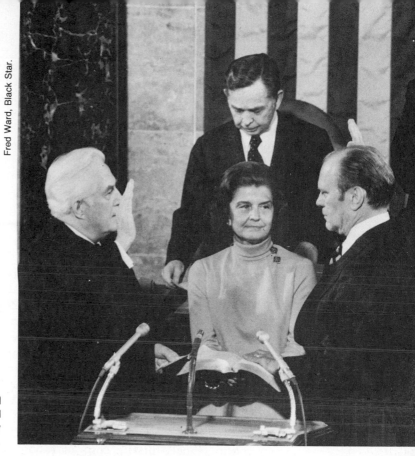

Despite the proclaimed separation of church and state, Bibles are routinely used in political ceremonies.

grounds of public safety, the Supreme Court has sustained a New Jersey statute permitting free bus transportation for school children to parochial and other private schools as well as to public schools. And in a highly controversial decision in 1968, the Court upheld the constitutionality of New York's use of tax revenue to provide secular textbooks to children in parochial schools.[48]

Church property used for religious purposes is exempt from taxation by all 50 states and the District of Columbia. A citizen of New York, claiming that tax exemption for church property resulted in higher taxes on his property, challenged the exemption in New York courts as a violation of the First Amendment prohibition on establishment of religion. The U.S. Supreme Court, hearing the case on appeal, found "no genuine nexus [connection] between tax exemption and establishment of religion." Chief Justice Burger viewed it as merely an expression of the state's "benevolent neutrality" toward religion.[49] Because only Justice Douglas dissented, tax exemption of church property has thus been legitimized as public policy.

In recent years, Congress has passed numerous laws providing for loans and grants for buildings and educational programs in institutions of higher

[48] Pierce v. Society of the Sisters of Holy Names of Jesus and Mary, 268 U.S. 510; Everson v. Board of Education, 330 U.S. 1 (1947); Board of Education v. Allen, 392 U.S. 236 (1968).
[49] Walz v. Tax Commission of the City of New York, 397 U.S. 664 (1970).

427

428

PART 4
outputs of the
political system:
who gets helped,
who gets hurt?

learning, including sectarian colleges and universities, with the provision that the public funds not be used for religious purposes; e.g., chapels. In 1965, for the first time, Congress extended national aid to elementary and secondary church schools in poverty areas. Much of the attention of the Burger Court in church-state questions has been directed to the constitutionality of these governmental programs of financial assistance to religious education.

In a 5-to-4 decision in 1971, the Court upheld the Higher Education Facilities Act of 1963 under which the national government made grants for the construction of college buildings, even though colleges with religious affiliations were included. The Court held that so long as the buildings were used solely for secular educational purposes, the grants did not violate the First Amendment.[50] The Court extended this interpretation in 1973[51] and 1976[52] from national to state grants that included religious institutions. Justice Blackmun concluded that "Religious institutions need not be quarantined from public benefits that are neutrally available to all."

In a somewhat contradictory line of reasoning, the Court has been far less permissive with regard to state aid to church schools at the secondary and elementary levels. It invalidated New York grants to nonpublic schools for maintenance and repair, reimbursement of tuition for children from low-income families in parochial schools, and tax credits for tuition payments by parents not at the poverty level.[53] Justice Powell defended this decision on the ground that the repair grants might be used for religious facilities and that the tax and tuition grants created an "entangling relationship between church and state." On the same day, the Court invalidated a law which paid nonpublic schools for the costs of record keeping required by state law.[54] Expressing continuing concern about the excessive entanglement of the government with church schools, the Court found unconstitutional a Pennsylvania law allowing the state to loan them instructional equipment or to provide them with auxiliary staff.[55]

In the late '70s, the Court tried to apply a three-way test to the financial transactions between state governments and church-related education. The law in question must

1. reflect a clearly secular legislative purpose
2. have a primary effect that neither advances nor inhibits religion
3. avoid excessive government entanglement with religion

Although the test seems straightforward enough, it has proven to be somewhat less than easy to apply. Other questions and future litigation remain for the Court of the '80s to answer in establishment of religion cases.

[50] Tilton v. Richardson, 403 U.S. 672 (1971).
[51] Hunt v. McNair, 413 U.S. 734 (1973).
[52] Roemer v. Maryland Board of Public Works, 423 U.S. 736 (1976).
[53] Committee for Public Education and Religious Liberty v. Nyquist, 413 U.S. 756 (1973).
[54] Levitt v. Committee for Public Education and Religious Liberty, 413 U.S. 472 (1973).
[55] Meek v. Pittinger, 421 U.S. 349 (1975).

The First Amendment protects religious convictions, but whether it protects convictions based on conscientious feelings *not* grounded in religion is a matter of long controversy. Every draft law has provided for exemption of conscientious objectors, with the specification that such objectors must believe in a "Supreme Being." In a 1965 case, however, the Supreme Court interpreted the "Supreme Being" clause as including any belief which was sincere and meaningful and occupied a place in the individual's life comparable to a belief in God.[56] In 1968, in order to narrow the interpretation of the Supreme Court, Congress struck the "Supreme Being" clause from the revised Selective Service Act. It specified instead that no one should be exempted because of a merely personal code or for political, sociological, or philosophical views but only "by reason of religious training and belief." Nevertheless, the Supreme Court held in 1970 that all persons whose consciences are spurred by deeply held moral, ethical, or religious beliefs are entitled to exemption even if they expressly disavow any religious basis for their objection to participation in war.[57]

The defendant's rights

Justice Frankfurter once said that "the history of liberty has largely been the history of observance of procedural guarantees." The constitutional requirements of due process of law in the Bill of Rights are quite specific. They represent the procedures under English common law that were considered basic to a "government of laws and not men."

These requirements are set forth in the following amendments:

IV. The right of the people to be secure in their persons, houses, papers, and effects, against unreasonable searches and seizures

V. Indictment by grand jury for capital or otherwise infamous crime, the restriction upon double jeopardy, and immunity against self-incrimination

VI. The right to a speedy and public trial, by an impartial jury in the state and the district where the crime was committed, the right to be informed of the nature and cause of the accusation, the right of the accused to be confronted with the witnesses against him, the right to obtain witnesses in his favor, and the right to counsel

VIII. Protection against excessive fines and cruel or unusual punishments

The Supreme Court has assumed that since the Fourteenth Amendment guarantees, "nor shall any State deprive any person of life, liberty, or property, without due process of law," the "liberty" includes the rights of the First Amendment in the cases discussed above. The Court has never been willing to concede, however, that all the procedural rights from the Bill of Rights (quoted in the paragraph above) are included in the Fourteenth Amendment's guarantee of "due process of law."

[56] U.S. v. Seeger, 380 U.S. 163 (1965).
[57] Welsh v. U.S., 398 U.S. 333 (1970).

429

CHAPTER 12
government
impact on the
rights and
liberties of
Americans

430

PART 4
outputs of the
political system:
who gets helped,
who gets hurt?

In 1937, in the case of *Palko v. Connecticut,* Justice Cardozo attempted to define and explain the procedural rights in the American federal system.[58] A rather unsavory character, Frank Palko had been tried for first degree murder in a Connecticut court, was convicted of murder in the second degree, and sentenced to life imprisonment. Under Connecticut law, the state was able to appeal the case and secure a new trial. Palko objected to a new trial on the ground that it would constitute double jeopardy within the meaning of the Fifth Amendment. Nevertheless, he was retried and sentenced to death. Palko's lawyer appealed to the Supreme Court that "whatever is forbidden by the Fifth Amendment is forbidden by the Fourteenth also." The Supreme Court rejected the appeal and accepted the verdict in the second trial.

Justice Cardozo perceived a "wavering and broken line" between the guarantees in the Bill of Rights that were binding on the states and those that were not so binding. As he explained it, those guarantees that are of "the very essence of a scheme of ordered liberty" were absorbed by the due process clause of the Fourteenth Amendment, but those less fundamental in the Anglo-Saxon tradition of justice were not carried to the states by that amendment. To Justice Cardozo, the fact that Connecticut placed one of its citizens in double jeopardy "is not cruelty at all, nor even vexation in any immoderate degree." To Frank Palko, however, double jeopardy meant the difference between life and death. He was executed.

Even before 1937, the judges had held that due process of law in the states need not include grand jury indictment, jury trial in either criminal or civil cases, or protection against self-incrimination, although these are constitutional rights against the national government. Relying on the Palko decision, states could continue to follow their own practices in the administration of justice so long as these practices did not "shock the conscience of the community" or violate the canons of "civilized decency." For almost a quarter of a century, Justice Cardozo's opinion swayed Supreme Court decisions, although some of the justices maintained that the double standard of justice (demanding for the national government, more lax for the states) was a wrong interpretation of the Constitution. In many dissenting opinions they argued that the Fourteenth Amendment was intended to nationalize all of the privileges, protections, and safeguards granted by the Bill of Rights.

Beginning with the 1960s, a new spirit of judicial activism altered the double standard. Case by case, the Supreme Court began to nationalize the procedural rights in the Bill of Rights. In 1961, the Court held that the Fourth Amendment's protection against unreasonable searches and seizures extended to the states; therefore, evidence unlawfully seized could not be used as evidence in state courts.[59] Justice Clark observed that the exclusionary rule (the exclusion of evidence illegally seized) "makes very good sense. . . . There is no war between the Constitution and common sense." But what looks like common sense to one Court may look like "coddling criminals" to another.

[58] 302 U.S. 319 (1937).
[59] Mapp v. Ohio, 367 U.S. 643 (1961).

Chief Justice Burger expressed strong objections to the manner in which the exclusionary rule was applied by the Warren Court. As a result, he has been instrumental in significantly limiting the rule's application. It is his hope that it will be used only "for a small and limited category of cases." Thus, the Court has weakened the exclusionary rule by reducing the number of situations in which it is applied (not applying it, for example, to evidence presented to grand juries) and by permitting more "harmless error" to enter into proceedings even when the rule does apply.[60] In more than a dozen cases, the Burger Court has made significant departures from the Warren Court's expansion of Fourth Amendment rights, creating, according to the dissents of Justices Marshall and Brennan, "the continual evisceration of Fourth Amendment safeguards."

In 1962, the Supreme Court in effect nationalized the Eighth Amendment's guarantees against cruel and unusual punishment. At issue was a California statute that made drug addiction a crime punishable by a mandatory jail sentence. Justice Stewart, who delivered the opinion for the Court majority, felt that jailing a person for drug addiction was akin to jailing someone for mental or physical illness—"a cruel and unusual punishment."[61]

In the celebrated case of Clarence Gideon, the Court reversed a decision it rendered 21 years earlier. It ruled that a state must furnish counsel (a lawyer) to poor persons accused of noncapital offenses.[62] Gideon had been sentenced to serve a 5-year term in a Florida prison after he had unsuccessfully conducted his own defense in a jury trial. He was charged with breaking and entering a poolroom, with intent to commit a misdemeanor. Without funds of his own, he had been unable to hire a lawyer; and under Florida law, only a person charged with a capital offense was entitled to a public defender. The Supreme Court ruled that "in our adversary system of criminal justice, any person haled into court, who is too poor to hire a lawyer, cannot be assured a fair trial unless counsel is provided for him." Gideon's case was sent back to the Florida court for retrial with counsel, and Gideon was found not guilty. Right of counsel now extends to all proceedings in which the defendant could spend time in jail, but does not cover charges in which the only punishment is a fine.[63] It is also required for each stage of the proceeding, from arrest through appeal.[64]

431

CHAPTER 12
government
impact on the
rights and
liberties of
Americans

[60] For some of the many opinions see U.S. v. Calandra, 414 U.S. 338 (1974); U.S. v. Janis, 428 U.S. 433 (1976); Stone v. Powell, 428 U.S. 465 (1976).

[61] Robinson v. California, 370 U.S. 660 (1962).

[62] Gideon v. Wainright, 372 U.S. 335 (1963) *reversed* Betts v. Brady, 316 U.S. 455 (1942). Gideon had made his petition to the Supreme Court in a handwritten note on prison stationery. *In forma pauperis* (in the manner of a pauper) is a proceeding whereby any citizen has a right to proceed in any federal court without payment of fees upon execution of a pauper's oath. The best-seller *Gideon's Trumpet,* written by Anthony Lewis, former Supreme Court reporter for *The New York Times* (New York: Random House, 1964), helped to celebrate the case.

[63] Orgesinger v. Hamilton, 407 U.S. 25 (1972).

[64] Brewer v. Williams, 430 U.S. 387 (1977); Geders v. U.S., 425 U.S. 80 (1976); *but the Burger Court held that no appointed counsel is required on discretionary appeals:* Russ v. Moffit, 417 U.S. 600 (1974).

432

PART 4
outputs of the
political system:
who gets helped,
who gets hurt?

In 1964, the Supreme Court did away with still more of the double standard. Overruling longstanding precedents, the Court held that safeguards against self-incrimination were also incorporated in the Fourteenth Amendment. In a Connecticut case, a prisoner convicted of gambling was ordered to testify further in a court-ordered inquiry into gambling and other criminal activities. When the prisoner claimed constitutional rights against self-incrimination, Connecticut judges informed him that the Fourteenth Amendment "extended no privilege to him." But a majority of 5 justices on the U.S. Supreme Court took a different view.[65] In the words of Justice Brennan, who spoke for the Court:

The Fourteenth Amendment secures against state invasion the same privilege that the Fifth Amendment guarantees against federal infringement—the right of a person to remain silent unless he chooses to speak in the unfettered exercise of his own free will, and to suffer no penalty . . . for such silence.

The Supreme Court unanimously decided that "the Sixth Amendment's right of an accused to confront witnesses against him is likewise a fundamental right and is made obligatory on the states by the Fourteenth Amendment."[66] The decision overruled a Texas conviction partly based on transcribed evidence by a witness who had moved out of the state. The witness therefore did not appear at the trial.

In *Miranda v. Arizona*, the Supreme Court reviewed the whole issue of police court procedures relating to constitutional rights.[67] The majority of the Court ruled that individuals held for interrogation have a right to a lawyer and to have that lawyer present the first time they are questioned. Moreover, if the suspects cannot afford a lawyer, the court must appoint one for them. The individual must be informed of these rights. To be accepted as evidence, confessions must be given freely and voluntarily, after the accused has been allowed counsel.

Conservatives protested this expansion of the rights of defendants in criminal cases. After the election of Richard Nixon they hoped for a reversal of Warren Court decisions. In this regard the Burger Court has been mildly disappointing. It has not expanded criminal defendant rights, but neither has it overturned Warren Court precedents. It *has* increasingly put restrictions on the Warren Court rulings. For example, it has drawn back from a full application of *Miranda,* holding that statements made by a defendant not informed of his rights could be used in court under limited circumstances to show that the defendant was lying.[68] With some anger, Justice Brennan has warned that the 5-member majority is undoing what the Warren Court achieved in requiring police to follow the Constitution when arresting suspects. Despite the Brennan view, the Court continues to allow incriminating evidence

[65] Malloy v. Hogan, 378 U.S. 1 (1964).

[66] Pointer v. Texas, 380 U.S. 400 (1965); *also* Davis v. Alaska, 415 U.S. 308 (1972).

[67] 384 U.S. 436 (1966).

[68] Harris v. New York, 401 U.S. 222 (1971).

based on statements made without observance of the full rights specified in the *Miranda* case.[69] It has thus nibbled away at defendants' rights without going as far as "get-tough" advocates had hoped.

The Burger Court's most momentous struggle has been with the question of the death penalty. The court split 5 to 4 in *Furman v. Georgia*,[70] declaring that capital punishment as practiced in all 50 states was unconstitutional— "cruel and unusual punishment in violation of the Eighth and Fourteenth Amendments." But all four Nixon appointees were in dissent, and the 5-man majority stopped short of declaring capital punishment, as such, cruel and unusual. Justices Brennan and Marshall could not convince the other three members on the majority to join them in declaring the death penalty *inherently* unconstitutional. In an eloquent statement against all capital punishment, Brennan wrote:

The punishment of death is inconsistent with . . . four principles: Death is an unusually severe and degrading punishment; there is a strong possibility that it is inflicted arbitrarily; its rejection by contemporary society is virtually total; and there is no reason to believe it serves any penal purpose more effectively than the less severe punishment of imprisonment. The function of these principles is to enable a court to determine whether a punishment comports with human dignity: death, quite simply, does not.

The Court majority would not follow the absolute ban. Instead, it ruled that existing state laws gave judges and juries so much discretion in handing down the death sentence that it has been imposed "wantonly and freakishly." It became "cruel and unusual in the same way that being struck by lightning is cruel and unusual." After this decision, 35 states passed new capital punishment laws, some making the death sentence required for certain crimes, others specifying clearer standards to guide judges and juries in deciding when the death penalty should be imposed.

Congress added to the support for capital punishment in 1974 by passing a law that allowed the death penalty for hijacking an airplane if someone died as a result of the hijacking. In 1976, the Supreme Court upheld the death penalty in three cases in which state laws (of Florida, Georgia, and Texas)[71] set forth clear standards, but the Court also ruled unconstitutional two mandatory death penalty laws (of Louisiana and North Carolina).[72] A mandatory death sentence departs from current concepts of human dignity and decency in that it is "unduly harsh and unworkably rigid." On the other hand, with a majority of states and Congress having passed new laws calling for capital punishment, the Court concluded that "it is now evident that a large proportion of American society continues to regard it as an appropriate and necessary criminal sanction." The Court did rule that the death penalty for rape of an adult woman was excessive and implied (but did not rule) that the death penalty may be properly imposed only in crimes resulting in the

---

[69] See Michigan v. Tucker, 417 U.S. 433 (1974) and Oregon v. Hass, 420 U.S. 714 (1975).

[70] 408 U.S. 238 (1972).

[71] Gregg v. Georgia, 428 U.S. 153 (1976); Proffitt v. Florida, 428 U.S. 242 (1976); Jurek v. Texas, 428 U.S. 262 (1976).

[72] Woodson v. North Carolina, 428 U.S. 380 (1976); Roberts v. Louisiana, 428 U.S. 325 (1976).

433

CHAPTER 12
government
impact on the
rights and
liberties of
Americans

Amid intense opposition, a majority of state legislatures have passed new capital punishment laws.

death of the victim.[73] Whether the evolving concepts of dignity and decency will some day reject killing as "cruel and unusual punishment" remains to be seen. In these cases, the Court threw that determination back to the people and their state legislature. Since the decisions, the people of Utah and Florida have executed two prisoners.

EQUAL PROTECTION OF THE LAWS

Like the liberties we have considered to this point, the right to equal protection of the laws is guaranteed in the Constitution. Among other things, the Fourteenth Amendment says, "No State shall . . . deny to any person

[73] Coker v. Georgia, 53 L.Ed.2nd. 982 (1977).

within its jurisdiction the equal protection of the laws." This guarantee differs from those in the original Bill of Rights, however, in two ways: it was adopted to protect people against abuse by state governments rather than by the national government; it is more broadly stated than the more specific guarantees in the Bill of Rights. As a result of both these features, the promise of "equal protection of the laws" has been used to expand the rights of all individuals, but especially the disadvantaged, in relation to state governments.

435

CHAPTER 12
government
impact on the
rights and
liberties of
Americans

Equal protection by court decisions

The guarantee of "equal protection of the laws" was designed to extend the same civil rights to all persons without regard to race or color. Specifically, Congress intended to remove any doubts about the constitutional validity of the civil rights legislation it had passed during Reconstruction, to protect blacks. Ironically, the Supreme Court subsequently denied this specific intent in the *Civil Rights Cases* (1883).[74] In these cases, the Court held unconstitutional the Civil Rights Act of 1875, which guaranteed the right of persons within the jurisdiction of the United States to the full and equal enjoyment of hotels, public transportation, theaters, and other places of amusement.

The logic of the Court in nullifying the Civil Rights Act of 1875 seems tortured. The justices of that day (all, of course, white) denied that the Fourteenth Amendment gave Congress power to deal directly with violations of civil rights by private individuals or businesses, even those offering public accommodations. Instead, they narrowed the meaning of the amendment to permit Congress merely to enact corrective legislation that might be needed to counteract state laws violating civil rights (as if the courts were not obliged to declare such state acts unconstitutional). The Fourteenth Amendment was thus reduced to a protection against state governments only, not against private establishments, and the Congress was reduced to the role of overturning unfair state actions rather than being allowed to protect civil rights in a positive way.

In its own rulings on matters of race relations, the Supreme Court long bowed to the preferences of the dominant white elements in southern states. So long as the letter of the Constitution was observed in a formal sense, blacks could be singled out by law for different treatment, including state-enforced segregation. For many years, southern states counted on the courts to hold that laws requiring separate facilities for "white" and "colored" met the constitutional standard of equal protection of the laws so long as the facilities seemed to be equal. The leading case was *Plessy v. Ferguson*, which involved a Louisiana statute that required white and black passengers to ride in separate railway carriages. Plessy, a citizen of the United States, described as having "seven-eighths Caucasian and one-eighth African blood," attacked the constitutionality of the act. Plessy had been arrested for refusing to leave a coach reserved for whites and to take a seat in another coach assigned to blacks. He claimed

---

[74] Civil Rights Cases, 109 U.S. 3 (1883).

436

PART 4
outputs of the
political system:
who gets helped,
who gets hurt?

that such a legal requirement violated his constitutional rights under the Fourteenth Amendment. The Court upheld the Louisiana law, declaring that *"in the nature of things* [the Fourteenth Amendment] could not have been intended to abolish distinctions based upon color, or to enforce social, as distinguished from political, equality, or a commingling of the two races upon terms unsatisfactory to either."[75]

The justices of the Court made no effort in *Plessy v. Ferguson* to document their own sense of "the nature of things" with the findings of sociology, psychology, or philosophy. Instead, they relied on their own assumption that racial prejudice cannot be overcome by constitutional restrictions. They simply bypassed the argument that Plessy was seeking restrictions on behavior rather than beliefs. Justice John Marshall Harlan, the lone dissenter, was "of opinion that the statute of Louisiana is inconsistent with the personal liberty of citizens, white and black, in the United States."[76] The doctrine of separate but equal, established in *Plessy v. Ferguson*, long gave constitutional support, however, to laws of southern states that required racial segregation (with "equal accommodations") in public transportation, public schools, and public meeting places.

Beginning in the 1930s, under the New Deal, black groups began to press their claims in a whole series of lawsuits for equal protection of the laws. The first major breakthrough came in the field of public education. In 1938 the Court held that a state must offer equal educational facilities to blacks and whites and do so within the state. The states—Missouri in this case—could no longer claim to be treating blacks "equally" by giving them scholarships to go out of state for professional training available to whites within the state. The Court ruled that a state must give all its citizens equal privileges regardless of race.[77] The effect of this decision was to improve educational facilities for blacks in the southern states, though the facilities were still kept separate and were still, in fact, inferior instead of equal.

In 1950, the Supreme Court virtually abandoned the doctrine of "separate but equal" in higher education. It upheld the claim of a black graduate student at the University of Oklahoma that he had been denied equal protection. Although allowed to attend the university, he had been required to sit apart from white students in the classrooms, the library, and the cafeteria. The Court conceded that these restrictions were "in form merely nominal," a concession that would seem strange today except in South Africa. Nevertheless, it ruled that the student had been substantially handicapped in the pursuit of his graduate work because much of education consists of discussion and association with fellow students.[78] In the same year, the Court held that the establishment of a separate law school for blacks in Texas did not provide "equal protection," since the new law school for blacks was inferior to the

---

[75] Plessy v. Ferguson, 163 U.S. 537 (1896). *Emphasis added.*

[76] *Little more than half a century later, Justice Harlan's grandson, also named John Marshall Harlan, was to join in a unanimous opinion of the Supreme Court in 1955 which turned the "brooding spirit" of his grandfather into the "intelligence of today."* 349 U.S. 294 (1955). *This was the implementation opinion for* Brown v. Board of Education.

[77] Missouri *ex rel.* Gaines v. Canada, 305 U.S. 337 (1938).

[78] McLaurin v. Oklahoma State Regents, 339 U.S. 637 (1950).

437

CHAPTER 12
government
impact on the
rights and
liberties of
Americans

University of Texas Law School for whites. In its evaluation, the Court employed criteria such as the prestige of the faculty and the position and influence of alumni.[79] Under criteria of this sort, factors considered by any prospective student, *no* racially segregated school could possibly meet the equal protection standard. Racial separation had not been rejected as such, but it had been subjected to a test that it could never pass in a specific case.

The Supreme Court heard 5 cases in 1952 involving segregation in public schools below college level. In the earlier cases on higher education, the Court had avoided passing directly on the "separate but equal" doctrine. In these new cases, however, the blacks did not argue that facilities were unequal—simply that they were separate. The Court's decision, stated by Chief Justice Earl Warren in 1954, was unanimous: "We conclude that in the field of public education the doctrine of 'separate but equal' has no place. Separate educational facilities are inherently unequal." Unlike the earlier decision in *Plessy v. Ferguson,* which it finally reversed, the decision in *Brown v. Board of Education* cites learned journals in sociology and psychology in support of its reasoning.[80]

Finally, in 1955, the Court handed down its decision on how desegregation was to be carried out. It ordered a "prompt and reasonable start toward full compliance" but left it to the federal district courts to supervise this process in the local communities. Although no deadline was fixed, the Supreme Court ordered that desegregation proceed "with all deliberate speed." The *Brown* case focused on segregation in public schools. One week after that decision, the Court extended the principle of desegregation to other public facilities such as parks, theaters, and playgrounds. Earlier it had held state segregation laws an unconstitutional burden on interstate transportation. Obviously, the Court was giving general application to a policy decision that segregation, whether enforced or merely permitted by state laws, is a denial of equal protection of the laws.

Public reaction to litigation

Enforcement of the Court's new policy with respect to equal protection of the laws was to have nationwide effects, but its immediate massive impact was on the southern states. At first, white political leaders in the South all opposed desegregation. The issue thus did not lend itself to political compromise. The token responses to the new law of the land that did occur could be explained more in terms of the social and economic characteristics of southern counties than in terms of their political characteristics.[81] White Citizens

[79] Sweatt v. Painter, 339 U.S. 637 (1950).

[80] Brown v. Board of Education, 347 U.S. 483 (1954).

[81] See Donald R. Matthews and James W. Prothro, "Stateways versus Folkways: Critical Factors in Southern Reactions to *Brown v. Board of Education,*" in Gottfried Dietz, ed., *Essays on the American Constitution* (Englewood Cliffs, N.J.: Prentice-Hall, 1964), pp. 139–56; and a companion study, Donald R. Matthews and James W. Prothro, *Negroes and the New Southern Politics* (New York: Harcourt, 1966).

438

PART 4
outputs of the
political system:
who gets helped,
who gets hurt?

Councils and other groups were organized to enlist public opinion against official compliance. Hundreds of new laws and ordinances were passed throughout the Deep South to prevent, restrict, or control school desegregation. A variety of tactics were used to avoid integration in other public facilities. Public golf courses were converted to private clubs, public swimming pools were closed for extended repairs, and picnic facilities were removed from public parks.

Racial tensions grew more critical within the region, but interracial cold war in the 1950s generally followed a strategy of nonviolent resistance. As white southerners counted on state and local legislation, so black southerners countered with suits in federal courts.

By the 1960s, it was clear that litigation as a means of obtaining equal rights was not going to fulfill black expectations. The courtroom victories were dramatic, but somehow they seemed to have little effect on patterns of behavior in most communities. Biracial conferences, committees, and councils made even less impression on community relations. "The time was ripe for rebellion—rebellion against white domination and segregation, against legalism, against gradual reform through governmental action, against established Negro organizations and leaders."[82]

New black leaders taught the tactics of direct action and civil disobedience, massive street demonstrations, and communitywide boycotts. Most eloquent and probably most influential was Dr. Martin Luther King, Jr., who headed the Southern Christian Leadership Conference (SCLC), a loose confederation of ministers who carried the black cause northward and into areas of interracial contact such as open housing and equal employment opportunities. It is estimated that demonstrations for civil rights legislation were staged in more than 800 cities and towns across the country in 1963. In the light of increasing demands and obviously mounting support (and also in fear of violence), decision makers in Washington were forced to produce a more positive nationwide policy in the form of civil rights legislation.

Equal protection by legislation

How did the President and Congress react to desegregation rulings by the courts? When black school children were endangered by riotous white adults in Little Rock, Arkansas, in 1957, President Eisenhower ordered the use of troops to enforce national court orders. In 1962, President Kennedy took similar action when Governor Barnett of Mississippi personally barred the entry of a black student at the University of Mississippi, despite a national court order requiring his admission. These were, however, isolated incidents; neither President Eisenhower nor President Kennedy used full presidential powers to bring about desegregation of the public schools in line with Supreme Court decisions.

As for Congress, it simply sat tight and took no action, though individual

---

[82] Matthews and Prothro, *Negroes and the New Southern Politics,* p. 411.

439

CHAPTER 12
government
impact on the
rights and
liberties of
Americans

members expressed strong opinions in continuing debate on the issue of civil rights. Congress did pass in 1957 and 1960 two modest Civil Rights Acts which pertained mainly to rights of suffrage and discrimination in voting practices. The Supreme Court meanwhile held that a privately operated restaurant within a public facility (a bus terminal) could not discriminate among customers. It later went further to determine that a privately owned restaurant could not choose to serve only white customers, even though public policy in the local community, express or implicit, required or permitted segregation. But not until 1964, a decade after the initial decision in the *Brown* case, did Congress attempt to back up court decrees, executive orders, and administrative rules with a comprehensive Civil Rights Act that would make equal protection of the laws a positive national policy.

The 1964 act finally placed the authority of Congress and the executive branch of the national government behind the attack on racism. It outlawed discrimination in privately owned places of public accommodation such as hotels, restaurants, gasoline stations, sports arenas, and theaters. The Attorney General was authorized to bring federal action against establishments not in compliance, and hundreds of complaints poured into the Department of Justice. The public accommodations section of the act was extremely controversial. Opponents claimed that it violated rights of private property, and supporters claimed that it protected basic civil rights. But the Supreme Court quickly declared the public accommodations section of the act constitutional;[83] and thousands of private institutions, formerly closed to blacks, began to accept them as well as whites.

In addition to a liberal and broad interpretation of the 1964 Civil Rights Act, the Court held that the Thirteenth Amendment gave power to Congress to legislate against racial discrimination by private individuals, through its powers to outlaw all forms of involuntary servitude. The restrictive interpretations of the nineteenth century have thus been turned around. In fact, the Court has relied on the old Civil Rights Act of 1866 to approve federal action against private discrimination, including housing, employment, and education in private schools.[84] Thus, both through interstate commerce powers (the basis of the 1964 act) and the Thirteenth Amendment, Congress and the courts moved to outlaw many forms of private discrimination.

Title VII of the 1964 act, together with judicial interpretations, executive orders, and other statutes, outlawed racial discrimination in employment practices and established the Equal Employment Opportunity Commission to receive complaints and ensure compliance. Because the elimination of job discrimination was necessary to blacks' efforts to enter the mainstream of American economic life, black leadership viewed Title VII as critical in their struggle for equality. Unfortunately, both at the outset of implementation and later after executive orders had supplemented the act, the problems were so vast and complex that EEOC was never adequate to its vast responsibility.

[83] Heart of Atlanta Motel v. U.S., 379 U.S. 421 (1964).

[84] Jones v. Mayer, 392 U.S. 409 (1968); McDonald v. Santa Fe Trail Transportation, 427 U.S. 273 (1976); Runyon v. McCrary, 427 U.S. 160 (1976).

440

PART 4
outputs of the
political system:
who gets helped,
who gets hurt?

Discouragement about the lack of progress in employment was a primary reason for racial tensions in the late '60s and '70s.

Although the courts had long been concerned about protection of voting rights of racial minorities, the most significant breakthrough finally came from Congress with passage of the 1965 Voting Rights Act. Unlike earlier legislation, which relied primarily upon the courts for protection, the 1965 act authorized federal agents in the Justice Department to register voters and protect their right to vote. Outlawing the much abused literacy tests, the law was first applied in counties with a history of racial discrimination. Its effect was dramatic, with millions of black voters registering to vote for the first time, enhancing not only their impact on public policies but permitting the election of black officials as well. Declared constitutional by the Supreme Court, the Voting Rights Act promised to become of long-term consequence in American politics.[85]

Having belatedly addressed public accommodation, employment, and voting, Congress joined with the courts in 1968 to eliminate discrimination in housing through the Fair Housing Act. Although the act gave limited exemption to some private housing, its coverage was broad, forbidding most owners from selling or renting with racial, sexual, or religious bias. It also required real estate brokers and banks to follow nondiscriminatory practices. Although the impact of the act has been far less than hoped for, it has provided a legal mechanism by which minorities can increase their access to suitable housing, especially in America's cities.

Busing: positive efforts for integration

By 1969, the Supreme Court was disgusted with the long delays in eliminating racial segregation in schools. Desegregation had not come with the "deliberate speed" called for by the Court over a decade earlier. Rather, there were numerous examples of district judges cooperating with segregationist interests in their districts. Thus, the Court firmly ordered that delay was no longer constitutionally permissible. "School districts must immediately terminate dual school systems based on race and operate only unitary school systems."[86] For some time, both the courts and other decision makers had recognized that elimination of illegal segregation would not, in and of itself, achieve integration or racial balance in American institutions. If integration was to be achieved, if access to equal opportunity for minorities was to be a reality, something more affirmative and positive would have to be done. Officials implementing the 1964, 1965, and 1968 Civil Rights Acts moved to positive action along with the courts.

The most controversial tool to achieve racial balance was busing, encouraged by HEW and required by some district judges. In the face of continuing

---

[85] South Carolina v. Katzenbach, 383 U.S. (1966). Extended twice since 1965, the Voting Rights Act is law under present legislation until 1982.

[86] Alexander v. Board of Education, 396 U.S. 19 (1969).

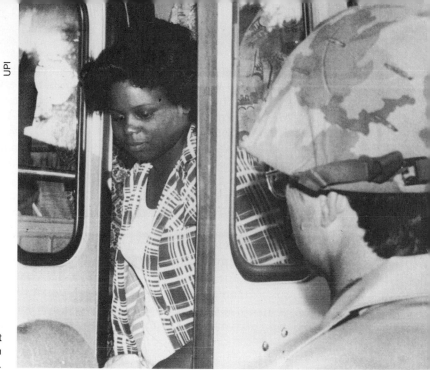

National Guardsmen were called out
to protect school children
from antibusing demonstrators.

racial imbalance in schools, the Supreme Court held that school busing, racial balance ratios, and redrawing of school district lines were all acceptable methods for school officials to adopt in order to eliminate dual school systems and the vestiges of state-imposed segregation.[87] Acknowledging that such severe measures might be "administratively awkward, inconvenient, and even bizarre," it concluded that they were acceptable as an interim corrective measure. Chief Justice Burger, speaking for a unanimous Court, declared that "desegregation plans cannot be limited to the walk-in school." The Court repeatedly noted in its opinions that it was giving limited approval to busing and specified that it was to be required only in districts that were victims of state laws requiring segregation in the past. Later it held that a district was not obligated to keep changing students from school to school once it had implemented a racially acceptable plan.[88]

Racial imbalance, of course, is a problem not confined to states that once had segregation laws. Many districts outside the South had actual *(de facto)* segregation, even with no history of "legal" *(de jure)* segregation. In 1973 the Court spoke for the first time to the school districts where racial segregation had never been required by law. In a divided and unclear decision, the Court seemed to say that schools within the district should desegregate if school board policies, past or present, produced the racial imbalance. The Court placed the burden of proof on school boards to show that segregation was not intentional.[89]

[87] Swann v. Charlotte-Mecklenburg County Board of Education, 402 U.S. 1 (1971).
[88] Pasadena City Board of Education v. Spangler, 427 U.S. 424 (1976).
[89] Keyes v. Denver School District No. 1, 413 U.S. 921 (1973).

442

PART 4
outputs of the
political system:
who gets helped,
who gets hurt?

Facing increased opposition in Congress and among the electorate, the Court drew the line on busing when it overturned a lower court order to Detroit schools. The order required busing across city, county, and district lines in order to desegregate the schools of Detroit. In still another sharply divided (5 to 4) decision, Chief Justice Burger declared that the lower court would have to find that all of the districts involved were responsible for the segregation before they could be required to bus children on such a massive scale.[90] "Without an inter-district violation and inter-district effect, there is no constitutional wrong calling for an inter-district remedy."

Later in the decade the Court disapproved three systemwide busing orders in systems with *de facto* segregation.[91] As a result of these decisions, it is unclear whether the Court wishes to use busing only in those schools legally segregated in the past or if it will also require busing to end segregation outside the South, where the practice was not required by law. Separate schools for blacks and whites are not permitted in the South; but in the absence of an earlier intent to segregate, predominantly black schools and white schools *may* be permitted to operate outside the South. The picture remains unclear.[92]

Affirmative action: the step beyond discrimination

Busing was but one policy designed to overcome centuries of discrimination. The courts had opened the doors for equal opportunity, but intellectual preparation, motivation, financial resources, and skills competitive with those of whites prohibited most members of minorities from entering higher education. They were also seriously underrepresented in skilled employment and had little real opportunity for upward mobility.

One response to this dilemma was a variety of affirmative action programs, active efforts to recruit minorities and females into education and occupations in which they had been traditionally underrepresented. Established first by President Johnson in 1965 by Executive Order, affirmative action plans were developed for bureaucratic agencies, the education system, and private industry. Many were implemented with target time periods for bringing a certain percentage of minorities and females into particular enterprises.

Affirmative action plans met intense opposition and were quickly challenged in the courts as discrimination in reverse. Few constitutional questions in recent history have stirred so much legal debate and public attention. Because the issues are complex and contentious, it is not surprising that the courts have given uncertain judgments on the constitutionality of such programs.

In 1974 the Supreme Court was faced with a major attack on affirmative action when Marco DeFunis challenged the right of a law school to use race

---

[90] Milliken v. Bradley, 418 U.S. 717 (1974).

[91] Dayton Board of Education v. Brinkman, 433 U.S. 406 (1977); Austin School District v. U.S., 429 U.S. 990 (1976); School District v. United States, 433 U.S. 667 (1977).

[92] For current state of the law on busing see Martin Shapiro and Rocco Tresolini, *American Constitutional Law* (New York: Macmillan, 1979), pp. 490–96.

Minorities objected to the Bakke decision, fearful
that it would destroy Affirmative Action programs.

as a factor in admission.[93] DeFunis argued that he had been denied admission
to the University of Washington law school in violation of equal protection
of the law because less qualified minority students had been admitted on a
preferential basis. The Court refused to decide the case on its merits and
declared it moot (not a real dispute) because DeFunis had later been admitted
and was about to graduate from the University of Washington law school.[94]
Unable to reach a judgment or unwilling to announce one, the justices were
aware that the conflict would have to be confronted directly in the near future.
The center spotlight was soon taken by Alan Bakke.

Alan Bakke, a 32-year-old white veteran, had been turned down for admission to 11 different medical schools, including the University of California at

[93] DeFunis v. Odegard, 416 U.S. 312 (1974).
[94] For full discussion see Allan P. Sindler, *Bakke, DeFunis, and Minority Admissions* (New York:
Longman, 1978).

444

PART 4
outputs of the
political system:
who gets helped,
who gets hurt?

Davis. In 1973 and 1974 the Davis medical school had reserved 16 places in its entering class for "disadvantaged students." This policy was specifically designed to encourage admission of minority students, many of whom had lower Medical College Aptitude Test scores than white applicants. Bakke argued that he was a victim of racial discrimination, and the California supreme court agreed with him. On appeal to the Supreme Court, the central issue had to be faced squarely: could an affirmative action program legally enhance opportunities for minorities under the equal protection clause of the Fourteenth Amendment?[95] The case was scheduled for argument in 1977, and almost sixty amicus curiae ("friend of the court") briefs were filed, an all-time record for a single case, recommending a particular decision or line of reasoning for the judges. In 1978, the Court handed down a judgment that sought to placate both sides of the Bakke dispute. A 5-man majority (Powell, Brennan, White, Marshall, and Blackmun) held that Title VI of the 1964 Civil Rights Act did *not* prohibit taking race into account and that race can be considered along with other factors in giving special consideration to members of minority groups to remedy past discrimination. But because the Davis medical school used race as the only criterion for admission to its 16 positions, because the number of positions was rigid, and because candidates were not considered competitively with other special factors taken into account, Justice Powell left the majority when determining if the Davis plan itself was constitutional. Because Powell rejects quotas, he joined the group of Burger, Stevens, Rehnquist, and Stewart and ruled that Bakke must be admitted to the Davis medical school.[96]

Both sides in the controversy claimed victory; both were disappointed. Although some supporters of affirmative action found comfort in the verdict, other commentators saw the decision as "straddling," "confused," and "expedient." Although the Justices did commend the Harvard admissions plan as an acceptable form of a "race among other factors" model, it remained unclear as to how lower courts and federal bureaucrats were to adjust existing programs to make them constitutional.

Additional confusion came in 1979 when the Supreme Court upheld in a 5-to-2 vote the right of private employers to take "race-conscious steps to eliminate racial imbalances in traditionally segregated job categories."[97] Brian Weber, a white worker in the Kaiser Aluminum Plant in Louisiana, was denied admission to an on-the-job training program because half of the openings in the program were reserved for black employees. He claimed that he was a victim of discrimination, because some of the minority employees admitted to the program had less seniority. Although the lower courts agreed with Weber, the 5-member majority on the Supreme Court found that although the Civil Rights Act of 1964 prohibited racial discrimination in employment, it "does not condemn all private, voluntary, race-conscious affirmative action plans." Although Justice Brennan was unable to say where "the line of demar-

[95] See Nathan Glazer, *Affirmative Discrimination* (New York: Basic Books, 1976).
[96] Regents of the University of California v. Bakke, 98 S. Ct. 2733 (1978).
[97] United Steelworkers v. Brian V. Weber, 99 S. Ct. 2721 (1979).

cation between permissible and impermissible affirmative action plans" might be drawn, he did conclude that the Kaiser plan "falls on the permissible side of the line." Justice Rehnquist led a strong attack on the majority, accusing them of "totally ignoring" the civil rights laws. Comparing the majority to "escape artists such as Houdini," he said that the opinion "eludes clear statutory language, uncontradicted legislative history, and uniform precedent in concluding that employers are, after all, permitted to consider race in making employment decisions."

445

CHAPTER 12
government
impact on the
rights and
liberties of
Americans

Because the lines between permissible and impermissible plans have not been drawn by the court, no one can be certain about how such policies will fare in future litigation. Both the *Bakke* and *Weber* opinions suggest that the Court will approve programs that are racially attentive (influenced by considerations of race). These decisions are also important for sex-bias cases, because executive orders and amendments to the Civil Rights Acts encourage the inclusion of women in affirmative action programs. But fixed racial or sexual quotas in employment or admissions have not been approved by the judiciary. Thus, one can expect protracted conflict in the future over plans that claim to be racially or sexually "attentive" but are challenged because they have sexual or racial quotas. If the soft majority of the Court is able to hold its voting members in future challenges, one may find a clearer rule of law on these issues by the 1990s.

Equal protection for the majority: women's rights

Although the Civil Rights Acts and affirmative action plans were originally designed to protect the rights of racial minorities, they were soon expanded to include protection for a majority who were victims of discrimination, American women. Sexism is as difficult a problem to solve as racism, for discrimination against women is a deeply engrained attitude and practice of American society. It is especially manifested in employment opportunities. The earnings gap between men and women is staggering: men average 75 percent more income than women; in age groups 30 to 44, for example, women average $3,000 less a year than men with similar education and careers.[98] Faced with a clear denial of rights and inspired by the civil rights movement of the '50s, women have organized to claim equal protection of the laws, achieve passage of favorable legislation, and win court decisions.

In 1963, Congress passed an Equal Pay Act for the benefit of women in a few occupations, and a 1972 amendment greatly extended the coverage. The 1964 Civil Rights Act included women as a category under its protection, and executive orders have tried to expand protection by outlawing sexual discrimination in government employment and by government contractors.

The courts have followed an uneven course in extending equal protection of the laws to women. Certainly the judiciary (almost always male) was not

---

[98] Department of Labor, *The Earnings Gap Between Men and Women* (Washington, D.C.: Department of Labor, 1976).

Sam C. Pierson, Jr., Photo Researchers, Inc.

Supporters of the Equal Rights Amendment regard its adoption
as essential to the elimination of sexism in American law.

helpful in the early battles against sexual discrimination. For example, it upheld a law in 1948 prohibiting a woman from being a bartender unless she
was the wife or daughter of the owner of the bar.[99] Since that time the justices
have changed their viewpoint to overturn many laws as sexually discriminatory.
The Supreme Court has found that the Civil Rights Act of 1964 would not
permit a hiring policy that discriminated against the mothers of pre-school
children[100] and has invalidated a state law that automatically preferred a father
over a mother as executor of a child's estate.[101] The Court also overturned
a national law requiring women in the military to prove their husband's dependence on them in order for the husbands to receive dependents' benefits,

[99] Goesaert v. Cleary, 335 U.S. 464 (1948).
[100] Phillips v. Martin Marietta Corp., 400 U.S. 542 (1971).
[101] Reed v. Reed, 404 U.S. 71 (1971).

447

CHAPTER 12
government
impact on the
rights and
liberties of
Americans

without requiring the same proof for wives of military men.[102] In this case, four members of the Court (Brennan, Douglas, White, and Marshall) argued that any laws based on sexual classifications should be viewed as inherently suspect, but the full majority has not yet adopted this strict interpretation as Court policy. It has held that the Equal Pay Act of 1963 requires men and women to be paid equal wages for performing equal work, whether it is performed during the day or night,[103] overturned mandatory maternity leave policies that require teachers to stop teaching 5 months before the expected birth of a child,[104] and overturned a state law exempting women from jury duty.[105]

In other rulings, the Court, by holding against sexual discrimination, has extended benefits to males, confirming the claims by many women's groups that sexual discrimination has negative consequences for men as well as women. Thus the Court overturned a state law that presumed that an unwed father was an unfit custodian for a child,[106] struck down a law prohibiting the sale of beer to males under 21 but to females under age 18,[107] and invalidated a provision of the Social Security law which gives survivors' benefits to widows but not widowers with small children.[108] In some instances, however, the Court has given support to laws that give advantages to women. It upheld a state law giving special property tax exemption to widows, but not to widowers, on the ground that women were more likely to be left in difficult economic conditions.[109] It has also permitted women to receive greater social security benefits than men, to compensate for past economic discrimination.[110]

Women have been generally but not uniformly successful in their court challenges. In 1974 the Court upheld a California disability insurance program that did not cover loss of wages resulting from a normal pregnancy.[111] The Court declined to hold that such an exemption violated the Fourteenth Amendment or the 1964 Civil Rights Act. In 1979 women lost the court battle to overturn veteran preferences in hiring, even though they demonstrated that such preferences created great employment disadvantages for women.

Although the United States has achieved significant progress in equal protection, problems of racism and sexism clearly remain. All areas of the country contribute to inequality in education, employment, income, and housing. To some degree, the easy decisions have been made. How to achieve the more difficult balance between needs of minorities and the rights of the majority is the critical question for the rest of the century.

[102] Frontiero v. Richardson, 411 U.S. 677 (1973).

[103] Corning Glass Works v. Brennan, 417 U.S. 188 (1974).

[104] Cleveland Board of Education v. LaFleur, 414 U.S. 632 (1974).

[105] Taylor v. Louisiana, 419 U.S. 522 (1975).

[106] Stanley v. Illinois, 405 U.S. 645 (1972).

[107] Craig v. Brown, 429 U.S. 190 (1976).

[108] Weinberger v. Wiesenfeld, 420 U.S. 636 (1975).

[109] Kahn v. Shevin, 416 U.S. 351 (1974).

[110] Califano v. Webster, 430 U.S. 313 (1977).

[111] Geduldig v. Aiello, 417 U.S. 484 (1974).

The ideology for American civil liberties is from the Declaration of Independence—that every human being has certain inalienable rights. The Bill of Rights and the Thirteenth, Fourteenth, and Fifteenth Amendments made these rights more specific. The federal courts have assumed the major responsibility for deciding what these rights mean and for resolving conflicts between rights. In recent years the Burger Court has had difficulty establishing a firm civil rights policy, but it has generally been more conservative than the Warren Court on defendants' rights and First Amendment liberties.

The Fourteenth Amendment gave the first constitutional definition of citizenship: a person born in this country is a U.S. citizen; U.S. citizens are automatically citizens of the state where they live. The Constitution states that Congress may enact laws of naturalization by which immigrants can become citizens. The basic civil rights guaranteed by the Constitution apply to aliens as well as citizens; however, aliens may not vote or hold office.

A preferred position has been given to the freedoms guaranteed in the First Amendment: freedom of speech, press, assembly, and religion. Obscenity is not protected by the amendment, and the courts have had great difficulty establishing a standard to determine what is obscene. Freedom of the press and the rights of the press to protect news sources and cover pretrial hearings are current concerns of the court. Freedom to differ in one's political beliefs was under attack during the McCarthy period of the 1950s and the Vietnam protest period of the 1960s. The Court has handled many cases involving freedom of religion, but most recent litigation has focused on the prohibition of laws "respecting an establishment of religion," including school prayers, Bible reading, and financial aid to parochial schools.

Defendants' rights are a special concern of the judiciary. A person accused of a crime now has expanded rights, for evolving concepts of human decency and dignity change the meaning of phrases such as "cruel and unusual punishment."

Equal protection of the laws has come to mean much more than in the early twentieth century, when southern states required separate facilities for blacks and whites. States can no longer require segregation on the basis of race without violating the right to equal protection of the laws. Nor may private establishments legally discriminate on grounds of race. The struggle of racial minorities for equality in education, employment, and housing has been joined by women, whose legal and political efforts have raised the consciousness of a male-dominated society. Affirmative action plans and school busing are two especially controversial policy results of these struggles.

policy: the purpose of politics

13

450

PART 4
outputs of the
political system:
who gets helped,
who gets hurt?

No public policy is perfectly fixed or permanent, because politics—the attempt to influence policy—never stops. It never stops because laws are never neutral. The conflicting needs and views of various groups are constantly changing. Every election, every law, every administrative ruling, and every court decision reflects some combination of conflicting claims, pleasing some political interest groups, displeasing others. And in a democracy the losers are free to do what they can to modify or change the decision. Although this practice may distress those who seek permanence or neutrality in government, it is the essence of politics.

We have seen that the Constitution itself reflects the continuous struggle over policy. The framers simply *began* the debate over the meaning of the Constitution; they did not complete it. The anti-Federalists at first denounced the document, warning that it would bring about the complete consolidation of the states into one government. Once the Constitution had been adopted, however, they reversed their argument and insisted that the Constitution was really only a compact among states that still retained their sovereignty (complete and independent power). Ever since, the dominant groups in each generation of American politics have interpreted the document to correspond to their views. Minimum wage laws were regarded as unconstitutional in the 1920s not so much because of the "intention of the framers" or the objective meaning of the Constitution, as because of the way in which the groups then controlling American politics viewed the public interest—and their own. Minimum wage laws finally became constitutional in the 1930s, not because of any change in the intentions of the framers or in the words of the Constitution, but because of *the Supreme Court's response to the new conditions and the new power relations* that had developed in the current generation.

Politics is the pursuit of power, and policy is the expression of power. All groups do not have equal power over every decision of government; policies therefore affect various interests differently. Since few groups in a democracy are willing to accept a lesser role—or a "raw deal"—forever, policy becomes the center around which politics continuously revolves. Policy making knows no end.

In this chapter we shall consider both politics and policies, as we have in all the preceding chapters. But here our focus will be primarily on policies—their functions, their scope, how they are used, and some of their consequences.

The government's role in perspective

In examining the people and practices through which American government establishes and enforces policy, we focused on 6 specific functions of the political system that were outlined in chapter 1. On the input side are (1) identification of interests, (2) selection of leaders. On the output side: (3) rule making, (4) application of rules, (5) settlement of disputes. As both input and output: (6) political socialization. At the more general level of government, we said in chapter 1, "the basic output functions of the political system are fairly obvious: the system must furnish some general rules or policies to *maintain order* and to *satisfy demands* on the system." Those are the key output functions: maintaining order and satisfying demands. The specific functions and activities of government can be put in perspective by returning to these basic functions: maintaining order (the negative function of protection) and satisfying demands (the positive function of service).

Basic functions of policy

Even primitive people cannot exist without government. As Aristotle recognized centuries ago, human beings are social creatures who, from the beginning of their lives, depend on others for their survival. They depend on social life, on living together; and to live together, they must have some means of establishing and enforcing rules of behavior—in a word, *government.* Their minimum need is the survival of the group, but other institutions and a variety of human attributes are necessary for social life. The sociologist or anthropologist might point out that a person cannot survive without the family. The economist would remind us that survival depends on some system of creating and allocating essential goods and services. The psychologist may say that if human beings could not communicate, social life would be impossible. Specialists tend to overstate the importance of their specialty.

Granting that all these institutions and attributes are necessary, we still look for the special function of government. Without government, group existence would be constantly threatened by disorder—disorder so extreme that life itself would be endangered. The gullible, the weak, the unsuspecting, the envied, the trusting—all would be in danger of attack and possible extinction. We would have to give up many of the things we need and enjoy, including pasteurized milk, garbage disposal, national defense, fire protection, passable highways, social security, and safe working conditions.

This consideration of what our lives would be like without government points to the two basic functions of government policies emphasized above: (1) *the negative function of protection* and (2) *the positive function of service.* The purpose of the United States government, as declared in the Constitution, is to accomplish these minimum functions. Here, purpose and effect are the same. The framers demonstrated their political insight by emphasizing the two essential functions or effects of government in their declaration of purpose. The Preamble begins with a statement of the negative function of protection, "We the People of the United States, in Order to form a more perfect Union, establish Justice, insure domestic Tranquility, provide for the common defense . . ."; and it concludes with a statement of the positive function of service, ". . . promote the general Welfare, and secure the Blessings of Liberty to ourselves and our Posterity, do ordain and establish this Constitution for the United States of America."

The specific policies through which we realize these underlying functions are constantly challenged and frequently changed. Government must provide some kind of protection and some kind of service if people are to live together. On that, everyone agrees; but many disagree on what form these activities

Without the expansion of government protection and service, popular liberties could not have been sustained in the United States.

should take. To ensure "domestic Tranquility," is it necessary that murderers, horse thieves, and false advertisers be arrested as criminals? If they are guilty, should they be hanged, drawn and quartered, imprisoned, or fined? Does the promotion of the "general Welfare" require government sponsored roads, schools, social security, and health insurance? If it does, on what scale? It is over policy questions of this sort that bitter controversies have raged since the early days of the Republic; indeed, action by the government emerges from conflict among private interests, not from agreement.

Expanding functions of government policies

Government acts in response to dominant elements of society, even though the elements that lack power may protest bitterly. Since the social and economic environment constantly changes, government policies must also constantly change. For one thing, new conditions may lead the powerful interests themselves to change their minds about what they once championed as desirable policy. So they change the policy and develop a new one. Economic and social changes may also give rise to new coalitions of interests with different views and with enough power to redirect policy to their own ends.

In the early days of the Republic, businessmen and industrialists favored strong national government, for they felt that they needed constitutional provisions that would protect contracts and provide uniform regulation of commerce, tariffs, land grants, and other subsidies. Later on, when the country had become highly industrialized (partly because of these very provisions), big business interests made an about-face and began to favor states' rights policies. Their change in attitude occurred when smaller interests (farm, labor, and local businesses) decided that they, too, could use the federal government to promote their endeavors and to regulate the larger business that had fostered the strong government, in the first place. Extended suffrage, increased literacy, and new forms of organization in labor and agriculture thus changed the power structure so much that corporate interests found national power, on balance, more threatening than promising. They then began to support different governmental principles to serve their new policy needs.

Life in America, far more complex than it was in past centuries, multiplies the needs and controversies that give rise to government action. Government must always provide protection and service, even for the simplest community, but the policies it uses for a modern urban, industrial society cannot be the same policies it used when the society was rural and agrarian. In 1790, if the owner of a shipbuilding firm underpaid a worker or if the worker threatened to quit unless his wages were raised, the issue was handled as a local, personal problem. Nowadays, if the General Motors Corporation underpaid its thousands of employees, the workers' reduced purchasing power would have an effect on the whole country. If the United Automobile Workers Union were to go on strike, the halt in automobile production would threaten the entire economy. Consequently, the government guarantees minimum wages, protects labor's right to organize for collective bargaining, and prohibits unfair practices by labor or management.

In recent years, government's regulation of industry has been aimed primarily at management. This trend reflects the increased political power of labor and the effect of that power on government policy. As we would expect, the policies have emerged from bitter power struggles rather than from consensus. In the 1930s, management called it "class legislation," warned that it would destroy democracy, and otherwise condemned the government's guarantee of minimum wages and labor's right to organize. In 1947, labor denounced the Taft-Hartley Act as "slave labor law" because it restricted the right to strike.

In an industrial economy and an urban society, each of us is dependent on others in almost everything we do. Yet, in spite of this dependence, our relations with others are highly impersonal. Again the effect is to expand the role of government. In 1790, when about 95 percent of the population lived in rural areas, each family produced much of its own food or could purchase anything that was not home-grown from other families nearby. If a family did not raise pigs or cows, it would buy meat from someone whose cleanliness was well known. But today, city dwellers buy meat that has been produced by someone they will never know, processed in a plant they will never see, and labeled, priced, and marketed by one or more companies that

454

PART 4
outputs of the
political system:
who gets helped,
who gets hurt?

they see only in the person of an anonymous salesperson. In 1906, Upton Sinclair's best-selling novel, *The Jungle,* described slaughtering practices with such shocking realism that sales of meat dropped sharply. Partly because of the impact of that book, a long fight for government regulation culminated in passage of the Food and Drug Act of 1906. In the absence of personal contact between consumer and producer, the government had to intervene to ensure a purchaser of canned beef, for example, that the can would not contain horse meat or diseased beef.

The expansion of government has thus been closely related to general social change and to new needs and power relations that have grown up among the people. These needs and power relations, in turn, are related to the interdependence and impersonality that are characteristic of an urban society. Once industrialization had concentrated power in the hands of private groups, notably business and labor, "big government" became inevitable. With government making policy for society as a whole, it must have more power than any private group. When we remember that the AFL-CIO has a membership about five times as large as the entire national population in 1790, and that corporations like Exxon have assets greater than those of most of the state governments, it becomes clear that either the functions of the national government had to expand or the power of the public at large would have been overshadowed by the power of private groups. Robert MacIver underlines the inevitability of this development:

Wherever technology advances, wherever private business extends its range, wherever the cultural life becomes more complex, new tasks are imposed on government. This happens apart from, or in spite of, the particular philosophies that governments cherish. . . . In the longer run the tasks undertaken by governments are dictated by changing conditions, and governments on the whole are more responsive than creative in fulfilling them.[1]

The idea of an expanding national government, of course, was at odds with the antigovernment bias of early Americans. But the government has expanded all the same. To begin with, Americans are more pragmatic than ideological. They are too practical to hold onto an abstract idea when it begins to get in the way of something they want to do. As Samuel Lubell says, the tenement dweller was quick to reject the idea that all will be well if the government "leaves things alone." He discovered that, "If only God could make a tree, only the government could make a park."[2] When enough people want a service they cannot achieve in any other way—whether it is a city park or a Tennessee Valley Authority—government is obliged to move into a new role. Moreover, Americans are more willing to tolerate governmental authority than they are to put up with the irresponsible use of private power. The general bias against expanding government seems to persist, but Americans are quite ready to make exceptions whenever the exercise of private power appears to be threatening their basic freedoms.

[1] *The Web of Government* (New York: Macmillan, 1947), pp. 314–15.
[2] *The Future of American Politics* (New York: Harper, 1951), p. 33.

The old belief that the "least government" is the "best government" has delayed but not stopped the adjustment to new conditions. In 1886, Grover Cleveland vetoed an act that would have appropriated $25,000 to buy seed for drought-stricken Texas farmers:

I can find no warrant for such an appropriation in the Constitution, and I do not believe that the power and duty of the general government ought to be extended to the relief of individual suffering . . . though the people support the government, the government should not support the people.[3]

Here the dogma is still firm and unyielding.

In 1930, Herbert Hoover, who seemed strongly dedicated to "least government," brought himself to approve an appropriation of $45 million to save the livestock of drought-stricken farmers in Arkansas. But he opposed a grant of $25 million to feed the owners of the livestock, explaining that such relief "would have injured the spiritual responses of the American people." Here the dogma has been cracked, but not broken; direct aid to cattle is all right, but not direct aid to human beings.

One generation later, in the administration of the next Republican President, Dwight Eisenhower, the national government owned about $8 billion worth of surplus farm goods, which had been purchased for the benefit of farmers after private customers had refused to buy them at high enough prices. Here the dogma has been shattered, with vast sums of public money being spent to help farmers. The people—meaning mostly city dwellers—still support the government just as Cleveland said they should, but now the govern-

[3] *Congressional Record*, Vol. 18, Part 2, 49th Cong., 2d sess. (February 17, 1887), p. 1875.

456

PART 4
outputs of the
political system:
who gets helped,
who gets hurt?

ment does much to support the farmers. And such aid stimulates highly favorable responses, even though they are not the "spiritual responses" that
concerned Hoover. Farm pressure groups insist on aid for the "rugged individ-
ualists" of the soil, and each political party boasts that it can do the most for
the farmer. The service state is here to stay.

Examples of expanding policies

We found that the American creed stresses equality and individualism.
The concept of individual equality includes more than the equal right of each
person to strive for material success; it also includes the equal right of each
person to use the government for protection against private individuals with
great economic power. Late in the nineteenth century, when industrial technology created a new economy dominated by corporate giants, Americans
were quick to show their resentment. According to "natural economic law,"
the pursuit of profits should have led to competition, but actually it seemed
to bring about combinations or "trusts" that restricted competition. To many
Americans, irresponsible private control of the economy seemed just as bad
as irresponsible government. So widespread was this opinion that, in 1890,
a Congress otherwise sympathetic toward "big business" passed the *Sherman
Antitrust Act* with only one dissenting vote.

The Sherman Act outlaws any "combination . . . or conspiracy, in restraint
of trade or commerce among the several States" and makes it illegal to try
"to monopolize any part of the trade or commerce among the several States."
Violators of the act are subject to criminal prosecution, injunctions to stop
their illegal activities, or damage suits by injured parties. This act has been
on the books for over 90 years, but during much of that time it has been
little more than "a piece of paper with a number." Attempts to enforce it
have been spotty, and some Presidents have shown little interest in carrying
out its aims. Indeed, the first time it was applied, under Grover Cleveland,
was against labor unions!

The long-range effect of the Sherman Act is hard to determine. Some
say it has checked the trend toward monopoly, while others point out that
economic power is more concentrated now than it was in 1890. It can be
used to prevent the outright purchase of competing firms, or formal agreements among "competitors" to limit output and fix prices, but it is less useful
in attacking such informal practices as "price leadership," in which a dominant
firm like U.S. Steel sets the pattern for an entire industry.

Walton Hamilton, an outstanding economist and student of public affairs,
believed that, "In antitrust we are meeting the great economy with a weapon
of control designed for petty trade. . . . The direction of industrial activity
to public ends is a constructive, not a punitive task."[4] It takes years to fight
an antitrust action through the courts; and by the time one practice has been
declared illegal, technological change or good lawyers will have produced a

---

[4] *The Politics of Industry* (New York: Knopf, 1957), p. 144.

substitute. Hamilton quoted a lawyer skilled in antitrust lawsuits as saying, "Like all things of earth, the practices of my corporations are not free from error. But I can count on a period of three or four years at the very least before the courts outlaw them. By that time I will have worked out a new set of practices."[5]

Comments of this sort leave many Americans uneasy in the face of large-scale industrial empires. Justice Louis Brandeis' assumption that bigness is a "curse" still crops up from time to time, even in the Supreme Court.[6] However attractive the idea of decentralization and a return to the simpler forms of small business may be, it is difficult to imagine such a program being achieved in the twentieth century. Luckily, since bigness seems to be inevitable, it also appears to be neutral. Complex and difficult though the job may be, the most practical aim of government economic policy is to direct economic power into constructive channels rather than to destroy it.

One of the powers under which government control of the economy has expanded is the power of Congress to "regulate Commerce . . . among the several States." This clause has been used to justify some of the major policies adopted by the United States in its attempts to adjust to an industrial economy. The establishment of *minimum standards of wages and hours* in the 1930s illustrates how the commerce clause applies to modern problems.

American workers lagged more than a generation behind workers of most other industrial countries in putting through legislation for minimum wages and maximum hours. Contributing to the delay were opposition of the business community, constitutional limitations on government interference with property rights, and the preference of the AFL (as a craft union of skilled workers) for collective bargaining rather than general legislation.

In the early 1930s the situation was highly confused. The Supreme Court had upheld state regulation of working hours for special classes of workers such as children, women, and those in hazardous industries. But it continued to regard the guarantee of minimum wages as unconstitutional. In 1923, a conservative Supreme Court, speaking through George Sutherland, President Harding's former campaign adviser and a new appointee to the Court, invalidated a minimum wage law for women. It was viewed as an interference with freedom of contract, contrary to "due process of law." The employee was protected in her freedom to agree with the corporation, as her bargaining equal, to work for as little as she pleased.[7] Since the Fourteenth Amendment extends the due process limitation to the states, just as the Fifth Amendment limits the national government, minimum wage legislation was stalled.

Human needs and political forces, however, were about to produce a new reading of the commerce clause. Faced by the mass unemployment of the Great Depression, the AFL had decided to support national wage and hour legislation. In addition, the CIO's organization of semiskilled and unskilled workers gave them a new voice in politics. When, in 1936, the Supreme

---

[5] *Ibid.*, p. 146.

[6] See his *The Curse of Bigness* (New York: Viking, 1935).

[7] Adkins v. Children's Hospital, 261 U.S. 525 (1923).

Efforts to regulate child labor were long delayed by
court decisions supporting business interests.

Court again stated that regulation of wages and hours was beyond the power
of the state or national governments,[8] the Democratic party responded with
a platform promising national action even if it required a constitutional amendment. Influenced perhaps by the overwhelming Democratic victory in the
1936 election, by President Roosevelt's plan to "reorganize" the Court, and
by the mood of workers as revealed in "sit-down" strikes (workers barricading
themselves inside plants), the Supreme Court reversed its earlier stand and
upheld a state minimum wage law in 1937.[9]

[8] Morehead v. New York *ex rel.* Tipaldo, 298 U.S. 587 (1936).
[9] West Coast Hotel Co. v. Parrish, 300 U.S. 379 (1937).

This decision encouraged those favoring a national law to push the *Fair Labor Standards Act* through Congress in 1938. The act extended the power of Congress to include the regulation of working conditions in factories producing goods for interstate commerce. Through the commerce clause, then, minimum national standards were finally achieved. In addition to illustrating the way the powers granted to Congress by the Constitution can be adapted to modern conditions, the fight for passage of the bill illustrates several other features we have found to characterize American politics:

1. *The President as chief legislator.* President Roosevelt urgently requested passage of such a bill in a special message to Congress, and on the same day virtually identical bills were introduced in both houses.

2. *American parties as imperfectly united, but with Democrats generally more liberal than Republicans.* Neither party was perfectly united for or against the bill, but the Democrats furnished the chief support and the Republicans the chief opposition.

3. *Labor pressure groups as champions of the welfare state, despite their own disagreements on details.* In committee hearings on the bill, labor testimony supported the general aim of the bill, although the AFL and CIO differed sharply on details.

4. *Business pressure groups as opponents of welfare-state aid to labor groups.* Representatives of the National Association of Manufacturers, the Chamber of Commerce of the United States, the Cotton Textile Institute, the Anthracite Institute, and similar business groups appeared in opposition.

5. *Power of the House Rules Committee, and cooperation across party lines between southern Democrats and northern Republicans.* A combination of southern Democrats and Republicans on the House Rules Committee refused to bring the House bill to the floor.

6. *Ability of an insistent and well-organized majority to overcome minority opposition.* Proponents got enough signatures on a petition to discharge the Rules Committee by threatening to block farm legislation if their rural colleagues failed to sign.

7. *Independence from national public opinion enjoyed by members of Congress from "safe" districts.* Senator "Cotton Ed" Smith of South Carolina announced that 50 cents a day was enough to live on reasonably and comfortably in his state.

8. *The laborious nature of the legislative struggle, and the ability of powerful minority groups to win concessions.* The bill was passed after 13 arduous months, with almost countless amendments and with numerous exemptions, such as agricultural workers and employees of most small-town newspapers.[10]

The Fair Labor Standards Act established a minimum wage of 25 cents an hour, to be raised to 40 cents in 7 years, for workers employed by (nonexempt) industries engaged in interstate commerce. Maximum hours were set at 44 hours a week, to be reduced to 40 in 3 years; for any work beyond the maximum, employees must be paid at "time-and-a-half" rates. In 1970, the minimum wage was raised to $1.80 an hour for employees already covered

[10] See John S. Forsythe, "Legislative History of the Fair Labor Standards Act," *Law and Contemporary Problems,* 6 (Summer 1939), 464–90.

460

PART 4
outputs of the
political system:
who gets helped,
who gets hurt?

by the Fair Labor Standards Act. The coverage of the law was also extended, and the floor keeps rising: $2.65 in 1978; $3.35 in 1981.

Like all laws, this one was the work of political forces working within the framework of the Constitution. Just as Congress had to tailor the law to fit the Constitution, the Supreme Court was called on to test the law's legality against the wording of the Constitution. In 1918, the Court had decided that Congress did not have the power to forbid shipment of the products of child labor in interstate commerce, because "the powers not expressly delegated to the national government" were reserved to the states or the people.[11] On rereading the Constitution in 1941, the Supreme Court had discovered that although the national government was restricted to "expressly" conferred powers under the Articles of Confederation, no such restriction could be found in the present Constitution. The power to regulate commerce became, in substance, the power to regulate the national economy. "Congress, having . . . adopted the policy of excluding from interstate commerce all goods produced for the commerce which do not conform to the specified labor standards, it may choose the means reasonably adapted to the attainment of the permitted end, even though they involve control of intrastate activities."[12]

Types of public policies

Just as there is no end to public policies, there is no end to political scientists trying to classify them. Among dozens of classification schemes, one of the most interesting is Theodore Lowi's classification of policies according to their expected impacts on society. He identifies three arenas of public policy: *distribution, regulation,* and *redistribution.*[13]

Distributive policy includes decisions about giving rewards such as jobs or government contracts to particular individuals or firms. All decisions to grant fairly specific favors are thus distributive, including "most contemporary public land and resource policies; rivers and harbors ('pork barrel') programs; defense procurement and R & D [Research and Development]; labor, business, and agricultural 'clientele' services; and the traditional tariff."[14] Decisions in the distributive policy arena tend to be highly individualized, each more or less isolated from the other. We said in explaining our scheme of a political system (in chapter 1) that all policy decisions include both rewards and deprivations, but that in some decisions deprivation might be present only in the sense of differential rewards. Such is the case with distributive policies: the deprived and the rewarded may never confront each other in conflict. If the deprived are those who get a smaller piece of the pie or those who are out of this particular policy arena and who support the distribution in their tax payments, they may not even have a sense of deprivation.

[11] Hammer v. Dagenhart, 247 U.S. 251 (1918).

[12] U.S. v. Darby, 312 U.S. 100 (1941).

[13] "American Business, Public Policy, Case-Studies, and Political Theory," *World Politics,* 16 (July 1964), 677–715.

[14] *Ibid.,* p. 690.

Decisions on the routes of interstate highways are examples of distributive policies.

In the *regulatory* arena, deprivations are as clear as rewards. When Congress enacts a statute on labor-management relations, the deprived parties are as aware of their loss as the rewarded parties are aware of their gain. "Regulatory policies are distinguishable from distributive in that . . . the regulatory decision involves a direct choice as to who will be indulged and who deprived."[15] Here, too, decisions tend to have specific and individual impact. Each decision, however, involves the application of a general standard, which tends to carry over to others who are subject to the regulation. A regulatory policy is accordingly more nearly a general policy, whereas a distributive policy is merely lots of individual decisions.

Redistributive policies are similar to regulation in their application to broad categories of people and in the interrelation of individual decisions. But redistribution applies to much broader segments of the population and carries still greater rewards and deprivations. "The categories of impact are much broader, approaching social classes. They are, crudely speaking, haves and have-nots, bigness and smallness, bourgeoisie and proletariat. The aim involved is not use of property but property itself, not equal treatment but equal posses-

[15] *Ibid.*, p. 690–91.

462

PART 4
outputs of the
political system:
who gets helped,
who gets hurt?

sion. . . ." Professor Lowi's only examples of redistributive policies in the United States are the income tax and various "welfare state" programs, and he concedes that these are only mildly redistributive. Nevertheless, "the aims and the stakes involved" render these policies redistributive.

What, then, are the differences among the three policy arenas? The most important difference is that each seems to correspond to a different interpretation or "theory" of the policy process. Distributive politics appears to be best explained by the *log-rolling interpretation*, which explains policy as the product of a decentralized bargaining process among various groups that want some piece of the pie. The competition is not over any general policy question but simply over who gets in on the action. Most members of Congress will be indifferent, for example, about whether or not some district in another state gets a new post office building. But they may be happy to vote for such an appropriation if that district's representative will support their own pet projects. Thus policy is put together in piecemeal fashion by people who are pretty much indifferent to everything except getting their share.

The primary political unit affected by distributive decisions is an individual or a particular firm or corporation. The Public Works Committee of the House, for example, decides billion-dollar issues with reference to rivers and harbors, but these are broken down into a series of million-dollar and thousand-dollar decisions. This kind of policy making multiplies the number of interests involved and creates a relationship of mutual noninterference ("you work your side of the street, and I'll work mine") within a coalition whose members have nothing in common except a desire for some share of the rewards. The goals of distributive policies lead not to conflict but to a structure of mutual accommodation among the key decision makers and their supporters—"you scratch my back and I'll scratch yours." Power relations are involved here, of course, and the relative strengths of pressure groups vary. But when thousands of separate and obscure decisions are merely packaged together as a "policy" of rivers and harbors development or of defense subcontracting or of natural resources development, those who have access to the key decision makers will tend to support them. The result is a stable power structure dominated by key decision makers and their supporting groups. The primary site of decisions in these cases is generally specialized agencies, such as congressional subcommittees and executive bureaus.

The policies that have been most widely studied by political scientists are regulatory. Regulatory policies, the ones most widely studied by political scientists, are best explained by *group*, or *pluralistic, theory*. In group theory, conflict among groups—each with different interests—replaces mutual noninterference. Majority coalitions (alliances) must be formed on each issue. But many powerful individuals and groups will not join in the coalition-building effort. They spin in their own orbits, decentralize power, and create an unstable, competitive situation.

A regulation goes beyond rewarding or depriving an individual or firm; it deals with conflicts among people with similar interests. Principally, it affects the organized special interest groups described in chapter 6. When labor or management is regulated because it engages in "unfair" practices, the decision affects more than a single firm or union. Furthermore, the decision may lead to conflict among many people with common interests. They may bargain and form coalitions because of the regulation; and from their coalition-building, a power structure will be formed. It will be an unstable power structure, however, because the interests of the various groups in the coalition may change. Conditions of the economy or of an industry may lead to changed attitudes and objectives.

When we discussed distributive policy, we mentioned that it included awards of government contracts or jobs to firms or individuals. Those distributive decisions are usually made in specialized agencies or congressional committees. Regulatory policies, from time to time, are fought out on the floor of Congress, the policy arena that political science best explains. Lowi sees policy as something formed by what is left after the smoke clears away. "Within this narrower context of regulatory decisions, one can even go so far as to accept the most extreme pluralist statement that policy tends to be a residue of the interplay of group conflict."[16]

Since the log-rolling interpretation has been applied to the distributive arena, and the pluralistic, or group, interpretation applied to the regulatory arena, only one interpretation is left for redistribution—the *power-elite theory*. This theory views the distribution of power as centralized, taking the shape of a pyramid, with those at the top of the pyramid—particularly those in the highest industrial, military, and political positions—making all the key decisions. Their resources are overwhelmingly greater than those of lower-status people, and the theory assumes that the power elite unanimously applies those resources. Also according to the theory, people for these top positions are chosen because they are likely to agree with one another, and they are placed in a way that will reduce any basic conflicts among them. Policy can thus be settled by informal, courteous agreement, without formal debates and votes. Group conflict and coalition building occur, but only on relatively unimportant issues and among people at the middle levels of power.

Professor Lowi interprets redistribution policies in power-elite terms. He sees redistributive issues (income tax and welfare programs) as dividing the participants into "money-providing" and "service-demanding" groups. With one elite for each side, the only negotiation that is possible is on increasing or decreasing the impact of redistribution. (What would be the effects of increasing taxes? Of reducing welfare payments?) Decisions here tend to be made by top leaders in the executive and in peak associations, not on the floor of Congress or in specialized agencies. Because the broad class structure in the United States remains about the same, year after year, and because of what Lowi calls the "impasse (or equilibrium)" in the relations between classes, he concludes that the power structure of redistribution is also highly stable.[17]

We think this interpretation of the redistributive arena is strained. Although we agree with Lowi's imaginative analysis of the distributive and

16 *Ibid.*, p. 695.
17 *Ibid.*, p. 711.

464

PART 4
outputs of the
political system:
who gets helped,
who gets hurt?

regulatory arenas, we cannot agree with his view that the power-elite theory explains the redistributive policy arena.[18] But we agree that some kind of elite control can exist within the pluralistic, or group, theory.

What, then, takes the place of the power-elite theory? The orthodox pluralist theory? It does not fill the gap. Pluralists choose to study issues on which conflict occurs, so they discover conflict in decision making. They also choose issues that are decided by officeholders in the formal political system, so they miss potential issues that were barred from presentation.

Future research may show that distributive, regulatory, and redistributive policy arenas are not so different in the way they make decisions, but the redistributive arena distinguishes itself in the way it *prevents questions from being presented* for formal decision. Sometimes there is a "standing decision" that a certain practice is beyond debate.[19] In shaping that standing decision in a community or in the nation, pressure groups and other unofficial agencies may be more important than the official decision makers who are bound by it. As Schattschneider put it:

All forms of political organization have a bias in favor of the exploitation of some kinds of conflict and the suppression of others because organization is the mobilization of bias. Some issues are organized into politics while others are organized out.[20]

Bias may be mobilized indirectly—even subconsciously—to take some issues out of politics. Picture a member of Congress who decides that the way to deal with the energy crisis is for the government to assume ownership and control of the major oil companies. A representative with this conviction would recognize, if prudent, the futility of introducing such legislation. Here a decision is made, a decision not to raise an issue, but it is made outside the formal system. For the formal political process, then, it is a nondecision, an issue never raised. Questions that challenge the private enterprise system, fundamental constitutional arrangements (and how many other policies?) are usually "defined out" of the political system.

Is American politics under the control of a small ruling elite? In the distributive and regulatory arenas, no. An upper-class bias is not the same as direct rule by a narrow elite. In the redistributive arena, the necessary research for a confident answer has yet to be carried out. When such research is undertaken, it will have to include a consideration of the process by which issues are suppressed as well as the process by which they are resolved once they are raised.[21] At this stage of our knowledge, we are confident that the

---

[18] See Nelson Polsby, *Community Power and Political Theory* (New Haven: Yale University Press, 1963).

[19] For the concept of the "standing decision," see Todd Gitlin, "Local Pluralism as Theory and Ideology," *Studies on the Left,* 5 (Summer 1965), 21–45.

[20] E. E. Schattschneider, *The Semi-Sovereign People* (New York: Holt, 1960), p. 71.

[21] For a statement of what such research should investigate, see Peter Bachrach and Morton S. Baratz, "Two Faces of Power," *American Political Science Review,* 56 (December 1962), 947–52; also see their book, *Power and Poverty: Theory and Practice* (New York: Oxford University Press, 1970).

mobilization of bias favors upper-status groups. Indeed, it would be truly amazing if the dominant values and rules of procedure in a stable society did not favor those in more powerful positions. But we are not at all confident that this bias can be equated with positive control by a narrow power elite. Some hybrid theory (biased pluralism or multicentered elitism) may be the answer.

Consumption of governmental policies

Processes of government that bring forth public policies are obviously political. Less obvious is the fact that when we use or "consume" these policies of protection and service we are also engaging in political acts. Our feelings about some policies and how they are delivered have great impact on the support we give the political system. With the great expansion of governmental policies, the people are always receiving and responding to outputs of government.

Political participation has often been defined narrowly. The number of people who campaign, hold office, or contribute to campaigns is a standard measure of participation.[22] A much more universal form of participation is the citizen-government contact that results from the use of government services.[23] Consumption activities have increased greatly. Depending on and demanding more and more governmental policies, we have become closely tied to, and involved in, the political system. Herbert Jacob cites census statistics to show that as early as 1960, "55 million people or almost half of the adult population . . . consumed governmental outputs which were central to their life style."[24] With new policies pouring forth from government each year, it is likely that using and reacting to public policies is the most frequent contact most of us will have with the political system. Furthermore, using and reacting to public policies usually has an immediate effect upon us—much more immediate and apparent than the result of our vote. Reward or punishment—the specific help or hurt—will probably have more visible importance to us very soon after the policy is instituted: military service, school busing, a change in the minimum wage law.

Large sectors of the population are not highly aware of political institutions and specific governmental policies. Less than half the adult population pays attention to recent Supreme Court rulings. Citizens find it difficult to make abstract judgments of governmental outputs; but when policy actions touch them directly, helping or hurting, they do make judgments and transmit their feelings as either support or nonsupport for the system.

[22] For discussion of this type of participation, see William H. Flanigan and Nancy H. Zingale, *Political Behavior of the American Electorate,* 4th ed. (Boston: Allyn and Bacon, 1979).

[23] For a complete discussion of this type of contact see Herbert Jacob, *Debtors in Court* (Chicago: Rand McNally, 1969). The following material is drawn from Darlene Walker, Richard Richardson, Oliver Williams, Thomas Denyer, and Skip McGaughey, "Contact and Support: An Empirical Assessment of Public Attitudes Toward the Police and Courts," *North Carolina Law Review,* 51 (November 1972), 43–79.

[24] Jacob, *Debtors in Court,* p. 4, note 1.

466

PART 4
outputs of the
political system:
who gets helped,
who gets hurt?

DOONESBURY

Copright, 1978, G. B. Trudeau.

Obviously, public policies are not the only basis upon which people make judgments about government. As we have shown in our discussion of political socialization, long before public policies are visible or real to a child, attitudes shaped by age, class status, family, and school are already present. We therefore are not political innocents when we look at the actions of public officials and policies of public agencies. We are well-developed political beings when we are first exposed to public policy; and because of our political upbringing, we have a context or frame of mind within which we evaluate a policy. If a mother's food stamps are cut off, for example, she will react to this change in policy by thinking back to other discriminations or hurts that she has suffered from the system. If, on the other hand, a federal tax policy allows her to deduct $2,000 on the purchase of a new home, she will evaluate this new help in the context of all the other goods and bads that have come to her from government.

Feelings of support, therefore, are not necessarily directly related to the use of a service or the protection enjoyed. Earlier feelings, developed from status, race, income, age, and education, are among other factors that enter in.[25] Another factor is the condition under which our contact with the policy arises. Perhaps the most important condition is whether we seek the service or protection or whether it is imposed; that is, whether our use of the public policy or program is voluntary or nonvoluntary. If you are arrested by the FBI because of federal policy on interstate sale of stolen securities, you will probably have negative reactions. If, on the other hand, your call for FBI assistance results in the return of your kidnapped child, you would be more likely to have positive reactions.

[25] For evidence of this in law enforcement see President's Commission on Law Enforcement and Administration of Justice, *The Challenge of Crime in a Free Society* (Washington, D.C.: Government Printing Office, 1967).

by Garry Trudeau

467

CHAPTER 13
policy:
the purpose
of politics

Another condition that will shape a citizen-government exchange is how satisfied the citizen is by the experience. Was the official courteous? Did the public service give you what you needed and expected? Was the treatment (even if not voluntary) reasonable, fair, and done with as little damage to you as possible? We may find a federally enforced 55-mile-per-hour speed law inhibiting, but we can still conclude that in its purpose and application, our experience with it has been satisfactory.

We have pointed throughout this book to numerous instances of imbalance in the helping and hurting in American society. These imbalances lead to the expectation that dissatisfaction with public policies would be worse than it is. We have pointed to evidence of declining trust in political institutions and to evidence of opposition to public policy; for example, the widespread and bitter opposition to the policies pursued in the Vietnam War. As we saw in our analysis of political attitudes of children, differences among groups do exist even at an early age. But the overall context of evaluation of public policies seems to be a favorable one.

Legal justice policy

Seeing the consumption of public policies as political acts is an intriguing idea. Herbert Jacob, who applied this view to the legal system,[26] compared the political attitudes of those who had their day in court and those who had never been in court. They differed significantly. The people who went to court had either declared themselves bankrupt or were there because of garnishment proceedings (their wages had been deducted to pay a debt). Both classes of litigants were much more politically aware than were people

---

[26] *Debtors in Court.*

468

PART 4
outputs of the
political system:
who gets helped,
who gets hurt?

who had no court contacts. People with voluntary court contact (bankruptcy) were more favorable to the courts and the broader political system than were those with involuntary court contacts (garnishment).

Thomas Jahnige proposed a similar theory with regard to more common court experiences such as divorce proceedings and hearings on traffic violations. He maintains that the average citizen goes into the judicial arena with high expectations of objectivity and fairness, but is often disappointed. "To the court professional the rough and tumble manner of a proceeding may seem obvious. . . . To litigants and witnesses, however, this may be an extremely disturbing experience. . . litigants, witnesses, and jurors may leave the courtroom psychologically dissatisfied and with their respect for the courts greatly lowered."[27] Thus, Jahnige suggests that the contact the average person is likely to have with legal justice policies may lower support for the judicial system, because its procedures and outputs do not measure up to the idealized standards or expectations.

The most recent work done on the interrelationships between public policies, contact, and satisfaction has involved the public and the police. In the legal system, people become receivers of legal services when they report a crime or call the police for help. They have important nonvoluntary contact when they receive a traffic ticket, are stopped by the police for questioning, or are arrested. All of these deliveries of public policies are capable of playing an important role in feedback for the political system.

Studying blacks' and whites' perceptions of justice, Jacob found that contact with the police and courts affects attitudes.[28] In a statewide study of public attitudes toward police and courts, a team of North Carolina political scientists demonstrated "that the extent of public contact with these agencies is broad and the level of support is high. The data persuasively show that the satisfaction and dissatisfaction of citizen contacts is strongly related to specific, changing opinions . . . and to more enduring, generalized public attitudes."[29]

Murphy and Tannenhaus have looked at public attitudes toward the Supreme Court. They concluded that "there can be no doubt about the character of issues apt to be salient. They are clearly the ones that can be viewed in an intensely personal fashion."[30] To this conclusion, Barth agreed from his research. "The degree to which the citizen perceives the outputs of the Supreme Court is closely related to the degree to which the citizen perceives his interests to be involved in the decisions."[31] Thus, contact with civil rights

---

[27] "A Note on the Implications of Legal Rules and Procedures," in Thomas Jahnige and Sheldon Goldman, eds., *The Federal Judicial System* (New York: Holt, 1971), pp. 94–99.

[28] Herbert Jacob, "Black and White Perceptions of Justice in the City," *Law and Society Review,* 6 (August 1971), 67–89. For similar findings see David Bayley and Robert Mendelsohn, *Minorities and Police* (New York: Free Press, 1969).

[29] Walker, et al., "Contact and Support," p. 79.

[30] Walter Murphy and Joseph Tannenhaus, "Public Opinion and the United States Supreme Court," in Joel Grossman and Joseph Tanenhaus, eds., *Frontiers of Judicial Research* (New York: John Wiley, 1969), p. 279.

[31] Thomas Barth, "Perception and Acceptance of Supreme Court Decisions at the State and Local Level," *Journal of Public Law,* 17 (1968), 319.

and desegregation decisions had dramatic impact on both blacks and whites. School prayer and Bible reading decisions touched sensitive nerves across the society, affected large numbers of school children, and were, therefore, received as important.

The public policies that spill forth in a democracy are, one hopes, some reasonable output of a political struggle that gives the people what they need and want. Often, we know, they are not. As we shall note later, there are some complex reasons why policy often does not fit need or desire. However imperfectly public policy is devised or applied, it has profound consequences for stability of the political system. We have sought to demonstrate this by looking at the receiving and evaluation of public policy as political acts of major dimensions. In the end, one is helped or hurt not by the political struggle itself but by the products or outcomes of the struggle.

UNANTICIPATED CONSEQUENCES AND IMPERFECTIONS OF POLICY

One of the aspects of public policies most frustrating both to policy makers and consumers is that policies seldom turn out as designed. Even when decision makers are able to understand what the public wants and even when they try to make decisions that reflect these wants, they often design imperfect policies with imperfect results. Why is this the case?

Certainly one of the central reasons is the *fragmented nature of the American policy-making machinery.* As we have seen, the constitutional system was designed with many decisional points. President, legislatures, courts, bureaucrats—all check and balance each other, each contributes a share of policy decisions and policy confusion. In the federal context, the process is multiplied fiftyfold. In answering the question, "Who's running this show?" the answer has to be, "Lots of folks." No person or institution is responsible for policy in the United States. That's the way we want it, because we fear concentration of power. But the result is that public policy making is partial, seldom coordinated, and often poorly supervised.

Policy is imperfect because it is always a *compromise* with interests constantly working to *maximize benefits* or *reduce injuries.* Few public policies emerge from the decisional process as their supporters designed them at the outset. The give-and-take of deliberations requires that all sides give a little before the end product, and there are multiple points along the way where the losing side can nibble away at policy decisions. Few policies are *made* at one point in time. The policy process is unending because the forces particularly affected by policy decisions continually try to improve their position. Long after the general public has lost interest in a policy decision, organized interests continue to bargain at each new stage for their concerns. Thus, years later, when the policy again hits the headlines, often radically transformed, a puzzled public asks, "What happened?"

470

PART 4
outputs of the
political system:
who gets helped,
who gets hurt?

Imperfect policy outcomes also result from the *decentralized nature of their administration*. National policy is administered through regional and district offices or through the states. Although there may be a national "decision," it must be carried out by regional and district offices of the national bureaucracy or by state agencies. Thus, there is seldom a national policy, but a great variety of national policies as defined by those officials who administer them in the states. A classic case of this was seen in implementing the Supreme Court's decisions on desegregation. Implementation and interpretation powers were given to the federal district court judges. These judges, usually local, born and trained in their districts, gave a variety of colorations and local values to their decisions. The result was not only delay in, and avoidance of, desegregation, but almost as many desegregation policies and plans as there were cases. National poverty policy and crime control policy are additional examples of the variations one finds because of the dependence on state machinery for implementation and administration.

The American commitment to put a man on the moon was so costly that it had unanticipated consequences for other public policies.

NASA

A public policy may also have an imperfect outcome or undesired impact because it conflicts *with the objectives of other policies* being pursued with equal vigor. The same combination of interests does not win on all policy decisions, and victory on decision A may be offset by loss on decision B. Additionally, two policies, both designed to promote the general welfare, may conflict. A national policy to reduce pollution and gasoline consumption may conflict with a policy on full employment. A public policy to rehabilitate prisoners will often conflict with a policy desire to punish them. Efforts to desegregate educational institutions may have the undesired consequence of destroying most black educational institutions and black academic leadership. One can hardly think of a policy decision that does not have consequence for other policy judgments. When this occurs, the outcomes of both policies become interlocked, sometimes conflicting, with often unanticipated results.

This conflict of purpose is often made more acute by the *vagueness* of policy objectives and the *range* given to their interpretation. Laws, decisions, administrative orders are often worded in general, nonspecific language, in order to get them through political compromises required for their passage. This kind of language is desirable also for flexibility in dealing with changing problems and new political coalitions. But the very vagueness of policy wording makes variation and change in intent highly likely. What does "substantial interstate commerce" mean? Or "all deliberate speed"? For that matter, what is "cruel and unusual punishment"? These words mean different things to different groups; and although embodied in the law and part of public policy, they are subject to continuous change and interpretation.

If vagueness is a problem for policy forecasting, *lack of information* and *misinformation* is an even greater difficulty. In an age in which there is information in abundance about everything—from sex habits to planet temperatures—it is amazing how much in the dark policy makers feel about the decision they are making. They have little precise, solid, focused information that will enable them to forecast accurately the outcome of a policy. In part, this scarcity is attributable to a shortage of time and staff. In part it is a lack of skills or knowledge to forecast impacts accurately. Finally, it is a result of information that is colored or skewed by the special interests that transmit it. Those who develop policies often ask advice of people who will be affected by the policies. The practice reduces conflicts and builds strong constituency ties, but it is not a very good way to obtain objective information. Choosing among several good guesses on the outcome of a policy may be all that a decision maker can do.

With all the constraints on public policy making, it is not surprising that our successes are partial, our failures many, and that almost all of our efforts bring forth unanticipated results. We drift into a Vietnam War; we do not want it but cannot stop it. We conduct another "war" on poverty, yet hunger persists. We seek to regulate an activity, only to find that the "regulated" are making the regulations. Only because our failures are offset by our successes does the policy-making process of American society continue to challenge us and continue to receive our support.

SUMMARY

Society would not exist without government, which performs the essential functions of protection and service. Without government we would have extreme disorder.

Policies are always changing in response to changing demands and environmental conditions. The larger, more interdependent and impersonal our society has become, the more regulatory responsibility the government has taken on in behalf of the citizens. Examples of expanding government policies include the Sherman Antitrust Act, the establishment of minimum wages and hours, and the Fair Labor Standards Act.

There are three general types of public policy: distributive, regulatory, and redistributive. As citizens, we are most likely to be aware of policies that affect us directly, and our reactions to these policies help us make judgments about the government. Policies, however, seldom turn out as designed. They are formed by many people, usually through a series of compromises, and are then carried out through regional or district offices or through the states. Policies may conflict with each other because of the vagueness of their objectives and the lack of information that went into their formulation; but among all the weaknesses of policy making, one strength emerges: perpetuity. Policy making never ends.

misconceptions
and
concepts
in
perspective

474

PART 4
outputs of the
political system:
who gets helped,
who gets hurt?

If we were to list everything we hope you have learned from this book, we would have to repeat every generalization we have offered in the preceding thirteen chapters. Education is not just a matter of gaining new understandings; it is also a process of unlearning, of ridding one's self of false conceptions. With the help of the concepts developed in the book, we conclude by returning to the misconceptions about politics that we looked at in chapter 1. We hope we can clear them away when they are false and make them more accurate when they are merely distorted.

"The founding fathers were above politics"

Some patriotic organizations seem to have the notion that schools can produce good Americans only if they present a "depoliticized" picture of our first great politicians. Perhaps a somewhat idealized version must be presented at the secondary level, but to give students a false picture of democratic government is misguided patriotism. Countless Americans still have an image of George Washington, Thomas Jefferson, Alexander Hamilton, James Madison, Patrick Henry, and others marching forward in perfect unison, shoulder to shoulder, toward sunrise. Pictured as being above petty politics, these leaders are supposed to have been followed by all right-thinking men in adopting the Constitution (which Henry called "the most fatal possible plan for the enslavement of a free people"!) and to have launched the ship of state on calm waters, without bickering over mere political differences.

Most of our founding fathers were in fact great politicians. They were quite capable of expressing their disagreements in clear-cut terms and of throwing themselves into power struggles as lively as any that occur today. Only by understanding the special interests, the conflicting ideas, and the political strategy of the founding fathers can we appreciate them as real human beings, and then we can apply that understanding and appreciation to a consideration of contemporary politics. In the real political world, different experiences and conflicting interests inevitably lead even the best-intentioned people to rational (and irrational) disagreements.

The tragedy of the "nonpolitical" view is that it sacrifices accuracy for the sake of patriotism and is still a poor means of molding loyal citizens. The idea that a democratic leader should be "above politics" is as ridiculous as the notion that the Pope or the Archbishop of Canterbury should be above religion. But the false image of the founding fathers, coupled with the great respect they enjoy, leads to disillusionment when the citizen of today evaluates the performance of current officeholders and discovers that they are "mere politicians."

"All politicians are corrupt"

Reverence for the founding fathers is often coupled with contempt for current politicians, a contempt that leads some to believe that all politicians are crooks.

This misconception is easy to understand. We do not perfectly live up to our highest ideals in any area of life, and politics is no exception. In 1976, revelations by the Senate Intelligence Committee demonstrated repeated violations of the law by the FBI under both Republican and Democratic Presidents. Abuses of power reached a new high under Richard Nixon, but they were certainly not confined to his administration. No one today can deny that illegal activities by officeholders have been widespread in recent years. Skepticism in regard to politicians is therefore realistic.

The extent of corruption among today's politicians is, however, probably exaggerated. The idea that *all* politicians are corrupt is certainly a misconception. Although no one is perfect, three factors seem to produce an exaggerated image of the imperfections of politicians. First, politicians make decisions of importance to many people, and someone is always disappointed by every decision. The losers often respond to their disappointment by claiming that they "got a dirty deal." Second, politics necessarily involves compromise, and it is the politicians who must make the compromises that enable people to live together peaceably. The rest of us can afford the luxury of inflexible principles and the feelings of superiority that go with them. Third, Americans appear to have a double standard of morals, condemning politicians for behavior that they take for granted in their own lives. Newspaper headlines indict the public official who is given a favor by a business contact, but many of the most indignant private citizens seek similar favors themselves. The "wheeling and dealing" that we applaud on the part of the enterprising business person is considered disgraceful in public life. True, we have a right to expect higher standards of government officials, but we should at least be aware of the sacrifices we expect of them.

"The American way is the only democratic way"

Any thinking person should be able to detect blind provincialism, or narrow-mindedness, in political discussions. Love of country can be kept separate from an irrational rejection of everything strange or new. Whether unfamiliar institutions deserve to be rejected or not, they should at least be evaluated on intellectually defensible grounds. Such practices as legislative supremacy (instead of separation of powers), multiparty politics (instead of the two-party system), and socialism (instead of capitalism), for example, may be un-American without being undemocratic.

The reverse side of this same coin, which pictures everything American as essential to democracy, is equally counterfeit. In a democracy, government leaders must be responsive to the people. Our leaders are responsive enough to satisfy that requirement, so we can infer that none of our key institutions is absolutely incompatible with democracy. But to conclude from this that every one of our institutions is *essential* to democracy is shabby logic. Separation of powers and checks and balances, for example, were designed by men who were alarmed at the prospect of popular control over policy. Despite these barriers, not because of them, we have achieved a remarkable

476

PART 4
outputs of the
political system:
who gets helped,
who gets hurt?

degree of democracy. To claim that institutions such as these were designed in the interest of popular control is to misunderstand separation of powers and checks and balances and to misinterpret the aims and ideas of the men who helped create them.

"Ours is a government of laws and not of men"

This idea, often heard during the American Revolution, has inspired the struggle for responsible government everywhere. It seems to be a misconception only in the literal sense. In both Europe and America, those who fought for democratic government resented the unpredictable and arbitrary power of rulers, from kings to local magistrates. Like any propagandists engaged in a serious political struggle, the American revolutionists exaggerated the evils they were trying to do away with—the purely personal nature of irresponsible decisions—and the improvements they could offer—the impersonality of government under law. Without eliminating personal favoritism or malice entirely, democracy has greatly reduced the exercise of personal caprice (whim) by limiting public officials to known procedures, rules, and punishments. So in a sense we have achieved what would have been regarded in the age of monarchy as something close to "a government of laws and not of men."

To carry this concept to the extreme, to believe in a government conducted by laws only, becomes both false and dangerous. Our government is made up of men and women, and our Constitution and laws are made, applied, and interpreted by men and women. Literal belief in a government of laws and not of people is dangerous because it leads either to blindness or disillusionment. Anyone who thinks that judicial decisions are or should be impersonal products of "the Court," for example, must either ignore split decisions or else conclude that some of the justices have lost their reasoning powers or have become scoundrels. A realistic appraisal of the Court requires an awareness that people differ on political issues and that political decisions must be made by human beings. By giving more people a voice in making laws and establishing procedures for their enforcement and interpretation, we have moved toward "a government of laws [reflecting popular preferences] and not of [a few irresponsible] men."

"Free elections ensure majority control of public policy"

This idea is older than democratic government itself. In America, for example, Sam Adams dissolved the political machine through which he had controlled Boston politics before the Revolution, because he saw no need for such an organization once freedom had been won. Popular suffrage seemed to promise a solution for the whole problem of making government responsible to the people. Emphasis on the vote is not misplaced, for the effectiveness of all the other means of political influence stems from the basic right to vote. When the Supreme Court's repudiation of the "white primary" enabled large numbers of black southerners to vote, that basic right soon enabled them to use other techniques of political pressure more effectively.

For the individual citizen to cast a vote is not enough in itself, however, for individual votes are not automatically translated into public policy. If millions of Americans were to vote as so many separate individuals, the results would be almost meaningless. Hundreds of candidates would receive votes, and pluralities as high as 10 percent would be unusual. When winners were announced, there would be no way of judging what policies had been endorsed. To give meaning to the vote, intermediary organizations—pressure groups and political parties—standing between the citizen and the government are necessary in every democracy. Political parties and pressure groups serve a "middleman" function in identifying popular interests and selecting leaders. These agencies are mentioned nowhere in the written Constitution, but they are as much a part of American politics as Congress, the President, or the Supreme Court.

Voting does not ensure, by itself, popular control of public policy.

Irene Springer.

PART 4
outputs of the
political system:
who gets helped,
who gets hurt?

"Policy reflects consensus"

Some people assume that official policy in a democracy always reflects consensus or general agreement. Margaret Mead, an anthropologist, found that this assumption was quite accurate in the rigidly traditional Balinese civilization. Every issue there is resolved by a simple process that boils down to asking, "What is the place of this new proposal in our pattern of decreed and traditional behavior?" Americans, however, who become emotionally involved in public issues, find it difficult to imagine "a society in which issues as vital as migration or war are settled as formally, from the standpoint of public opinion, as is the date of Thanksgiving Day."[1] Certainly none of the policies we have discussed in preceding chapters reflected consensus. Policy in the United States represents the victory of one coalition of interests over another, with the losers protesting so loudly that no one can doubt their displeasure.

Balinese differ from Americans, not in having an accepted tradition, but in having a tradition that produces unquestioned answers to specific problems. Their tradition answers questions; ours provides a method of seeking answers. Any stable society requires wide acceptance of basic political procedures, and democratic government is impossible unless most of the losers as well as the winners are willing to accept policies determined by "consent of the governed." But this is quite different from *policy* by consensus. Not all Americans agree on even underlying elements of our politics such as the rules of Congress or the powers of the national government. What we *agree* on, essentially, is a method of governing in which policies reflect widespread interests without destroying the right to *disagree*. This is radically different from the idea that specific policies reflect consensus.

The danger in the expectation of consensus is that it can be turned into acceptance of minority control. Various devices that block or delay the achievement of policies with majority support—devices like the seniority system in Congress or the filibuster in the Senate—are thus defended on the ground that they promote government by consensus. But this is the pursuit of a will-o'-the-wisp. A device like the filibuster gives the minority a veto over policy; it does not give us consensus. When a majority of those participating in politics are prevented from enacting a policy they want, what we actually have is minority control over policy.

A decision to continue an old policy is just as binding—just as much an act of government—as a decision to modify that policy. If a minority keeps an old policy in effect when a majority wants to change it, the majority is forced to accept the preference of the minority. This is no less frustrating for the majority than the requirement of observing the new policy would be for the minority. The question is not how to get consensus, but who is going to be frustrated—the majority or the minority? The seniority system and the filibuster may be justified on the ground that they give strategic minorities a negative control over policy and that they make more than ordinary

[1] Margaret Mead, "Public Opinion Mechanisms Among Primitive Peoples," *Public Opinion Quarterly,* 1 (July 1937), 7.

majorities necessary to change policy. But with majorities frustrated in the first case, and with minorities frustrated in the second, this is hardly consensus.

"Government is neutral"

A somewhat similar misconception is that government is neutral. This is a tendency to confuse preferences with realities. You may think it would be nice if the government were neutral, but the notion simply does not fit the facts. The idea of neutral government is really a contradiction in terms. Government is not called upon to make policy in the absence of controversy. By its very nature, the act of governing involves settling issues. Without a dispute, there is no issue; without an issue, there is no need for government to decide and enforce policy.

Granted that government action is called for only when people disagree, some will be disappointed and others will be pleased whatever the outcome. To analyze government, then, the most useful device we have found is to ask of any governmental arrangement or proposal: (1) What are its effects or consequences for people? (2) Who is hurt and who is helped by such consequences? The facts of American government are constantly changing, but a permanently useful yardstick to be taken from this book is to be found in these two analytical questions. Whatever the changing circumstances of politics, you can always decide whether or not to get interested in an issue and which side to join if you apply the "who-gets-helped/hurt" test.

"Government is inherently evil"

The idea that government is inherently evil is more basic than the view that today's politicians are corrupt. If we are troubled by corrupt politicians, we can "turn the rascals out" and hope for something better. If government is evil in its very nature, all we can do is try to minimize it. Communist regimes go so far as to promise that, as Karl Marx said, government will eventually "wither away." The more common idea in the United States is that government is necessary, but the complete phrase is "a necessary evil."

We call attention to the inappropriateness of applying the "necessary evil" label to government alone among the powerful institutions of modern society. If government is evil, other institutions must be equally or more so. Our government is made up of fallible human beings; it differs from other organizations in that all citizens can have a say in selecting its leaders. Compared with a corporation, a labor union, a church, a university, or any other organization, the government of a democracy can convincingly claim that it comes closest to representing the interests of the general public.

"The national government is worse than state or local governments"

A nationwide organization like the United States Steel Corporation is "the industrial family that serves America" and the AFL-CIO is made up of "the

480

PART 4
outputs of the
political system:
who gets helped,
who gets hurt?

nation's workers," but our national government is "the Washington bureaucracy." Many Americans seem to have this impression: all politics is dubious, but local government is best, state government is second best, and national government is the worst of all.

The old Jeffersonian idea that local government was the most efficient, honest, and responsive to broad public needs seems to be an exact reversal of the facts of modern political life. A different conclusion seems called for today. Inefficiency, dishonesty, and minority domination are probably found most often in local governments. Conditions improve in state governments, and they are probably at their best in the national government.

The persistence of the old attitude is not easy to explain. Perhaps it is simply a case of the survival, after the facts have changed, of what may once have been a good theory. Whatever the situation may have been in Jefferson's time, our problems today are national or international in scope, and the most exciting government decisions are made in Washington. As a result, politicians find a greater challenge there than in county offices, and the press and public follow decisions in the national government more closely. Moreover, the constituencies of national officials are broader and include too many different interests for any one special interest to dominate policy. In short, the pressures of politics encourage statesmanship in governors more than in members of a city council; in Presidents more than in governors.

"Tyranny of the majority is a threat to freedom"

First conceived as an argument against democracy itself, the threat of majority tyranny has served as an effective weapon in opposing every extension of popular power, from universal suffrage to stronger political parties. When examined in the light of actual experience in democracies, however, the threat disappears.

First, just what does the term mean? *Tyranny* is the imposition by rulers of severe deprivations upon those ruled, combined with the denial of any legal way (such as propaganda and election efforts) to eliminate those deprivations. When citizens pay their taxes or are required to drive within fixed speed limits or are forbidden to engage in specified business practices, they may feel a sense of deprivation. But we do not regard them as victims of tyranny, because they are neither treated with capricious severity nor denied an opportunity to try to change the law.

The interests and viewpoints of Americans are extremely diverse—so diverse that a majority cannot be united behind any narrowly tyrannical program. A majority coalition can be created only by a broad program representing compromises among the aims of countless minority groups. With overlapping group membership and with general commitment to popular freedom, no tyrannical policy can win majority endorsement. In the United States, truly tyrannical schemes have been heard only from the lunatic fringe.

Justice under law remains the product of fallible human beings.

482

PART 4
outputs of the
political system:
who gets helped,
who gets hurt?

"The incapacity of the people causes many malfunctions of American government"

This belief is the final retreat of those who really do not like democracy but find themselves in an era when they cannot openly admit their feeling (perhaps even to themselves). Unable to reject democracy directly, they do so indirectly by denying the capacity of the average person for self-government. If the ordinary people are, as Alexander Hamilton said, a "great beast," then whatever is wrong with the system must result from the people's bungling.

In a sense, this belief is true: a system that is reasonably democratic gives the people a formal right to correct ills, to change things to their satisfaction. But the real, as opposed to the formal, chance to correct the wrongs in the system is not great.

Throughout this book we have found that the resources needed to influence policy are unevenly distributed, with a small percentage of the population having tremendous advantages over most of the rest. And we have found that official and unofficial agencies of politics are organized to the advantage of the "haves" over the "have-nots." The one resource in which the majority of the people have the advantage is sheer numbers—they can outvote any minority. But these millions of ordinary people are dependent on political parties to give them clear and helpful choices. In a less immediate way they depend on such agencies as the mass media and the schools to give them the background for judging the choices they are offered. If parties and candidates appeal to emotions rather than to logic, the only possible outcome is an election based on the feelings rather than the thoughts of the voters.

The choices that the mass of the people make for the political system cannot be of higher quality than those they are offered. If politicians, the media, and textbooks are geared to the belief that people cannot understand complex or subtle reasoning, for example, they will treat all issues at the intellectual level of comic books and television commercials. In a horrible self-fulfilling prophecy, the assumption that people cannot digest meaty intellectual fare may reduce their capacity to the point that they can handle only pablum. Should this come to pass, the responsibility will lie with the politicians, with those who speak for the media, and with the authors of textbooks, more than with the people whom they address.

People are capable, we believe, of thinking. We also believe they are capable of handling as much responsibility and power as they are encouraged to develop. This is simply to say that we think more democracy is possible.

The Constitution of the United States

WE THE PEOPLE OF THE UNITED STATES, in Order to form a more perfect Union, establish Justice, insure domestic Tranquility, provide for the common defence, promote the general Welfare, and secure the Blessings of Liberty to ourselves and our Posterity, do ordain and establish this Constitution for the United States of America.

Article I

Section 1. All legislative Powers herein granted shall be vested in a Congress of the United States, which shall consist of a Senate and House of Representatives.

Section 2. The House of Representatives shall be composed of Members chosen every second Year by the People of the several States, and the Electros in each State shall have the Qualifications requisite for Electors of the most numerous Branch of the State Legislature.

No Person shall be a Representative who shall not have attained to the age of twenty five Years, and been seven Years a Citizen of the United States, and who shall not, when elected, be an Inhabitant of that State in which he shall be chosen.

Representatives and direct Taxes shall be apportioned among the several States which may be included within this Union, according to their respective Numbers, *which shall be determined by adding to the whole Number of free Persons, including those bound to Service for a Term of Years, and excluding Indians not taxed, three fifths of all other persons.*[1] The actual Enumeration shall be made within three Years after the first Meeting of the Congress of the United States, and within every subsequent Term of ten Years, in such Manner as they shall by Law direct. The Number of Representatives shall not exceed one for every thirty Thousand, but each State shall have at Least one Representative; and until such enumeration shall be made, the State of New Hampshire shall be entitled to chuse three, Massachusetts eight, Rhode-Island and Providence Plantations one, Connecticut five, New-York six, New Jersey four, Pennsylvania eight, Delaware one, Maryland six, Virginia ten, North Carolina five, South Carolina five, and Georgia three.

When vacancies happen in the Representation from any State, the Executive Authority thereof shall issue Writs of Election to fill such Vacancies.

The House of Representatives shall chuse their Speaker and other Officers; and shall have the sole Power of Impeachment.

Section 3. The Senate of the United States shall be composed of two Senators from each State, *chosen by the Legislature thereof,*[2] for six Years; and each Senator shall have one Vote.

Immediately after they shall be assembled in Consequence of the first Election, they shall be divided as equally as may be into three Classes. The Seats of the Senators of the first Class shall be vacated at the Expiration of the second Year, of the second Class at the Expiration of the fourth Year, and of the third Class at the Expiration of the sixth Year, so that one third may be chosen every second Year; *and if Vacancies happen by Resignation, or otherwise, during the Recess of the Legislature of any State, the Executive thereof may make temporary Appointments until the next Meeting of the Legislature, which shall then fill such Vacancies.*[3]

No Person shall be a Senator who shall not have attained to the Age of thirty Years, and been nine Years a Citizen of the United States, and who shall not, when elected, be an Inhabitant of the State for which he shall be chosen.

The Vice President of the United States shall be President of the Senate, but shall have no Vote, unless they be equally divided.

The Senate shall chuse their other Officers, and also a President pro tempore, in the Absence of the Vice President, or when he shall exercise the Office of President of the United States.

The Senate shall have the sole Power to try all Impeachments. When sitting for that Purpose, they shall be on Oath or Affirmation. When the President of the United States is tried, the Chief Justice shall preside: And no Person shall be convicted without the Concurrence of two thirds of the Members present.

Judgment in Cases of Impeachment shall not extend further than to removal from Office, and disqualification to hold and enjoy any Office of honor, Trust or Profit under the United States: but the Party convicted shall nevertheless be liable and subject to Indictment, Trial, Judgment and Punishment, according to Law.

---

[1]Throughout, italics are used to indicate passages altered by subsequent amendments. In this instance, for example, see 14th Amendment.

[2]See 17th Amendment.

[3]See 17th Amendment.

Section 4. The Times, Places and Manner of holding Elections for Senators and Representatives, shall be prescribed in each State by the Legislature thereof; but the Congress may at any time by Law make or alter such Regulations, except as to the Places of chusing Senators.

The Congress shall assemble at least once in every Year, and such Meeting shall be on the first Monday in December, unless they shall by Law appoint a different Day.[4]

Section 5. Each House shall be the Judge of the Elections, Returns and Qualifications of its own Members, and a Majority of each shall consitute a Quorum to do Business; but a smaller Number may adjourn from day to day, and may be authorized to compel the Attendance of absent Members, in such Manner, and under such Penalties as each House may provide.

Each House may determine the Rules of its Proceedings, punish its Members for disorderly Behaviour, and, with the Concurrence of two thirds, expel a Member.

Each House shall keep a Journal of its Proceedings, and from time to time publish the same, excepting such Parts as may in their Judgment require Secrecy; and the Yeas and Nays of the Members of either House on any question shall, at the Desire of one fifth of those Present, be entered on the Journal.

Neither House, during the Session of Congress, shall, without the Consent of the other, adjourn for more than three days, nor to any other Place than that in which the two Houses shall be sitting.

Section 6. The Senators and Representatives shall receive a Compensation for their Services, to be ascertained by Law, and paid out of the Treasury of the United States. They shall in all Cases, except Treason, Felony and Breach of the Peace, be privileged from Arrest during their Attendance at the Session of their respective Houses, and in going to and returning from the same; and for any Speech or Debate in either House, they shall not be questioned in any other Place.

No Senator or Representative shall, during the Time for which he was elected, be appointed to any civil Office under the Authority of the United States, which shall have been created, or the Emoluments whereof shall have been encreased during such time; and no Person holding any Office under the United States, shall be a Member of either House during his Continuance in Office.

Section 7. All bills for raising Revenue shall originate in the house of Representatives; but the Senate may propose or concur with Amendments as on other Bills.

Every Bill which shall have passed the House of Representatives and the Senate, shall, before it become a Law, be presented to the President of the United States; if he approve he shall sign it, but if not he shall return it, with his Objections to that House in which it shall have originated, who shall enter the Objections at large on their Journal, and proceed to reconsider it. If after such Reconsideration two thirds of that House shall agree to pass the Bill, it shall be sent, together with the Objections, to the other House, by which it shall

[4]See 20th Amendment.

likewise be reconsidered, and if approved by two thirds of that House, it shall become a Law. But in all such Cases the Votes of both Houses shall be determined by Yeas and Nays, and the Names of the Persons voting for and against the Bill shall be entered on the Journal of each House respectively. If any Bill shall not be returned by the President within ten Days (Sundays excepted) after it shall have been presented to him, the Same shall be a Law, in like Manner as if he had signed it, unless the Congress by their Adjournment prevent its Return, in which Case it shall not be a Law.

Every Order, Resolution, or Vote to which the Concurrence of the Senate and House of Representatives may be necessary (except on a question of Adjournment) shall be presented to the President of the United States; and before the Same shall take Effect, shall be approved by him, or being disapproved by him, shall be repassed by two thirds of the Senate and House of Representatives, according to the Rules and Limitations prescribed in the Case of a Bill.

Section 8. The Congress shall have Power To lay and collect Taxes, Duties, Imposts and Excises, to pay the Debts and provide for the common Defence and general Welfare of the United States; but all Duties, Imposts and Excises shall be uniform throughout the United States;

To borrow Money on the credit of the United States;

To regulate Commerce with foreign Nations, and among the several States, and with the Indian Tribes;

To establish an uniform Rule of Naturalization, and uniform Laws on the subject of Bankruptcies throughout the United States;

To coin Money, regulate the Value thereof, and of foreign Coin, and fix the Standard of Weights and Measures;

To provide for the Punishment of counterfeiting the Securities and current Coin of the United States;

To establish Post Offices and post Roads;

To promote the Progress of Science and useful Arts, by securing for limited Times to Authors and Inventors the exclusive Right to their respective Writings and Discoveries;

To constitute Tribunals inferior to the Supreme Court;

To define and punish Piracies and Felonies committed on the high Seas, and Offences against the Law of Nations;

To declare War, grant Letters of Marque and Reprisal, and make Rules concerning Captures on Land and Water;

To raise and support Armies, but no Appropriation of Money to that Use shall be for a longer Term than two Years;

To provide and maintain a Navy;

To make Rules for the Government and Regulation of the land and naval Forces;

To provide for calling forth the Militia to execute the Laws of the Union, suppress Insurrections and repel Invasions;

To provide for organizing, arming, and disciplining, the Militia, and for governing such Part of them as may be employed in the Service of the United States, reserving to the States respectively, the Appointment of the Officers, and the Authority of training the Militia according to the discipline prescribed by Congress;

To exercise exclusive Legislation in all Cases whatsoever, over such District (not exceeding ten Miles square) as may, by Cession of particular States, and the Acceptance of Congress, become the Seat of the Government of the United States, and to exercise like Authority over all Places purchased by the Consent of the Legislature of the State in which the Same shall be, for the Erection of Forts, Magazines, Arsenals, dock-Yards, and other needful Buildings; — And

To make all Laws which shall be necessary and proper for carrying into Execution the foregoing Powers, and all other Powers vested by this Constitution in the Government of the United States, or in any Department or Officer thereof.

Section 9. The Migration or Importation of such Persons as any of the States now existing shall think proper to admit, shall not be prohibited by the Congress prior to the Year one thousand eight hundred and eight, but a Tax or duty may be imposed on such Importation, not exceeding ten dollars for each Person.

The Privilege of the Writ of Habeas Corpus shall not be suspended, unless when in Cases of Rebellion or Invasion the public Safety may require it.

No Bill of Attainder or ex post facto Law shall be passed.

No Capitation, or other direct, Tax shall be laid, unless in Proportion to the Census or Enumeration herein before directed to be taken.

No Tax or Duty shall be laid on Articles exported from any state.

No Preference shall be given by any Regulation of Commerce or Revenue to the Ports of one State over those of another: not shall Vessels bound to, or from, one State, be obliged to enter, clear, or pay Duties in another.

No Money shall be drawn from the Treasury, but in Consequence of Appropriations made by Law; and a regular Statement and Account of the Receipts and Expenditures of all public Money shall be published from time to time.

No title of Nobility shall be granted by the United States: And no Person holding any Office of Profit or Trust under them, shall, without the Consent of the Congress, accept of any present, Emolument, Office, or Title, of any kind whatever, from any King, Prince, or foreign State.

Section 10. No State shall enter into any Treaty, Alliance, or Confederation; grant Letters of Marque and Reprisal; coin Money; emit Bills of Credit; make any Thing but gold and silver Coin a Tender in Payment of Debts; pass any Bill of Attainder, ex post facto Law, or Law impairing the Obligation of Contracts, or Grant any Title of Nobility.

No State shall, without the Consent of the Congress, lay any Imposts or Duties on Imports or Exports, except what may be absolutely necessary for executing its inspection Laws: and the net Produce of all Duties and Imposts, laid by any State on Imports or Exports shall be for the Use of the Treasury of the United States; and all such Laws shall be subject to the Revision and Controul of the Congress.

No State shall, without the Consent of Congress, lay any Duty of Tonnage, keep Troops, or Ships of War in time of Peace, enter into any Agreement or Compact with another State, or with a foreign Power, or engage in War, unless actually invaded, or in such imminent Danger as will not admit of delay.

Article II

Section 1. The executive Power shall be vested in a President of the United States of America. He shall hold his Office during the Term of four Years, and, together with the Vice President, chosen for the same Term be elected as follows:

Each State shall appoint, in such Manner as the Legislature thereof may direct, a Number of Electors, equal to the whole Number of Senators and Representatives to which the State may be entitled in the Congress but no Senator or Representative, or Person holding an Office of Trust or Profit under the United States, shall be appointed an Elector.

The Electors shall meet in their respective States, and vote by Ballot for two Persons, of whom one at least shall not be an Inhabitant of the same State with themselves. And they shall make a List of all the Persons voted for, and of the Number of Votes for each; which List they shall sign and certify, and transmit sealed to the Seat of the Government of the United States, directed to the President of the Senate. The President of the Senate shall, in the Presence of the Senate and House of Representatives, open all the Certificates, and the Votes shall then be counted. The Person having the greatest Number of Votes shall be the President, if such Number be a Majority of the whole Number of Electors appointed; and if there be more than one who have such Majority, and have an equal Number of Votes, then the House of Representatives shall immediately chuse by Ballot one of them for President; and if no Person have a Majority, then from the five highest on the List the said House shall in like Manner chuse the President. But in chusing the President, the Votes shall be taken by States, the Representation from each State having one Vote; A quorum for this purpose shall consist of a Member or Members from two thirds of the States, and a Majority of all the States shall be necessary to a Choice. In every Case, after the Choice of the President, the Person having the greatest Number of Votes of the Electors shall be the Vice President. But if there should remain two or more who have equal Votes, the Senate shall chuse from them by Ballot the Vice President.[5]

The Congress may determine the Time of chusing the Electors, and the Day on which they shall give their Votes; which Day shall be the same throughout the United States.

No Person except a natural born Citizen, or a Citizen of the United States, at the time of the Adoption of this Constitution, shall be eligible to the Office of President; neither shall any Person be eligible to that Office who

---

[5]Superseded by the 12th Amendment.

shall not have attained to the Age of thirty five Years, and been fourteen Years a Resident within the United States.

In Case of the Removal of the President from Office, or of his Death, Resignation, or Inability to discharge the Powers and Duties of the said Office, and Same shall devolve on the Vice President, and the Congress may by Law provide for the Case of Removal, Death, Resignation or Inability, both of the President and Vice President, declaring what Officer shall then act as President, and such Officer shall act accordingly, until the Disability be removed, or a President shall be elected.[6]

The President shall, at stated Times, receive for his Services, a Compensation which shall neither be encreased nor diminished during the Period for which he shall have been elected, and he shall not receive within that Period any other Emolument from the United States, or any of them.

Before he enter on the Execution of his Office, he shall take the following Oath or Affirmation: — "I do solemnly swear (or affirm) that I will faithfully execute the Office of President of the United States, and will to the best of my Ability, preserve, protect and defend the Constitution of the United States."

Section 2. The President shall be Commander in Chief of the Army and Navy of the United States, and of the Militia of the several States, when called into the actual service of the United States; he may require the Opinion, in writing, of the principal Officer in each of the executive Departments, upon any Subject relating to the Duties of their respective Offices, and he shall have power to grant Reprieves and Pardons for Offences against the United States, except in Cases of Impeachment.

He shall have Power, by and with the Advice and Consent of the Senate, to make Treaties, provided two thirds of the Senators present concur; and he shall nominate, and by and with the Advice and Consent of the Senate, shall appoint Ambassadors, and other public Ministers and Consuls, Judges of the supreme Court, and all other Officers of the United States, whose Appointments are not herein otherwise provided for, and which should be established by Law: but the Congress may by Law vest the Appointment of such inferior Officers, as they think proper, in the President alone, in the Courts of Law, or in the Heads of the Departments.

The President shall have Power to fill up all Vacancies that may happen during the Recess of the Senate, by granting Commissions which shall expire at the End of their next Session.

Section 3. He shall from time to time give to the Congress Information of the State of the Union, and recommend to their Consideration such Measures as he shall judge necessary and expedient; he may, on extraordinary Occasions, convene both Houses, or either of them, and in Case of Disagreement between them, with Respect to the Time of Adjournment, he may adjourn them to such Time as he shall think proper; he shall receive Ambassadors and other public Ministers, he shall take

Care that the Laws be faithfully executed, and shall Commission all the Officers of the United States.

Section 4. The President, Vice President, and all civil Officers of the United States, shall be removed from Office on Impeachment for, and Conviction of Treason, Bribery, or other high Crimes and Misdemeanors.

Article III

Section 1. The judicial Power of the United States, shall be vested in one supreme Court and in such inferior Courts as the Congress may from time to time ordain and establish. The Judges, both of the supreme and inferior Courts, shall hold their Offices during good Behavior, and shall, at stated Times, receive for their Services, a Compensation, which shall not be diminished during their Continuance in Office.

Section 2. The judicial Power shall extend to all Cases, in Law and Equity, arising under this Constitution, the Laws of the United States, and Treaties made, or which shall be made, under their Authority; — to all Cases affecting Ambassadors, other public Ministers and Consuls; — to all Cases of admiralty and maritime Jurisdiction; — to Controversies to which the United States shall be a Party — to Controversies between two or more States; — *between a State and Citizens of another State*[7]; — between Citizens of different States; — between Citizens of the same State claiming Lands under Grants of different States, *and between a State or the Citizens thereof, and foreign States, Citizens, or Subjects.*[8]

In all cases affecting Ambassadors, other public Ministers and Consuls, and those in which a State shall be Party, the supreme Court shall have original Jurisdiction. In all the other Cases before mentioned, the supreme Court shall have appellate Jurisdiction, both as to Law and Fact, with such Exceptions, and under such Regulations as the Congress shall make.

The Trial of all Crimes, except in Cases of Impeachment, shall be by Jury; and such Trial shall be held in the State where the said Crimes shall have been committed; but when not committed within any State, the Trial shall be at such Place or Places as the Congress may by Law have directed.

Section 3. Treason against the United States, shall consist only in levying War against them, or in adhering to their Enemies, giving them Aid and Comfort. No Person shall be convicted of Treason unless on the Testimony of two Witnesses to the same overt Act, or on Confession in open Court.

The Congress shall have Power to declare the Punishment of Treason, but no Attainder of Treason shall work Corruption of Blood, or Forfeiture except during the Life of the Person attainted.

Article IV

Section 1. Full Faith and Credit shall be given in each State to the public Acts, Records, and judicial Proceedings of every other State. And the Congress may by gen-

486

eral Laws prescribe the Manner in which such Acts, Records, and Proceedings shall be proved, and the Effect thereof.

Section 2. The Citizens of each State shall be entitled to all Privileges and Immunities of Citizens in the several States.

A Person charged in any State with Treason, Felony, or other Crime, who shall flee from Justice, and be found in another State, shall on Demand of the executive Authority of the State from which he fled, be delivered up, to be removed to the State having Jurisdiction of the Crime.

No Person held to Service or Labour in one State, under the Laws thereof, escaping into another, shall, in Consequence of any Law or Regulation therein, be discharged from such Service or Labour, but shall be delivered up on Claim of the Party to whom such Service or Labour may be due.[9]

Section 3. New States may be admitted by the Congress into this Union; but no new State shall be formed or erected within the Jurisdiction of any other State; nor any State be formed by the Junction of two or more States, or Parts of States, without the Consent of the Legislatures of the States concerned as well as of the Congress.

The Congress shall have Power to dispose of and make all needful Rules and Regulations respecting the Territory or other Property belonging to the United States; and nothing in this Constitution shall be so construed as to Prejudice any claims of the United States, or of any particular State.

Section 4. The United States shall guarantee to every State in this Union a Republican Form of Government, and shall protect each of them against Invasion; and on Application of the Legislature, or of the Executive (when the Legislature cannot be convened) against domestic Violence.

Article V

The Congress, whenever two thirds of both Houses shall deem it necessary, shall propose Amendments to this Constitution, or, on the Application of the Legislatures of two thirds of the several States, shall call a Convention for proposing Amendments, which, in either Case, shall be valid to all Intents and Purposes, as Part of this Constitution, when ratified by the Legislatures of three fourths of the several States, or by Conventions in three fourths thereof, as the one or the other Mode of Ratification may be proposed by the Congress; Provided that no Amendment which may be made prior to the Year One thousand eight hundred and eight shall in any Manner affect the first and fourth Clauses in the Ninth Section of the first Article; and that no State, without its Consent, shall be deprived of its equal Suffrage in the Senate.

Article VI

All Debts contracted and Engagements entered into, before the Adoption of this Constitution, shall be as valid

---

[9]See 13th Amendment.

against the United States under this Constitution, as under the Confederation.

This Constitution, and the Laws of the United States which shall be made in Pursuance thereof; and all Treaties made, or which shall be made, under the Authority of the United States, shall be the supreme Law of the Land; and the Judges in every State shall be bound thereby, any Thing in the Constitution or Laws of any State to the Contrary notwithstanding.

The Senators and Representatives before mentioned, and the Members of the several State Legislatures, and all executive and judicial Officers, both of the United States and of the several States, shall be bound by Oath or Affirmation, to support this Constitution; but no religious Test shall ever be required as a Qualification to any Office or public Trust under the United States.

Article VII

The Ratification of the Conventions of nine States, shall be sufficient for the Establishment of this Constitution between the States so ratifying the Same.

Done in Convention by the Unanimous Consent of the States present the Seventeenth Day of September in the Year of our Lord one thousand seven hundred and eighty seven and of the Independence of the United States of America the twelfth. In witness whereof We have hereunto subscribed our Names.

ARTICLES IN ADDITION TO, AND AMENDMENT OF, THE CONSTITUTION OF THE UNITED STATES OF AMERICA, PROPOSED BY CONGRESS, AND RATIFIED BY THE SEVERAL STATES, PURSUANT TO THE FIFTH ARTICLE OF THE ORIGINAL CONSTITUTION.

Amendment I

[Ratification of the first ten amendments was completed December 15, 1791.]

Congress shall make no law respecting an establishment of religion, or prohibiting the free exercise thereof; or abridging the freedom of speech, or of the press; or the right of the people peaceably to assemble, and to petition the Government for a redress of grievances.

Amendment II

A well regulated Militia, being necessary to the security of a free State, the right of the people to keep and bear Arms, shall not be infringed.

Amendment III

No Soldier shall, in time of peace be quartered in any house, without the consent of the Owner, nor in time of war, but in a manner to be presecribed by law.

Amendment IV

The right of the people to be secure in their persons, houses, papers, and effects, against unreasonable searches and seizures, shall not be violated, and no Warrants shall issue, but upon probable cause, supported by

Oath or affirmation, and particularly describing the place to be searched, and the persons or things to be seized.

Amendment V

No person shall be held to answer for a capital, or other infamous crime, unless on a presentment or indictment of a Grand Jury, except in cases arising in the land or naval forces, or in the Militia, when in actual service in time of War or public danger; not shall any person be subject for the same offence to be twice put in jeopardy of life or limb; nor shall be compelled in any criminal case to be a witness against himself, nor be deprived of life, liberty, or property, without due process of law; nor shall private property be taken for public use, without just compensation.

Amendment VI

In all criminal prosecutions, the accused shall enjoy right to a speedy and public trial, by an impartial jury of the State and district wherein the crime shall have been committed, which district shall have been previously ascertained by law, and to be informed of the nature and cause of the accusation; to be confronted with the witness against him; to have compulsory process for obtaining witness in his favor, and to have the Assistance of Counsel for his defence.

Amendment VII

In Suits at common law, where the value in controversy shall exceed twenty dollars, the right of trial by jury shall be preserved, and no fact tried by a jury, shall be otherwise reexamined in any Court of the United States, than according to the rules of the common law.

Amendment VIII

Excessive bail should not be required, nor excessive fines imposed, nor cruel and unusual punishments inflicted.

Amendment IX

The enumeration in the Constitution, of certain rights, shall not be construed to deny or disparage others retained by the people.

Amendment X

The powers not delegated to the United States by the Constitution, nor prohibited by it to the States, are reserved to the States respectively, or to the people.

Amendment XI

[January 8, 1798]

The Judicial power of the United States shall not be construed to extend to any suit in law or equity, commenced or prosecuted against one of the United States by Citizens of another State, or by Citizens or Subjects of any Foreign State.

Amendment XII

[September 25, 1804]

The Electors shall meet in their respective states and vote by ballot for President and Vice President, one of whom, at least, shall not be an inhabitant of the same state with themselves; they shall name in their ballots the person voted for as President, and in distinct ballots the person voted for as Vice President, and they shall make distinct lists of all persons voted for as President, and of all persons voted for as Vice President, and of the number of votes for each, which lists they shall sign and certify, and transmit sealed to the seat of the government of the United States, directed to the President of the Senate; — The President of the Senate shall, in the presence of Senate and House of Representatives, open all the certificates and the votes shall then be counted; — The person having the greatest number of votes for President, shall be the President, if such number be a majority of the whole number of Electors appointed; and if no person have such majority, then from the persons having the highest numbers not exceeding three on the list of those voted for as President, the House of Representatives shall choose immediately, by ballot, the President. But in choosing the President, the votes shall be taken by states, the representation from each state having one vote; a quorum for this purpose shall consist of a member or members from two thirds of the states, and a majority of all the states shall be necessary to a choice. And if the House of Representatives shall not choose a President whenever the right of choice shall devolve upon them, *before the fourth day of March next following*,[10] then the Vice President shall act as President, as in the case of the death or other constitutional disability of the President. — The person having the greatest number of votes as Vice President shall be the Vice President, if such number be a majority of the whole number of Electors appointed, and if no person have a majority, then from the two highest numbers on the list, the Senate shall choose the Vice President; a quorum for the purpose shall consist of two-thirds of the whole number of Senators, and a majority of the whole number shall be necessary to a choice. But no person constitutionally ineligible to the office of President shall be eligible to that of Vice President of the United States.

Amendment XIII

[December 18, 1865]

Section 1. Neither slavery nor involuntary servitude, except as a punishment for crime whereof the party shall have been duly convicted, shall exist within the United States, or any place subject to their jurisdiction.

Section 2. Congress shall have power to enforce this article by appropriate legislation.

Amendment XIV

[July 28, 1869]

Section 1. All persons born or naturalized in the United States, and subject to the jurisdiction thereof, are citizens of the United States and of the State wherein they reside. No state shall make or enforce any law which shall abridge the privileges or immunities of citizens of the United States; nor shall any State deprive any person of life, liberty, or property, without due process of law;

---

[10]Altered by the 20th Amendment.

nor deny to any person within its jurisdiction the equal protection of the laws.

Section 2. Representatives shall be apportioned among the several States according to their respective numbers, counting the whole number of persons in each State, excluding Indians not taxed. But when the right to vote at any election for the choice of electors for President and Vice President of the United States, Representatives in Congress, the Executive and Judicial officers of a State, or the members of the Legislature thereof, is denied to any of the male inhabitants of such State, being twenty-one years of age, and citizens of the United States, or in any way abridged, except for participation in rebellion, or other crime, the basis of representation therein shall be reduced in the proportion which the number of such male citizens shall bear to the whole number of male citizens twenty-one years of age in such State.

Section 3. No person shall be a Senator or Representative in Congress, or elector of President and Vice President, or hold any office, civil or military, under the United States, or under any State, who, having previously taken an oath, as a member of Congress, or as an officer of the United States, or as a member of any State legislature, or as an executive or judicial officer of any State, to support the Constitution of the United States, shall have engaged in insurrection or rebellion against the same, or given aid or comfort to the enemies thereof. But Congress may by a vote of two thirds of each House, remove such disability.

Section 4. The validity of the public debt of the United States, authorized by law, including debts incurred for payment of pensions and bounties for services in suppressing insurrection or rebellion, shall not be questioned. But neither the United States nor any State shall assume or pay any debt or obligation incurred in aid of insurrection or rebellion against the United States, or any claim for the loss or emancipation of any slave; but all such debts, obligations, and claims shall be held illegal and void.

Section 5. The congress shall have power to enforce, by appropriate legislation, the provisions of this article.

Amendment XV

[March 30, 1870]

Section 1. The right of citizens of the United States to vote shall not be denied or abridged by the United States or by any State on account of race, color, or previous condition of servitude.

Section 2. The Congress shall have power to enforce this article by appropriate legislation.

Amendment XVI

[February 25, 1913]

The Congress shall have power to lay and collect taxes on incomes, from whatever source derived, without apportionment among the several States, and without regard to any census or enumeration.

Amendment XVII

[May 31, 1913]

The Senate of the United States shall be composed of

two Senators from each State, elected by the people thereof, for six years; and each Senator shall have one vote. The electors in each State shall have the qualifications requisite for electors of the most numerous branch of the State legislatures.

When vacancies happen in the representation of any State in the Senate, the executive authority of such State shall issue writs of election to fill such vacancies: *Provided,* That the legislature of any State may empower the executive thereof to make temporary appointments until the people fill the vacancies by election as the legislature may direct.

This amendment shall not be so construed as to affect the election or term of any Senator chosen before it becomes valid as part of the Constitution.

Amendment XVIII

[January 29, 1919]

Section 1. After one year from the ratification of this article the manufacture, sale, or transportation of intoxicating liquors within, the importation thereof into, or the exportation thereof from the United States and all territory subject to the jurisdiction thereof for beverage purposes is hereby prohibited.

Section 2. The Congress and the several States shall have concurrent power to enforce this article by appropriate legislation.

Section 3. This article shall be inoperative unless it shall have been ratified as an amendment to the Constitution by the legislatures of the several States, as provided in the Constitution, within seven years from the date of the submission hereof to the States by the Congress.[11]

Amendment XIX

[August 26, 1920]

The right of citizens of the United States to vote shall not be denied or abridged by the United States or by any State on account of sex.

Congress shall have power to enforce this article by appropriate legislation.

Amendment XX

[February 6, 1933]

Section 1. The terms of the President and Vice President, or acting as President, during the term within which this Article becomes operative from holding the 3rd day of January, of the years in which such terms would have ended if this article had not been ratified; and the terms of their successors shall then begin.

Section 2. The Congress shall assemble at least once in every year and such meeting shall begin at noon on the 3rd day of January, unless thay shall by law appoint a different day.

Section 3. If, at the time fixed for the beginning of the term of the President, the President elect shall have died, the Vice President elect shall become President. If a President shall not have been chosen before the time fixed for the beginning of his term, or if the President elect shall have failed to qualify, then the Vice President elect shall act as President until a President shall have

---

[11]Repealed by the 21st Amendment.

qualified; and the Congress may by law provide for the case wherein neither a President elect nor a Vice President elect shall have qualified, declaring who shall then act as President, or the manner in which one who is to act shall be selected, and such person shall act accordingly until a President or Vice President shall have qualified.

Section 4. The Congress may by law provide for the case of the death of any of the persons from whom the House of Representatives may choose a President whenever the right of choice shall have developed upon them, and for the case of the death of any of the persons from whom the Senate may choose a Vice President whenever the right of choice shall have devolved upon them.

Section 5. Sections 1 and 2 shall take effect on the 15th day of October following the ratification of this article.

Section 6. This article shall be inoperative unless it shall have been ratified as an amendment to the Constitution by the legislatures of three-fourths of the several States within seven years from the date of its submission.

Amendment XXI

[December 5, 1933]

Section 1. The eighteenth article of amendment to the Constitution of the United States is hereby repealed.

Section 2. The transportation or importation into any State, Territory, or possession of the United States for delivery or use therein of intoxicating liquors, in violation of the laws thereof, is hereby prohibited.

Section 3. This article shall be inoperative unless it shall have been ratified as an amendment to the Constitution by conventions in the several States, as provided in the Constitution, within seven years from the date of the submission hereof to the States by the Congress.

Amendment XXII

[February 26, 1951]

Section 1. No person shall be elected to the office of the President more than twice, and no person who has held the office of President, or acted as President, for more than two years of a term to which some other person was elected President shall be elected to the office of President more than once. But this Article shall not apply to any person holding the office of President when this Article was proposed by the Congress, and shall not prevent any person who may be holding the office of President, or acting as President, during the term within which this Article becomes operative from holding the office of President or acting as President during the remainder of such term.

Section 2. This article shall be inoperative unless it shall have been ratified as an amendment to the Constitution by the legislatures of three fourths of the several States within seven years from the date of its submission to the States by the Congress.

Amendment XXIII

[March 29, 1961]

Section 1. The District constituting the seat of Government of the United States shall appoint in such manner as the Congress may direct:

A number of electors of President and Vice President equal to the whole number of Senators and Representatives in Congress to which the District would be entitled if it were a State, but in no event more than the least populous State; they shall be in addition to those appointed by the States, but they shall be considered, for the purposes of the election of President and Vice President, to be electors appointed by a State; and they shall meet in the District and perform such duties as provided by the twelfth article of amendment.

Section 2. The Congress shall have power to enforce this article by appropriate legislation.

Amendment XXIV

[January 23, 1964]

Section 1. The right of citizens of the United States to vote in any primary or other election for President or Vice President, for electors for President or Vice President, or for Senator or Representative in Congress, shall not be denied or abridged by the United States or any state by reason of failure to pay any poll tax or other tax.

Section 2. The Congress shall have the power to enforce this article by appropriate legislation.

Amendment XXV

[February 19, 1967]

Section 1. In case of the removal of the President from office or of his death or resignation, the Vice President shall become President.

Section 2. Whenever there is a vacancy in the office of the Vice President, the President shall nominate a Vice President who shall take office upon confirmation by a majority vote of both Houses of Congress.

Section 3. Whenever the President transmits to the President pro tempore of the Senate and the Speaker of the House of Representatives his written declaration that he is unable to discharge the powers and duties of his office, and until he transmits to them a written declaration to the contrary, such powers and duties shall be discharged by the Vice President as Acting President.

Section 4. Whenever the Vice President and a majority of either the principal officers of the executive departments or of such other body as Congress may by law provide, transmit to the President pro tempore of the Senate and the Speaker of the House of Representatives their written declaration that the President is unable to discharge the powers and duties of his office, the Vice President shall immediately assume the powers and duties of the office as Acting President.

Thereafter, when the President transmits to the President pro tempore of the Senate and the Speaker of the House of Representatives his written declaration that no inability exists, he shall resume the powers and duties of his office unless the Vice President and a majority of either the principal officers of the executive departments or of such other body as Congress may by law provide, transmit within four days to the President pro tempore of the Senate and the Speaker of the House of Representatives their written declaration that the President is unable to discharge the powers and duties of his office. Thereupon Congress shall decide the issue, assembling within forty-eight hours for that purpose if not in session. If the Congress, within twenty-one days after receipt of the latter written declaration, or, if Congress is not in session, within twenty-one days after Congress is required to assemble, determines by two-thirds vote of both Houses that the President is unable to discharge the powers and duties of his office, the Vice President shall continue to discharge the same as Acting President; otherwise, the President shall resume the powers and duties of his office.

Amendment XXVI

[June 30, 1971]

Section 1. The right of citizens of the United States, who are eighteen years of age or older, to vote shall not be denied or abridged by the United States or any state on account of age.

Section 2. The Congress shall have the power to enforce this article by appropriate legislation.

index